The Birth of the RAF, 1918

The Birth of
the RAF, 1918

The World's First Air Force

RICHARD OVERY

ALLEN LANE
an imprint of
PENGUIN BOOKS

ALLEN LANE

UK | USA | Canada | Ireland | Australia
India | New Zealand | South Africa

Allen Lane is part of the Penguin Random House group
of companies whose addresses can be found at
global.penguinrandomhouse.com

First published 2018

001

Copyright © Richard Overy, 2018

The moral right of the author has been asserted

Set in 12/14.75 Dante MT Std
Typeset by Jouve (UK), Milton Keynes
Printed in Great Britain by Clays Ltd, St Ives plc

A CIP catalogue record for this book is available from the British Library

ISBN: 978-0-241-27421-7

www.greenpenguin.co.uk

MIX
Paper from
responsible sources
FSC® C018179

Penguin Random House is committed to a
sustainable future for our business, our readers
and our planet. This book is made from Forest
Stewardship Council® certified paper.

Contents

List of Illustrations

Preface

The Royal Air Force was formally activated on 1 April 1918, April Fools' Day. It was an inauspicious date on which to launch the world's first independent air force, and there were hesitations about choosing it. Perhaps the army and the Royal Navy, both for their own reasons wary of the fledgling service, quietly approved the choice of date, hoping that a separate air force would soon prove itself a joke. They certainly both hoped that the RAF and the new Air Ministry it served would not last beyond the end of the war. In this they were soon to be disabused. The RAF survived victory in 1918 and has survived regular calls for its dissolution since, and now celebrates an uninterrupted hundred years.

The birth of the RAF was surrounded by argument and controversy. There already were two air services fighting Britain's aerial contribution to the First World War: the Royal Naval Air Service and the army's Royal Flying Corps. The establishment of an entirely new branch of the armed forces was a political decision, prompted by the German air attacks on London in 1917, not a decision dictated by military necessity. The politicians wanted a force to defend the home front against the novel menace of bombing, amidst fears that the staying power of the population might be strained to breaking point by the raids. From the politicians' viewpoint, the air defence of Great Britain was one of the principal charges on the new force, and it is the defence of the home islands twenty-two years later in the Battle of Britain that is still remembered as the RAF's 'finest hour'. The reality of the past hundred years has been rather different. The RAF has principally served overseas and for most of the century was a force dedicated to bombing and to ground support for the other services. This future was anticipated in the final seven months of combat in 1918 when the RAF, building on the legacy of its two predecessors, contributed substantially to the air support of Allied armies in Western Europe and the Middle East, and organized the Independent Force (independent of the front line) for the long-range bombing of German industrial towns. By the time of the Armistice in November 1918, the shape of RAF doctrine was already in firm outline, even if its future as a separate force was thrown into doubt once the fighting was over.

The birth pangs of the RAF are the subject here. Founding a new service in the midst of a bitterly contested conflict raised all kinds of practical questions which had to be resolved, from the colour of uniforms to the very name itself. The long history of the RAF as an institution was given shape in the earliest days of its existence. There are numerous records to help reconstruct those early days and a wealth of memoir and historical literature to draw on. I am grateful for the help I have received in the archives and libraries I have exploited and for the encouragement of the staff at the RAF Museum at Hendon, where I have been privileged to chair the Research Board. This volume is a small contribution to the wider programme of commemoration in which the museum is engaged. My thanks as ever to my agents, Gill Coleridge and Cara Jones, and to Simon Winder and the team at Penguin, and particular thanks to one of my colleagues on the Research Board, the Head of the Air Historical Branch, Sebastian Cox, for his sound advice on an earlier draft. Needless to say, the views expressed throughout are my own, as are any errors of fact or interpretation that might remain.

Richard Overy,
Exeter and London, 2017

Britain and the War in the Air

A fixed determination to attack and win will be
the surest road to victory.

RFC Training Manual, 1913

In 1908, only five years after the Wright brothers' first powered
flight in December 1903, the British novelist H. G. Wells published *The War in the Air*, in which he imagined a near future
when aircraft would decide the outcome of modern war. The
novel's hero, Bert Smallways, watching the destruction of
New York by German airships, reflects on Britain's vulnerability: 'the little island in the silver seas was at the end of its
immunity.'[1] Aircraft changed the whole nature of war. Writing twenty-five years later in his autobiography, Wells noted
with a grim satisfaction that he had written the novel 'before
any practicable flying had occurred', but he had been correct
to predict that aircraft would abolish the traditional divide
between a military front line and the home population, and so
erode the distinction between combatant and civilian. With
the arrival of aircraft, Wells concluded, war was no longer a
'vivid spectacle' for the home front, watched like a cricket or
baseball match, but a horrible reality for ordinary people.[2]
Only seven years separated Wells's novel from the first bombs

to fall on British soil and only ten from the establishment of the Royal Air Force, set up to try to protect Britain's vulnerable people from an air menace described so graphically by Wells at the dawn of the air age.

One of the many remarkable consequences of the coming of powered flight was the speed with which the armies and navies of all the major powers sponsored the development of aircraft –both dirigibles and aeroplanes – for military purposes. The technical development of aircraft in the decade following the Wright brothers was exponential and knowledge of the new invention universal, but for the British people, all but immune to invasion for a millennium, aviation posed a particular strategic threat. This perhaps explains why the evolution of military air power in Britain in the age of the Great War was strongly influenced by public opinion and political pressure and was not solely a result of the military need to respond to innovation. Critics at the time and since have blamed military conservatism for the slow development of organized air power in Britain before 1914 and have assumed that public disquiet, noisily expressed in the popular press, prompted a grudging army and navy to explore the use of aircraft despite harbouring strong prejudices against their use.

The army and navy were, in truth, less narrow-minded than the popular image suggests. The first powered flight in Britain was only made in 1908 by A. V. Roe, who managed a distance of just 60 yards (55 metres). A mere three years later the army began developing a military air arm when the Royal Engineers established an Air Battalion consisting of a company of airships (still considered a major factor for the future of air warfare) and a company of aeroplanes. On 13 April 1912 the King issued a Royal Warrant for a new service, and a month later, on 13 May, the battalion was replaced by the Royal

Flying Corps (RFC), the direct ancestor of the future RAF. The Corps consisted of a military wing, a naval wing, a Central Flying School and a reserve, loosely controlled by an Air Committee with representatives from the two services.[3] A small cluster of soldiers and seamen who had qualified as pilots joined the force. The RFC adopted a modified khaki army uniform and the Latin motto *Per ardua ad astra* ('Through adversity to the stars'), still the motto of today's air force.[4] The intention was to keep a unified corps serving both the army and the Royal Navy, but when Winston Churchill became First Lord of the Admiralty in 1913, he exploited his personal enthusiasm for flight to insist that the navy should have a separate air force.[5] The first commander of the Royal Naval Air Service (RNAS) was Captain Murray Sueter, the director of the Admiralty's Air Department. In July 1914 the RNAS was formally divorced from the RFC just as Europe was about to plunge into war. A year later the Admiralty assumed full responsibility, a bifurcation that was to lead to endless friction between military and naval aviation until united as awkward rivals in the RAF in 1918. In the same month that the RNAS was created, a Military Aeronautics Directorate was established by the War Office to oversee the military wing of the RFC under one of the pioneers of army aviation, Major-General David Henderson.[6]

Both the navy and the army understood that aircraft were likely before long to become assets indispensable to their operations. 'In view of the fact that aircraft will undoubtedly be used in the next war,' wrote the Chief of the Imperial General Staff in 1911, 'we cannot afford to delay . . .' The army Field Service Regulations published in July 1912 were the first to contain reference to the use of aircraft, and in the 1912 field exercises two airships and fourteen aircraft were used for reconnaissance purposes. The observer in one of the aircraft was Major Hugh Trenchard, the man later regarded as the 'father of the RAF'; commander of one of the armies in the exercise was Douglas Haig, who later formed a close working relationship with Trenchard on the Western Front. By the summer of 1914, on the eve of the Great War, a major RFC training exercise saw experiments in night flying, flight at high altitudes, aerial photography, and the first attempt to fit machine-guns to an aircraft. The RFC Training Manual issued the year before stressed the need for offensive aviation well before the means were available.[7]

It was nevertheless true that the RFC was a considerable way behind the development of aviation elsewhere. In France, Austria and Germany rapid progress had been made in military aeronautics; the small Bulgarian air force was responsible for inventing the first modern aerial bomb; and in 1914 the Russian engineer Igor Sikorsky developed the multi-engine *Ilia Muromets* Sikorsky Type V aeroplane, the first modern heavy bomber. British services were slower to respond, partly because they did not anticipate a major European war, partly because public and government were fixated on the battleship arms race, and partly because the British army was so much smaller and less politically powerful than its Continental rivals. When war broke out in August 1914, the RNAS possessed only six airships and ninety-three aeroplanes, many of which were unserviceable, and could field only one flying squadron (the word chosen in 1912 to describe the small air units being formed). The RFC arrived in France with the British Expeditionary Force (BEF) with just four squadrons totalling approximately sixty aircraft. There were 105 officers and 755 other ranks. The French army put twenty-three squadrons in the field, the German army twenty-nine.[8]

The first two years of war provided a steep learning curve for air forces on all sides. Aircraft technology improved all the time, but aircraft remained fragile objects, subject to frequent damage and repair. They were constructed chiefly of wood and fabric, carried a heavy metal engine and were held together with wire or wooden struts. Some idea of the nature of early aviation engineering can be gleaned from the trades assigned to each RFC squadron, which included two blacksmiths, six carpenters, four coppersmiths, twenty-one riggers and four sailmakers.[9] Flying was an exceptionally hazardous undertaking with few base facilities, primitive navigational instruments, and the constant threat posed by sudden changes in the weather. Naval aviators were occasionally sent off over the sea never to be seen again. Diaries kept by servicemen in the RFC talk repeatedly of the cold. Aloft in an open cockpit, thousands of feet up, the temperature was debilitating. The RFC Training Manual in December 1915 listed the clothing pilots and observers were expected to wear to combat the intense cold: two pairs of thick long drawers, a woollen waistcoat, a British 'warm coat' with a waterproof oilskin over it, a cap with ear pads, two balaclavas, a flying helmet, goggles, a warm scarf, and two pairs of socks and gloves.[10]

Although the RFC manuals stressed that aircraft could accomplish little or nothing in 'heavy rain, fog, gales or darkness', pilot records show that flying continued even in cloudy, cold conditions with limited visibility. Advice on weather in the air force Field Service Book was rudimentary: 'Red at sunset . . . Fair weather'; 'Red at dawn . . . Bad weather or wind'; 'Pale yellow at sunset – rain'.[11] Crashes and accidents were as a result routine occurrences. British air forces lost 35,973 aircraft through accident or combat during the war, and suffered the loss of 16,623 airmen, either dead, or severely injured, or prisoners of war. A diary kept by an air mechanic during the later war years gives a vivid description of a typical accidental death:

> Lt. J. A. Miller was taking off in an S.E.5 when he crashed, his machine caught fire & he was burned to death, we were powerless to help him, the ammunition in his guns & boxes was exploding & bullets were flying around, soon the fire died down and his charred remains were taken out of the machine & buried in a wood close by, a wooden cross made out of a propeller marks his grave.[12]

The situation in the first years of the war was not helped by the poor level of training of novice pilots, many of whom would have only twenty hours flying time or less before being posted to operations, where only two hours would be spent learning to fly the frontline aircraft assigned to them. A young John Slessor, later Chief of the Air Staff in 1950, recalled that he was commissioned as an RFC pilot with just twelve hours solo flying, and was fortunate to survive.[13] There were no parachutes.

The RFC and the RNAS were military midgets compared with the other branches of the army and navy, and it was still not entirely clear what aircraft might achieve in the context of a major war. All experience prior to the war suggested that the principal function of aircraft, whether aeroplanes or airships, would be reconnaissance of an enemy's military or naval forces, and for much of the four-year conflict the supply of intelligence became an essential and central function of all air force operations, military and naval. 'The most important role of aeroplanes in war,' according to the 1915 Training Manual, 'is reconnaissance.'[14] Moreover, as one senior RFC officer claimed in 1917, 'Aircraft reconnaissance is the most perfect and the most complete it is possible to obtain in war.'[15] This was true only to an extent, since reconnaissance operations were often interrupted by poor weather, while aircraft could be destroyed by ground fire and hostile planes, or disappear altogether at sea. Reconnaissance involved observation of enemy troop movements and dispositions, but, as trench warfare set in, aircraft were also used to spot enemy artillery and to direct the artillery fire of their own forces. This became an increasingly sophisticated operation as the war went on. Aircrew used either the 'target-battery line', when they could see both the objective of fire and the guns doing the firing, signalling by wireless the number of yards the shells were wide, short or long, or the 'clock code' system, where the observer placed the enemy target at the centre of an imaginary clock face 1,000 yards wide and signalled back the 'time' and distance to the gunners on the ground, who had a map and a clock-face disc to enable them to locate the target with greater precision.[16] On a static front line, with artillery duels a regular feature, directed gunfire became indispensable.

Reconnaissance was nonetheless only one of the functions aircraft were expected to perform. In the first days of war RFC pilots and observers practised using pistols or rifles to attack enemy aircraft engaged in observation. Soon, machine-guns were fitted to most aircraft so that those on reconnaissance could protect themselves from attack. By the end of 1915, RFC manuals classed counter-force operations ('fighting against other aircraft') as a key function, without which other duties could not be carried out. The relentless offensive against the enemy air force became a primary objective as the war continued. The third major task was support of surface forces, whether ships at sea or troops on the ground. For the RFC this involved 'destruction of matériel, and demolition at vulnerable points on the enemy's communications' and 'offensive action against troops on the ground'.[17] Ground support operations were conducted using bombs and machine-guns, but from very early in the wartime career of the RFC it was assumed that the impact on the morale of enemy troops was more important than the physical destruction possible with small 20lb bombs, an assumption that came to be embedded in British air doctrine for a generation.

Independent bombing operations, however, were still not regarded as a significant element in air warfare. The RNAS is generally credited with launching Britain's strategic bombing when, at Churchill's prompting, a handful of naval aircraft attacked the sheds and repair facilities of the German Zeppelin airships. On 22 September 1914 four planes attacked targets in Cologne and Düsseldorf, with little effect; on 8 October, two more attacked and struck a Zeppelin hangar, destroying airship LZIX; on 21 November the Zeppelin factory at Friedrichshafen was attacked by a number of small Avro 504 single-seat aircraft, capable of carrying just four 20lb bombs. It was, Churchill told the House of Commons, 'a fine feat of arms', and indeed it was remarkable that targets were found and attacked so far from the front line, given the limitations of current aviation technology; but the raids were tiny and the impact in the end insignificant.[18] The RNAS continued to plan for independent bombing operations against German military targets. In May 1916, No. 3 Wing was established to undertake long-range bombing more systematically, but the Battle of the Somme that summer forced the diversion of RNAS aircraft into assisting the army. Between October 1916 and April 1917 the wing undertook twelve small raids on targets in Germany, but was then disbanded with little achieved and the aircraft again diverted to the land battle.[19] Where bombing mattered in the first years of war it was against targets at or near the front, but even here its effect was marginal.

As the air services grew rapidly in size in the first two wartime years, new organizational structures had to be created. In November 1914 the RFC was divided into two wings, the First Wing supporting the British First Army, the Second Wing supporting the Second Army. A third headquarters wing was added in April 1915. Each Army had an 'aircraft commander' attached to it to maximize coordination between army and air force. The level of expansion made it necessary to create brigades, composed of at least two wings, and eight were formed between 1916 and 1918. Each wing was made up of two or more squadrons, each squadron of three flights of four aircraft each. Brigades were retitled 'groups' after the war, but the basic organizational structure of the later RAF was already in place well before its formation. The headquarters of the RFC was established in northern France at St Omer, near the Channel coast. The site was a small chateau, overcrowded and improvised. There were no electric lights, and inadequate accommodation for serious staff work. 'My main recollection,' wrote Maurice Baring, recently appointed to the RFC staff, 'is a stuffy office, full of clerks and candles and a deafening noise of typewriters . . . a perpetual stream of guests and a crowd of people sleeping on the floor.'[20] Among the uncomfortable guests was Lt.-Colonel Hugh Trenchard, commander of the RFC (Military Wing) at home, but in November 1914 made commander of the newly formed First Wing. Baring met him at the quayside at Boulogne to take him to St Omer, 'a tall man, with a small head and a Scots Fusiliers cap on'.[21]

Trenchard played a central role in the history of both the RFC and the RAF, but in autumn 1914 he might just as easily have ended any prospect of a major new air service when, as Commander of the Military Wing, he had recommended, with support from Sefton Brancker, Henderson's deputy in London, that the RFC be divided up between the army corps and divisions, each with their own assigned air units, and with no central commander or headquarters.[22] The proposal was quashed after protests from Henderson and his chief-of-staff, Lt.-Colonel Frederick Sykes, who had been Trenchard's predecessor as commander of the Military Wing. There was little love lost between the two men. Sykes was a punctilious military intellectual, at home in the world of politics and diplomacy, more than capable of articulating his views on air strategy and organization, and confident that his view was the right one. He was regarded by some as aloof, cold and devious, by others as too able for his own good.[23] Trenchard, Sykes claimed in his memoirs, was an officer with 'a forceful personality and great drive', but he thought on the bigger issues Trenchard was 'fundamentally wrong' not only in 1914, but later in the war when the two men, one after the other, became chief-of-staff to the fledgling RAF.[24] Trenchard in turn thought Sykes 'secretive . . . kept everything hidden, and never spoke to anyone', though he did concede that Sykes 'was a hard worker and had some brains'.[25] Sykes' dislike of Trenchard persisted long into retirement. He was the only one of Trenchard's surviving contemporaries who refused in the 1950s to be interviewed by Trenchard's biographer.

Other airmen had more generous opinions of a man affectionately known as 'Boom' because of his deep resonant voice. After army service in the Royal Scots Fusiliers in India, South Africa and Nigeria, Trenchard learned to fly at the age of 39 and became Deputy Commander of the Central Flying School, run by the naval aviator Godfrey Paine. When his future chief-of-staff John Salmond arrived at the school as a young trainee pilot he later recalled seeing 'a dark, glowering man with a parchment coloured face and a light behind the eyes'. It was not long, Salmond continued, 'before I knew what the fire meant'.[26] Trenchard was respected as a commander who worked fearlessly without flagging, cared for his crews despite the sacrifices he demanded of them, and single-mindedly defended the organization he commanded. He attracted great loyalty, but colleagues learned that at times he could display a harsh temper and a deliberate brusqueness of manner, masking a lonely inner self. Unlike Sykes, he was ill-at-ease in the world of politics, and instinctively distrusted civilian interference in military affairs. He has always enjoyed the reputation of being inarticulate, in speech and on paper, though he generally knew what he wanted. 'I know I am an untidy talker,' he told his biographer, 'and you may say I have an untidy brain, but in my mind I am persistent and consistent.'[27] His commitment throughout the war was to pursue strategies that would facilitate army victory. As it turned out, he was an unlikely 'father of the RAF'. Up to the last he opposed the formation of the new service in 1918, even after he had reluctantly been pressured into accepting the role of chief-of-staff. Trenchard for his part regarded David Henderson, first Director of Military Aeronautics, as the true father.[28]

In August 1915, Trenchard replaced Henderson as Commander-in-Chief of the RFC in France. His rival Sykes had been posted to the Mediterranean theatre two months before, at the request of the Admiralty, in order to resolve the problems facing the RNAS in the Gallipoli campaign. Henderson had poor health and had relied heavily on Sykes as his chief-of-staff, though, for reasons still not entirely clear, Henderson, like Trenchard, came to distrust his ambitious lieutenant and was happy to see him go.[29] In December 1915 General Douglas Haig, Trenchard's commander when he had been in charge of the First Wing, was appointed Commander-in-Chief of the BEF, and for the next two years a close relationship was forged between the two men as each pursued his own version of the offensive as the only key to victory. Trenchard, like Haig, was prepared to accept high losses as long as the momentum of the offensive could be maintained. 'Air superiority' became the intermediate objective of offensive airpower, because the achievement of superiority would allow aircraft to perform their other critical duties of reconnaissance, artillery spotting and close support without the threat of enemy interception. When Trenchard arrived to command the RFC, however, air superiority was still a distant hope against a German enemy now equipped with the Fokker E.I fighter (or scout, as they were called), which was armed with a forward-firing machine-gun, synchronized with the rotation of the propeller. Losses of aircrew and machines outpaced their replacement. News of the crisis facing the RFC reached the press at home, and for the first time in the war Britain's air services began to catch the attention of politicians and public.

The 'Fokker scourge' as it came to be known in the press was just one of the factors that brought aviation more fully into the limelight. On the night of 19/20 January 1915 the first bombs fell on British soil, when Zeppelin airships attacked the east coast towns of Great Yarmouth, Sheringham and King's Lynn, killing four people and injuring sixteen. The authorities had expected airship raids for some time, but had done little to prepare for them. Over the course of 1915 there were twenty raids in which thirty-seven tons of bombs were dropped, killing 181 people and wounding 455. The first raid that managed to reach London took place on the night of 31 May, when a single airship, LZ38, dropped eighty-nine incendiaries and thirty aerial grenades on the East End, killing nine people.[30] The attacks were indiscriminate, since airships flew at a great height, in the dark, and subject to the vagaries of wind and weather, their crews in a regular state of anxiety about the safety of their isolated airborne station, while fighting against the cold and the occasional lack of sufficient oxygen.[31] As a result of largely random bombing, almost all the casualties were civilians, many of them children, many killed where they lay in bed. Small though the human cost was compared with the campaigns of the next war, the sheer novelty of attacks on British soil against British civilians explains the exaggerated reaction of press and public. After the first modest raid *The Times* condemned an enemy that practised 'ruthless and inhuman destruction', and throughout 1915 there was growing anger at German bombing and deep disquiet about the apparent failure of the armed forces to do anything at all to combat or deter the attacks.[32] There was no way of knowing when a raid was coming. The government and the police were against early warning of impending raids from fear that this would simply create widespread and perhaps unnecessary panic, particularly among war workers; it was also assumed that an audible warning would act as a lure for the airships. Worse still, Zeppelin raids proved a spectacle that encouraged crowds of onlookers, exposing them to the very threat they clustered to watch.

Air defence was not yet a recognized branch of air warfare. The defence of the coasts and inland towns was entrusted to the RNAS in an agreed demarcation between the naval and military wings in 1914, but the Admiralty had given little thought to what air defence entailed. In May 1915 just one anti-aircraft gun, a converted artillery piece, defended London, and there were very few aircraft. The entire RNAS home defence organization even by 1916 employed only 17,341 servicemen and 110 aircraft.[33] Night air defence was rudimentary and dangerous for the crews and, because of the height and speed of the airships, entirely ineffective. Only after the introduction of aircraft with a higher operational ceiling and the development of deadlier explosive and incendiary ammunition did it prove possible on occasion to find and destroy an airship, but most went undetected or unmolested. Against twenty-nine raids counted from 1914 to 1916 there were 166 sorties by British defending aircraft, but 145 never saw the enemy; twenty-one out of the twenty-nine raids were conducted without being sighted at all.[34] The wave of protest against the failure of air defence led to the transfer of home defence to the army in February 1916, with the RFC responsible for all home-based aircraft except those guarding fleet installations. Gradually, over the course of 1916, a more extensive and better-armed air defence system was constructed. In May 1916 the first home defence squadron was activated, and by the end of the year there were eleven squadrons and one night-training squadron. They were eventually formed into 6th Brigade Home Defence, with six wings, eighteen squadrons and ten night-training units.[35] Under army control, a system of lighting restrictions and air raid warnings was introduced. A network of 'Warning Controls' was set up, one for Scotland, six for England and Wales, each run by a Warning Controller who was also the local anti-aircraft defence commander. Cordons of observer posts were set up around London and other industrial centres, linked to the RFC and anti-aircraft commanders by priority telephone, a system not unlike the one later used in the Battle of Britain. Warnings were issued to key personnel, however, not to the public. Some local communities did deliver audible warnings, against police advice, but there remained great confusion over what sounds were permissible if an enemy airship were overhead. Church bells and clock chimes were prohibited, and there were even proposals 'to prohibit singing, whistling or shouting in the streets, even the barking of dogs'. Not until July 1917 did the government finally relent and permit the use of sirens, rattles, whistles and bells.[36]

A dedicated air defence suggested the need for an air force operating independently of the army in the field. The same was true of the long-range bombing of targets beyond the enemy front line, which also implied the possibility at some point of a strategy separate from the army's campaigns on the Western Front and in the Middle East against Turkey. Throughout 1915 and 1916 the RFC and RNAS had conducted small raids against more distant objectives, but the scale was tiny. The Zeppelin raids encouraged the public to call for reprisals and the development of a dedicated bombing force, but the army and navy resisted the idea of attacks carried out simply for revenge. From 1915 onwards senior officers in both services began to explore the possibility, when the technology was available, of conducting long-range raids against industrial and military targets in Germany, with the object of limiting the supply of munitions and reducing the scale of German air attacks. This was the origin of an idea that dominated postwar thinking in the RAF: that the best defence against air attack was an air offensive against the enemy.[37] Even Trenchard, in command of the RFC in France, came during the course of 1916 to accept the idea that aircraft might be used to attack the sources of German supply on the home front and so reduce the pressure on Allied armies. Neither home defence nor long-range bombing necessarily required an air service distinct from the army and navy, but they both involved air power functions that were difficult to reconcile with the insatiable demands of the navy and army for all the aircraft they could get for the direct support of their operations. This emerging sense that airmen would soon be pursuing strategies that did not fit easily with the war on land and at sea prepared the ground for the arguments in 1917 and 1918 over the formation of the RAF, but it did no more than that.

No factor mattered more in preparing the way for a separate air ministry and air force than the damaging competition that developed in the first war years between army and navy demands for aeronautical equipment. Both needed large numbers of aircraft and engines because of the sustained wastage rate, but they competed independently for engineering and industrial resources from a limited number of manufacturers, who indulged in the production of a bewildering array of prototypes. The RFC alone developed or used over 140 different aircraft models and variants.[38] There was no effective coordination of the naval and military air programmes, little standardization, and a persistent war of words between the two sides over allegations of privileged access to contractors. The two services did indeed require different armament, yet competition between them compromised the capacity to produce enough specialized equipment for either force. The alarm over losses in combat spilled over into public concern at the state of the air industry, and in February 1916 Asquith's government established a Joint Air War Committee under the War Minister, Lord Derby, to try to resolve the struggle for resources between the two services. It possessed almost no power to act, and after eight abortive sittings, during which the contest for procurement was aired but not altered, Derby resigned and the committee was wound up.[39] In May, the government decided to appoint an Air Board under the Conservative Leader of the House of Lords, Lord Curzon, but the board was again given no real power to intervene in the disputes between the two services. It did have the effect of demonstrating publicly how far apart the army and navy were on the issue of reconciling their air power aspirations and how dim was the prospect of satisfying public concern about Britain's air policy.

On 23 October Curzon presented the Cabinet with the Board's first and, as it turned out, only report. He used the occasion to lambast the Admiralty in less than diplomatic language for obstructing all efforts to produce a more rational allocation of resources or to take the Board seriously. The RNAS was, in Curzon's view, 'the least efficient branch of the Royal Navy', while the Sea Lords regarded the Board 'as an intruder if not an antagonist'. The First Lord of the Admiralty, Arthur Balfour, rejected Curzon's censure. 'I do not suppose,' he responded, 'that in the whole history of the country any Government department has ever indulged so recklessly in the luxury of inter-departmental criticism.' Curzon had the last word, warning the Cabinet that the Admiralty not only failed to provide assistance to the Board as he had been promised but had displayed throughout a 'resolute antagonism'.[40] The exchange launched almost a decade of remarkably candid, occasionally vituperative, exchanges between the navy and the rest of the air force establishment over the future organization of British military aviation. The conflict was suspended while David Lloyd George succeeded Asquith as Prime Minister in December, but Curzon's objections did not go unheeded. In early 1917 Lloyd George began a radical overhaul of the British air effort that culminated more than a year later in the formation of the RAF. The decision was taken to allocate responsibility for the production of all air equipment to the Minister of Munitions, who was to enforce a rationalization of planning and production. For the first time, there appeared the prospect that an air ministry might be needed to oversee air policy. Lord Curzon had already suggested together with his Board that a single imperial air service and an air ministry would be needed after the war, but it was feared that their creation in the midst of a major conflict would cause too much dislocation.[41] However, in December 1916 the New Ministries and Secretaries Bill decreed that the chair of the Air Board should enjoy equivalent status to a minister, and when a second Board was formally constituted on 6 February 1917 its chair, the industrialist Lord Cowdray, expected that his Board would have proper executive power to influence the evolution of British air policy.[42] In this the new Board was to be disappointed.

The creation of the two Air Boards revealed the extent to which the future organization of British air power was to be governed by political interests as much as by military necessity. For the government, the air mattered first because fear of being bombed might affect public opinion on the war effort, second because the chaos in aircraft production was an issue for the home front economy and the civilians who organized it. For the army and navy, on the other hand, aircraft were overwhelmingly regarded as an auxiliary extension of naval and military power. By the end of 1916 both the RFC and the RNAS were still small branches of their respective services, bearing little comparison with the size or significance of other specialized services such as the Royal Artillery, or the cavalry, or the fleet's gunnery branch. The RFC had 5,982 officers and

51,945 other ranks; the RNAS comprised 2,764 officers and 26,129 supporting personnel.[43] In 1917 both forces were to grow to be much larger, but, although some senior airmen on both sides of the service divide had begun to think that a separate unified force might be desirable, the RAF was not yet visible on the horizon.

2
Battles in the Sky, Battles in Whitehall

For the essential truth on which the Flying Service must be
founded is that only aviators understand aviation. The great gain
of a separately organized Air Service would be its emancipation
from the control of the Admiralty and the War Office, who are
very apt to think they know more than they do.

Hugh Cecil MP, August 1917[1]

On 1 March 1917, German Gotha G.V bombers, flying from air
bases in German-occupied Belgium, dropped nine high-
explosive bombs on the Kent coastal town of Broadstairs,
three of them falling in the sea. On 5 April the Kent coast was
hit again: four bombs fell on Broadstairs this time, one on
Ramsgate and three near Sandwich. No one was killed. These
probing raids against easy-to-reach coastal targets signalled
the onset of a German bombing campaign by aeroplane rather
than by airship. Insignificant as the first raids proved to be, the
War Office worried about the implications of operations that
'exhibit entirely new possibilities in aerial warfare'.[2] More than
any other factor, it was the German decision to begin this
small-scale bomber offensive that triggered the British government's move to form an independent air service.

The decision by the German High Command to switch

from airship to aeroplane bombing coincided with the authorization in February 1917 of unrestricted submarine warfare against Allied shipping. Both were gambles in a year when the German war effort was stretched taut, and military leaders searched for less-orthodox strategies in order to put pressure on the British government and public to withdraw from the war. The gamble rested on the hope that even with a modest number of aircraft – there were just twenty-three Gotha bombers at the start of 1917 – a crisis of morale might be triggered among the war-weary British population. The same calculation had persuaded German leaders to allow Lenin and his revolutionary entourage to travel in a sealed train across Germany to Russia following the overthrow of the Tsarist regime in February 1917, in the hope that revolutionary crisis would undermine the Russian war effort too. But by the time the first major bombing raid was launched in daylight on 25 May, with all twenty-three Gothas attacking targets on the Kent coast, the United States had declared war on Germany, making it even less probable that bombing seaside towns would quickly eliminate British belligerency. The raid on 25 May caused severe damage and killed ninety-two people. Although RFC and RNAS aeroplanes were sent up to intercept, the Gothas flew too high and none was hit. The next raid, by twenty-two aircraft, struck the Thames Estuary on 5 June. Finally, on 13 June fourteen bombers reached London in mid- morning, where they dropped their load in a broad swathe across the central and eastern areas of the city, out of range of anti-aircraft guns and enemy aircraft. One bomb hit a school in Poplar and exploded in an infant class, killing all the small children inside. It was the deadliest raid of the war, unexpected and without warning. A total of 145 people were killed, 382 injured, most of them in a handful of East End boroughs, but nothing matched the horror expressed across the capital at the slaughter of the eighteen infants in Poplar. Their funeral a week later sparked a deep emotional response and fuelled an outburst of popular anti-German sentiment and calls for reprisals in kind.[3] Anger was directed equally at the military authorities for the complete failure of the air defence system and at the government for maintaining their refusal to issue warnings of oncoming raids. The Home Secretary announced in the House of Commons on 28 June that it was still considered impracticable to issue adequate warnings, but the result was to increase public fear that the raids would only get worse.

The raids in fact developed very slowly as aircraft were repaired or new ones introduced, and the right meteorological conditions were essential. Not until 7 July 1917 was London attacked again, but this raid has generally been taken as the point at which the government, alarmed by the growing public protest, began a search for a solution that ended with the creation of an air ministry and the RAF. There is no doubt that the second major raid on London did finally prompt the government to react to the public's uneasy anger at the supine response to this and earlier raids. The Home Secretary at last agreed that warnings could be issued, signalled by 'sound rockets' or 'sound bombs' fired from police and fire stations or by policemen with whistles and rattles. On 16 July the Local Government Board announced that welfare aid and compensation would be paid to surviving victims of the raids.[4] Although the raid inflicted fewer casualties than the one in June (fifty-three dead and 182 injured), once again the failure of the guns or defending aircraft to inhibit the raiders exacerbated the sense of outrage in the capital. Rioting and looting were directed at any premises that looked alien. The press called for tough reprisals against the German civil population. On 10 July Parliament met in special session to discuss the raids, and the following day Lloyd George established a small committee to investigate the whole air situation, consisting of himself and the South African Lt.-General Jan Smuts, who had come to Britain as an invited member of the Imperial War Cabinet.[5] The Prime Minister's Committee on Air Organisation and Home Defence Against Air Raids was further reduced to a one-man show once it became clear that Lloyd George intended to play only a passive role. It was Lloyd George's intention to ask the MP Hugh Cecil to join the committee, but Smuts persuaded him that all that was needed was a secretary, and he proposed the Conservative MP Leo Amery. For expert advice Smuts relied chiefly on the Director General of Military Aeronautics, David Henderson.[6]

Smuts has often been regarded as an odd choice for an assignment that raised significant political and military issues for Britain's continued war effort. He arrived in Britain from South Africa in April after two years in command of British Empire forces in East Africa. Although he was a former enemy in the South African War of 1899–1902, he was a distinguished political and military figure who had played an important part in healing the rift between Dutch and British colonists when South Africa became a unitary state in 1910. He had a reputation as something of a military intellectual. He arrived in Britain at a point of mounting pessimism among Britain's political and military leadership about the outcome of the war and the social costs it imposed on the population.[7] For Lloyd George, Smuts seems to have been a respected outsider, whose advice would be fresher and less prejudiced than that of his military leaders and political colleagues, but he turned down the prime minister's offer to take up command in the Middle

East on the ground that he did not want to run an essentially defensive campaign, and as a result he was present in London when the first bombs fell.[8]

He was interested in air power because, like other air enthusiasts, he believed that the air effort properly directed might have 'decisive importance' for the outcome of the war. On 5 June he met Winston Churchill, who had been out of office since the Dardanelles disaster. He tried, almost certainly at Lloyd George's instigation, to persuade Churchill that, if he were to be offered the choice of running the Ministry of Munitions or a proposed Air Ministry, he should accept the latter, where his 'constructive ability and initiative' would prove more useful. Smuts reported to Lloyd George that Churchill would take the offer only if he were given real scope to develop a new 'Air Service' and control over appointments.[9] Lloyd George, after much hesitation given the opposition of many of his coalition partners, finally did offer Churchill the choice of Munitions or Air, without informing Lord Cowdray, who already held ministerial rank as President of the Air Board. 'I said at once,' Churchill later wrote, 'that I preferred Munitions.'[10] The appointment was announced on 18 July, and for the moment the creation of an air ministry was postponed. It is evident that Smuts was already involved in political discussions about changes to the organization of British air power even before the raids in June and July, which makes his appointment to run the new air committee less anomalous. Two days after his meeting with Churchill, Smuts watched the first major Gotha raid from the roof of the Savoy Hotel in the Strand, where he was staying. He later toured the bombed areas.[11]

Smuts produced for the War Cabinet two reports, not one, as is often suggested. The first was circulated on 19 July 1917 and concerned the question of more effective defence for London. The Army Commander-in-Chief of Home Forces, Field Marshal John French, had already written to Henderson following the 7 July raid to express the army's disappointment at the failure of guns and aircraft to obstruct the attack; the Army Council recommended a single centralized air defence system, bringing together observation, communication, anti-aircraft artillery and aeroplanes under one commander.[12] This view was almost certainly passed on by Henderson to Smuts, whose first report also recommended to the War Cabinet a unitary defensive system for London. A month later the London Air Defence Area was established under the command of Brigadier-General Edward Ashmore, a career artilleryman who learned to fly in 1912 and was briefly commander of an RFC wing under Trenchard.[13] The Second Report was presented on 17 August 1917, and it is this document that is usually referred to as the 'Smuts Report'. The conclusions clearly owed something to views that Smuts already had about the future possibilities of air power, but the recommendations that British air policy and air operations would best be handled by an air ministry, an air staff and a unified air service were arrived at only after Smuts had listened to and accepted the arguments of others.[14] Henderson was a key contributor. On 19 July he drafted a lengthy memorandum on the 'Organisation of the Air Service' for the committee, which laid out the long history of friction between the RFC and the RNAS and the limitations imposed on the second Air Board by the determination of the army and navy to keep air policy in their separate hands. Henderson concluded that the only way to overcome an illogical situation was the formation of 'a complete department and a complete united service dealing with all operations in the air', a recommendation that formed the hub of the later report. Henderson ended with a warning that proved only too prescient: there would be 'the most violent controversies over the petty details'.[15]

Of the two major recommendations, the creation of an air ministry with a consultative board, equivalent to the Admiralty and the War Office, was the least contentious. The idea of a separate air ministry had circulated among politicians since it was first raised in the House of Lords by the air enthusiast Lord Montagu of Beaulieu in March 1916, where his motion in favour was defeated.[16] Even among those who supported the idea, including the President of the First Air Board, Lord Curzon, and Lord Cowdray, President of the Second Board, the view prevailed that the creation of a new ministry at the height of the war effort might prove too disruptive. But in July 1917, Cowdray wrote at length to Smuts to explain that his Board had simply been unable to establish any control over policy and to recommend that an air ministry with its own war staff should after all be set up at once.[17] Churchill, now in overall charge of aeronautical supply as Minister of Munitions, discussed the whole issue with Smuts and Cowdray in early August and endorsed the idea of a new War Staff for a strengthened Air Board or ministry, a view that he passed on to Lloyd George two weeks before the Second Report.[18] What both meant by a 'war staff' or what responsibilities it might have were unclear, but the army and navy leadership assumed that an air ministry would act simply as a 'trainer and provider' of air crew and equipment rather than direct operations, while the army and navy would retain absolute control over selecting and utilizing the naval and military air forces assigned to them. The War Office accepted the proposal for an air ministry only on the proviso that the army would still decide what air supplies it needed and should be 'free to use them in their own way without any interference from the Air Ministry'.[19]

The more radical proposal in the Second Report was the creation of a single unified 'Air Service' run by an Air Staff. Here Smuts relied almost entirely on Henderson's advice, since neither Cowdray nor Churchill, otherwise staunch supporters of the idea of a new ministry and staff, argued for the creation of an entirely new service, to be created under the extreme conditions of a war that Britain might still lose. The argument for a separate air service rested in the end very little on the importance of providing more effective air defence, even if that was what Lloyd George had expected. Instead, the issue of a unified service rested on the contention, strongly supported by Smuts, that aircraft technology had now reached the point where it was possible to inflict long-range 'independent' damage on the German home front. The report concluded with the well-known speculation that 'continuous and intense pressure against the chief industrial centres of the enemy as well as on his lines of communications may form the determining factor in bringing about peace'. Smuts also endorsed bombing in the Middle East theatre. He hoped that Allied air superiority would enable air forces to cut Turkey's fragile communications network and finally 'wrest victory and peace' from the dangerous stalemate that currently existed. For Smuts and his advisers, as for the German leadership, air power seemed to offer a way out of the strategic dead end both countries had arrived at in 1917.[20]

Supporters for the idea of a long-range bombing campaign could be found in both the navy and the army, although the military and naval leadership assumed that long-range operations would be designed to help surface forces achieve their goals more effectively, rather than usher in a new age of

independent air power. Arguments in favour of bombing multiplied in the autumn of 1917, not least because it would at the
same time assuage public demands for retaliation against German raids and dampen down social protest. In the discussions
before the Second Report was published, it was widely
assumed that there would be an aircraft surplus the following
year, thanks to the effort of Sir William Weir, the Scottish engineering industrialist who had been recruited in January 1917
to run the aeronautics branch of the Ministry of Munitions.[21]
The 'Surplus Air Fleet', as it came to be called, was something
of a phantom, since the army and navy would happily have
taken all the aircraft available, rather than see a fraction of
them siphoned off for independent operations. Weir did succeed during the course of 1917 in more than doubling the
output of finished aircraft – 14,168 against 6,099 in 1916.[22] This
was done by cutting back the very large number of different aircraft models in production, from fifty-five in spring 1917 to
thirty a year later. Aircraft firms were compelled to shift from
the haphazard and small-scale pattern of production to more
efficient manufacturing units, each one monitored by a Production Officer to ensure prompt delivery and good practice. For
1918 Weir promised to deliver more than 11,000 aircraft between
March and June, from which the 'Surplus Air Fleet' could be
supplied alongside the demands of the army and navy.[23]

The plans for bombing Germany transformed the way
modern warfare was conceived. They made explicit the idea
that the civilian home front was ineluctably linked with the
overall national war effort and could legitimately be regarded
as an object for attack. Military and industrial targets supplying the means to wage war were a priority, but from the outset
the campaign against domestic civilian targets was also expected to have a demoralizing effect on the enemy workforce,

although the result in London had been to make the population vengeful and angry rather than despondent. The effect, it was hoped, would be to reduce war output through interruptions caused by alarms and raids and a consequent increase in absenteeism, as German bombing had achieved, if only briefly, during 1916 and 1917.[24] Like Smuts, those who pressed for independent operations saw bombing as perhaps decisive for the outcome of the war. Rear-Admiral Mark Kerr, one of the navy's foremost advocates of bombing, warned the Air Board that 'the country who first strikes with its big bombing squadrons of hundreds of machines at the enemy's vital spots, will win the war.'[25] Victory, wrote Kerr in a separate note, was now about interrupting or destroying the supplies and communications of the enemy, not about defeat in the field. In these early arguments about the independent use of aircraft lay the roots of what soon came to be called 'total war', a struggle between entire societies, soldiers and civilians alike. Air power exercised independently meant waging war, as the Liberal MP Sir Henry Norman put it, 'upon new strategic principles'.[26]

The Second Report produced by Smuts was acted upon almost at once. On 24 August, in Lloyd George's absence, a meeting of the War Cabinet was called to reach a decision on whether or not to accept it. The minutes show strong support for the creation of an air ministry, but more guarded judgements about the creation of a unified air service. Churchill was strongly supportive, not least because he hoped that American entry into the war would mean additional aircraft for the 'Surplus Air Fleet' and United States participation in the air war. Strongly opposed was the First Lord of the Admiralty, Eric Geddes, who on the advice of the Admiralty Board rejected both a ministry and a united air force on the grounds that the air war at sea was fundamentally different from the air support given to the British armies. The Chief of the Imperial General Staff, Sir William Robertson, wanted the War Office to retain the right to determine its own aerial requirements, but his proposed amendment along those lines was rejected. Both army and navy were overruled. The Cabinet voted to accept the report; a new committee was to be set up, again under Smuts, to arrange the coordination and amalgamation of the RNAS and the RFC, together with the necessary legislation.[27]

There is little record of Lloyd George's own motives in initiating the two reports, though they were almost certainly expedient. It seems likely that he thought the change might be no more than a wartime improvisation that would not need to survive the end of the war. His priorities were short-term and political: first, he wanted to be seen by the public to be responding to popular anxiety about the air war, and to be exploring new strategic avenues away from the stalemate in the trenches, currently exposed in the brutal and ineffective offensive at Passchendaele; second, the decision to take back political control of the air services under an air ministry run by civilians was a further episode in the contest between military and civilian direction of the war effort, which Lloyd George wanted to see resolved in favour of the politicians. For both of these reasons, the creation of the Air Ministry and the RAF must be understood as a direct product of political calculation, not of military insistence.

Smuts now found himself as the busy chair of four further committees: an Air Raids Committee for issues of civil defence, an Air Reorganisation Committee for drawing up the necessary legislation and organizational structures for the combined air service, the Air Policy Committee for addressing the question of what aircraft were needed and for which roles, and finally on 8 October 1917 a War Priorities Committee to decide where resources should best be allocated for strategic impact, which Smuts, with Weir's support, used as a platform to argue the case for shifting resources to the new air arm.[28] Nevertheless, the Cabinet decision did not create overnight either a ministry or a new air force. The flurry of activity masked a growing confusion about how a new ministry should be set up and with what responsibilities, and over the extent to which the new unitary air service would or would not still be subject to the navy and army that they served. Throughout the year, both the navy and the army air services had grown in size and competence in their roles as auxiliary to surface forces. The RFC won back air superiority over the British section of the front in France during the course of 1917; the RNAS had improved aircraft and tactics for the anti-submarine campaign, which was a strategic priority for 1917. Neither service wanted a situation where these improvements in air support might be compromised.

Of the two branches, the navy was most hostile to the decision for amalgamation, though not uniformly so. Admiral David Beatty, Commander-in-Chief of the Grand Fleet, told Geddes before the Cabinet meeting that the Royal Navy was 'too parochial' in its views and that he broadly favoured the new ministry and the new air force. But Beatty also assumed that where air and fleet operated together, the air service must always be 'an adjunct and servant' of the navy, controlled and commanded by the naval staff.[29] The First Sea Lord, Admiral John Jellicoe, was adamantly opposed to what he viewed as a 'mistaken organisation', in which nothing would be gained and a great deal lost once an air staff had begun to redirect aircraft supplies away from the army and navy to meet their own independent needs.[30] The detailed and lengthy memoranda generated by the Admiralty response to the Smuts report highlighted the navy's concern that the specialized and specific functions in air-sea warfare could only be managed by naval personnel who understood the training and operational requirements of a naval air force. This was not an unreasonable position, given that the RNAS did require a different kind of training for long oversea flights, difficult landings on the first improvised seaplane and aircraft carriers, and a high level of navigational skill. A few days before the Second Report was submitted, the captain of HMS *Campania*, one of the first converted aircraft carriers, complained to the Admiralty that the pilots supplied by the joint training scheme were hopelessly unprepared for naval work. Most had never flown with a passenger and found it difficult to accommodate the observer's needs; most had little familiarity with the use of a compass; few actually knew how to start their engine, or how to throttle down and stop it.[31] The need for specialized and prolonged training remained a central argument for the Royal Navy throughout its long postwar efforts to kill off RAF control of their aircraft.

The attitude of the army to the new flying service was governed by rather different concerns. By 1917, offensive counter-force operations and ground support for troops had assumed much greater significance. Operational summaries for the RFC in 1917 show aircraft engaged in reconnaissance, aerial photography, artillery spotting and extensive bombing of enemy air bases and rail communications.[32] The RFC was constantly in combat, where for the RNAS combat at sea was a rarity. RNAS squadrons stationed on the French Channel coast flew regularly in support of army operations, where they acted like RFC squadrons. In May 1917 the RNAS aircraft assembled in No. 3 Wing for bombing targets in Germany were disbanded and sent to assist the land battle.[33] The BEF leadership wanted to maintain the momentum of operational success in the air and, like the navy, wanted to control air units attached to the army and to be able to determine how many aircraft were needed. But in contrast to the RNAS, the RFC was larger and better endowed by 1917 with aircraft and air crew and an extensive logistics system. Amalgamation might well mean, as the navy feared, that naval aviation would become a junior partner. Army attitudes were as a result ambivalent in all except one significant case. Douglas Haig, the Commander-in-Chief of the BEF, was an enthusiastic champion of the RFC and firmly in favour of developing a greater long-range bombing capability, and he did not actively oppose the conclusions in the Second Report. Even with a separate air force, Haig assumed that he would still be able to dictate what the army wanted the air force to do, an argument that the Chief of the Imperial General Staff had tried to get the Cabinet to accept in August.[34] The idea that air power might end the war on its own, however, Haig dismissed as 'mere assertion unsupported by facts'.[35]

The sternest opponent of the proposal for a separate air force was Hugh Trenchard. In this there is a profound irony, because two years later Trenchard was instrumental in ensuring that the RAF retain its independence from the army and navy, and subsequently became the champion of the air force against all efforts to break it up. In 1917, however, Trenchard saw the situation differently. By the autumn he had succeeded in turning the RFC into a force capable of retaining air superiority, armed with a clutch of improved aircraft and poised, if the promised supply of 'surplus' equipment materialized, to conduct long-range bombing operations in order to weaken German resistance at the front. His priority was to assist the army in achieving a victory on land under his command, and to resist reforms that threatened to undermine that aim. In late August he sent a detailed memorandum to Robertson setting out 'reasons against creating a separate Air Service'. His principal concern was the effect on military efficiency brought about by the creation of a third competitive service after years of strife with the RNAS. Worse still was the introduction of political control of aviation:

> An Air Ministry with a civilian head and uncontrolled by any outside Naval and Military opinion, exposed as it would inevitably be to popular and fractional clamour, would be very liable to lose its sense of proportion and be drawn towards the spectacular, such as bombing reprisals and home defence, at the expense of providing the essential means of co-operation with our Naval and Military Forces.[36]

In another report a few weeks later, Trenchard returned to the theme that union would not only undermine the principle that the navy and army should necessarily control their own auxiliary air force, but would inevitably lead to 'friction and serious danger of loss of efficiency'.[37] Nor could Trenchard understand why no senior RFC officer had been invited to attend Smuts' committee on the Air Service. He deplored the probability that the new service would be imposed on him willy-nilly: 'I do not quite understand why these changes are continually going on in the Air Service when there is nothing wrong with the Service except the quantity of material supplied.'[38] When his chief-of-staff, John Salmond, was appointed to replace Henderson in October as Director General of Military Aeronautics, Trenchard reminded him that his priority was to serve the needs of the military: 'Remember that we are part of the Army and are not trying to run a separate show at their expense.'[39]

It is unlikely that Trenchard could have prevented the creation of the new air service, much though he might have wished it, because he neither wanted nor sought political support in London for his views, nor an alliance with naval critics. The committees set up under Smuts worked away to resolve the many practical and administrative issues involved in amalgamation. In September Smuts established an Air Council which would replace the Air Board once the Air Ministry and an air service had been approved by Parliament, but progress was slow.[40] The factor that ended any uncertainty in the minds of the politicians about the wisdom of the decision taken in August was supplied once again by the German enemy, when the Gotha bombers, accompanied now by the new four-engine Zeppelin-Staaken R. VI aircraft, whose huge size earned it the nickname 'Giant', returned in late September to recommence the campaign. The raids began on 24 September and continued with one interruption until 1 October, but the bombers came this time at night rather than during the day. What came to be called the 'Harvest Moon Raids' had a much greater impact than the two major raids in June and July because they continued night after night, with the bombs scattered quite indiscriminately, just as they had been in the earlier Zeppelin raids. The raids were nevertheless modest in scale. Few of the attacking aircraft, as in June and July, actually reached London. During the first raid, on 24 September, only three aircraft bombed the capital: one dropped three 50 kilo bombs and six incendiaries, two more between them dropped ten 50 kilo bombs and eleven incendiaries, one of which destroyed a gallery in the Royal Academy's Burlington House. The remaining raids were small-scale and random. Most incendiaries were observed to fall harmlessly on roadways, backyards and open spaces. Casualties as a result were remarkably low, given the unpredictable nature of the raiding, with forty-seven deaths and injury to a further 226 (though six deaths and sixty-seven injuries were caused by the debris from anti-aircraft shells).[41] The impact on public morale was nevertheless as disconcerting as it had been in the summer.[42]

Rumours had circulated for some time that the German air forces were planning an obliterating attack on the capital, a fantasy from which the military were not immune. In October 1917 Rear-Admiral Kerr, relying on intelligence supplied by Britain's Italian ally, warned the Air Board that the Germans were planning a knockout blow with 4,000 bomber aircraft (more like forty, Trenchard scoffed, who was much closer to the truth).[43] The popular view was pessimistic. After the first raid, thousands of Londoners searched every night for shelter in tunnels or basements, or camped out in Richmond Park and other open spaces. They also began to congregate in stations on the London Underground – an estimated 120,000 on the second night of raiding. On two nights when there proved to be no raids, queues had already formed by 5.30 in the evening. The Home Office assumed that many were 'the poorer type of aliens' from London's East End. 'They not only went there in entire families,' claimed a later report, 'diminutive girls or boys carrying the latest baby, but they took with them supplies of provisions, pillows and bedding . . . together with their cat or their dog, their parrot or their pet canary'.[44] By the end of the raids, an estimated 300,000 clustered into the stations each night. The effect on production was temporary but severe. At one of the country's major clothing companies in the East End, workers failed to turn up during the day, and output sank from 40,000 suits to 5,000. The managing director uncharitably attributed the crisis to the fact that 90 per cent of his employees were women, 'easily frightened and liable to panic', and the other ten per cent Jewish aliens 'who were even more liable to panic than the women', though the fears were more than justified because the factories were almost entirely constructed of glass to allow more light and had no available shelters. Even at the Woolwich arsenal, better prepared for disruption, more than 70 per cent of the workforce was absent during the raids, cutting output to a fraction.[45]

This time the War Cabinet was more alarmed by the public response. On 1 October Trenchard was summoned back from France to attend a meeting to discuss the retaliatory bombing of Germany. He was asked to set up a unit of bombers at Ochey, near Nancy in eastern France, to bomb German industrial targets in the Saar region. On 2 October Henderson wrote to Haig informing him that, in response to the bombing of London, the War Cabinet insisted on inaugurating the long-range bombing of Germany at the earliest moment possible. With some reluctance, since neither the bases nor the aircraft were yet in place, Trenchard and Haig complied, though Trenchard even on this issue could not refrain from voicing his objections: 'the weather may break, the moon is going, and we are being rushed into doing it with short range machines which will not have the desired effect on PRUSSIAN towns.'[46] On 16–17 October a force of twenty-two aircraft in two raids dropped sixteen bombs on factories in and around Saarbrücken. The crews claimed that at least eight bombs had fallen on the Burbach ironworks, causing fire damage, but effective intelligence on the results was almost non-existent.[47] The tiny force was organized as the 41st Wing (later 8th Brigade) and placed under the command of Lt.-Colonel Cyril Newall, the future RAF chief-of-staff at the start of the Second

World War. As Trenchard had predicted, its achievements were negligible. The standard light bombers, the De Havilland DH4 and the Farman Experimental F.E.2B, with its open-sided fuselage, could carry little more than 250 pounds of bombs.[48] To fly in difficult winter weather, principally by night, against distant targets, was a considerable challenge; 'no great accuracy,' concluded a GHQ report on the campaign, 'can be expected . . .'[49] The 41st Wing had only three squadrons, one of them from the RNAS, until the formation of the RAF in April 1918. Over the period from October 1917 to June 1918, the force dropped just 129 tons of bombs (fifty-four tons by day, seventy-five by night), and suffered accumulating losses of 13 per cent of the aircraft employed. Intelligence surveys of the damage concluded that material effects on enemy rail traffic 'cannot be said to have been very great', nor the damage to the Saarland steel industry and the bombed chemical works ('material damage has been small').[50] The raids were nevertheless reported in the British press as evidence that the RFC was now retaliating in kind to the German bombs.

The September raids also ended any hesitation about the merits of establishing a new air force and a new ministry. The necessary legislation was drafted and submitted to Parliament, where it was debated on 12 November. 'It is the spirit and object of this Bill,' the Attorney-General, F. E. Smith, told the Commons, 'that the Air Service shall be recognized as an entirely distinguishable Service . . . all the conditions of warfare have been revolutionized by the calling into existence of a new arm.'[51] The Air Force (Constitution) Act was passed into law on 29 November 1917. The preamble stated that 'It shall be lawful for His Majesty [George V] to raise and maintain a force, to be called the Air Force . . .' but the personnel were in the first instance to be recruited for a period of no more than four years, a decision that was to hamper postwar efforts to maintain the RAF as a separate service. The Act empowered the creation of an Air Council presided over by the new Secretary of State for Air, both to be in place by January 1918, when the Second Air Board would relinquish all its functions and personnel to the new ministry.[52]

There remained the politically awkward issue of who would become the first Air Minister. After Churchill's refusal, the natural choice was the current president of the Air Board, Lord Cowdray, who had worked successfully to turn the Board's organization into a semi-ministry. For reasons which remain unclear, Lloyd George decided to sound out Lord Northcliffe, the press baron, as a possible candidate. Northcliffe was an odd choice, given the persistent hostility to the government displayed in his newspapers, and it may be that Lloyd George was less interested in his qualifications for running an air ministry than in securing Northcliffe's collaboration. This proved a profound misjudgement. On 16 November 1917 Northcliffe took the tactless path of publishing a letter in *The Times* publicly declining the prime minister's 'repeated invitation' to take charge of the new department. 'I can do better work,' he continued, 'if I maintain my independence and am not gagged by a loyalty that I do not feel towards the whole of your Administration.'[53] Cowdray learned only by the letter in *The Times* that he was to be replaced; he resigned the same day, making sure his resignation letter was published in the same paper. Lloyd George apologized on behalf of the War Cabinet, but the damage was done and Cowdray left public life (though he later endowed the RAF Club in London's Piccadilly with £100,000). It was not to be the only time that political and personal controversy surrounded the new offices created by the legislation.

Lloyd George then offered the post to Northcliffe's brother, Harold Harmsworth, Lord Rothermere, owner of Associated Newspapers and the successful proprietor of the *Daily Mirror* and the *Sunday Pictorial*. Northcliffe had shown a keen interest in aviation, but Rothermere's qualifications for the job were minimal. He had helped to run the army clothing department in 1916–17, a role in which he was regarded as a success. Lord Beaverbrook, his fellow press baron, later suggested that Rothermere accepted the offer as a token of political appeasement after Northcliffe's brusque rejection, but his motives still remain unclear.[54] His appointment was confirmed following the formal announcement of Cowdray's resignation on 26 November. Lloyd George may once again have hoped that recruiting one of the Harmsworth brothers might stifle press criticism, but Rothermere had little political experience and only a layman's grasp of the way air power had developed over the course of the war. His newspapers were used to agitate for heavy retaliatory raids on Germany, beyond any operational possibility.[55]

The obvious choice for the new post of Chief of the Air Staff was Trenchard, but his opposition to a new air service and his complete lack of experience in the world of politics and administration made him a difficult choice. When the post of Director General of Military Aeronautics had become vacant following Henderson's retirement through ill-health, Trenchard rejected the idea that he should replace him: 'I am no good in an office, and I am afraid that I would not carry through the work at home with all the different departments as well as other men would.'[56] Rothermere and Northcliffe invited Trenchard to a meeting at the Ritz Hotel in central London on 16 December 1917, and after hours of often bitter argument, he accepted the post against all his better instincts. His parting shot as he left the room at 3.00 in the morning was to remind his hosts that 'I am neither a good writer nor a good talker.'[57] He later claimed that he had accepted the post only to forestall a newspaper campaign against Haig's conduct of the war, a man for whom he had unreserved respect. 'I thought by doing this,' he wrote, 'I might be able to help Haig and victory.'[58] But it is clear that he also believed a senior airman was needed to secure the future interests of the air services in the face of political intervention and that no one else had the necessary rank or experience to be able to do so. Trenchard and Haig both hoped that he would be allowed to retain command of the RFC as well as his role as chief-of-staff. Salmond was sent back to France to act as Trenchard's deputy, but on the eve of his new appointment Trenchard still saw himself as commander of the RFC. The War Cabinet rejected the idea, despite Haig's insistence, correctly as it turned out, that the following four months might be the 'most critical of the whole war'.[59] On 18 January Trenchard was confirmed as the new Chief of the Air Staff, with Rear-Admiral Mark Kerr as his deputy. John Salmond became the new commander of the RFC.

The task facing Rothermere and the new Air Council and Air Staff was a formidable one. No other fighting power established an independent air force during the war. The new service rested heavily on established practices and personnel from both the RNAS and the RFC, both of whose commanders would be on the new Air Council. This did not prevent the Admiralty from continuing its efforts to torpedo the new organization by insisting on retaining as much control as it could over the use of naval aircraft and the command and discipline of naval air personnel. The creation of a single service, as Geddes wrote some months later, was only accepted 'against [the Admiralty's] own views and under protest'.[60] In January the new Air Ministry complained to the Admiralty that the navy's request to keep the right to command and discipline all airmen engaged on operations with the fleet would make the ministry 'a controlling body . . . with nothing to control'.[61] Efforts at compromise still left the Admiralty on the eve of the transfer to the new air service in command of all airmen engaged in operations, and subject to naval discipline, while a newly created Admiral Commanding Aircraft would run the air service of the Grand Fleet with advice from an Air Force officer – in effect creating a naval service within the air service. The Air Council failed to modify the Admiralty claims, and in consequence the tension between the navy's view of the new air force and the claims of the Air Ministry remained unresolved even after its official formation.[62]

The Air Council nevertheless worked on the assumption that a unitary air service was a possibility, even if it would take months to work out the necessary details on discipline, pay, ranks, pensions and administration. As David Henderson had observed the year before, the devil was in the details. The first problem was to try to accommodate the new Ministry. Rothermere inherited the Hotel Cecil on the Strand in central London, where the Air Board had been housed. The requisitioned hotel gave the whole enterprise a more temporary character than it needed. Rothermere later complained that the hotel was a model of inefficiency, with a myriad of small bedrooms on endless corridors, with the result that 'supervision is difficult', and much unnecessary communication was needed between offices that were physically too far apart.[63] To add to the problems, Weir, appointed as the Ministry of Munitions representative on the Air Council, requisitioned the upper floors of the nearby Savoy Hotel (leaving the restaurant still functioning) but with hundreds of administrative officials and technical officers spread across the hotel's bedroom accommodation.[64] The most pressing issue facing the Council was to decide when the new air service should come into operation, but the unpredictable nature of the many obstacles to establishing a new service in wartime made it difficult to be precise. As late as early March the Council was still debating when it might happen, though the beginning of April was the preferred date. Trenchard warned that acting too hastily 'might cause dislocation on the Fronts', which he was always anxious to avoid. Perhaps aware of the drawback to April Fools' Day as the choice, Godfrey Paine, one of the RNAS representatives, suggested midnight on 31 March, if the Treasury agreed that this was the official start of the new financial year. Not until 8 March did the Council finally confirm that 1 April would be the date when the new air service would begin.[65]

There was again uncertainty about what the force should be called. Most of those involved talked and wrote about an 'Air Service'. The legislation for the first time defined it as an 'Air Force', a term that had been used rarely. But because the Act had specified 'His Majesty's Air Force' there was no possibility of adding 'Royal' without the king's warrant. The Air Council wondered whether, like the Royal Navy, where the 'Royal' had been accepted by usage rather than royal approval, the Air Force could simply add the extra adjective. Legal advice was sought to see whether or how the King might authorize the use of 'Royal', or to learn if it could be done informally without the King's explicit consent.[66] The title clearly mattered given the atmosphere of insecurity surrounding the new service, but the issue assumed an exaggerated importance. On 19 February the Council was informed that the King had happily consented to the title 'Royal Air Force', the name it has borne ever since.[67] A royal warrant was prepared for the new service, and on 22 March the King approved an Order in Council uniting the two air services and authorizing the transfer of personnel from the navy and army for a period not exceeding four years.[68] After a complex gestation, the Royal Air Force was to be born ten days later, on 1 April 1918.

The intervening days saw the new force plunged into drama. On 19 March Trenchard had unexpectedly tendered his resignation after just two months in his new office. He told Rothermere the day before that he could not tolerate the fact that air force matters, which he regarded as properly the concern of the chief-of-staff, were discussed or decided on without his advice or his presence. He cited several examples to illustrate that, in his view, 'the situation created is an impossible one'. Although Rothermere tried to assure him that he had great confidence in his chief-of-staff, a view at odds with the awkwardly hostile relationship evident between the two men, Trenchard asked to be relieved of his position.[69] Rothermere invited him to wait for formal acceptance of his resignation until after the founding of the RAF on 1 April to avoid public concern, and Trenchard reluctantly agreed. The explicit reasons for his decision to resign lay in his frustration at Rothermere's practices as a minister. In January, he complained to Haig that Rothermere was 'quite ignorant of the needs or working of the Air Service'; Haig noted in his diary Trenchard's judgement that 'the Air Service cannot survive as an independent Ministry.'[70] Weeks before sending his resignation letter, he had considered abandoning a job he had not wanted. On 10 February he wrote to his replacement as the commander of the RFC, John Salmond, complaining that the ministry he now worked for was 'ridiculous' and 'inefficient' in the way its numerous offices were set up.[71] Three days later, he sent Salmond a second private letter, regretting what he had done, and deploring the decision to create a separate air force:

> I come against snags every day in making this Air Service and the more I think of it the more I think what a ghastly mistake has been made in trying to make an Air Service during this war. It is almost an impossibility to run . . . I miss very much the small self-contained Staff in France . . . It is impossible for me to impress myself on them as a Dictator. I hope to do this in six or eight months' time . . . I am still on the brink of stopping, but if I do I do not know whether I shall be doing right to the Flying Corps.[72]

Rothermere's treatment of Trenchard might well have been the straw that broke the camel's back, but Trenchard had been right the year before when he said 'I am no good in an office', and the first few weeks in the Hotel Cecil had confirmed his judgement. He was a natural commander, used to military structures of command. In a ministry, even one devoted to a military service, command was elusive. On the Air Council he was one voice among many, with less influence, so he thought, than the ministerial appointments, and always subject to the veto of the new minister. He was, Rothermere observed after Trenchard announced his resignation, a prime case of 'a square peg in a round hole', though Trenchard could well have returned the compliment.[73]

The commander in Trenchard must have longed to be back in France when, two days after he had sent his resignation letter, the German army launched the last major offensive on the Western Front, the *Kaiserschlacht*, the Kaiser's battle. The British length of the front was pushed back in disarray, and every squadron of the RFC was in action giving ground support to the retreating army, joined by those RNAS squadrons stationed near the coast, uniting the two services in the field through the military crisis. Trenchard was briefly back in his element, communicating with Salmond and the RFC staff without reference to Rothermere or the Air Council.[74] The Council minutes, as a result, give little or no sense of the crisis in France. Nor did the air forces, battling away in French skies, have any hint that Trenchard was about to resign. The creation of the RAF was eclipsed entirely by the desperate efforts to stem the German tide. A separate or independent air force in April 1918 was an irrelevance to the army commanders and RFC staff engaged together in the ground campaign in France and would remain so even when the name was changed.

3

April Fools' Day 1918

Today I find myself a Colonel RAF though I don't
feel particularly exhilarated by the thought.

Richard Peirse, diary, 1 April 1918[1]

There was a great deal of uncertainty on 1 April 1918 about
what the change to a separate air service might entail. It was
not only April Fools' Day but an Easter Monday. The young
RNAS officer, Richard Peirse, later to serve as Commander-in-
Chief of Bomber Command in the early years of the Second
World War, found himself stationed at Dunkirk with the 65th
Wing when the changeover occurred. On Easter Day he dined
with No. 2 Squadron, soon to become the 202nd squadron RAF
following the decision that RNAS squadrons should be re-
numbered by adding 200 to their original designation. The men,
Peirse noted in his diary, 'had a large gathering to celebrate
the departing hours of the RNAS and a general rough-house
ensued after dinner'. Two days later he found himself attacking
'stacks of papers and new RAF procedures and manuals . . .'[2]

There were no fanfares or ceremonies to mark the day
when the RAF was born. The formal changeover was indicated by the simple device of a new rubber stamp. 'Royal Air
Force' in a large rectangular box was affixed to operational

reports over 'Royal Flying Corps'. RNAS reports were also altered on the first day when squadron record books were signed 'Officer Commanding RAF' rather than simply 'Squadron Commander/Commanding Officer'.[3] The Air Council worried in March that the supply of rubber stamps sent to the RFC Middle East would not arrive in time. Making the RAF immediately visible was a detail that evidently mattered, but the changeover made little impact at first. The development of a new service, with its own doctrine, its own ethos, and its own material presence took a great deal longer.

The new force consisted of 25,000 officers and 140,000 men, most of them technicians, mechanics or drivers. Only 8 per cent of the new force actually flew.[4] The RNAS had 5,300 officers and 49,000 men in March 1918, though not all of them joined the RAF; the rest came from the RFC units stationed in Britain, France and Italy, and from the Middle East Brigade, which ran British air forces in East Africa, Egypt, Palestine, Mesopotamia and Salonika. The personnel were all transferred on a temporary arrangement, for a period not exceeding four years, because no decision had been made about the future of a postwar air force. All of those transferred had the right within three months to register their objection and to return to their original army or navy service 'without prejudice', though it is not clear how many did so during the war.[5] The RAF stationed in Britain was divided between five commands, each under an officer with the rank of major-general, each responsible for a number of RAF groups. The commands were based in London, Salisbury, Birmingham, York and Glasgow (the latter also responsible for Ireland); any units attached to the Grand Fleet remained, however, under control of the Royal Navy.[6] Although the new Air Ministry directly owned only one of the sites, the plan in April 1918 was to establish at least thirty permanent bases after the war, with a further sixty-six temporary bases for training purposes, lighter-than-air craft and kite balloons. 'Is this very excessive?' minuted one official, to which the reply came back that 'London will remain the prime object of attack' in any future war, and deserved effective air defence.[7]

These changes made little difference to the air forces engaged in fighting in the war zones. The RNAS units that were not deployed to help combat the German offensive continued anti-submarine patrols and long and exhausting oversea reconnaissance flights against an enemy that, as it would turn out, had no intention of bringing out the German fleet to face the Royal Navy after the indecisive battle of Jutland in 1916. The operational reports of squadrons detailed to fly on long sea patrols show little change across the period when they became RAF units. In contrast to the costly fighting going on in France, former RNAS squadrons were still finding little to do. No. 4 Squadron (No. 204 as an RAF unit) filed regular daily summaries with 'nothing to report'; it saw real action only in October 1918 when it was sent on line patrols in Belgium and France, bombing and machine-gunning the retreating Germans.[8] For other squadrons, the changeover meant flying south to join former RFC units in ground combat, or to assist with the 8th Brigade in its long-distance bombing campaign. The foreboding in the Royal Navy that the RNAS would be swallowed up by the former army air service was not entirely misplaced. The Admiralty complained in May to the Air Ministry that 'our fears as to the desirability of the transfer are being confirmed as time goes on', citing the reduction in naval representation on the Air Council, and the transfer of naval bombing squadrons to army service.[9] In July Beatty complained that naval aircraft and trained pilots for the Grand

Fleet were simply not being produced. Though he had been promised 100 of the new torpedo-carrying Sopwith aircraft by July, there were only three; instead of the thirty-six trained pilots, there was none. Beatty had initially approved the change to the air services, but this time he suspected that the independent Air Ministry was diverting aircraft to other uses and neglecting the essential needs of the navy.[10]

The army on the other hand played a major part in the new RAF, where the majority of officers and other ranks had been former army personnel. Ranks in the new air service were army ranks, which is why Richard Peirse found himself to be a colonel on 1 April, when he had been a Squadron Commander RNAS. In October 1918 the Air Ministry explored the possibility of calling the most senior RAF officer 'General-in-Chief', a title that the King himself then appropriated.[11] Until a new uniform was decided on, airmen wore army khaki. Former naval airmen with the fleet could keep their dark blue uniforms, but there was some confusion over whether those airmen would keep their naval rank, or adopt the new army nomenclature, as the land-based units had done. The army also supplied canteens for the RAF, as well as supplying clothing, quartering and rations for RAF units at home and in the field.[12] Above all, the urgent necessity of coping with the German offensive in the spring of 1918, and the subsequent drive to breach the German defensive 'Hindenburg Line' in the autumn, meant that the main priority of the Air Ministry and the Ministry of Munitions was to keep the army supplied with aircraft and pilots. Losses were exceptionally severe, averaging 670 aircraft a month (one third of the force on the Western Front), so that re-supplying army squadrons soaked up much more of the expanded aircraft programme than had been expected.[13] It was here over the trenches on the Western Front that the RAF effectively began its long career fighting side by side with the army and the anti-aircraft artillery in noisy, dangerous combination. In July 1918 RAF Air Mechanic Thomas Spencer witnessed one spectacular episode of the air war over the base of No. 65 Squadron:

> Last night was one of the worst nights I have seen out here, Jerry came over at about 6,000 ft, the searchlights got him at once & the guns opened out. Twenty batteries banging shells at him at once, the air was full of shells, shrapnel, & the noise deafening to add to the row, he dropped 4 bombs & then loosed the remainder all at once, about 16 of them, you cannot imagine what it was like, the earth shook, the shells bursting & the bombs exploding & threw off dense clouds of black smoke, the noise was terrific . . . so Jerry got away . . . so ended one of the most thrilling airfights I have seen.[14]

By October 1918 the army on the Western Front had eighty-four squadrons in direct support, four on the Italian front, and thirteen in the Middle East Brigade, more than half of all the new RAF units.[15] If the sixty-four squadrons working with the navy in fleet support and anti-submarine patrols are added in, an overwhelming proportion of the separate air force was engaged as before on auxiliary operations for the navy and army.

Such a situation was predictable in the midst of a major war in which aircraft serving naval and military needs were already an established fact. But it placed into question exactly what the RAF had been formed for in the first place. The months following 1 April were spent trying to establish a clearer identity for the new service. The most urgent requirement was to find a settled leadership following Trenchard's decision to resign and Rothermere's own hesitation over whether to continue in an office in which his role was increasingly uncomfortable. The news of Trenchard's decision was published in mid-April after Rothermere had told Trenchard on 10 April that the War Cabinet had approved it. Rothermere's formal letter accepting the resignation was a deliberately harsh indictment of a man he found 'perfectly impossible'.[16] 'I cannot say I do so with any particular reluctance,' he wrote to Trenchard. ' . . . I believe your act in resigning your post as Chief of the Air Staff twelve days before myself and the large staff here were going into action to accomplish the gigantic task of the fusion of the Royal Naval Air Service and the Royal Flying Corps is an unparalleled incident in the public life of this country'.[17] The shock of Trenchard's impending departure had prompted Lloyd George to summon Smuts once again to review the crisis between the minister and the chief-of-staff, but Smuts, who had first-hand experience of Trenchard in action on the Air Policy Committee in 1917, recommended that he should be allowed to go. On the same day that Rothermere accepted the resignation, Smuts wrote to Lloyd George recommending as the best man for the job Frederick Sykes, Trenchard's nemesis.[18] Sykes arrived at the Hotel Cecil to take over; Trenchard cleared his desk and walked silently out of the building to temporary unemployment.

The crisis did not abate with the appointment of Sykes. He accepted the post despite his reluctance to abandon entirely his new role as an adviser at Versailles to the Allied Supreme War Council in favour, as he wrote in his memoirs, of 'the vortex of the Hotel Cecil'. He thought his task 'formidable', not least because the army and navy still saw air power as auxiliary and not as a third service 'with widespread functions of its own'.[19] He was more at home in a ministry than Trenchard, though he too thought that the ministerial officials were too many and their efficiency as a result too low – 'the repository for discarded members of other Ministries and the happy hunting ground of the careerist'.[20] Sykes was able to avoid too much time in the Hotel Cecil because he retained his role at Versailles, dividing his time between the two. But less than a week after his appointment, the vice-president of the Air Council, Lt.-General David Henderson, resigned on the grounds that it was not in the interest of the air service for him to work with someone he had disliked and distrusted since the beginning of the war, citing the 'atmosphere of intrigue and falsehood' that now permeated the ministry as one of his reasons for leaving. He left Rothermere and Smuts with his 'very unfavourable opinion' of the new chief-of-staff.[21]

The resignation of two men widely regarded as the architects of the army air service hinted to the public of a deeper crisis in the newly founded RAF. Some pointed the finger of blame at Lord Rothermere, who had already considered his own resignation on grounds of ill-health and his personal devastation at the death in February of his eldest son from wounds sustained in action. He had told Trenchard as much in their discussions in March. Trenchard later recalled that his first reaction had been 'Thank God', but his second a more cautious 'Is this true? I don't trust you to resign.'[22] Rothermere himself did hesitate over inflicting what would be a third blow to the infant service, but in the end the rumours and criticism circulating over the loss of Trenchard and Henderson pushed him to the final decision, and on 25 April 1918 his resignation was announced. In a letter to Lloyd George, Rothermere admitted he was 'suffering much from ill-health and insomnia' brought on, according to his friend Lord Beaverbrook, by the stress of overwork and trying to master his private grief.[23] Rothermere had not been popular with career airmen. Salmond complained in a letter to his parents in April about the 'arch blighter' in charge of the Ministry. 'His point of view,' Salmond continued, 'is no good for a soldier.'[24]

The third resignation prompted a flurry of speculation about what malaise lay at the heart of the new ministry. Beaverbrook judged that Rothermere 'was not the man to grapple with a political crisis', brought on it seemed by renewed tension between the military and the politicians. Lloyd George suspected that the resignations of Trenchard and Henderson were linked in some way to a broader conspiracy by senior military figures to undermine the government. He speculated that a cabal consisting of Trenchard, Haig, Lord Jellicoe and General William Robertson, recently replaced at the War Office, was orchestrating a showdown with his administration, but there was little or no substance to the charge. The government survived the debate on Rothermere's resignation in both houses. Lloyd George chose as Rothermere's successor a more neutral appointment.[25] On 27 April, Sir William Weir, the director of aeronautical production in the Ministry of Munitions and a member of the Air Council, was offered the post. His condition for acceptance was to be granted a peerage, because he felt ill-at-ease at the prospect of facing the tough debating techniques of the Commons. The King reluctantly agreed to yet further wartime ennoblement and he was created Lord Weir of Eastwood. He was a more rational choice than Rothermere, partly because he had no political experience or familiarity with the intrigues and posturing that had governed the creation and establishment of the ministry, partly because in his role at the Ministry of Munitions he had displayed a clear grasp of the needs of a modern air force and had succeeded in overcoming the prolonged feud between army and navy over production priorities. Weir was also a knowledgeable enthusiast for aviation, rather than an amateur.[26] The appointment of Weir, with Sykes as his chief-of-staff, stabilized the political crisis that surrounded the creation of the RAF and brought to office two men who were committed to making a single air service work.

For those airmen keen to establish a distinctive branch of the armed forces, there had to be clear material differences between the RAF and the other services. The most conspicuous way in which service identity could be established was to have a uniform that set the air force apart. The short period of time in which the new force had to be prepared, and the pressing issues of pay, discipline and administration that the Air Council had had to deal with before April, meant that the creation of a new uniform was still not settled by the time the RAF was inaugurated. A modified version of army uniform was introduced first, but it proved unpopular, undermining, according to the Air Council minutes, the new 'esprit de corps' that the air force needed. The new commander of RAF North-West reported 'evil effects' on the men who had to wear what was essentially still army dress.[27] A light blue uniform with much gold braid was the preferred option, and was finally approved in late May, and given royal sanction on 21 June, but there was a shortage of the necessary blue cloth. This, too, was not popular with the force. It was the kind of uniform, recalled John Slessor, 'which brought irresistibly to mind a vision of the gentleman who stands outside the cinema'. The sky-blue 'Ruritanian' costumes, as another RAF officer later put it, remained at first a rarity.[28] It was agreed that, in the field, RAF personnel could still wear khaki; officers who could not afford to pay for the new blue dress were permitted to continue to wear khaki uniform until it wore out, with the result that the RAF looked a motley force throughout 1918.[29] In the Middle East and India, it was recommended that khaki be worn in the hot season, and the blue uniform when it grew colder. Only by November did it prove possible to supply an adequate number of blue uniforms and to suspend the wearing of khaki by officers, except for overcoats. They were permitted to wear the dark blue naval overcoat or the army khaki coat until October 1919.[30] By this time the negative attitude towards sky blue and gold had had its effect. A darker grey-blue cloth was found, first for work uniforms then, on 15 September 1919, for all RAF dress. Non-officer ranks had to wait until 1921 before they were all able to wear grey-blue because of the large quantity of khaki still held in RAF stores.[31]

The search for a distinctive flag for the RAF proved even more difficult, provoking a long-running feud with the Admiralty. The Air Ministry proposed in May using either a white ensign without the red St George's Cross (to distinguish it from the principal flag of the Royal Navy) or a pale blue ensign, which better matched the new uniforms. The Admiralty immediately rejected the idea of a 'mutilated white ensign', or an ensign in red or blue. The naval view was that ensigns belonged only to the Royal Navy, 'by virtue of their origin and of long association', and asked the RAF to use the Union Jack flag with some appropriate emblem in the middle.[32] In July, Weir tried again to persuade the Admiralty to allow a white ensign for the RAF but was told by the First Lord that it was against the Defence of the Realm Act to fly an ensign on land without Admiralty permission, which would not be given. The Air Ministry persevered nevertheless and proposed in October to submit to the King a white ensign design or a Union Jack with an RAF badge superimposed, only to be told that the Union Jack violated Board of Trade regulations. When the white ensign was again proposed to the naval authorities as the RAF preference, the Admiralty remained utterly opposed to the idea that an ensign design could be appropriated by another service. The Air Ministry sought legal advice, to be told that the Admiralty's stubborn defence of the ensign was covered by Orders in Council from 1864, giving the Royal Navy exclusive right to use it.[33] When the navy found that two RAF stations had been observed already flying an ensign, the Air Council was told to have them removed at once.[34] There followed a long lull while the RAF focused on more serious issues for its peacetime survival, but in June 1920 the Admiralty was informed that a blue ensign had finally been selected, with the distinctive RAF red, white and blue roundel (first used as a recognition symbol on RAF aircraft in 1915 and known then as the 'target'), set on the pale blue background. The roundel was chosen, it was claimed, to honour the RAF dead; the small Union flag in the corner of the ensign to show it was a British service. The navy objected once again to a flag too close in design to the naval ensigns, and consulted the College of Heralds, responsible for authorizing flags and coats of arms, which confirmed that no flag could be approved which contained two different shades of the same colour, in this case light and dark blue. The Board of Admiralty prepared at once to inform the King, but their sense of triumph was short-lived. The RAF hurried to get to the monarch first. George V liked the new flag and approved it without demur, after more than two years of Air Ministry efforts.[35]

Another distinctive feature was the introduction of a women's component of the RAF, to supply auxiliary staff for air stations and air force administration, as well as women who could train as fitters and drivers to release men for active service, and who would owe their allegiance to the new force. The navy and the army had already organized a women's branch, and some of them now served with the RFC and the RNAS. The proposal was raised early in 1918 and the title 'Women's Royal Air Force' (WRAF) finally approved on 5 March and activated on 1 April, drawing 9,000 women from the existing army and navy women's services on a voluntary basis. The Director of Manning, Lt.-Colonel W. Bersey, was insistent that 'no pressure of any kind is to be used', for reasons that remain obscure.[36] The WRAF was from the start divided between women regarded as 'immobiles' and those regarded as mobile. Since accommodation was difficult to find – a situation made more complicated by the insistence that women should not be housed in proximity to men – preference was given to 'immobiles' who lived no more than three miles from an air station and could reach air stations by bus or rail. Mobile women were generally posted to France after initial training, where they worked in a range of clerical and auxiliary roles in a male-dominated world. The list of possible posts for women included familiar female jobs such as typist, cook, waitress and laundress, but also fifteen technical trades, from acetylene welder to tinsmith. The requirement for a 'Vegetable Woman' and a 'By-Product Woman' must have been understood at the time by the manning department, even if their function today is less obvious. Women also had the right to drive light vehicles of all kinds, but under no circumstances to drive a heavy tender.[37]

Lady Gertrude Crawford was recruited as the first Chief Superintendent of the WRAF, but she too joined the list of senior figures who left in April when it was decided that she should be replaced by a well-respected civil servant, working as a National Insurance Commissioner in Wales, Violet Douglas-Pennant. Her claim to fame was to have equipped a hospital with 500 beds in a single day during the first week of the war. She took the post in June 1918 with some reluctance following an exploratory month, and set about trying to create a better organization for a service where there were no effective welfare or health facilities and too few officers to run the corps – seventy-three in charge of 16,000 recruits at 500 air stations.[38] She contemplated resigning almost at once because she found the whole establishment 'hopelessly bad', but was persuaded again that she was witnessing the teething troubles of a new service and should persevere.[39] What followed remains open to dispute. After ten weeks in office she was brusquely dismissed without explanation by the recently appointed RAF Master of Personnel, Brigadier-General Sefton Brancker, her dismissal confirmed when she met Lord Weir a few days later. Weir reacted to pressure from the Minister of National Service, who threatened to stop allocating personnel to the WRAF because of allegations that it was failing to function effectively under a commander regarded as 'grossly unpopular'. The allegations, it was discovered, had been brought by a former clerk in a Newcastle toy shop, Katherine Andrew, who had been denied promotion in the newly created WRAF, resigned in protest and denounced Douglas-Pennant to Weir as a 'disreputable woman'. The Air Minister insisted on his right to dismiss officers who undermined the service (although it would have been surprising if the officer had been a man), and refused to reinstate her. Weir was convinced that she had been a mistaken appointment and that the problems facing the WRAF were largely her responsibility.[40] Her successor was Helen Gwynne-Vaughan, the controller of the Women's Army Auxiliary Corps in France, who coped more effectively than her predecessor but who prudently refused to reinstate Katherine Andrew to the service.

Douglas-Pennant did not go quietly. The interview with Brancker, who had just arrived back from the United States to take up his post as Master of Personnel, was a travesty of procedure. An officer relieved of his or her position was entitled to a period of notice and a detailed report justifying the decision. Brancker told her to leave on the day of the interview without a proper explanation. When he tried to shake her hand at the end of their brief exchange, she justifiably refused, though Brancker saw this as some evidence that the rumours about her personality might be correct.[41] In early September 1918 Douglas-Pennant requested a full enquiry into her dismissal, which Lloyd George refused. Her case rested on the obstruction she had found from the men running the stations and the manning directorate, who disliked taking orders from a woman. Bersey, whose role it was to oversee manning in general, insisted that Douglas-Pennant would always have to go through his office rather than communicate directly with the male commanding officers at air force stations. The conditions in the camps, she told Churchill in February 1919, were 'extremely bad, in some cases scandalous', but the men held her attempts at reform at arm's length.[42] Her chief drawback was her completely civilian background and lack of experience. An attractive and energetic woman, she saw herself, with evident justification, as the victim of male prejudice. Her case continued to attract support into the 1920s, with enquiries set up by the House of Lords, but not until the 1930s was she finally exonerated. The birth of the WRAF, like its parent service, was surrounded by an unanticipated level of intrigue and argument.

The real issue of identity for the RAF was not to be found in uniforms or flags, or in the more trivial efforts to establish difference by adopting a unique form of saluting, or the formation of RAF bands (both of which occupied valuable Air Council time in 1918). The critical test for all those who had argued the case for a separate service was to establish a body of air doctrine that made the contribution of air power strategically distinct from the functions of army and navy. A particular air strategy had been anticipated in the political efforts to establish a ministry and the new air force. Both air defence of the United Kingdom and long-range bombing of Germany were ideas cemented in Smuts' two reports in the summer of 1917, and both were used after April 1918 to demonstrate that the RAF was more than an auxiliary prop for the established services. Nevertheless, the RAF began its new career with doctrine that was borrowed from the RFC and RNAS in their auxiliary role. One of Rothermere's many complaints about Trenchard was his apparent failure to produce a coherent strategy for the new air force in his three months as chief-of-staff. In reality, the problem was not that Trenchard lacked a strategy, simply that it was a strategy tied to the offensive use of aircraft in support of the army or, in Sykes's uncharitable view, 'battering-ram tactics'.[43] Trenchard's ideas were closely reflected in the army General Staff pamphlet 'Fighting in the Air', republished in April 1918 from its March 1917 edition. The priority was to achieve 'ascendancy in the air' against the enemy air force: 'To seek out and destroy the enemy's forces must therefore be the guiding principle of our tactics in the air.'[44] For the air units supporting the army, active counter-force patrols were to be combined with direct ground support using bombs and machine-guns against enemy troops, billets and transport, and longer range bombing of communications and production facilities. Those attacks on rear areas deemed most useful 'were in connection with operations on the ground'.[45] Defensive aviation, on the other hand, was not regarded as useful either at the fighting front or at home. 'In the air even more than on the ground', concluded another General Staff study, 'the true defence lies in attack . . .'[46] Squadron record books describe day after day of 'Offensive Patrols' or 'Patrolled Army Front', sometimes achieving little more than scaring German aircraft back to base, sometimes engaging in 'indecisive combats', only occasionally recording an enemy aircraft shot down or the loss of comrades in action ('Lt. White last seen over Grillancourt 8.45 p.m.').[47] The air war, like the ground campaign, was a slow war of attrition, less thrilling and more mundane than the popular image of aerial combat.

One of Sykes's first tasks as chief-of-staff was to strengthen the air and anti-air defences around London and what he called 'other nerve centres'. By June 1918 there were 469 anti-aircraft guns (in comparison with a handful in 1915) and 622 searchlights, manned by 6,000 officers and men, together with 6th Brigade RAF, which comprised 376 aircraft (166 service-able), 660 officers and 3,500 other ranks. Squadrons based in north-east France and Belgium were also detailed to try to intercept German bombers on their approach or return. The RAF now had available a trio of effective fighter aircraft: the Bristol F.2B, the Royal Aircraft Factory's S.E.5a and the Sop-with F.1 Camel. The extensive and improved resources available may well have discouraged further German in-cursions. The last raid was on 19 May 1918, when seven from the small number of Gotha bombers available to German air forces were lost, six to guns and fighters, one to accident – 25 per cent of the attacking force.[48] The enlarged air defence system may have given the RAF an independent strategic function, but until 1940 it was never properly tested. More sig-nificant at the time and for the future development of the RAF was what Sykes called in his memoirs his 'cherished project' for the strategic bombing of the German homeland. While it is true that Sykes put much of his energy as chief-of-staff into establishing a bomber force that was not tied to control by the army on the ground, there was nothing original about his strategy. Long-range bombing of the German industrial cities within aircraft range had been mooted for several years, and detailed plans developed. The stumbling block to initiating a campaign was the short range of British bomber aircraft and the remorseless demand for air equipment generated by the land battle.

The evolution of a practical bombing strategy in fact owed little to Sykes. Both Smuts and his chief adviser, David Henderson, favoured bombing the German homeland and pressed this as a possibility in the summer of 1917. By the autumn of that year the RNAS too had a coherent programme for what would later be called 'strategic bombing'. In September 1917 Lt.-Commander Lord Tiverton (later Viscount Halsbury) sent to the Air Board a 'Scheme for bombing German Industrial centres' that defined four groups of probable targets: the Düsseldorf group, Cologne group, Mannheim group and the Saar Valley. Bombing the Ruhr–Rhineland area was regarded as the priority, because a large proportion of German iron, steel, coal and engineering production was concentrated there. Tiverton and his colleagues in the RNAS analysed the kind of aircraft needed, the scale of the force, the probable bomb loads required, the differences between night and day operations and the material and moral impact of bomb destruction.[49] The Director of Flying Operations added a detailed list of objectives in order of importance: Grade C comprised the capital cities of the Central Powers (Berlin, Vienna, Sofia and Constantinople); Grade B included German communications;

objectives given the top Grade A included the major industrial sectors, chemicals, iron and steel, aero-engine and magneto works, submarine bases and shipbuilding yards, gun shops and engine repair depots.[50] The War Trade Intelligence Department of the Admiralty supplied Tiverton and his RNAS colleagues with detailed target information to be used when bombing became a technical possibility.

The RNAS preparations for bombing contributed to the operational planning for the 41st Wing established in October 1917 on the instructions of the War Cabinet to undertake bombing of the Saarland area. Trenchard, despite his reservations about the practical difficulties of achieving very much in winter weather with a tiny force, did see long-distance bombing as one way of wearing down the German war machine to make the task at the front easier. In October 1917 his memorandum on 'Future Air Organisation' suggested that thirty squadrons would be needed in 1918 for bombing German manufacturing centres if there were to be any serious effect on munitions output and 'sufficient effect on the inhabitants to destroy their confidence and break down their morale'.[51] The 'moral impact' of bombing has long been associated with Trenchard's postwar strategy for the RAF, but its roots can be found in his wartime writing. In November 1917 he returned to the theme that the moral impact of bombing was likely to be considerably greater than the material results, but this could only be achieved with better bombers capable of reaching targets deeper inside Germany 'in order to secure the all important moral results of bombing purely German towns' and creating what he called a 'sustained anxiety'.[52]

Sykes was fortunate that he came to office just as a new generation of heavy bombers was made available. The Handley Page O/400 entered service in April 1918. Britain's largest wartime aircraft, with a 100-foot wingspan, the bomber was capable of carrying up to 2,000 pounds of bombs and utilized a newly developed MkIA bombsight to increase accuracy. During the time Sykes was chief-of-staff 400 were produced, with a further 170 manufactured under licence in the United States. The bomber began its operational career supporting the British army as it tried to stem the German March Offensive, but by the summer was available for long-range operations into Germany. Sykes was also fortunate that in Lord Weir he found a firm advocate of attacks on the German home front using a force deliberately set aside from the 'Surplus Air Fleet' that Weir had hoped to create for 1918. On 14 May 1918, two weeks after assuming office as Air Minister, Weir provided the War Cabinet with what he regarded as his inaugural statement of intent: a rapid development of aerial strength devoted to the weakening of German civilian morale and the interruption of the German industrial effort. Weir thought it not unrealistic that bombing would contribute materially 'towards bringing about a definite demand for peace' from the German enemy.[53] Sykes himself finally gave shape to his own thoughts on the role of an independent RAF in June 1918 when he submitted to the War Cabinet a long statement on air strategy in which he suggested that air power was capable of transforming the way the war, and future wars, would be fought.Modern war, Sykes argued, was now a war of 'national attrition', and the best way for the new RAF to contribute to that process was to engage in long-range offensives against the 'root industries' of the German war effort, and 'to break down the moral [sic] of his nation'. The 'wholesale bombing of densely populated industrial centres', he continued, 'would go far to destroy the morale of the operatives', an early iteration of what would later be called 'area bombing'.[54]

The search for a clear strategic identity for the RAF resulted in May 1918 in the creation of the so-called 'Independent Force' for the long-range bombing of German targets. On 13 May the Air Council was given approval by the Supreme War Council to undertake a long-distance bombing programme, and the following day the Army Council was informed that a new Independent Air Force was to be set up under the direct control of the Air Ministry, not the British Expeditionary Force, the first clear statement of the separate status the RAF had gained in April.[55] This was a solution neither Haig nor the French high command liked very much, since support for the struggle on the Western Front was paramount, while French leaders worried that German aircraft would retaliate against French industrial centres. The War Cabinet was also unenthusiastic about the idea that the Air Ministry should control any air forces, but it allowed the new formation to go ahead on a provisional basis. The new force was in effect a military-political instrument designed by Weir and Sykes to demonstrate that air power could be exercised separately from the activity of the army and navy and thus justify the creation of both the Air Ministry and the RAF.

There remained the issue of who would command the independent element. To Sykes' discomfiture, Weir decided to offer the post to Trenchard, despite his private disapproval of Trenchard's 'very indefinite reasons' for resigning.[56] The former chief-of-staff was not an obvious choice given his view that the needs of the army came first, and his sceptical judgement about the adequacy of existing bomber forces. Nor did Trenchard accept the post easily. On 14 April, the day of his formal resignation, he had applied to the War Office for permission to return to an army career with his former regiment, in charge of a battalion of infantry. Rothermere supported the application, no doubt relieved to see Trenchard at a safe distance. But the War Office turned down the application, perhaps because Trenchard was too conspicuous and contentious a figure to be given junior command. He was offered instead command of a division, but Trenchard thought he lacked the experience.[57] Haig was keen to have him back in some capacity or other but offered nothing concrete. On 1 May, the day Weir began in office, Trenchard wrote to assure the new minister that he wanted to help the RAF 'to the utmost of my power' and suggested that he might be a General Officer Commanding of the whole RAF with a seat on the Air Council, giving advice on policy and touring the RAF stations overseas. This was a strange request, not only because it would pit him face-to-face with Sykes, but because he had resigned only weeks before from a very similar post. Not surprisingly Weir refused and instead offered Trenchard a choice of one of four roles: Inspector General of the RAF overseas; Inspector General of the RAF at home; RAF Commander-in-Chief Middle East or Commander of the Independent Force in France. Trenchard havered on them all. The role of Inspector General he thought would give him no responsibility and no power of command. He remained doubtful that independent bombing would achieve very much and, like Smuts in 1917, saw the Middle East as a military dead end. On 6 May Weir lost patience and told him to choose one or have nothing. For two days Trenchard continued to dither, and his final decision to accept command of the new bomber force on 8 May was done with scarcely concealed reluctance: 'I have already stated my objections several times, and which I think will lead to efficiency being lowered. But since you are set on it and need a commander, I will accept.'[58]

On 13 May the Air Council notified Trenchard that he was

now General Officer Commanding the Independent Force, and charged him with the task of attacking German industrial targets of military importance, though no mention was made of the expected moral effects on the workforce. On 24 May the War Cabinet accepted the decision to inaugurate the new force with Trenchard in charge.[59] On the way to his new command based around Nancy, where the 41st Wing operated, Trenchard stopped at RAF headquarters where, he observed, 'everyone seemed opposed to the formation of the Independent Force', much as he had been.[60] He arrived in Nancy on 20 May, and assumed command on 5 June; on 15 June the transfer from control by Haig and the BEF to control by the Air Ministry was completed.[61] The force he found was anything but a flagship for the RAF. There were four squadrons available, their operations divided between assistance for the army and the bombing of the Saarland when weather permitted. The force was supposed to grow to twenty-four squadrons by October, well below the figure of sixty-six squadrons for long-range bombing that Haig had requested the previous November. The slower expansion of output in 1918 and high losses at the front compromised even the more modest figure of twenty-four. In June, the force had five squadrons, by August seven and at the end of the war in November only ten, one of which consisted of fighters.[62] This was not the force that Trenchard had been expecting to command. In an interview many years later he complained that the 'high-sounding name' of the Independent Force was so much moonshine: 'What I commanded was a few squadrons. I was not anybody very much.'[63]

Shortly after his assumption of command, Trenchard sent a report to the Inter-Allied Aviation Committee at Versailles to explain what he saw as his role. Aircraft could only be diverted to long-range bombing, he argued, once German aviation was defeated. Once air superiority was established then surplus machines would be freed 'for fighting the Germans in GER-MANY'.[64] A counter-force offensive was, in Trenchard's view, a critical factor if bombing were to succeed at all. The plans he laid down for 1919, had the war continued, divided the operations of the Independent Force equally between attacks on enemy aerodromes and long-range attacks against industrial targets.[65] This was sound advice, given what is now known about all bombing offensives, but it was not what Weir and Sykes had had in mind. Trenchard allowed his small force to be diverted to attacking the German air force and German communications to the front, turning it into a force that appeared to be part auxiliary, part separate. This diversion was evident from the regular operational résumés sent to the Air Ministry from Trenchard's headquarters. On 8/9 July the force dropped five tons of bombs, by day on the aerodrome at Bühl and railway sidings at Luxembourg, by night on aerodromes at Boulay and Freisdorf and on two trains. On 19/20 July, bombs were dropped on the munitions works at Oberndorf by day, and at night on aerodromes at Freisdorf, Boulay and Morhange, trains near Saarbrücken and Rémilly, and three industrial plants in Mannheim. On 12/13 September, six tons were dropped on Courcelles, Orny and Verny rail junctions, and railways at Metz (using four of the squadrons).[66] That month, Brigadier-General Percy Groves, director of operations in the Air Ministry, complained to Sykes that in defiance of RAF policy, Trenchard's campaign 'amounts to the diversion of maximum effort against targets of subsidiary importance.'[67] However, the pattern of operations remained the same down to the armistice in November. Once again in command, Trenchard followed his own strategic instincts.

Bombing at long distance was a difficult and risky operation in the conditions of 1918. Bombing by night presented a severe challenge once German blackout regulations were in place. Bomber aircraft dropped clusters of parachute flares which illuminated an area up to a quarter of a square mile, but they carried the risk that the wind would float them away. It was calculated that one third of aircraft failed to find the designated objective at night (and 18 per cent by day).[68] Bomb-aiming was still a primitive skill, even with an improved bombsight. Flying at between 10,000 and 15,000 feet, close observation of the target and of the results of bombing was difficult; it was later found that one third of the bombs failed to explode.[69] The weather played a major part in limiting operations or in increasing the risks pilots faced as they tried to operate through cloud or high wind. In October 1918, mist, fog and low cloud meant that on nineteen days and twenty-two nights no operations were possible at all.[70] Even when flying was possible, technical problems could force aircraft to return to base or attempt an improvised landing. In a raid on Thionville station on 6 June, six out of eleven DH.9 bombers had to return with engine trouble. Losses due to non-combat damage were high, usually higher than losses to the enemy. In August 1918, when the weather allowed 100 tons to be dropped on enemy targets, fifty-four machines were wrecked and written off. Aircraft missing, either to crashes or enemy action, totalled twenty-seven.[71]

Enemy aircraft were nevertheless an ever-present menace, which is why suppressing the German air forces was Trenchard's priority. As the bombing became a regular feature, so the German high command moved to establish proper air defences, as the British had done. By 1918 there was a network of 400 searchlights and 1,200 anti-aircraft guns, and a number of nighttime decoy targets, illuminated amidst the blackout. An Air Warning Service was established, using a combination of ground and aerial observation.[72] Aircraft were diverted from the front, and by August 1918 there were sixteen home defence squadrons of Albatross, Fokker and Pfalz fighters, a total of 240 planes. They were supported by at least ninety aircraft stationed on the Alsace-Lorraine front which, like the RAF units based in Belgium to cut off German bomber raids, tried to intercept the bombers on their way to their more distant targets.[73] The RAF bombers flew in close formation, usually in groups of six. When possible they would have an escort of fighters by day. German aircraft attacked when they could in large numbers, to inflict heavy losses, but they also hunted in smaller groups to pick off any stragglers from a bomber formation. Success was sometimes almost total. On 31 July 1918, a force of nine DH.9s was attacked by forty single-seat fighters and all but two destroyed; on 26 September, seven bombers were attacked by a larger fighter force and only one returned with a wounded pilot and a dead observer.[74] In turn, casualties could be imposed on the German enemy either by escorting fighters or by the machine-guns of the bomber formation. In August 1918, the Independent Force claimed nineteen enemy aircraft shot down, but this was scant compensation for the overall loss that month of eighty-one of the small force available.

Sykes was unperturbed by the difficulties and the small scale. His aim was to expand the Independent Force into an Inter-Allied Air Force using French, Italian and United States bomber units alongside those of the RAF.[75] The anxiety of the French high command that bombing long-distance would divert effort away from the front line was heightened by June, when it was evident that the German army on the Western Front was facing crisis and might crack under continued pressure. Sykes tried to persuade the Inter-Allied Aviation

Committee in late May that an Allied force would have more impact on the German home front than the RAF operating alone, but the French remained unconvinced, although a meeting in early June face-to-face with Georges Clemenceau, French President of the Supreme War Council, did elicit for Sykes what he described as a 'hearty endorsement' from the French leader.[76] In August Weir wrote to Clemenceau explaining that long-distance bombing was not merely in a narrow sense military, it was also political, being 'an attack on the morale of the industrial population with the object of reducing output and of producing a tendency towards peace'.[77] The French high command might well have asked for the recall of the Independent Force, because it operated outside the overall command structure, led by the French Marshal Ferdinand Foch, who was unenthusiastic about strategic bombing and hostile to Trenchard.[78] The Independent Force survived largely because it was an increasing irrelevance once Allied efforts were devoted to exploiting the optimistic prospects on the Western Front against a crumbling enemy. To prevent French leaders from insisting on terminating the RAF experiment, Weir and Sykes agreed that overall control of the Independent Force should pass to Foch, who could use its resources in any emergency in the ground war.[79] Only in October did the French leaders agree that an Inter-Allied Independent Air Force could be created, and on 26 October Trenchard was notified that he would be its commander. The decision was overtaken by events, for within three weeks the Germans had sued for an armistice.[80]

The plans to develop an Inter-Allied force highlighted the growing collaboration between the RAF and the American Air Service, established in Europe since the United States declaration of war in 1917. American and Canadian volunteers were already a feature of the RFC. A group of 210 United States university students came to train in Britain to join the RFC, and 115 of them became casualties.[81] During the war 1,239 Canadian air officers and 2,750 other ranks were seconded to the RFC, RNAS and RAF; with Canadian volunteers, the total number who served was 8,000. In August 1918 a separate Canadian flying corps was finally established.[82] The new United States Air Service was attached to the American Army expeditionary force in Europe. The overall commander, General John Pershing, shared the view of Haig and Trenchard that offensive operations in support of the ground armies was the best use of America's still very limited air resources. Even American air officers keen on bombing as a distinct strategy still saw the operations as essentially raids on tactical targets behind the front to assist the army.[83] Two officers, Major Raymond Bolling and Lt.-Colonel Edgar Gorrell, were more committed to the maximum view that air power might yet prove decisive. Bolling headed the American Air Mission to Europe in June 1917, where he discussed air strategy with British airmen; Gorrell was made Chief of the Strategical Section in November 1917. The Bolling mission recommended 260 American squadrons by 1919, including sixty dedicated to long-range bombing.[84] In summer 1918, Gorrell increased the planned scale to 358 squadrons, 110 of them for bombing, and the War Department authorized the plan in June. Production was planned for 17,500 bomber aircraft, to be produced in the United States from British and Italian designs, but by the time of the Armistice only sixty bombers had reached the front. Those American aircraft that did make it to France served like the RAF, chiefly in close support of the ground army.[85]

The balance-sheet showing the achievements of the 'independent' elements of the RAF in the months of its wartime existence is unimpressive. The limited results help to explain why after the Armistice the new service faced such strong political and military pressure to terminate what many regarded as a purely temporary, wartime expedient. It is worth observing that the Royal Navy's hostility to the RAF and defence of the established role of the RNAS was scarcely justified by what air-sea aviation achieved during the war. Research showed that Royal Navy aircraft sank only three small German vessels: one torpedo boat, one tug (which was raised and repaired) and one small harbour boat. Not a single German merchant vessel was sunk, while three small Turkish ships were torpedoed, with unverified results; only two German submarines, U32 and U59 (the latter bombed in a dry dock), were in fact destroyed by seaplanes, although the RNAS claimed during the war to have sunk 100.[86] There were throughout the war only twenty-nine combined sea-air operations in the North Sea; in 47 per cent of cases seaplanes were unable to take off from the water, and out of twelve aeroplanes used, three failed to take off from ship decks and five were lost at sea. [87] The use of aircraft at sea was most successful in the role of observation and reconnaissance, in forcing submarines to submerge, and in bombing enemy ports and naval installations, but the days when air-sea warfare could be based around high-performance aircraft carriers and radar-directed operations were still far in the future.

Nonetheless, the achievements registered by the air defence and anti-aircraft structure set up during the war were every bit as modest. One postwar calculation showed that of the thirty-nine German raids recorded over the mainland in 1917–1918, only twenty-one were sighted at all by British aircraft; out of the 1,737 sorties by defensive aircraft, 1,592 (91.7 per cent) never saw the enemy.[88] Statistics compiled on the wartime casualties inflicted on enemy bombers were equally modest: thirteen aircraft were brought down by anti-aircraft fire, three by day, ten by night; nine were accounted for by British fighter aircraft, five by day, four by night. British losses amounted to two aircraft shot down by British anti-aircraft guns, five by enemy aircraft, and twelve written off when they crash landed.[89] The evidence of just how difficult it was to intercept enemy aircraft was later used by the army to justify returning the air force to army and navy control. Like the air war at sea, effective air defence depended on the advent of more advanced equipment and radar intelligence.

The greatest disappointment came from the performance of the Independent Force, on which Sykes and Weir had staked their claim to a separate air service. During the five months of its operational existence the Force dropped just 537 tons of bombs, 160 by day and 377 by night. Of this quantity, 220 tons were dropped on railway targets in support of the ground army and a roughly equal quantity on enemy air bases and air force installations. The tonnage dropped on targets more than eighty-five miles from the front line (a distance adopted by the RAF as a measure of long-range bombing) was just forty-seven tons.[90] Most of this tonnage fell on the German city and port of Mannheim-Ludwigshafen (twenty-four tons); some five tons were dropped on Koblenz, five tons on Frankfurt. Other cities hit with much smaller loads included Bonn, Cologne, Darmstadt, Düren, Stuttgart and Wiesbaden.[91] The whole bomb tonnage could be carried in the Second World War by a dozen Lancaster bombers. Over the course of 1918 the RFC/RAF dropped 321,000 bombs, but only an estimated 5,000 of this total were dropped by the Independent Force on German towns. The independent campaign contributed just 8 per cent of the total bomb tonnage dropped between 1915 and

1918 by British aircraft.[92] This result was dictated by the small size of the Independent Force, starved as it was of an adequate number of aircraft and personnel by the demands of the fighting fronts, but also by Trenchard's own preference for tactical rather than strategic targets. In November 1918 only ten out of ninety-nine squadrons in France and 140 out of 1,799 aircraft were allocated to Trenchard.[93] At the war's end he issued a communiqué for his force praising them for bombing Germany with such vigour that they assisted 'in bringing about the demoralization that has produced this Armistice'. His private view, consigned to his diary the same day, was more in keeping with his own ambivalence about an independent campaign: 'A more gigantic waste of effort and personnel there has never been in any war'.[94]

Postwar surveys of the damage done to German targets confirmed that the bombing had had little material effect. German officials found the bombing of railway communications 'annoying'; the directors of those blast furnaces subjected to raids insisted that the bombing was inaccurate and ineffective. The psychological impact on the bombed population, on the other hand, was regarded by German officials as substantial. In postwar interviews, the mayors of the bombed cities agreed that the moral effect had been 'very considerable'. Once casualties mounted, 'panic became general'. This had been one of the aims of the offensive. In August 1918 the Air Ministry, citing letters from home found on German prisoners, observed that the population in the bombed regions was apparently 'unsettled and terrified'. From this a conclusion was drawn that was to influence British bombing strategy down to the end of the Second World War: 'it is certain that the moral of the German population becomes lower as the range and power of our bombing squadrons increase'.[95] In his despatch on the work of the Independent Force, Trenchard famously enshrined this conclusion in RAF strategic culture when he claimed that 'at present the moral effect of bombing stands undoubtedly to the material effect in a proportion of 20 to 1 . . .', an assertion for which no firm quantitative evidence existed, or was likely to exist.[96]

The aerial assault on the war-willingness of the German population raised significant ethical issues about the violation of civilian immunity. The German bombing of British cities had provoked widespread outrage at an enemy regarded as manifestly criminal. 'The cowardly wickedness of such raids,' wrote one diarist in November 1917, 'is almost incredible; to think of defenceless, innocent women and children and old men and boys being ruthlessly murdered and mutilated by these devils in the air . . .'[97] Bombing of German cities could be interpreted as legally justified reprisal against a barbarous enemy, though the Air Staff was anxious that British raids should not be seen as a mere response in kind but instead 'as a definite war campaign', so Weir informed the War Cabinet in August 1918, worked out with 'elaborate preparations'.[98] There is little evidence that bombing to demoralize civilians was regarded as morally unacceptable or illegal either at the time or since, although the German mayors interviewed in 1919 did condemn the deliberate bombing of 'workmen's colonies' as a possible war crime. In his memoirs, Sykes was at pains to claim that British bombing was not an example of 'frightfulness' (the term widely used to describe terror bombing), but simply a reflection of the harsh reality that it is 'impossible to humanize modern warfare'.[99] Trenchard had no doubt that killing German civilians was part of his policy. In early November 1918 he explained to Salmond, RAF commander in France, that he preferred to use high explosive rather than incendiary bombs against German targets 'to create moral effect and to kill'.[100]

The bombing by both sides in the war technically violated the intention in the Hague Conventions of 1899 and 1907 that explosive projectiles from balloons, airships or any other flying vehicle should be prohibited, but the extent to which this had the force of international law was open to interpretation, since a final decision had been postponed until a third Hague Conference, which never materialized, and most of the major powers refused to ratify the bombing clause.[101] Article 25, which prohibited the bombardment by whatever means of undefended 'towns, villages, dwellings or buildings' was taken to apply to aircraft too, but this clause left open the awkward definition of what was meant by 'undefended'. This was a matter of judgement for armed forces, but the prevailing sentiment during the Hague discussions was that modern states would observe the generally accepted notions of civilized warfare. These were vague limitations, far from legally binding. When the Imperial General Staff called for a formal legal opinion on aerial bombing in April 1918, they were informed that since none of the enemy powers had ratified the Hague Convention of 1907, they could not expect their enemy to abide by international agreement. More significantly, France had failed to ratify either. In a coalition where one power had not signed international legal instruments, the allies were also released from their obligation.[102] This was so much legal sophistry, but it confirmed that RAF bombing of distant civilian targets could not be considered illegal. When in 1919 the British Committee of Enquiry into Breaches of the Laws of War considered whether German airmen should be arraigned for bombing British 'undefended towns', Trenchard himself told the War Cabinet that his force had done much the same. In October

1919, the War Cabinet decided not to pursue the principle that bombing was contrary to law.[103] Not until the Geneva Convention of 1949 were restrictions on bombing civilians and the civilian milieu first introduced. Despite initial government prohibition in the late 1930s and the first months of the Second World War, the RAF was to return to civilian targeting in the bomber offensive of the next war, and with broadly similar reasoning.

If the independent operations of the new RAF showed little evidence that a separate service had really been necessary, the triumphant end to the ground campaigns on the Western Front and in the Middle East underscored the extent to which British military aviation had come of age as a successful tactical air force. The pursuit of a beaten enemy gave the RAF the opportunity to demonstrate how important counter-force and ground support operations had become. In addition to suppressing German air forces, RAF aircraft bombed and strafed German troops on the move or in trenches, attacked transport columns and bombed incoming supplies and ammunition dumps. Statistics compiled for 1918 claimed that the RAF destroyed 12,000 enemy artillery batteries, destroyed 1,150 gun pits, took 256,000 reconnaissance photographs and fired 321,000 machine-gun rounds.[104] Reliable or not, the figures display a sense of the scale of RAF ground support operations that absorbed the activity of the great majority of the personnel. In the Middle East, RAF units hounded Ottoman forces in the final offensive through Palestine and Syria. Aircraft hovered around Turkish aerodromes, dropping a bomb every time there was a sign of movement, and machine-gunning the hangars at the end of each sortie. Troops on the ground were pursued by air attacks as they withdrew, and subjected to repeated bombing and strafing. Salmond's brother and RAF commander in the Middle East, Brigadier-General Geoffrey Salmond, sent a grim report back to the Air Ministry about the carnage his air force inflicted on the Turkish retreat: 'I have been all through these columns and I have never seen anything so appalling and sickening. Gun piled against gun, horses underneath mixed up with oxen, motor lorries abandoned without stopping the engine and running amok and then, finally, overturning, dead Turks, smells indescribable.'[105] Against a beaten enemy, the remorseless activity of the RAF contributed to the final victory on the ground more certainly than any independent campaign.

The day and night before the war ended, on 10/11 November 1918, the Independent Force was, ironically enough, engaged solely on army support operations. Nine tons of bombs were dropped on railway sidings at Ehrhange, on the Metz–Sablon railway, and on air bases at Morhange, Lellingen and Frescaty. The first of a new generation of heavy long-range bombers, the Handley Page V/1500, was ready but arrived too late for operations. Weir and Sykes had planned for a great offensive in 1919 against the German homeland, but the plan was overtaken by events. On the cusp of proving itself more than an auxiliary arm, the RAF, with its 22,647 aeroplanes and seaplanes and 198 squadrons, was still tied to its parent services. The birth of the RAF in April 1918 gave no guarantee that the infant would survive into peacetime adolescence.

4

'A Very Gruelling Business': Saving the RAF

We contend that the British policy is to develop the independent
conception of the air as an art, as an arm, and as a service; and that
this method alone will secure that qualitative ascendancy and
superiority which the safety of the country requires . . .

Winston Churchill, October 1921[1]

In June 1933 Air Vice-Marshal Brooke-Popham gave the after-
dinner speech on 'The Spirit of the Air Force' at a special
event organized to celebrate twenty-one years of the Royal Air
Force. The date actually commemorated was the founding of
the Royal Flying Corps in 1912, but the RAF elided the two
organizations together as if there had been a continuous
history of an independent flying arm. Brooke-Popham's
remarks made evident that the naval air service was a historical
detour. The RFC-RAF lineage was paramount. Brooke-
Popham had wanted to mention famous names from the
wartime years but realized that they had almost all died in
combat and that this might give the air force an unnecessarily
morbid image. Nevertheless, dead or alive, the airmen contributed by their 'courage and determination' to creating the
soul of the RAF, which after twenty-one years Brooke-Popham
regarded as 'permanent and fundamental'.[2]

The speech marked a particular historic moment for the RAF, but Brooke-Popham's seamless narrative masked a very different reality. The RAF was created out of bitter arguments over its necessity, and for half a decade after 1918 the future of the RAF as an independent service, separate from the army and navy, hung by a thread. The principal advocate of an end to air power independence remained the Admiralty, which might explain the absence of the navy in Brooke-Popham's talk, but by 1921 the army too began to have grave doubts about whether it made strategic and budgetary sense to keep the RAF. This was a far cry from the optimistic expectations of the Air Staff when the war ended that the RAF ought to play an expanded role in the defence of the motherland and the Empire. On 9 December 1918, a month after the Armistice, Sykes drew up a memorandum for the Cabinet on 'Air Power Requirements of the Empire'. He urged the government not to demobilize the air force too rapidly, because specialized air forces were essential to the future security of Britain's imperial territories. Air power, he continued, had tremendous potential, so that in peace or in war 'the nation which thinks in three dimensions will lead those still thinking in two'.

What followed was a classic description of a strategy that has come to be known as 'Douhetism', after the Italian airman Giulio Douhet, who argued in his book *Il dominio dell'aria* (*The Command of the Air*), first published in 1921, that any future war ought to begin with an annihilating air strike against the enemy's cities and civilians as a swifter and ultimately more humane route to victory than the four costly years of attrition between 1914 and 1918.Sykes 'strategic considerations' anticipated Douhet by some years:

Future wars between civilized nations will be struggles for life in which entire populations, together with their industrial resources, will be thrown into the scale. Evolution has brought about the creation of air fleets to meet the demands of such warfare. These will consist of home defence units and striking forces. The objectives of striking forces will be nerve centres, the armies and navies of the opponent, the population as a whole, his national moral [sic] and the industries, without which he cannot wage war.[3]

In early January 1919 Sykes even initiated discussions with the Admiralty to get the navy's agreement that the achievement of 'Command of the Air' was the responsibility of the RAF, while command of the sea was the navy's business.[4] Although Sykes was to remain in office for only a few more weeks, the strategic principles he outlined at the end of the war came to dominate RAF strategic thinking down to the start of the next, without reference to Douhet. Home air defence and strategic bombing gave to the air force a unique strategic profile. Sykes recommended a peacetime establishment for the two strategic forces of thirty-seven squadrons, twenty for defence, seventeen as the air striking force. The addition of squadrons for air-sea cooperation, empire defence and support for the army brought the total recommended by Sykes to 154 squadrons, not far short of the number at the end of the war.[5]

Sykes was to be swiftly disillusioned about the possibility of maintaining a substantial air element at the heart of British strategy. By 1920, the whole RAF consisted of just twenty-eight squadrons, twenty-one of which served in Empire areas overseas, with just seven for home defence.[6] Demobilization was carried out rapidly and thousands of aircraft were written off and destroyed, or sold to third parties abroad. The Aircraft Disposal Company, set up in 1919, handled 10,000 aircraft and 30,000 aero-engines.[7] RAF personnel at the end of the war numbered 30,122 officers and 253,410 other ranks. They had signed on for four years but no longer. Men could return to the navy or army if they wished, but there was now no guarantee of a post as the entire military apparatus contracted to peace-time levels. Financial stringency was imposed at once to try to limit the financial fall-out from four years of the costliest war in history. Thousands of officers assigned from the former RNAS abandoned the air force, either to return to the navy or to civilian life.[8] The remaining RAF officer corps was drawn heavily from men who had served in the RFC before April 1918, but most found themselves demobilized. By the autumn of 1919 the RAF had already shrunk to just 35,000 men, one tenth of its size at the conclusion of the war, with 1,500 officers, three quarters of them on short-term commissions for two to five years. The element working with the fleet, much to the dismay of the Admiralty, was reduced to just 140 officers and 4,000 other ranks.[9] The Air Council had hoped to retain the WRAF with a peacetime strength of 6,000 – the women's branch, the Council president suggested, 'would accord with the spirit of the times' – but Parliament rejected the idea. By March 1920, when the WRAF was wound up, there were just 376 women left in the force.[10] The small scale of the surviving air service in 1919 served to emphasize the temporary status of the wartime RAF and encouraged those military and naval predators who hoped to devour the air service for their own purposes.

The case for keeping the RAF as a permanent peacetime service was thrown again into jeopardy by a renewed crisis surrounding its leadership. Trenchard gave up command of the Independent Force on the day of the Armistice and handed his units back to John Salmond, commander of the RAF in France attached to the British Expeditionary Force. Trenchard's future in the RAF was entirely uncertain, and he doubted that any senior role would be granted him with Sykes as chief-of-staff. A few weeks later Lord Weir also announced his resignation. He told Lloyd George that he did not want in peacetime 'the collective and political responsibility of the whole Ministry'. He returned to his business interests and never held political office again, although he remained through to the 1930s an important adviser to governments on air force matters.[11] Weir's resignation was made on the day of the General Election called by Lloyd George at the end of the war, which was won overwhelmingly by his Liberal–Conservative coalition. The return to postwar conditions might have made it possible for Lloyd George to terminate the Air Ministry as a wartime improvisation, as other wartime ministries were wound up in the year following the Armistice. Instead he offered the post to Winston Churchill in tandem with the War Office, as Secretary of State for War and Air. This was not Churchill's first choice. At the end of the war he told Lloyd George that he contemplated leaving the Coalition government unless he was offered a 'key post' in the reconstructed Cabinet after the election.[12] Lloyd George preferred to have Churchill in the government rather than outside, and in late December offered him the choice of the War Office or the Admiralty, the post he had held at the start of the war. 'You can take the Air with you in either case,' Lloyd George is quoted as saying; 'I am not going to keep it as a separate department.'[13] Churchill replied that the choice was easy –'my heart is in the Admiralty' – but he suggested that the Air Ministry and air force would best be attached to the Admiralty and Royal Navy instead of remaining independent. Aircraft, Churchill wrote, 'will never be a substitute for armies', but they would become an 'economical substitute' for ships, an argument that would hardly have been welcomed by the navy's high command.[14] In the end, Lloyd George insisted on Churchill at the War Office with the Air Ministry added in. On 10 January Churchill accepted the joint appointment and took up his office four days later.[15]

If Lloyd George had hoped that fusing the army and air force under one ministerial appointment would eventually see the disappearance of the ministry and the RAF, Churchill became a sudden enthusiast for a separate air force. On 8 February he informed the Admiralty that 'the future independence of the Air Force and Air Ministry will in no way be prejudiced' by his appointment.[16] It is not clear why Churchill changed his mind, and later in the year he had second thoughts about whether it would not be more economical to divide the air forces between the army and navy, until he finally came out in full support of the idea that the air force might at some point 'obtain the primary place in the general conception of war policy' and ought to remain independent.[17] It seems unlikely that Churchill decided to support the air force in the prospect of enhancing his political reputation, since the Air Ministry was still a temporary institution with a low public profile. More probable is the role played by his almost boyish enthusiasm for flying, first expressed before the war when he flew with naval aviators 'for sheer joy and pleasure' and renewed in 1919 when he hoped to get a pilot's licence. His flying ended only after a crash on 18 July during a training flight at Croydon aerodrome, which left him severely bruised and his instructor with a broken leg. He was persuaded that flying was too dangerous an occupation for a senior minister of the Crown.[18]

1. RFC carpenters' repair shop

2. Frederick Sykes and the RFC administrative staff, 1912
3. Crashed RFC aeroplane, 1917

4. Observer with camera, 16th Wing Photographic Section

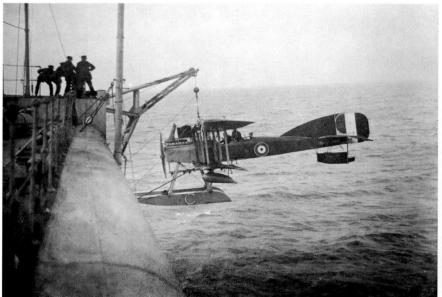

5. Hugh Trenchard and Herbert Asquith at the Western Front, 1916
6. Hoisting an RNAS seaplane on board

7. Temporary accommodation on the Strand outside Hotel Cecil
8. Aerial view of bombing of London, 7 July 1917

9. Jan Smuts and Arthur Balfour, July 1917

10. RFC cadets at dinner in Christ Church, Oxford, October 1917

11. King George V and John Salmond at RFC HQ

12. Farewell dinner in the sergeants' mess
13. Funeral of Von Richthofen, the 'Red Baron', April 1918

14. Women of the WRAF servicing an engine

15. RAF mechanics preparing targets for gunnery practice

16. Handley Page O/400 heavy bomber, 1918
17. Training US officers in aerial gunnery

18. Cranwell at the end of its construction, 1922
19. Churchill and Trenchard at the Hendon Air Show, 1920

20. RAF Sopwith Snipes in Germany, March 1919
21. Siskin aircraft lined up at Hendon Air Show, 1929

22. Vickers Victoria landing at Abu Seir, Iraq, 1929

23. Fleet Air Arm Fairey Swordfish torpedo bombers above the Solent

In the first week of February 1919 Churchill invited Trenchard to attend a meeting. Weir had advised reinstating the former chief-of-staff, despite the effective collaboration he had had with Sykes. Churchill wrote later that he had been happy to have Trenchard back, partly because he sympathized with his reasons for leaving his post in 1918, partly because in his view Trenchard had 'outstanding qualities' as a leader.[19] Trenchard was astonished to be offered the role he had resigned from almost a year before. He protested that Sykes was already in office, but Churchill told him that he had already decided to divide the military and civilian sectors and that Sykes was to be Director General of Civil Aviation. Trenchard then objected that he was unlikely to agree with Churchill's view of the RAF's future, but when he submitted a paper describing his policy for the RAF Churchill agreed to it, and Trenchard accepted the post. Why he did so is open to speculation. Trenchard's own recollection of the decision is brief and laconic: 'He said I must accept, and he pressed me to, so I agreed to come back as CAS.'[20] He did so, he told an RAF audience a few years later, 'with a good deal of alarm . . . I thought my effort likely to end in failure'.[21] Until that point, Trenchard's attitude to the new ministry and a separate air force had been almost entirely negative, even when he occupied the role of chief-of-staff briefly in early 1918. He found ministerial life uncongenial and was candid about his incapacities in the world of political and bureaucratic infighting. His view of the Independent Force he had commanded for five months was dismissive. The decision to accept the post must have owed something to Trenchard's own poor career prospects without a senior role, even though there was no certainty that a Chief of the Air Staff would still be in post later in 1919. He may have liked the fact that the War Office and the Air

Ministry were now under one portfolio, given his earlier preference for army aviation. The sidelining of Sykes also meant that Trenchard, as the most senior and experienced officer in the force, was free for the present to shape the air arm the way he wanted. Perhaps aware that his change of heart needed some justification both for himself and for others, he later wrote in notes for his biographer, in capital letters, 'I LEARNT AS I WENT ON'.²² Whatever his motives, he was altered by his decision from an ambivalent observer of the young RAF to its foremost champion.

The force that Churchill and Trenchard now directed was in a state of turbulent dissolution. One of Churchill's first acts was to try to rescue a separate identity by insisting that the army ranks adopted by the RAF in April 1918 should be replaced by ranks that were particular to the air service. This Trenchard opposed without success, testament to his continued identity with the army he had served for more than twenty-five years. The adoption of army ranks in 1918 had simplified the transition to the RAF for the majority of the new force serving with the RFC. However, a tentative list had already been drawn up in 1917 employing a mix of army and navy ranks as well as ranks peculiar to the projected new air force – Air Marshal, Air Warden and Vice Warden, Commodore, Commander, Major, Captain, Lieutenant and Ensign – but it was not acted upon. Later in 1918, when the Air Ministry considered the size and distribution of a possible peacetime officer corps, the ranks were still the basic army categories from general down to lieutenant.²³ In early 1919, Churchill asked the Air Staff for their proposals for air force ranks, against the insistence by the Royal Navy that none of theirs should be appropriated and the army's preference for retaining the existing army nomenclature. The first attempt was little better than the suggestion of 'Air Warden' and 'Vice Warden' two years earlier: Air Marshal, Ardian, Squadron Ardian and Flight Ardian, titles loosely based, it was claimed, on the Gaelic words *ard* ('chief') and *eun* ('bird'). These were certainly more elegant than the suggestion that the equivalent rank to navy captain and army colonel should be 'Grouper'.[24] In the end, the agreed ranks reflected very closely the practice in the RNAS, with the exception of the senior ranks of Marshal of the Air, Air Chief Marshal, Air Marshal and Air Vice-Marshal. There was strong army opposition to the idea that 'air marshal' should mimic the title of 'field marshal' ('the ruination and degradation of a great name and a great rank' complained the Chief of the Imperial General Staff); the original request to the Crown to approve Marshal of the Air as the most senior rank was rejected by the King, who thought Marshal of the Air as pointless as 'Admiral of the Atlantic'.[25] The most senior rank was changed to Marshal of the Royal Air Force, though the King disliked this too and preferred the title 'Chief of the Air Force', which he used thereafter. The other ranks were modelled on the naval air service: Air Commodore, Group Captain, Wing Commander, Squadron Leader, Flight Lieutenant, Flying Officer, Pilot Officer. By Air Ministry Order 973 on 1 August 1919 the new ranks were confirmed as permanent, and have survived ever since.

The new ranks were applied to a rapidly shrinking body of officers, men and women. The Ministry plan in 1918 envisaged a small elite force of no more than 2,000 officers, with four generals, six colonels, twenty-five lieutenant-colonels, and so on. With the coming of peace, the officers all on temporary commissions were invited to apply for permanent status. Some 6,500 applied, but the Cabinet approved only 1,500 and the Ministry finally selected 1,005 on grounds that were inevitably arbitrary. Some officers were selected without difficulty, based on their wartime record. The future Commander-in-Chief of Bomber Command, Arthur Harris, was confirmed as a Major (soon changed to Squadron Leader) in the RAF on permanent commission early in 1919, against his expectations.[26] Yet it was also possible for a senior officer, with a fine war record, to struggle for permanent status. Acting Brigadier-General Percy Groves was chief-of-staff in the RFC Middle East Command and then, after the formation of the RAF, Director of Flying Operations in the Air Ministry. In September 1918 he applied for a permanent commission according to the instructions issued to the temporary officers in the RAF, which he assumed would be something of a formality. He was told only in May 1919, with his status uncertain, that he still had only a temporary commission, by which time he was representing the air force at the Versailles Conference. He was then informed that his rank as acting Brigadier-General was to be downgraded to Group Captain RAF, consistent with his formal army rank of Colonel, but Groves strongly objected to the change on the ground that the Europeans he negotiated with would not regard him seriously if he was a Captain rather than a General. He was granted a permanent commission only in March 1920, on condition he that he give up his commission in the army. In 1922 a frustrated Groves resigned his new rank as Group Captain, became a prolific author on air matters, and continued to call himself Brigadier-General. His correspondence from the early 1920s shows that he was not the only officer alienated by the change in rank title and the slow and unfathomable process in deciding who would and who would not hold a permanent commission.[27]

The Air Ministry was anxious, despite the problems surrounding demobilization and rank change, to establish a system of entry into the peacetime RAF that would bring in a fresh generation of young airmen who had not experienced the transition from one service to another. A committee on the 'Preliminary Education of Candidates for Royal Air Force Commissions' was set up under the air force officer and MP Hugh Cecil. Its report was submitted in March 1919. The first requirement was that every officer candidate should be physically capable of flying, even those destined for the scientific or administrative branches. Beyond that, the Committee focused on qualities of mind and temperament. 'A certain amount of intelligence is indispensable,' ran the report, but also 'a certain moral temper', summed up, it was suggested, by that ineffable English term 'a gentleman'. If possible, the successful officer candidate should have 'a high standard of courage, self-control, and honourable conduct, and seemly and considerate manners and deportment'. While not excluding men of 'small means and humble origins', the report recommended selecting from the universities and the public schools, including those 'who have a literary taste' as well as those with a scientific background.[28] The reputation of the later RAF for promoting men from public-school backgrounds, although less deserved as the air force became more technically advanced, was rooted in the initial preference for gentlemanly qualities. In November 1919, a cadet college was opened at Cranwell in Lincolnshire, where these qualities could be fully tested.The bias in favour of boys from public schools even extended to the first RAF Apprentice Scheme, established in 1920 to train a new generation of workers for the aero-engine, airframe and wireless trades. A dedicated educational programme for other ranks was in itself an innovation, and the most successful apprentices could move on to become commissioned officers themselves. Six years later, Trenchard told a gathering of RAF officers that his purpose was to recruit 'the intelligent class, who can learn quickly and absorb quickly'. Standards of entry remained high for the RAF through to the Second World War.[29]

The changes in personnel took place in a context where the very existence of the new service as a permanent feature of the defence establishment was called into question. Since commissions were at first still temporary, the whole organization suffered from a sense of impermanence. Survival through the early months of 1919 depended largely on inertia. The government faced a wide range of domestic problems, crisis across many areas of the Empire, and the large task of contributing to the peace settlement in Europe and the Middle East. The army and navy were faced with their own problems of large-scale demobilization, which postponed any renewed attempt to reabsorb air forces under their control. Churchill was heavily occupied with his responsibilities at the War Office and left his other portfolio largely in peace. The Air Ministry and Trenchard's staff took advantage of this moment of immunity to solidify the institutional structure of the air force, which had now moved out of the Hotel Cecil into permanent premises in nearby Kingsway, appropriately christened Adastral House. One of the first tasks was to establish all the ancillary branches that had been borrowed from the other services. These included medical and sanitary welfare, meteorological units, rationing, billeting and clothing. At the same time the ministry drew up the formal conditions for permanent commissions, rates of pay and pensions. This mundane work ensured that dismantling the whole operation would become an increasingly costly and legally complex task. The exact status of the RAF had nevertheless not yet been fully established. It existed in peculiar limbo, neither elevated to a secure future, nor yet dismantled as a redundant relic of the recent conflict.

In August 1919, Trenchard and his staff set out to establish the RAF on a more formal and permanent footing. In a memorandum on the 'Status of the Royal Air Force', prepared for a committee on national expenditure chaired by Eric Geddes, the chief-of-staff raised the central questions that had dominated the debate on a separate air force since 1917: should the RAF be capable of conducting its own independent operations under air force command? Or should it simply provide air force contingents 'as ancillary services' to the army and navy, under army and navy command? Trenchard now argued that the air force needed to be independent because multiple control by all three armed services 'reduced efficiency', the very argument he had used two years before against the idea of a new air service. The Air Ministry, he concluded, should have the right to allocate aircraft to the navy and army and to its own independent long-distance operations, a condition essential to an independent RAF.[30] The issue of permanence assumed a greater urgency when, in September, Churchill wavered briefly over the question of whether the cost of an air force was justified after the government had decided that defence expenditure should be cut back, based on the assumption that there would be no major war for at least ten years – soon to be popularly dubbed the 'Ten-Year Rule'. When Trenchard learned of Churchill's possible change of heart, he stormed into Churchill's office and engaged in a shouting match with his minister over the future of the force.[31] Later the same day, 11 September 1919, he drafted a second document that addressed the problem of the temporary character of a force set up in conditions of war 'owing to the great popular outcry' in 1917 about the state of the air services. This time he argued that a separate air force was essential to 'encourage and develop airmanship, or, better still, the Air spirit, like the Naval spirit, and to make it a force that will profoundly influence the strategy of the future'. The air force, he continued, had not had the luxury that the army and navy had had to develop over centuries, but had condensed 100 years of development into five short years, giving it a status that matched the other services. He concluded with a rhetorical question that once again sat oddly with his earlier arguments against change: 'how can you really progress in the Air except by a separate Air Force . . . ?'[32]

Churchill did not in the end renege on his initial commitment to maintain an independent ministry and air force. In late November the Air Staff drew up a third memorandum on the reconstruction of a permanent RAF, which they sent to Churchill for his approval. 'I agree,' he scribbled hurriedly on the draft.[33] Trenchard then produced a final document outlining the achievements so far in founding the force, the problems still to be overcome ('not one single permanent barracks', no government-owned stations except Cranwell), and the speculation that the role of an independent air force might become 'more and more the predominating factor in all types of warfare'.[34] This document was reproduced on 11 December 1919 for the Cabinet, prefaced with a covering note by Churchill, under the portentous title 'Royal Air Force: Permanent Organisation of the Royal Air Force'.[35] No political objections were raised, and the RAF at last achieved permanent status.

It turned out to be a fragile victory. Real independence for the air force proved to be a red rag to the bulls in the army and navy. What ought to have been the conclusion to an unstable period of construction was transformed by service rivalry into the starting point for years of fractious efforts to undo what Trenchard and his staff had achieved by the end of 1919. The ensuing conflict with both the navy and the army over the survival of an independent RAF was anticipated by Trenchard as he drew up the new terms of permanence. In November 1919 he informed the First Sea Lord, David Beatty, about the contents of his memorandum, promising that a portion of the air force would serve with the navy, a portion with the army, but the main portion would comprise an independent central core, likely to become the largest part. 'What is wanted in the Air Service,' he concluded, 'is a period of freedom from criticism by Parliament and the public' and the endless discussion by 'the large number of Naval and Army officers . . . who consider that the Air Force should be broken up'. At a face-to-face meeting with Beatty and the army Chief of the Imperial General Staff, Henry Wilson, Trenchard was able to extract a grudging year-long truce, but no promise that either service would abandon their intention to dismantle the RAF if they could.

The truce lasted a full year before the latent conflict resurfaced, but the sentiment of distrust and hostility did not disappear. Wilson noted in his diary in May 1920 after Churchill had agreed to allow the RAF to take a leading position in the pacification campaign in the League Mandate of Iraq, 'The sooner the Air Force crashes the better . . . It is a wicked waste of money as run at present'.[36] When in February 1921 Churchill, now Colonial Secretary rather than Secretary of State for War and Air, proposed to extend RAF responsibility throughout the Middle East, the army and navy joined forces to try once again to eliminate an independent RAF. The army General Staff prepared a memorandum for the new Secretary of War, Laming Worthington-Evans, setting out in detail their objections to the continued existence of the RAF: 'Aircraft at present and for many years to come must act as an auxiliary arm to the Naval and Military Services and as such should be organized, trained and employed as integral parts of these Services.' The army pointed out that no other country had adopted the British pattern, citing a comment from Franklin D. Roosevelt, former Assistant Secretary for the Navy in Washington, that the RAF was considered internationally as a 'costly failure'.[37] In forwarding the memorandum to the Committee of Imperial Defence, Worthington-Evans added that Marshal Foch, architect of victory in 1918, held strongly to the view that 'the principle of the absolute independence of the Air Service is inadmissable'. Neither the Committee of Imperial Defence nor the Cabinet were impressed by the arguments, but in September Wilson returned to the fray when Geddes was once again investigating possible cuts in national expenditure: 'we deprecate the divorcement of the Royal Air Force from the Army and Navy . . . we want as much Air Force and as little Air Ministry as we can get for our money'.[38] Trenchard for his part deplored this 'still more intemperate attack' and added 'the imagination of the soldier has evidently severe limitations', an accusation that might at one time have been directed at him. In preparing papers for Geddes' Committee, the Air Staff condemned the older services for seeing no further 'than their own limited horizons'.[39] Geddes' final report in December vindicated the RAF as good value for money but, ironically enough, cut the money available for navy and army cooperation.[40]

In 1922 the campaign against the RAF was renewed, but this time the chief antagonist was the Royal Navy. The Admiralty had since early 1919 always insisted that the navy respected the principle of a separate air service. But this principle did not exclude the strong desire to win back complete control over that portion assigned to work with the navy, particularly those units working directly with the main fleet. In March 1922

Beatty complained to Churchill that the navy disliked a situation in which their air equipment and personnel was supplied by another service 'over which we have no control'. A few months later he reiterated to Churchill the Admiralty view that a naval unit of the fighting fleet 'must be manned, administered and controlled by the Navy'.[41] Trenchard rejected what he saw as the navy's dissimulating claim: 'The Admiralty, and you can camouflage it how you will, are asking for a separate Air Service'. The Air Staff remained utterly opposed to what they saw as an attempt to turn the clock back to the situation in 1914.[42] The intransigence of the two services over the future of air power at sea was finally resolved by Lloyd George's successor as prime minister, Andrew Bonar Law, when a committee was set up under Lord Salisbury to investigate the taut relations between the three armed services. In July 1923, the committee found in favour of the RAF on the dispute between the air force and the navy over personnel and equipment. For the time being, the Air Ministry kept overall control over naval aviation and a unitary RAF.[43] The following year Trenchard and Vice-Admiral Roger Keyes negotiated a final agreement that gave the Admiralty operational authority over what was called the Fleet Air Arm, a branch of the RAF on permanent secondment to naval vessels at sea. The Fleet Air Arm was formally constituted on 1 April 1924.[44]

There are a number of ways in which the repeated efforts of the naval and military high commands to break up the RAF might be explained. The most straightforward is simply a question of service jealousy. In the current climate of close collaboration between the three armed services, it is difficult to understand why in the early twentieth century the services saw each other as competitors rather than colleagues, each guarding its own role and identity, each scrambling for a share of the limited defence budget. In this case, however, rivalry was based on more fundamental issues. The two areas in which the RAF assumed a leading role after the war, in home defence and imperial policing, were both the traditional responsibility of the older services. The idea that British imperial territory and the British homeland could better be protected or policed by aircraft was a radical departure, certain to arouse resentment and argument over the merits of the upstart service.

The role of aircraft in imperial security was an unpredictable outcome of the rapid wartime development of British air power, summed up in Sykes' memorandum at the end of the war on the future of the RAF when he suggested that the 'Air Force must be the first line of defence of the British Empire'.[45] The first use of aircraft for the defence of empire was modest enough. In May 1919, aircraft were used in the Third Afghan War in raids against the cities of Dakka and Jalalabad. One raid was made on the Afghan capital of Kabul by the only operational Handley Page V/1500 heavy bomber, the aircraft originally intended for a bombing offensive against Germany in 1919. Though the damage was slight, the raid encouraged the Afghan leaders to abandon the war. However, the campaign that provoked the first fears of the older services about RAF ambitions was conducted against the so-called 'Mad Mullah', the Somali religious leader Mohammed Abdulla Hassan, and his Dervish supporters. Two squadrons of just eight aircraft were sent to British Somaliland and began a five-day bombing campaign in January 1920 before army units moved in. The pacification was a limited success at best, but there followed an argument between the air force and the army over who might claim it. For Trenchard and the fledgling service, the air control of the empire opened up important possibilities, not only justifying an independent air force, but also demonstrating that air power was a much cheaper way of policing Britain's global territories than army expeditionary forces and naval intervention.

Over the following two years, with Churchill's strong support at the Colonial Office, the RAF developed a scheme for the policing of the Middle East, where Britain now had additional territorial responsibilities in Palestine, Transjordan and Mesopotamia (modern-day Iraq) following the granting of mandates from the League of Nations. Iraq was the most important of the three because of widespread resistance to British control, but here was a case where army responsibility had been clear. The decision of the Cabinet to approve the air policing of the territory, under an RAF Supreme Commander, challenged military prerogatives, and occasioned the long campaign in 1921 and 1922 to break up the air force. Air control in Iraq began on 1 October 1922 under the command of the former Commander-in-Chief of the RAF in France, John Salmond, who used aircraft ruthlessly not only against insurgents but also at times to enforce the payment of taxes.[46] The army chafed at the bit over the limitations imposed on its own operations, but the Air Ministry argument that air policing saved the taxpayer substantial sums was vindicated when a committee under Lord Colwyn, established in August 1925 to investigate RAF expenditure, confirmed the air force claim.[47] To demonstrate the apparent effectiveness of the RAF's new imperial role, the annual RAF tournament at Hendon aerodrome in north London climaxed with a flight of aircraft dropping small incendiary bombs on a model of an African village.

Service jealousy, though real enough, was not an argument. Both the older services found solid reasons to question the real effectiveness of aircraft acting independently. Postwar investigation of the long-range bombing campaign provided no evidence that the raids had made any difference to the outcome of the war, while the navy insisted that bombing civilian areas was contrary to international law. In 1921, the army General Staff dismissed the idea that bombing could possibly be decisive, though in terms that must have worried the politicians who read it: 'London might be laid in ruins, the House of Commons, the Admiralty and the War Office might have to function in disused coalmines or other subterranean refuges, the national life might be dislocated to an unprecedented degree, but that would not of itself force a decision . . .'[48] Air defence was also rejected by the army General Staff as a justification for a separate air force. The original aim in 1917 to establish an air force to defend Britain, and London in particular, against air attack was shown by the official statistics to have been in their view largely a failure.

For their part, the Royal Navy deprecated the loss of their principal role in defending the home islands from possible attack. In January 1919 the navy informed the War Cabinet that the response to the threat of invasion of the home islands was their responsibility, and consequently that it made sense to give them control of coastal aircraft to work with the fleet in repelling enemy air and sea operations. Air attacks on inland centres, the Admiralty gracelessly conceded, 'would appear to be the responsibility of the Air Ministry'.[49] The navy argument that any enemy crossing the sea ought sensibly to be engaged first by the fleet and by supporting aircraft under naval command rumbled on for some years thereafter. There were good grounds for doubting the capacity of the RAF to deliver effective Empire defence. At one point early in 1920 there were only two fully serviceable RAF squadrons available for home defence, a puny force to meet any possible air attack on the United Kingdom, unlikely though it might have been. In India the RAF was starved of aircraft, spares and mechanics, and the small handful of aircraft available were for the most part not serviceable. In Ireland, the limited number of aircraft allocated for the 'Defence of Ireland Scheme' were poorly maintained; at one station in the west of the island there was for a time only a single serviceable aircraft. The men lived mostly in tents in conditions described after one investigation as 'squalid to the last degree'.[50] Under these circumstances, the argument that the air force ought to supersede the other services in defence of the homeland and Empire seemed at best unconvincing.

The Air Staff and their combative chief did not take the arguments of the other services lying down. In response to naval claims that the Senior Service should be responsible for defending the home islands, the Air Staff counterattacked by circulating a memorandum on the 'Big Ship Controversy' that foresaw the disappearance of the old-fashioned capital ship once enough resources had been devoted to the air. 'In the past,' the document continued, 'one of the roles of our Navy has been to protect these islands from invasion: the Air Staff has no hesitation in saying that the Air Force of the present . . . is an adequate counter to this menace.'[51] The Fleet Air Arm, claimed a later memorandum, is an integral part of the RAF, not 'part of the Navy'. Trenchard told Churchill in March 1922, at the height of the naval controversy, that he started from the basis, 'from which we cannot depart, that the Air Service is one complete whole', not one to be divided up to suit the other services.[52] Nevertheless, the RAF position remained vulnerable. Most of the assertions about air power lay in the future, as the army and navy both realized. In autumn 1922 the Lloyd George coalition collapsed and a Conservative administration under Andrew Bonar Law took its place. By fateful coincidence, Sykes had married Bonar Law's eldest daughter. When his father-in-law asked for advice on the future of the Air Ministry, Sykes mischievously suggested that the RAF should be broken up and returned to the other services. The new Air Minister, Samuel Hoare, was told that he might not occupy his new portfolio for very long. In late October that year Trenchard wrote to one of his senior commanders about the latest crisis: 'frankly I think (though I may be wrong) that I may not be much longer in office'.[53]

Why did the RAF maintain an independent existence in the face of so much pressure to return to the pre-war defence establishment? The simple answer is that the RAF was saved by the politicians, a conclusion that Trenchard, with his inveterate distrust of the world of politics, would have been reluctant to endorse. Trenchard himself proved to be a more adroit political operator than his diffidence about office work or his reputation for blunt talk, serial resignation and muddled thinking might have suggested. Yet time and again when it seemed the future of the RAF was seriously in doubt, senior political players were willing to campaign on its behalf. In 1919 the key figure was Churchill, despite his occasional doubts. It was Churchill who defended in Cabinet the change to permanent status for the RAF in December 1919; it was Churchill at the Colonial Office who insisted in 1921 that the RAF draw up a plan for air policing in the Middle East. Churchill told Trenchard, according to a later account, that it was his chance 'to establish the Air Force as a separate service beyond doubt'.[54] In the renewed crisis over the future of the force in 1922, it was Churchill who wrote to the Foreign Secretary, Austen Chamberlain, in March that year explaining that the uncertainty surrounding the future status of the RAF was damaging the service and asking him to state categorically in a Commons debate that there was no intention of winding it up. Chamberlain obliged with a parliamentary statement on 16 March that made the present government's position clear: 'Believing, however, as we do that the Air Forces have immense potentialities of their own, and in their own element . . . we consider that it would be a retrograde step at this time to abolish the Air Ministry and to reabsorb the Air Service into the Admiralty and the War Office.'[55]

The advent of the Bonar Law government in August 1922 led to a brief renewal of the argument about a separate air force, but the new Secretary of State for Air, Samuel Hoare, became an instant supporter of an independent service. He held the office, except for a brief interlude in 1924, for seven years, the longest-serving air minister, and with his unstinting support the RAF survived the investigation into service co-operation instigated by Bonar Law in March 1923. The Sub-Committee of the Committee of Imperial Defence under Lord Salisbury, the Lord President of the Council, reported in July that year, confirming once again the political preference for an independent RAF. Inter-service collaboration, which had been one of the objects of investigation, was to be maintained by the recently established Chiefs-of-Staff Committee, an initiative that Trenchard had helped to set up deliberately in order to ensure that the RAF would sit on an equal basis with the navy and army to decide Britain's defence strategy.[56] Hoare's Principal Private Secretary, Christopher Bullock, recalled that 'ministers found the Air Ministry case unanswerable.' Trenchard admitted years afterwards that the survival of the RAF 'owed a lot to the Salisbury Committee'.[57] This was not yet the end of the story. The Admiralty refused to accept the terms of the Salisbury report, and Hoare battled on the RAF's behalf to prevent any further attempt to subvert the clear decision that the naval air forces were part of the RAF. Finally in 1926, Stanley Baldwin, the Conservative prime minister, lost patience with naval intransigence. He told the House of Commons that the organization of imperial defence was now based on 'three co-equal services', sharing responsibility for British security: 'controversy upon this subject must now cease.'[58] After eight years of what the RAF Director of Intelligence described as 'a very gruelling business' – fighting the army, the navy and the Treasury – the RAF no longer faced an uncertain future.[59]

Political support for the RAF continued the tradition established in 1917 when Lloyd George overrode military objections to force through the inauguration of the new service. The British constitutional system required that a reform of this magnitude should be the responsibility of Parliament, but it also meant that the older services had no real power to affect the politicians' decision. Churchill reminded Austen Chamberlain in March 1922 that the RAF was created by Act of Parliament and the statute could only be undone by a parliamentary decision to repeal it, not by what Churchill called 'mischievous inter-departmental agitation'. In Parliament there existed a strident lobby on behalf of British air power which would, in Churchill's words, 'oppose and obstruct to the utmost any measure of repeal'.[60] Moreover, the formal creation of the RAF had been the responsibility of the monarch, George V, who now bore the title 'Chief of the Air Force' and who was not likely, given the support he had already displayed for the RAF, to relinquish the title lightly.

The King was a regular guest at the Hendon Tournament (later the 'air pageant'), an event that grew in popularity with the spread of what was called 'airmindedness'. The first tournament in 1920 attracted more than 40,000 people, with additional crowds gathered outside the airfield to watch the displays of mock combat and aerobatics. Aviation was big news in the 1920s, whether long-distance endurance flights, or exploration of the little known areas of the globe, or air circuses and displays. The Air Ministry was also responsible for organizing the development of British civil aviation in the 1920s. The novelty of regular commercial flight for those who could afford it helped to shape an increasingly sympathetic public opinion after the critical attitude toward British air performance during the war. It also meant that the future of Britain in the air was a civilian as well as a military issue.

The popular interest in aviation was reflected in the willingness of the politicians to exploit the air as a novel solution to difficult issues of imperial security. Even before the end of the war, the British Viceroy in Ireland, trying to cope with the threat of a national uprising, was calling on the RAF to use bombs and machine-guns to 'put the fear of God into these playful young Sinn Feiners'.[61] Though the 'Defence of Ireland Scheme' drawn up by the RAF in 1919 was difficult to operate with any success, the politicians saw the air force as an instrument capable of overcoming the limitations of the army presence. The RAF was sent to Russia as a contribution to the anti-Bolshevik campaign waged in 1918–19 by the Allied powers. The development of air policing of the Empire was welcomed by the government not only as a way to cut costs, which was a prime consideration, but because the exercise of air power was shown to work. Henry Dobbs, the British High Commissioner in Iraq, and an early sceptic about the value of an RAF campaign, concluded in 1924 that air control had been 'brilliantly, magnificently successful'.[62] The financial argument for governments that were committed to defence retrenchment in the 1920s was unassailable. The cost of the military occupation of Iraq in 1920–21 had been £32 million, in 1921–2 it was £23 million; in the year following the assumption of RAF command in the region, the cost was £6.6 million and by 1927–8 that sum had been reduced to just £1.65 million.[63] The fiscal implications helped to underwrite the growing awareness that air power was a cost-effective way of maintaining empire security. 'I think the Air Force,' Churchill later claimed, 'was a great economy in maintaining order in these wild countries.'[64]

Finally, the political appeal of the RAF was bound up with public and government anxiety in the early 1920s that the rapid demobilization of the air force left Britain vulnerable to any possible attack from the air. The fear of the 'knock-out blow', as it came to be known, was evidently exaggerated, since no neighbouring air force in the early 1920s was capable of delivering such a blow even if it were feasible, while the evidence from the bombing during the war showed that the effects of bomb attack were much more limited than the postwar fantasies suggested.[65] The fear, nevertheless, was real enough. In 1922 the Committee of Imperial Defence discussed the possibility that an enemy air force could drop 300 tons within 48 hours, and 100 tons per day for a month thereafter. There was talk of putting the population under martial law if this happened, with absentee workers treated as 'deserters'.[66] The prospective 'enemy' in this case was France. A year before, the Committee had been presented with tabulated statistics showing the air strength of the major powers. French air forces now dwarfed the RAF, and, even if a sudden French air strike seemed implausible, British leaders considered the possibility that the French government might use the threat of a bombing campaign to make Britain a more pliant onlooker as France came to dominate the European continent. Arthur Balfour thought that in the face of the French menace Britain was 'more defenceless than it has ever been before'. [67] That year the Defence Committee established yet another sub-committee on the 'Continental Air Menace', the product of a similar paranoia that had fuelled the naval race against Germany before 1914. The French 'Air Division' set up to perform strategic tasks was known to possess almost 600 fighters and bombers. Intelligence assessments added the thirty-four other French squadrons and French civil aircraft to paint a gloomy picture of Britain's helpless plight in the air. The menace, fanciful though it proved to be, helped to change Bonar Law's mind about the RAF. Having flirted with breaking the air force up, he came to see its expansion as a pressing response to the temporary imbalance of air power against Britain's erstwhile wartime ally. One of the recommendations of the Salisbury Committee when it reported in July 1923 was to endorse a planned RAF home defence strength of 600 aircraft to match the French 'Air Division'.[68]

There seems little doubt that Trenchard and the Air Staff played up the idea of Britain's vulnerable position in the air against France to win political support for a larger air force organized independently of the other services. The result was a political victory for the RAF in its struggle for recognition. In mid-1922, Trenchard drafted a revised scheme for home defence to meet the current alleged danger. In place of the three squadrons currently available to defend the British Isles, he recommended a force of twenty-three squadrons. Consistent with the view he and other senior airmen had held during the war that the best defence was offence, the force was divided between fighters intended to defend against incoming bombers, and day and night bombing squadrons to inflict a counter-blow against the enemy.[69] In August that year the Cabinet accepted what came to be called the Home Defence Air Force. The RAF argument that only a strong air force could counter the strategic vulnerability of the country was accepted by the politicians, and on 9 July 1923 the force was formally approved by the government with wide public support, giving the RAF a rationale that neither the army nor navy could challenge. The Home Defence Air Force proved difficult to establish quickly, given the financial constraints and the failure under Trenchard's leadership to move fast enough out of the biplane age. In 1925 the government postponed completion of the force until 1935 under the 'Ten-Year Rule', by which time the French 'menace' had evaporated and the force seemed less urgent. Nevertheless, the policy decisions in 1922–3 ensured that the RAF would be regarded by the politicians as the primary means of defending the heart of the Empire.[70]

One central question ran through all the arguments and counter-arguments in the years after the end of the war: what was the RAF for? In the last months of the war this question was never fully answered, since most aircraft continued to give direct support to the army and navy, despite the expectation that home defence and strategic bombing would really give the RAF a claim to full service independence. In April 1919, a convalescent Trenchard wrote to Churchill with brief thoughts about the postwar air force. The most pressing need, Trenchard wrote, was to define 'for what purpose we are and with what object is the RAF being maintained'.[71] This proved to be a difficult proposition. RAF doctrine, to the extent that it was understood at the time, remained unclear, contradictory and speculative for much of the inter-war period. The main difficulty, a profound one for Trenchard as the great wartime champion of air support for the army, was to disengage the RAF from its principal wartime role as an auxiliary to the older services. The failure to do so would open up the objection that the air force was better off divided by function, part for the air-sea war, part to support the land war. This was how the air service was organized in all other major states where there was no separate air service. As the world's first independent air force the RAF faced the problem of creating a body of doctrine that justified that accolade. Whether airmen liked it or not, the situation pushed the RAF to argue for bombing and home defence as their strategic preference and to abandon as central aims the counter-force and ground support tactics deployed with great effect during the war, but both of which tied the air force too closely to the other services.

This doctrinal choice emerged only slowly, and with much uncertainty, in the early years of the new air force. When Trenchard set out the case for a permanent RAF in late 1919 he still suggested that a portion of the air force would be assigned to the army, a portion to the navy. A naval Fleet Air Arm did develop after much argument about who really controlled naval aviation, but the naval dimension of the RAF featured little if at all in Air Staff discussions about the nature of air strategy. By the time the Fleet Air Arm was finally assigned to Admiralty control in July 1937, British naval aviation was far behind those navies with a dedicated naval air force such as the United States and Japan. An army cooperation element remained largely on paper until the creation of what proved to be the painfully obsolescent Advanced Air Striking Force in autumn 1939, sent from Bomber Command to support the army in France after the declaration of a second world war, alongside a small number of fighter squadrons.

The German Air Force by contrast was almost entirely dedicated to supporting the ground offensive and destroying the enemy air force. Although support for surface forces and counter-force strategy did not disappear as an element of air doctrine, they were relegated to a back seat. The Manual of Combined Operations published later in the 1930s conceded only that 'the Army may need help . . .' in advancing against the enemy on land, not that air–ground collaboration was a vital dimension of modern war. Only three and a half pages out of 272 were devoted to air–army cooperation, one third of those to 'Control of Semi-Civilised Tribes within our own Jurisdiction'.[72] Until 1939, the prevailing hope in government was that a major land war in Europe could be avoided, which explains the low priority given to tactical air power. In March 1939 the Air Ministry finally drew up a specification for an aircraft that could do for the army exactly what they had done in the Great War ('close and distant tactical reconnaissance by day, observation of artillery fire, photography, low-level or shallow dive-bombing, and supply dropping'), but the slow two-seat design was obsolete even on paper, and never materialized.[73] When it became necessary to prepare for possible ground support against enemy troops, a mere seven pilots were trained in shallow dive-bombing, dropping just fifty-six bombs in practice. The Director of Plans at the Air Ministry, John Slessor, expressed a view common among airmen that 'the aeroplane is not a battlefield weapon'.[74] Before the Battle of France, when the AASF was also supposed to prepare for bombing operations against the enemy air force, RAF commanders continued to insist that this was an ineffective use of air resources, which ought to be directed at larger and more vulnerable industrial objectives in Germany itself. Unlike 1918, when Trenchard regarded the suppression of enemy air power as the first call on air resources, the RAF went to war in 1939 convinced that counter-force was no longer a viable strategic option. [75]

From the onset of imperial air policing, when light bombers were used to coerce recalcitrant tribesmen, long-range independent bombing came to be seen as the characteristic strategy for a modern air force. Once Trenchard was allowed to construct the Home Defence force, he openly campaigned along with his staff for a striking force to attack the enemy home front as the quickest and most effective way of compelling an enemy to give up. This remained a matter of faith, since there was no evidence to support the argument. Like Douhet in Italy, the British Air Staff simply assumed that, for modern urban populations, bombing on a large scale must be unendurable. In a speech to War Office staff in April 1923, Trenchard spelt out his vision of what air power ought to achieve:

> It is probable that any war on the European Continent in which we might be involved in the future would resolve itself, virtually, into a contest of morale between the respective civilian populations. By this is meant that there would be a tendency for the nationals of the power which suffered most from air attack, or which lacked in moral tenacity, to bring such pressure to bear on their government as to result in military capitulation.[76]

To army and navy objections that the true nature of strategy was to engage and overcome the enemy armed forces in combat, the air force countered that air power directed at an enemy's national centres 'is not to avoid fighting, but to win the war'. This meant choosing targets that would have 'the greatest effect on enemy will power' and would bring the war to an end in the shortest time.[77] These were assertions rather than strategic principles, but the idea that air power could shorten wars, or even win them single-handedly, had an appealing logic to a force determined to demonstrate its strategic independence. When the army and navy challenged the RAF in 1928 to define more precisely what was the 'War Aim of an Air Force', on the grounds that bombing in the Great War had been both ineffective and illegal, the Air Staff persisted with the idea that bombing the enemy's home front was the RAF's principal aim. Trenchard argued that air power afforded the opportunity to attack the enemy where he was weakest, rather than where he was strong. Enemy cities and industry were 'the points where defence is most difficult for him and where he is most vulnerable to attack by the air weapon'.[78] This speculation remained the central element of the RAF's approach to future war right down to 1940, when in May of that year the first long-distance raids against German cities began.

The emphasis on the offensive nature of air power meant that RAF commanders were much less interested in the issue of air defence at home, even though, to satisfy popular and political anxieties, the Home Defence Air Force was also designed to act as a shield against an enemy's air incursions.[79] Home defence could not be ignored, but the view that Trenchard had held in the war, that the best defence was a counter-offensive, remained another article of faith. When in the 1930s successive governments insisted that the RAF develop a major defensive capability, the Air Staff thought there was too much emphasis on defence. In a paper drafted in the summer of 1938, the staff returned to the question that Smuts had posed in his reports in 1917 about how to win a war. Defence did not win wars; instead, the paper continued, 'we must regard the Air Striking Force as constituting not only a strong deterrent and insurance in peace, but also as our only means of imposing our will on the enemy in war.'[80] This claim highlighted a strategic paradox that ran through all the interwar years: air defence was supposed to blunt any enemy bombing campaign, but an enemy would not in turn be able to prevent an RAF counter-offensive. In spring 1939 the Commander-in-Chief of Fighter Command, Air Chief Marshal Hugh Dowding, wrote to the Chief of Air Staff, Cyril Newall, claiming that any German bombing campaign against Britain 'would be brought to a standstill in a month or less' as a result of the casualties imposed by the air defenders.[81] At the same time the Air Ministry was preparing the so-called Western Air Plans, in which bombing German industrial centres played a central part, on the assumption that German air defences would not do the same as Fighter Command. Neither assumption proved correct, though Dowding was much closer to the truth, but the RAF retained well into the Second World War its paradoxical commitment to the view that offence and defence would be equally effective.

By this stage the RAF had been reorganized into functional categories that reflected the priority of an independent air strategy. In 1936, the force was split between Bomber Command, Fighter Command and Coastal Command. There was no dedicated tactical air force and no command for air–army cooperation. The legacy of the Great War, when counter-force and ground support had been paramount, had to be learned anew in the Second World War. When it was, British tactical air power arguably became the most important and successful development in the history of the RAF during its second major war. Bombing the home front, on the other hand, had not been well prepared and proved to be strategically dubious, lengthy rather than the swift knock-out blow, and costly to both friend and foe. British tactical air campaigns also demonstrated that institutional independence and service cooperation were not incompatible. When the war began, the one element in the RAF's new organization that was technically up to date and reasonably prepared was the fighter defence of the British Isles. By a peculiar irony the pressure of the politicians in the 1930s to find an effective defence against bombing brought the air force back full circle to the crisis in 1917 that had prompted the call for a separate service in the first place. The Battle of Britain was in this sense the fruit of a long gestation from the feeble defences of 1917–18 to the sophisticated air defence system of 1940.

Another twist of fate that year brought to power Winston Churchill, whose support for the fledgling RAF had played such an important part in the survival of an independent force. That support wavered at times again in the Second World War as it had in 1919, but in a speech in Boston, Massachusetts, thirty years after his brief spell as Air Minister, Churchill returned to the theme that air power was the future: 'For good or ill, air mastery is today the supreme expression of military power and Fleets and Armies, however necessary, must accept a subordinate rank.'[82] If Churchill's prognosis did not quite work out as he expected, the air service that he championed years before lit the flame for all the independent air forces that followed.

Notes

1. Britain and the War in the Air

1 H.G. Wells, *The War in the Air* (London: George Bell & Sons, 1908), p. 208.
2 H. G. Wells, *Experiment in Autobiography* (Boston: Little, Brown, 1934), p. 569.
3 Andrew Whitmarsh, 'British Army Manoeuvres and the Development of Military Aviation, 1910–1913', *War in History*, 14 (2007), pp. 326–7; Liddell Hart Archive Centre (LHA), Brooke-Popham papers, 8/3, 'A Brief History of the British Air Service, 1910–1935' (n.d.), pp. 1–2.
4 Frederick Sykes, *From Many Angles: An Autobiography* (London: Harrap, 1942), pp. 95–7. The motto is also used by the Australian, Canadian and New Zealand air forces, and was used by the Indian air force until 1947. The translation of *ardua* as 'adversity' is the preferred RAF version, but it can also mean 'struggle' or 'effort'.
5 Churchill College Archive Centre (CCAC), CHAR 13/6B/265, Churchill to Capt. Murray Sueter, 31 May 1914. Churchill wanted the title to be the Flying Wing.
6 The National Archive (TNA), AIR 1/727/149/1, Maj.-Gen. Sefton Brancker, 'Home Defence and Reorganisation of the RFC, 1914–1917' (n.d.), pp. 1–2.
7 Whitmarsh, 'British Army Manoeuvres', pp. 329–36; LHA, Brooke-Popham papers, 8/3, 'A brief history', p. 5.
8 LHA, Brooke-Popham papers, 1/8, RAF Staff College Notes, Dec 1924, 'Air Strength on the Western Front: Development and

Order of Battle'; 8/3, 'A Brief History', p. 5; TNA, AIR 1/718/29/8, Cmd. 100, 'Synopsis of British Air Effort during the War', Apr 1919, p. 16; Christopher Luck, 'The Smuts Report: Interpreting and Misinterpreting the Promise of Air Power', in Gary Sheffield and Peter Gray (eds.), *Changing War: The British Army, The Hundred Days Campaign and the Birth of the Royal Air Force, 1918* (London: Bloomsbury, 2013), pp. 150–51. RNAS figures are from Stephen Roskill (ed.), *Documents Relating to the Naval Air Service: Volume I, 1908–1918* (London: Navy Records Society, 1969), p. 747.

9 LHA, Brig.-Gen. Percy Groves papers, Box 2 (a), lecture by Groves on 'The Organisation and Work of the Royal Flying Corps', 3 Feb 1917, p. 3.

10 LHA, Brooke-Popham papers, 8/2, Training Manual, Royal Flying Corps, Part II (Military Wing), p. 82.

11 LHA, Brooke-Popham papers, RAF Field Service Book, Apr 1918, p. 74; 8/2, Training Manual, Royal Flying Corps, p. 28.

12 Royal Air Force Museum, Hendon (RAFM), B2717, transcript of diary kept by Air Mech. 2, Thomas Spencer, 66th Squadron RFC.

13 Paul Marr, 'Haig and Trenchard: Achieving Air Superiority on the Western Front', *Air Power Review*, 17 (2014), p. 32; John Slessor, *The Central Blue: Recollections and Reflections* (London: Cassell, 1956), p. 24. See too Trevor Nash, 'Flight Training in the First World War and its Legacy', *Air Power Review*, 19 (2016), pp. 38–41.

14 LHA, Brooke-Popham papers, 8/2, Training Manual, Royal Flying Corps, pp. 27–8.

15 LHA, Groves papers, 2 (a), 'The Organization and work of the Royal Flying Corps', 3 Feb 1917, p. 6.

16 Ibid., pp. 7–10.

17 LHA, Brooke-Popham papers, 8/2, Training Manual, Royal Flying Corps, Dec 1915.

18 CCAC, CHAR 13/29/194, draft statement by Churchill to House of Commons, 23 Nov 1914; R. D. Layman, *Naval Aviation in the First World War: Its Impact and Influence* (London: Chatham Publishing, 1996), pp. 37–8.

19 Roskill (ed.), *Naval Air Service: Volume I*, pp. 179, 309, 408–9; Layman, *Naval Aviation in the First World War*, pp. 74–5.

20 Maurice Baring, *Flying Corps Headquarters, 1914–1918* (London: Buchan & Enright, 1985), p.66.

21 Ibid., p. 64.

22 Basil Collier, *Heavenly Adventurer: Sefton Brancker and the Dawn of British Aviation* (London: Secker & Warburg, 1959), p. 46.

23 Russell Miller, *Trenchard: Father of the Royal Air Force* (London: Weidenfeld & Nicolson, 2016), pp. 100–102.

24 Sykes, *From Many Angles*, pp. 144–6.

25 Cambridge University Library (CUL), Boyle papers, Add 9429/1B/265, Trenchard to Major Lockhart (his first biographer), 3 Feb 1953.

26 RAFM, papers of MRAF Sir John Salmond, AC 71/20/B2644, 'C.F.S. Reminiscences', p. 2.

27 CUL, Boyle papers, Add 9429/1B/268 (i), 'Notes on a chapter written by Major Lockhart', 18 Jan 1954, p. 1.

28 Ibid., 1B/273 (i), Trenchard to Lockhart, 10 Oct 1958.

29 Eric Ash, *Sir Frederick Sykes and the Air Revolution 1912–1918* (London: Frank Cass, 1999), pp. 65–7.

30 Jerry White, *Zeppelin Nights: London in the First World War* (London: Bodley Head, 2014), pp. 125–6.

31 For the best recent account see Guillaume de Syon, *Zeppelin: Germany and the Airship, 1900–1939* (Baltimore, MD: Johns Hopkins University Press, 2002), pp.103–6.

32 Susan Grayzel, *At Home and Under Fire: Air Raid Culture in Britain from the Great War to the Blitz* (Cambridge: Cambridge University Press, 2012), pp. 25–31.

33　Layman, *Naval Aviation in the First World War*, p. 71.

34　TNA, AIR 9/5, note by the Chief of the Imperial General Staff on Mr Balfour's Memorandum, 16 Sep 1921.

35　TNA, AIR 1/718/29/8, Cmd. 100, 'Synopsis of the British Air Effort during the War', Apr 1919, p. 10.

36　TNA, AIR 1/721/46/4, Home Office, Home Defence Anti-Aircraft Precautions (Civilian), 1914–1918 (n.d.), pp. 3–4, 40–53.

37　LHA, Brooke-Popham papers, 8/3, 'A Brief History', p. 5.

38　J. M. Bruce, *The Aeroplanes of the Royal Flying Corps (Military Wing)* (London: Putnam, 1982), passim.

39　TNA, AIR 8/2, Brig.-Gen. David Henderson, 'Memorandum on the Organisation of the Air Service', 19 Jul 1917, pp. 2–3; AIR 9/5, 'Note by the Air Staff on the reasons for the formation of the Royal Air Force' (n.d., but 1921), pp. 1–2; Malcolm Cooper, 'Blueprint for Confusion: The Administrative Background to the Formation of the Royal Air Force, 1912–19', *Journal of Contemporary History*, 22 (1987), pp. 438–9; Peter Gray, 'The Air Ministry and the Formation of the Royal Air Force' in Sheffield, Gray (eds), *Changing War*, pp. 135–6.

40　TNA, AIR 8/2, 'First Report of the Air Board', 23 Oct 1916; Balfour for the Cabinet, 'A Reply to the First Report of the Air Board', 6 Nov 1916; Lord Curzon for the Cabinet, 'Last Words on the Air Board Controversy', 15 Nov 1916.

41　TNA, AIR 9/5, 'Note by the Air Staff on the reasons for the formation of the Royal Air Force' (1921), p. 3; AIR 8/2, Curzon, 'Last Words', p. 1. Curzon claimed that he had been given assurance not only that the Air Board's powers would be strengthened, but also that it would eventually be turned into an air ministry.

42　Gray, 'The Air Ministry', pp. 136–7; Cooper, 'Blueprint for Confusion', p. 439.

43　TNA, AIR 1/718/29/8, 'Synopsis of the British Air Effort', p. 16.

2. Battles in the Sky, Battles in Whitehall

1 TNA, AIR/1/718/29/9, memorandum by Hugh Cecil for Trenchard, 26 Aug 1917, p. 3.

2 TNA, WO 158/947, Intelligence Section, GHQ, Home Forces, 'Air Raids 1917', Jul 1917, pp. 3–4.

3 Jerry White, *Zeppelin Nights: London in the First World War* (London: Bodley Head, 2014), pp. 211–13.

4 Susan Grayzel, *At Home and Under Fire: Air Raids and Culture in Britain from the Great War to the Blitz* (Cambridge: Cambridge University Press, 2012), pp. 72–3; White, *Zeppelin Nights*, p. 214.

5 Christopher Luck, 'The Smuts Report: Interpreting and Misinterpreting the Promise of Air Power', in Gary Sheffield and Peter Gray (eds.), *Changing War: The British Army, the Hundred Days Campaign and the Birth of the Royal Air Force, 1918* (London: Bloomsbury, 2013), pp. 153–4.

6 Parliamentary Archives (P.Arch), Lloyd George papers, LG/F/45/9, Smuts to Lloyd George, 11 Jul 1917; RAFM, Henderson papers, AC71/4/4, 'Notes on Relations of Air Force with Navy and Army for Consideration by General Smuts' Committee' (n.d.).

7 See on this Brock Millman, 'A Counsel of Despair: British Strategy and War Aims 1917–18', *Journal of Contemporary History*, 36 (2001), pp. 244–50; Richard Toye, *Lloyd George and Churchill: Rivals for Greatness* (London: Macmillan, 2007), pp. 173–4.

8 P.Arch, LG/F/45/9, Smuts to Lloyd George, 24 and 31 May 1917.

9 Ibid., Smuts to Lloyd George, 6 Jun 1917.

10 Winston Churchill, *The World Crisis, 1911–1918: Volume II* (London: Odhams, 1938), p. 1170; Toye, *Lloyd George and Churchill*, pp. 178–80.

11 John Sweetman, 'The Smuts Report of 1917: Merely Political Window Dressing?', *Journal of Strategic Studies*, 4 (1981), pp. 155–6.

12 RAFM, Henderson papers, AC71/4/4, C-in-C Home Forces to Henderson, Jul 1917.

13 Raymond Fredette, *The First Battle of Britain 1917/18* (London: Cassell, 1966), pp. 89–90.

14 For the Second Report see RAFM, Trenchard papers, MFC 76/1/2, 'Committee on Air Defence and Home Defence Against Air Raids, Second Report', 17 Aug 1917.

15 TNA, AIR 8/2, 'Memorandum of the Organisation of the Air Service', 19 Jul 1917, pp. 8–9, 13.

16 Stephen Roskill (ed.), *Documents Relating to the Naval Air Service: Volume I, 1908–1918* (London: Navy Records Society, 1969), pp. 315–16, correspondence between Lord Montagu and Lord Derby, March 1916.

17 Ibid., pp. 497–9, Lord Cowdray to General Smuts, 28 Jul 1917, on 'Duties and Functions of the Air Board'. On Cowdray's role see H. A. Jones, *The War in the Air: Volume VI* (Oxford: Oxford University Press, 1937), pp. 7–8.

18 P. Arch, LG/F/8/1/8, Churchill to Lloyd George, 2 Aug 1917.

19 TNA, AIR 1/718/29/9, War Office to Trenchard, 2 Sep 1917.

20 Roskill (ed.), *Naval Air Service: Volume I*, p. 513, 'Second report of the Committee on Air Organisation and Home Defence', 17 Aug 1917.

21 W. J. Reader, *Architect of Airpower: The Life of the First Viscount Weir* (London: Collins, 1968), pp. 57–9. See too Neville Jones, *Origins of Strategic Bombing: A Study of the Development of British Air Strategic Thought and Practice up to 1918* (London: William Kimber, 1973), pp. 137–40; Sweetman, 'The Smuts Report of 1917', pp. 163–4.

22 Reader, *Architect of Airpower*, p. 63. On the 'Surplus Air Fleet' see the discussion in Cowdray's memorandum for Smuts on 28 Jul 1917 in Roskill (ed.), *Naval Air Service: Volume I*, pp. 489–90.

23 Reader, *Architect of Air Power*, pp. 60–63.

24 See the details in LHA, Brooke-Popham papers, 1/8, RAF Staff College Notes, 1924, 'Air Raids on England; Report by the Home Office on the Effect of Air Raids (9.3.22)', pp. 3–14.

25 RAFM, Henderson papers, AC71/4/4, 'Memorandum for the President of the Air Board', 11 Oct 1917, p. 3.

26 CCAC, WEIR 1/2, memorandum by Sir Henry Norman for the Air Minister, 'Long-range Bombing', 25 Mar 1918, p. 2.

27 TNA, AIR 8/2, War Cabinet 223, draft minutes, 24 Aug 1917.

28 Luck, 'The Smuts Report' in Sheffield and Gray (eds.), *Changing War*, p. 159; Reader, *Architect of Air Power*, pp. 65–6.

29 Roskill (ed.), *Naval Air Service: Volume I*, pp. 520–22, Beatty to Geddes, 22 Aug 1917.

30 Ibid., pp. 497–9, Jellicoe, 'Remarks on a Scheme of an Imperial Air Policy', 14 Aug 1917.

31 Ibid., pp. 491–2, Captain O. Swann to Director of Air Services, Admiralty, 9 Aug 1917.

32 TNA, WO 158/35, Royal Flying Corps, Summary of Operations 1917, reports for 1 May, 22 Jul, 3 Sep.

33 R. D. Layman, *Naval Aviation in the First World War: Its Impact and Influence* (London: Chatham Publishing, 1996), pp. 74–5.

34 TNA, AIR 1/718/29/9, Lord Derby to Trenchard, 2 Sep 1917.

35 Luck, 'The Smuts Report', p. 158.

36 TNA, AIR 1/718/29/9, Trenchard to Chief of the Imperial General Staff, 30 Aug 1917.

37 Ibid. 'Memorandum on Future Air Organization, Fighting Policy, and Requirements in Personnel and Materiel', 10 Oct 1917.

38 Ibid.,Trenchard to Lt.-General L. E. Kiggel, 21 Oct 1917.

39 John Laffin, *Swifter than Eagles: A Biography of Marshal of the RAF Sir John Salmond* (Edinburgh: Blackwood, 1964), p. 95.

40 TNA, AIR 8/2, memorandum by General Smuts for the War Cabinet, 18 Sep 1917.

41 Details of raids from TNA, WO 158/950, Report on Air Raids, 24 Sep–1 Nov 1917, pp. 5–11,107, 108.

42 White, *Zeppelin Nights*, pp. 215–18.

43 RAFM, Henderson papers, AC71/4/4, 'Memorandum for the President of the Air Board', 11 Oct 1917; Russell Miller, *Trenchard: Father of the Royal Air Force* (London: Weidenfeld & Nicolson, 2016), p. 181.

44 LHA, Brooke-Popham papers, 1/8, RAF Staff College Notes, 'Effect of Air Raids on Railway Traffic', pp. 2–3.

45 Ibid., 'Report by the Home Office on the Effect of Raids', 9 Mar 1922.

46 RAFM, AIR 69/2651, RAF Staff College Notes, 'The War 1914–1918', XV, 'The Independent Force'.

47 TNA, AIR 1/2085/207/5/3, Approximate results, 41st Wing RAF, 'Résumé of operations', 16/17 Oct 1917.

48 Francis Mason, *The British Bomber since 1914* (London: Putnam, 1994), pp. 67–74.

49 TNA, AIR 1/725/97/6, GHQ Report (RAF) for 1 Jan–31 Jul 1918, p. 7.

50 LHA, Brooke-Popham papers, 8/5, Air Ministry, 'Report of Air Raids on Germany, January 1–November 11 1918', Jan 1920, pp. 1–3, 64; 1/8, RAF Staff College Notes, Dec 1924, Policy Report No. 5, 'Statistics of Independent Force, Work Carried Out'.

51 TNA, AIR 8/2, minute for Trenchard, 'Supplementary Note on the Intentions of the Government in setting up a unified Air Service in 1917'.

52 TNA, MEPO 2/1622, Air Force (Constitution) Act, 1917, 29 Nov 1917, pp. 1, 2, 4.

53 Reproduced in Roskill (ed.), *Naval Air Service: Volume I*, pp. 581–3.

54 S. J. Taylor, *The Great Outsiders: Northcliffe, Rothermere, and the Daily Mail* (London: Weidenfeld & Nicolson, 1996), p. 229; Lord

Beaverbrook, *Men and Power, 1917–1918* (London: Hutchinson, 1956), pp. 217–18.

55 Miller, *Trenchard*, pp. 186–9.

56 TNA, AIR 1/718/29/9, Trenchard to the War Office, 6 Oct 1917.

57 Taylor, *The Great Outsiders*, p. 230.

58 Miller, *Trenchard*, pp. 189–90; CUL, Boyle papers, Add 9429/1B/209 (i), 'Notes by Trenchard for Major Lockhart' (n.d.), p. 3.

59 RAFM, Trenchard papers, MFC 76/1/18, Trenchard to Haig, 31 Dec 1917; Haig to Lord Derby, 10 Jan 1918.

60 Roskill (ed.), *Naval Air Service: Volume I*, pp. 670–71, Geddes to Lord Weir, 22 May 1918.

61 Ibid., p. 619, Air Ministry letter to Admiralty, 19 Jan 1918.

62 Ibid., pp. 641–2, extracts from Admiralty Weekly Orders, 19 Mar 1918.

63 RAFM, Sykes papers, AC73/35/3/4/1, letter by Lord Rothermere in the *Daily Telegraph*, 15 Apr 1918.

64 TNA, AIR 6/12, Air Council minutes, 3rd, 6th and 8th meetings, 11 Jan, 22 Jan, 29 Jan.

65 TNA, AIR 6/12, Air Council minutes 13th meeting, 16th meeting, 17th meeting, 19 Feb, 5 Mar, 8 Mar 1918.

66 TNA, TS 27/58, Air Board minute 12 Jan 1918; letter from Air Board to the secretary of the Air Council, 8 Jan 1918; Air Council to Sir John Mellor, 14 Jan 1918.

67 TNA, AIR 6/12, Air Council minutes, 2nd meeting, 13th meeting, 8 Jan, 19 Feb 1918.

68 RAFM, Sykes papers, AC73/35/3/4/1, Secretary of the Air Ministry to the Air Council, 21 Mar 1918.

69 RAFM, Trenchard papers, MFC 76/1/19, Trenchard to Rothermere, 18 Mar 1918; Rothermere to Trenchard, 19 Mar 1918; Trenchard to Rothermere, 19 Mar 1918; Miller, *Trenchard*, pp. 198–200.

70 Beaverbrook, *Men and Power*, p. 221.

71 RAFM, Trenchard papers, MFC 76/1/92, Trenchard to Salmond, 10 Feb 1918.

72 Ibid., Trenchard to Salmond, 13 Feb 1918.

73 Miller, *Trenchard*, p. 204.

74 Ibid., p. 202.

3. *April Fools' Day 1918*

1 RAFM, AC71/13/15, journal of Richard Peirse, 22 Mar 1918–15 Apr 1918, 65th Wing RNAS, Dunkirk.

2 Ibid, entries for 29 Mar, 3 Apr.

3 TNA, AIR 1/1679/204/118/2, Record Book No. 4 Squadron RNAS, 10 Mar 1918–20 Jan 1919; AIR 1/2085/207/5/3, 41st Wing RAF, Résumé of operations, night of 12/13 Apr 1918.

4 Peter Dye, 'The Bridge to Air Power: Aviation Engineering on the Western front 1914–1918', *Air Power Review*, 17 (2014), p. 11.

5 TNA, AIR 2/78, 'Order of the Air Council for Transferring and Attaching Officers and Men to the Air Force', 22 Mar 1918.

6 TNA, AIR 2/78, 'Royal Air Force Units at Home, Summary of Arrangements; Memorandum on the Organisation of the Royal Air Force in the United Kingdom', 21 Mar 1918.

7 TNA, AIR 2/78, 'Permanent Royal Air Force Stations, Approved by the Chief of the Air Staff', 12 Mar 1918.

8 TNA, AIR 1/1679/204/118/2, No. 4 (No. 204 RAF) Squadron Record Book, 10 Mar 1918–20 Jan 1919.

9 Stephen Roskill (ed.), *Documents Relating to the Naval Air Service: Volume I, 1908–1918* (London: Navy Records Society, 1969), pp. 670–71, 672–3, Geddes to Weir, 22 May 1918; Admiralty to the Air Ministry, 22 May 1918.

10 Ibid., pp. 684–6, Beatty to the Admiralty, 30 Jul 1918.

11 TNA, AIR 8/5, minutes of Air Members' Meeting, Air Ministry, 25 Oct 1918; CUL, Boyle papers, Add 9429/1B/132 (i), J. C. Nerney (Head AHB) to Trenchard, 11 Oct 1952.

12 TNA, AIR 2/38, 'Minutes of Inter-Departmental Conference on Transfer of Duties to the Air Ministry', 1 Feb 1918 (the War Office confirmed the agreement to supply and quarter the RAF on 6 Dec 1917).

13 Malcolm Cooper, 'Blueprint for Confusion: The Administrative Background to the Formation of the Royal Air Force, 1912–1919', *Journal of Contemporary History*, 22 (1987), pp. 448–9.

14 RAFM, B2717, transcript of diary of Air Mech. 2 Thomas Spencer 1916–1918, entry for 1 Jul 1918.

15 TNA, AIR 1/718/29/8, Cmd. 100, 'Synopsis of the British Air Effort', Apr 1919, p. 16.

16 Russell Miller, *Trenchard: Father of the Royal Air Force* (London: Weidenfeld & Nicolson, 2016), pp.202–3.

17 RAFM, Trenchard papers, MFC 76/1/19, Rothermere to Trenchard, 13 Apr 1918.

18 P. Arch, Lloyd George papers, LG/F/45/9, Smuts to Lloyd George, 13 Apr 1918.

19 Frederick Sykes, *From Many Angles: An Autobiography* (London: Harrap, 1942), p. 215.

20 Ibid., pp. 217–18.

21 Miller, *Trenchard*, p. 205; Lord Beaverbrook, *Men and Power, 1917–1918* (London: Hutchinson, 1956), pp. 378–9, Appendix IV, letter from Henderson to Rothermere; letter from Henderson to Bonar Law, 26 Apr 1918.

22 CUL, Boyle papers, Add 9429/1B/209 (i), notes by Trenchard for Major Lockhart (n.d.), p. 3.

23 S. J. Taylor, *The Great Outsiders: Northcliffe, Rothermere, and the Daily Mail* (London: Weidenfeld & Nicolson, 1996), pp. 231–2, 228–30; 'Beaverbrook, *Men and Power*, pp. 228–30.

24 John Laffin, *Swifter than Eagles: A Biography of Marshal of the RAF Sir John Salmond* (Edinburgh: Blackwood, 1964), p. 116.

25 Beaverbrook, *Men and Power*, pp. 222. 251.

26 W. J. Reader, *Architect of Air Power: The Life of the First Viscount Weir* (London: Collins, 1968), pp. 68–70.

27 TNA, AIR 6/12, Air Council minutes of meetings, 26th meeting, 28th meeting, 10 May and 23 May 1918.

28 John Slessor, *The Central Blue: Recollections and Reflections* (London: Cassell, 1956), p. 31; P. G. Hering, *Customs and Traditions of the Royal Air Force* (Aldershot: Gale and Polden, 1961), p. 214.

29 TNA, AIR 8/5, Air members' meetings, 27 May 1918, 21 Jun 1918; AIR 6/12, Air Council minutes, 28th meeting, 23 May 1918.

30 TNA, AIR 8/5, Air members' meetings, 17 Jul 1918, 4 Nov 1918.

31 TNA, AIR 6/14, Air Council minutes, 24 Mar 1919; AIR 2/223, 'Proposed Scheme for clothing other ranks RAF as from 1 July 1920'; 'Proceedings of Conference on Revision of Clothing for Other Ranks, Royal Air Force', Director of Equipment, May 1920; Hering, *Customs and Traditions*, p. 215.

32 TNA, ADM 1/2493, Director of RAF Quartermaster Services to Director of Stores, Admiralty, 11 May 1918; Secretary, Admiralty, to Secretary, Air Ministry, 31 May 1918; Admiralty minute 20 May 1918.

33 TNA, TS 27/67, minute from Sir Alfred Dennis for the Treasury Solicitor, Oct 1918.

34 TNA, ADM 1/12493, Admiralty to the Air Ministry, 12 Oct 1918, 8 Nov 1918.

35 Ibid., Air Ministry to Admiralty, 29 Jun 1920; Admiralty Board minutes, 8 Jul 1920; Admiralty to the Air Ministry, 26 Jul 1920; CUL, Boyle papers, Add 9429/1B/132 (i), J. C. Nerney (Head

AHB) to Trenchard, 11 Oct 1952, encl. letter from T. Marson to the Secretary of the Air Ministry, 18 Jun 1920.

36 TNA, 6/12, Air Council minutes, meetings of 1 Mar, 5 Mar 1918; AIR 1/106/15/9/284, memorandum by Lt. Col. Bersey, 1 Apr 1918, 'Women Employed in the Royal Air Force', pp. 1–3.

37 TNA, AIR 1/106/15/9/284, WRAF: Conditions of Service in the Immobile Branch; RAF Publication no. 14, 'Constitution and Regulations of the Women's Royal Air Force', p. 3.

38 Basil Collier, *Heavenly Adventurer: Sefton Brancker and the Dawn of British Aviation* (London: Secker & Warburg, 1959), p. 96.

39 CCAC, WEIR 2/7, Godfrey Paine (Master of Personnel RAF) to Douglas-Pennant, 9 Jul 1918.

40 TNA, PREM 1/205, Notes on the WRAF case (n.d.); Reader, *Architect of Air Power*, pp. 76–81.

41 Collier, *Heavenly Adventurer*, p. 23.

42 CCAC, WEIR 2/7, Douglas-Pennant to Churchill, 28 Feb 1919; Douglas-Pennant to Lloyd George, 2 Sep 1918.

43 Sykes, *From Many Angles*, p. 220; Miller, *Trenchard*, p. 204.

44 LHA, Brooke-Popham papers, 8/3, Army General Staff, 'Fighting in the Air', Apr 1918, p. 1; TNA, AIR 1/725/97/8, 'Policy for Operations 1918', p. 1: 'the primary task of the RAF must be to gain and maintain superiority in the air, as without such superiority the effective co-operation of aircraft with other arms is hindered . . .'

45 Ibid., pp. 1–3.

46 LHA, Brooke-Popham papers, 8/3, General Staff paper, 'Offence versus Defence in the Air', Oct 1917.

47 TNA, AIR 1/175/15/163/4, 65th Squadron Record Book, Jun 1918.

48 Sykes, *From Many Angles*, pp. 223–4; H. A. Jones, *The War in the Air: Appendices* (Oxford: Oxford University Press, 1937), p. 170.

49 TNA, AIR 1/462/15/312/121, Tiverton to Capt. Vyvyan (Air Board), 3 Sep 1917, pp. 1–13; AIR 1/460/15/312/97, memorandum

by Wing Commander Randall for Capt. Stopford, 4 Dec 1917;
Tiverton to Rear-Admiral Mark Kerr, 1 Dec 1917.

50 TNA, AIR 1/460/15/312/97, DFO memorandum, 'Strategic
Bombing. Objectives in Order of Importance' (n.d.).

51 TNA, AIR 1/718/29/9, 'Memorandum on Future Air Organisation, Fighting Policy, and Requirements in Personnel and
Materiel', 10 Oct 1917, p. 5.

52 TNA, AIR 1/725/97/7, memorandum, 'Long Distance Bombing',
26 Nov 1917, p. 5.

53 CCAC, WEIR 1/6, 'Memorandum for the War Cabinet on
Certain Lines of Main Policy involving the activities of the Air
Ministry', 14 May 1918; Lord Weir, 'Memorandum of Independent
Air Force Command for long-range bombing of Germany', 25
May 1918.

54 TNA, AIR 9/8, Chief of Air Staff, 'Review of Air Situation and
Strategy for the information of the Imperial War Cabinet', 27
Jun 1918, pp. 2, 6.

55 RAFM, AIR 69/2651, 'The War of 1914–18', RAF Staff College
Notes, 'The Independent Force'.

56 CCAC, WEIR 1/6, private memorandum, 27 Apr 1918.

57 RAFM, Trenchard papers, MFC 76/1/19, Trenchard to the War
Office, 14 Apr 1918; Rothermere to Lord Derby, 14 Apr 1918. See
too Miller, *Trenchard*, pp. 209–10.

58 RAFM, Trenchard papers, MFC 76/1/20, Trenchard to Weir,
5 May 1918; Weir to Trenchard, 6 May 1918; Trenchard to Weir,
8 May 1918.

59 Trenchard papers, MFC 76/1/28, Air Ministry to Trenchard,
13 May 1918; memorandum for the War Cabinet from Lord Weir,
22 May 1918.

60 Miller, *Trenchard*, p.213 (citing Trenchard's private diary).

61 RAFM, AIR 69/3, 'Despatch from Major General Sir Hugh
Trenchard on the Work of the Independent Air Force', p. 1.

62 RAFM, Trenchard papers, MFC 76/1/28, memorandum by Lord Weir for the War Cabinet; 76/1/3, letter from Haig to the War Cabinet, 20 Nov 1917; LHA, Brooke-Popham papers, 8/5, Air Ministry, 'Results of Raids on Germany, January 1st–November 11th 1918'.

63 TNA, AIR 8/179, 'Interview with Lord Trenchard on the Independent Air Force', 11 Apr 1934, p. 6.

64 LHA, Brooke-Popham papers, 1/8, RAF Staff College Notes, 'Memorandum on the Bombing of Germany submitted to the Inter-Allied Aviation Committee of the Supreme War Council, 23 Jun 1918'.

65 RAFM, AIR 69/3, 'Despatch from Major General Sir Hugh Trenchard . . .', p. 4.

66 TNA, AIR 1/2085/207/5/3, 'Independent Force: Approximate Results, 9 July 1918–11 November 1918'.

67 TNA, AIR 1/460/15/312/97, Groves to Chief of the Air Staff, 11 Sep 1918.

68 LHA, Brooke-Popham papers, 1/8, RAF Staff College Notes, Memorandum No. 3, 'Notes on Night Reconnaissance and Bombing, July 1918', pp. 1, 5; Memorandum No. 5, 'Statistics of Independent Force'.

69 RAFM, AIR 69/3, lecture by Air Vice-Marshal Brooke-Popham, 'The Air Force in its Role as a Separate Service' (n.d.), p. 3.

70 TNA, AIR 1/2085, Independent Force communiqué for Air Ministry, 1 Nov 1918.

71 TNA, AIR 1/718/29/5, 'Report on Operations August 1918, Independent Air Force', 1 Sep 1918; AIR 1/2085, Independent Force Communiqués, 5/6 Jun 1918.

72 Edward Westermann, *Flak: German Anti-Aircraft Defenses, 1914–1945* (Lawrence, KA: Kansas University Press, 2001), pp. 18–27.

73 RAFM, AIR 69/3, Sq/L Drummond to Sq/L Mackay, 11 Dec 1923, reference query on IAF casualties.

74 Ibid., 'Independent Air Force, Notes by Air Vice-Marshal Brooke-Popham', pp. 5–7.

75 RAFM, Sykes papers, AC 73/35/3/5/1, minute by Chief of the Air Staff, 'Independent Bombing Command', for the Prime Minister, 1 Jun 1918.

76 RAFM, Sykes papers, AC 73/35/3/5/1, memorandum of a conversation between Lloyd George, Clemenceau and Sykes, 3 Jun 1918.

77 RAFM, AIR 69/2651, RAF Staff College Notes, 'Note from Lord Weir to M. Clemenceau', 26 Aug 1918.

78 Eric Ash, *Sir Frederick Sykes and the Air Revolution 1912–1918* (London: Frank Cass, 1999), pp. 161–3.

79 RAFM, Sykes papers, AC 73/35/3/5/1, 'Note on the Inter-Allied Bombing Force Problem', British Section, Supreme War Council, 23 Jul 1918.

80 Sykes, *From Many Angles*, pp. 232–3.

81 Laffin, *Swifter than Eagles*, p. 97.

82 CCAC, WEIR 1/5, Air Ministry, 'Synopsis of British Air Effort', p. 12.

83 Richard Overy, 'Strategic Bombardment before 1939: Doctrine, Planning, and Operations', in R. Cargill Hall (ed.), *Case Studies in Strategic Bombardment* (Washington, DC: Air Force History Program, 1998), pp. 21–2. The best account of Anglo-American thinking about strategic bombing is Tami Davis Biddle, *Rhetoric and Reality in Air Warfare: The Evolution of British and American Ideas about Strategic Bombing 1914–1945* (Princeton, NJ: Princeton University Press, 2002).

84 M. Maurer, *The U.S Air Service in World War I*, 4 vols. (Washington, DC: Office of Air Force History, 1978), Vol. ii, p. 132, 'Report by Major R. C. Bolling to Chief Signal Officer, 15 August 1917'.

85 National Archives and Records Administration, College Park, MD, RG 18/11, Division of Military Aeronautics, 'Accomplish-

ments and Program Requirements under Maj. General Wm L. Kenly April–November 1918', 1 Jul 1919, p. 8.

86 R. D. Layman, *Naval Aviation in the First World War: Its Impact and Influence* (London: Chatham Publishing, 1996), pp. 86, 209–11.

87 TNA, AIR 9/2, 'Combined Naval Operations in the North Sea 1914/1918' (n.d.). Out of sixty-six seaplane sorties, thirty-one failed to rise from the sea.

88 TNA, AIR 9/5, note by the Chief of the Imperial General Staff, 16 Sep 1921. Modern calculations can be found in Christopher Cook and E. F. Cheesman, *The Air Defence of Britain, 1914–1918* (London: Putnam, 1984), pp. 418–19.

89 LHA, Brooke-Popham papers, 1/8, 'Statistics on German Air Raids on England. Results of German Bomb Raids'.

90 Brooke-Popham papers, 1/8, RAF Staff College Notes, 'Statistics of Independent Force, Work Carried Out', pp. 1–2.

91 RAFM, AIR 69/2651, RAF Staff College Notes, 'The War of 1914–1918', Appendix 3, 'Weight of Bombs dropped on Targets more than 85 miles from the Front Line'.

92 Peter Dye, 'The Bridge to Air Power: Aviation Engineering on the Western Front 1914–1918', *Air Power Review*, 17 (2014), p. 13; Alan Morris, *First of the Many: The Story of Independent Force, RAF* (London: Jarrolds, 1968), Appendix A.

93 Cooper, 'Blueprint for Confusion', p. 448.

94 TNA, AIR 1/2085, 'Communiqué to all Personnel of the Independent Force', 11 Nov 1918; Arnold Harvey, 'The Royal Air Force and Close Support, 1918–1940', *War in History*, 15 (2008), p. 420.

95 LHA, Brooke-Popham papers, 8/5, Air Ministry, 'Results of the Air Raids on Germany January 1st – November 11th 1918', Jan 1920, pp. 1, 3.

96 RAFM, Air 69/3, 'Despatch from Major General Sir Hugh Trenchard on the Work of the Independent Air Force', 31 Dec 1918.

97 Susan Grayzel, *At Home and Under Fire: Air Raids and Culture in Britain from the Great War to the Blitz* (Cambridge: Cambridge University Press, 2012), p. 85, citing a diary by Ethel Bilbrough, 4 Nov 1917.

98 Ash, *Sir Frederick Sykes*, p. 162.

99 Sykes, *From Many Angles*, p. 231.

100 TNA, AIR 1/725/97/7, Trenchard to Salmond, 4 Nov 1918.

101 Heinz Hanke, *Luftkrieg und Zivilbevölkerung* (Frankfurt/Main: Peter Lang, 1991), pp. 6–8.

102 Joel Hayward, 'Air Power, Ethics, and Civilian Immunity during the First World War and its Aftermath', *Global War Studies*, 7 (2010), pp. 118–22.

103 TNA, AIR 8/3, War Cabinet minutes, 16 Oct 1919.

104 Dye, 'Bridge to Air Power', pp. 12–13. See too David Jordan, 'The Genesis of Modern Air Power: The RAF in 1918' in Gary Sheffield and Peter Gray (eds.), *Changing War: The British Army, the Hundred Days Campaign, and the Birth of the Royal Air Force, 1918* (London: Bloomsbury, 2013), pp.192–203; Harvey, 'Royal Air Force Close Support', pp. 466–70.

105 LHA, Groves papers, Box 2 (a), Brig.-Gen. Geoffrey Salmond to Groves (n.d.).

4. 'A Very Gruelling Business': Saving the RAF

1 TNA, AIR 9/5, Note by Winston Churchill at the Colonial Office on a 'Separate Force', 24 Oct 1921, p.1.

2 LHA, Brooke-Popham papers, 9/ 5, Brooke-Popham to H.A. Jones, 6 Jun 1933; Jones to Brooke-Popham, 9 Jun 1933; Draft of speech, Royal Air Force dinner, 23 Jun 1933.

3 TNA, AIR 8/6, 'Memorandum of the Chief of the Air Staff on Air Requirements of the Empire', pp. 1–4.

4 TNA, ADM 116/1836, 'Minutes of a conference held between Admiralty and Air Ministry on Jan 2 1919', p. 8.

5 Eric Ash, *Sir Frederick Sykes and the Air Revolution 1912–1918* (London: Frank Cass, 1999), p. 176.

6 LHA, Brooke-Popham papers, 8/3, 'A Brief History of British Air Services 1910–1935', p. 10.

7 John Laffin, *Swifter than Eagles: The Biography of Marshal of the RAF Sir John Salmond* (Edinburgh: Blackwood, 1964), p. 146.

8 R. D. Layman, *Naval Aviation in the First World War: Its Impact and Influence* (London: Chatham Publishing, 1996), p. 196.

9 TNA, ADM 116/1836, Admiral Commanding Aircraft to commander-in-chief Atlantic and Home Fleets, 14 Apr 1919; AIR 6/14, Air Council minutes, 18 Mar 1919, p. 6; CUL, Boyle papers, Add 9429/1B/207-15, report of lecture by CAS to officers of the RAF, 22 Jan 1926.

10 TNA, AIR 6/14, Air Council minutes, 18 Mar 1919, p. 6; Beryl Escott, *Women in Air Force Blue: The Story of Women in the Royal Air Force from 1918 to the Present Day* (Wellingborough: Patrick Stephens, 1989), p. 295.

11 W. J. Reader, *Architect of Air Power: The Life of the First Viscount Weir* (London: Collins,1968), p. 81.

12 P. Arch, Lloyd George papers, LG/F/8/1, Churchill to Lloyd George, 7 Nov 1918; Churchill to Lloyd George, 9 Nov 1918.

13 Stephen Roskill, *Hankey: Man of Secrets: Volume II, 1919–1931* (London: Harper Collins, 1972), p. 46.

14 P. Arch, LG/F/8/1, Churchill to Lloyd George, 29 Dec 1918.

15 CCAC, CHAR 2/105/3, Churchill to Lloyd George, 10 Jan 1919.

16 CCAC, CHAR 16/1, Churchill to the Admiralty, 8 Feb 1919.

17 David Omissi, *Air Power and Colonial Control: The Royal Air Force 1919–1939* (Manchester: Manchester University Press, 1990), p. 8.

18 Winston Churchill, *Thoughts and Adventures* (London: Macmillan, 1942), pp. 153, 158, 166–7.

19 CUL, Boyle papers, Add 9429/1B/219-57, Churchill to Hilary St George Saunders, 7 Jun 1951.

20 Russell Miller, *Trenchard: Father of the Royal Air Force* (London: Weidenfeld & Nicolson, 2016), pp. 236–7.

21 CUL, Boyle papers, Add 9429/1B/207-15, report of lecture delivered by CAS to officers of the RAF, 22 Jan 1926, pp. 1–2.

22 Ibid., 1B/268 (i), Notes on chapters by Major Lockhart, 18 Jan 1954, p. 1.

23 TNA, AIR 8/5, minutes of Air Members' meeting, 17 Jul 1918.

24 TNA, AIR 6/14, Air Council minutes, 18 Mar 1919; P. G. Hering, *Customs and Traditions of the Royal Air Force* (Aldershot: Gale and Polden, 1961), p. 22; H. A. Jones, *The War in the Air: Volume* VI (Oxford: Oxford University Press, 1937), p. 25.

25 CUL, Boyle papers, Add 2429/1B/132 (v), note by Trenchard, 27 Oct 1952; Hering, *Customs and Traditions*, p. 23.

26 Henry Probert, *Bomber Harris: His Life and Times* (London: Greenhill Books, 2006), pp. 45–6.

27 LHA, Groves papers, 6/3, Groves to Secretary, Air Ministry, 7 Apr 1919; Groves to Air Ministry, 16 Apr 1919; Air Ministry, Master of Personnel, to Groves, 13 May 1919; Groves to Trenchard, Jan 1920; Trenchard to Groves, 10 Feb 1920; Air Ministry to Groves, 31 Mar 1920.

28 LHA, Brooke-Popham papers, 8/3, E. Halford Ross, 'Report of the Committee on the Preliminary Education of Candidates for Royal Air Force Commissions', 15 Mar 1919, pp. 1–3.

29 CUL, Boyle papers, Add 9429/1B/207-15, report of lecture delivered by CAS, 22 Jan 1926; John James, *The Paladins: A Social*

History of the RAF *up to the Outbreak of World War* II (London: Macdonald, 1990), pp. 109–11.

30 TNA, AIR 9/5, Trenchard memorandum 'on the Status of the Royal Air Force', 14 Aug 1919.

31 Miller, *Trenchard*, p. 245.

32 TNA, AIR 1/718/29/2, 'Memorandum on Why the Royal Air Force should be maintained as separate from the Navy and Army', 11 Sep 1919, pp. 1–2, 4.

33 TNA, AIR 1/718/29/7, Trenchard to Churchill, enclosing draft 'Memorandum by the Air Staff on the Reconstruction of the Royal Air Force', 22 Nov 1919.

34 TNA, AIR 1/718/29/8, memorandum by the Chief of the Air Staff, 25 Nov 1919.

35 LHA, Brooke-Popham papers, Cmd. 467, 'Royal Air Force', 11 Dec 1919.

36 Omissi, *Air Power and Colonial Control*, p. 22.

37 TNA, AIR 9/5, 'Memorandum prepared by the General Staff for the Committee of Imperial Defence', 26 May 1921.

38 TNA, AIR 9/5, 'Note by the CIGS on Mr. Balfour's Memorandum', 16 Sep 1921.

39 Ibid., 'Draft notes by the Chief of the Air Staff for the Secretary of State', Sep 1921; 'Notes by the Air Staff on the main policy Observations by the Committee on National Expenditure', Oct 1921.

40 Omissi, *Air Power and Colonial Control*, pp. 28–9.

41 TNA, AIR 8/17, Beatty to Churchill, 19 Mar 1922; Beatty to Churchill, 17 Jul 1922.

42 Ibid., Trenchard to Churchill, 'The Question of Air Personnel Working with the Navy', 24 Mar 1922; Trenchard memorandum, 19 Jul 1922; AIR 8/2, Air Staff, 'History of the Establishment of a Separate Air Force and its Relations with the other Services' (n.d.).

43 TNA, AIR 8/3, 'Note on Agreement between the First Lord of the Admiralty and the Secretary of State for Air', 26 Feb 1923; Omissi, *Air Power and Colonial Control*, pp. 31–3.

44 CCAC, TRENCHARD 4, Cabinet paper 394(24), relations between the Navy and the Royal Air Force: note by the Lord Chancellor, 1 Jul 1924; Trenchard and Keyes to Lord Haldane, 4 Jul 1924, encl. Cmd 1938 on air–naval cooperation.

45 TNA, AIR 8/6, 'Memorandum by the Chief of the Air Staff', 9 Dec 1918, p. 1.

46 Jafna Cox, 'A Splendid Training Ground: The Importance to the Royal Air Force of its Role in Iraq, 1919–32', *Journal of Imperial and Commonwealth History*, 13 (1984–5), pp. 169–76.

47 Omissi, *Air Power and Colonial Control*, pp. 10–15, 25–6, 31–6. See too Sebastian Ritchie, *The RAF, Small Wars and Insurgencies in the Middle East, 1919–1939* (Northolt: Air Historical Branch, 2011), esp. pp. 78–83.

48 TNA, AIR 9/5, Notes by the Air Staff on the main policy observations by Committee on National Expenditure, Oct 1921, p. 3.

49 TNA, ADM 116/1836, memorandum by Admiral R. Wemyss for the War Cabinet, 'Postwar Functions of the Air Ministry and Postwar Strength of the Royal Air Force', 7 Jan 1919, p. 2.

50 John Laffin, *Swifter than Eagles: A biography of Marshal of the Royal Air Force Sir John Salmond* (Edinburgh: Blackwood, 1964), pp. 150, 156; David Richardson, 'The Royal Air Force and the Irish War of Independence', *Air Power Review*, 19 (2016), pp. 15–16.

51 TNA, AIR 9/2, Air Staff memorandum, 'The Big Ship Controversy from the Air Point of View', 20 Jan 1921, pp. 5, 8–9.

52 TNA, AIR 9/2, Air Staff memorandum, 'Is the Fleet Air Arm part of the Royal Air Force?', 26 May 1926, p. 2; Air 8/17, Trenchard to Churchill, 24 Mar 1922.

53 Omissi, *Air Power and Colonial Control*, p. 31; Miller, *Trenchard*, pp. 274–5.

54 CUL, Boyle papers, Add 9429 1B/95 (i), Wing Commander T. Marson to Trenchard, 8 Jul 1954.

55 CCAC, TRENCHARD 1, Churchill to Chamberlain, 11 Mar 1922; TNA, AIR 8/2, Extract from Hansard, 16 Mar 1922, p. 5.

56 Omissi, *Air Power and Colonial Control*, pp. 33–4.

57 CUL, Boyle papers, Add 9429/1B/68, Trenchard to Lord Hankey (Secretary to the Cabinet in 1923), 8 Feb 1952; 1B/283 (ii), notes by Sir Christopher Bullock on his years at the Air Ministry (n.d.), p. 4.

58 TNA, AIR 9/5, Statement by the prime minister, 25 Feb 1926; AIR 8/2, Sir Christopher Bullock, (PPS to Hoare), 'Supplementary note on the Intentions of the Government in setting up a unified Air Service in 1917', 11 Feb 1926.

59 CUL, Boyle papers, Add 9429/1B/333, John Steel to Major Lockhart, 24 Mar 1955.

60 CCAC, TRENCHARD 1, Churchill to Chamberlain, 11 Mar 1922.

61 Richardson, 'The Royal Air Force and the Irish War of Independence', p. 12.

62 Omissi, *Air Power and Colonial Control*, p. 35.

63 Cox, 'A Splendid Training Ground', p. 175.

64 CUL, Boyle papers, Add 9429/1B/219, Churchill to Hilary St George Saunders, 7 Jun 1951.

65 Brett Holman, 'World Police for World Peace: British Internationalism and the Threat of a Knock-out Blow from the Air, 1919–1945', *War in History*, 17 (2010), pp. 314–7.

66 Michele Haapamaki, *The Coming of the Aerial War: Culture and Fear of Airborne Attack in Inter-War Britain* (London: I. B. Tauris, 2014), pp. 40–41.

67 John Ferris, 'The Theory of a "French Air Menace": Anglo-French Relations and the British Home Defence Air Force

Programme of 1921–25', *Journal of Strategic Studies*, 10 (1987), pp. 65–7.

68 Ibid., pp. 70–73.

69 TNA, AIR 8/6, 'Note by the CAS on a Revised Scheme for the Provision of a Home Defence Force', Jun 1922, p. 1.

70 Cox, 'A Splendid Training Ground', pp. 165–6; Ferris, 'The Theory of a "French Air Menace" ', pp. 70–72, 74–7.

71 CCAC, TRENCHARD 1, Trenchard to Churchill, 25 Apr 1919, encl. 'Post War Air Force'.

72 TNA, AIR 2/1830, Revision of 1936 Manual of Combined Operations, 1938, para. 28.

73 TNA, AIR 16/108, 'Air Staff Specification A 7/39', Mar. 1939; 'Minutes of a Meeting of Operational Requirements Committee to Consider Army Cooperation Aeroplane', 29 Mar 1939.

74 TNA, AIR 14/181, Commander, Advanced Air Striking Force to Bomber Command HQ, 5 Mar 1940. Slessor comment in Peter Smith, *Impact: The Dive Bomber Pilots Speak* (London: William Kimber, 1981), p. 34.

75 See for example TNA, AIR 9/99, HQ Bomber Command to Air Ministry (Plans), Dec 1939; 'Note, The Attack of Air Force on the Ground', 9 May 1940; Plans (Ops), 'Attack of German Air Force on the Ground', 6 Sep 1939.

76 TNA, AIR 9/8, Speech by the Chief of the Air Staff to the War Office Staff Exercise, Buxton, 9–13 Apr 1923, p. 3.

77 RAFM, AIR 69/3, speech by Brooke-Popham, 'The Air Force in its role as a Separate Service' (n.d.), p. 9.

78 TNA, AIR 9/8, 'Note upon the memorandum of the Chief of the Naval Staff, Paper no. COS 156', p. 3.

79 Neville Parton, 'The Development of Early Royal Air Force Doctrine', *Journal of Military History*, 72 (2008), p. 1167.

80 TNA, AIR 8/244, Air Staff memorandum, 'The Role of the Air Force in National Defence', 5 Jul 1938.

81 TNA, AIR 16/261, Dowding to Newall, 24 Feb 1939.

82 CUL, Boyle papers, Add. 9429/1B/110 (i), Air Ministry pamphlet 317, John Slessor, 'Place of the Bomber in British Strategy', 31 Dec 1952.

The RAF in 1918:
Command Areas and Combat Groups

N

Group 28

N.W. AREA

Group 20

Glasgow

Group 22

Group 17

Group 18

N.W. AREA

Group 11

N.E. AREA

York
Group 16

Group 14

Group 12

MIDLAND
AREA

Birmingham
Group 13

Group 3

Group 4

Group 2

Group 7

London

Group 1

S.W. AREA

S.E. AREA

Salisbury

Group 8

Group 5

Group 9

Group 10

Command Headquarters

0   100 miles
0   100 km

Commentary on Plate Section

1. A carpenters' repair shop for the Royal Flying Corps. Their skills were essential to keeping the vulnerable wooden aircraft flying.
2. Major Frederick Sykes (*centre*), later chief-of-staff of the fledgling RAF, with the administrative staff of the RFC shortly before the outbreak of war. Trenchard thought he was 'a hard worker and had some brains', but the two were bitter rivals.
3. A crashed aeroplane on the airfield at Longavesnes. Accidents were routine with the first experimental aircraft, and survival a matter of luck.
4. An RFC observer of the 16th Wing Photographic Section holding his camera. In the early years of air power, reconnaissance was an essential function.
5. Liberal Prime Minister Herbert Asquith (*centre, in dark civilian clothing*) watching a returning flight of aircraft land at RFC headquarters at Frevillers. To the right, with shooting stick, is General Hugh Trenchard, commander of the RFC, whose negative view of politicians seems captured in the image.
6. Hoisting an RNAS seaplane on to the sea for its flight. In 47 per cent of cases in North Sea operations the seaplanes failed to take off from the choppy surface.
7. The view from the Hotel Cecil of temporary accommodation built in the Victoria Embankment Gardens to house part of the Ministry of Munitions. The Hotel housed the Air Board and later the Air Ministry, but it developed a wartime reputation for intrigue and incompetence.

8. An aerial photograph taken by German raiders of the bombs falling on London on 7 July 1917. The raid finally triggered a government response that ended with the founding of the RAF. St Paul's Cathedral is clearly visible towards the right of the image.

9. Jan Smuts (*right*) and British Foreign Secretary Arthur Balfour after attending an Allied conference in Paris, 27 July 1917. Smuts was invited by David Lloyd George two weeks before to report on air defence and the future of British air power.

10. RFC cadets in November 1917 share a dinner in the Great Hall of Christ Church, Oxford, where they were posted for officer training. Many air officers shared a background from British public schools and the ancient universities.

11. King George V was an enthusiastic supporter of the decision to create a separate air force. Here he takes leave of Major-General John Salmond (*left*), commander of the RFC after Trenchard departed for the job of chief-of-staff.

12. A farewell dinner in the sergeants' mess of No. 49 squadron, RFC, before the transition to the new RAF.

13. An RAF chaplain leads a procession of men from No. 3 Squadron, Australian Flying Corps, carrying the coffin of Manfred von Richthofen, the legendary German air ace, to the cemetery at Bertangles. He was the most prominent early victim of the renamed RAF when his aircraft was shot down on 21 April 1918.

14. Women of the recently formed Women's Royal Air Force servicing an engine in 1918. Although thousands of women played a vital role in the new service during the war, Parliament decided in 1919 to terminate the branch, which was only revived at the start of the next world war.

15. RAF mechanics prepare drawings of German aircraft for gunnery practice in 1918. By the end of the war, fighter offensives against enemy aircraft had come to replace reconnaissance as the principal activity of the air force.

16. Major John Simon (a later Chancellor of the Exchequer) inspecting one of the new heavy bombers, the Handley-Page O/400, at Ligescourt in August 1918. The aircraft was poised to become the mainstay of the independent bombing campaign.

17. American airmen are instructed at the British Aerial Gunnery School on how to hit a rapidly moving target. American participation in the air war after 1917 took time to develop and relied heavily on British and French assistance.

18. The RAF College at Cranwell, shortly after its completion in 1922. Trenchard wanted to attract 'the intelligent class' into the air force, and cadets had to meet stringent standards.

19. Winston Churchill, the Air Minister, and Trenchard at the first Hendon air pageant in 1920. The two men cemented a relationship that saw Churchill defend the independence of the RAF against attacks by the army and navy.

20. A row of Sopwith Snipe aircraft lined up next to an ambulance at Beckendorf, near Cologne, in March 1919. The Allied occupation of western Germany was one way of reinforcing the eventual peace settlement.

21. Armstrong-Whitworth Siskin aircraft of No. 29 Squadron, RAF, lined up at the Hendon Air Show in 1929. The RAF remained committed to biplane designs under Trenchard's leadership, when faster monoplanes were already in development.

22. A Vickers Victoria III of No. 20 Squadron, RAF, landing at the Iraqi airfield at Abu Sueir with the British High Commissioner on board. The 'air policing' of Iraq from 1921 onwards helped to promote RAF claims to be an independent service.

23. A flight of Fairey Swordfish Mark I biplanes flying from RAF Gosport over the Solent Estuary on the English south coast. Naval aviation became the poor relation as the RAF developed, though in this case the robust Swordfish had notable success in the first years of the war despite its slow speed and ungainly appearance.

Index

When Mountains Walked

When ⚜ Mountains ⚜ Walked

Kate Wheeler

HOUGHTON MIFFLIN COMPANY
Boston   New York

For information about permission to reproduce selections from
this book, write to Permissions, Houghton Mifflin Company,
215 Park Avenue South, New York, New York 10003.

Library of Congress Cataloging-in-Publication Data
Wheeler, Kate, date.
When mountains walked / Kate Wheeler.
p.   cm.
ISBN 0-395-85991-3
1. Americans — Travel — Peru — Fiction. 2. Medical
personnel — Peru — Fiction. 3. Married women — Peru
— Fiction. 4. Earthquakes — Peru — Fiction. I. Title.
PS3573 H4326 W47   2000
813'.54 — dc21   99-051324

Printed in the United States of America

Book design by Robert Overholtzer

QUM 10 9 8 7 6 5 4 3

Part of this book was published as "Future Shock,"
in *Granta* 54 (The Best of Young American
Novelists), Summer 1996.

For my father

ACKNOWLEDGMENTS

This book could not have been written without the help of the National Endowment for the Arts, the John Simon Guggenheim Foundation, and the Mrs. Giles Whiting Foundation. Their support meant far more than just the money over five years of writing. Similarly, Ian Jack and other writers associated with *Granta* called me a novelist when I wasn't sure.

My writing group — Pamela Painter, Jim Mezzanotte, and Tom McNeely — gave freely of their ideas, suggestions, and encouragement. Their ideas are built into every chapter. In particular, Pam helped me selflessly and incisively throughout. Her honesty and insight rescued this work from abysms of various kinds. Janet Silver, my editor at Houghton Mifflin, saved the second half. Without her help and that of Heidi Pitlor, her assistant, who held my hand through one or two difficult moments, this book would not exist. Thanks also to Denise Shannon, my agent and my friend.

My father, Charles B. Wheeler, proposed changing Johnny Baines from a volcanologist to a seismologist because more people would be interested. My sisters, Margaret B. Wheeler and Jan Krissy Wheeler-McInvaille, gave medical information and devised health-related plot twists. David Guss suggested the name "Black Rainbow Movement," renamed characters, tolerated my writing schedule and the desperate or elated moods associated with it. I'll never forget sitting on a French train listening to Sharon Salzberg and Anne Millikin work out Maggie's name and the details of her life. Brian Rawlins and Martha Bardach helped at, and with, the ending. Joseph Olshan and Margaret Edwards helped early on.

Wolfgang Schuler of La Paz kept me on track. Wendy Weeks, Adela Arenas, and Adolfo del Álamo, of Ollantaytambo, Peru, gave me a home away from home when I was starting to write. Some of the stories they told found their way into my imagination and this text. Peter Yenne, Jesús Briceño, and, again, David Guss got me to places I needed to be. I wish I could thank personally all of the friends whose *cariño,* humor, and encouragement have meant so much to me during this writing.

My parents, Charles B. and Jan M. Wheeler, and their parents in turn, brought me to South America and gave me geologic antecedents. Katherine R. and Orby C. Wheeler's lives were a central inspiration, though altered quite a bit. My lost grandmother, Mary Margaret McCullough, provided one of the mysteries that fuel the narrative. May she be well, wherever she went.

Thank you all.

Only fools get out alive.

— Wolf Zimerman Lustik, "El Lobo"

1

THE ROSARIO was the deepest canyon in the world. Four thousand meters, twice as deep as the Grand, cut by a fast, north-flowing river of the same name which eventually turned eastward to braid itself into the Amazon. A chasm full of sky, too vast to think about. Even those times when Maggie was actually standing on the Rosario's top rim, she could never quite withstand the sight of it. She always had the same unbidden thought: This cannot be real. So much void, full of so much hazy hanging light; and the opposite wall striped like a tiger (Cretaceous limestones, according to her grandfather, who had been the first to map them); and past it, the black horizon; and past even that, the rain forest, invisible on the back slopes but sending up sweet white puffs of cloud in the afternoons. The rain forest, full of ruins and bones and gold but uninhabited, stretched endlessly, the local people said, or anyway as far as the Atlantic Ocean.

At the bottom of all this was Piedras, barely clinging to the slim gravelly terraces of the Rosario River, which was cutting all too quickly through soft rock, rushing to attain the level of the sea. In Piedras, where Maggie and her husband, Carson, were living, all was airless heat and flies and bushes coated in dust. Somehow it never seemed to have sufficient reason for existing, let alone the importance it had possessed in Maggie's imagination ever since she was a child.

✤

Back in February, when she and Carson had first arrived, Maggie had known immediately that she would never get used to the bus ride. It was near the end of the rainy season, and the road from Cajamarca had only recently been reopened after a section fell off during a torrential December rain. Going over the canyon's western lip, the bus had tilted like a roller coaster, and her stomach had dropped away.

She could not see the bottom of the canyon, just the road like a limp string flung impossibly far across the dark shoulders of the mountains. The canyon was vast, unexpected, a hole in the ground bigger than any idea of it could ever be. Then its east wall rose up, suddenly contradicting everything, a frozen angry-looking wave of black stone. Distant details were clear, grainy as in an excellent photograph, so that Maggie felt she could have picked out a fly on a cliff face.

"Cliff tombs," she said to Carson, "waterfalls!" Her grandmother Althea had told stories of the strange things hidden in the canyon's folded cliffs. Tombs, waterfalls where you could take a shower. Maggie could almost feel a rope of frigid water shattering against her own skull, driving out every thought, and how it would feel, then, to step out onto the bare, bright, burning trail again: clothing drying instantly, skin staying cool.

Carson was making a guess that the canyon sides were about twelve miles apart.

Twelve miles, Maggie thought. How far was that? How did Carson think he knew?

She started shivering.

A cold wind whistled through the cracked window as the bus began threading its way down through standing rocks that looked like a demolished, or about to be constructed, Inca fortress, of the type she and Carson had visited last week in the southern part of the country. They'd taken a honeymoon in Cuzco and Machu Picchu before settling down to a year of serious work, reopening Piedras's medical clinic.

"So then don't look," Carson said as Maggie gripped his thigh. But she couldn't stop. The chasm drew her in; its emptiness exerted a suction. In comparison, the road was too narrow. For the first time she realized what defined the edge of any mountain road. Nothing.

Nothing was fine on its own terms. That was exactly what was wrong with it.

The road here was slimy white mud with big rocks in it and turns without protection, all causing the driver to manhandle the wheel, hand over hand; and to anticipate in the application of the brakes. The bus was overloaded and topheavy, too, partly because of Maggie and Carson's gear tied to a rack on the roof. They had purchased a small refrigerator in Cajamarca and had it reinforced with iron straps. If only this refrigerator could be sacrificed, she thought, they'd all have a chance to survive.

The road grew worse as it went down, mostly because the mud got deeper. Though it hadn't rained in a week, none of the mud had hardened. It did change from white to red, and brown, and yellow. Some places were as badly churned as if an army had recently retreated along them, full of ruts and hoofprints and the tracks of the heavy equipment that had gone down to repair the bad section, which was still ahead. Steering and braking would have been difficult under the best of circumstances, Maggie thought, but now the driver seemed desperate, wrestling with the wheel. Likely this bus had things wrong with it, such as thin brake shoes, loose tie rods. Often she felt the wheels leave several feet of muddy skid. What if another vehicle came at them around these blind, unprotected curves? Fortunately, the bus was going downward; because of this, it stayed next to the mountain's body instead of the edge. The road was barely wider than one lane, so the bus would push any opponent off, but Maggie found little comfort in that idea. One day she'd have to leave, and it would be her turn on the outside.

Carson pointed out a wooden cross on the shoulder. "Third World warning sign," he joked.

"Comforting, aren't they?" Maggie said sarcastically. Grateful for an excuse to talk, she told him how, when she and her sister were little, in Mexico and in Colombia, they'd ritually crossed themselves each time they'd passed a roadside memorial, despite not being Catholic.

"The maids taught you how," guessed Carson.

"You know me well." Their Colombian maid, Gloria, had sat in the middle of the back seat, telling stories so enthralling that Maggie and Sonia had never needed games, nor pinched each other.

The bus heaved up to the point of a curve where a thicket of crosses surrounded a hutch of raw cement. With her right hand, Maggie performed a series of quick figure eights, fingertips swooping just short of her lips. "Bad spots are a lot of work," she said, though she couldn't remember any place as bad as this one. A whole bus must have gone off the edge here.

Carson leaned forward to peer at Maggie from the front. She was doing the crossbar backwards, he said. "That's Greek Orthodox or something." He ought to know: he had been brought up Catholic. Gently he corrected her, brushing his fingertips across her breasts. Left to right, opening her heart like a door — or closing it, depending on which side she imagined the hinges.

She crossed herself Carson's way at the next bend, kissing her fingertips at the finish, then let her hand fall into her lap. Despite the dire reminder, she was glad to see the crosses. They returned her to herself. It was curious too, she thought, how Carson saw them in reference to safe, North American highway warning signs.

He'd grown up in Baton Rouge, in the same house all his life. When he spoke, she could feel his childhood inside him, a solid grid of hamburger stands, summer lawns, blacktopped highways sticky in the sun.

Maggie Goodwin had been born in Mexico. She'd lived there until she was five, and then the family moved to Colombia. She was ten and her sister Sonia thirteen when their father's shoe factory had failed unexpectedly. Calvin Goodwin's Colombian partner had suggested to the authorities that they might inspect the books, enforce certain laws that protected against imperialism. Calvin's capital became the fine. By coincidence, Sonia had caught typhoid in the same month when Maggie's mother had begun firing the servants, packing some things, selling others. Her parents were euphemistic about what had happened, so Maggie first blamed her older sister and then her mother, Julia, for their departure. Julia kept insisting she was overjoyed to go back to the United States. She'd had it with the chaos, envy, and dishonesty that ruled the rest of the world.

Then Maggie had known that her mother was betraying herself, not to speak of everybody else in the family. Julia had been born in

Bengal, and brought up in all the most unstable places, Peru, Turkey, Chile, India, and Afghanistan, where her father, a seismologist, had studied the world's most grievous faults. Maggie's grandmother Althea could always draw a protest from Julia by joking that Julia's dark hair and fathomless eyes came from all the Indian sun Althea had absorbed while pregnant. Maggie's features were almost the same.

Maggie liked to think of India as an explanation for her own thin ankles, and the way her skin turned yellowish when she was tired, and for the tiny hook at the tip of her nose, comparable to a drop of water beginning to form under a faucet. Julia wouldn't hear it, any of it. Her father, Johnny Baines, had always attributed Julia's coloration to a Cherokee great-grandmother of his. To the end of his life, he'd called Julia his Indian princess, Princess Oh-What-a-Part-o-Me.

Princess indeed: as soon as she'd reached ninth grade, Julia asked to leave Ecuador, where Johnny was inspecting the Cotopaxi volcano, and go to a Swiss boarding school instead. Not long afterward, arthritis and financial stress put an end to Johnny's geological explorations. Despite his reputation for eccentric thinking (he was determined to produce a theory predicting earthquakes), he'd gotten a job lecturing at Harvard, based on his work measuring tension in stable rocks.

Maggie was the opposite of her mother. She'd always been glad of her dark hair and eyes, jealous that her parents had given Sonia a name that was the same in Spanish. She blamed the United States for causing her to be a foreigner in every place she'd ever lived, including, eventually, itself.

As for her father, Calvin Goodwin, Maggie had always understood how hard he had fought to escape from Connecticut. Through all her childhood, he'd seemed a foreigner in the family, paler than his wife and daughters, the red-haired gringo Julia married. They'd seen him as if from a distance, slurping his dinner cold long after the girls and their mother had eaten, alone in the dark kitchen, late home from his factory. He'd sit worrying over his papers on a Sunday in his study, his presence defining the farthest room in every house. She'd been shocked to realize that it was Calvin who had held them in particular places on the surface of the earth; when he'd lost his grip, the rest must lose theirs, too. He'd been happiest in Colombia, but in the end he'd been lucky to get a job in his family's hardware distribution business, outside Bridgeport. His snake-proof boots grew mold in the closet.

❖

Around noon, the bus reached the bad section of road: even softer mud than elsewhere, nothing but a few tons of new dirt dug out of the hillside and pushed together. Carson said, "Maggie, look." There was the old road, a small landslide spilling down for about a hundred yards before it reached the edge of a cliff and disappeared.

To Maggie's relief, the bus got stuck here, in an awesome slough where some kind of quicksand lurked at the bottom of a puddle twenty yards long. The driver and his helper donned rubber boots and first tried tossing some cabbage-sized rocks under the wheels. Soon they had to ask all of the men to get out and push. Maggie would have liked to help, but she was told to sit inside with the other women.

At least, she thought, there was little danger of the men's pushing the bus too far. She watched as her new husband took off his hiking boots and rolled up his jeans as far as he could, revealing calves as pale as fish and covered with long, dark, fine French hairs. She told him she was worried that he'd cut his foot on something sharp.

"Pfft," said Carson, stepping into calf-deep, murky water.

Despite twenty men's heaving, the bus rocked only slightly. The driver's boy stuck his head in to announce that the women must get out, too, in order to lighten the burden. Maggie declined his offer to be carried piggyback across the puddle, but the other two women accepted. She took off her shoes and waded through the opaque brown water. The bottom was silky, safe, the water cold.

Oh, it was grand to stand on solid ground again. Soon the bus was high and dry, a matter of rocks and ropes and grunting. Several men celebrated, sipping from a flat bottle. Carson had a slug, then came up to where Maggie stood on a tussock of muddy alpine grass that seemed to have been chewed down by sheep.

"What was it?" she wanted to know.

"Anisette. Pure sugar. It's coated all my teeth." He wiped one hand across his beard. His forehead already bore a streak of war paint. "Whew, that was rough. You okay? You look kind of pale."

"I wish I had an excuse to walk the rest of the way."

"Want to go home?"

He meant it, she saw. "No."

"Good!"

Maggie didn't speak to him again until they had sat down and the bus had begun to roll. Then she said, in a carefully quiet tone, "I can't wait to get to Piedras. It's just that I hate being trapped inside this box. I'd rather be in a truck I could jump out of."

"If we die, we die, that's my attitude," Carson said.

"If?" Maggie said. She returned to gazing out the window.

How dare he think he belonged here more than she did! She had no home, unless it was ahead of her. Even if she hated the road, she already loved the canyon. Its immensity drew her into a focused, particular joy, so that she felt she had discovered it herself. In fact, she had rights over it, at least compared to Carson. Her uncle had been conceived in Piedras, according to an intricate and perhaps unreliable story of her grandmother's. That was why, when she and Carson had been searching for a place to do health work together, and the name of Piedras had scrolled down the computer screen in white letters on royal blue, Maggie had stood up and looked for an atlas, then phoned her grandmother. First thing the next morning, she'd called up Catholic Charities, begging them to modify the job to accommodate two North Americans: a physician's assistant and an administrator-trainee. They agreed, perhaps because the post had gone begging for so long, or because Maggie had insisted, as her grandmother Althea was famous for doing, that two could live on the salary of one.

Getting to Peru must be the greatest achievement of her life so far — the only deed, Maggie thought, that had ever flowed from her own true character. She hoped happiness would ensue, of course, though she knew happiness was often too much to expect. This trip was an experiment, to see what resulted from acting purely on the intuitions of one's heart.

Her friends approved of her leaving Larry; they just thought she should have stopped there, rather than remarrying and running off to South America two weeks after the divorce was finalized. "Far," and "away," Maggie had argued, were relative concepts. Far from what? Away from what? In her own mind, she was running toward something. From the point of view of Piedras, it was the United States that would seem distant and bizarre.

Moreover, she loved Carson and he loved her, and she was pretty sure of both these things even though they'd known each other less than a year and had married mostly in order to satisfy Catholic Charities, which would not have allowed them to work together otherwise. Maggie hadn't revealed this detail to her mother, for whom Carson's willingness to marry her questionable daughter was his chief merit. Julia Goodwin believed that a wedding band was a woman's first line of defense, all over the world, beginning in her own house. She'd even pushed for Maggie to take Carson's name, Miller, but Maggie had refused, claiming she disliked the initials MM, which was true. She told Julia she'd do it the grand old Latin way, "Maggie Goodwin de Miller," and left it to her mother to recall how good it was that Maggie had never let herself become "Mrs. Larry Fabularo."

People made big changes all the time, Maggie thought. There would always be voices, inside and out, shouting reasons why one shouldn't. If this venture didn't work, she could always go back and make peace with a half-life, like everybody else. Until then, she couldn't identify any one thing she had to lose. Until then, at the very least, she and Carson were in this together.

She jerked her head back, a reflex, for her window had come within inches of an outcrop. The bus had not ceased to fling its passengers violently about, lurching unpredictably on several tilt-axes at once, as if attempting to dislodge their vital organs. Carson turned away and stuck his long legs into the aisle to avoid crushing his knees against the steel back of the seat ahead of him. Absurd, under these conditions, to wish for him to kiss her. If she wanted a kiss, the back of his neck was available, but then she ran the risk of crushing her lips between Carson's spine and her own incisors.

She picked out a dark spot on the opposite wall of the canyon, a cave, or maybe just a huge black spot of mildew that had dripped from the roots of the hanging vegetation. This scenery justified everything it had taken to reach it.

"Carson," she said, turning to him again and finding, happily, that he was facing in her direction. She asked permission to lick a speck of mud off the corner of his eyebrow. "No," he said, but he was tickled, she could see; he permitted her to rub it off with the ball of her thumb while with the other hand, invisible to the other passengers, she caressed his penis. He clamped her hand between his legs for a few seconds. "Dirty girl," he said approvingly.

By now both of their clothes were dry. Halfway down, still before you could see the river bottom, the canyon had suddenly turned into a desert. A rain shadow, Maggie explained: the upper slopes took all the moisture. Cactus and mesquite grew here, just like in a western, but there were orchids in the jacaranda trees. Nothing smaller than trees grew from the bare yellowish dirt.

The road here was no less bad, except for being dry. All by itself, the mud on their jeans began cracking off and falling to the floor. Dust came in the windows until Maggie's teeth were gritty.

She exulted when the bus finally rattled off the wall of the canyon onto the relief of the river flats. She pinched her husband's biceps. "We're here. I can't believe it. I'm totally happy."

Carson pinched her back, more gently. "Yeah, I know."

They were entering a mango grove, surely the same one her grandmother had talked about. You could hear the river even in the bus. These crumbling buildings must belong to the hacienda, maybe the same one where Althea and Johnny might have taken shelter after their raft broke up in the whirlpool, back in 1932 or so — her grandmother was bad at years. "Piedras, Arenas, Aguas, Piedras. Yes," Althea had said. Did Carson remember hearing about the raft that had the live cow tied to the back of it? He did not, even though Maggie was sure she had mentioned it, high among the marvels of her grandparents' trip. What could have distracted him? The cow's fate had worried her deeply as a child. Which was worse, she had kept trying to decide: drowning tied up or having your throat slit by someone who had taken care of you all your life? She'd asked her grandparents about it again and again. Sometimes they didn't remember. Other times they just said whatever came into their heads — that they had sold her to someone before they reached the whirlpool, that they had eaten her somewhere downstream. Even today, with a fervor strong enough it could almost alter the past, Maggie still hoped that the cow had swum to shore.

"Points for spotting our first patient. See that guy on the veran-dah?" Carson pointed out. The man, about sixty, was staring at the bus. His clothes were so old they had turned the color of river water.

"Why is he our patient? What does he have?"

"Cataracts!"

"I didn't see them," Maggie said. "What could we do for him? You can't operate, right?"

"We'll get a doctor down here. Line up all the cases, guy comes down for a few days? The surgery's easy."

"Great. I'll write the letters, translate the interviews." Maggie saw herself in the modest dark skirt she'd brought for formal purposes, persuading the Cajamarca health officer, a fat bureaucrat in aviator sunglasses, to disburse some tiny amount of funds.

"We'll do it," Carson promised.

Satisfied, Maggie went back to inspecting the hacienda, which consisted of several buildings and many walls. A trio of ragged chil-dren stood in a doorway. They might have been the same children who appeared in all villages. Maggie waved at them. The littlest one balled up a fist and lifted it halfheartedly to her mouth.

This hacienda must have been abandoned by its owner in the agrarian reform, then taken over by local families. Its stuccoed build-ings still showed decrepit remains of grace. Through the trees, Maggie glimpsed the chapel where Grandma Althea had looked into the glass eyes of the saint.

Here was an iron bridge, the only means of crossing the river for many days' travel in either direction.

They crossed, the bus tires loud on dusty planks, and almost im-mediately passed a low adobe building with a corrugated roof. It stood far from its neighbors, between the road and the river, and was painted a thick, shabby government-green with a blood-red cross. "That's it," Carson cried, "that's our clinic!" Shuttered for years, the building didn't offer any encouragement.

"Looks pretty well closed," Maggie observed.

It had been shut down five years ago, due to generalized subversive activity in rural Peru. Maggie had checked carefully, finding a few bombings and assassinations in Cajamarca, the nearest big city, but nothing in the Rosario area. Piedras was remote from everything, in-cluding terrorism.

Now most terrorist leaders were in jail, and even the worst parts of the mountains had been officially pacified. After years of internal warfare and lack of foreign investment, the new government couldn't afford to run its rural health care system, so international organizations had stepped in. Carson and Maggie had a one-year contract with Catholic Charities. If things went well, it would be renewed, but eventually the goal was to replace the gringos with Peruvians.

Now they were arriving in what they would soon call downtown Piedras. On the left side of the road, against the mountains, were more mango groves, and cane fields and corn and some low leafy stuff, probably vegetables. All this must be irrigated from the river. The first houses were half hidden behind a long fence of living cactus and hibiscus plants that were choked with road dust. No one came out to wave. One woman was trudging alongside the road. She stood aside, turning her back and putting her hand over her face against the bus's passing.

So this was Piedras: two dozen houses crammed between the river and the east wall of the canyon. Call them adobe or mud brick, they were of mud plastered together with mud, most of them unpainted, with corrugated roofs, shaded by mango trees and papaya trees with fruit like giant milky breasts. The stringy road ran in one end of town and out the other along the river's terrace. Skinny dogs slept curled up in the soft dust at the bottom of potholes. If a truck or the bus came (all year, there would be only one car), the dogs got up leisurely, inches ahead of the oncoming wheels, and sauntered off not looking back. At the center of town was the general store, with a small area of beaten earth in front of it, the main arena for Piedras's social life. On that first day, as on most days, the store owner had set out a lawn chair and collapsed into it, so relaxed that when Maggie first caught sight of him, she had felt with a little thrill of fear that he must be the local AIDS patient.

But he was only Don Nasir, the Syrian. As Maggie would soon learn, he was a person who did not rise to occasions unless rising was profitable.

The bus shuddered to a halt. So this was the center of town. Maggie spied a man sprawling face-down in the sun next to the door of the general store, inert as death.

Suddenly she felt a gut-sinking certainty that, having confirmed the existence of the canyon, river, hacienda, chapel, and mango grove, she had already done all that was possible for her here. The bus would leave, and she and Carson would stay, and there was nothing for them. No school, no phone, no post office, no movie house. No doctor other than Carson, and Carson was only a physician's assistant, though he'd worked for twenty years overseas and knew more about wounds and tropical diseases than many M.D.s.

"Oh, God, I'm sorry," she whispered, almost involuntarily.

"What?" Carson was watching the drunk struggle to his feet, revealing a face half covered with bright fresh blood. He turned. "What did you say?"

"Nothing."

The passengers were crowding into the aisle all at once, pulling bags and boxes with them. The drunk fell down onto his hands and knees.

"Terrible," Maggie said.

"*He's* the reason we came." Carson began pushing forward through the struggling passengers. Maggie wondered whether she should follow, translate, but he'd left her with all their hand luggage. Besides, he hadn't asked for help. Before coming here, he'd requested that Maggie not hover excessively or worry about translating for him. He knew how to make himself understood; he'd done it in Thailand, India, Angola.

The drunk struggled to his feet again and zigzagged toward the bus, each step correcting a severe mistake made by the previous foot. He laughed at the disembarking passengers, who insulted him in return. A short, barrel-shaped, brown, indestructible-looking person. Maggie didn't like to think this way, but his face looked coarse and corrupted. His lips were purple, turned inside out. His forearms covered with blurring tattoos — one was a tick-tack-toe.

He and Carson met at the bottom of the bus's stairs. Maggie saw Carson step down onto the ground and raise his right hand tenderly toward the drunk man's cheek, indicating the bleeding wound. The drunk pulled his head back like a boxer and said something that gave his face an ugly look. Carson gathered a couple of supporters who seemed to be trying to explain to the drunk that he was offering help. At some point the message reached the drunk man's central nerve ganglion and he made an even uglier face than before. He put out his hand, insolently begging for money.

At this, Maggie slung all of the hand luggage about her body and squeezed forward through the aisle, straps catching, bags banging against the seats.

Carson had given up and gone around the back of the bus to unload their larger bags. The drunk was gripping the handrail at the bus steps, swaying as if a wind were blowing from the opening of the door. Clearly he intended to climb the steps and was only waiting for Maggie to start down them.

She waved at him to get on and he did. His smell was complex, shocking.

The bus driver explained to Maggie that this man was a *minero* and had spent the weekend drinking in Piedras. He had drunk, and fought, and slept, and his paycheck was gone, and now he wanted a ride back to La Tormentosa, the gold mine eight hours uphill, but he had no money left.

"This man is from Huancayo," the bus driver concluded. "He is not from our zone."

"Here you don't drink like that?"

"Oh, no, here we drink until we crawl home on all fours! Get on," he said to the drunk. "Sit down, you man without a conscience."

Maggie thanked the driver and got off. She found Carson standing behind the bus, trying to slow the boy helper, who was flinging their bags and boxes from the roof of the bus directly onto the ground. Three men struggled to lift down the refrigerator, but having completed this task, they disappeared.

The bus drove off, leaving Maggie and Carson standing amidst an immense amount of stuff. Together, they dragged their suitcases and boxes closer to the store. The refrigerator was a small one, but very heavy with its lockable iron straps, so they left it in what, now that the bus had pulled away, had again become the middle of the road.

The man in the lawn chair watched them, still immobile. A boy with a shaven head was fanning him with a folded glossy magazine.

They walked into the store wondering who was responsible. The air smelled edible, thick: motor oil, cheap perfume, dust, rancid flour, sunlight, cigars, and last night's frying onions. Voices could be heard from the back room. This was a restaurant, too: it had two long tables covered with plastic, with vases of dirty plastic flowers and napkin holders stuffed with sharp triangles of wax paper. A couple of used tumblers remained at the end of one table, with two related chairs pushed back at careless angles. A poster of a fat, garish baby decorated one wall. Carson said it looked like an ad for contraception.

They leaned over the glass counter, peering into the kitchen. It seemed deserted. Under the counter they saw wax matches and cigarettes, sold one by one from an open box. Carson pointed out a tiny brass scale, a miniature of the one used by blindfolded Justice; soon they'd learn that it was used for weighing gold dust. Maggie liked the dried piranha, apparently not for sale; and the loops of PVC joints, faucets, and machetes clipped to nylon ropes, festooned diagonally under the ceiling. Shovels, pickaxes, and hoes leaned in a corner. There were stacked boxes of yellow and blue batteries, hinges and chisels, open sacks of rice and flour and coarse gray salt, and a small shelf of items where the beautification of women commingled with good and bad sorcery: jasmine soap, bleaching cream, Florida water, myrrh, envelopes smelling of sulfur with dollar signs on the front, love soap, lucky soap, soap to get rid of devils.

Carson called out, "Hey! *Hola!*"

Eventually a woman came out. She was about four feet tall, stout, and her face had a kind expression. She wore a green-and-white-checked pinafore.

Maggie explained in her best voice that this was her husband, a doctor, el Señor Doctor Miller, and that she was his wife and assistant and trainee, Señora Margarita Goodwin de Miller. They were here to open the clinic. They had brought many things with them but would purchase more. Just now they needed transport. Was there a taxi, any kind of vehicle for hire?

"Nasir!" the woman howled, and went back into the kitchen.

At last the man unfolded from his chair. He smiled, showing incisors rimmed in silver. His shiny skin and small mustache reminded Maggie of a card shark; in another life, he would have worn a Panama hat. "Nasir," he said, offering his hand to Carson, but not to Maggie. She stepped forward and put her own hand out. With some surprise, Nasir took it.

❖ 14 ❖❖

While she repeated their introduction, Nasir smiled and actually rubbed his hands together. At the end he said he had a truck that he would rent to them for fifty *soles*.

"Fifty!" Maggie said. This was almost twenty dollars. The clinic was a thousand yards away.

"Tell him we expect a discount," Carson said. "Tell him we'll be buying all our food from him for a year. And tell him we may need to rent his truck at other times. Maybe, you know, we'll have some emergency and we'll have to drive someone up to Cajamarca Hospital in it. Oh, and ask him if we can borrow a crowbar and a hammer."

"You're so smart," she told him. Yesterday, the Cajamarca health officer had announced that there was no longer a key for the Piedras clinic.

"The padlocks are Chinese," Nasir told them. Taking one from under the counter, he showed where to strike it so that the lock sprang open.

"Descuento," Maggie reminded him. "On the truck."

Nasir said he paid to have all of the gasoline trucked here from the city. Surely they appreciated his difficulties.

"Ten *soles*," Maggie said, wondering why Nasir didn't drive the truck to Cajamarca and load it with barrels of fuel.

They agreed on fifteen.

The truck was stoutly chained into its own dark shed, a monster rarely allowed to emerge. When it did, it was so enormous that Maggie almost understood why Nasir had wanted fifty *soles*. He could have charged five just to look at it.

Its rust-brown cab had a tall oval grill like whale baleen. Its windshield was two dull eyes separated by a piece of metal, shielded by a narrow aluminum eyebrow. The gas cap was a petroleum-soaked rag that converted the whole thing into a rolling bomb. Tent cloth had been draped over part of its back platform, which was wood planks, surfaces white and eroded soft as suede. The planks were so long that Maggie was sure Nasir had stolen them off the bridge, which, she recalled, had been missing several.

The bridge had not existed when Althea was here, Maggie was sure of that.

2

THE RIVER SWELLED more strongly against the raft's prow in the afternoons. Green-brown, it was dangerous to drink, even though it looked perfectly clear and clean squishing up between the soft logs of the raft. Lighter than paper, the long white logs felt like suede under Althea's bare feet. Balsa. A gigantic tree that grew in the rain forest, Johnny said.

Johnny Baines stood at the prow wearing his cane cutter's straw hat so that his face was hidden in a wedge of shade. First he'd peer up at the canyon walls with his binoculars, then quickly take notes on his pad in minute, irregular handwriting. He had a contract from Standard Oil to map the strata, see if these were continuous with others where the company was drilling. Johnny wasn't an exploration geologist but he was good at mapping. Years later, on another continent, he'd make a crucial contribution to World War II. Just now, in Peru, on his own account, he was trying to understand just why these rocks that had been so far underneath the ocean could end up high in the air. They'd floated, Johnny believed. When he explained Wegener's theory to Althea, it made her think of baked Alaska.

At times they'd beach the raft so that Johnny could chip off samples. Sometimes he sent the oarsman's fifteen-year-old boy up a cliff, barefoot, with the geologist's hammer. The oarsman and the boy were interested in the rocks too. Some were full of fossils which Johnny said were crinoids, and the oarsman, roses.

Althea's place was to recline against a fifty-kilo sack of rice under a small canvas awning built just for her. If not for the smell of the cow tied just behind her, she would have felt like Cleopatra on her barge. Who knows why, but some sections of the river had more flies than others; here she fanned herself with a palmetto leaf the boy had cut down to size when he saw the lady from the Estados Unidos swatting at the air around her face like a crazy woman. If the boy would fan her, if the boy were wearing golden cobra armbands, then she truly would have felt Egyptian.

Althea sighed, imagining herself pregnant, her belly bloated like the rice sack, but precious, the most precious thing floating up this river. Floating toward what? Thebes, or an Inca ruin? More likely, one more lost Peruvian town, all shanties made of sticks.

The country of hills and thorn scrub where they'd started was two days behind them now; the walls of the Rosario Canyon were beginning to rise, close in. All morning they'd glided along, the brown man moving the raft with one long, narrow oar. Early in the afternoon there began to be small dramas, a rapid or a boulder ahead. The oarsman would pull the raft onto the bank, and then he and his boy and Johnny would scramble up to whatever eminence they could in order to chart a path through the next stretch of river. Usually Althea amused herself collecting rocks and stones, leaving them in a pattern on the sand when they started up again. She never bothered showing them to Johnny; he had his own rocks, collected under his own criteria. At night he painted white dots on them, then code numbers in India ink, fine as insects' legs.

The river beaches were small, each one a revelation nested in the arms of its cliff. They seemed untouched and useless to man, so that Althea imagined her footprints were the first since the world was made. She liked it that the beaches offered so little to do, although she was sorry to ruin them with her messy traces. Sometimes a bush with a red bird in it, sometimes a dead thing rotting on the sand or at the edge of the water, or a jam of driftwood like forked, naked corpses tossed into a pile. She was beginning to identify the smell of Peruvian dirt: it was rich, like dried beans, but not exactly pleasant.

Mostly she was dreaming about the baby whose sweet, dusty blue eyes she could see in the air in front of her. It had fair, thin, whitish hair. Though it wasn't clear whether it was a boy or a girl, she could feel it, as palpable a person as any on this boat. It loved her, she loved it. Already she could imagine things that it might say, all the ways it would surprise her.

"All aboard! Darling? We've figured it out," Johnny would shout to her, proudly, and kiss her brusquely on the cheek. Who is he, she wondered.

Then they'd get on again, the cow rolling her eyes in fright at the roaring and splashing of the water. Sometimes she'd quiver and shit in fear, and try her best to escape from the ropes that held her. Althea would stand up then, put her hand flat against the sweating hide, and say things that seemed to soothe the cow for a second or two. The first morning she'd thought the oarsman cruel as he tightened the gray rope around the cow's horns and neck. Now she saw his mercy, for the cow was suicidal.

Meanwhile, the oarsman plied his oar, his boy toiled with a long pole, straining every muscle to get them all past the obstacle. Up front, Johnny peered down into the water, shouting warnings and gesturing with his arms. Right, left. Water washed up through the logs, everything was soaked in spray. Althea admired the oarsman's knotty calves, his feet like a monkey's; Johnny said he could walk on tacks or coals. Yet she was afraid, too, of his pulsing brown body, covered with shiny drops of sweat and river water, at work so close to her. It was difficult to accept his hand when he held it out to help her onto shore, but she always took it. The man must be about sixty. Everything about him was pure strength. He was missing two knuckles from his right forefinger.

Why?

When the waters were calm she went up front, sat next to Johnny, let her feet slide into the water. Once, she whispered that she was afraid of them. The man, even the boy. Johnny teased her, being her same old Johnny Baines, saying the oarsman's father had been a cannibal in the Amazon jungle. Again, she believed whatever he told her, until he removed the curse.

That night they camped on a bigger beach. They came to it at three o'clock and Johnny wanted to go on — too early to stop. He said the oarsman was shirking, but the man stubbornly explained they'd not find a better place before dark. He wanted to scout the next stretch of river before morning; there was dangerous water ahead. Besides, it was hot between the canyon walls. Here there was shade, a bit of long grass for the cow, driftwood for a fire, and a waterfall with clean cold water for bathing and drinking.

Althea watched the boy untie the cow. She sank her muzzle into the river for a long time, then he took her to the grass and hobbled her. She was a young cow, too young to have had any calves yet. She was quite stupid, Althea realized, but she emanated some kind of emotional warmth. She seemed to recognize Althea, so that Althea felt the two of them were similar. Females, future mothers, one destined to devour the other.

While the men were making camp, she took her things up to the waterfall and let the cold, cold water blast down upon her head. Gasping, she looked down at her white body, the belly round as a shell. Maybe the cold would shock her womb into fertility. Tonight, she thought.

That night around the campfire, the oarsman spoke to Johnny in urgent, despairing tones. The river was terrible ahead, unnavigable. The Señor had agreed to turn around when they reached this point. The river was accursed, and many people had drowned in it. Johnny barked back, disagreeing. He expected a full six days of travel upstream. They'd spent two days before even reaching the beginning of the canyon, and only one day now below the clear rock walls. The oarsman defied Johnny to climb up the cliff with him and see, tomorrow morning. Johnny insulted him, said he was superstitious and a coward.

All right, the oarsman said. We will go on, then. But you will double my pay and we must leave the cow, she is too heavy. We'll get her on the way back.

What will we eat, Johnny said. What will my wife eat?

Fish, the man said. If we are alive enough to be hungry.

Okay, we leave the cow. But forget the double pay. Either this or nothing.

In the tent that night, Althea asked Johnny why he didn't listen to the oarsman. Domingo was his name. Domingo was a riverman, even if he didn't know this section. Johnny said local men always did this. Porters, mule drivers. The trip was not their own quest. They wanted to get their money and go home as soon as possible to their wives and children.

Althea said she understood wanting to get home to a family. Besides, she said, if the raft breaks up, Domingo will have no more way of making a living.

He can make another raft in a week, Johnny said. That's the beauty of these people's lives.

What about me, Althea thought, but she didn't say anything. She'd begged hard not to be left behind in horrible, cold Huaraz, where they'd been living for three months. Johnny was finishing his Ph.D. dissertation, trying to find the fault that was responsible for the mountain's falling on the town again and again. People in Huaraz were unfriendly, mountain people passing by all wrapped in their blankets and never changing their expressions. If Althea greeted them, they turned their faces away from her. Stone people, Johnny said, was their name for themselves in Quechua.

That night Johnny lay awake on his folding cot, thinking and thinking. From a foot away, Althea could hear the noise inside his skull. Near midnight, she reached across the gap between them, lifted the sheet, and touched Johnny's side with her finger, but he didn't pay any attention.

The next day was almost continuously terrible, the raft bucking, awash. The ropes that held the logs together began to bite and loosen. Johnny stood in the bow; the oarsman and his boy worked in such a deep silence that Althea worried they might do something to cause Johnny to fall in. It would have been easy as they negotiated whirlpools with rocks underneath them. Once, the boy got out and towed them up a rapid as long as a giant's bowling alley. Afterward there was no more calm river. Althea got soaked to the skin, no longer reclining but standing, hanging on to the ropes of her canopy. The bread got wet and so did Johnny's drawing paper, even though it was encased in two waterproof canvas bags.

"I'm not finding anything, that's the hell of it," Johnny shouted. "These oilmen, they claim to be scientists, but they shoot the messenger if there isn't anywhere to drill." He had wanted to work for the oil company a few more times, to save money for his own, less profitable seismological idiosyncrasies.

The child, Althea thought. What will I feed it when there's no money? "We've got to go on," she said.

"That's my girl," said Johnny.

A boy, Althea thought.

By four o'clock, the shadows were beginning to creep down the canyon walls, and they had not yet found a beach wide enough for tents. Domingo suggested they could tie the raft to any overhanging tree, or stake it on any patch of dirt, but Johnny wanted just to get around the corner of the next cliff. Luckily, there was some flat water there, almost a lake but for the deep pulling current.

Even if Althea had felt like making love, it was no night for romance. Menace hung in the darkness, as if this beach were haunted by the evil spirits and ghosts Domingo said lived in the upper parts of the Rosario River. At two in the morning, Johnny heard a rustling noise like voices and put his head out of the tent. He reached back and grabbed his hunting rifle by the barrel, sliding it out of its long ugly holster, then slid through the flap and was gone. Althea heard him shouting in Spanish, but she was too afraid to go and see what was happening. She got off the cot and lay on the canvas floor instead, just in case.

The oarsman had been trying to slip away in the darkness, abandon them. Johnny said he was so mad he wanted to shoot the bastard and his kid right there and then, except that if he was going to shoot them, he might as well have let them go. So he tied them to a tree instead, and covered them with their own blankets against the cold.

It was a matter of principle now, Johnny said. The vein on his forehead was pumping, and Althea could see the lines where he gritted his jaw. Half a day more upriver, then they could call it quits. He seemed to be defying Althea to join the rebellion herself, but she was quelled by his gray eyes, sharp as picks. Johnny left Domingo's kid tied to the tree while he and the oarsman walked up as far as they could, to see what was coming next. They crossed the river on a series of gravel bars, wading in thigh-deep water, Johnny keeping the gun above his head. Then the two of them disappeared around a long bar of rock. They were gone an hour and Althea began to half listen for a shot, to worry that the oarsman had overpowered Johnny. She'd be left with the boy, maybe the boy and his father. She imagined the fate worse than death. Would she be able to love that kind of baby? She didn't think so. It was a certain person, this pale child who wanted to come to her. When she felt his presence — and it had been given her to know he'd be a boy — she knew her husband would come back in one piece.

Soon he did. Ahead was not as bad as yesterday, Johnny said. He'd offered Domingo double pay to continue, just until noon. Johnny wanted to find one or two familiar strata, but if he didn't, he had to be able to say he'd gone twenty miles up the canyon.

Domingo seemed satisfied, if a little grim; he admitted there was an hacienda up this way; they should already have reached it.

Johnny kept the rifle in reach, though wrapped in oilcloth.

Indeed, it was not as hard as the day before, until eleven A.M. They began negotiating a combination of problems, not nearly as bad as others they'd seen even that morning, when the nose of the raft got pulled under by a wave roaring off one boulder, and the tail of the raft slued sideways and hit another boulder. The oar caught and flipped, throwing Domingo into the air, and then the raft began falling rapidly back toward the whirlpool. While the accident was happening they entered another kind of time, faster and slower at once, so that Althea later remembered Johnny shouting, but at the time everything was one simultaneous shouting, her ears full of inward and outward sound. Johnny was shouting to warn her about a long tree trunk jammed sideways, four feet above water level; it knocked Althea between the shoulders and suddenly she was in the water, water the color of dying leaves, water full of light and motion. She kicked, hoping to propel herself upward — no resistance, her foot was out in air. Twisting like a fish she wriggled, poked her head out, saw a steep beach the size of a bed, and swam to it without thinking of anything or anyone else.

Eventually she and the boy and Johnny were squatting together on that rocky sand. Domingo had disappeared. He didn't know how to swim, his son said. Maybe he'd been swept down to last night's campsite, where he could get himself to shore, Althea suggested.

They were all soaked and shivering. They could not stay where they were. Cautiously they swam around the corner of the cliff to another small beach. Then, froghopping boulders, swinging from trees, avoiding the water, in less than an hour they reached the beach where they'd camped last night. The boy was crying. It was no longer difficult for Althea to accept a hand as he helped her negotiate certain gaps. The cow was here, cropping grass, but Domingo was no-where.

At the beach's southern end the boy discovered a faint trail leading away from the river, and they decided to follow it. Soon Althea's legs were covered in red-brown dust. Her bare feet began to bleed, so Johnny ripped his shirtsleeves off and tied them around. How can this be happening to me, she thought over and over, finding herself helpless, stripped, alone, crawling over the body of the awesome world.

And in this way, Althea and Johnny Baines, together with the boy, Wifredo Sánchez Aliaga, reached the Hacienda Chigualén on August 1, 1931.

3

A DESICCATING WIND blew through the canyon, thickening the gringo doctors' hair with dust. They stood at the front door of the clinic, locked and bolted since four years ago.

"Five years without aspirin," Nasir intoned. "Thus we lived the people's revolution."

Wham! Wham! The Chinese lock resisted the first blow of his hammer, but not the second. Sliding aside the thick iron bolt, Nasir stood back and kicked his heel against the crack between the clinic's narrow double doors, which popped open instantly. *"Pedazo de mierda,"* he growled, fingering the snap lock that had held the doors, like a button holding together a knitted shawl.

"He says 'piece of shit,'" Maggie translated for Carson.

Carson practiced *"mierda"* under his breath while Nasir permanently disabled the snap lock with a chisel, explaining that the nurses had installed it in order to come and go at any hour, independent of one another. "You, Doctores, are decent people, and will not need it."

Carson fingered the hand-forged sliding bolts, one inside and one outside. "What's he say?"

"He says we're decent people because we intend to sleep on the same side of the door." In Spanish, Maggie defended the bad, unmarried women to Nasir. "Maybe they only wanted to *independizarse.*"

Nasir grunted disapprovingly. "Ask yourself, Señora — freedom, for what purpose?"

Carson observed that anyone could come along and bolt the door from the outside, thus trapping them in the clinic.

This was the instant Maggie would have regretted leaving Cambridge, Massachusetts, but the clinic stood open now before them, full of all the possibilities of the year to come. There was nothing to see at first except for a scintillating body of dust, raised by the canyon wind and the doors bursting open. As it thinned and fell, Maggie saw that the room was nearly bare. The floor was of cured cement. A broom leaned in the corner, a black comma worn to the stitching. The examining table was homemade, draped with a coarse grubby sheet. Against the far wall was a counter and a stool and a set of wooden shelves, empty but for a stack of folders and scattered debris: brown medical bottles, tiny boxes, balls of hair.

On Maggie, the vacant space exerted an ecstatic pull. She glanced at Carson.

"I've seen better," he said, lacing his fingers through hers. His voice was low and flat, reminding her that, once upon a time, he'd tried to leave this kind of life behind. She hoped she'd been right to convince him to drop out of Harvard Divinity School. "I've also seen worse."

As he spoke, she saw the room's ugliness and filth. She let Carson drag her by the hand across the room, not pausing to inspect a single thing. They passed through an opening in the far wall, into the living quarters, the back half of the house. Nasir opened a barred window at the end of the hallway, admitting light and the roar of the river.

In the kitchen lay a mouse's bones, a black, exploding aureole of decay.

Nasir preceded them into the bathroom. The toilet was a tall box painted red, with a seat and cover. "The jewel of Piedras," said Nasir, lifting the lid.

Maggie couldn't resist peering over his shoulder. She saw a dry cement trough with a fossilized human turd sitting at the bottom.

"*Mierda!*" Carson uttered his new vocabulary word.

"*Correcto,*" said Nasir, letting the lid slam shut. River water should be flowing here, but someone must have diverted it. The toilet was a luxury, a sanitary achievement; Nasir wanted one, too.

"Not sanitary! *Sucio,* dirty," Carson said. He was standing in the shower. "Tell this guy about fecal-oral transmission downstream."

"Ugh, do I have to?"

Carson glared. "Please, that's the point." According to Catholic Charities, education and prevention were duties equal to the treatment of disease.

As she began, uncomfortably, to explain to Nasir (taking refuge in the formula "My husband says . . ."), Maggie inadvertently stepped back and kicked over a plastic wastebasket which spilled out liverpink screws of toilet paper and an ancient sanitary napkin. Her stomach contracted painfully. She turned and left the room.

Nasir hadn't been listening anyway, she told herself in the hall.

Carson came out. "You okay?"

"A little queasy." Her stomach clamped again.

"You'll get used to squalor." He put one cool palm on the nape of her neck. "We'll get the place cleaned up. I'll dig a toilet outside."

She said she was fine, happy; she didn't really mind. It was true: even nauseating filth was interesting, far better than the subtle dread she'd grown familiar with in Cambridge, a feeling that she must have done or said something reprehensible quite recently but couldn't remember what it was.

"It's okay even if you do mind," Carson said.

"I do mind, a little bit," she said to please him.

In the bedroom more dust, the color of ground bones, covered everything: the wooden chair; the metal *armario* for clothes; and the two uneven iron bedsteads, with their rolled mattresses and knotted, clubbed mosquito nets. Here the floor was wood, darkened by the kerosene that was used to wash it and prevent termites. A faint reek still pervaded the room; its walls were so hot, Maggie wondered why the clinic had not caught fire spontaneously.

"Reminds me of summer camp," said Carson.

"Really?" Maggie said. The beds should have had skeletons in them.

"Camp Gimme My Mommy."

It took her a few seconds to realize that Carson had never gone to such a camp. During that time, he and Nasir left the building to unload the truck, leaving Maggie to perform female tasks inside the house. Instead of airing the mattresses or starting to sweep with the evil broom, she selfishly went into the kitchen, hoping to open the back door and admit the sight and sound of the river. This door, too, was locked. She kicked at it, not hard, for it was massive, some rain forest hardwood, more solid than the wall.

There was a window, though, high up. Small and square, it was just the size to lead Maggie to wonder whether her hips could fit through in an emergency. Standing on one of the kitchen chairs, she opened its brass latch on half blue infinity, half canyon wall.

She went back to the bedroom, unhooked the dire mosquito nets, and dragged them outside to air. Next, the mattresses, but these were stuffed with extremely heavy, rotting foam rubber, so when she tried to embrace the first one, it slipped from her arms and bounced back onto the bedsprings. How she hated the intractable weight of large objects, the nightmarish sensation that she could not hold on.

She plunked herself down abruptly on the edge of the metal bed frame, and might have burst into tears except that when she hung her head she spied, down through the spiral grid of bedsprings, a comic book on the floor. Its hot-pink cover was laden with soft furry dust. She made out a busty woman kneeling on a bed, fully clothed, hands pressing at the sides of her screaming mouth as a dark man fled the room with a pistol in his hand.

He Killed to Save Her Honor.

She shook it, and, holding it from its spine, carried it to the doorway where there was light, and read it from cover to cover. Men in turtlenecks argued with each other. Women wept, and kissed them. Maggie felt lifted into another life, simpler and more fantastic, where it was no longer necessary to be herself.

Now Carson and Nasir came tromping back inside, shouting for her help. They were carrying the refrigerator and needed her to dust the counter so they could put it down.

The first important thing Carson had said to Maggie was that she did not seem to belong in the United States. How had she gotten trapped in Cambridge? At first, she'd been embarrassed to admit that she'd never considered settling anywhere else. As she spoke to him, however, she realized she hadn't felt entitled just to go and live in someone else's country. Carson had replied that, in his opinion, she'd closed the door too firmly behind her. If a missing piece of her soul resided in South America, why not go reclaim it?

Soon she'd returned the favor, pointing out that Carson should listen to himself, and go back to the work he'd been born for, the life he knew was real.

He'd been one of her ex-husband's graduate students. Older than most, he was part of a special program for people who'd run upon the rocks and shoals of life and needed time to think. They spent a year, or two, writing a long paper about the reason for suffering, or where was God in an imperfect world. At the end they had master's degrees in divinity but were discouraged from leading congregations. Maggie worked in the divinity school administration, and for some reason she had identified with these students and looked forward to their visits to the office. One man, whose brain had been damaged in a car accident, could not stop himself from sharing his deepest emotions with strangers. A black M.D. had a son who'd disappeared. The daughter of an infamous billionaire had changed her name, renounced her fortune. Even the aging ladies who'd left their husbands after thirty-three years, hennaing their pageboys, were full of a sense of adventure.

Like all other first-year students, they were required to take a course in Religion and History, taught by Dr. Larry Fabularo, Maggie's ex-husband. Larry designed his curriculum to destroy a broad spectrum of wrong thoughts. He punctured creationists, materialists, and idealists with equal glee, brought empty nesters up to academic speed. In the case of older students, Larry felt a special mission to disabuse them of the idea that life should have a meaning. To wish for meaning was a source of torture, Larry believed. Maggie had observed that this belief was at least an equal torture to Larry, but that he felt less pain when he was inducing others to adopt it.

Larry often said he envied his wife because she had a passion for experience, experience for its own sake. One of his pet theories, based on a study of infants grabbing toys, correlated the highest intelligence with a lack of ambition, pure curiosity. Maggie was flattered by his analysis, but when she turned thirty, she'd begun to wonder what she was becoming. It wasn't Larry's fault that she'd adopted his opinion of her; yet as long as she was with him, she didn't know how to figure out whether or not she was the person they'd agreed on.

She'd married him right after graduating college, taking this job he'd found for her, to pay bills while she chose a graduate school. First she'd tried counseling psychology, but soon it was clear she'd lose her mind if she were to be locked in a small room with one neurotic after another for the rest of her life. In reaction, she'd gotten certified in massage. She'd loved feeling the ghostly sensations of her fingers on her own legs and shoulders as she kneaded her patients' flesh, but then afterward, for a few unnerving hours, she became the person she'd been touching: she smelled, felt, thought as they did. Often her clients dreamed of her on the night after a treatment. Kinesthetic possession, Larry called it.

Another year she took up night photography, long exposures in the dark with a moving penlight, but this was not a career.

Everyone in the divinity school office was similar. Overeducated, or anyway too intelligent for the third-grade skills required, they'd unofficially decided it took ten years to give up the idea of ever becoming anything. Their salaries were nearly as good as the professors'. Shoats locked on to the teats of Mother Harvard, they shared an airy, pleasant pen, an office with high ceilings, and windows looking out on a tidy oak-treed lawn. Boredom and lack of prestige were the main job stressors; otherwise, working there was a bit like playing "school," licking stamps and answering the phones.

The fall Carson arrived, two people in the office decided to have crushes on him. He stood out, a craggy, self-conscious, almost comically louring romantic presence, the overseas health worker now stalking the long, wainscoted hallways in his battered leather jacket, jeans, and boots. His hair was dark. His skin was pale. His nose was thin. He spoke with a slight accent, Southern, mixed with the kind of forgivable affectation people picked up overseas. He looked either Dutch or French. The head administrator, Brian (he edited gay porn videos on the side), and the departmental secretary, Rita (she had a black belt in tae kwon do, two kids, and a restraining order against her husband), both found devious ways of summoning Carson into the office to fill out forms or straighten out his scholarship. He'd lean over the counter and play with the doodads on Rita's desk, guessing which was a gift from which professor.

Maggie took the scoffer's position, saying Carson was too conspicuous — too, too *something*. But she noticed his hands, the long fingers fitting together as if never to let anything run through them uselessly. Rumors said he'd been under bombardment in Angola; his girlfriend had recently died of brain cancer; he'd been cured of leprosy, of exposure to chemical weapons. Bit by bit, Brian and Rita drew him out, proving most of the rumors true. He'd worked in seven countries, seen famines, wars, epidemics, refugee camps, the worst poverty. His British girlfriend, Maxine, had died — of breast, not brain, cancer. He'd held her in his arms at the end.

Carson entertained them with his wicked opinions. Women in Boston had the worst hairdos on earth. The summer heat reminded him of Bangladesh. But Harvard! He'd feel more useful mopping floors at a homeless shelter. The main thing taught here was that education took away your right to speak. Even if a hundred people agreed a cat was gray, none of them could say so. They had to ask the cat. If the cat didn't feel like answering, too bad. Obviously if those same hundred people confronted a gray building, they were in deep, deep trouble. This way of thinking was a disguised intellectual blight, death to compassion and imagination, and its chief perpetrator was Professor Larry Fabularo. Fabularo's stance was forgivable only because he was clinically depressed. "Untreated," Carson called him.

That day Maggie hid her face behind a ream of laser printing paper, recognizing her husband's cat lecture, one of his most provocative. When, later, her co-workers had commiserated with her, she'd said Carson wasn't the first to have such thoughts. Lately Larry had fallen away from himself in some deeply dismaying way. His book was five years overdue; he couldn't resolve the last chapter. He'd smoke pot for inspiration and end up losing heart, let the sun set without turning on the lights, then play computer games so obsessively he'd had to get a wrist brace. Maggie hated walking past his office door in the evenings, seeing him silhouetted in the sick glow of the screen. Once she'd asked him to consider getting help, and he'd retorted that her request was self-centered. After that, she'd been unable to consider leaving him.

He always gave a cocktail party in the middle of the fall semester. For days beforehand, Maggie cooked, arranged flowers, and ironed tablecloths, the way her mother Julia had taught her. Maggie's spread was famous. Everybody came; useless to expect Carson not to. Larry had aimed him right at Maggie, saying, "You'll be interested in talking to my wife. She grew up in South America. Maggie, this is Carson. Carson has lived everywhere."

She began by apologizing for not identifying herself in the office. In turn, Carson said he hoped he hadn't been insensitive, but Maggie should know he'd said all the same things to Larry's face, in class. Now, if it was okay to change the subject, he *would* like to hear about South America, a place he'd never been. How had she felt growing up there? Didn't she find the United States harsh and hellish in comparison? Here, the myth of progress poisoned everything, Carson believed. You could never be satisfied because you always had to be improving. "This myth of the successful self," he said. "My God, it's narcissistic!"

Maggie wanted this man to know she'd gone to El Salvador, two years ago, with Larry. They'd lived six weeks with a village family, part of the Witness for Peace program. The man they'd been escorting, supposedly protecting with their presence, was assassinated a month after they left. He'd come out in the newspaper, dead, with a sign around his neck.

"You kept him alive as long as you were there," Carson interrupted.

"Our intervention killed Santiago, that's what Larry thinks."

Carson gripped her arm. "When you do this work, you have to believe your intentions count for something."

Maggie quoted Larry on naive, imperialist do-gooders.

Carson said, "Whose opinion matters more, yours or his?"

"We're exactly the same," Maggie said, too quickly.

"You should listen to your own opinions a little more, I think."

"Now there's a scary idea," Maggie told him, laughing.

She'd considered all this to be high-level party chat, no deep soul-baring — until the next morning, when she'd awakened on fire, as if a spark had smoldered while she slept. Larry's shoulders had been hunched and still, turned away from her as usual, a monadnock under the blanket.

She didn't belong where she was.

Strange how words of insubstantial breath, long since absorbed in silence, could have revolutionized her life.

❖

Going to pee behind the clinic, she ran across a dirty, wide-mouthed basket in which the nurses must have collected their trash. Garbage here must be burnt, unless fed to livestock or buried. She was surprised at the depth of her pleasure in figuring out how things worked. When she was younger, hearing her grandmother speak about tombs, ruins, and mummies, she'd wanted to become an archaeologist. This must be the pleasure archaeologists felt, yet hers was deeper, proving she belonged here, in this place.

She filled the basket with detritus, rummaged in boxes until she found the blue-headed wax matches. A widespread Peruvian brand, they could easily be the same matches her grandmother had used. With everything assembled, Maggie walked out, around, down toward the river rapid. The water was past fifty yards of waste ground littered with eroded rocks and jimsonweed. The shore was irregularly terraced by past floods and still had no permanent vegetation. Between the bigger boulders were jams of driftwood draped with dried grass like long, dun-colored wigs. When she came upon the ring of blackened stones where the nurses had burnt their garbage, five little birds flew up, startled at her approach.

The trash lit with a single match. Barefoot on a rock, Maggie watched transparent orange flames devour the toilet paper and cardboard boxes and balls of human hair, finally reducing all of it to ash. Things were simpler here, fewer, and from the space between them an invisible light shone forth. Was this feeling the definition of home? A place where things fit easily inside you? Or was her exultation proof that she was just a tourist? People in Piedras would never exult in burning garbage; surely they'd prefer it to disappear from the curb without their intervention. Unless they understood all the other things they'd have to put up with — but by the time they'd found out, it would be too late.

This was an illogical train of thought.

She heard Carson's faint voice, calling from the other side of the clinic.

She ran to him, leaving her shoes on a rock.

"You're awful chipper," he teased as she twined one leg behind his thigh, reporting her deeds of housework. Mattresses beaten, airing. Rooms all swept. Trash burnt. "Honey, you ought to keep your shoes on." There could be *Strongyloides* in the sand, worms that sneaked in through bare soles. First they gave you a dry cough, then ate holes in your guts, and you died of a massive infection.

"Don't be a bossy doctor."

"If you died, you'd mess up my life."

"I'm not planning to die."

"It's part of my job to stop you." His face looked etched. He must be thinking of Maxine.

✦

"There's chicken soup," Doña Albita said, her voice trailing off, discouraged.

"Great!" said Maggie.

Carson scowled.

Under the next table sat an orange dog with yellow eyes, watching all their moves.

They ordered chicken soup and a liter of Coca-Cola which they drank immediately. Through the half-open door of the kitchen, Maggie watched Doña Albita ladling up the soup, her arms shining in the heat. The shave-head boy came out with two flat bowls, setting them down so carefully he spilled them both.

Yellow liquid with pale, hairy boiled chicken parts submerged. Hulks of yam, white potato, and hominy corn on the cob stuck up from the surface, where flecks of blackish-green cilantro jerked about like water insects. The dog ventured forth, sniffing the air above its head, until the boy swatted it with a broom and it slunk behind the legs of a chair.

The boy returned with a plastic saucer of condiments: small round limes cut in half, raw hot peppers, and a mound of coarse damp salt.

"Oh, God, I'd forgotten Third World cuisine," groaned Carson.

"Shh, he'll understand your tone of voice."

"The soup's cold," Carson announced, putting down his spoon.

"How can it be cold?" It was lukewarm. Alone, Maggie would have eaten it without complaint.

"Hey, kid." He signaled for the boy.

"*Disculpen,*" the boy said, excuse me. Maggie wanted to apologize too, but instead she pushed her bowl along with Carson's to be reheated.

They stared at the table catatonically. Their last meal had been in a previous eon, hard rolls and coffee in the Cajamarca bus station. Even longer ago, Maggie thought, she'd believed that Carson knew how to live well anywhere in this world.

"*Gringos, no lo creo!*" Gringos, I can't believe it! Silhouetted in the doorway stood a local woman, medium height with long iron-gray braids. She wore a faded aqua shift and canvas pumps. Night had fallen, closing the world behind her. Advancing into the room, she said she'd come to confirm a rumor that *norteamericanos* had arrived in Piedras.

"*Buenas noches!*" Maggie said, and stated the obvious. "Yes, that's us."

Encouraged, the new customer sat down at their table and, turning her chair toward the kitchen, yelled for Nasir. She was in late middle age, with a thick waist and stout hard body. Below the hem of her skirt, her calves were smooth and muscled like a gymnast's — from walking up and down the mountain trails, Maggie decided.

"*Qué es esto?*" Nasir came out in an undershirt and jeans. "Doña Fortunata, what a joy to see you!" Fortunata was an important personage, he told them. This day could never have finished without Fortunata registering their arrival.

"Why?" Maggie asked. Did she hold some official position?

Both Peruvians ignored her. Fortunata was feigning a further convulsive shock. "Nasir, by God, but these are gringos!" she cried. "Bring them some bread at least. Gringos, are you lost? Are you Germans? Have you taken the wrong bus?"

Nasir said, "These are our new doctors. They are going to reopen the clinic."

"*Gracias a Dios!* We miss our nurses, even though they were useless."

Maggie asked how many gringos had come here in the past.

The boy set down a plate of the same cementlike rolls they'd eaten in Cajamarca. Carson made a sandwich of margarine, salt, and raw hot peppers. While Maggie watched in admiration, he bit into it, wiggling his eyebrows at Maggie, who hurried to translate everything that had been said.

"I knew you were not *turistas*," Fortunata went on with authority. "*Turistas* are afraid of us. They think we are terrorists and savages. They don't know that today we want capitalism and progress! The only tourists we ever saw in Piedras were some Californians. Your *compatriotas,* yes?"

Yes, but, said Maggie. California was far away, another coast, another country.

Fortunata agreed. The Californians had been large and golden, beautiful and very spoiled. (Not dark and long and earnest like us, Maggie thought.) They'd stayed at Nasir's for weeks, eating vitamins and playing in the rapids in their kayaks while people stood watching from the shore. They'd loved the dangerous waters so much, they'd decided to set up a rafting center here in Piedras. "We're still waiting for them to come back with all the money they said they'd bring. Why are you not their representatives!" She laughed mockingly and said, with real suspicion, that some people believed the Californians had secretly panned for gold, and had exported enough gold dust so that they did not need to return.

After this there was a silence, into which Maggie was tempted to utter denials.

Her name was Fortunata Rosas de Carrión, and tonight her husband had gone to get drunk at a party up the mountain, and she did not expect him home. In revenge, she would get as drunk as he. "Beer! Don Nasir, bring that frigid blonde!" Nasir said he'd see her money first, and Fortunata put her hand into the furrow between her breasts, drew out a knitted bag, and disdainfully dropped a few *soles* into Nasir's outstretched hand.

"What's she saying?" Carson had finished all the bread. "'*Bodracho,*' I recognize that." He mispronounced the word for drunk, but Maggie praised him anyway.

Fortunata said, enunciating fully, "I am not *borracha,* sir, not yet."

Carson looked at Fortunata, then at Maggie, and then he began to laugh.

Fortunata laughed with him. "Welcome to Piedras, Doctor Calzón! What a rare name you have! When is the inauguration?"

"Carson," Maggie translated in two directions. Fortunata had just offered him his new nickname: Doctor Underwear.

Carson said, "Tell her I don't wear underwear. Underwear is for sissies." Fortunata was delighted. "Now just tell her our doors are open. Anyone can come, no charge."

Maggie did.

At this, Fortunata was disappointed. "You will have no act of opening? I can supply cooked foods. Chickens, any number, at one day's notice. Papas a la Huancaína, suckling pig? Not just to say so, but I have fame as a cook." Her voice lowered. "Doña Albita is a terrible cook. Even Nasir admits it. *Claro,* they can sell you the beer. Everyone will come!"

Carson shook his head. "They'll say we're getting peasants drunk so we can sterilize them. We'll be kicked out," he predicted. He wagged his finger at Fortunata. "No way."

"*Qué esta diciendo?*" Fortunata asked. What is he saying?

"He hates parties," Maggie told her. Carson had never wanted to be the head of a program. Heads of programs spent all their time kissing babies, making sure their funding got renewed. Carson would rather lance a boil. Lately, though, he'd realized there was one reason to run your own outfit, which was to avoid being supervised by some idiot like his last boss, Suzette Fauchon.

Remembering things her father had said about not neglecting protocol in South America, Maggie asked Fortunata whether they should present themselves to the mayor, but Fortunata explained that the town council had voted itself out of existence.

So that was that. The beer arrived in a tall brown liter bottle. Fortunata poured a tumblerful and handed it to Carson. "Here, Señor, drink with a Peruvian. Sit down, Nasir, drink with us!" Nasir pulled up a chair.

Carson took a sip, set down the glass. "*Gracias.* I still wonder, where's our soup?"

"Ya, ya, it's coming," Nasir said, while Fortunata instructed Carson how to drink: "No, Doctor, *seco,* drink it down." Carson obeyed, slamming the tumbler on the table. Fortunata cried out, "Yes, like that!" and refilled the glass for Maggie. "*Salud,* Doctora!"

The soup arrived, steaming fiercely.

"Now but *I* can make a soup," boasted Fortunata, peering into the bowls.

Thus they acquired their cook.

✦

During their first week in Peru, when they'd gone to register at the U.S. embassy in Lima, a man behind a bulletproof window had warned them against visiting the Rosario Canyon. He had shown them a photocopied map where Piedras lay under heavy, blurred crosshatching, an unpacified zone. He'd said, "I hope we don't have to send in a Marine division after you."

As they left the embassy, whose thick cement walls were obviously designed to withstand a small missile, Carson had fumed, "He enjoyed scaring you. They all do that. Sadists. I've been warned against every country where I've ever worked."

Having seen the look in the man's pale eyes, Maggie knew Carson was right. Still, the official *had* succeeded in frightening her, at least temporarily. She'd wanted to blurt out that she'd changed her mind, but it was much too late for that.

Shovel, broom, mop, bucket, machete. Soup pot, laundry soap, dishrag, mousetrap, insecticide, disinfectant. Salt, sugar, oil, instant coffee, canned milk. Bags all sticky with cane syrup from the shattered jar. Kerosene, gasoline, matches, butcher knife. Fortunata was helping Maggie unpack the supplies she and Carson had bought at the Cajamarca market.

She was disappointed that the gringos' boxes contained nothing but familiar, Peruvian goods. "How much did all this cost?" she nonetheless wanted to know.

"A lot, because we had to buy it all at once," Maggie prevaricated. It was strange to find herself managing the servant. Neither her mother nor her grandmother would have hoped for Fortunata's friendship, nor cared about her good opinion.

"How much?"

"Six hundred *soles*."

Fortunata sucked air through her teeth, though six hundred was a gross understatement. Maggie was grateful for Carson's decision to own nothing that would draw attention to their privileges. She'd already hidden their air tickets between two overlapping roof sections in the bedroom, and Carson's guns under a floorboard by the wall.

One thing her friends would never understand was how Carson, the healer of humanity, could possibly be into guns. Maggie rather enjoyed their discomfiture. Carson came by his interest honestly, hunting muskrat and deer with his father and his uncles in the Mississippi Delta as a boy. Plus, she could see how firearms could be a comfort in most places Carson had lived and worked, now including Piedras. He'd never had to shoot at anyone, but he'd cemented friendships going hunting with chieftains and officials. He tried to have a gun in every place he worked, prevailing on embassy friends, shopping locally, or simply smuggling. In Peru, incredibly enough, he'd learned that incoming baggage wasn't x-rayed; he'd packed a pistol and a shotgun into one of his aluminum medical supply trunks.

"How much was this machete?" Fortunata slid it from its leather scabbard. "Ah, Bolivian. It is superior. Fifty *soles*. What about the refrigerator? Why don't we place it in the kitchen?"

"It's not personal," Maggie said. "It's for antivenin, and vaccinations."

"We have no vipers here."

Maggie filed this away to tell Carson. "The refrigerator is for medical uses."

"Beer is curative," Fortunata argued. "Milk, eggs, butter feed the bones."

"True, but this *nevera* belongs to the Catholic Church."

"You condemn it to be like a nun. Empty and cold inside. What about vitamins, did you bring some? Those Californians ate capsules full of seaweed, and live bugs."

"No." Maggie laughed, recognizing spirulina, acidophilus. "Fortunata, is this what Nasir meant about how you register everybody? Or was it something more official?" She'd been waiting to ask this question.

"I am always counting," Fortunata replied, rummaging in the next box. "Counting things and people. Doctora, you forgot floor wax and a scrub brush. The clinic floor is *inmundo*, filthy. You will buy those things from Nasir." She got to her feet and bustled off, saying she would now help Maggie's husband.

The electricity went off at eleven. Maggie and Carson each lay under their own mosquito net, watching the filaments turn orange, fade, and disappear. Soon their bedroom was dark as a cavern. Maggie could smell the dust of the mosquito net, filtering all her air. She experimented with her hand in front of her face: an inch or a foot away, there was nothing to see.

She began relating the day's events. In such a darkness she sensed all the edges of her voice; if Carson stopped listening or fell asleep, she'd know immediately. "Fortunata is so nosy. Could she be planning to rip us off?" She hated to impugn the cook, but felt a duty to report misgivings to her husband.

His voice came, oracular, from the dark. "People always want to know what things cost. It's no sin to lie, but you've got to let the servants steal a little. If you're too strict, one day they run off with everything."

His reasoning astonished Maggie, but she saw its logic. Her mother had always said the opposite, that you couldn't let them get used to thievery or they encroached more and more. Maggie preferred Carson's attitude, cynical on the surface but generous and soulful underneath. She went on: she didn't want to be paranoid, but she worried that Fortunata had been sent to spy on them or set them up. Did he remember Nasir saying she was an important personage?

"If they feel like killing us, they'll just swoop down and do it."

Maggie reflected silently on this possibility.

"I'm joking, honey," Carson said. "Sort of." Everyone in town must have been implicated in some way or other with the terrorists. If Nasir was still alive, they couldn't have been too bloody. Nasir was a foreigner and Piedras's official capitalist. Maggie could ask him for a character reference on Fortunata, if she wanted.

She was reassured. "She wanted the Californians back, remember? That's a good sign."

Without warning, Carson came crawling under the edge of her mosquito net, breathing and hairy, like some animal. She couldn't see even an outline of his body. "Who are you?" For an answer, he clamped his teeth onto her earlobe and pulled her T-shirt up. Their bellies rubbed against each other, rosinous with today's dried sweat. Their smells mixed together, salt and bread and vinegar.

The best sign, Maggie believed, was that she was still so attracted to him after a whole year. With Larry, it had taken only a few months before she'd begun to dislike the shape of his upper lip, among other things. Carson had been shocked that she'd stayed married seven years to a man she didn't like to sleep with. He'd made her vow that with him, passion would never be replaced by more mature emotions.

Whatever the reason, her body kept trying to reach him, as if closing an indefinable gap that she hoped would never disappear. The gap was love, she thought. Still, she knew that on the scale of things, even on the scale of marriages, a year was not very long.

Afterward, he rolled away to lie on his own bed, under his own mosquito net pavilion. "G'night." Seconds later he was snoring.

Maggie groped for their new fake-fur blanket, drew it up from the floor where it had fallen. Her bed had cooled too quickly. How could five inches of empty space (three horizontal, two vertical) sever her utterly from mental balance, human warmth, and physical safety?

"You have to love me," she said into the darkness, glad that Carson couldn't hear.

"Fortunata sent me," the visitor said.

"Do you feel bad?" Maggie asked him in Spanish.

Behind her, Carson was trembling like a spaniel on scent. "What's his complaint?"

"I am a carpenter." The man looked ready to flee. His eyes were shining, triangular under a jutting brow.

"Don Zoilo made the kitchen furniture," said Fortunata, coming out of the kitchen. "The table, the door, and the chairs."

"He's not sick?" Carson said.

No, he was offering to build a matrimonial bed to replace the metal torture racks on which the government nurses had slept. "You have complained, Señora."

Much as she hated nurses' beds, particularly the gap between them, Maggie couldn't remember saying anything. Yet she didn't have the heart to send away this threadbare, hundred-pound man who stood before her, twisting in his hands a pale gray hat that might have been worn by a New Jersey *paterfamilias* of 1950. She led Don Zoilo into the bedroom, where he took measurements with a piece of string and promised a bed in eight days.

"Trade him for the metal ones," said Carson, suddenly appearing at the doorway.

"They're government property!"

"We'll leave the new bed for Peru," said Carson. Don Zoilo was eager for the deal. He needed beds for his children.

"Tomorrow, bring us a patient instead!" Carson said to Fortunata when the carpenter was gone.

❖

Ofelia was nine, the daughter of Fortunata's female cousin. On the back of one of her skinny, sturdy legs, a pig had bitten her. Her mother half carried her in.

There was little blood. Carson scolded the mother for waiting since morning. He put Ofelia up on the table and inspected the dirty, heaved-up wound. Maggie brought a stool so the mother could sit holding her daughter's hand, but the woman fluttered, too nervous to sit.

Carson gave Maggie's arm an encouraging squeeze and asked if she'd like to clean the wound, inject the subcutaneous anesthetic. He'd talk her through it, and then he'd do the stitches and the antibiotics. Maggie had been studying medical manuals every day since they got married, and it was time for her to learn some hands-on skills.

Ofelia's calf grew paler as Maggie gently washed it. She tried to keep her voice steady as she explained how they'd kill the germs outside the cut with soap, and the ones inside with another medicine. While Carson got out the lidocaine and a disposable needle, the mother watched intently. "What color was the pig?" Maggie asked the child.

"Sow. White with black spots." The family had been fattening a sow for the fiesta. The bigger she got, the hungrier and meaner she became, fighting with her own babies over food. She'd attacked Ofelia this morning when the girl had gone out with a pan of scraps.

"*Ingrata,*" Maggie said. Ungrateful.

Ofelia's father had shot the animal to stop her from tearing the child to pieces. Fortunately the fiesta wasn't until October, so they could still fatten one of the sow's three children for the promised feast. Maggie translated all this, requiring Carson to repeat simple words in Spanish. "*Chancho, chancha,*" he said, to the child's delight. Then he got distracted, pulling liquid into the hypodermic.

"*Dí, dí 'colmillo,' dí,*" cried Ofelia, urging him to continue. Say "fang." She half sat up, turned, and saw the needle. Was this the poison he was going to put inside her?

"Yes, *sí,*" said Carson, misunderstanding.

"No," Maggie corrected. "This is *medicina* to stop your leg from hurting. Next we kill the germs with powder, *polvo antibiótico.* It's poison against microbes, not against a person. Señora, please, help Ofelia to lie facing down."

Ofelia's mother grabbed her daughter's head and, mashing it into her bosom, sank toward the floor. In a high, frightened voice she begged Ofelia to stay calm, yet she was pulling the girl's whole torso off the table. Maggie placed one hand on Ofelia's ankle, hoping her grip felt warm and secure. The needle in her hand began to waver as she looked more closely into her first major wound: churned, raw meat with a lot of charred-looking black stuff down inside it. Dirt? Blood? She gulped, wondering where to place the first injection.

The mother tightened her grip on Ofelia's head. The child emitted a whimper.

"It's easy." Maggie spoke to a fear she saw behind the mother's eyes — the same black eyes as Julia's, the same fear as Maggie's own. "You pierce the skin shallowly, as if lancing an *ampolla.* Anyone can do it." She held up the needle. Ofelia's mother shrieked "No!" and let go of Ofelia's head to wave both hands frantically in front of her face, whereupon Ofelia fell off the table. Her mother scooped her up just before she hit the floor. Now they clung to each other at the edge of the examining table like victims of a shipwreck, the mother babbling, "No, no, no, Doctora. I cannot, you give the injection, you, that is why I came."

Carson grabbed the needle out of Maggie's hand. "Here." He pried mother and child apart, pushed Ofelia flat on the table. "Lie down," he commanded in English. "Maggie, grab her legs."

The mother, instantly calm, sat on the stool and took her daughter's hand.

After the anesthetic had taken hold, Carson directed Maggie to squirt saline into the wound while he gently sponged. The damage to the calf muscle went surprisingly deep. He'd put in stitches and a cannula. The mother was looking calmer now, so Maggie explained to her, in case of any future accidents, that boiled water with salt was the best way to clean any wound.

Not looking up, Carson said, "Maggie, shut up for just one second, please." He threaded the long, curved needle. As it entered flesh, the child stared at the wall, reporting that she felt a pulling sensation. Her mother inhaled sharply, but didn't speak.

Finally Carson held the black thread taut above the puckered seam. "Snip this here. No, I said lower down, goddamit!"

Maggie snipped, resentfully. Carson was speaking to her the same way her dentist back in Cambridge spoke to his assistant, a way she very much disliked. She reminded herself that Carson was her boss, that this was surgery, that planes crashed when pilots didn't bark their orders.

"Tell them to come back in five days," Carson said. "Scare 'em a little. You know, keep the bandage on, keep it clean, or else her leg falls off." He left the room. They could hear him in the kitchen, washing his hands.

When Maggie walked Ofelia and her mother to the door, the child looked up at her with shining eyes, boasting that the needles hadn't hurt. Maggie couldn't resist patting the top of her head. "You're a woman of *coraje*," she told the child, not looking at the mother. After refusing the faintly offered payment, Maggie gathered up the instruments. In the kitchen she began rinsing them and putting them into an enamel box which she would later seal, place in a pot, and boil on the cooktop. Her heart was pounding. *Coraje*, she told herself.

Carson was writing his report at the kitchen table. He said, "I am sorry to say this and I know it will be hard to hear, but if you can't behave more like a doctor . . ."

"If you'd waited one more second," Maggie blurted out, but from his blank, angry stare she decided her best hope lay in appealing to his indulgence. It was only her first time, she said. She'd learned a lot by watching Carson. She hoped he'd give her another chance.

He shrugged, shut his notebook, and walked toward the front door. On its threshold he turned around. "You. And they. Are not. The same!" Then he walked outside.

4

INSIDE MAGGIE'S HEAD a furious conversation began, which lasted, off and on, until Ofelia's next appointment. Was Carson turning all authoritarian now that he was responsible for a clinic? Or was she overreacting? His behavior was justified by its results — as soon as he'd taken over, Ofelia's mother had calmed down. But was it necessary to flatten a child so roughly?

Carson was right, she needed to maintain a distance. But how? And really, why? She wanted to be one of them; he'd seen that. Was that so bad? She felt ashamed. If her desire was illegitimate, she couldn't think how to change it.

Had she been living in Cambridge, she'd have telephoned a friend, and they would have talked for an hour, dissecting everyone's motivations and stress levels, establishing what Maggie might productively say to Carson next time. Had she still been married to Larry, they would have chewed at the Ofelia incident until they were exhausted, ending up feeling worse than ever.

But she was no longer in Cambridge, nor married to Larry. She was here, with Carson, living at the bottom of the deepest canyon in the world. There sat her husband, eating a stew of goat, tomato, and onion by the light of one bare bulb that left all corners of the room in shadow. If she looked at him with a naive, painter's eye, he was laughably scary, eyes glittering at the depth of two inky hollows. She could assume that her own face looked just as wild.

Who was he? She'd thought she'd brought him here, but now everything had tilted and reversed itself, so that she was living in her husband's shadow. She'd thought they shared one common purpose, but now it seemed clear that the purpose was Carson's and that she, Maggie, must find one of her own, or else stifle in the bell of solitude available at his side.

She refused to let her marriage be ruined within three days of arriving. How had her grandmother Althea followed a man all over the world?

Carson and Johnny Baines had much in common, she had decided this already. They both were men with missions. On the surface, Maggie's grandfather had seemed more driven and fanatical, especially from the point of view of the child Maggie had been when she knew him. Everybody said how he adored his wife, though; and his half-mad dream of predicting earthquakes showed how deeply he'd felt the death of his and Althea's first child, a son. That baby had not been discussed too often. Maggie had only confirmed his existence during her junior year in college, when she'd learned his name was Christopher and that he'd died of cholera after an earthquake in Huaraz, Peru. She'd have visited the grave this year, with Carson, had the cemetery not been buried in a landslide sometime in the fifties. Thus Johnny's mission was intimately connected to Althea, less ingrained in his character than Carson's drive to heal the sick and suffering in Godforsaken places, an inclination that seemed to have been born inside him and had then been fed and watered by his Catholic upbringing — martyrdom, transcendence, the first last, the last first. Maggie had practically worshiped it up to this morning, when it had suddenly shown itself capable of becoming her most implacable enemy.

Enemy? That might be too much. She must learn to take Carson's corrections at face value — he was her boss, after all. Even so, he was a more modern husband than Johnny Baines, who'd never let Althea accompany him on field trips. Once, Althea had locked herself into a convent for nine months while Johnny traipsed off to Mongolia. Whatever had that meant?

Maggie had always believed that her grandmother had done exactly as she pleased all her life; now she began to wonder what daily bargains Althea had made. Perhaps it had never been that easy to be somebody's wife, not even fifty years ago.

Carson gestured with his fork, talking about endemic malaria and hepatitis, extending to her the same cordial assumption as usual, namely that she wanted to learn about diseases. And she did. Knowing about diseases was fundamental to this life she'd chosen.

He *was* superior, she decided. Nothing was grinding away at him from the inside.

"Do you adore me, Don Calzón?" she interrupted him.

"What? What brings *that* on?"

"I want to know if you adore me."

"I adore you. Sure, of course I do, of course, but Jesus! Are you okay?"

After dinner, she said she wanted a breath of air. It was hot inside the clinic, but Carson was tired and didn't want to come. He would if she insisted; she didn't want to insist. She walked a little way down the road, out of range of the light from the clinic's door. The walls of the canyon were darker than the sky, towering and towering, imprisoning even the sound of the river.

That night it was Maggie who crawled under Carson's mosquito net. She felt lucky when he took her, squeezed her in his rugged arms.

❖

In the afternoons, it was usually too hot to stay inside, so the men and women of Piedras would find a tree, sit down in the dirt with their backs to its trunk, set fire to a little pile of dry horse or cow dung in a hubcap or a flattened tin can, stretch their legs out straight, and, safe from horseflies, enter a state of consciousness Maggie wasn't sure was sleep.

"Why can't you just laugh at them," Carson said. "So what? You aren't going to hell for it. Or do you think so?"

Maggie didn't want to give herself the right to think that the people around her led pointless, wasted lives.

"Christ, you're hard on yourself," said Carson. "In the end you're hard on them. Maybe it's true, they have nothing better to do."

"You're preaching again," Maggie remarked.

"What about the way they blow their noses?" Carson imitated the local gesture, pressing one nostril closed, honking out the other. "What about the way they shit in corners? Let babies crawl around eating dirt?"

"Stop it!" Maggie was laughing, outraged. That morning they'd seen a baby cramming dirt into its mouth with both fists, not because it was hungry, just because it was curious. Its mother had been gazing off in the other direction.

"It's cultural," she said lamely. Strange that Carson should mention that baby, since when she'd seen it, she'd been pulled by a weird new desire to release one of her own, to crawl around eating dirt beside the first.

Carson was reminding her to respect her own opinions, claim her feelings. It was a helpful lecture he often gave her. Maggie considered her own insight, that feelings were conflicting and misleading. It was easy to feel someone else's emotions, or to be indoctrinated by an evil government. That seemed important to remember.

"Oh, so what. It's us who are wasting our lives." Carson sighed. "They don't want us."

She scratched his scalp. "Don't worry." Trust would come, but until it did, all they could do was to live blamelessly in the presence of the people of Piedras.

Her earliest memory was of flying up through the air toward something white and full and soft, like a spinnaker. No words in her mind at all; her mind was not yet divided into words. Mystery, ecstasy, safety, risk, love were united in one lifting movement, up toward white. Years later, Maggie saw a photograph of her family — her parents, her sister, herself — on the steps of the house in Mexico City where she'd lived the first years of her life. Behind them, as in photographs from the nineteenth century, were all of the people who worked for the Goodwin family: a cook and a maid and a gardener, and Maggie's father's driver with his brushy mustache. The cook wore an apron, which Maggie had immediately identified as the spinnaker of her memory.

Her name had been forgotten. "We fired her, though," said Maggie's mother. "She threw all the kitchen scraps behind the stove and we ended up with rats."

On the third day when there was no water, Maggie went along with Carson to dig out the channel, blocked each night by the family upstream. Since the nurses left, they must have gotten used to irrigating their peppers and tomatoes. Yesterday the lady of the house had come out to yell and shake her fist, surely protesting that the gringos were wasting good water just to wash away their shit.

"Thief, jerk," Carson called her.

"But you basically agree," Maggie argued. "You say you're going to dig a toilet."

"The clinic needs water," Carson reasoned. "I can't dig ditches. I have to be the doctor."

You're not a doctor, you're just a physician's assistant, Maggie thought, even though she knew what Carson meant. "Let's go talk to her."

Today, when they arrived, the little house was padlocked from the outside. No one answered Maggie's knock. Made of rammed, unpainted earth, it qualified as a hovel, but it was beautiful, too, harmonious with the landscape, composed of nothing besides mud, grass, stones, and water. Its roof was dark grass thatch, two feet thick, with watermelons trained to ripen on it and a spattering of orchids never planted by human hands.

Carson dug and swore, removing the messy dam of earth and stones that had been pitched into the channel.

"We could let her take the water just at night," Maggie suggested.

What if a stab wound came in at midnight, Carson wanted to know.

Maggie saw the victim, staggering out of Nasir's. "I'll help her dig her own channel."

"That's insane."

"Let's consult Nasir," Maggie suggested when the ditch flowed freely again.

They hiked up to the road on a path beaten by the water-stealing family. Where the terraces grew steep and the path got narrow and rocky, Carson slid wordlessly ahead. Maggie resented him at first, and then decided it was not all bad, being second. All she had to do was to place her foot where Carson's heel had been.

Nasir served hard rolls and enamel mugs of instant coffee, and sat down to discuss their *problema*. Both wrists on the table, he leaned forward so that his hairless, concave chest was visible all the way down his shirt. His fingers moved constantly; if he'd been an animal, he would have been a fox or a lemur. He said that woman was a *desgraciada,* capable of anything, but maybe she'd listen to Doña Fortunata.

Why Fortunata, Carson asked.

"Fortunata knows her," Maggie answered.

"Translate," Carson insisted.

"Fortunata knows her," Nasir said. He smiled, incapable of much sincerity.

Maggie asked *how* Fortunata knew this woman.

"Everyone knows everyone. But Fortunata? *Everyone* knows *her.*"

"She's hard to ignore," Maggie encouraged him to go on.

Nasir barked, "Character! Under the rebel government, she appointed herself an official. She sticks herself into everything."

"The rebel government," Carson urged. "See what he's willing to tell us."

Nasir didn't hesitate. He told them the whole *rollo.*

Piedras had been lucky in its terrorists, for they were educated men who spoke to the people with respect. They never executed teachers or the mayor, and they had permitted the government nurses to return safely to their homes and families on the coast. They came down the mountain one afternoon, ten men and two women, full of weapons, hand grenades hanging from their ribs like papayas. They entered Nasir's store, clattered their *armas* against the wall, and announced a people's assembly.

Afraid to come, afraid to stay away, four hundred *campesinos* arrived in front of the store. The rebel spokesman was a sexy woman with big meaty hips, looking great in her uniform with many leather belts. She spoke atop this very table, dragged outside. Back then, there was no electricity for small canyon towns like Piedras. Even in big cities the light was often cut off, when terrorists bombed the transformers. That night, bonfires and torches were lit so that all could see.

The rebels raised a banner with their insignia: the silhouette of the last Inca emperor, Atahualpa, cut in two, his severed head and headless body, with a black arc above. Everyone was rapt as the leader retold the legend that summed up the rebel goals. The Inca's head and body were growing toward each other underground. When they met, the emperor would rise again. Nasir would not forget the cry: "We, all, are Atahualpa! Our hands are his hands, our heart his heart! But we have been separated! Let us come together!" Nasir had joined the roar, a great roar as if they had all been turned into lions.

The group called itself Movimiento del Arco Iris Negro, the Black Rainbow Movement, after the sign that appeared in the heavens when the last Inca emperor was murdered by the Spanish. Ever since Atahualpa's death, Peru had been ruled by outsiders, murderers and thieves. The Black Rainbow Movement stood for Inca principles, dignity and self-sufficiency and work. The rebels invited everyone above the age of ten to vote whether they wished to participate in an experiment to revive the ancient way of life. Piedras would repudiate the central government. Peasants would establish their own laws, administer their own justice. The people had voted, overwhelmingly, yes. Nasir too, though he was influenced by certain doubts about the advisability of voting no.

The rebels had moved on, leaving one behind, Comandante Oquendo, to guide the experiment. Just two days later, word came that the others had all been killed in a police ambush. Comandante Oquendo offered to end the experiment, but the Piedrasinos refused.

In those days Peru was different. Yet another president was robbing the treasury, but there existed a hope that poor people could arise and create a new reality. Even the intellectuals in the universities were seduced by that movement called the Shining Path, Sendero Luminoso; it spoke about justice and equality and dignity for everyone. Too late they learned how the Shining Path had shot thousands of peasants in the head. Still, before the disillusionment, Peru had burned with a revolutionary idealism that gave birth to many groups. Some, like the Black Rainbow, had been more idealistic, less bloody and vicious, than Sendero. The word "love" resounded in all Black Rainbow speeches.

Comandante Oquendo sent a letter off to Lima, which caused the valley to be designated a red zone and hastened the closing of the mine. Both things were inevitable anyway, since the Sendero controlled the highways, and any place far from the capital was assumed to be under terrorist control. All those years, the rich in Lima were afraid to drive one hour to the beach.

Why not repudiate a government that only takes and never gives? The peasants of Piedras and Piedad, El Mirador, and Piedras Baja proudly formed their own indigenous government. Humble men and women exercised all charges. At the people's assemblies, laws were created, work crews assigned, and justice done. Today's water problem would have been decided in favor of the clinic, not because the Doctores were superior people, but because the clinic served all the community. A work crew might be assigned to help the family dig their own ditch, but the mother, as head of a thieving family, would have been forced to perform some humiliating reparation, such as scrubbing the clinic floor on her hands and knees.

Meetings often ended with a public whipping. In this way crime soon disappeared. Bad elements departed or learned to control themselves. Even wife beating was punished.

Comandante Oquendo had brought prosperity and order. His great act as a leader was to persuade all of the canyon's villages to co-operate in rebuilding the road, which had fallen into such disrepair that only mules and people on foot could use it. It was Peru's misfortune that he was now a fugitive.

"It sounds like a paradise," Maggie said. Nasir's description of the Black Rainbow reminded her sharply of old friends in El Salvador. Such humble beliefs and wishes, so much firepower aimed at crushing them. The men and women killed at the roadblock had probably been university students. Unbidden, she imagined herself, sexy in crossed bandoliers.

"There was a proposal to rename Piedras Paraíso, Paradise," Nasir said. A corner of his mouth lifted ironically. "The two have letters in common. But there are things missing, and others left over."

"Tell Nasir you were wondering if Fortunata was a spy," Carson said.

Nasir shook his head. "Señores Doctores, speak to her of those days if you want to spend hours listening to a hymn of glory. She will always spy, it is her nature, but nowadays she can only report to other, gossiping women." He simpered and, turning his head to one side, said in a thin, high voice, "'And what little thing does the male gringo use for underwear?'"

❖

Their cook was asleep in the shade of a thorn tree across the road from the clinic, lying on her side with her knees drawn up. When she heard the gringos' footsteps she covered her face with her hands, rubbed her eyes, then sat up.

Maggie apologized for being late, and asked Fortunata to speak with the Señora upstream.

Fortunata stood up heavily, slapping the dust from her dress. That woman lived alone with her children, two big sons who didn't help. They took after the husband, a drunken *desgraciado* who had run off with a fifteen-year-old.

"That explains a lot," Maggie said.

She would have liked to go along, enter the house overgrown with watermelons. Instead, she followed Carson inside to finish yesterday's jobs. He was setting up a filing system while Maggie cleaned the floor. Yesterday, she'd spent all her psychic energy trying to hold on to the conviction that washing the floor was as important as Carson's paperwork. The floor was unsanitary and unsafe, a threat to patients — so even Fortunata had said, and Maggie had confirmed it a thousand times as she crawled around, scrubbing at nameless smears that released shitty, decaying reeks when wetted. Meanwhile, Carson towered above her on a stool. With great effort, she'd refrained from reminding him that paperwork was officially her job; that she was the one who'd invented the filing system, modeled after a database she'd used at Harvard; and most of all that Carson had once used floor scrubbing as a criterion of existential value, back when he'd been tired of Harvard and had said — remember? — he'd feel more useful scrubbing floors at a homeless shelter. She'd begun to wonder how she'd adopted this trivial remark of his. On top of everything, this morning Nasir had offered floor cleaning as an example of a punishing, humiliating task.

Walking back from the store, she got a minor inspiration. She took off her shoes, tied a large rag to the bottom of each foot with string, daubed the rags with orange wax, and began skating up and down. She embraced the air with her arms, pantomimed singing.

"What are you doing?" Carson asked, looking up from his folders.

"Waxing. My new method."

"It's kind of distracting."

"Then go in the kitchen," she said. "I can't exactly move the floor."

"I'm done anyway," Carson said, slamming the folder. "What we need now is a patient."

"No kidding."

Maggie heard him crash onto the bed, and felt guilty for her pettiness. Only briefly. Then she moved the stool and examining table outside, and strode up and down like a speed skater. Why was this method not widely known? She was pushing her toes into corners by the time Fortunata returned, accompanied by the water thief. This woman had the same blocky silhouette as Fortunata, but her cheeks were soft and brown, not hard and pink. She might have been as young as forty: there was no gray at all in her coarse, wavy black hair. Fortunata introduced her as Doña Ema, her *comadre*. Maggie was afraid to ask what a *comadre* was. It resembled the word for "weasel," but perhaps it meant sister-in-law, or midwife.

Carson came in, rumpled from lying down. Maggie could see his brightness fading when he recognized the woman who'd yelled at him. "What's her problem?" he said. In Maggie's translation, he offered a warm welcome.

Doña Ema had her own lie: her two sons hadn't noticed that the clinic had reopened. They'd believed their dam was being washed away by heavy rains upstream. She'd come to apologize, to ask permission to dig a branch from the clinic's main ditch. It would take only a little of the flow. As she promised this, Doña Ema took small steps back and forward, leaving pale dusty shoe prints on the fresh wax, like a cha-cha diagram in a book.

"Forget it," said Carson.

"He says, 'How could it be worse than now?'" Maggie translated. As the women laughed, she argued to Carson in English, "If we get rid of the toilet, like you say we should, we'll only need half our water."

He grimaced. Maggie insisted: Ema was a single mother.

"Suit yourself," said Carson.

Maggie told the women that her husband felt great sympathy, and he even invited Doña Ema to see the clinic's famous *sanitario*. Doña Ema and Fortunata both giggled and said yes, Doña Ema would love to see the Jewel of Piedras. Her sons had seen it years ago.

"She wants to see our toilet," Maggie told Carson.

"Our main attraction," Carson said gloomily. He ran his fingers quickly through his hair, a gesture Maggie had often seen at Harvard. She still found it appealing; it made her wish he'd brought his leather jacket.

Ema and Fortunata giggled like schoolgirls going to the bathroom together. Maggie decided not to follow. Left alone with Carson, she couldn't think what to say. Luckily, the time was short before a door slammed and Fortunata came back. "Doña Ema wanted . . ."

"Christ," Carson said. He went over to the counter and began flipping nervously through the pages of *Where There Is No Doctor*, looking for a cartoon to illustrate germ theory.

Fortunata cried, "Oh, what a floor! The Doctora is a super housewife. Those nurses never cleaned. They were coastal girls. Flies." She made rapid, nervous hand movements. "They didn't know anything. They hated Piedras. They killed one baby, giving it seven shots of penicillin. Everyone rejoiced when they went back to where they could talk on the telephone and look for husbands and buy tunafish in cans."

This cheered Carson up. With Maggie's help, he and Fortunata held a brief conversation about the corrupt stupidity of government-service nurses. Then he flipped through the manual to show Maggie how to diagnose pneumonia. Fortunata peered over their shoulders, moving her lips to the English text. Eventually Doña Ema came back, sparkling with amusement, arms wet to the elbows. Carson wanted to teach her sons to dig pit toilets, but Maggie didn't translate. "Can I invite her to stay for coffee?" she asked instead.

"Go ahead," Carson said.

"Care to join?"

"Nah."

But Doña Ema could not stay.

"She will return," Fortunata predicted. "Every day she passes twice, going to pray at the chapel in Piedras Baja and coming back."

"So religious?" Ema didn't seem the type.

Fortunata explained that Doña Ema asked for a miracle, that her husband would leave his teenage lover, return to her, and give her a child. She and the husband had wanted one more baby, but after a year of trying, he'd run off. Now he lived with the girl and her parents up in El Mirador. Doña Ema prayed and took herbal baths every day to improve her womb in case he ever came back.

Maggie asked whether the fifteen-year-old was pregnant.

"No."

"Do they use birth control?"

"He would never!"

"Why does Doña Ema assume she is the infertile one?"

Fortunata's eyes grew round.

"I can think of a solution more direct than prayers. I'm not recommending it, I'm only saying it exists," said Maggie. There, she'd accomplished something at last.

"Not recommending, only saying," Fortunata repeated.

On the appointed day, Ofelia did not appear for her follow-up visit. Maggie suggested a house call, but Carson said it was better for the patient to come to the clinic. Maggie didn't argue; Ofelia remained a delicate topic. She knew Carson would prefer to keep digging at his pit, a job that offered unambiguous progress. In two days it was already half done, a meter square and a meter deep, with a large pile of rocks beside it. He'd bought a twelve-foot crowbar from Nasir, in order to pry out boulders, and he'd refused Maggie's offers of help, saying there was not enough room in the hole for two. Even standing next to it was dangerous, the way he flung out dirt and stones without looking.

Maggie went into the kitchen, where Fortunata was chopping a pile of small pink onions. "Do you know where Ofelia lives?" As a child, she'd cringed when Julia had ordered servants about. This hinting, though, was almost worse.

"*Claro!*" Fortunata wiped her hands on her apron, happy to interrupt her task.

Across from Nasir's, Fortunata led her up a stairway embedded in the stone retaining wall, laughing at Maggie's speculation that the stairs were Inca stonework. The steps and walls had been built under the rebel government. "We made many improvements," she said. "We were similar to the Incas, yes."

This was the path to the heart of Piedras. No dwellings were visible from the road, but after passing through a deep band of thorn brush and fruit trees gone wild, they came to a warren of houses connected by dirt trails. The main path, wider than the rest, wound up and up. Fortunata walked fast, and Maggie had to concentrate on keeping pace. The path was six feet wide, with a runnel down its center eroded by the rains; in this season it was only occasionally dampened by dishwater or urine. Junctions and switchbacks were reinforced with stones to prevent them from washing away. Small fuchsia-colored *cantú* flowers overhung the bamboo fences. The poorer houses were of wild cane plastered with mud, the richer ones of rammed earth or adobe; the richest were plastered and painted in colors.

Why couldn't Maggie and Carson live up here instead of on the deserted highway? Here children stood tongue-tied on the path, wearing no pants. Men sat on rocks, and women spread clothing on grass to dry. Though the hill was steep, somehow the cook had breath for laughing and waving and telling everyone who Maggie was. Her affability reminded Maggie of certain people back in Cambridge who walked expensive dogs on leashes, and were only too glad to explain their provenance to anyone caring to listen, or even those who didn't. This trip was good P.R. for the clinic, she decided, waving at people who gave back no more than stony glares.

After twenty minutes' climb, Fortunata finally stopped at an open, dark doorway and yelled inside that they were looking for Ofelia. A woman's voice cried, *"Más allá!"* They climbed a hundred yards more, crossing paths with two people who stared at the stones at the edge of the trail, letting them pass, not offering any greeting. Maggie's skin prickled with rejection. Had Fortunata not been with her, she'd have fled, choosing all downhill paths. She could never have come here alone, nor without Ofelia as justification.

They came at last to a woman sitting on a bench under a papaya tree, suckling a baby. This was Ofelia's aunt. Behind her was a house surrounded by a sturdy, pretty bamboo fence, its top half draped with heavy vines. Below the vines Maggie could see the faces of several young pigs peering out between the close-set bamboo, their fore-heads comically encrusted with mud.

"Ofelia is not here," the aunt said guardedly.

Fortunata gave Maggie a look. "Wait for me, Doctora." She disappeared around the corner of the fence.

Maggie stood awkwardly for a few seconds before venturing to admire the baby's abundant hair. To her surprise, the aunt invited her to sit down, rest, rest. She had a piping voice and no teeth at all.

Maggie sat down at the far end of the bench. It commanded a beautiful view of river and canyon walls, which helped her not to stare at the woman's translucent melon-colored breast, the sheen of saliva as the child turned around to see who had come, then turned back to the breast with a rejecting finality. It was a girl, too old for breast milk, Maggie thought.

"Why are you looking for Ofelia?" the woman asked.

"Her leg," Maggie said, pointing at her own calf.

"Yes, yes, her leg," the woman said, resettling her haunches on the bench.

"How is it?"

"It got bad. Her father is curing her."

Maggie hoped Fortunata was getting to the bottom of this situation. She admired the suckling child anew. Hearing itself spoken of, it turned and gaped, showing a complete set of teeth stolen from its mother's body.

This baby was two years old, the mother said. "She is my last, my *benjamina*. I can't harden myself to wean her."

Calcium, Maggie thought, unable to think of any food to recommend.

Fortunata came bustling out. "Let's go, go." She ran just ahead of a man who must be Ofelia's father. He was carrying Ofelia over one shoulder. Maggie could see the back of Ofelia's leg, where the thick gauze bandage was deeply stained with black dirt and brown blood. It sagged messily. Clearly it had been removed and replaced. No sign of the cannula.

They hurried downhill as if Ofelia's father were in danger of changing his mind.

At a wide spot in the trail, Maggie hung back to get a look at

Ofelia's face. It was stiff, thinned by pain and fever. Still, the child grinned at Maggie. "It swelled, so they tied a lizard on me. The lizard died but my leg stayed hot so they put mud."

❖

That night, Maggie told Carson she wanted to write a letter to her friend Vivian after dinner. "Fine," he said. "I'll lie in bed and read."

She sat at the kitchen table, lit a candle to even out the gaps in the wavering electric light. The kitchen wiring was faulty, gnawed by mice or something. Maggie began by describing this room, where her shadow palpitated on the uneven mud-brick walls. Since she liked getting letters that described the immediate surroundings, she put in the rushing sound of the Jewel of Piedras, the grain of the kitchen table. "Everything here is alive."

Then she wrote about Ofelia. Tablespoons of pus, the color of French mayonnaise, had burst out when Maggie pressed her leg with the back of a spoon. Far from being disgusted, Maggie had felt exultant, tender, fierce. "My first true medical moment," she wrote, speculating that at last she understood the emotion that drove most of Carson's personality.

A little later, he came in, asking if she was interested in going to bed. Curled over her letter, Maggie said, "I'm almost finished." She was writing about how Carson had scolded Ofelia's father, yelling with a vehemence no false translation could ever have disguised. She twisted a bit in her chair, to look at him standing there, his pajama pants barely hanging on below his belly. "He could have killed her," Carson said.

"I know!" Maggie said, deciding this was his apology. She promised to come to bed in a minute. After he'd left, a doom of tenderness struck her heart. She thought of her husband, the quixotic Don Calzón, a knight in cardboard armor, fighting ignorance and all the other windmills that turned in the wind whistling up and down this canyon.

She sealed the envelope, carried it to the sink, and put a match to its corner, watching the long orange flame sear up toward her fingers, releasing her complaints into the darkness. She dropped the burning thing at the last instant, rinsed flat black flakes of ash down the drain, into the river. Lastly, standing on a chair, she opened the square window to let out the bitter smoke.

A gust of fresh damp air heaved in, then out, as if the house had breathed.

The hallway felt humid, intimate, as she felt her way down one wall to where Carson lay asleep. It had been good to burn that letter. This was only the tenth day in Piedras. The letter would not have been mailed for months. By then, different things would be true.

She lay down quietly in her own bed, slid her hand under the nets, and touched Carson's hand in the darkness. A silky red edge of her heart unfolded toward him, like the mantle of a shell underwater when the tide is right. She hoped she could continue to extend her mercy toward her husband, that it was responsive to her will. Never forget, she told herself, seal it with lead and cement. As she began to sink toward sleep, though, certain images floated into her mind, illustrations she'd cultivated as a child, flat and bright and rimmed with a definite edge of black. Rather than slipping quickly down into nothingness, as she'd hoped, the brightly colored pictures entranced her and disturbed her for a while.

Althea and Johnny Baines had visited the Goodwin family once a year at least. They clattered and shouted their way into the house, bearing many heavy bags full of Johnny's instruments and books and blasting caps, clothes for all weathers, gifts from overseas. If Johnny was between grants, they'd stay for weeks or months. Maggie was a little afraid of her grandfather Baines, with his thick black-rimmed glasses, his opinions expressed in a booming voice that grew louder as Johnny aged. He claimed he needed to hear himself think. He spread his notebooks all over the house — in case he had an idea, he could write it down immediately. Everyone in the family knew Grandpa Johnny was trying to find a formula to predict earthquakes, and that it was a secret, because if his colleagues found out, they'd say he was insane. Earthquake prediction was placed on a par with witchcraft, but Grandpa Johnny still wanted to make it scientific. There were forces in the earth. Rocks had a breaking point. When force was divided by breaking, the result would come out as a number. His problem was defining the quantities; they were huge and hard to measure. There was a third factor, which he called "the coefficient of creep." "Creep" was an activity, not a kind of person, but after his explanation Maggie never could remember what he'd said it was, nor where "creep" went after being turned into a number — above, below, or beside the fraction line.

Althea always tried to compensate for the inconvenience they caused. She'd start frangipani cuttings in glasses of water, dust and vacuum endlessly, take Maggie to the park and her sister to the movies, and shoo Julia out of the kitchen, saying, "You, rest!" Althea made each recipe only once, never learning from her mistakes. Tomato aspic, pheasant in sauerkraut, beef and peaches stewed inside a pumpkin. Julia complained about one bean dish that had left the kitchen reeking of skunk or armpits. Althea had retorted that she'd learned the recipe from the man whom Julia ought to respect more than anyone in the world, Brother Jesūnandā, without whom Julia would never have existed.

Julia had screeched and left the room, saying her mother was a crackpot, a religious nut.

That was the day Maggie learned that her grandmother had once locked herself up in a convent. It was in India. Priests and nuns in robes fed the naked, shoeless poor; they taught them to grow bananas, make rope, and raise milk cows. Althea had lived there while Grandpa Johnny had gone off to feel the earth shake, then gotten trapped in Russia and Shanghai by the war. The priest of this convent had been the most wonderful man on earth, after Grandpa Johnny, according to Althea. How she wished her granddaughters could have met him! "Brother Jesūnandā used to wash the beggars' feet every morning."

That did seem a sign of goodness. "Did Mommy know him?"

"She wasn't even a twinkle." Althea explained Julia's evolution, from nothing, to twinkle, fetus, infant, child, teenager, woman, wife, and finally mother of Sonia and Maggie. Between nothingness and twinkle, the priest had intervened, gladdening Althea's heart so she could have another baby. "You'll be mothers one day. Then you'll understand."

"Never!" Maggie's young mind had reeled.

"Nonsense," Julia had said minutes later. "A child comes from its parents."

Maggie's imagination had gotten caught in the time before Julia had been a spark, a time when Althea's priest had been the illustration of an angel. His flowing hair was black, he wore a peach-colored belted gown; and though he lacked wings, he sometimes had a silver sword and helmet. He knelt before Grandma's chair holding her bare foot, as the prince held Cinderella's. "Did that priest ever wash your feet, Grandma?"

"Do I look like a beggar to you?"

5

WITHIN TWO WEEKS, they'd given up fabricating work for themselves in the afternoons and began taking naps like everybody else. After all, it was roasting hot, and they were in South America. Of course, it would have been preferable to loll outdoors like most people, wreathed in cow dung smoke. The smoke was like incense, plus they could have taken advantage of whatever microscopic breezes were available. Unfortunately, the gringo doctors had dignity to uphold, so they sweltered indoors, breathless and naked under the mosquito nets.

They couldn't bear to touch each other, nor even sleep with their own legs together.

Pulsing, vivid heat emanated like another wall from the wall at her side. Maggie began to hear the river rapid, roaring and breathing like a burning furnace. The very sound was stifling. She felt herself underwater with her grandmother, fighting for air in this same river. "I'm hearing it," she'd eventually say, knowing she'd cause Carson to begin to hear it too. Strange how quickly they'd learned to ignore the sound; strange, when hearing it, that they'd ever been able to ignore it at all.

Carson said you simply had to forget the noise. It was too goddamned loud.

She envied his economy of mind.

Her own mind was more like the river. Everyone warned her not to go in past her knees. Nasir and Albita's son had drowned at age eighteen. His tomb was behind the store, a hump of river cobbles cemented together, painted blue and white, with sad plaster lambs and a marble plaque and a small round window like a submarine's, to look in upon his coffin. The Rosario became safe only two days downstream, below the hydroelectric plant. At Piedras it was full of whirlpools and rapids and deceptive smooth spots where the surface roiled with deadly currents. The water was opaque, a brownish gray that changed to slate at twilight, yellow in strong light. People got sucked down, swept away. Rafts broke in pieces, boats got dashed on rocks.

The river carried many secrets, Fortunata said. Maggie was proof that one, at least, was true. Her grandparents had swallowed its water fifty years ago, and this was why she'd been drawn to return. Now, though it was boiled and tamed, she drank nothing but river, river, every day.

Nobody came to ask for help. Maggie tried feeding the neighbors' dogs, Bobby, Chocolatín, and Bestia, buying friendship to replace their snarls. Once, as she turned to go back inside, Chocolatín ran up behind and tried to bite her.

She wrote no more letters. During the days, she read every adult comic book in Nasir's lending library and told the far-fetched plots to Carson, who scoffed at her addiction to crime and romance. She sat on a rock beside the river, staring at the water, at the canyon walls. Watched the haze of morning give way to the stark, killing sun of noon. She asked the natural world whether it was friendly, and she thought it said it was.

For two hours each morning, she studied medical manuals, memorized the symptoms of diseases, and took notes to educate herself. When the matrimonial bed arrived, she sewed a double mosquito net with bright yellow fabric bought from Nasir. Then she and Carson slept together, like pies on display at a roadside café.

Doña Ema's irrigation ditch reduced the clinic's water to a trickle, some days to nothing, but Maggie insisted they must tolerate this. Don Calzón, as he'd occasionally begun to call himself, finished his toilet pit and enclosed it in a screen of leafy branches that quickly dried, becoming a rattling, fragrant bower. Using rocks he'd dug out, he built a low wall in front of the clinic, to keep out road dust from the buses and trucks that went by, bearing passengers and cargo but never stopping at the clinic. Behind this wall, Maggie planted flower seeds guaranteed by Nasir to sprout. They did, but fell flat overnight. Carson plastered the kitchen and painted the whole building stark white inside, freshly government-sea-green outside. He made a plywood tent sign and propped it in the road. Then he dragged a chair and table to the clinic door and sat facing outward, daring people to come in.

Days passed slowly, slowly, like crawling across a plain of gleaming knives. Maggie wanted to kiss the nights when they descended, bringing coolness, the scent of leaves, wet dirt, and flowers, and dissolving the canyon walls. Often she couldn't sleep, and she'd sit in the kitchen until four A.M., staring at the stars in the square window, finding shapes in the monstrous shadows cast by a single candle.

She told Fortunata about her grandparents' visit to Piedras, and their meeting with the eccentric *hacendado* who owned a mummy and had written a book about herbs and cures. Before coming to Piedras, she and Carson had agreed that finding the *hacendado*'s herbal encyclopedia would be a nice project for Maggie. She might even publish a little article in some magazine back home.

"Nasir is educated, Nasir might know," Fortunata said.

"I did ask him." The shopkeeper's incuriosity had been complete. "I even said there might be money in it."

Fortunata guffawed. The mummy had been sold, had it existed, but perhaps she and Maggie could find a book. It might prove useful for humanity. Next, Fortunata wanted to know why Maggie's grandparents had come to Piedras. Had they been doctors too?

"My grandmother was just a woman, my grandfather a geologist."

"A geologist. That explains it. He was looking for gold, like all foreigners."

"Not me and Carson!"

"Doctora, you are not a foreigner. You have an uncle buried in Peru."

Maggie invited Carson to come along on the Don Héctor expedition, but failed to persuade him to close the clinic even for a few hours. How could he take time off when he had not yet worked? Walking out the door, Maggie was angry with him for agreeing that she was superfluous. Still, they both knew it was dumb for two people to sit there waiting for no one; and if one had to stay, it was obvious which. Maggie told herself she must enjoy her freedom, since it was hers, and it was all she had.

She and Fortunata headed north, up the rutted dusty road. Crossing the bridge, walking onto the grounds of the hacienda, Maggie felt time ratcheting backwards, displacing her arrival into the past. The yellow dust had a strange smell, like roasted rotting beans.

In the dappled shade of the enormous mango grove, it was cooler, and there were clouds of mosquitoes. All walls were dyed bright ocher halfway up, from being splashed with mud during the rainy season. Here it seemed everything could be true, and that a young Althea could be hiding among the thick green lizard-skinned trunks of the mango trees. When her grandmother had come to Piedras, she was younger than Maggie was now.

Peering around corners, through holes in the broken walls, they soon spotted the old man with cataracts, the same man she and Carson had seen from the bus window on their first day. He still sat on his verandah, wearing his suit of dun-colored river water. His jacket sleeves were composed entirely of patches, his ancient shirt buttoned tightly at the neck. In a tender, drifting voice he said, "No, little gringa, no gringos, never, no."

His cataracts facing the sky reminded Maggie that she would one day be wiped from the earth.

This *anciano* was more than old enough to remember the days before the agrarian reform, but he claimed not to know the hacienda's name. Anyway, it was no longer an hacienda, it was just a place. Now its name was Piedras Baja.

"I know," Maggie said. "Do you live here, in Don Héctor's house?"

"Yes," he said, "yes."

"Are there things inside? Books?" Maggie asked.

The *anciano*'s hand waved in no particular direction.

"Who else lives here now?" Fortunata prodded.

"In this house," he began. Then he closed his lips and chewed once, silently.

He had lived all his life in slowness, Maggie decided.

She walked over to the French doors and peered inside. The room had a floor of patterned tiles, yellow and red and black and white. It was vacant except for a pile of mules' pack-saddle frames and braided rawhide reins. Maggie stepped inside, thinking that even now the hacienda would make a nicer clinic than the low, bleak building where her husband sat waiting for no one.

The next room was also tiled, and it had plaster garlands all around its upper walls. What must its furniture have been, mirrors and clawfoot sofas? Through its doorway Maggie spied a small, ornate marble fireplace and, in the far corner, a straw mattress. From under messy blankets, a man's bare foot peeked out.

"There is no one," Fortunata declared.

"But yes, someone is sleeping," Maggie whispered. "See his foot?"

"Let's go to the chapel," Fortunata insisted.

"But who is it?"

"Oh, someone," said Fortunata. "Anyone. Let's go."

They walked to the chapel, their feet swishing up a moldy, rainy smell from the dry leaves. Its lower walls were stones held together with mud, a foundation bowed and crumpled outward, like a stomped-on shoebox. The windows were shuttered, too high for looking into. Fortunata described the blue walls and huge gilded altar full of columns and compartments. If Maggie wanted to join the Pentecostals, she could see all this. Otherwise, no priest would come until the saint's day in October.

"I could come and pray with Doña Ema," Maggie joked, giving rise to a sharply curious glance from Fortunata.

"Pray for what?"

Maggie didn't answer.

The *hacendado*'s tomb, in the cemetery behind, was a low tunnel the size of a doghouse. Inside the chamber was a framed portrait of the man at thirty. His skin was dark, and there were water stains under the glass, so his features were unclear, but Maggie could tell he had been civilized, thick hair combed back. In her imagination she'd never seen him young. She caught herself hoping that these might be the wrong bones, that her grandmother's *hacendado* had borne a different name: Don Enrique, Don Fernando. Years ago, in Rome, she'd felt a similar disquietude inside the main cathedral. It hadn't seemed right for Saint Peter to be confined, even in that most splendorous tomb.

She and Fortunata walked home, Maggie yakking about how medical researchers in the United States were learning to respect herbs and traditional cures. "Yes," Fortunata agreed, "before the Spanish ruined us, we had our own medicine, our own science."

Maggie's legs felt limp and heavy in the heat. Had Fortunata tried to steer her away from that innocuous, slender foot? She'd forgotten how to reach conclusions, just like everyone else in Piedras.

Don Calzón greeted them at the clinic door, asking if they wanted to hear great news. "No news is good news, right?" No patients had come in.

Carson told Maggie that everything felt regurgitated, days chewed over one by one, without refreshment. "Join us in the kitchen," she invited him. Fortunata was always ready to interrupt her duties for coffee and a chat, but Carson said this wasn't appropriate. His self-importance irritated Maggie.

Each night, she tried to entertain him with what she'd heard. She suspected Fortunata of making up half of everything she told, but her stories were good ones, full of ghosts, coincidences, thievery, in-fidelity, bigamy, and drownings. Under the river was another world, where the beautiful *encantados* lived. The mountains were full of nonhuman beings, souls cast out from Heaven at the time of Luci-fer's rebellion. Many had landed here, among the deserted crags. Flat, legless monsters flapped up from the surfaces of lakes, look-ing like enormous pieces of leather. Lightning bolts defended treas-ures; women's voices called men to walk off the edges of cliffs. The most imposing monster was the Pishtaco, a large blond gringo who dressed up in a military uniform and stomped around the trails on moonless nights, seeking children's fat to eat. "Doesn't he just explain everything?" Maggie asked Carson. "Doesn't he?" She ex-tracted his responses, sometimes embarrassed at her need to do so — and sometimes angry, Carson's silence proving that she pleaded with a stone. At other times she was glad she'd made the effort, rewarded with his agreement, his genuine laughter.

Fortunata must herself be one of Piedras's scandals. Despite being

Pentecostal she drank to excess, though nowhere near as much as her appalling husband. She'd converted to Pentecostalism because the congregation met on Saturday night, her husband's biggest drinking night. Now he beat her Sundays instead. Maggie suggested the husband talk to Carson about alcoholism. Knowing the message would not be delivered, she was almost glad: she'd never meet him.

One Monday Fortunata came in saying proudly, "I gave back as good as I got. Whacked him in the forehead with a wooden ladle he had carved himself." And she imitated the movement of her arm, rising and falling more times than Maggie hoped was true.

Fortunata never turned off the radio; batteries became a major expense. She forgot to burn the trash. She had a dream in which Maggie gave birth to a baby. She stole food, too. Bags of macaroni vanished. Anytime Maggie invested in a chicken, it was always surprising how few pieces ended up in the soup. Fortunata had a peculiar way of cutting up a bird so that no piece was identifiable. Maggie was unable to reconstruct the original chicken to determine how much was actually missing. Once, she fished out all of the chunks and put them together. They formed a heap about the size of a softball.

"What are you doing?" Carson said.

"Trying to see how much of the chicken Fortunata steals. Look."

"Don't sweat it," Carson said. "One chicken is more than enough for the two of us." With his fork, he began picking apart Maggie's softball, choosing the bits he wanted.

What in the world could make a person so self-contained, Maggie wondered.

He caught her staring at him, and gave her a wink.

"You're a mystery," she said, slightly dazzled.

"I'm not."

Past the outhouse of Don Calzón, the trail meandered flat through scattered thorn scrub, then plunged across a stagnant stream and into the band of castor bushes and mesquite that marked the riverbed's margin. Here was the fork, one tip branching southeast toward the upper fringes of Piedras where Fortunata's cottage was. The other branch ran north, parallel to the river, sloping up sharply to come out on the open hillside where it joined a goat path knitted with cloven-hoof prints. A kilometer on, it shouldered around a ridge, descended to cross a forsaken field of stones and stunted bushes. Here lived a naked dwarf, according to Fortunata, with hot-pink skin and curly hair, in a nasty hole below the cliff. His presence explained why Maggie had always turned back, scared. She'd thought it was from losing sight of the clinic.

The boulder field did seem a good place for a cast-out soul to land. Maggie had never before dared to cross it. Again a slight fear trembled in her belly, distracting her from the scenery; but she had vowed to urge herself on longer hikes, if only to expand her life. At the shoulder of the mountain, she took one last look down toward the clinic and saw the transparent wall that had confined her within a hundred yards' radius. Carson was inside, pacing up and down the clinic's long empty room, his eyes rotting at the backs like a tiger's in a zoo. Behind the building, facing the river, she discerned a tiny Fortunata sitting on her tiny bench with a sequin-sized glint beside her. She must be shelling fava beans into the dishpan.

The sound of grasshoppers or locusts accentuated the heat. Maggie crept across the haunted field, recognizing a place where unwary girls found unhappy destinies and men and women arranged to meet unseen. No one bothered Maggie. She stopped under the cliff with cheesy holes. One hole seemed to have a wall blocking its front, unless it was an old landslide. If it was a cliff tomb, Don Héctor must have sent his workers down on ropes from above, endangering their lives to bring out feather crowns, shriveled corpses, and other worthless treasures.

A faint track forked downhill toward the river. Following it, Maggie came to a bend protected from the worst currents: a pool below two rocks that had accumulated a stack of driftwood the size of a small house.

She took off her dusty sandals and, hanging on to a tree's bare silver arm, stepped into the shallow water. It pulled coolly at her insteps, inviting her to risk her life.

Had Althea depended on the fiery particulars of this world as acutely as this?

She stepped forward, fully clothed. The sandy bottom suddenly dropped hip-deep into a lenticular depression. The current was green here, solid, and far stronger than she'd expected; it frightened her with an instantaneous, invincible pull, forming an audible suck-hole behind her waist, pulling her feet up from the bottom, so that she had to grip the branch for all her life as legs and feet swung out toward the stream. Making sure of her grasp, she dipped her face into the water, past her ears. The roar was as loud as she needed it to be. Opening her eyes, she saw nothing but a grayish blur. After a few seconds she raised her head, to calculate how to get out. She swam her legs over to a shallower spot, near the bank, and stood up quickly, crookedly, gripping at stones with her toes.

A grasshopper clicked, thrummed. Pebbles slid down from the hill. Someone watching, maybe. Afraid to look, she bolted uphill, dust sticking to her pants legs so that they thickened, slowed her, like trying to escape from terror in a dream. In the middle of the dwarf's boulder field it became obvious no one was chasing her. She stopped, stood panting. Ahead the trail ran like dry white woolen yarn amongst the boulders, so opaque and burning that they reminded Maggie of the fake asbestos rocks in the bottom of Calvin's gas grill in Connecticut. It was roasting hot. She wished she had somewhere else to go, another home besides the clinic.

By mid-June they had treated a total of eleven people. Six were repeat visits by Fortunata Rosas de Carrión, who was susceptible to headaches and sour stomach. The rest were coughs and colds, cuts and bruises, the pig bite, an earache, and a sprain. Maggie searched the *Merck Manual* and wrote down the worst-sounding diagnoses, but she wasn't going to fool Catholic Charities. Eleven patients was not enough; if the dearth continued, their contract would not be renewed and they'd have to find work elsewhere, and Carson would have failed at his first responsible post.

"Why don't you bring your children for lunch?" Maggie had asked this of Fortunata many times, each time hearing a different excuse. Each time, Fortunata swore and promised they'd come, and Maggie encouraged her to make extra food, and again the children never arrived. Then, on one such day, when Carson had gone to Nasir's for something or other, Doña Ema arrived instead, at three P.M., with her sons, Boris and Limbert, aged seventeen and fourteen.

The boys had wide, soft jungle faces; their father was from Pucallpa, in the lowlands. They stood hulking in the kitchen until Maggie offered them the lunch leftovers, half the enamel pot full of cooked spaghetti. Doña Ema heaped her own plate. After eating, the younger son strode down the hall, peed long and loud into the Jewel of Piedras without closing the door, returned, and sat down as if daring Maggie to object. Soon both boys left without having said a word. Doña Ema hung back, so Maggie offered coffee.

Tilting the can of condensed milk over Doña Ema's cup, Maggie asked how the prayers were going. Doña Ema cocked her head sideways and put out the tip of her tongue as she watched a thick column of sperm-colored sweetness flow into her coffee.

Only when Maggie stopped the flow of milk did Ema tell her story. She was well and truly pregnant, by God's grace, and praying for a girl. Last week, in a dream, Jesus came to her wearing a brown dress saying, "Doña Ema, thou hast prayed upon thy knees for a year, thou hast drunk, hast bathed in herbs, and hast cleaned thy heart and womb. Thy *promesa* is fulfilled. Now cometh my obligation."

Maggie strained her chin toward one corner of the ceiling so as not to break into a giggle. "And so?"

"My husband returned," she said. "The next day."

"*Qué bueno!* Everything is good again between you?"

Doña Ema hugged herself, describing the miracle of renewed affection.

Maggie saw that Fortunata was suppressing a smirk, so she asked how Doña Ema could be sure that she was pregnant. Wasn't it rather soon?

"I have sensation," said Doña Ema, placing a palm across her bulging lower belly. "Does this clinic have a test?"

"No," Maggie said. "Come back in two weeks."

She put Doña Ema on her list, patient number twelve. Doing well in the first trimester of pregnancy.

Fortunata howled with laughter as soon as Ema left. How her *comadre* lied! Surely she was pregnant — women always knew — but did Maggie want to hear the true story?

Doña Ema had followed the Doctora's good *consejo* and found herself a lover, a young truck driver who took supplies to the mine. For weeks they'd carried on, trysting shamelessly in Ema's house, the truck parked on the road, until one day the truck driver had spoken sharply to Doña Ema's son Boris. Boris had run to El Mirador to complain to his father, who had already been trying to ignore the rumors. All he needed was one spark of confirmation to set fire to the jealousy that had been seething. Half out of his head, he'd saddled his mule and galloped to Piedras, stopping at Nasir's to buy a liter of cane spirits which he drained in two gulps. At his old home, his wife saucily announced that if he had the right to take a young lover, so did she. Unfair! The husband went out of his head. He decided to commit suicide. He ran outside, determined to throw himself from the bridge into the river. It was a long way to run, but he was very determined, for he was still in love with her. When he reached the bridge he ran breathlessly off the center span, thinking to land where the water was deepest, but he'd forgotten the large pylon of stones there, supporting the bridge's legs. The carcass of a pig happened to be stuck on these rocks. It must have died of disease, and its *campesino* owner had pitched it in upstream. A miracle indeed, for upon this pig the husband fell. Rotten and filled with gas, the carcass saved his life. As it exploded, he came to his senses and returned to Doña Ema.

✣

"What is the name of the herb she bathed in?" Maggie came into the kitchen with her notebook a few minutes later.

Fortunata was husking corn, holding the tin *palangana* between her knees. "*Ruda*. Do you want some? I have it in my garden." When she described it, a blue-green herb with a rank smell and a little yellow flower, Maggie recalled seeing some in a glass on Nasir's counter.

"*Ruda* does everything a woman wants," Fortunata declared. "For a business it attracts money." *Ruda* increased fertility; boiled in milk, it also induced abortions. Fortunata looked up from her task to gauge Maggie's expression. "Which is your purpose?"

"Well, if *ruda* does whatever a woman wants, then I want *ruda*," Maggie joked.

"We always believed you used birth control, Doctora," Fortunata said. "Do you have the other problem? Why don't you have children?"

Maggie shrugged. "My husband . . ." She was starting to explain that she and Carson had agreed not to be parents because they believed there were already enough children in the world, and that people should take care of the ones who were already here.

"Your *husband?* Who is he? Are you not the woman?" Fortunata wanted to know. "Who will have the baby, him or you? Don't you like children?"

"I adore them," Maggie said firmly. Time to change the subject. "Why don't you ever bring your children here?" While Fortunata dished out lame excuses, Maggie ran through the chilling implications of her line of questioning. What if Fortunata was spreading a rumor that the gringos were cold and heartless? Child-devouring Pishtacos?

That would be unfair, since maternal feelings had blossomed in Maggie since arriving. More precisely, they'd roared through her, laying waste to her ideas of herself. Whenever she saw the families of Piedras walking on the road, father, mother, little ones, she felt a pull as strong, as mindless as the river. The whole world changed at the sight of a young father carrying his daughter on his shoulders, home from the soccer field. In this, Maggie saw life's meaning, a beauty most exquisite.

Some nights she lay in bed quivering with a strange and inconvenient kind of lust, knowing from the calm odor of his body that Carson did not share it. She had vowed to understand him and to love him as he was. When once she'd experimented with a veiled allusion to her new vision of the world, he'd shrugged and said that bliss was hardly the definition of the family lives she'd learned about so far. Why imitate the Piedrasinos? He was right: she'd had the same thoughts herself.

Besides, her feelings were so overwhelming that she resented and mistrusted them on principle. They invaded her like a curse, or spell, exhaled from the very earth. No wonder you want to reproduce, she'd told herself, now that you're feeling bored and superfluous in this Catholic valley.

Had she believed in *ruda*'s omnipotence, Maggie would have eaten a whole bush, only to be returned to the simple way she'd felt before.

And then the wish would whisper once again, insidious, intelligent, compelling arguments. Motherhood must be a richer, warmer life. Why fight desire?

She'd have liked to confide in someone — but Fortunata was hardly unbiased, and besides, conspiring with a servant against a husband seemed to violate an obvious rule of life.

Fortunata pursued the issue. "*Pero* Señora, what kind of a husband is he?"

"He's good," Maggie said. "He's my Don Calzón," and she explained all that Carson's nickname had come to mean, the romance and futility of good intentions.

In July, three more patients came in, sprains and cuts and bruises. A review was due in September; more and more, Maggie began to want to fudge the numbers. With an effort of will, she left out Doña Ema's frequent visits, because Carson so disliked her, even though Ema almost counted as a legitimate patient, proudly recounting each twinge of early pregnancy, beginning with headaches and nausea. The soul of the child had landed from above, and would descend slowly over nine months, causing discomforts all the way, especially at the end.

Maggie diagnosed herself with amebiasis, and treated herself with Flagyl, carefully noting in her folder that she was clinic staff. The pills made her mouth and breath taste of metal, yet she wondered whether she'd diagnosed herself correctly or whether she was merely entertaining herself, fattening her lists. When she mentioned this doubt to Carson, he laughed and said anyone who would take Flagyl recreationally belonged in an asylum.

"This whole canyon's an asylum," she said, voicing a judgment she was sure was his. Sometimes it scared her how many of her thoughts consisted of conversations with him that weren't occurring in real life.

Carson agreed. They both felt a sneaking, existentially unhealthy sensation. They'd lived openly, as if on stage, letting people decide whether to trust them, but there was no audience to justify their efforts, so their play grew falser by the day, until it seemed by now that no one should ever be convinced. They weren't fighting, yet Maggie felt a forced, superficial quality in their conversations. She teased

Carson; he responded in a silly falsetto, as if to announce that his real self had retreated far inside, leaving a small, kind imp behind. He never raged, never blamed her for dragging him to Piedras. Maggie supposed she should be grateful, but she wasn't.

At last she asked why he never got upset. Didn't he care?

"I'm giving it until September." Carson's nose looked straighter than usual, as if he were smelling something bad. Perhaps she'd offended him with the very question, whether he cared. "But we were told there were forty-eight thousand people who needed health care," she cried, outraged on his behalf. "Where are they?"

"Somebody's keeping them away," said Carson.

"Do you really think so? Why didn't you say so earlier?"

He shrugged. "Just a theory."

She kissed the back of his neck, kissed it again because he'd cringed a little, hunching his shoulders to get away from the sensation. Maybe the canyon was stripping them of all of their illusions. Only when they'd both been reduced to nothing would it lift them up again.

❖

"You see my husband, Fortunata, see he's *desesperado?* No one's coming to our clinic. Help us. You are our only friend. Why do they not come?"

Fortunata's eyes rolled up under her lids and fluttered, showing only the whites, the way the eyes of a friend of Maggie's, who had gone to Smith, rolled back when she expressed a superior conviction. "I explain to them," Fortunata said, "but they don't listen. Perhaps they are afraid."

"Afraid? Of what?"

"Of the foreigner. The Pishtaco." Fortunata recounted a rumor about forced sterilizations at one gringo hospital she'd heard of.

Maggie groaned. She told Fortunata about El Salvador, where everyone had seen rapes, kidnappings, torture, murder. They'd all been hurt by the cruel war the U.S. government was sponsoring, and yet they never saw Maggie as a representative of violence. People had opened their hearts to her; they'd met her at the simplest human level, without false humility or pride.

She tried to keep the preaching and the yearning out of her voice, describing how it had felt to sit around a table with Dorotea and Santiago. Fortunata wanted to know whether Maggie had returned to see those people.

No. Returning was impossible. Coming to Peru had been her way of returning.

"What did you think about their revolution?" Fortunata asked.

"I wanted them to win," Maggie said. "Had I been born in Peru or El Salvador, I wonder what choices I would make. I might have joined the Sendero Luminoso. Often I wonder why the poor don't all rise up to kill the rich."

"Don't talk like that, Doctora," Fortunata warned her. "You don't know what you say. The Shining Path was *sangriento, sin piedad.*" Bloody, heartless. "They would have hung you up, the day of tomorrow, just for your blond hair."

"It's brown, dark brown," Maggie insisted, as she'd done many times before. In Cambridge, people had even called it black.

Blond, repeated Fortunata, and still the Black Rainbow Movement would not have hanged her. The Rainbow had been good, good for the people. If the Doctores were interested, one day they could meet the former leader. Comandante Oquendo lived a few hours' walk upriver, past El Mirador. People maintained respect for him.

"I wish he would advise us," Maggie said. She told Fortunata that she, herself, Maggie, would happily meet the Comandante, but she'd need Carson's permission. As foreigners, they had to be careful not to become involved in any way with revolutionary groups, or the Peruvian government would deport them. At the same time, Maggie wished it known in Piedras that she and Carson both understood how the definition of a terrorist often comes from a corrupt and violent authority. In Maggie's mind, the Black Rainbow wasn't terrorist, since nobody had been terrified. "If we met, I think Comandante Oquendo would see that he can trust us," Maggie said. She scooped up the sugary, undissolved condensed milk from the bottom of her coffee cup and savored it on her tongue. Then she ran outside to share the news. Carson shrugged, again, but at least he didn't disagree with what she'd done.

6

"*DREENK*," Don Héctor Saavedra Ibáñez said in English. The Baineses were sitting in his astonishing parlor, full of antique spotted mirrors and furniture with curved legs. The hacienda owner poured hot yellow water from a chipped enamel kettle. "In the keetchen they are giving thees to your boy." He served Johnny first.

"What is it?" Johnny asked, making a face before he touched his lips to the glass.

This tea was the color of urine, Althea saw. She drank a sip, and then another. Mint had been added to cover the taste of roots, musky and bitter. Her thighs began to quiver all over again with cold. She hadn't been able to say much since arriving here, so she finished the cup without asking more about its ingredients.

Herbs for removing shock, for restoring warmth to the heart, Don Héctor explained, as if he'd heard her wondering. Valerian from the high passes; and another herb, a bitter reddish succulent that grew only in ruins. The ancients had planted it. He waved a small, dark hand and told how he walked everywhere, all over these hills, gathering plants and specimens. Talking to people about their cures. He tested most remedies on himself, except for those that had to do with childbirth and retrieval of the soul. Most were very effective. Others, like rubbing a sick person with a black guinea pig, or tying a puppy onto a broken bone, relied perhaps on faith. Don Héctor was reluctant to discount them entirely. A power was required that he did not possess.

He was a small man with a long, creased face and the hairiest arms Althea had ever seen. She thought he would easily fit into one of the wee suits of conquistador armor she had marveled at in Lima.

She drank the bad-tasting liquid in two gulps, then set down her teacup on the oval mahogany table. It was calming her, she thought. Whatever her eyes fell upon, she felt she was seeing it quite clearly. The table, now. She felt a vague wonderment about where it had come from, how it had arrived here, but mostly she saw the way the light ran in a long finger along its top. Light with dust in it, light so white it was almost bluish, as if it had been washed.

This parlor might have been a delirium of Heaven. A Venetian mirror, horsehair sofas, portraits of Don Héctor's family hanging near the ceiling in oval frames. One old lady with a trap mouth: Althea tried to be charitable and suppose it had set that way during the endless photographic sitting. A lot of color had been added to her cheeks, a failed attempt to make her look more pleasant. No wonder he wanted to live here, if this was his mother-in-law. Then there was a prosperous family posed against a background of urns and busts and boats traversing lakes. The wife filled a large chair, the mustachioed husband pressed one hand down on her shoulder, while two little sons in striped socks sprawled in coy poses at their feet pretending to play with two toy dogs on wheels. Could these have been Mr. and Mrs. Saavedra in their youth? The strangest photo was one of an infant in a long white dress, held up by its Indian wet nurse: she stood behind the child with a black shawl over her face, so that only her brown hands were identifiable.

Don Héctor's rug was a spotted cowhide; its leathery smell comforting, fatherly. The tiles beneath it, red and yellow and white and black, looked like a child's fingerpainting.

He'd fed them veal soup and plantains; he had produced dry clothes. Althea was wearing a tucked shirtwaist dress belonging to his wife — when his wife was thinner, Don Héctor said — and a pair of her tan, pointed Mary Janes. Who could consider heels as country shoes? Althea would have preferred to wear Don Héctor's oxfords; his feet were about the same size as hers. These Parisian imitations must pinch Mrs. Saavedra's toes just as frightfully.

The Señora, her husband explained, disliked the country life, where she felt surrounded by the stupid and the ignorant. She was not interested in nature, and had visited the hacienda only once, just after the big house was built. The Señora de Saavedra, whose full name was Inés Monroy Bastos de Saavedra y Arce, lived in her family's palace in the city of Trujillo with the couple's four children, who, Althea was sure, were separated in age by the same intervals as Don Héctor's annual three-month-long visits to the coast, which he undertook during the rainy season.

Or perhaps the woman had a lover, Althea thought, some fancy man in a striped suit and vest, more her style than Don Héctor. Don Héctor did not seem to keep a picture of his wife anywhere. Perhaps he had his own lover here, a warm brown woman.

Her gaze now fell on Johnny's feet. Bare, long, pale, bony as the feet of crucified Jesus. Fortunately he had not lost his boots. They were drying on the verandah along with his notebook, out of reach of the many hungry-looking dogs who roamed outside. Lucky thing Johnny kept his notebook inside his shirt, in a double thickness of oiled cloth, or his work would have been lost.

Doubly lucky, Don Héctor chortled. Not just because of the notes but because of the boots. No one in Peru had ever seen size 44 feet! It would be possible to cut him a pair of leather sandals, but boots were better, especially for one whose feet were soft, unaccustomed.

"Do you feel the effects of the tea?" Don Héctor asked, looking at Althea.

Her thighs had stopped trembling. She nodded but didn't explain. Couldn't. The things around her were very interesting, and if she did not continuously hang on to them, she would begin inside her head to see and hear the yellow-brown water. She could see it from underneath, opaque with the light coming through it, and from above, roiling and giving back no evidence of the oarsman. She could remember small pieces of what had happened so quickly, including the sight of the oarsman flying into the air. The worst was the long absence afterward, when she could not account for where the boy's father had gone — he had so recently been a person. When she tried to think about this, the water began to roar.

Perhaps they wanted to sleep, Don Héctor said. The Señora must be fatigued after the ordeal. Johnny looked at Althea, who did not want to be alone with the sound and color of the water, especially not in the lugubrious canopied bed where she sensed Mrs. Saavedra's ancestors being born and dying. So she shrugged, no. Johnny voiced the no for both of them, not yet, but if Don Héctor had work to do? No, no, Don Héctor said. It was so seldom he saw anyone from outside, let alone foreign visitors, and despite these tragic circumstances he hoped they could recognize his gratitude for their presence. What did el Señor Baines think about the poetry of the Señor Walt Wheetman, the national poet of the United States? El Señor Baines had not drunk his tea.

He pronounced Baines as "Byness." Would Señor Byness like to drink a coffee brandy and discuss? Johnny accepted a small cup and drank it off, then confessed he couldn't remember much of the poetry he had learned in school. However, he said, Whitman could have used a dose of modesty.

"*El hombre cósmico,*" Don Héctor said.

"Listen, Don Héctor," Johnny proposed, mangling the man's name as badly by pronouncing Don "Dawn" (surely he took it for the short form of Donald). "Listen, you're a naturalist. Let's talk about something else. Do you believe the earth is shrinking?"

"That is what we accept," Don Héctor said, clearly intrigued. "As our planet cools, the crust remains too large, and so the mountains are formed. Like an apple."

"You've got a good education, sir." Johnny began to talk about Wegener's theory, which was all the rage at the University of California, where Johnny was to defend his Ph.D. dissertation in geology. "Did you ever notice how your continent fits together with Africa?" As Johnny went on, Don Héctor laughed aloud. At the end of Johnny's lecture, he said, "Bravo, bravo. It takes a genius to state what a child can see. It is a revolution that you bring to me." He rose from his chair, extended a hand. "Come, come."

Althea had fallen into a reverie, absorbed in the pattern of spots on the cowhide rug, which resembled a galaxy of stars but in reverse, black on white. When Johnny touched her shoulder, she said, "Huh?" as if she'd been asleep.

"Come, darling."

Don Héctor ushered them into his study. It was lined on one wall with shelves of books and on another with glass cases, which contained his specimens, gathered in the hills.

It was like a museum, Althea thought. Yards of patterned cloth, broken clay pots with brown designs on them, a frame full of butterflies on pins. Over the door was a badly stuffed black and white bear's head, raccoonish, with eyes of folded black leather. Don Héctor said he had stuffed it himself, with saltpeter, following a book. His own ineptitude had made him marvel at the ancients who had dared to preserve the human dead. In the center of the room was a large glass box, and in it sat a large ball of loosely woven, white cotton cloth. Althea took it, at first, for a giant ball of string. This was a mummy, Don Héctor said. His workers had brought it from a cliff tomb. If Don Héctor did not offer a bounty for such specimens, the workers would loot all of the tombs anyway, breaking everything looking for gold. But there was no gold there, Don Héctor said, only in the ground and in the river. In the cliff tombs were these crude, unpainted pots, a few feather decorations, beautiful fabric, and the dead.

The mummy had been buried in the fetal position. Althea remarked that perhaps it was a child. Oh ho, no, no! An adult, Don Héctor said, a woman of age.

He offered to unwrap her. Althea said no, but simultaneously Johnny said yes, and so Don Héctor, apologizing to the Señora, opened the case and gently pulled out the body. It looked light as a bird in his small hands. He set it on the desk and lifted the veil. Althea stood riveted to the spot as the face was revealed, a face screaming in eternal pain with her hands lifted to her two cheeks as if at some last awful sight. Teeth showed in the open distorted mouth. The lips had shrunk back. She had long, long yellow fingernails that had grown after she was dead, Don Héctor explained, tilting the body to show how the left hand's nails had grown out through the back of the fist. Her skin was rawhide. Her hair was black, unkempt as a horse's tail; it had grown like the nails, Don Héctor said.

She smelled. "Was she buried alive?" Althea wanted to know.

Don Héctor again apologized to la Señora de Byness for the disturbing sight, but he begged to explain that the mummy's horrible expression came only from the way the jaw had fallen open and the lips had drawn back as they dried. She was a woman of the elite, a priestess or a queen. She had been prepared after death, then buried high on a cliff, facing the rising sun. One day, he said, the studious ones would be able to tell us what the thoughts in her mind had been. Until then, Don Héctor would keep her safe in this glass case.

As close as he could get to her thoughts was this shoe: Don Héctor showed it to Althea. It was braided wool, impossibly fine. She sat in a chair to look at it. Try it on, Don Héctor said. She put it on one foot and stood.

The shoe fits, Cinderella, said Johnny. His face was open, soft with love and admiration.

Althea took it off, ending the instant in which she'd wished she could have lived that other life.

Certainly this Indian princess had suffered. Before or after dying. In her face no beauty remained.

And now, Don Héctor said, would Johnny like to see the geological samples? Johnny said yes, yes. Although he had not lost his notes, his case of fossils, so carefully marked in white paint and India ink, had sunk to the bottom of the river.

Don Héctor said that he had many duplicates. Johnny could study his collection and perhaps regain what he had lost. Perhaps too, since Johnny was a professional geologist, he could offer Don Héctor a more precise idea of what these animals had been, their habitat and names.

They began pulling out drawers, looking at brachiopods and crinoids. "This conodont marks a horizon," Johnny said.

Althea said she would go now to rest. She left the two men discussing the Cretaceous period.

Doors seemed to open in front of her and close behind her. Looking at the strange engulfing bed, she decided that only Johnny's presence there could protect her from ghosts. The French doors of the parlor pulled her through themselves. She walked outside, down the colonnade of arches to the end of the outer verandah. The house was shaded by many mango trees whose large leaves littered the ground like varicolored boats. A hundred yards away she spied a small chapel. It might help to pray, Althea thought, for the oarsman's life, or at least his soul. Though her father had been a Foursquare Baptist who hated Catholics, and she herself had been baptized in a river, she sometimes crossed herself when passing cemeteries. It felt good to have something to do at those times.

The chapel was not locked, but its heavy brown doors were stiff and ill fitting, hard to push. Inside, it smelled strongly of dust. The walls were bright turquoise, the floor of stone. There were hard benches for the humble and a plush padded one for Don Héctor and the family who never came. The altar was wood, painted gold, flanked by columns like wrung towels. Fat, painted angels' heads pouted from the four corners of the ceiling. There were Gospel animals, and slaves groaning under the altar; beside it lay a litter with a tiny throne on it and an angel Gabriel dressed in grubby satin knee pants. In the central compartment of the altar stood a woman in a blue velvet dress who must be Mary, wringing her hands and looking up to the sky for help. On one side of her was a knight on horseback in a cape, and on the other side some gentler saint with a dark beard who looked down at her with his blue glass eyes full of tears.

What is wrong with you, little one, the saint seemed to be saying.

My husband just as good as killed that oarsman, Althea answered. He might as well have shot that man. And I didn't stop him.

The oarsman is with us now, the saint said. In our hole under the river, in our secret place under the mountain. He is happy, with us.

What about his boy, Althea asked.

Pray for Johnny, the saint said.

Althea prayed, but it did not seem to be enough.

It's not enough, she told the saint.

Sacrifice, said the saint. You are right. You will pay, and your husband too. There is an order that cannot be escaped. If you wish, though, you can pay a little more.

I wish, Althea said. Her hands went to her belly and she curled over. It felt as if she had been kicked in the stomach.

And another thing, the saint said. You will have a baby soon.

"That child was a miracle," Althea had said to Maggie. "Chahld," and "murkle." She never lost her Texas drawl, despite having traveled to the far ends of the earth. "That's what I'd say if I were a religious woman. But I'm a scientist's wife, so I say I got that chahld from Johnny Baines."

"Maybe the truth lies somewhere in between," Maggie remembered saying. It was her junior year at Brandeis, the year she'd lived with Althea, and she was taking a course in critical theory. Thinking was a novelty. She loved it when the professor said you couldn't ascribe just one cause to any situation. At the time of this conversation with her grandmother, she hadn't yet understood that multiple causality was not the same as having things both ways.

"Julia, now, Julia was a different type of miracle," Althea said quietly. She looked down, stirring the tea in her cup. Her face was in a shadow; more than ten years later, her granddaughter would wish she'd seen its expression.

Maggie was still struggling to absorb the new, traumatic version of the canyon trip, with the oarsman sacrificed to Johnny's well-known stubbornness. At the moment it didn't seem preferable to the old version, a fairy tale whose repetition she and her sister had demanded all through childhood. The young couple bathing in waterfalls, climbing up a cliff to find mummies; the raft barely eluding whirlpools, and the oarsman wrestling and straining to bring them safely ashore at the hacienda.

Maggie thought, At least they didn't barbecue the cow.

It was late on a November afternoon in Cambridge. She remembers how the shadows crept out from under the furniture and the long mirror acquired a lugubrious white sheen. How cold the house was! Her grandmother never turned the thermostat above sixty-two. Maggie was amazed at this old woman sitting on the couch, talking, wearing one thin cardigan for insulation. After a lifetime in the tropics, how could she be immune? Later, when Maggie had followed more of Althea's route through life, she would know just how bone-chilling the tropics can be, how at night the mountains and the forest were cold in a way that makes a person yearn for a straightforward low temperature.

Althea often lay in wait for Maggie, wanting to chat a little before sending her up to study. They'd sit and talk and drink tea or wine while the evening fell. Althea turned on the lamps at seven, then Maggie was free to go. Darkness and cold were the drawbacks to living with her grandmother. Twenty years ago, when Althea and Johnny had bought their house, the neighborhood had been disreputable. Now values had multiplied tenfold and snobbish cars gleamed in the newly bricked driveways. Althea could be miserly and abrasive, but Maggie forgave her, for in all other ways she was more amusing, more advanced than Julia. Althea hid her Burmese ruby in the sugar bowl; she declared to Maggie that she believed in sex.

That day Maggie tucked the moth-eaten alpaca blanket more tightly under her own feet, and was quiet, letting Althea tell how she and Johnny had stayed six weeks at the hacienda. Johnny had written his report, relying on Don Héctor's rock collection. Althea had loved their dinners with the *hacendado,* listening to Don Héctor's tales. The Franciscan priests had failed to civilize the mountains. Seeing male and female Indians dressed in shifts, they'd believed Satan had sent a parade of women to tempt them to break their vows. Don Héctor was a Catholic, but he also believed in exorcisms and coincidences, in hoards of gold guarded by malignant rainbows. He'd tickled Johnny by recounting the Andean theory about earthquakes. They were caused by a gigantic boa shifting underground: black, with a squashed head, it could also turn itself into small, small worms and suck the life from children.

He'd sent his *peones* downriver to seek the oarsman or his body, but nothing was ever found. Come the time for his North American guests to leave, he had loaned them mules; they'd ridden as far as Cajamarca, then taken a car to the coast. When they'd reached Huaraz again, their servants had given up on them and had divided all of their belongings. Most of the servants came back to work, with deep apologies for the things they'd taken.

"I didn't tell Johnny I was pregnant for a long time. I knew it, standing in front of that statue, but I wanted evidence before I told Johnny.

"I sometimes like to think the oarsman was waiting for his boy at home. Not drowned at all." She smiled a faint smile. "Your uncle Christopher. He'd be fifty this year. Sometimes, child, I believe I can see just what he would have looked like. My firstborn. But I lost that boy. He died," she said. "He died in Huaraz before he turned two."

There was always cholera after an earthquake, from the bad water. The rivers could run green and yellow, red and black. Poisons seeped from inside the earth. Impossible to prevent a baby from putting its mouth on anything. Harder still to cure a young child of cholera when there was no good water, no wood to boil what water there was.

Now that she was studying medicine, Maggie learned how the child's body would have been placed in a sling with a hole in it, because the diarrhea was constant, leaving him too weak to cry. Shit would have run like water through the hole into a bucket. Clear as water that rice had been boiled in. The body wasting, pale. The eyes sinking, like a fish left too long on melting ice.

Maggie could not conceive what it would mean to lose a child. Nor how she'd feel if an earthquake came while Carson was away, collapsing the Rosario Canyon's walls, turning the river into a fissure full of neon lava.

During Althea's earthquake, Johnny Baines had been away in Lima buying supplies. All the roads had been destroyed; it had taken him a week to return; by then his son was in the ground. Althea had wanted to keep the body, poor Christopher, poor angel, but the Peruvians took him away from her. It sounded crazy now, but she couldn't bear to put him in his little white coffin before Johnny had said goodbye to him, too. He lay rotting, ugly in his crib. Peruvians came: a woman held Althea in an embrace of iron, pinning her arms while the priest lifted up the corpse. She went to the church, begging for Christopher to have a paper crown and wings, like the other infants who had not been baptized. The priest said Christopher was too old. He'd had the power of speech. Althea insisted the saint had given her a child in order to take him away again, and so he deserved the angel costume. The priest agreed. All Peruvians believed such tales. Johnny would have stopped it, but Christopher went into the ground as an angel, in that cemetery which was to be buried in the next earthquake, when the face of the mountain again fell on Huaraz.

Soon Johnny came back. After visiting his child's grave, he stood in what had once been the plaza and shouted out his exhortation: "Move your town! Don't repeat the disaster!"

The Peruvians pretended to listen, because they felt sorry for him. Where should they go? The town was here.

Johnny couldn't work in Peru anymore. Althea never wanted to leave.

✤

"I told him, why should they move their whole town for one white child when so many of their own had died?"

Maggie had made quick calculations in her head. "I guess you didn't feel like having another baby for a while?" Julia was vague about her age, but it still seemed to have taken at least six more years before Maggie's mother had come along.

Althea sighed heavily. She'd had Julia in 1940, in the British hospital in Calcutta. "Julia's so unhappy with me," said Althea with a glimmer of enthusiasm. "You'd think I'd be used to it by now, but I've always wanted someone to hear my side of things. You seem to be the only one I can speak to."

"Grandma, you can tell me anything."

"Watch out," Althea had cackled, "I might just say your mama was a Hindu."

That evening, Maggie had called her mother on the telephone. She understood Julia so much better, and wanted to capitalize on this new sympathy. Julia had grown up in an angel's shadow. No wonder she was such a perfectionist. Of course Maggie hadn't been planning to say any of this; even if she had, she'd have been prevented, for she and her mother had instantly become embroiled in their typical difficult conversation. Maggie mentioned that Althea had told her old stories of Peru, things she'd never heard before. "Don't believe everything you hear," Julia had snapped. "My mother ought to write bestsellers." Mother and daughter had fought on from there, submerging all nuances of the conversation with Althea.

The next year, her senior year, Maggie had taken an apartment closer to campus. Her visits to Althea had predictably diminished. Then she'd met Larry. By the time she recalled a fleeting expression crossing Althea's face, and wondered what her grandmother might have said, or meant, or tried to say, she was in Piedras, forced to wonder what she had remembered, what invented.

7

ON THE MORNING of the first of August, six months
to the day after they'd arrived in Piedras, sixty-three
years after her grandmother had crawled out of the waters, Maggie
Goodwin began the day as usual by studying medical books.

Today's lesson was from chapter 27 of the *Emergency Medical
Technicians' Manual*. She submerged herself in the text, then took
the quiz at the chapter's end, hoping never to forget the difference between the two kinds of diabetic attacks.

Meanwhile, her husband worked on his educational mural. Since
his clinic still stood empty, the Señor Doctor had begun a slightly
vengeful prevention and education campaign, covering the north
wall of the clinic with cartoon images no one could avoid or misinter-
pret as they walked past or arrived on the bus from Cajamarca. Today he would complete the final, hellish scene, showing where flies
had walked before they landed on your food, how they laid their eggs
and worms then hatched to gnaw you from within.

For lunch they ate fried Spam and onions, fried eggs, white rice,
and hot peppers. Fortunata stood with her back to them, rinsing
yams at the black sink; she'd eat when her employers finished. Carson sat down raising his arms, bent, as a surgeon does whose hands
are scrubbed and ready. He was splattered to the elbows with many
colors of cheap enamel paint, purchased from Don Nasir. Paint
looked bad on a doctor, he said, so he was glad no patients came
today.

"El Señor Doctor converts himself into a peasant," the cook said graciously.

"*Yo no campesino,*" said Carson in his broken but improving Spanish. "*Yo no doctor! Yo loco! Don Calzón!*" Spreading his napkin in his lap, he took a couple of bites before testing his wife on her morning studies. He never confined himself to one topic, but asked her random questions: How do you treat a laceration? Where is the acromion? Which type of diabetes needs an immediate dose of sugar?

Then she and Carson and the cook all discussed his plans for one more mural, having to do with water. Carson wanted to put it on the south wall of the clinic, showing a man shitting in an irrigation ditch with a big red X over his backside. He was obsessed with fecal matters, Maggie teased. She didn't want that image on the same bedroom wall she slept inside of every night. Fortunata, however, was in favor. The image was educational and funny; there was no kinder way of illustrating that bad habit. She did agree with Maggie that Carson mustn't paint it onto his own clinic, lest people begin to make a certain type of joke. For a small consideration, Nasir would surely let him use the retaining wall of his tomato field on the east side of the road, halfway to town.

Coffee was under way when they heard a truck barreling up the river road, too fast. Carson worried aloud that the driver was drunk and would crash into the boulder that sat where the road curved a little, leaving downtown Piedras. Last month, they'd had three patients from just such an accident. They'd rushed outside to see men rolling in the road uttering loud moans, but soon it was clear that they'd been saved by their own drunkenness, which had made them limp as rag dolls as they'd bashed against the insides of their truck. They'd been drinking their way from Nasir's to the house in Piedras Baja where a woman sold her own cane liquor at one *sol* per liter. After Carson had released them, splinted and bandaged, they'd driven off, one wheel making a frightful noise against the dented fender, only to crash again just as harmlessly into a ditch a hundred meters farther on. This time the doors popped open and an astonishing number of empty bottles had rolled out.

Today's truck successfully negotiated the curve. Seconds later, it came to a screeching halt in front of the clinic. A door slammed and someone came running in, someone heavy. Carson leaped up and met him halfway. It was the mine director's driver, a man nicknamed Cantinflas because of his scruffy disordered air and low-riding trousers.

Cantinflas said there had been a small accident at the mine. *Accidentito*. He chopped at his calf with the side of his hand. *Dinamita*. His hands exploded in the air. Rock had flown, a man had broken his leg.

"Why didn't you bring him?" Carson said angrily in English, then translated his own question while Maggie overrode him, more politely. Cantinflas replied as Maggie had expected, that the road was too rough for a man with a shattered calf. The Canadian mining company maintained the east-side road with its own machinery, yet it was worse than the west side, because it rained more on the east side and the mountains were steeper. Eight hours down and the patient would have been screaming.

Carson started packing his kit. Maggie followed him from room to room. "You can't leave me here," she said. It had been their cardinal rule: Carson went no farther than half an hour from the clinic.

"No shots," Carson said, stuffing gauze into a zip-lock bag. "'Take two aspirin, call me in the morning.' Cures most things." He laughed.

"I know, I know," said Maggie. "Doesn't the mine have its own doctor?"

"No!" Carson glared at her now. "You want me to sit here painting flies on piles of *mierda?*"

Maggie had no answer. She let him go into the kitchen alone, to wash his arms with turpentine.

"Bye, darling. You can handle it." He climbed into the mine director's pickup and cranked up its smoked purple window, staring ahead into his own individual future. Before he could shut it entirely, Maggie hung her forearms into the cab, hoping he'd kiss her goodbye, but he didn't, even though Cantinflas was taking his time fussing with cassette tapes. She pleaded to come along, her hands gripping the edge of the open window. If he'd agreed, she would have dived straight in. But he didn't. He promised, with exasperated patience, to return as soon as possible, late that night or the next morning.

Cantinflas turned the key. "Bye," her husband said. "Good luck," said Maggie, still wishing he'd kiss her. Instead, he cranked up the purple window, forcing her to remove her fingers. A legitimate defense against the dust, Maggie told herself. The muffled sound of Cantinflas's tape player came through the glass, playing the first strains of a song. "Billie Jean, she's not my lover," Michael Jackson grunted. As soon as Maggie had recognized the song, the singer, the truck roared off.

The fact that the song was old and bad only made her envy of Carson more humiliating. She stood in the road watching the slender silver Toyota disappear into its own brown cauliflower of dust; stood in the silence until she began to feel the canyon walls towering and towering, making her smaller and smaller.

It was one o'clock when she looked at her watch and decided it was time to go back inside. She could have sat in the kitchen with Fortunata, listening to Andean songs, but she was afraid she'd either burst into tears or say something disloyal, so she passed by, not looking in. From her bedroom she heard Fortunata clattering pots, an invitation. It touched Maggie's heart, but she was grateful to have the childish luxury of refusing. Soon the cook gave up, and turned the radio louder so that Maggie could hear it from the bedroom.

Tired by now of all her comic books, she lay on her belly under the mosquito net rereading the dog-eared Russian novel her husband had suggested she bring along for the new life overseas. She kept losing her place, her attention wandering from the anguish of the characters back to her own certainty that Carson's absence would somehow cause a dire case to arrive.

It was three-thirty when Fortunata appeared in the bedroom doorway saying *"Pacientes."* With a weird relief, Maggie sat up in bed, threw back the mosquito net, and felt with her toes for her shoes.

Let it be a clean machete slash to the foot, she thought.

They were already planted in the middle of the clinic room's polished cement floor, a man and woman. The woman held a baby, wrapped so tightly in its gray blanket Maggie couldn't see its hair. It looked inanimate. The man seemed to be in his late twenties. Maggie noticed he was tall for a Peruvian, almost as tall as she was, and that he exuded physical strength, a kind of glow shining through the absurd, faded orange T-shirt that proclaimed him, in English, "World's Greatest AUNT!" On his head was a little white plastic cowboy hat.

Seeing Maggie, he jerked it down nervously. Country people could be so shy, she thought, touched.

His wife had dressed up for the visit in a gray A-line skirt, an electric-blue sweater, and dusty black pumps. Her face was hard and pure, Andean. She looked ten years older than her husband, but Maggie knew she wasn't.

"*Sí?*" Maggie said to them. The man shifted his body behind the woman, preventing her from running out of the room. He glanced at Maggie from under his hat, and she felt his dark gaze strike her cheek, burning as if he'd slapped her.

Something solidified in her chest, a deep, pulling sensation indistinguishable from dread.

Where was the Doctor? the man asked brusquely. Away, Maggie told him, but before she could elaborate, he shrugged and said to his wife, "*Vámonos, pues,*" let's leave, then.

In a loud voice Maggie began to talk, trying to hold them in one long sentence explaining that the Señor Doctor had gone to the gold mine, leaving her in charge, *in charge,* and since this child was obviously very, very sick, she had the clear duty to ask them not to leave. She was authorized, trained, ready to offer treatment. "*No pueden irse,*" she concluded, you can't go. She addressed the husband, who'd stood shaking his head the whole time she'd been talking.

"Far is the mine," the woman whispered. "Eight hours." Then she cried out, "Doctora!" and thrust the infant forward so that Maggie had to accept it or let the bundle drop to the floor.

Maggie lifted a flap of blanket and saw the baby's face, opaque, white, and rough as a plaster cast. It was limp, so light in her arms that if the upper lip hadn't fluttered slightly at the touch of the air, she'd have thought it was already a ghost.

The mother leaned over Maggie's shoulder. She smelled of wood smoke, and faintly too of urine. "*Ve, ve,*" she said, see, see — as much to comfort the baby as to communicate with Maggie.

The man began explaining. *Hace tres días,* three days ago, the baby became sick. *Anoche,* last night, she got worse. *Fiebre,* fever.

Why had they waited so long to bring her to the clinic? If the baby died, they'd say, The *Doctor norteamericano* wasn't home, and his wife, who doesn't know anything, she killed our child.

"*Pulmonía*," the man said firmly. His wife was nodding. "*Pulmonía.*"

"I will examine her." Maggie's arms shook as she tipped the infant to peer inside its nostrils. Blocked and green. She tried to find a pulse, fingering the tender flesh of the neck, behind the ear, but she felt nothing and was afraid to press too hard. The baby definitely seemed to be alive, though barely lukewarm. Did she feel pain?

Surely I will kill her, Maggie thought.

Putting her ear to the baby's lips, she tried to feel, or hear, her breath. Was that a tiny sigh or Maggie's imagination? Suddenly the baby inhaled, shuddering in her arms, but the baby's eyes stayed closed.

"*A veces no respira*," the mother said apologetically. Sometimes she doesn't breathe.

Maggie saw it was going to be impossible to get her to swallow oral medicine.

"*Inyección,*" she said.

"*Penicilina,*" the mother said at once.

Maybe this woman knew what to do; maybe she'd had other children treated for pneumonia. Pneumonia was one of the most frequent killers in any poor mountains, carrying off the old, the young, the weak. Carson's admonitions rang in Maggie's mind: Don't give shots. Never cave in when patients write their own prescriptions, especially if they're illiterate peasants. Never, never. Never, never. "*Pulmonía, inyección,*" Maggie at last agreed, her thin voice shouting in her own ears, barely overriding Carson's. Now, what should be in the needle? Hadn't the government nurses killed a baby just like this one? Would an infant's treatment be in one of Carson's medical manuals, and if so, which one?

The mother stood aside, a jittery shadow, clamping her arms across her breasts. Maggie wondered how many other children she had, how many she had lost. They hadn't named this baby yet. It was a seven-week-old infant. Maybe they were waiting to see if she would really grow up to be a person.

God help me if the child's allergic, Maggie thought, she'll turn red, swell up, and die. No one would care about her good intentions. The terrorists would swoop down . . .

Steam from a kettle and a hot water bottle would be as important as the antibiotic.

"We'll go to the kitchen," Maggie announced. "Boil water, and hold the infant in the smoke" — she couldn't remember the word for steam — "while I prepare the *inyección.*"

Both parents watched, black eyes inhaling light. The father's eyes were clear, untroubled, intelligent. He'd agreed to Maggie's plan. "*Vamos,*" he ordered.

The mother nodded. Her face was relaxed, almost sleepy, as Maggie handed the baby back to her. With a routine gesture, she flipped the blanket back down over the baby's face. Keeping her warm was good, but Maggie hated seeing her face disappear again like that.

The three of them passed down the dark narrow hall, through the ridged green plastic fringe that hung in the kitchen door. The kitchen was full of people.

"*Buenas tardes,*" the baby's father said. He took his hat off, smiled a wry, lopsided smile.

"*Ah! Ah! Perdón!*" Fortunata jumped up from the table where she'd been sitting with Doña Ema and Ema's two sons. Such guilt was unnecessary, Maggie thought, although she did wonder when the visitors had come in. Somehow she hadn't heard them.

Fortunata and Doña Ema both began to babble incoherently. The boys continued sitting, staring inches before their eyeballs, like students asked a question, until Fortunata barked, "*Váyanse!*" They and their mother filed out, mumbling perfunctory goodbyes. At the door of the kitchen, the older boy, Boris, turned back, smiling, as if he planned to stay and watch.

"Chss!" Fortunata shooed him, like a dog. Then she hastily swept up the greasy plates into the sink while the transistor continued a weak, scratchy *pasillo* ballad. The baby's mother sat down at the table.

Fortunata asked Maggie whether the patients had introduced themselves.

"No — this is an emergency! Fortunata, we need hot water!"

"*La bebita está muy mal,*" the baby's father explained. "*Tiene pulmonía.*"

Maggie asked Fortunata to fill both kettles and heat them on the stove, but the cook was riveted to the middle of the floor, saying she was so sorry the Doctor was not here. While the husband told her sharply not to worry, everything was fine, *correcto,* the Doctora was sufficient, Maggie walked between them and filled the kettles herself, feeling momentarily invincible, like Carson, cutting through whatever obscure emotions were paralyzing others.

"Mi amor es inocente," a radio baritone revealed. *"Mi amor es un volcán."* By the smears on the plates, Maggie saw that Fortunata had fed her guests the same lunch as the Doctores had eaten: Spam, eggs, rice, *ají.* When she turned around, Fortunata was bustling aimlessly, rearranging chairs so that the husband could sit down too.

"Fortunata, *fuego!"* Maggie commanded, but Fortunata seemed to have forgotten how to dominate the cooktop. She lit a match, whose head flew off. She burnt her finger on a second, and still the stove wouldn't light.

The baby's mother pulled the blanket-bundle up to her face. Coarse wool, it looked as if it had been gathered from mouse nests. She pressed her lips on it, murmuring to the infant inside. Fortunata pumped the stove, her fat arms wobbling. She wasted several more matches before discovering that the fuel valve was closed; when she opened it, kerosene sprayed all over the walls and ceiling. Fortunata dabbed at the liquid with a rag while the kerosene kept spraying.

"Carajo!" Maggie cursed, then added gentler words, to the effect that all were scared.

The father got up and closed the valve. Fortunata thanked him profusely, and they stood waiting for the pressure to diminish. The transistor began another Ecuadoran ballad. Dead flowers, ashes, tombs, it was perfect for the occasion. The baby's mother warbled unconsciously, nervously along under her breath, directing her song to the child.

Kerosene had collected in the ring below the burner. Too much: when Fortunata touched the pool with a lit match, blue and yellow flames poured across the stovetop, down onto the floor. Maggie jumped back shouting *"Cierra!"* The father wrenched shut the valve that led to the kerosene tank, and they all stared in awe at the flames on the stovetop and the floor, burning without visible support.

Maggie should have given the injection long ago. She had no idea whether the baby was still alive, or, if it was, how urgent the timing might be.

"*Lo haré yo*," the husband said, I'll do it. The flames were a small blue tiara on the cement. He stomped on it negligently and squelched it into nothing. The mother seemed in shock, her long jaw hanging open. If the baby was dead in her arms, surely she'd say something.

The man opened the valve slightly and struck a match, and the burner lit with a ripping sound.

"*Ya,*" said Fortunata, as if claiming credit.

Maggie ran into the clinic, where it was a relief to be alone. Unlock chest. Get vial, unwrap hypodermic. Needle pointing in air, she leafed furtively, hurriedly through the *Merck* and *Where There Is No Doctor,* feeling like she was cheating at school. Carson's notes on drugs were tucked into the back of one of these books. Here, at last, she found that the pneumonia drug was Rocephin. No baby dosage on the ampule, nor the box, nor in the circular's fine print. She decided to administer half a vial and hope the baby was not allergic.

Fortunata came in, eyes like Ping-Pong balls. "It's him, it's him, Black Rainbow, Comandante Oquendo, don't say anything," she said in a stage whisper, and ducked out again.

Maggie barely heard her through the pounding that began in her ears. She should have known. She knew. Or did she? She'd called him; he had come. Again she felt the slight, pulling dread she'd felt on first seeing these people. It's down to me, she thought. Moving with infinite patience, she swam down the hall back into the kitchen, where the mother handed her the baby again. The infant was really not moving sufficiently and Maggie would never forget how she felt, too small, bones mobile under the skin. The skin on her forearms wanted to twitch, the backs of her knees. Poor wee mite.

"*Todavía no hierve,*" Fortunata mumbled, the water's not boiling yet. The mother now put both hands over her face. Maggie decided not to look at the man again, not yet. The terrorist who scared no one except herself. Was he really the baby's father? She wished his foot wasn't showing in the corner of her visual field, for it reminded her of something. After years in rubber-tire sandals, most men's feet around here resembled large clods of mud. This man wore the same coarse sandals but his feet had delicate, visible tendons. No, she could not remember. She must move on, concentrate, concentrate on this dying child.

She opened the blanket and peered at the baby, white as a Victorian photograph she'd seen once of a baby lying in state. In the photograph you could see how the infant's cheeks had started to rot. Maggie laid her out on the kitchen table. The soft skull thwacked dully on the wood and she didn't even whimper. Bad sign. Flipping the blanket open, Maggie saw the baby dressed in one of those fake-fur union suits she'd seen in the Cajamarca market. Orangish brown, matted polyester, a gorilla costume the color of a malnourished orphan's hair. Unzip, pull, twist, expose the baby's skinny, cold bottom. Spike diaphragm. Pull plunger, suck transparent liquid into the barrel of the needle. Swab, stick. She was amazed how the flesh didn't resist, just like butter in its texture. The baby said, *"Ih!"* More breath than voice. But breath.

When Maggie turned her up again, her eyes flew open for an instant, counterweighted.

Fortunata handed her a pint whiskey bottle full of warm water, and Maggie closed the blanket over it and the child. The baby drew two huge breaths, her nostrils flaring. *"Eunhh,"* she exhaled wearily.

"Vive," the terrorist declared. She lives.

"Casi," Maggie said, almost. The infant was breathing with a heavy desperation, chest and belly seesawing. The mother reached for her, but Maggie didn't let go, not yet. She clung to the child, to the returning life, wanting to hold it forever. Meanwhile, the full kettle had started to hiss and rattle menacingly. Before it steamed, Maggie showed how far from the spout to hold the infant.

Fortunata suggested adding eucalyptus leaves to the kettle. *"Perfecto,"* Maggie said. She was tired. She wished they would all go home now. They could cut branches on the way. If the baby was no longer in her arms, it could slip away and start to die again. If so, she didn't want to watch, or even know about it.

"Fortunata will cut," the man said. Fortunata took the knife, slipped out. The closest eucalyptus tree was half a kilometer uphill. The speed of her exit, Maggie thought, disproved Fortunata's boast that she'd never been scared of Comandante Oquendo.

Maggie restated the prescription for home treatment, looking the Comandante flatly in the eyes, pretending to impress details upon him. This might be the only moment when she could ever look at him without being seen in return. He did not appear dangerous. His skin was velvety; the few lines in his face seemed to belong to the normal range of human expressions. His face was widest at the cheekbones. There was humor in it, intelligence. The density of his hair amazed her.

He grinned, or rather his eyes sparkled at her slightly — he'd seen her trying to inspect him, and was, again, amused. How could she think he wouldn't notice?

Quickly Maggie turned to the mother and repeated not to scorch the baby in the steam, and to test the water in the whiskey bottle too. Her heart pounded. He knows I know, she thought.

The terrorist pointed to the half-full vial of antibiotic on the counter. He pinched and waggled the baby's foot again, to show that it was still limp. The baby's face was still cement-colored. Maggie wondered whether Rocephin was dangerous. She hadn't read the side effects listed on its wrapper. Maybe, since she was sure this was pneumonia, it was best that all concerned should feel she hadn't held back treatment.

"Muy bien," she said, and laid the baby out again on the table. She was acquiescing. Doing just what this man told her, just what Carson told her not to. Where was her own judgment, and what could guarantee it? She was tempted to jab the baby through her clothes, to get it over with, but she forced herself again to unwrap her. The little body was quite warm now, thanks to the hot water bottle. This time, as the needle went in, the infant managed an "Ah" that was close to protest.

The mother took the baby and wrapped her up again, covering her face. Maggie shrugged. *"Ahora, manda Dios,"* she said, pointing to the ceiling, above which chance and law played freely across the sky.

"La voluntad de Dios," Comandante Oquendo said lightly. God's will.

Maggie agreed. She wondered what Carson could be doing. She left the room with what she hoped was an air of responsible authority.

The clinic looked even starker and longer than usual. There was little to clean up. Maggie tossed out the drug circular, then fished it out of the wastebasket for later study, then threw it out again. The idea of poring over all that small print gave her a headache, and she knew she'd learn more by simply asking Carson. For a third time she fished it out and put the box and circular on the counter, an answer to his question: Are you sure?

No point in praying or nail-biting. She logged the case, checking the date on their calendar, a gift from the hardware store in Cajamarca: it showed a pudgy Caucasian baby sitting behind a basket of apples, a fruit that did not grow well in Peru. Today was the day of San Celsio — the inventor of the thermometer or a martyr boiled to death?

No-name Baby was their sixteenth patient. An auspicious number, Maggie thought. The baby must not die. If it did, Maggie hoped to feel something different from the cascade of selfish paranoia that had begun to shake her mind. It mattered most deeply to the baby whether it lived or died, and since the baby did not yet know this, Maggie must not forget it.

The kitchen sounds were turning frisky, festive. Fortunata had turned up the radio, which was playing a *huaynito*. The terrorist said something that made the women laugh.

Just as Maggie was deciding to retreat to the bedroom, Fortunata called, *"Doctora Maggi! Ven!"* She always pronounced Maggie "Ma-hee," like the Swiss powdered soup or the Hawaiian sushi fish.

They'd hung a bedsheet over the kitchen door opening. The pot and kettle were boiling, each with a large messy branch of eucalyptus sticking out. Dry, comma-shaped leaves littered the floor. Piedras's afternoon heat had thickened, and so the kitchen's air was doubly thick, fragrant as hot jelly. The Peruvians were all huddled around the table drinking coffee. Their foreheads glistened.

"Now you must be presented to Don Vicente Quispe Cruz, and this is Doña Luz María." Maggie shook their hands. The man, Vicente, announced that the baby had been saved. Luz María uncovered her at last. *"Duerme,"* she announced, and leaned back so Maggie could examine the tiny face. Asleep indeed, and she'd turned the proper color, weak milky tea. Maggie gently touched her hair.

In the time it took to walk them to the door, Maggie remembered over and over again that she'd saved this life. Carson would be proud. She was tempted to take the afternoon at face value, decide that their work in Piedras had begun, and start to believe that she and her husband would never endure another afternoon when they chirped and teased each other, pecking at a frozen, amputated silence between them.

She thanked Luz María, told her the child would wake up hungry. Luz María gave her a look that was loving and pitying and grateful all at once; it made Maggie want to jump out of her skin, as if she must now do some further, impossible thing. "Keep her warm," Maggie insisted, "keep boiling eucalyptus."

Vicente gripped her hand strongly. "*Gracias, Doctora.*"

"Not Doctora," Maggie said.

"Señora. Doña Maggie," Vicente said. "How much?"

"*Gratuito.*"

He stood there and made a little speech about poverty and humanity and understanding. Everything he said was true, though she hated how he said the gringos didn't understand the people, their farms, their animals, their trees, their sufferings. To her relief, he concluded by saying that Doña Maggie had shown true human compassion, and if God willed, they could all reach comprehension, here in the valley of the Rosario.

Maggie asked for permission to repeat the speech to Carson. Vicente nodded and said, "You will tell him everything."

On impulse, Maggie leaned over and kissed the baby's head. It was fuzzy and fragrant, like a geranium leaf. "Congratulations, baby with no name."

Luz María said, "I cannot choose! Do you like 'Lady'?"

"It's beautiful," Maggie said. In fact "Lady" sounded false, a kind of brand name for a child. What did it have to do with Peru?

"I'll name her 'Lady Maggy,'" Luz María teased, smiling a gummy smile. "You will baptize her, be her godmother. You and I will be *comadres*. Okay?"

Maggie smiled, but didn't say yes or no. On the one hand were Luz María's feelings; on the other, educational expenses and unforeseen obligations. Somewhere else, both closer and farther away, bulkier uncertainties shifted.

"*Ya,*" Fortunata said, "you saved her. You will stand at her baptism. When the priest comes in October."

Maggie promised to consider the idea. Meanwhile, night had crept out of the river and up the sides of the mountains. She watched Vicente and Luz María walk north toward the iron bridge and pass into the dove-colored shadow that had fallen across the road. They were going back into the land of Althea, she permitted herself to think.

8

ALTHEA WOULD NEVER forget watching her child's face change: how the bruises of rot spread and bloomed, from the edges of his nostrils, from under the skin of his cheeks; how his lips hardened and his stillness grew deeper and deeper, the stillness of death that was worse than anything, evil and unmistakable, stiller than a wooden doll, stiller than stone or anything that had never been alive, until she no longer could remember what her living child had looked like. Yet she knew that if she was ever to find Christopher again he would be there, in Peru, nowhere else. Thus it amazed her that she allowed Johnny Baines to take her hand and pull her into the dark car, leaving Christopher behind in his shining white sliver of a coffin, there under the high valley's too blue sky, in the graveyard surrounded by its white wall: stacked sarcophagi like apartment houses in the center, young eucalyptus trees shivering in the wind, newly planted in the earthquake victims' section. As the car drove away, Althea turned again and again to look back, but the rear window was always full of the snowy, misshapen peak of Huascarán, with the new dent in its face where the avalanche had come from. Thanks to Johnny and geology, she knew the mountain was already starting to collapse again.

She was relieved when the road curved and the walls of the valley rose and she could no longer see the mountain.

Within the week, Christopher's parents had shipped to New Orleans through the Panama Canal, then flown to California where Johnny defended his dissertation. As a doctor of geology, uninterested in petroleum, he obtained work in India, mapping for the British Crown. India would be a little like Peru, he reassured Althea, who thought she'd be glad if it wasn't.

India: a hazy flatland the color of lions. It was white, or yellow, or brown, the color of eternal dust. It could almost have been West Texas, Althea thought, except that its mud-brick towns and patchwork fields were not green, not irrigated. A geometry of monotone shadings, scratched into or built up out of the earth.

Not a river to be seen. No mountain, no ocean.

They had traveled for so long her eyeballs felt dirty, cracked, the roots of her hair swelling grease into her scalp. Her insteps had puffed to bonelessness and were sticking out of her shoes. Nights and days had run together into one dull, irritated mass: San Francisco, Hawaii, Singapore, each place stranger than the previous one.

Landing in Delhi, she felt gravity catch her, focusing her into this new place which was the farthest away of all. It must be opposite her hometown of Amarillo on the globe. Opposites attract, she thought, having each other in common. She'd never believed in Chinamen hanging upside down in hats. Here below them a double row of large, dark green spreading trees lined a narrow, precise stripe of road. The trees were bigger than oaks, wider than cottonwoods, solider than mesquite; they were impressive from the airplane; they'd found a way to grow in a dry landscape. Soon she would see how each tree would shelter a world of shade and singing birds, and monkeys, and women with water jars who rested, chatting together, until they'd regained the strength to hoist the heavy, shapely brass urns back onto their heads or hips and carry the water home to husbands and flocks of children.

Johnny scratched her companionably between the shoulder blades. She was startled to realize he was asking for her attention by this gesture. She sat up, vacating his view out the window.

"We'll be all right here," he said, pleading for her acknowledgment.

She forced herself to smile and nod, but she could not say yes.

She was to take comfort, in this country of skinny, desperate people, in seeing how the bones of life were bare and no one turned away. There was nowhere to turn, but still they didn't try. It was a land where babies died and women wailed for them. Not like the

States, where each house built up its lie that life was complete, for other people.

Johnny's job was in Bihar, the dry, hot desert heart of the subcontinent. A train from Delhi all night, then two hours on a cart drawn by a pony the size of a poodle, whipped mercilessly by a wizened ancient who wore a dirty white turban on his head and a sagging diaper of the same color to cover his private parts. A clean white beard grew out of his black face. He was not a Negro but an Indian person. Althea felt uneasy around him. He reminded her of the boatman who had drowned, though he and Domingo didn't look at all the same.

She was uneasy in Bihar, generally, though Johnny had told her its rocks were stable. She disbelieved: the ground didn't feel right to her; it felt as if one day or night it could suddenly begin to squirm as the ground had done in Huaraz. She actually felt better after hearing, from the British women at the club, that Bihar too had had its earthquake, back in the 1900s, hot sand spouting from the barren ground. After that, she could make love with Johnny, cautiously.

She didn't go with him to the field, but instead grew versed in seeing him from afar.

All day he was a tiny stick figure drilling holes and provoking explosions. At dusk he trudged across some range of darkening hills while the sun spilled crimson devastations, orange wealth across the sky. She was not allowed to go with him, so it was only in her mind that she lay on the cot in Johnny's olive-green tent, watching him log the day's measurements by kerosene lantern, worrying about his eyesight until he came to her and they fell asleep together, once more, in the circle of one shared horizon.

After two months he was finished. His independent research on the tensions in stable rocks was well received, and good for his reputation. Next he would work in Assam, where a fault called the Chedrang had shifted. Two British tombs had left their plinths and leapt to touch, a distance of one and a half meters. A road had moved aside so that the view from a curve improved. Johnny was excited about measuring these displacements. Althea wondered what it meant that Chedrang's earthquake, Assam 1897, had broken a single crystal wineglass in Leghorn, Italy. Beauty, an opera singer's voice singing from far; but from near, cracks in the earth had opened, closing with great force, buildings had collapsed in unhearable noise, leaving ten thousand dead, crushed and bleeding, burnt and diseased. The mountains had lifted twenty-six feet. Althea dreaded going to Assam, where she'd have to see the many British graves, shaded by cedars near the stone Episcopal churches, for she counted herself among grieving survivors. But she'd have only an absence, not even a stone.

She didn't sadden him with her true feelings. Instead, she told him she'd be happier in a big city. He rented a cottage in downtown Calcutta, which they'd call home for nearly two years. It had a high wall in front of it and a garden full of trees. When Johnny was out of town Althea rarely left the place, afraid of the broken beggars thrusting their stumps in her face, of the crowds teeming like ants. She sent the cook to market, and received one or two visitors a week.

Johnny happened to be "home" when the Altai quake was announced on the BBC, but Althea had been the first to hear of it. She sat in shifting, mottled bougainvillea shade, writing next week's menu and bazaar list for Madhukar the cook. In Calcutta she'd discovered an English news broadcast that she could sit down with every day, when there was electricity. It was so nice to be accompanied by a voice. Within reason, it was her duty to improve her mind as well. She found it strangely pleasant to allow the world to form its garish backdrop to the ordering of her own small realities. Things in Europe were rotten and falling down.

"Monday. Meat loaf. Buffalo, eggs, tomatoes, crumbs," she wrote in her neat, round hand, placating Madhukar, who had worked ten years for a British family and was proud of his bland cooking. She had pleaded with him to display the fiery delicacy of his own Indian cuisine; he agreed to cook one curry per week.

The last strains of a ponderous Mahler symphony throbbed in the hot green air.

"Tuesday. Fish curry." She loved this dish of Madhukar's, tiny river fish fried in mustard oil with potatoes, yellow turmeric, and hot red, green, and black peppers.

This just in. A massive earthquake has taken place in the Altai Mountains of Outer Mongolia, the announcer said. *The report by Radio Moscow this morning claims a magnitude of eight point six. No greater earthquake is possible.*

"Wednesday. Peeled," Althea wrote, and forgot cucumbers as her stomach went cold. Though the reporter was speaking from Moscow, she could hear behind his voice the roar of mountains collapsing, the smell of burning rocks. And in her belly the feeling of atrophy that would last forever and a day.

Few deaths are reported, but the geologic crisis is of an almost unbelievable magnitude, the announcer went on. *A trench sixty-five feet wide and two hundred miles long has opened in a remote area of these legendary mountains. Fortunately, most of the shepherds of the Altai are nomadic, and have been moving southward to avoid the winter temperatures, which average sixty degrees of frost. Twelve people are reported dead so far, but it is difficult to assess reports due to the extremes of climate and geology. Strong aftershocks are expected over the next weeks.* An international team of scientists was assembling in Ulan Bator. The Soviet government had offered travel permits as a courtesy to the scientific team, but it was not known whether the intractable climatic and geological conditions would permit the mission to reach the affected area. *Wishing them warm toes, this is BBC Moscow correspondent Nigel Jones.*

The reporter sounded smug, world-weary, as if the reason he was glad of the small number of deaths was that it permitted him to report from the relative comfort of Moscow. Althea imagined his Communist apartment with a cheap but ostentatious glass-front cabinet full of cut-glass decanters. Sweating cement walls alive with buried microphones, the reporter drinking vodka to blur his vision of the world as teetering between boredom and disaster. Drunk, he might talk to his walls, pretending to be more than one person, giving misleading information. Althea decided she disapproved of Nigel Jones, though he would make an entertaining guest at a dinner party. She was beginning to understand there were lots of characters like him in foreigners' enclaves overseas, morally degenerate but full of amusing stories about Cairo, Capri, and Sumatra. Their only remaining innocence was their belief that they'd seen it all. Blue martinis, talking frogs.

She'd seen plenty of wonders here in India, and the mummies in Peru. She'd followed Johnny to the mining camps of the Chilean Andes, two miles high, where her heart flipped in her chest like a dying fish and the wind cut her earlobes until they bled, and she'd watched the dark-skinned men go down into the earth to suffocate and die.

For some reason it was from these heights that Johnny had studied the unreliable coast.

Mongolia must be twice as cold as that, unimaginable.

All the more right and necessary that men should go there, to ennoble the mountains and make their collapse worthwhile. She knew better than to believe there might be hidden worlds, nor even the red molten quick at the bottom of the earthquake's crack. She had seen cracks and they were dry mouths. Still, that stark fissure cutting two hundred miles across the frozen landscape, now that would be almost glorious. At least instructive. Morally.

For what was a worse false faith than stupid trust in the ground underfoot? The ground rose up and killed forty thousand people every year, Johnny said. If he could warn them to move out of the way just for a few days while the earthquake came, at least some of them would be saved. But Johnny did not know the true nature of that which he would warn against. You could not know until you had felt it. And even so, you were doomed to trust the earth — where else were you to go?

Oh, she and Johnny had felt the earth tremble three or four times, slightly, and slightly more than slightly. A blue glass lemonade pitcher had fallen on its side, rolled to the edge of the table, and shattered on the floor. The pictures had swayed on the wall as if at sea. Johnny had yelled, "Up, out, go! Get under the door!" He'd told her afterward how she'd sat smiling as though she enjoyed it.

A doorway had saved her in Huaraz, the house collapsing behind her. She'd nearly squashed little Christopher, holding him too tight. She had watched lights coming out of nothing in the ground. Waves of earth advancing like surf across the patio, then shaking in a pattern of squares and diamonds like water shaken in a flat pan. The roar in her ears was like a million trains. Days later, living in a tent with Peruvian women, the earth had not stopped trembling. People wandered shaking their heads, and when a new tremor began they screamed. The river ran black, bile and metal from the body of the earth. They filtered the water through shirts. No wood to boil it; the few trees were buried in the landslide. They had mixed water and raw flour to eat, and everyone had gotten sick from the poison in the water.

When Johnny talked of geology he talked of slowness, the earth like half-melted butter heaving in its sleep. Slowness was pleasant in the imagination, making the mind so vast. The fast part of geology was more difficult. Johnny's calculations encompassed awful things — how many ergs it would take to twitch a road aside from its destination, to lift a slow green river into a series of foaming waterfalls — but this was all afterthought. He still believed that his geologic mind could know the way the earth was. In his mind, science left no room for terror. He'd shown her pages of equations in which S was strength, E was elasticity, B was the breaking point of rocks. Althea was afraid for him.

She wanted to save him from his colleagues, too, who laughed at his ambition. On their scale of geologic thoughts, earthquake prediction was at once too vast and too microscopic. How could you be accurate about one day, even one year, out of an eon? How could you hope to predict the arrival of the unpredictable? Johnny was careful, canny. He was building a small, visible, and acceptable career upon his genius for mapping and his descriptive studies of fault systems in remote parts of the world, primitive and unstable areas where tens of thousands of people died in earthquakes every year, so many that no one in the States could ever imagine them as people, but saw them instead as ants under a mudslide. Places where there was cholera, dysentery, and tuberculosis; where other Western geologists — much less their wives — were reluctant to spend their lives. He got paid by companies and governments to do their kind of work; his own work he carried on at night, by oil lamp, or candle, or weak bulb.

Johnny would go through any hardship to learn what he needed to know; this was one of the things Althea liked about him. He was fond of saying that there was no further use to be extracted from beetles crawling across the windowpanes of Oxford University, that the Japanese and the Californians didn't need earthquake prediction because they could afford to engineer houses to withstand the movements. No, it was Peruvians and Turks and Indians whom Johnny wanted to save. Besides his wife, they'd been the last to see his son alive. He'd make it worth Althea's while that she'd stood in that doorway to save herself. He knew she had sometimes regretted it.

In general, Johnny didn't believe in filtering his data through the soft cracks of any human brain. He had been in Belgium during the Great War, and his body had stopped reacting to the whistle of incoming bombs, as if it had finally understood something bodies rarely did: that death was not a choice but rather a matter of uncontrollable timing. Later in the war, he was hit by a sniper and lay wounded in snow until an enormous white pigeon's breast lowered itself upon him. Waking up in the dark, pain was visible as a line of steely light gleaming along the rail of his hospital bed. In the morning, he began a second, unexpected life. Purple centipede tracks crisscrossed his belly. The Alps had been white and perfect outside his window. His first sight on returning from the dead. Mountains became his gods. He went to school to learn them.

What would he do when the mountain fell? Althea could still feel Huaraz breaking things inside her. A shaking beyond the contours of her body. It had been a year. It was not just Christopher, not just the sacrifice of a child that had turned her and broken her. Earthquakes were terrible, and terrible in being unknowable. Suddenly they were there; when you were in one, you could not perform all of the necessary knowing.

Maybe Johnny could find a way to trap the shaking in an equation. He already had an idea about the continents' motion. If you could measure the growth of mountains, the spread of coastlines, you might find out how many earthquakes were necessary in a year, or one hundred years, or one hundred thousand years. Johnny had the mind for that, if anyone did.

But he would have to suffer first. He'd need to feel what it was when the solid earth became untrustworthy. Not just untrustworthy: when it turned against you, against itself, revealing a part of its nature that was demonically strange. One day there might be a symbol for that demonic exhalation; no one had caught it before. A curl across a page. If Johnny wanted this, Althea had to give him his chance. She didn't know whether she was helping his theory or trying to bury it.

Before the news report had ended, she had decided to fire their two servants and let go of this bungalow house. As she stood up she had already begun to miss the waxy red tile floors and this bougainvillea the size of a coral reef, but she'd long since learned that these were the worst moments of missing, when departure had been announced but had not yet begun. Things sat innocently in their positions. She had betrayed the objects around her, made some tragic admission that all the love which their mute existence bore toward her was not enough to stay her here among them. By her departure, the objects' helplessness was terribly revealed, as was her own failure to have cared for them sufficiently. The table with its chipped green paint, the whitewashed river rocks encircling the rosebush, now looked so stripped and defective that there was nothing to do but run away from them. She had endured this awful juncture dozens of times since marrying Johnny. Soon enough, she knew, the spasms of sweaty effort would begin, too chaotic and detailed to leave room for sadness. Boxes would be packed, the furnishings disappear, servants cry and press her hands, and somewhere amidst it all, grief would give way to anticipation. The heart was corrupt in healing. New things would absorb her; she'd reckon their superiority or inferiority to the ones left behind, learn their quirks, submit to their fascination, allow them to fill her existence until she could very nearly forget that she would leave these things, too, in their turn. It was horrible, all of it.

Still, if she'd never left West Texas, following Johnny, Althea would not have known that the world cannot be foreseen. Each new place was unimaginable from the point of view of the one before. Once she left, the places changed behind her, too. Even Texas. For example, Texan skies were the only skies on earth with a sense of humor: row on row of lambs hanging from blue rafters on invisible threads. She hadn't understood that until she left them, and saw that northern skies were full of dread, tropic ones were often stark white, and the skies over Kashmir's high mountains were silken, tinted. How could all this shrink down to numbers?

She would stay at the Christūnandā Convent, which she'd twice visited. It was a few hours' train ride north of the city. Johnny could go away knowing she was quite happy and protected. No servants to manage, no work beyond strolling very slowly along the warm shadowy paths of the banana plantation like a glamorous invalid. The notion of sleeping in a bed from which rules excluded Johnny felt a little unwifely, but it could hardly be called improper in a nunnery. It was a temporary measure, she reminded herself.

Mère Anandī, the mother superior, was French. Had she been Indian, Althea would have been afraid to stay at her convent. But foreigners understood about boiling the water, and understood each other's foreignness. Mère Anandī had a standing invitation to all foreign ladies, tea on the first Sunday of each month. She was not judgmental like the British wives; Althea wondered what kind of life she'd had before renouncing it. She offered cookies baked with lard and sugar, fat red bananas, and Darjeeling tea that was never quite strong enough. Althea spooned in gray sugar coarse as gravel, added lots of grassy milk from the convent's cows, but the tea's thin, overdelicate edge could not be blunted and usually gave her a headache as soon as she tasted it.

On both of Althea's visits, Mère Anandī had not failed to welcome her to spend a quiet week or two at the convent, any time Johnny was out doing field work, but so far Althea had refused. She did not want to assert her solitude while Johnny was out of town. It would be disloyal — her place was at home, waiting for his return.

Convent guests lived for free, and what Althea and Johnny saved on food, rent, and servants would pay Johnny's airplane fares to Moscow and Mongolia. Living on the economy, Althea had always managed to stretch Johnny's oil company money and his university grants for nearly twice as long as they'd ever been intended to last. Sending him off to the Altai would be a brilliant twist, a final flourish, justifying her scrimping that sometimes made Johnny so impatient, bordering on insulted. "This tea bag's dead. What are you saving the money *for?* I can always get another grant." She didn't know how to begin to explain to him how doubling his money made her feel: as if she had earned it over again herself, by her own intelligence.

She took it as a sign that the plan fell together so perfectly in her head. At noon when Johnny came home for lunch she could not wait. The idea burst out of her mouth as soon as he set foot on the verandah, even though he looked dirty and tired, in no mood for major announcements. "I heard on the radio the biggest earthquake just happened in Mongolia, and they're sending scientists to study it, and I've figured out how you can go!"

"Are you crazy? It's winter there," Johnny said.

She followed him into the bedroom. He started taking off his shirt. While his face was hidden in khaki she found courage to go on. "The whole Altai range was lifted, I know, but tell me again how you calculate the weight of mountains."

"Estimate, not calculate," Johnny said.

"But they say they know," Althea said.

❖ ❖ III ❖

"They don't. They're only guessing."

Her ankles, then her calves began to quiver, as if Huaraz were rumbling up through this very ground. "Why don't you go? You'll notice something important they won't see. How something falls in, or fits together."

In the morning, Johnny had woken up repeating her words — how something fits together — and he raised his voice, imitating hers. "The world is not falling in, it's fitting together. Actually, Althea, you have summed up the ideological mistake of a generation of geologists." Althea raised her eyebrows, but Johnny did not elaborate. She could not blame him. He was embattled; even the great Richter himself had once dismissed his work. Since then he had hidden his light. She always told him she was certain of his greatness. He could have done his research as part of a team in California, but after Richter's remark he'd rather make his own mistakes, and take all the credit.

Now Johnny rolled on his side and pulled her leg over his waist. His arms were so strong they still frightened her, even after four years of marriage. His strength had never understood Althea; it would never allow her image to inhabit its density. Just before eight in the morning, it was already hot, airless under the mosquito net. "*We* fit together," he said, "don't we?"

"Of course," Althea said.

He sat up. She raised herself on her elbow and watched while he carefully rolled the condom onto his penis. "Now," he said. She lay down again, envying him the automatic solace he found in her body. It gave her a sad, distant feeling that this joy did not seem to be in her power to offer as her own gift, but came from beyond her and went to him directly. And it had so much more import for Johnny than any of the more painstaking, maneuvered offerings she could ever make with words. He stole warmth from her flesh without the mediation of her soul. She didn't speak. She had to enter her own state where she could feel the pleasure of hurtling forward, abandoning herself so as to find where Johnny was, a place of warmth such as there was none in her. So as not to be left alone, after she reached him, at last she looked back at herself to discover Althea, whom Johnny loved.

She could feel his happiness beginning to glow out of the open pores of his skin. I'm close, he said. Close! Are you? Immediately she began to condense herself willfully onto a single dark, intensely material point. She grew smaller and smaller, denser and denser, until she could bear it no more, and imploded.

Opening her eyes, she saw him looking into them, smiling, and she saw on his dreamy face that he believed she was an angel, a far kinder and more beautiful person than she knew herself to be (a person with the black hole inside her creating ever more strange ideas). She didn't care about earthquakes at all. She didn't care about saving anyone. She just wanted to bring Johnny into the same evil, magnificent world she lived in. Then he could truly save her.

"I'll go," he said. "You're right."

They rolled onto their backs. Their mingled sweat began to dry into fine tidal grains, but without the slightest cooling. Althea turned her head toward the window, which was shaded by thick hibiscus leaves. Dimness offered no mercy. The sun's blunt heat pressed down, trapped under the corrugated roof.

There was a thinness in the air between them, and Althea realized that Johnny had taken Mongolia from her, taken it for his own. Now there would be hurry. Today had just become the last day of gardener. The last day of cook and of maid. She would have to tell them, pay them all. Time began racketing forward again, a heavy metallic momentum. She slipped out from under the limp mosquito mesh and stood for a moment enjoying the larger, unconfined air. Then into the bathroom to splash water from the bucket over her back. Wet toeprints, drops, smears followed her footsteps, looking bloody on the dark red tiles.

Later, on the day they left their bungalow, she saw a fire at the bottom of Johnny's eyes, saw his body move with the contained elasticity of a stalking cat, like a soldier's whose goal was killing. She hadn't seen him so focused in a year, yet she felt neither relieved nor indulgent. He ordered her out of the bedroom while he stuffed handfuls of already dirty clothing into his duffel bag. She told herself of course he ought to be excited — he was visiting the greatest earthquake of all time, Altai 1938. Instead of reproducing Johnny's emotions within her own, as she was used to doing, she began to be afraid of this departure, which up to now had belonged to her.

9

PEELED, BOILED POTATOES with cheese sauce, fried chicken, and a salad of avocado, tomatoes, and lime — Fortunata produced a surprise banquet to celebrate Maggie's triumph. She'd made food enough for six, so Maggie invited her to stay. They sat eating like friends in a restaurant, sharing a liter of beer.

The night bus to Cajamarca roared by. "You can no longer escape," Fortunata observed.

Maggie said she did not desire to.

"The Comandante liked you," Fortunata said. "What a good idea to invite him."

"Truly?"

"Truly!" Fortunata had been afraid he'd never come. He was a fugitive; he'd suspect a trap. Even during the Rainbow, he'd rarely shown himself. His philosophy was to let the people rule themselves until a problem came along.

"I'm a problem!" Maggie joked. She wished there were a second bottle of beer to share. "So what should we do next?" The idea of the future was unexpectedly exhausting.

Fortunata told her to wait with confidence.

What if the gringa hadn't saved that baby? Would Comandante Oquendo exact some retribution?

"Tch! Don't talk like that, Señora."

Now they realized it was Saturday, for they heard the Pentecostal preacher howling faintly, all the way from Piedras Baja. Behind him was a mini-beeping rhumba of programmed electronic rhythm. The congregation must finally have bought its sound system. Standing up, Fortunata imitated the preacher, looming over Maggie, intoning, *"Saca! Saca! Diablos!"* Out! Out! Devils! She invited Maggie to come and experience the electrified service, with artificial lightning and the sounds of a storm at sea.

Tonight of all nights, Maggie would have loved to see people falling down in ecstasies, and to fall down herself, exorcised and pure. Alas, she'd feel too self-conscious to enter any trance, especially knowing Carson might come home in the middle of it.

With her own forefinger she smeared toothpaste on her friend's incisors, to cover the sinful scent of alcohol, then sent Fortunata off. She locked the inside bolt with the gigantic padlock she'd bought at a motorcycle shop in the States, on recommendation of a friend who traveled. It had cost her fifty dollars. Tonight, its rippling coils and red, uncrushable viper's head seemed fully justified.

She washed all the dishes, swaying to radio *huaynos,* then got into bed and tried to sleep. Her eyes kept flying open, hard and shiny as a China doll's, and in the darkness, just as blind. Would Carson return tonight or in the morning? Or after some unforeseeable interval of days? She turned on the light and tried to read her Russian novel, but by now all the characters were snarled in awful fates. She wished she'd brought along the British country farce her mother had recommended, something light or, God forbid, even inspirational.

Cheer up, she told herself. She'd saved a baby today. She'd made new and important friends for the clinic. Why feel that doom and retribution were due to land upon her? Why feel guilty that Carson hadn't been there? He'd had his own case, the mine accident, to deal with. This situation had been hers. She rolled flat on her back, nearly gasping with excitement as she recalled Fortunata's nervousness when the couple first stepped into the kitchen, and how Luz María had thrust the baby into her arms, and the way Vicente's eyes had met hers. Best of all had been the way the infant had gasped alive the second time Maggie stuck her with the needle.

Surely, if there was danger, Fortunata was friend enough to warn her. It was best that Carson had been away, and not just for Maggie's ego. He might have made a ruinous remark. He'd never believed the Black Rainbow was as innocent as everybody said. After tearing a thumbnail prying out rocks, he'd concluded that force, only force, could have obtained all that road-building cooperation for which Comandante Oquendo was so famous. Maggie had argued that peasants didn't find rock-moving as onerous as Carson did. To end the argument, she'd admitted that Carson might be right, that Nasir and Fortunata could have lied, each for their own reasons.

Today, though, had been a real victory, even Carson would have to admit. A baby had been saved. The Comandante had brought a patient. Why torture herself with speculations? That would be Carson's advice.

She turned on her belly resolved to sleep, to rest, to have a dream; but instead spent the next hours corkscrewing in the sheets. Around two A.M. she began to hear the faint sound of an engine. It came and went phantasmally at first. Twenty minutes later, the truck pulled up. She leapt from bed, ran to the door. First a banging fist, then Carson's voice came shouting: "It's me, babe, let me in!" She slid aside the bolt. Barelegged under her T-shirt, she didn't care how Cantinflas's truck headlights seared her exposed thighs. Let them see, she thought, my husband is here, the only man on earth with rights over my flesh. Nevertheless, she skipped into a shadow when he pushed both doors wide open.

He dropped his bag on the clinic's counter. "What a trip!"

Maggie cried, "Tell all," as she ran into the bedroom to pull on her jeans. When she came back, dressed, Carson was bolting the door, Cantinflas having raced off to Cajamarca with the patient strapped down in his truck bed with a saline IV and a leg splint. Carson had stabilized the wound, but the man needed surgery and Cantinflas was driving to Cajamarca Hospital, twenty hours straight through from the mine, chewing coca leaves to stay alert.

Carson was starving. Maggie uncovered the enamel bowl and watched him wolf down the leftovers of Fortunata's banquet, talking between bites. He still fascinated her unreasonably, down to the way he scattered pinches of damp coarse salt so carefully over his avocado. There had been no rock fall. It was a gunshot wound, with a bad exit and a shattered tibia. From what he could gather, it had happened during a gang fight. "Wish you'd been there to interpret, honey," he said. "I understood about half of what Ignacio was explaining."

"Ignacio?"

"The mine director. I made friends with him." Ignacio said the canyon was fraught with a tension far more significant than any residue of stamped-out terrorists. The wounded man was from Huancayo. He'd been shot by a local. When the Canadians reopened La Tormentosa, they'd hired almost no Rosarinos. Instead, they'd trucked in professionals from Cerro de Pasco, Huancayo, and Ayacucho, violent hardhats whose families had mined for generations, loyal to the death, underground. Conditions were terrible, but wages were forty dollars a week. Locals vainly insisted that since La Tormentosa was not a shaft mine, there was no reason for the company to prefer shaft miners. La Tormentosa used new methods of extraction, profitable in grams of gold per ton of rock. The Canadians were grinding up a whole mountain, crushing it, and dissolving it in acid. Their machines were huge mountain-eating monsters with titanium teeth. There was no time to hire ignorant farmers. Some of the ignorant farmers resisted this idea, thus the envy and the fight. Sadly, typically, the miners harmed each other rather than uniting against the administration. "Get this, though," Carson said. Going up, he'd looked down upon a gorgeous blue alpine lake, half covered by a white plume. Cyanide. They were using the lake as an effluent basin.

"Cyanide," Maggie repeated. The word had an evil sound.

"Mercury, too, I bet. Arsenic. The fish are gone. No trout, even in the river. Stuff ends up down here. We're drinkin' heavy metal." He drained his water glass, slammed it on the table for effect. "Can't boil that shit out. Good thing we're adults. We'll just get liver cancer." Wiping his lips, he predicted defective babies. All the fault of the new president and his gung-ho policy toward foreign exchange. "They won't regulate. Those Canadians have their pristine wilderness up north. Peru? Who cares?"

Maggie hadn't seen him so animated in months. Carson described the mining camp, a raw scarred mountainside covered with the shabby tents and grim cement houses of the workers. They had recreated a village from the central highlands, complete with livestock and women cooking in pots outdoors. Lots of kids and dogs underfoot. There was a cinderblock school and a health post, both unstaffed; and a long barracks for the soldiers who guarded the operation and rode on the trucks that once a month carried the gold out to

Cajamarca, whence it was flown to Lima on a plane rented from the Peruvian air force, thence to Geneva or elsewhere.

The mine director was okay, surprisingly. Ignacio García, a city boy in a fancy leather jacket. He must be the son or nephew of a minister, or a bureaucrat who licensed mine operations. He lacked any skills for this post, but the Canadians didn't care; they'd hired him because a Peruvian was less likely to ruffle feathers or be the target of an expensive kidnapping. Ignacio knew it. He was not a stupid man, even if it had taken him six months to notice that a gringo doctor was available. Ignacio's job was to do nothing. He devoted his time to studying chronicles and myths of the eastern slopes of the Andes. Last night, he'd gone on and on about lost aviators, gold, and the failed Franciscan missions. Despite his pedantry, Carson had found Ignacio far more human than most such officials he'd met during his travels, almost human enough to be shocked by the miners' misery. Carson kicked himself for not listening to Maggie, not going up the mountain sooner. "We talked about setting up a clinic, once a week. Any objections?" They wouldn't pay, but Ignacio might provide supplies out of some slush fund or other. "He's got TB up there."

Objections? Maggie stared at Carson's wrist, its hairs, and the corner bone half hidden in his shirt cuff. Why would she object? "What would I do, stay here?" she asked. To be left behind seemed a kind of punishment, though she knew she shouldn't feel so, not after today.

"We didn't talk details." Carson pushed his plate away. "Ah. Thanks. Right now I'm exhausted, darling. How was your day, anyway?"

"You'll never guess."

"Heap big terr'ist came to visit. No — no, wait. You saved somebody's life." He touched her cheek. "Were you okay, all alone?"

"I did, I saved a baby," Maggie declared. "I had to give her a shot."

"What kind?"

"Rocephin. I kept the box."

"Tell me how you made the diagnosis."

She followed him as he walked into the bedroom, stripped off his clothes, and hung them on the chair, his male body shining. He praised her medical work; before she'd finished he apologized, asked to hear the rest in bed. Maggie agreed. After all, he'd spent sixteen hours riding up and down the mountain, and it was past three A.M., and she'd been talking for a while already. She lay on the bed. His neck was getting burnt, leathery, but the rest of him had stayed transparent, skin like a painting by El Greco. She reached to touch the small, hairy hollow in the center of his chest. "Let me just take a shower," he said.

She tucked the mosquito net in place, took off her own jeans again, pulled up the sheet. His shower was quick. When he came down the hall, into the bedroom in his towel, damp and smelling of pink Lux, Maggie forgot what else she was going to say, because he was standing close enough to the bed for her to pull his towel off.

She admired him with all his dark-haired mystery hanging right at her eye level. "What's the big idea?" he said.

"You," she said.

"You," he said. He looked down at her as she kissed him, and he said what a pretty sight she made. She grabbed his ass and pulled its halves gently apart, which caused his knees to buckle. Quickly she slid aside to let him duck under the net.

They didn't wake up until ten, when Maggie gradually felt the sunlight trying to penetrate the wall beside her. She stretched and lay contented; her small waking movements woke Carson too. "Today is going to be not boring," she predicted.

"Let's hope," said Carson.

She could have told him about Vicente, but they made love again instead.

Despite yesterday's dramas, the clinic smelled more than normally of dust, as if it wanted to return to its years of hibernation. Carson agreed to lock up and walk to Piedras Baja, find Luz María, and give the baby his official bill of health.

"We worked," Maggie exulted aloud. "Both of us." They posted a note, promising to return by two.

The sky was the deep, opaque turquoise of a fifties postcard. Tons of light fell out of it. On the white dry road, they held hands except where rocks or ruts prevented them. For some time they stood on the bridge, twenty feet above the river's brown rush. Maggie considered telling about the Comandante here, but the waters were too loud and the world felt too complete around her. Carson said it was amazing how this water could look so natural, combing and seething around the rock pylons, when it was also full of poison. As soon as they stepped on dry land, he told Maggie she had to go up to Cajamarca right away and report the mine effluent to the authorities. He'd filled a Coke bottle with lake water and it needed to be analyzed.

Maggie didn't want to leave the valley just yet. Was Carson sure there was a problem?

Carson believed she ought to go — there was a bus that afternoon. Their friend Klaus Wechsler would know how to get the water tested and what to do with the report.

They'd begun to walk under the first wall of the hacienda's *casco*, tall and thick as the wall of a prison. Maggie said, "There's something I've got to tell you." In one sentence she divulged the visit of Comandante Oquendo. "We should ask him what he thinks."

Carson stopped walking. "Hold it, wait, no way." He hoped Maggie saw the folly of dragging the Black Rainbow's leader out of retirement. Given that he hadn't revealed himself, it might even be dangerous to let on that they knew who he was.

"I think he knows I know."

Carson rolled his eyes. "I kinda hope not."

"He's probably already aware of this problem. Maybe he has some ideas!"

"Yeah, like blowing up the mine. This is serious, dear. We've got to bring Klaus Wechsler in on this. He'll help us figure out what to do. About the water and about your newfound friend."

Klaus Wechsler was famous as the gringo who'd stayed on teaching at Cajamarca University even while nine Peruvian professors were murdered by the Shining Path. Carson had gotten his number at a cocktail party in Lima. "He's this crazy German," the man had said. "Nice guy, though. Wife's Argentine. He's going to be your only other gringo in the area, and he's lived there forever, so you'll want to get to know him." Of course, it had turned out that Klaus and Carson had several friends in common.

Maggie admitted that Klaus might have some ideas.

"Look, I know the bus ride is a pain," Carson went on, "but you'll have fun with Klaus and Liliana. You need a vacation."

"Then so do you," Maggie retorted. One day she'd cease to be infuriated by the calm, reasonable way Carson told her about herself.

"You know I can't go," he said in a heavy, falling tone. "Don't be so insecure. Look at it this way, this could be a bigger contribution than we ever hoped to make. The most important mission of your life, honey." They could save hundreds of people, without even making them say "Ah" or take their clothes off.

Don't condescend to me, she thought. In this grove, the mango trees were in flower, darkly-bright green crowns surrounded by a coral haze. Pollen drifted thickly on the ground. If she left Carson in Piedras, everything that happened to him would be real, her own experiences barely worth remembering.

Among the dirty stucco buildings, squadrons of extra-small mosquitoes hung aimlessly until the foreigners drew near. Then they hummed excitedly, zeroing in on the fragrance of unfamiliar blood. The gringos wandered amongst courtyards, threshing floors, pillars, and mazy walls, waving their arms against the bugs, until at last they came across a little boy who said he'd lead them to Luz María, who lived with her mother in what must have been an overseer's cottage or a guest house, connected to the main house by a pillared walkway. Maggie and Carson stood disconnectedly outside the open door while the boy went inside.

Enormous hen-and-chick plants, green and pink, grew from the tops of all the walls. Deep in the house, a radio faintly played. Maggie peeked into the cool and gloomy front room. Just inside the door was a life-sized saint in a glass case, with fake flowers and tinsel and a slitted wooden box for donations. Fortunata had mentioned how this family of devotees had rescued him ten years ago, when the priest had stopped coming and the church had fallen into disuse. Maggie stepped inside, wishing he'd speak to her as he must have spoken to her grandmother, but his blue glass eyes just stared obliquely into nothing. Had he lost his power? She prayed anyway, if yearning for resolution could be called a prayer. Outside, Carson yawned and waved his hand across his face to dispel mosquitoes.

Just then Luz María appeared clutching her baby, again wrapped tightly in its blanket. "I decided on Lady Maggy as a name," she cried with false cheer. "It repeats my initials! Are you coming to say you'll be her godmother?" Carson made a small, wry mouth while Maggie introduced him formally.

"She's well," Luz María said to the Doctor. "She sleeps." She uncovered Lady Maggy's face, submerged in its own fat cheeks. Maggie saw the tenderness of this life, how it had burgeoned and made room for itself. All at once the canyon seemed to arrange itself around the baby's body, not exactly to protect it but to celebrate it.

Carson made a small movement of impatience, and Luz María led them back through the house to a walled courtyard. It had a packed-dirt floor where chickens scratched and a litter of puppies roistered, trying to catch their mother dog. When the puppies all turned at once to see the new arrivals, the bitch shook them off and raced around a corner. Corn cobs were drying on looped strings against one wall. There was a cement sink with an iron bucket standing in it, and a pigsty behind a fence, which stank. A radio blared away, connected to a long, dangerous-looking, twisted red and blue electrical cord coming down from a second-floor window. At the center of everything sat Luz María's mother on a rocking chair. She was a widow in black, with a set mouth, who sat unraveling the sleeve of a pea-green sweater. She nodded at the gringos but didn't smile.

Carson put out his arms and said, *"Bebé."* His pronunciation of this word sounded a bit like Elvis Presley's, though no one except for Maggie would have known this. Luz María handed the child over, her face registering objection.

He took Lady Maggy in his arms with such an obvious tenderness that anyone could imagine the uncountable numbers of children he'd taken from mistrustful mothers all over the world. Nonetheless, Luz María clamped her arms over her breasts, just as she'd done yesterday in the clinic, watching narrowly as he lay her baby on a bench. First he put his face close to the baby's and asked her in English how she felt after her travails. Then he unwrapped her, gently scratched the bottoms of her feet, spread the palms of her hands, lifted her eyelids, upper and lower, and peeked into her tiny ears. Pushing her nose tenderly, he picked her up and cooed at her, moving his head from side to side. Lady Maggy opened her fathomless black eyes but didn't follow Carson's gestures; her eyes seemed not to register. Was theirs a darkness of surface or of depth, Maggie wondered. She was a little scared of babies, not knowing what to expect. The child was awfully young.

"You aren't watching me," Carson warned the baby. "She's been sick," he said in English to Maggie, "but she's also real small. Skinny. Unresponsive." He jiggled her foot again to prove this. Lady Maggy shut her eyes.

"Aren't Indian babies different?" Maggie said. Since childhood she'd seen them, riding impassively on their mothers' backs. She was grasping at straws; Luz María was mestiza and could have nearly as much European blood as Maggie.

"I could be wrong," Carson admitted.

"Maybe she's just a little slow. Like her mom!"

Carson shrugged. Smiling a big, toothy smile, he gave Lady Maggy back to her mother. "Tell her to eat well, feed this kid, and bring her in next week. Say we're keeping tabs on the recovery. We'll weigh her up, give her some vitamin drops. In a couple weeks we'll see clear signs of retardation, if they're coming, but don't mention that of course."

Maggie translated, sickened by the lies even a good cause seemed to require. Worse yet was her own selfishness. How could she have refused to travel to Cajamarca! Did she want more defective babies to be born? She managed a polite goodbye to Luz María. "And please give my *saludos* to your husband."

Luz María looked confused, then laughed. "Who? Oh, him! He's not my husband! Vicente visits me."

Her mother suddenly cried, *"Demasiado!"* Too often!

"Life is *complicado*," Carson said brokenly to Luz María, who shrugged, not even trying to understand. In the mango grove, he told Maggie it was tough to diagnose a child so young — even an expert would want a hair analysis. He kicked himself for leaving his neonatology books in storage.

"I'll have them shipped down when I go to Cajamarca," Maggie promised. Since deciding to go, her thoughts had taken a new and thorny path. "I want to confess my awful thought. I gave this baby a shot, right? Now she turns out retarded? I mean, I'm not saying . . ."

Carson knew exactly what she meant. Doctors always had to deal with superstitions and local mores; they reaped the mistakes of past practitioners. Even the States had malpractice mania, a related syndrome. There was one consolation, as awful as Maggie's thought: if his water theory was correct, Luz María's wouldn't be the only child with problems.

"Okay, then here's an even worse thought," Maggie said. "Say Oquendo has seen a few of these cases, and he's maneuvering us into a position to be blamed, and that's the reason why he came."

Carson sighed. "You invited him." Then he shrugged. "Look, he brought us a patient. She had pneumonia. You saved her. So far everything's cool."

"Do you, in this line of work — I mean, we have those guns, did you ever worry about getting killed?"

After a little while, Carson said, "Ingratitude. Ignorance. Misunderstanding." It was the first half of the title of his divinity school paper, which he'd abandoned. Larry had strongly criticized it, saying even its title sounded like Marie Antoinette's complaints.

10

MAGGIE WOKE UP gasping, her hands gripping the bar on the back of the seat in front of her. She'd slept only a few seconds, but during that time the bus had sailed off the tip of a curve and started falling, end over end, toward the bottom of the canyon. Luckily, her screams must have come out muffled, for her seat neighbor slept on stolidly, basket on lap, chin on chest.

Hard to believe that she wasn't about to die. The bus must be driving along the edge of a cliff, for there was nothing to see outside except the full moon nailed to the middle of the sky. Her face swam in the window glass, smeared and dim as a corpse coming up in a river. It seemed unfair that the nightmare hadn't exempted her from dying, that she'd have to die again, maybe in the next few hours. Even if the bus didn't crash, it was easy to be murdered by bandits. According to Fortunata they always worked at night. Put rocks across the road; stopped the bus; killed the driver and anyone else who resisted; and then stole everything from the passengers, down to their clothes and shoes, leaving them naked on the freezing *puna*.

Bandit season had just begun. It ran from harvest to planting. When there was less farm work to do, the men of the Rosario went up into the hills to scratch for gold. Each family guarded its own secret vein. Don Nasir kept a scale and blowtorch, but the more enterprising doubled their profits in Cajamarca, where gold was higher and market goods cheaper. Bandits knew the system. Some were farmers from the sad, mean villages just inside the *puna*'s lip, others were ex-terrorists, continuing violent careers without a political excuse. During gold season, they waited for the bus to pass.

Last year, they'd killed eighteen people on this very road. Because of them, the mine maintained its army platoon to guard each shipment and was even said to be building an airstrip to fly the gold direct to Lima. What bandits might do to a gringa, Maggie hated to imagine. There had to be one person on this bus with clothes sewn full of gold.

She stared ahead, out the windshield, alert for roadblocks or suspicious movements. The road looked stiff as plaster, weirdly oversubstantial in the headlights. Once in a while the lights bounced off an overhanging rock and shot back through the cabin, revealing the silhouettes of men's heads up front and the curling tendrils of smoke from a cigarette.

It gave her confidence that she remembered her way from the bus station to Cajamarca's main plaza, even without Carson. Down and down, then right. First, on the high road, she followed a mountain peasant woman in a tall straw hat and bunchy skirt, a gunnysack over her shoulders. Something small moved inside. Guinea pigs. The woman walked with a fast, rolling gait, like a partridge running away.

Her energy felt as thin and grating as the dawn that bleached the mountains, roof tiles, and high walls. It was miraculous to be alive and walking, light as a ghost, into the city. Bottle caps, torn plastic bags, dead leaves, broken glass, all the refuse of the road glinted with an edge of extra reality, as if she'd taken psilocybin. Useless to wonder whether she should have come as each foot hit the ground with a satisfying certainty. Her bag was light, and for the moment she knew where she was going.

This must be how Carson feels, she thought.

At a chopped-off corner she turned down into the skinny tilted streets where a few people hurried along the high, narrow, broken sidewalks. Explosions of rattling steel: store owners rolled up their iron curtains to show liquor, irrigation pipes, shovels, brooms, radios, blankets, hams. Clothing stores had horrifying Caucasian mannequins, male and female, made of plaster in long, un-Peruvian proportions. The men had flattop haircuts and leered with gorilla teeth; the women pouted like sex dolls. This one wore jeans and a cotton bra, that one showed off navy-blue elastic socks, one long one short, under a plaid school skirt. Her pink skin was chipped to white beneath, her breasts grubby at the tips from being pinched.

Nearer the town's center, buildings grew older. The sun turned to liquid gold with diagonal shadows.

A man drove up slowly behind her, murmuring in a voice full of meaning. In case Maggie didn't understand, he rolled down his window and showed his tongue, a magenta worm writhing in his blocky purple face.

She could not escape, she thought, no matter how purely transparent to the world she felt. Just as she was blond here, she was also tall.

How often Julia had complained without the slightest embarrassment about the incompetence, the gamecock vanity of foreign men; and laughed about how the Hindus cleaned their rear ends with their hands. Once, Maggie had dared to chide her mother for cultural arrogance. "Don't kid yourself," said Julia. "They think you're just as stupid and filthy."

"But Mom, you were born in India!"

"You don't think of yourself as Mexican! Do you?"

Sometimes, Maggie had retorted.

Right now she was aiming for a cup of coffee at the Restaurant Caribe, before the government offices opened, but she found its front door sealed by a screaming orange poster announcing it was closed for avoiding the new sales tax. The windows, too, were shuttered, padlocked.

She'd go back to the plaza, kill half an hour at Atahualpa's death stone. She and Carson had visited it together; it would be fun to tell him she'd gone back.

Even at this hour, a dozen young guys were draped around the fountain, chatting and smoking in a large patch of sun. To avoid them, she circled into the surrounding topiary zoo, wandering behind a snail, around a swan, past a green Inca's head six times as large as life. His cedar hair was due for a trim.

The air was mint cool, liquid in the shadows. Its smell put Maggie's teeth on edge, reminding her of the trip to Maine her family had made when they'd first come up from Colombia, and Calvin had proclaimed a vacation before they'd even found a house, before they'd left the Howard Johnson's.

✤

A log cabin! When the Goodwins' rented car pulled up and Maggie saw it, red under the bluish shade of sharp-needled trees, like a toy or an illustration, she half expected the door to swing open, revealing a pioneer woman in a long dress, mobcap, and apron: Abraham Lincoln's mother displaying a fresh-baked pie.

Inside, the logs were varnished, like the skin of a roasted, basted turkey. All very American. Julia lectured her girls about the rag rugs on the floor, representing industry and thrift. In the cupboard, Maggie and her sister discovered mismatched plates with pictures of sleighs and bridges and presidents. Sonia claimed the best one, a creepy green interior featuring an empty cradle. On TV, a peacock spread its rainbow tail.

Summer in Maine was colder than winter in Colombia. The bright sun gave no heat; the lake water turned lips blue-black, the same color as itself. Sonia and Julia didn't get wet. They built a fire and sat in the cabin all day, keeping the windows closed because Sonia was still delicate from her typhoid. When Maggie came in from watching red squirrels or loitering near the ice machine, the place smelled sickly of sour milk, warm Coke, and VapoRub. Sonia was a teenager now, eating whatever she pleased. Ice cream, Jell-O, so many sodas she let them go flat without even finishing. Maggie had needed three dental fillings on arriving in the States, so she could only sneak the dregs from Sonia's soda bottles. Fur thickened on her teeth. She didn't care.

Maggie was proud of her immunity to all things Sonia succumbed to. Amoebas, three kinds of worms, now typhoid fever. Staunchly she marched through bog and rain with her father, learning how to catch the slimy, pretty trout. She got credit for being brave about impaling worms, removing hooks, and slitting fish bellies. She tried to get credit beyond Sonia's by not whining, nor letting her poor father know that, the whole time, what she really wanted to do was run out into the walled garden of their old house in Cartagena and pick a green mango and eat it with salt. Knowing that her father wanted the same thing (or at least his version) was what gave her strength to follow him.

"Daddy's had trouble," Julia had admonished her two girls. "Be on your tippy-toes."

Tippy-toes was not enough. The day after they got back to Connecticut, their father said he was going to work, but he went to the airport instead and was gone for five months. When he returned, they were still living in the Howard Johnson's, but snow had fallen and the pool had frozen. Julia had forced the girls to go to school in discount snowsuits whose thin nylon shooshed like a washing machine, so that when she climbed onto the yellow school bus, Maggie could hardly hear her schoolmates' taunts. "Is this what people wear in South America?"

Calvin brought a stuffed caiman for Maggie, a fringed shawl for Sonia, and for their mother a rough emerald set on a golden heart. He swore he'd never leave again. Maggie was almost too big for his lap, but she crawled up on it to ask him why he hadn't taken everybody with him. She was thinking only of herself; perhaps her mother knew this, for Julia had laughed like a platter dropping on the floor.

Here was Peru's coat of arms, all carved in shrub. Cedar, blackish green and dense. It must have taken twenty years to achieve these shapes. The stone lay flat in the shadow of a spouting whale. A meter square, roughly cut. A plaque said this was the actual stone on which Atahualpa was garroted by the Spanish, not decapitated, as the ignorant *campesinos'* myths would have it.

Either way, Maggie would have been better prepared for a replica. How long to wash off the stains of blood and fire?

Four hundred years ago, twenty generations, the Spanish rode in one evening and found Atahualpa soaking in his spring-fed hot tub. That day he'd won a battle against his brother: they were having a civil war. Atahualpa was illegitimate, but his father's favorite. He'd received the tiny force of conquistadores with majestic distraction, flicking wet bangs out of his face. Hours later he was a captive, his army decimated. He ransomed himself with a roomful of gold, but the Spanish didn't have the slightest intention of setting him free.

Atahualpa hadn't prepared for the fact that they didn't consider him to have a soul. On this stone, he'd converted to Christianity, then, minutes later, they'd garroted him, pressing even his wretched cries back down into his throat. A black rainbow had appeared in the sky. Within weeks the Inca empire was gone forever, and the conquistadores were the richest men on earth.

People in Piedras loved to think about the caravans of gold that had been sent to ransom Atahualpa. On word of his execution, the gold had been thrown into caves and lakes as the Incas girded for the short and fruitless war. Yet the treasure was still theirs, hidden beyond the eastern crest of the hills, in the black rain forest where no one lived anymore.

The plaque was also engraved with a poem, supposedly Atahualpa's dream on the night before his execution. Maggie read under her breath in Quechua, trying to shape her mind and tongue to the emperor's despair.

Ima phuyun haqay phuyu	What cloud is that cloud
yanayasqaq wasaykamun?	Dark, that follows me?
Mamaypaq waqayninchari	Perhaps it is the weeping of my mother,
paraman tukuspa hamun.	Turned into the rain that falls.

"You meditate on the death of Atahualpa," a man's voice said. "What do you feel?"

Some plaza lout, not genuinely interested in history. Maggie whirled around, ready to defend herself, or vanish.

It was Comandante Oquendo.

"What are you doing here?" she cried, shocked even to recognize him here, and without his cowboy hat. Today he wore a collared shirt and black leather sneakers.

He squinted into the sun. "*Buenos días, Doña Maggie,*" he said pleasantly, reminding her of her manners.

"*Buenos días,*" Maggie said. What was his real name? She struggled to recall it.

He was attending meetings in Cajamarca. "Today I thought you might pass through this plaza, and so I waited for you here."

The health office wasn't open yet, and the Wechslers were hardly expecting her at any specific time. She could invite him to the Hotel

Imperial, where they made real cappuccino, and crepes with caramel jam, and there were tablecloths. But then she'd have to pay for both of them, because it was expensive. This would not be the right protocol for starting a relationship with a revolutionary, even one who was retired.

After the long ride, she told him, she'd been looking for a coffee, but didn't know where to go.

"The Caribe," he said. "It's good there."

"It's closed."

"No." He pointed up the side street where a man stood seemingly distracted, then glanced up and down and slipped inside.

Maggie had not noticed the child-sized door cut into the wood of a larger one, not sealed by the tax-evasion poster. Comandante Oquendo didn't bother with furtive maneuvers. He just ducked in, and she followed.

Inside, it was as dark as King Tut's tomb, illegal operations taking place without benefit of electricity. The place smelled of onions and steam. A few shafts of dusty light came in through the badly fitting shutters, like thin rays of hope in a dungeon or a church. Vicente walked to the back, weaving his hips between the tables. Maggie stood for a few seconds, afraid of bumping into something.

When her eyes had adjusted, Maggie saw a large woman sitting behind a counter piled with jars of candy and cartons of cigarettes. She wore a stained white smock and was obviously the tax-evading owner. Vicente was talking to her, leaning over, flirting the way a young man flirts with a woman past her prime. As Maggie walked up, he raised his voice slightly and introduced la Señora Doctora Maggie Goodwin de Miller, the nurse who with her husband was offering free medical services to all of the *gente* of the Rosario Valley. Maggie had saved a baby yesterday by giving it a shot.

"How good Don Vicente," the proprietress said. Maggie beamed stupidly, barely recognizing her own name and description. Her knees were cold with excitement. Vicente Quispe Cruz, that was his name. When had he left Piedras?

The café owner was Doña Maclovia, and she exuded an earthy, postmenopausal confidence, the kind of woman who was often painted on murals to remind people that birth and death are an eternal cycle. Doña Maclovia laughed when Maggie ventured a small joke about whether this restaurant was closed or open. "Now that we have a government, we must pay," she said. *"Verdad?"*

"Each living thing must eat," Vicente said. "The peasant as much as the president, the rat as much as the cat, the shark as much as the politician."

"Only in the glory will we receive our true patrimony," Doña Maclovia said.

"Sooner," Vicente said.

At the only empty table they sat with their backs to the wall, to maximize the light. Maggie felt they were in cahoots, passing judgment or handing out certificates to everyone else in the world. By now she could see quite well. The walls were sea green, soiled with smoke. Many small tables the size of her mother's bridge table were scattered across the floor. At them, a full quota of customers bent over, slurping soup. All men, their clothes and skin faded to the colors of smoke and earth.

Doña Maclovia's daughter came by, and they ordered chicken soup and coffee.

"So, how was your bus trip?" he asked.

"A nightmare." All Peruvians loved to hear complaints about their roads; it made them feel superior and brave. "And your meetings?"

They would take place that afternoon, Vicente said. He was consulting with a group of *campesinos* who were hoping to dismantle the system by which they became enslaved to the agricultural credit bank. Maggie asked how they planned to escape, and he said, rather sarcastically, "With strong infusions of American dollars."

Maggie laughed nervously.

"The small man carries the big man on his back."

Maggie nodded mutely, and regretted having come. She had nothing to say to this person, nor to anyone else in this place.

All at once, half a dozen men pushed back their chairs and filed toward their table. Leaving, the first one tipped his gray fedora. He was a dignified man wearing a jacket and a thinning blue shirt buttoned tightly at the neck, but his expression wasn't pleasant. Vicente nodded in curt acknowledgment. The next two men made eye contact with Vicente, then with Maggie. The fourth walked too close past their table, bashing into the edge where Maggie sat. He apolo-

gized with threatening insincerity, muttering something insulting —
Vicente selling himself to gringos, Maggie thought.

"*No te metas*," Vicente retorted. Mind your own business.

"*Cuídate*," warned the man. Watch out.

The fifth man stopped, and was introduced as Vicente's uncle. He
had a wide, smooth, pleasant face with small teeth, separated like a
smiling cat's. Maggie thought better of giving him a hand to shake.
He cut his eyes at her, and asked Vicente whether they still had an appointment.

"Don't worry, Uncle," Vicente told him. "This is Doña Maggie.
She looks like a gringa but is one of us. She and her husband are doctors in our valley."

"I don't see her," the uncle said.

"One o'clock," Vicente called after him. The uncle gone, Vicente
grumbled a bit about his former associates. They were lacking in intelligence, they'd gone sour, they could consider nothing new. He had
to leave them all behind.

"You're well known in Cajamarca," Maggie observed.

Vicente barked a laugh. "Too well. *Momentito*," he said, and got
up and went to the kitchen, where she could hear him scolding and
asking questions. Coming back, he shrugged and said that the soup
was all finished. "Because of me," Maggie said, "isn't it?"

"It doesn't matter." Vicente cleared his throat. "Doctora, you already know that I am Comandante Oquendo."

"Yes." Maggie shrank down in her chair.

"I know about you also. For example. You are divorced. Your uncle is buried in Huaraz. Your mother was born in la India, and if I
saw her photo, I would think she was a rich Limeña. You worked
with rebels in El Salvador. Your father had shoe factories in Mexico
and Colombia. *Correcto?*"

"His businesses failed," Maggie said. "Now he works in his
brother's hardware store."

"Making you a true South American," Vicente said teasingly. "I
was wondering why you would choose this work, as the daughter of
an international business owner."

"Citizenship of the heart," Maggie dared to say.

"So it is. Before I met you, I thought your cook liked you too
much," Vicente admitted. "Many say you have another motive for

coming to Piedras. Unfortunately, due to historical reality, in my country that is how we think. Those who say they want to help are either selfish liars or insane. Having observed you, I changed my opinion. I will stop the evil tongues."

The main one being his own, Maggie thought. He was too young to be a killer. Thirty-two, tops. His fingers were thin, his feet not much bigger than hers. But the killers of the world were often young. Their faces always surprised Maggie when she saw them in the newspaper. Vicente was listing all the motivations that local people attributed to Maggie and Carson. They were CIA. They were counter-terrorism experts sent to spy on, arrest the Piedras population. They were drug agents. They went out at night in a silent helicopter with an infrared scope to find Inca tombs, then secretly dig up the golden artifacts for sale at a huge profit on the global antiquities market. They were becoming millionaires in Piedras — buying babies for re-sale to sterile Europeans. They'd sterilize any adult man or woman who walked into their clinic. Children they'd anesthetize and secretly remove one kidney. Or else they'd just drug the children, or kill them, and freeze them in that child-sized freezer (visible on the counter if you looked in the front door), and shove the bodies into suitcases, to be mailed north and dismembered, the vital organs and limbs used to repair the bodies of sick old white people. Gringos were Pishtacos. Piedras mothers threatened to send their misbehaving offspring to the clinic to have a shot. Worse, a house call. "Be good, or I'll call that gringa to come and give you an injection."

Maggie's mind reeled. She was glad she'd never understood what enmity had surrounded her and Carson. To think they'd felt bored! She said, tremulously, and resenting it, "Is your real name Vicente? Or Oquendo, Comandante Oquendo? What may I call you?" She wished there were something to fiddle with on the surface of the table, but nothing had been provided. There was only thick transparent vinyl over a flowered plastic tablecloth, made in China, of appalling ugliness.

Vicente shrugged. "Oquendo was my name of war." The Black Rainbow days had been a game of adolescence, he said, and like adolescence they were gone. She must call him by the name his mother gave him, the name everybody used. Vicente.

Maggie said, "You'll send us patients, then, Vicente?"

"Have I not already done so?"

Maggie babbled, flustered, that she hadn't meant to discount the gift of Luz María's visit. She tried to reiterate that she and Carson were sincere; that besides a few medicines, sincerity was all they had to offer. They could cure accidents and diseases, but only if people asked for help. She managed to insert that they were splitting a salary offered by the Peruvian government for one person; they certainly had no dollars to offer, though Maggie knew that the lack of an economic base in Piedras was the most fundamental health problem everybody faced, blah blah.

Vicente said that the true wealth of this life was for human beings to live in love and friendship. For this reason he had met her here in Cajamarca, to confirm a sentiment, to apologize for having mistrusted her and caused her and her husband many problems.

Coffee arrived, hot and thick as Maggie remembered. Vicente loaded his cup with sugar and she followed his example. He asked whether it was true that her grandparents had arrived in Piedras on a raft, the only part of Fortunata's *relato* that seemed less than credible to him.

"They came from the north," Maggie told him. "After their raft broke up, they walked."

Maybe it was possible after all, Vicente said, since only after the building of the hydroelectric plant had the waters swelled upstream and the Rosario become innavigable. Piedras was once an *oroya* crossing, with a rope to stabilize a balsa raft. The mine owners built the first bridge in 1967 — a good thing, since nowadays the waters were too strong for any raft.

In the old days, that part of the river was known by the name of its hacienda, Chigualén. Most of the hacienda's workers lived in a clutch of hovels on the Piedras side, indentured servants without the right to vote, virtual slaves under the law. They crossed the river each day on the raft to work in the fields of their *patrón*. Don Héctor was not among the worst. He had a true love for his workers, and they in turn felt lucky to have him instead of someone else. When agrarian reform came in 1965, they did not kill him or destroy his property. Most other landowners returned to the coast, proving their lack of affection, but Don Héctor stayed on, keeping half of his house and the small plot permitted by the government, farming it himself, wearing rubber sandals like a *campesino*. He'd died in 1979 at the age of ninety-one, asking to be buried in the earth he loved.

People said he was a *brujo,* a witch, for day and night he walked the hills, gathering plants, bones, and stones. He cured his *peones* using Indian methods, which worked on them because they were Indians, or because there was nothing else. After he died, his fat book on local herbs had been taken away by one of his sons. His four children still lived on the coast, in the palaces and *quintas* of his wife's family. They'd left behind only his piano, which was too big to carry over the mountains, and so it remained in the chapel, one leg propped up by bricks. Yes, it was possible that Don Héctor Saavedra Ibáñez had had some magical powers. On the day agrarian reform was announced, he got so angry that he placed the gypsy curse on General Velasco. Within a week, Velasco was having his leg amputated.

As Vicente spoke, Maggie kept stifling a seditious thought: this uneducated peasant had a greater curiosity about the world than Carson, who'd had every advantage. She reminded herself that there were different kinds of intelligence, some that shone and others that bit down. She asked Vicente how he'd come by his interest in Piedras. He replied that anything was fascinating when sufficient attention was paid to it. This was what Maggie believed as well. She'd have listened to him for hours, but now he asked where she was going.

She was going to ask the health officer about pollution from the mine.

"Bad idea," he said, instantly serious. "You will be removed from your post."

"Ayúdame." Help me. Maggie blurted this out, as if he had stepped on her chest and this was the squeak that emerged. She told him about the cyanide plume. "Don't tell Luz María." Vicente nodded encouragingly, compelling her to continue. Like the walk of the drunk she had seen in Piedras, each statement seemed to become a mistake that must be corrected with another. Mercury, cadmium, lead, cyanide. Retardation. Deformity. Stillbirth. Cancer. Was Vicente Lady Maggy's father? She didn't dare to ask. He cocked his head, listening. He ticked his spoon against the enamel mug.

She felt her words drawn down and weighed.

"Don't we have to do something?" Maggie concluded.

"If your feeling is so great as you say, Doctora, you will not be able to avoid action."

She raised herself up in her chair and insisted that a person could not wait for certainty, nor for everyone else to decide to do what was necessary. It sounded as if she were willing to take up arms against the enemies of the people, yet it was not a statement she was willing to retract. It seemed important not to go back on her words, so she made herself stop talking.

"The problem in the waters may be grave," said Vicente. "Lamentably, in Peru it can be dangerous to involve the authorities." They'd been given extraordinary powers to fight against the Shining Path. These powers had gone to their heads, and had not yet been legally removed.

Maggie argued that as a gringa maybe she could accomplish things a Peruvian couldn't.

Vicente bit his lip. As gringos she and her husband might be able to bypass the bureaucracy completely. They must think carefully. A report today would not save Lady Maggy. Even if the health officer did not remove the Doctores immediately from the Rosario, he would ask for a laboratory analysis, a long list of confirmed cases. "When he receives the report, he will put it in a file. When the file grows fat, he will send it away to Lima. Doña Maggie, you and I should discuss this matter further, with your husband. Surely together we can design a full solution."

"Please do come, and meet Carson." She allowed herself to imagine the three of them at the kitchen table, plotting to take over the valley again. Peacefully. Legally. A water treatment plant, or at least a filter in every hovel. Medicines, literacy classes. Solar ovens and fruit cooperatives. Prenatal and well-baby care. An official pardon for Vicente.

Maggie looked into his black eyes and saw past the surface, saw at depth his intelligence, luminous and redemptive and detached and honest. His thin mouth smiled with dry, sly humor. No wonder he'd been able to manage a whole section of the canyon. He smiled at her more broadly, and she smiled back, almost willing to let go of her seriousness, though she knew she'd better not.

At this point Doña Maclovia threw open a window at the back and coarse, thin light the color of sheep's wool filled the room. The air from outside was cool and smelled of nothing at all. Only one man was left eating. The light bathed his creased forehead, whitened his unwashed shock of hair, and just then it seemed to Maggie that this place was more real and alive than anywhere she'd ever been.

"Thank you for your sincerity," Vicente said.

"And you for yours," said Maggie.

The other man finished his soup and left. Doña Maclovia called to Vicente, *"Mi vida,"* my life, and asked when he'd come back again. Alas, she was closing now.

"Not before you have died of love," he flirted.

Maggie and Vicente emerged blinking into the sun.

Maggie said, "I ask myself if I should be afraid of you."

"Only if we are left alone," said Vicente. Seeing her look of alarm, he said, "That is a *piropo,* mere flattery. Never be afraid of me, *jamás."*

Jamás. The most satisfying word for never, encompassing eternity both past and future. Never feel afraid of him. Fortunata had used this word. She looked at Vicente. She'd already decided that his face had an appealing subtlety or mildness to it, like that of her friend Katie's British husband, whose good looks Maggie hadn't particularly noticed until Katie had said she'd married him partly because she'd thought she could look at him without ever getting tired. Now Maggie decided she could trust Vicente's face, or what she sensed in it.

He said, "Yet, I want to ask for something more. I want to be trained as a medical assistant. Can you ask your husband?"

He was a supplicant, Maggie realized, recoiling. He stood before her, scrubbed, in his cheap clean clothes, squinting into the sun, and she recalled a man who had once come to the gates of the Goodwin house in Cartagena, a tattered man holding a baby deer he'd caught and was trying to sell. The tiny creature's eyes had been crusted, weak, but so had been the man's. Julia had sent him away, saying that such cruelties were not to be encouraged.

"You?" Maggie blurted.

"Doña Maggie, you cannot stay in Piedras forever. And I, I simply need a job."

In fact, their contract stipulated training a local successor; it was one of Carson's disappointments that they hadn't found a single candidate. She told Vicente this, but added that, to be quite honest, his qualifications might be considered negative.

Did she think all revolutionaries were thugs? He had studied at the university for five semesters. There everyone had been intoxicated by violent ideologies, but in the school of his own experience he'd unlearned them. Bombs and assassinations were as destructive as they seemed to be. Nowadays, thank God, they gave a bad name to any cause. He smiled ironically as he said it had long been time for Peru to build a healthy path to the future. Maggie must understand? A path as enduring as an Inca highway, but not one made of stone.

Yes, she said, yes. Still, wasn't it dangerous for him to take a job in public?

"I am as you see me, no more, no less. They won't bring me soup in a restaurant. I have no real profession. I sit in El Mirador raising trout and avoiding the authorities. If I walk a straight line, I hope they will consider me rehabilitated." When the new president was elected, Vicente had seen the handwriting on the wall, and had written a letter to Lima repudiating the Black Rainbow experiment. Perhaps this letter was the reason he'd never been arrested. "If not?" He shrugged. "One can waste one's life preserving it."

"I'll speak with Carson," Maggie promised. Ashamed to have underestimated Vicente's education, she resolved to push for him strongly, even if she had to give up part of her own salary. Well, there wasn't much to spend it on in Piedras. "He's the boss."

"*Claro, claro.*" Would she go now to the telephone office, to call her parents with whom she had not spoken in so many months? No? Then to the house of the Wechslers? "In either case, I must leave you here. When I visit Cajamarca, I am constrained to avoid certain places."

Maggie thought of movies she had seen. A message in a piece of bread. A whisper at the window. What was the worst that could happen? She hoped Vicente wouldn't ask her and Carson to kill anyone. How had he known the Wechslers' name?

11

ALTHEA COULD HAVE walked between these same stuccoed walls, broken by the stone portals of Spanish palaces. Pregnant with Uncle Christopher, she might have passed under this studded wooden gate, this one with a lion's head knocker which had surely hung on it since the turn of the previous century. This endless nunnery wall would have been scrawled with the same palimpsest of political slogans, some fresh, others barely visible under coats of whitewash. *Viva, Fuera, Muerte* — Long Live, Out With, Death To — then a name. Lower down, festoons of pee stains.

Maggie could hear her grandmother chuckling. Who pisses on a nunnery? Dogs and men.

The street grew steeper and narrower, its houses newer. It became a manmade canyon lined with cement walls and gates of welded sheet iron. Some houses were protected by broken bottles set into cement. Wealthier palaces had electrified barbed wire tiered outward, like jails. After this morning's encounter, Maggie felt rightly guarded against. Surely this was what Vicente felt, or even an Indian woman daring to walk up this street wearing her many short skirts of homespun wool.

The street had two axes of tilt, upward and sideways. The Wechslers' side was higher, walls rising so abruptly they seemed ready to topple onto the street. Their gate was starred with rust, painted a faded green. Maggie rang the bell.

The first night after Maggie and Carson had arrived in Cajamarca, the Wechslers had come for Pisco sours at their cheap, damp-smelling hotel and soon whisked them out to dinner at a steak place. By the end of the meal they'd persuaded Carson and Maggie to move into one of their children's bedrooms. Their driver, Muñoz, had showed up the next morning to fetch them. He'd bargained for them in the market, loaded the Wechslers' Jeep with boxes of supplies. Not wanting to create misleading first impressions, Maggie and Carson had refused the Wechslers' kind, repeated offer to have Muñoz drive them down into the canyon.

Carson and Klaus had hit it off. Klaus was a little older, but they'd led parallel lives, starting wild and ending up committed. Carson's traveling days had been spent in Goa and India and Bali and Nepal; Klaus's all over South America. Klaus had a wife and kids; at the Wechslers' it was impossible for Maggie to avoid thinking of Maxine, Carson's long-time girlfriend, as Carson's wife. And Carson and Maxine had believed in neither marriage nor procreation. Besides friends in common, the two men each had friends who'd died of overdoses, others who'd ended up in ashrams, still others who'd started businesses and now drove gigantic Saabs and Volvos plastered with progressive bumper stickers.

Maggie enjoyed listening to them reminisce, even though it made her feel like an appendix to Carson's real life. She'd never expected to be friends with Liliana, who was ten years older, was so well dressed, and had four children.

Recently, however, Liliana had floated into her mind as one example of a mother. On this next visit Maggie had planned to scrutinize her more carefully, to see whether a woman was a continuous person before and after giving birth. Back in the States, as soon as her friends had children, Maggie rarely saw them again. If she did, they mostly talked about their kids' precocities and problems, asking after Maggie's life in pitying afterthought. With the advent of her new sensations down in Piedras, Maggie had wondered belatedly whether she'd discounted her friends' new orientation too quickly, in ignorance of the reasons for it. What if having children *was* the true purpose of life?

Now, with all of the uncertainties and bloody possibilities (however distant) that had recently arisen at the clinic, Maggie decided to let the idea of motherhood slide for a few years. She hoped she wasn't just finding an excuse not to make a real decision. Well, but in the most extreme case — which Maggie, standing in front of the Wechslers' gate, was momentarily prepared to imagine — having a child might make her more vulnerable, more conservative, easier to suborn . . . Here, she stopped herself.

Either she was being responsible and realistic or else she'd gone a little cuckoo down there in the canyon. She could still observe Liliana in hopes of gaining some perspective.

Pichit, pichita, thin rubber flip-flops sounded on cement, approaching from the other side of the gate. With a rusty creak, the peephole flipped open to show the black eyes of the Wechslers' housemaid, Clorinda. She was smiling, Maggie could tell. *"Señora, hola, como está."*

Maggie was glad to be recognized. *"Hola,* Clorinda. Don't call me Señora. It makes me feel old."

"Very good, Señora." Clorinda giggled and shut the peephole. With some ungreased clattering and screeching, the gate now opened. *"Pas',"* she whispered. She was a short, round woman who always wore the tightest clothes she could find. Today she had on white stretch pants and a striped blue and white top over a torpedo bra. Since Maggie's last visit, she'd gotten a perm of crisp shiny curls like a doll's hair.

Maggie complimented her, forgetting her ruminations momentarily.

"Qué hay?" Clorinda asked. What's new? *"Y su esposo?"* And your husband?

"Lo he abandonado," Maggie teased, I have abandoned him. Clorinda made a sympathetic face, sucking air between her molars, and led her into the house, whose silent, immaculate rooms always had the deserted smell of fresh floor wax.

"Seño-o-ora!" Clorinda yodeled. Maggie enjoyed her insouciance. Last visit, they'd talked expansively, Clorinda exposing her husband problems, Maggie admitting she felt ashamed of her divorce. Would Clorinda have heard of Comandante Oquendo, of the Black Rainbow's ideal kingdom at the bottom of the canyon?

The memory of Vicente was like a secret intoxication, or an infection she was bringing into the house. Her skin itched with it.

No answer to Clorinda's yells. Clorinda explained that Liliana had just returned from Buenos Aires, where she'd deposited the older son and daughter in their boarding school. Just now she might be at the market. The Señor was working in the back, and the two younger kids, Laurita and Klaus Junior, were at school; they'd return later in the afternoon. Somehow, as Clorinda spoke, Maggie understood that the two older kids were *traviesos,* drug addicts who needed to be in the prison of a boarding school, that Liliana was easily cheated in the market, and that the Señor worked too hard. Clorinda might soon say of Maggie, "That skinny gringa came again from the Rosario in those ugly boots of hers, without her husband."

Liliana decorated her home in the style of long-term expatriates all over the world, with a bareness both elegant and rustic: pillows covered with local weavings, spotted cowhides on the floor, and a mask over the fireplace, a demon with mirror teeth. Her own paintings hung on all four walls. They depicted faceless figures tied down by many strings in a pale, abstract landscape. Maggie wondered whether these related to Liliana's life in Buenos Aires or some more recent form of social torture. The smell of oil paint was exhilarating, though, and she caught herself vowing to do some pencil sketches of the canyon. Last time she'd been here, she'd made and broken a thousand resolutions. To wear makeup all the time, modulate her tone of voice, keep cut flowers always in the house. She'd understood a phrase that had echoed through her childhood, bitterly repeated by her mother: that for most of Johnny's career, the Baineses had lived "on the economy." As a child Maggie had visualized her grandparents cresting an abstract wave of thrift, but now, living on the economy herself, she understood why Althea had felt insecure, displaced at British parties. This was a feeling she should treasure (and she thought again of Vicente), for it must resemble how poor people felt visiting the world of gadgets and advertisements. If only every afflicted soul could know that this disease was universal, a disease without a heart.

"*Qué tal, Señora, qué tal su viaje.*" How was your trip? Clorinda asked.

Maggie told how she'd sneaked into the Restaurant Caribe and unexpectedly run into a former patient from down in the Rosario. "*Oh, qué genial,*" Clorinda marveled. "*La Señora se vuelve revolu-*

cionaria." Oh, how fabulous, Madam is becoming a revolutionary. The Caribe was where seditious meetings were always held. Leftist professors, union leaders, students, unrepentant terrorists, and disgruntled members of the police reached agreements and disagreements in that café. It was never open, never closed.

"He invited me," said Maggie. "I didn't know."

"'He'!" said Clorinda, giggling. "Who is this 'he,' tell?"

"The father of a sick baby," Maggie said. "I forgot his name."

Shillong, northeast India, 1944.

Althea usually refused these invitations, but Johnny had been gone into Nagaland for weeks, and in recent days she and four-year-old Julia had begun recovering from the same serious cold, coughing in their damp chilly bungalow. A party would be nice. Possibly Julia could be turned loose in back bedrooms with other children; and maybe, just once, it would be fun for Althea to spend time with other women.

Mrs. A's houseboy opened the door, motioned Althea and Julia toward the sitting room. Julia sniffled and clutched Althea's hand as they reached the inner door. The place was just as Althea had expected, warm from a coal fire, smelling of freesia. The walls were yellow and the decor lavish: a silk-cushioned divan, oil portraits, a tiger-skin rug. Julia crouched to inspect the tiger's teeth — real fangs, shiny from crunching the bones of other animals. She touched one with a fingernail. "Smelly tiger," she said to her mother. "Pee-pee smell."

"Shh!" Althea bent down to confirm this observation, then agreed that tigers stank. More likely Wullie, Mrs. Abercrombie's horrid, nearly hairless terrier, had lifted his tight little hind leg above the tiger's snarling head, to prove who was superior. There lay Wullie, on his cushion by the fireplace, wearing his striped sweater. Julia was not allowed to pet him. She didn't want to. Once, she'd tried and he'd snarled at her, showing stumpy brown teeth.

Colonel Abercrombie's wife, the hostess, was not in sight. She was in the back of the bungalow, chugging her secret dose of paregoric. There were no children present. At scattered tables women with long upper lips and narrow chins sat talking, leaning toward each other, oblivious to the mother and child standing just inside the door. The volume of noise was double what it usually would have been. Althea paused, wondering what kept them so absorbed and excited. Generally they murmured, more genteel and boring than they'd ever be in England. Finally Mrs. Liddell stood up: "Oh! Dear!" She fluttered across the room, whispered to Althea, took her arm. In the next room was the sensation of the party, an Assamese soothsayer, see, there, installed in an armchair in the corner, surrounded by British ladies.

A few women's heads turned in time to see Althea stunned by the sight of this priest, a man in cotton robes with golden skin. He could have been Brother Jesūnandā's twin, except that he wore large rings on all his fingers — diamond, tiger eye, ruby, to harness the influences of the nine planets. Mrs. Liddell whispered the explanation. They'd brought him from a temple beside the Brahmaputra where they worshiped the menstruation of the earth. Althea must ask her husband why its spring ran red once a year. That made it a temple for women, its priests devoted to satisfying women's scandalous requests. Whoever dared approach this teller was told sometimes of a past life, sometimes of the future. Sometimes of the present: Sally Batchelor's husband was sleeping with an Indian girl he kept in town. Was Althea brave enough? Not all the ladies were. Some wondered whether he'd talked to their servants in advance. Almost all he said was true, some was useful. He'd flatly refused to predict anything about the war, especially who would come back and who not.

Bridget de Jager's cook was the thief who'd stolen a ring.

Seeing them talk about him, the soothsayer exclaimed a faint greeting, waving his long, translucent hand: Come! All the women watched as Althea towed her child toward him. Such a funny child, golden, small, her mouth set into a hyphen. Why did that woman insist on bringing her everywhere? Could the Baineses not afford an ayah? The husband was often away. Texan bloke, a grizzled Wild West prospector, he never found a thing.

Althea thought them all ridiculous, and their husbands, who ineffectually paraded on the maidan hoping to be called up to fight. Johnny's work was secret now, mapping jungle routes to Burma. The

Baineses enjoyed pretending he was a madman searching for gold under the jungle duff. An easy pretense, not so far from truth, they joked to one another.

Althea was tall and rawboned, pale eyes like a shooter's. She wore a blue paisley cotton dress, the same one in which she was often seen; it had pin tucks in front, its own cloth belt, and an ungenerous gathered skirt with a flat, slightly faded place behind showing where she sat on it. Her hair was streaked with gray and fell in lank, sandy waves to her shoulders. The child was finer. Even her ordinary frock adapted itself to her small body, as does the clothing of an aristocrat. She would be tall like her mother, yet Julia's sallow skin and moon face looked suspiciously Eurasian to the British. Mrs. Baines insisted that her daughter's looks came from French and Cherokee ancestors of her husband's, but with him gone so often and so long, and the way she avoided female company . . . who knew?

No Englishman would have found Althea attractive. Women also recoiled from a scraped rawness that shone from her face. This was what a woman became when she lived like a native — that is, did not have enough money. It happened to missionary wives, too, the ones who went off into villages and ate bugs and lost their husbands to poisoned arrows. White skin could not withstand native life. Measures must be taken or a woman's face grew over with fine, fine wrinkles. Her mouth puckered. She'd be old before her time.

The fortuneteller cried, "American lady!"

She went to him, her only welcome.

"This child," he said, taking Julia's hand. "She has the mark of the God."

"She was an answered prayer," Althea said. She and the priest gazed into each other's eyes for a moment that extended and extended, overlong. At last Althea whispered the name of the convent where she'd stayed.

Julia jerked her hand back and put it behind her skirt. She heard the man tell Althea that her husband would succeed in his life work, but in a way that would disappoint him. The goddess Durga would grant Johnny a vision, but when he tried to explain, no one would listen. His real mission was spiritual; he must find satisfaction inwardly. If he resolved this karma, he'd be reborn in the pure realm of those gods who have minds but no bodies.

What about me? Althea said.

"This child," the soothsayer told her, "will be as a stranger to you. She must walk her own path. Only in her daughter will you find your own true child."

Then the soothsayer took Julia's small face in his hands. "The lives of the God's children can be difficult," he said. "If you truly want to be the God's child, you must allow other people to be less perfect than you are. Forgive them. Remember, they are not like you."

Julia squinted at him. His teeth reminded her of Wullie's. He wore a diamond on his thumb, where rings should never be. She did not want to be the God's child. She had a real father and she wished him to come home.

"What did he say to you, your daughter?" the ladies all asked at once.

"He told Julia she was a chosen daughter of God." Althea laughed lightly, certain that India's pervading mysteries would protect her as she spoke a blatant, dangerous truth. "I wonder what it means? She must have a great destiny."

Julia hid her face in Althea's skirt while her mother lied about her. She was trained never to ask for anything in these houses, but her eyes drank up the details with an outsider's hunger: soft furniture, carpets, parquet floors. Going with her mother everywhere, she saw what Althea did not: how the other women invited her out of pity, the women whose chins tipped up, whose dresses were soft and new.

She kept her face scrunched in the blue cotton paisley until the women began to say, "Are you shy? Come, pretty girl! Little goddess! Have a piece of cake!"

Althea replied in the voice she expected her daughter to imitate: "Yes, thank you, ma'am."

Julia acquiesced, repeating the words as she stared down in mortification at Althea's dusty laced oxfords, counting the stitches around the sole. Six, seven . . . No, she did not want to be a child of the God.

Clorinda led Maggie all the way back to the roofed patio. Klaus sat working at a laptop computer at one end of the long, deeply varnished wooden table where the Wechslers ate their meals. A greenish light filtered in from the walled garden. Above the barbed wire Maggie could see the sky, a pale, lowering gray. Liliana's honeycreepers flitted in their cages. The parrot on its T-stand scratched its pale blue eyelid with one claw.

Klaus closed the computer. It beeped, turning itself off. He reversed the stack of papers and weighted it with a carved black stone that Maggie had once held in her palm. An obsidian alpaca, an offering to the Earth Mother, with a hole in its back for fat. Klaus often found Inca things in his test plots. In this country, he said, you could hardly scratch the ground without turning up some fragment of pottery, cloth, bone.

He stood up to greet her. "Maggie! What a nice surprise. You look wonderful." Harder to imagine Klaus naked on a beach, stoned out of his mind, than Carson. Klaus's hair was prematurely gray, and he dressed like a missionary, in khakis and a plain blue shirt.

"Liar," Maggie said, kissing the air left and right of his cheeks. "I haven't slept."

"I never lie." Klaus's English was so good that he avoided all the normal German mistakes, even rounding the tight corners of his *w*'s with a barely compressed whistling sound. No "vash-and-vear" from Klaus. "Where is Carson? How long do we have the pleasure of your company?"

"He's down at the clinic. I decided to take a break," Maggie lied. "Go back tomorrow."

"How can you call this a break? Twenty-four hours on a bus? No, stay longer!"

"The clinic's heating up," Maggie said, realizing the truth of this. Her life was becoming a rats' nest, which she'd created. "I sort of need to call my parents. It's been six months."

"That will be good," said Klaus. "Your mother calls every few weeks and gets a bit hysterical. Liliana keeps on saying you're fine, even though we haven't seen you. You have letters also. I don't know where Liliana has kept them."

"God, how embarrassing," Maggie said. "Sorry you've had to deal with Julia."

"All mothers are like that," said Klaus. "You should see Liliana. If the kids are late? Bwaaah!"

Liliana was out shopping. Klaus hoped Maggie didn't mind relying on memory to find her way around the house. His eyes flashed upward, and she was sure he was observing her hair, a solid slab of bus dust.

"I'd love to wash up." Hot water, European shampoo.

When she was clean she must come out for coffee on the patio.

At the bathroom sink, Maggie washed her face, neck, waist, and arms in warm water with green herbal soap from Germany. Grime had infiltrated everywhere. The soap smelled clean and delicate, not fake perfumey like Peruvian soaps. Still, she'd lived in this country long enough that its green flecks looked like defects that should have been removed. She felt proud of this perception and stored it up for Carson.

"Why don't you just take a bath?" Clorinda was standing in the doorway with fresh towels. Apparently she'd been watching for some time. Maggie almost lost her balance; she'd been standing on one leg, the other leg bent, holding her foot under the tap.

"Gringos are special," Maggie said preemptively. "Special" was a mild, teasing insult in Peru.

"Very special," Clorinda agreed, smiling rather darkly, Maggie thought.

Now they heard the front gate clatter, and the rumble of the Jeep. Clorinda made a caught-in-the-act face and sped off down the hall-way, and Maggie sat on the edge of the tub to put on her crusty, crumpled socks. In the living room Liliana was arriving, wearing her hat and sunglasses from the market. Behind her came the driver carrying two large baskets full of produce. "Maggie! You came!" Liliana cried, rushing toward her. "Oh, I'm so happy! Your mother is very worried. We were both wondering when we would ever see you again."

Maggie kissed her cheek, bright as metal. Liliana's hands on her shoulders were strong. It felt nice, all this enthusiasm. Where was Carson? Would she like something to drink? Breakfast? Did she need a shower? Rest? Panchito was at school in Buenos Aires, so Maggie could have his room for as long as she cared to stay. She hoped Maggie didn't mind a boy's room, the girl's was being used for storage.

Lunch was shredded flank steak and cabbage in a warm vinai-grette; boiled yams; a salad of watercress, red onion, farmer cheese, and tomato; French rolls and Gouda cheese and real butter, because Cajamarca was a dairy area; and Chilean wine thick as blood, furry from the heat of its desert. For dessert Liliana promised one of the guanábana meringue pies that made Clorinda irreplaceable.

As they ate, Liliana said that anorexia was the style in Buenos Aires — even Panchito was looking very thin. No, argued Klaus, he refused to believe Panchito had a psychiatric condition. He was just a slave of fashion.

Klaus's experiments were either failures or successes, depending on how you looked at them. In his most recent field test, he'd set loose a thousand beetles hoping they'd eat another type of beetle. In no time, a flock of birds had swooped down and devoured the good and bad species alike. An unexpected result, an experiment worth repeating! Then, when it was Maggie's turn to talk, the Wechslers were proud of her for saving a baby, but said she'd been brave or foolish to treat an infant all alone. Had it died, the villagers might have stoned her. Did she know that unattractive legend about the Pishtaco, a white man in uniform who ate the fat off children? Had she heard how mothers threatened their children: "Do what I say or else the gringa will come and give you an injection"?

"Along those lines . . ." Maggie told them about the Canadian mine and Lady Maggy's poor reflexes. She'd combed through every statement in advance to make sure it bore no hint of Vicente.

"Report to the health officer immediately," said Klaus. "For your own protection."

"But he won't do anything, and we aren't sure it's real."

"You know it is real," Klaus assured her. "How can it not be real? Even if he does nothing, if there is any complaint? Better he has your report."

"We'll get kicked out for interfering with foreign exchange."

Klaus and Liliana both admitted this was possible. "In Peru," Klaus began, but then he stopped because Clorinda had tiptoed in to remove the plates smeared with yellow and red oils. He continued speaking when the maid had barely stepped away. In Peru, he said, it was never important to find out the cause of a problem, only to assign blame.

Maggie had always hated this gringo habit of talking on, deprecating local flaws in the presence of the servants, even if the servants didn't speak the language. Now she saw that a sudden silence was just as damaging. There was no solution. Looking at Clorinda's bra strap cutting into her retreating back, she knew all of their existences to be unjustified.

She asked Klaus and Liliana how they'd navigated their lives here, especially during the years of violence. Had they never been tempted to leave?

"Klaus refuses," said Liliana, smiling brilliantly.

"I minded my business," Klaus said. Reaching for his wife's hand, he added that they were both lucky enough to lack personal enemies. Klaus also believed that the Sendero had noticed that his work benefited *campesinos*. He began a long story about how they'd sent a cell member to accost him at a bank window just as he drew his paycheck. Meanwhile, Liliana cut huge slabs of pie, and Maggie protested, and Liliana insisted she was too thin, as anorexic as Panchito.

Then Klaus declared: "You and Carson better buy a two-way radio."

"We'd need a mighty big transmitter to get out of the canyon walls," Maggie said, taking a bite of pie. The fruit had a slick, collapsing texture. It tasted like roses and corruption, smoke and perfume. Its slight bitterness was masked by four layers of sweet meringue.

"What are Mommy and Daddy giving you for Christmas?"

Klaus would never speak to Carson so disrespectfully. Maggie explained that Carson believed it better not to own a radio. "You know how people are. They already think we're from the CIA, the DEA, *and* the FBI." She changed the subject, inviting Klaus and Liliana down to visit, to see the clinic. "I'll get Fortunata to make her green corn soup."

"Green corn is not in season until January," said Klaus.

"Stuffed hot peppers, then."

He nodded and smiled, but Maggie didn't think he was agreeing.

"More pie," Liliana commanded.

"I have reasons for what I say," said Klaus.

"Klaus, this poor girl is eck-sausted," Liliana said. "Maggie, Klaus is right, but he will save his lecture for later on. Yes?"

Under clean sheets, beneath Panchito's poster of a sweating, straining Michael Jordan, Maggie fell asleep like a child come home from the wars. Even the smell of Panchito's sneakers, piled messily in the closet, was reassuring. When she woke up it was cold and the light had changed. Her first coherent thought was of Vicente. She couldn't remember whether he was staying in Cajamarca overnight or not.

Her watch said four-thirty. She dressed rapidly and went out to the patio, where Klaus was still working. Liliana had gone to pick up the children, and the government health office closed for the day at lunch. With some satisfaction Klaus told her that if she wanted to go to the phone office to call her parents, she could not, since a bomb threat had just been placed on all the Entel offices in the country.

"Whose threat?" Maggie tried to keep the urgency out of her voice.

"Who cares? They are all a *manga de tarados,* a bunch of morons," Klaus said. "They want attention but they have no program." In Cajamarca the bomb squad had found nothing, and surely the whole threat would be dismissed tomorrow. Entel was too expensive in any case. Maggie should make her calls from the house, though it was early yet. Maybe she wanted to read her mother's letters first.

Klaus led her into his study, just off the patio. This was a room she hadn't seen, ill painted an ugly, shiny tan color. Two long tables set at right angles supported a jumble of electronic equipment: a fax machine, a telephone, a radio telephone, a full-sized computer, an outmoded dot-matrix printer. All of the electrical cords played through two large, humming red boxes with luminous dials, voltage regulators. One wall was covered with maps of the departments of La Libertad and San Martín, stuck with pins that must represent Klaus's projects.

Maggie found herself wondering whether Klaus himself was in the CIA. She often had odd, Peruvian reactions to gringos, reactions that would have included her had she been standing outside herself. She stepped closer to find Piedras on the map. No sign of it — the map had not been revised since 1960. She found that it did show the *oroya* crossing, a tiny stylized canoe; and the Hacienda Chigualén, a maze of structures with one lone building set apart with a rounded end and a cross — the chapel. "You've got three pins in the Rosario," she observed.

"Oh, those are ten years old," Klaus said, leaning over her shoulder. "Potatoes and bananas. Did you and Carson visit El Mirador yet?" No. "You should. It's much more beautiful than Piedras. Their fiesta in April is quite interesting." He handed Maggie the stack of letters, which had been imprisoned under the claws of a stuffed armadillo. The vast majority had come from her mother. She feared their content, but found the envelopes reassuring, crackling blue tissue paper addressed in Julia's uniform, ladylike hand. Klaus recommended she station herself on the living room couch, to read them under the alpaca blanket.

12

March 13. Dear Maggie, How is everything down South? Sending loving thoughts to you each day. Excuse no paragraphs — must cram all on 1 sheet lest P. O. employees be tempted by fat envelope. Ye olde trichés of S. America. Tulips coming in here. Dad accepted at Longwood Club on 1st March. Happy as clam, alas hurt back same weekend, practicing for Spring tournament. Abed complaining 3 days, now hobbling & cheery until reminded of entry cancellation! (Yours Truly relieved, thinks tournament too competitive, no longer a game.) How are you adapting to new life? And Carson? Happy in his healing work? Hope you are not infected with yellow fever or worse. I do long for news. Friends ask, I don't know what to say. Please send a letter soon. Love, Mom. P. S. We phoned your Grandmother on her 79th. She forgot she had a granddaughter in Peru. Next yr. we'll have sm. party for her 80th (despite unpleasant age reminder! Better to unite loved ones in life than at graveside). Pls. return to our hemisphere B4 then. When vacation? You're v. v. important to us you know. TAKE CARE. Love, Mom and Dad.

April 10. Dear Mags: Sonia, Alexandre and boys here from Paris for 2 weeks. Left yesterday. Cal & I loved visit but now enjoying quiet. Boys sound like little geniuses speaking fluent French, tho' Alfred does poorly in 2nd grade. Your sis. thinks he'd be better off in U.S. school? Pipe dream, alas, as Alexandre cld not get licensed in U.S. They took away 5 suitcases of sneakers and appliances. Quite worried now, no word from darling youngest in over 3 mos. Hope you're enjoying self? All well, my letters coming? (Silly question, if not.) Spring rains, cold here, gray & damp, good for ducks, flowers. Love, your mother, Julia.

[Undated, postmarked April 28.] Dear Maggie, Hate to put such news into a letter but see no alternative. Your Grandmother is in hospital. She was suffering from dizzy spells & just like her told no one. Monday, fell getting out of bed. Luckily boyfriend (!) had spent night (!), & called an ambulance. What a way (!) to learn that my mother (your Grandmother!) is involved w/someone, but we must be grateful. Name: Lester Weeks. Married 4X (at their age I spose this matters less) w/ grown children from all xcept last wife. (She, short-term, bombshell, 35!!) Owns antique shop, downtown Boston. Flexible hours, loyal to your G.M. — always at hospital when I call. On wknd. I'll take train up to help G.M. reinstall self @ home. No bones broken. Drs. say elbow bruised with poss. nerve damage, awaiting further tests on heart & brain. How soon can you fly home? I called number you gave and Mrs. W. (lovely lady) kindly says that in a real emergency she can get driver to you in ½ a day. But she has not heard from you. If something happens (God forbid) to you, how is anyone to know? Your old Ma wishes you'd live near a phone, movie theater, grocery. What is the attraction of poverty, filth, danger? Things life is better without & most societies endeavor to outgrow. Where is nearest police station & do they have telephone? Cal reading papers, says Peru on good track. NYT, WSJ report phone share speculation! No kidding, I know rural areas are "underserved." I'll buy stock (joke). Cal & I wonder daily how you are. Pls, pls call or write ASAP. Love, Mom.

May 10. Dear Mag, Your Grandmother discharged from hospital after only 4 days, all tests neg., don't relax yet, see below. 1st the good news, Cal's back fully healed & he's having swing videotaped as preventive. Yr. 2 nephews building model space station in tiny Paris living room. Cal & I ordered from toy catalog, unaware of size, now Sonia unsure it will fit thru door! May have to hang from ceiling — boys forbid slicing. Here in CT, drought & heat. 'Tis but May, already given up on lawn, don't care what neighbors think! Yr Grandpa Johnny pooh-poohed climate change. Wish he were here to explain why shade plants die. I planted bachelor's buttons and African marigolds so at least we'll have some flowers. Does it ever rain on you? I try to imagine your S.A. honeymoon cottage. Tile roof? Bougainvillea? You, or maid, keeping spic and span? Tropical abodes are charming, tho' yrs. truly never liked small sharers (bats cucarachas lizards, r — — and s — —). Ok, now bad news, I did call Mrs. W. again but not wanting to mention family trials to stranger said nothing xcept when did she plan to see you. Again she did not know. If we don't hear from you by 31st May I must ask her to send driver down and fetch. Well here goes a 2nd page.

After what I saw at yr Grandmother's house it is my feeling and your Father's that she is deteriorating, despite tests, no longer competent to live alone. Says anything — filler for memory lapses — filth and impropriety — insulting fabrications, all symptoms of mental waning. For ex. while I was there, neighbor paid visit, professional woman, lawyer, to show off recently adopted baby from Colombia thinking G.M. would be interested. G.M. spoke Spanish to baby, made it cry, tho' 'twas only 10 months old, and then G.M. accused new Mother of slave trading! Rude, volatile is one thing but then also gets out in car and drives. Has killed the balsam in her drive w/ much backing into. House not thoroughly cleaned. ETC ETC ETC No sense of own condition. You'll believe when you see, if not from my lips. We must take steps before serious problem occurs. I am asking you to return to the U.S. no later than July 4 to help, advise. Will pay for Carson too if nec. (Flyer miles.) (Can hardly ask Sonia, considering job, 2 boys in school, plus recent long visit w/boys and hubby in tow.) Have not mentioned anything to your G.M., you know how stubborn she is & resistant. Am also thinking: soft spot for you, listens more to you than anyone, you can ease transition. Solution could be simple, hiring Salvadoran, free rent to a student as you had. Must also consider, visit homes, sunset villages, communities, nice older professional people lectures, activities, doctors, etc. Do keep open mind! Plan to stay at least 3 wks. American ticket counter at Lima has prepaid tix for you. RSVP-ASAP-PPP (extra p's = pleases). Your loving mother and father.

At five-fifteen, Laurita and Klaus Junior clattered in wearing school smocks. Maggie smiled and sat up, and the children greeted her as cheerfully as trained seals, but before she could think of something fun to say, they disappeared, backing swiftly from the room, as if she were a sick person they'd never met before.

Minutes behind them, Liliana found Maggie immersed in an anthropology book she had discovered in the wall unit. One of the Wechslers' few books in English, it explained all cultures in terms of their consumption of animal protein, even Aztec human sacrifices.

"*Qué tal?*" Liliana perched at the edge of an armchair, glancing at the envelopes and papers scattered across the coffee table. Now she was dressed in a nubbly, dark green silk pantsuit with a heavy silver necklace.

"I love this writer," said Maggie churlishly, hoping Liliana wouldn't see the stupid tears that had welled up at the children's rejection. "A chicken in every pot is all that matters to him."

Liliana kept gazing at her until Maggie let the book fall closed, and said, "My mother wants me to fly home immediately. She's taken my grandmother as a hostage. If I don't drop everything and go, she'll put her in an institution." This was an ungenerous summation, but Maggie would have been even more ashamed to describe the way she'd experienced her mother's letters. They'd made her yearn for snowflakes, new shoes, and her old Mazda sedan — even for Julia, with all her guilt trips and false certainties.

"I think your mami puts on you a lot of pressure," Liliana said.

"How can she get under my skin from such a distance?" Maggie complained. "It makes me not even want to call her." She was throwing herself on Liliana's mercy, acting like a child — and because Liliana was a mother, expecting her to understand. That wasn't fair. She sat up and put her feet on the floor and thanked Liliana for placating Julia, who, unsurprisingly, had called six times as often as she'd said.

"You have to call," Liliana reasoned, "but after talking first to Grandma. Check out the real situation. Your mother easily becomes hysterical. Maybe if you explain to her everything, she will tranquilize herself."

"That would be nice," Maggie said.

Mexico City, 1964. When the Goodwins left Mexico City on the airplane, Maggie sat on a woman's lap, a woman who was not her mother. A Mexican dowager in a wool suit, with varnished hair, orange skin, and enormous earrings like an Aztec emperor's. Maggie, five, didn't get a window, but she had learned the power of her own pert, North American cuteness, and now she prevailed on a stranger to help her see the view.

The woman squeezed Maggie, as if she might fall out as she looked at the various sights. Look, how small the cars. See the roofs of the houses, the avenues, the mountain ridges receding gray and yellow. The scratched thickness of the window seemed to separate them decisively from this dwindling, perfect, toy world which in any case was not the place Maggie was leaving behind.

As they banked over a residential section Maggie asked the lady to find her house for her. It was the one whose roof was covered with a red bougainvillea. It had a wall around it, with grass inside and an iron gate for the car.

The woman glanced helplessly across the seats at Maggie's mother. Julia shrugged and smiled, abandoning the Señora to her own devices.

"Choose any one, the most beautiful house for yourself," the lady said. She used the formal *usted*. Then she peered toward the window herself, gently pushing Maggie aside. "Oh, look, there's a big house for you. With a bougainvillea! That house is yours, *princesa*. The castle for your return."

Maggie knew this was a lie, the return most of all. The Goodwins were moving to Colombia. Lock, stock, and barrel, her father had said — a phrase that started with amusing clicks but at the end boomed shut behind you like a vault.

Maggie wriggled in the Señora's arms and looked down.

"Do you see it?" the Señora asked. "Or is it that one? Look, there, I see the red bougainvillea."

"Yes, there it is!" Maggie chorused with false agreement. Maybe the lady had seen it after all. Even if not, she wanted the lady to feel better, too. Scores of houses had ridged barrel tiles, all gleaming in the sun. It didn't matter which she chose. No house, from the air, was hers.

At their real house the bougainvillea was red-violet mixed with pure scarlet, a color that could set fire to midnight. The vine grew up one of the corner posts of the front porch. Its twisted greenish-brown trunks were the forearms of a giant who had plunged his fists into the dirt and was holding on tightly to something underground.

"My granddaughter's calling from where, the moon?" Althea said. "How are you, dear? And where?"

It was easy talking to Althea on satellite delay; she left a pause after her words into which Maggie could naturally answer. Perhaps it took an effort for her to speak. "In Cajamarca."

"Where? Can't hardly hear ye!"

"*Cajamarca, Peru!*" Maggie shouted.

"Oh, Cajamarca? Peru! I liked Cajamarca," Althea said. "It was green. Johnny and I ate cheese."

"That's right. You remember Cajamarca well, then?"

"Mm-hm."

"You know I'm living in Piedras!?"

"Where?"

"Piedras? Chigualén! The hacienda! Where you washed up, remember?"

"Oh, yes," Althea said, and seemed to be gathering breath for a further statement, but here the satellite took advantage of her pause. There was a clip on the line, then a long, enforced silence in which Maggie could hear the signal bouncing up into outer space and down again.

"What did you say, Grandma?"

"Maggie? Is this Maggie Goodwin speaking?" Fumbling sounds, a thump, as if Althea had dropped the phone. "Just a minute."

Maggie began the conversation again, shouting, "How are you feeling, Grandma?"

"Fine, dear."

"Mom said you fell. Are you okay?"

"*How boo how,*" Althea said.

"*How boo how?*" Maggie said. "What does that mean?"

"Chinese for 'Good, not good.'"

"You mean so-so?"

"That's pretty good where I come from."

"How was it in the hospital?"

"'Turn to the wall, Mrs. Baines!' Ha! They found what they deserved."

"Julia thinks I should come up right away."

"She'll boss you right around if you let her. Don't you worry about me."

Maggie wavered, wondering whether it was cowardly or prudent not to discuss Julia's more sweeping intentions. "So where did you learn Chinese, Grandma?"

"*Shan tsao-liao,*" she said. "That's 'earthquake.' Means 'the mountains walked.' There's my whole Chinese vocabulary. I learned it at an aftershock. With Johnny."

"I thought you stayed in a convent. I thought you weren't allowed to go into the field." A camp hand had tried to molest Althea early on, Maggie recalled; later, she'd had Julia.

"Near the end he took me along to Kansu. But even that was long ago. Well, *ka-ching, ka-ching, ka-ching,*" Althea said politely. She was no longer speaking Chinese, but imitating the sound of shekels dropping into the telephone. "Honey, so glad you called."

"I saw his grave, Mr. Saavedra's grave," shrieked Maggie, unable to contain herself.

"What's that?"

"Don Héctor? The hacienda owner?"

"Oh, yes. He'd be dead by now."

"I think about you all the time, Grandma. I'm following in your footsteps!"

"I'd think you'd find them kind of slow." Althea panted a little of her laughter into the phone while another person spoke to her from the background, a man. Lester? Maggie saw a dapper tweedy character with pink baby cheeks. "Well, I do hope you come visit, but not before Christmas," Althea said. "And it is lovely to hear from you, dear, and enjoy yourself, and give my love to your husband, whatever his name was, and boil your water, and please don't worry about your old grammaw. I don't want to waste any more of your money. So nice of you to call."

Click.

❖

"Let me tempt you to stay longer," Liliana said at dinner. "Tomorrow we can go to the baths. The market. I have found such a wonderful wood-carver. Horseback riding, if you are interested. You can get relaxed, then argue with your mami, and then you will need to rest some more. Stay all week, as long as you like. For us it is really nice. Me, I don't like any of the other wifes around here."

I guess I'm a wife, after all, Maggie thought with some discomfiture.

"Too many mining engineers coming in," Klaus grumbled. "They rarely bring their families, but if they do, the women aren't that interesting."

"Those wifes," said Liliana. "Canadians. Minnesotans. Fat and pale. They look eck-sackly like rabbits."

At this comparison, the children brightened. Klaus Junior stuck out his incisors and singsonged, "I am Mrs. Olaffsen!" They had been told to speak English at this meal, for the benefit of the guest.

"Never do that in front of her," Liliana told him with feigned severity. "Mrs. Olaffsen *is* a rabbit, but that is our secret, just between us."

The children nodded at each other, making bunny ears with their hands and wiggling their noses. Liliana told them that since they were bunnies now, they should nibble their peas and carrots, which they were permitted to do without utensils.

Maggie repeated that she was needed at the clinic, but she sounded feeble, even to herself. Just now she would have liked to live with the Wechslers forever.

"Carson can manage alone," Liliana insisted, reaching down the table to wipe the children's smeared faces one by one. "He will appreciate you more when you return. Men! He's just like my Klausito, who hardly notices me until I go away to Buenos Aires."

"Darling, how untrue!" Klausito said.

Maggie admitted she hadn't accomplished a thing since arriving in Cajamarca. Tonight she'd call her mother, get it over with, and send a fax to Carson's friend asking him to ship down a neonatology text. Most importantly, she had to find a lab to analyze her flask of lake water. This errand would mean missing the bus, which left before anything was open.

"You're staying, good," Liliana said. "Carson will understand."

First thing tomorrow, they'd go to the Baños del Inca, the place where Atahualpa had been soaking on the night the Spanish army arrived. It was a series of tubs cut into stone by a culture before the Incas, channeling the water of a hot spring. Maggie was surprised that

Liliana would dream of dipping even one painted toenail into the water; she'd heard the baths were filthy. Nowadays they were at the end of a public bus line.

"You must go early, to one special bath inside a house, where you pay more." Liliana wanted to know what else to plan for Maggie. Did she have errands, medicines to buy? Another nap, a movie, the market? Muñoz was available to drive them anywhere.

Maggie said that she might like to visit the contraband stall in the market, buy a two-dollar bottle of Chilean red wine for Carson, maybe a flat-weave bedside carpet, and a wooden tray.

"What else?" Liliana asked. Maggie couldn't think of anything, so Liliana turned to her husband and children. "Let's help Maggie. What special treats can she buy?"

"A whole salami, and apples, and blue cheese, and chocolate pudding, the kind that comes in a plastic bag, and onion bread, and a tin of Danish butter cookies," added the other Wechslers. "And milk jam, and a brass elephant, and, and, a dirt bike, and a pregnant mother bunny like we have, a computer game, a camera, boxes of bandages, and a holy painting, and a truck to carry it all."

"Don't forget a radio," Klaus said.

"We women need each other," Liliana said. Her golden body wavered under the water's smoking surface. "All women need to gossip for two hours each day. Otherwise, our teeth rot." She tapped an eyetooth with her fingernail. "Maggie, seriously. No woman can survive just talking to her husband. Children give you something, but in the end they are only children. You have none, you want babies, oh how I forgot! Ay, we worry about you, Klaus and I."

Last night, Maggie had made her phone call to Julia. Refusing to fly home had been just as wrenching as she'd expected. Hanging up, she'd felt a monster, unloving, unforgivable. Klaus had toddled off to bed pronouncing Althea perfectly able to defend herself, especially with help from Lester Weeks. If Maggie wanted to get involved, she must recognize her own decision, not merely succumb to her mother's manipulations. It was precisely what Carson would have said. Maggie and Liliana disagreed: Maggie might need to fly north and rescue Althea from the nursing home, but only after trying to influence and placate her mother from a distance. Julia needed more frequent doses of communication. Maggie must soon return to town, to make another phone call. Until then, Julia would receive a series of newsy, affectionate, generic, and cajoling letters, dated a week apart but composed by Maggie and Liliana in a rush of creativity that had lasted long past midnight.

Certain passages had made them scream with laughter.

Now it was not yet seven A.M., and Maggie couldn't think of anything to say to her new friend. Near dawn she'd been awakened by a dream: Vicente kicking in the door. He'd been wearing his little white cowboy hat with a veil firmly tucked into his shirt collar, but Maggie had recognized his eyes burning behind the gauze. The dream meant she was attracted to him sexually — not too surprising, though it made her feel dumb that she'd have to learn it in a dream.

Outside the bathing shack, there was faint laughter and cries from the people sitting in the open-air tubs downstream. They were bathing and washing clothes in her and Liliana's used water. On the other side of the humped dirt road, Muñoz waited in the Jeep, asleep with a newspaper over his face.

"You've helped me so much this visit," Maggie finally said. "Maybe it's your turn now?" She considered Liliana's likely woes.

"This whole visit is your turn," Liliana declared, touching Maggie's thigh underwater. "My life is calm for now. It was not always, and still I have my little things and problems. But you! When I saw you yesterday, I heard the wheels inside your head. Turning, *Rroom, vrooom!* I thought, *I* would go crazy in that canyon. How can that little girl continue?"

"I'm not alone," Maggie said. "I talk to my cook, and I have Carson. That's one more confidant than you, isn't it?"

"No-no-no. Your cook is not a friend!"

"Why not? I see her every day."

"Maggie, you can never be one of them."

And if I was, she thought despairingly, I could never prove it to anyone. She slid into the water, whose warmth gently spread her vertebrae apart. Beams and slabs of dusty light shot in between the planks. In her dream, Vicente had complained of heart trouble. The instant she'd touched him with a stethoscope, her flesh turned to bouncing rubber, powerless to resist as he swept her off her feet, out onto a bus that was passing by the clinic.

She shoved Vicente out of her mind, and said, "I find Clorinda pretty entertaining. She's smart, I think. I enjoy my talks with her."

Liliana sighed. "Clorinda! When we are traveling in the Cheep, Klaus and I, and we pass through a village like hers or yours, I ask myself, How can they live? Well for them, it is their life, and they have their fiestas and their burials and all their ways which are very picturesque, but for you and me it is pure delusion to think we can live like that. And you are helping them, giving them medical services, and yes that's nice. For them! Who is nice for you? Not your servants. That is certain. Servants never think like that. The more closer you feel, the more they cheat you in the end. It has happened to me many times. And our husbands, Klaus and Carson? Yes, they love us, but! Men carry their justification inside them. For a woman this part of a man is fascinating. How can he never think he will become someone else than who he is? But for us, in that way they are useless. That's also why I say, we women need each other."

"You're right," Maggie capitulated. She was inwardly horrified at Liliana's beliefs, though she suspected they were largely true and she, Maggie, too chicken to admit it. Momentarily she adopted Liliana's vantage point, or the vantage point she thought Liliana expected her to have, and from it considered Carson, his seriousness, his purpose. All of his traits seemed proper to a man, and just then she loved him as much as she had ever desired to love anyone. There was an admixture of guilt in this, surely — guilt and the magic of distance — still, in a burst of gratitude, she told Liliana that Carson had saved her. As long as she had Carson, she was okay.

Liliana snorted. "For some women it's okay to take her mission from the man. But for you? When I see you both together you seem — you don't seem completely yourself. Maybe you love him, but you are like this," and she stood halfway out of the water and hunched her shoulders slightly.

"Who wants to be myself?" Maggie said. "That's boring." Yet it felt good for Liliana to insist that she was a better, stronger person than she felt herself to be. She sank underwater, eyes shut, and listened to the suffocating throb of her own blood in her eardrums. She felt Carson's hands touching her belly, his tongue lapping urgently at the insides of her legs. At the very top it turned into Vicente's tongue, with Vicente's face close behind it. She felt him knowing her, as if he were thinking of her right now. She burst to the surface, pushing her wet hair back from her forehead and saying she was not afraid of her husband. Afraid of losing him perhaps.

"Same thing, no?" Liliana said. She stood up, the water surging around her waist, her nipples dilated like large dark rosebuds. Naked, her body was luscious and complete.

"Not at all," Maggie said gravely. At this Liliana laughed with satisfaction, asking what Maggie meant. Clearly, for Liliana, the conversation had at last begun. She must have had affairs, Maggie thought. A man in Buenos Aires? Did she regret staying in Peru for Klaus?

Maggie decided not to shift the conversation onto a safe topic, such as her wish to have a baby (anyway, they'd talked of it last night, Liliana advising Maggie to misplace her diaphragm, or store it amongst the needles of her sewing kit, speaking with such urgent sincerity that Maggie had yearned to translate her words directly into action). She suddenly saw that Liliana was right. To be seen and known was as necessary as breathing; a child could never know her, and maybe Carson couldn't either. That might be all right, yet the need would never disappear. Just now, in fact, she was in danger of displacing it onto Vicente Quispe Cruz, who would probably disappoint her, even worse than Carson. Better to reveal herself now, to Liliana.

"I am afraid of myself," she said. And even more afraid, she thought, of where things might be going, including this conversation. What was the difference between hope and fear? She held herself stiffly against the stone lip of the tub, awaiting the next generous intrusion, but for the first time Liliana seemed to suffer a blunting of her instincts; she just nodded and said that considering where Maggie lived, she must have to rely on herself abnormally, more than anyone should. She was talking about herself now, Maggie thought.

"The Rosario, no? You had that group — I forget — Rainbow? Don't you hear about them?"

"Black Rainbow Movement," Maggie said. "God, how everybody loved them."

"Of course, if they made everybody rich with drugs, I would love them too," Liliana said.

"What!"

"They had a cocaine business. You know that, right?"

"They aren't rich now," said Maggie disbelievingly.

"Indians don't know how to save their money." How did Maggie think the town of Piedad had bought its satellite dish? Had she ever been to El Mirador? She should see some of the houses up there. They were practically mansions, with red tile roofs and artificial trout ponds.

With a shiver, Maggie understood that Vicente's house was one of these. And how would Liliana know? Had she seen it? Or had Klaus? She recalled the pin in Klaus's map, Vicente's recollection of the Wechslers' name.

Liliana explained that even two years ago there had been an active airstrip at El Mirador, where small planes from Colombia had landed each day, taking away hundreds of pounds of basic cocaine paste per flight. An airstrip was not an uncommon way for a remote community or rebel group to subsidize itself. Being small, the Black Rainbow would have paid tribute to the Shining Path, yet there must have been plenty left to finance the golden age of Piedras. These makeshift airstrips on mountainsides and especially at the canyon bottoms were dangerous, however, so when the Peruvian military began to offer flatter, safer landings in the jungle, closer to the coca-growing region, even at a thousand dollars per landing Piedras lost the Colombians overnight. For a while the Shining Path had attacked the jungle bases, trying to get its business back, but the new Peruvian president had eventually crushed the rebels, guaranteeing the army's monopoly. "Klaus makes a study of this thing," Liliana concluded.

"So the Black Rainbow was basically a successful business," Maggie said. "Nice that they shared the wealth." No wonder there was a feeling in Piedras that everyone was waiting, waiting for the world to come back to them. Maggie told some white lies about Fortunata: how, as an ex-official of the Black Rainbow, she'd been instrumental in changing the clinic's image, and had even persuaded the ex-commander to inspect it. "He came in incognito. In fact one of his kids was really sick. Fortunata only told us a long time afterwards, so we never figured out which one he was, but we've been getting patients ever since. Don't tell my mom! Don't tell Klaus either, I guess."

"Now you really scare me," Liliana said.

"I'm not scared," said Maggie. "Carson's not scared. It's clear they're helping us." She reminded Liliana of what Klaus had said, that the Shining Path left him alone because his work was beneficial to the poor. "I mean, I really think there's a sincerity there, don't you?"

"Oh, Maggie, if you saw it here in Cajamarca just eighteen months ago! We never went outside the city. At night we remained indoors. You heard the car bombs once, twice a week."

And the shooting of Klaus's fellow professors, Maggie remembered. "You must have been terrified. But everyone in Piedras talks about how dangerous it was in Cajamarca and how peaceful it was down there. No car bombs. No murders, as far as I know. You should come visit. It's so beautiful, so vertical, like living at the bottom of a Chinese painting."

Liliana closed her eyes and let her legs float the length of the tub, so that Maggie had to do the same from the opposite end. With her eyes still closed Liliana said, "If you are not aware, you will not fear. If you are not in fear, you are in danger. When you are kidnapped, or dead, it is too late for your powerful government to protect you. I'm sorry to say it in this strong way. Nothing will probably happen, but I feel responsible."

"I just don't get why you think it's more dangerous than right here." Maggie could hear the silence of the canyon's walls towering above Piedras. She longed to go back there. "Look, even your maid says she doesn't understand where you and Klaus get all your money." On her last visit she'd tried to explain to Clorinda about nonprofit funding. Clorinda had been making free with her opinions, as usual — Maggie should tell Carson to shave his beard because it made him look depressing, like the conquistador Pizarro; and the Wechslers were too rich. No Peruvian university professor could ever afford a car or a house like this. And Klaus's experiments? Planting *ají* in the roots of a palm tree, or spraying laundry soap on potato leaves, or making bugs attack one another? Who'd pay for them? They seemed utterly unprofitable to Clorinda.

Liliana said, "Well . . . We are getting overboiled. We will get a headache."

They heaved out and sat on the stone edge, their private parts shielded from germs by Liliana's plushy towels. Their skin steamed, their thighs spread on the stone. Bronzy skin next to white. Liliana's pubic hair was thin and long like a beard. Maggie's was dark and thick like a mat. They both looked meaty and monumental, like the women in early Picassos.

"What did she say to you? We may have to fire her," Liliana mused. "Can you stand ten more minutes in hot water?"

"Sure, but I would hate it if you fired Clorinda. We were just chatting."

"Klaus and I have to be very careful."

"I told her Klaus got paid in marks."

Both their heads were pounding, so they threw pitchers of cold water on each other first, blowing and stamping their feet, then jumped back in. Maggie arranged her now pulpy limbs in the water, recalling that she was likely bathing in the same tub where Atahualpa had experienced his last happiness on earth.

"I think I have to tell you," Liliana began. "Klaus even decided not to say anything until he heard something more concrete." Last month the grapevine had begun to say that the Black Rainbow was springing back to life. Other groups were stirring these days, as the people began to notice that, after five or six years of capitalism, they were still as poor and desperate as when they'd undertaken the path of *terrorismo*. "Sometimes the people, they have no memory, so stupid. And in Peru everything is rumors, nobody knows which one is true. Klaus was thinking not to tell you. After this with your family, not to upset you if it was nothing, only say you should be careful. Now that your clinic is working, maybe they will want to take advantage of the gringos in some way. Then today you told me all this thing, and I am thinking what if *you* are the new life of the Black Rainbow? I am glad if you buy a radio, then Klaus and I can call you. You and I can chat a little also. But please don't say to Klaus I told you anything."

Maggie agreed to get a radio. She didn't want Liliana to worry about her. In return, she asked Liliana not to tell anyone about the Comandante's visit to the clinic, not unless there was some disaster and the information became important. She needed to trust some-one, and Liliana seemed the only candidate. It felt good to take her into confidence; having mentioned Vicente, she almost felt she'd told Liliana everything.

She stood up, her body a bright, ugly shrimp color. Vapor rose from her upper arms. She wished they could open a window, but there was none.

"Let's go and buy that radio," Liliana said.

Maggie demurred. She didn't have the money with her. Next time. It was a big expense; she had to mention it to Carson.

"Good, okay, then come back even sooner," insisted Liliana.

13

CHRISTMAS EVE, 1939. Christūnandā Convent, Bengal, India. It was because the sunset clouds were flat across the bottom that they looked like miraculous islands floating in a golden ocean, and because Althea's husband wasn't here that she'd stared at them long enough to notice. For nearly an hour tonight, and every evening since seventy days ago when Johnny had left her at the convent, outside the village of Meghā, whose name meant Clouds, Althea had stood at the window of her bungalow sending him love and protection.

She had soon discovered that there was little to do but pray, and so she did. Half of her praying was some kind of gazing, the other half was asking favors. To keep the earth from swallowing him up, a mountain from falling in on him, a boiling geyser from scorching him, and the wind from freezing him to death. To keep him from forgetting her. To give him joy and success in his work and scientific revelations. She'd stood here every evening watching day change to night, the sky turn from air to fire to liquid silver and finally to blood and darkness. She'd come to know this place, this hour, this light so intimately that, even if she were to be shocked out of a sleep begun on another continent, for the rest of her life she'd always be able to say, This is a Bengali sunset. That curl of bronze foil is the Kavita River, fringed by palm shadows. And this is the air that clasps the skin of my inner forearm, heavy and warm as a brass bracelet.

She had sent him away, not knowing how long it would take him to return. The festering, spreading war made travel daily more impossible. He'd gone from Calcutta to Moscow; now he was probably in Mongolia; he might return through Shanghai if the Japanese didn't invade it.

Imagining where he was, she used a mental version of Johnny's mapping calipers. He was gone so far that she had to lift the ball of the earth, so far around the curve that he could never see Althea's sunset breaking and spilling like red egg yolk across the horizon. For him it would be long past midnight, his sunset having fallen during the still white heat of Althea's afternoon. Althea had gone into the principal's office at the charity school to examine the globe that was kept there. Mongolia was north-northeast, wedged between the USSR and China. Mongolia! Outer Mongolia! Unreachably far away.

She imagined the freezing steppe wind slamming against Johnny's tent, so loaded with ice and yellow dust that it was like a careening wall of stone, almost heavy and thick enough to hold back the dawn. Darkness at noon, so Johnny had predicted, due to the tremendous dust of the collapsing mountains. Even in its aftermath, the earthquake was a disaster. Althea tried to think of Johnny's earthquake without reexperiencing her own.

Here, the sun slid away as peacefully as a coin into a magician's envelope, pulling from the earth a warm sigh of farewell that barely troubled the heavy leaves of the convent's banana plantation, whose rustling only seemed to deepen the ancient, living stillness of another Indian evening.

Johnny's earthquake was the biggest of all time. There was not one biggest but many: all of the world's biggest temblors were equal and the same. Any one could fling a hill into the air. These were convulsions beyond which the earth could bear and produce no more. The crust split. Deaths and losses varied depending on who lived in a place, what kinds of houses they built. It was worst if the earth shook at night while they slept. Of course, for the earth there was no day or night. Althea took comfort thinking that hardly anyone had been there for the Altai quake. A tremor with no one to experience it was wonderful. Aftershocks were another story. The original shock had been stronger than Huaraz's. Its aftermath would be what she had felt — thousands of nasty surprises, spread over months. For these, Johnny would arrive in time.

Althea hadn't heard a thing since his telegram from Moscow, which had arrived the first day of November, just two short weeks after he'd left Calcutta. He'd gone off with the names of the Russian seismologists whose work had been translated into English, with whose help he'd hoped to reach Mongolia. Now he'd written: WITH TADZIEFF FLYING ULAN BATOR TOMORROW STOP LOVE. Would he remember it was Christmas? Althea imagined a circle of men — Russian scientists, bearish, worn out and unshaven — passing a flat steel flask around a fire, vodka burning down their throats while faces seared. She hoped Johnny would think of her, and know she was sending her thoughts to him, at least today.

On his departure she had proposed a pact: to think of each other every day at sunset. Johnny had called her idea childish. He might see no sky at all, his nights would begin at different times, so he might as well just think of Althea whenever he thought of her. Which was constantly, darling, every minute.

She would have to be satisfied, but now she wished he could have lied more thoroughly and simply said yes. He'd disliked her request, though he'd shrugged and teased, saying why would she miss him when she was the one who was sending him away? Why indeed, she wondered. Had she pushed her husband from her? Since Christopher's death she'd been unnaturally dependent on trivial displays of affection. Johnny said she mocked the depths of his feeling. He'd turned the tables, saying as he left that he'd come back from Mongolia only if she could remember that he loved her, even if he did not comply exactly with her requests.

She had promised, she had lied. She'd wanted him to refuse to leave her. Too late.

Far across the convent grounds, she could hear a faint racket, which must be the Christmas Eve procession forming up in the kitchen compound. A drum rattle, inconclusive flute trill, bossy shouts. Then silence again. Christūnandā's head nun, Mère Anandī, had explained at tea how the procession would wind around the grounds, stopping to bless each building, dormitory, and cottage, even the dairy cows' enclosure. Althea's bungalow, built overlooking the river by the French priest who had founded the order, would be their first stop. A hundred converts, widows and orphans and old men, would sing in honor of the founder, then invite Althea to join the parade, to walk back through the banana plantation toward the Christmas feast.

In honor of the occasion, she'd put on a sari, for the first time in two years in India. Seven yards of starched white gauze were wrapped, pleated, folded, twisted around her body. Rolled in these bindings she felt stiff and delicate as a fever victim.

The convent was a hospital, site of Althea's delayed convalescence from Huaraz. In its quiet she knew more perfectly how the ground would writhe and buck underneath Johnny's cot, sending him running outside into a darkness that screeched like molars being ripped in half. Time could not be known as long or short; the violence would not fit into sense. Every morning she relived the mornings when the quake had not been finished. Thousands of tremors, as if the earth were dying slowly and the first shock had not already provided enough of a bad memory to taint the rest of her life. Some were terrifying replicas of the first shock, others so nightmarishly gentle that again she'd be taken unawares, wonder what was wrong with her leg, whether she had a charley horse in calf or thigh.

Days passed, the tremors didn't stop, the river ran black. Without wings, she was condemned to walk the unreliable earth. Her body could not be stopped from trembling.

The kitchen floor had wriggled and she'd run screaming from her doorframe, like Chicken Little, exposing her baby to the sky, appealing, begging: At least, sky, you won't fall in on us, will you? She'd wanted the air to pull Christopher away.

And then he had indeed been taken, not by earth or fire or air, but by water. By the small worms Don Héctor had mentioned, secret children of the earthquake's boa. All that was left of Christopher was his soft skull inside her own face and her womb turned into a desert and her brain a black hole that emanated stellar streams of thoughts, which were not as her own thoughts had been, but instead were the thoughts of a new and unknowable person whom she did not love as she had loved herself before. Herself. That was as big a disappearance as the unconscious never-questioned way she had trusted the earth to provide a place for her foot when it came down to stop the body's falling. Never again.

And that, all of that evil, was what she wanted Johnny to know; and to her shame, she wanted him to know far more than she wanted him to love her. She'd hate him until he found out.

✤

After he dropped her off at the convent, and his train had finally disappeared around the hills' green shoulder, leaving behind only its rippled black ponytail of smoke, she'd felt her stomach go hollow and she had known she might never see him again. He could easily be drowned in the ocean, crushed under a falling building, bitten by a microbe as Christopher had been, or even attacked by partisans, or Japs or Nazis or Mongolian bandits. What kind of woman sent her husband to a place where he might die? What kind of woman sent her husband away at all? Perhaps she had secretly intended to murder him?

Words were a form of violence she knew now how to use. Lying was one of her new and dark abilities. She had lied to Johnny, not outright but with wiles and tactics, the concealment of her own motives (had she even known what these were before?), the use of his own vocabulary to influence his judgment. Words like "measurements" and "observations."

Pressing Johnny to listen to the BBC announcer until he was caught by the story of the international scientific teams, forming and moving toward the area. She had felt proud then of her power, hypnotizing Johnny. She wanted him to be devastated, to realize that he was condemned to trust what he could not trust at all. Sending him was a vengeance.

She repented of it now. His absence was a vortex, an invisible eyeless hurricane. It was a mystery how this chair, this table, continued to exist without him. This was not the worst thing. The worst thing was how she'd plainly proven to herself that the center of her own study was Johnny, while Johnny's study was the world. This was insulting, and she could not change it.

By now he must have changed, making irrelevant all her study heretofore. She'd sent him off for this purpose, knowing the earthquake would succeed where all her words and wishes had not. She might have lost him, she now realized. His absence changed her too. Chairs and tables had not disappeared. They sat there proving Johnny's marginality. She slept differently in the bed, flinging her arms and legs wide in dreams, waking up stark in the middle, no longer leaving room for him.

She was comfortable here at the convent. Oh yes, she had fallen in love with the almost cruel simplicity of her barely furnished rooms, the chipped painted metal bed (white over green), the wooden washstand with its cool earthen jug, and the chair so plain it reached out to strip her of every clinging personal association. She was living in a doll's house, a small and manageable representation of life. This was simply a stronger version of the joy she'd felt when she had become used to making herself at home in shacks, hotels, and rented houses: places with holes in the floor for toilets, rooms whose unpainted cement walls seemed to collapse inward at nightfall. Why did she enjoy feeling like a stranger? Because strange rooms expected her to exist. Only when Johnny was home did she begin to feel she'd lost herself, dissipated into a mist.

When dusk crept in through windows, now, Althea began her so-called prayers. She was versed in calling Johnny to her mind's eye, vividly alive, as she imagined he existed to himself. Only rarely did he come to her lifelessly as a Catholic's repetitious litany. Once or twice he would not come at all — because he had not thought of her that day, she'd managed to decide. Perhaps an infidelity had drained the life from their connection. One night she'd dreamed he was on a Hawaiian island, eating from a hollowed pineapple, surrounded by fat brown women. On one or two recent evenings she'd felt certain he was dead, and would stay that way unless she could bring him to fuller life in her mind.

Tonight's sky had a hard yellow and orange skin. Johnny was outside it, far away in the freezing dark. The near sky was stiffening into a golden floor that looked almost solid enough for two people to walk across. Althea could feel it, cool metal clasping her ankles. If Johnny were here, she'd propose they hold each other's hand and run straight off the earth's flat edge. Skate across all that gold — avoiding those swirls of blood — and go, live out their dreams on a purple cloud island. Who would they be if they lived there? When Althea met Johnny, she thought Heaven was the promise of marriage. Again, when she had boarded the green and white Grace Line ship that would take them to Venezuela, she'd believed she was sailing for Eden.

She lifted her arm to show Johnny how the white choli sleeve was turning the color of tiger lilies.

The evening began to thicken, pressing on her its ancientness. Across the pale road, where several fishing families lived under roughly thatched pavilions, the spaces beneath the thorn trees were filling with a haze of fragrant smoke. Cooking fires of dung and wood, these were the same fires that had burned in India every evening since before time. Althea considered how easily she could have been born across the road, an Indian woman. She could have existed thousands of years ago instead of today. A camp follower heating rice for her mustachioed soldier — he'd come to her covered with wounds and dust, with blood on his saber, to rest while some battle for forgotten empires paused at dusk. Hindu thoughts were inherent in the smell of a dung fire. She must have been reincarnated ten thousand times to reach this hour, this place.

A toddler in a cotton shift ambled out of the trees, ran back and forth in the river sand until it fell down. It picked itself up, ran back under the trees. Where was its mother? Cooking, with an infant at her breast. The toddler seemed springy and independent. Had Christopher been like that child, he would not have died. She remembered his pale, fragile skin, the thinness of his skull.

Behind her, the sitting room was darkening, gray shadows pooling in the corners. Her shadow on the stucco wall was skinny and pyramidal, a Chinese mountain. She disliked being in this bungalow at dusk, where dead priests' ghosts floated out through the thinning surface of the daylight. Her only remedy was turning on the ceiling bulb, but its electrocuting glare was another form of hell. The French founder of the convent had died in this room; his brother, five years younger, was dying now, in his own identical cottage two hundred yards away. One night shortly after moving in, Althea had dreamed of one of them so vividly she took it for a visitation. Old man gasping for breath, so old his skin had turned to silver. He'd looked up at his nuns, seen angels' brown faces with white wings folded alongside rounded cheeks. Touched by women for the first time since a boy, he'd die convinced of Heaven.

With enforced dignity Althea walked out onto the verandah, letting the screen door slam because she did not want to turn her body, much less lift her arm. She'd draped the sari herself, and so it was in danger of falling off.

Outside, she could smell the cooking fires more strongly, hear the racket from the kitchen compound grow more insistent, the shouts more commanding. They must be lighting the torches. Soon they'd begin to walk.

She dreaded descending the steps, melting into the knotted crowd: people made of pure tendons, smelling of cow dung and burnt sugar. Crowding the narrow paths of the convent's banana plantation, jostling, trying to keep an eye on the ground in case of cobras, her sari might loosen, its folds relax, the cloth spiral off and down her body, revealing her glories to a hundred poor. They'd wonder what the white woman had done to make her husband punish her, send her away. She was not a nun.

Unnatural. Accursed. Once in a while, she believed it of herself.

Tonight she'd dine with Mère Anandī and Brother Jesūnandā in the beggars' banquet hall, on the floor. She already took two meals a day there, embedded in a long row of nuns who were separated by one screen from the priests, by two screens from the beggars. Nuns came along slopping rice, beans, sambar, and yogurt from steel buckets onto banana leaves laid down on the scrubbed bare floor. Everyone ate with their hands. Althea had discovered a fondness for this style, for green banana curry, too. But if she sat on the floor tonight, she'd never rise clothed. How did hill women climb trees in saris? They clung like monkeys with bare strong toes, reached overhead with iron blades to lop branches for firewood, turning trees into spears like huge amputated asparagus, but never unveiling their own brown trunks.

For the fiftieth time Althea retucked her sari skirt as the bazaar woman had shown her. Circling the waist, pleating the cloth between a stiffened thumb and little finger, tucking it under itself. She drew the remainder up around her breasts, back, shoulder, head. Mère Anandī praised saris with such intelligence that Althea had to agree: they were the most gracious female costume in the world. But Althea had not gotten the hang of it. The great bunchy ball at her belly was always threatening to burst open. She'd chosen an inexpensive kind, sheer cotton with a simple border of white embroidered daisies. Its low quality was showing: the cloth was rebellious, creased, and limp.

Poor as it was, she wished she'd worn it as her wedding dress. She and Johnny had been married by a justice of the peace in New Orleans, and Althea still regretted the lack of pomp. She'd worn a linen suit that had unfortunately matched the linoleum floor, which tried to look like coffee and cream but looked instead like mixed digestive fluids. Johnny's loud redheaded friend had been the witness.

It was unwifely, disloyal, to prefer over her wedding dress an outfit her husband had never seen; even more so to change her body from an American hourglass to a delicate Indian column without his consent — and not for him.

Still, she was in the convent, safe. She was looking forward to pleasing everyone, surprising them with her costume. Mère Anandī often said she wished she had been ordained here in India, so she could wear a sari like the local nuns. Then instantly she would deride herself: "Only a Frenchwoman still wishes for a sari after forty years in robes!" Althea didn't understand Catholics. It seemed to her that Mère Anandī should not admit desires in public, even small ones. "Your habit is perfect," Althea said, meaning it. Bride of Christ. Could married women ever shine that way, or were they all tarnished by rubbing against their husbands?

The sun's red yolk was fattening and flattening itself onto the black frying pan of India's dirt. Fully lit, on fire, Althea at last completed her promise to her marriage. Offering herself in the sari to her husband, she imagined herself floating free toward him, big and light, like a Christmas present or a meringue. A cumulus cloud full of sunlight. It might be Christmas morning where he was. If he was alive, he would rejoice among collapsing mountains.

Rejoice, Johnny, she told him. She offered him as gifts the sky and all things under it.

Now, after energetic quiet, the procession started singing all at once, a hundred untrained voices. They held n's so long they turned to vowels, then abruptly stopped, leaving an unexpectedly protracted silence. And just when Althea stopped waiting, thinking the song was over, they burst forth again, wild joy. And silence once again.

Sights — the reddish, crumbled earth of the convent's dairy pen. Its cows blurred into humps of pencil shadow under the palm thatch roof where they rested for the night on their sides, like derailed boxcars. The fishing shacks. The pale road where a boy in a turban was just passing through a shaft of last light, driving home a camel along with his family's buffalo and goats. The Kavita River's oxbow, all day a sludgy olive-green bend cluttered with washermen, now blazing in the color of the sky.

Shabik-*nnn!* A! Taqir *uuuu*-la! The procession was here, curving around the corner of her bungalow. First came a bunch of little kids, jumping up and down, clacking sticks together. Next came the oldest with rattles, soft-drink caps strung in wooden frames, made in the craft workshop. They sounded so happy, Althea wished she knew the language they were singing in.

Came the main body of the procession. First an ancient lady in a mud-colored sari whose pattern would have been impossible to see even in daylight. She wore no choli underneath, and Althea could see her skinny flat dugs hanging like flaps of softest calfskin. This crone leaned on a stick with one hand, and in the other she carried a lantern, raising it as high as she could to light the way for those behind. Following her, a tiny boy pulling at the forward corner of a white bedsheet, walking very slowly, conscious of the importance of his task. Three old blind men clutched the cloth's rear corners. Bodies gnarled like fig vines, chests parallel to the ground, they picked up and set down each foot in gentle deliberation, like chickens. Afraid of landing on a snake, Althea decided. A circle of boys surrounded the blind men, herding them away from the banana trunks.

Behind the blind men was the main chorus, a crowd of ordinary poor, with white nuns standing out. Althea hadn't seen a nun before she was nineteen and married, when she and Johnny had first gone to New Orleans to board the Grace Line boat for South America. There had been two of them on that ship, missionaries bound for Venezuela. Johnny said their heads were bald. Their bodies must be white as grubs; they were waistless under insistently ugly gray habits. Their underwear knitted from itchy thread, oxfords thick-soled for kicking sinners' shins. Not in India. In India nuns were beautiful. Even Mère Anandī, in her white cotton dress and Indian sandals, was light, bony, dry. On fire rather than putrid.

At the very rear Brother Jesūnandā held a torch which flickered over his face. He smiled. In the shadows he looked like a painting of the young Rembrandt. Althea could not get used to the beauty of Indian men, beauty palpable as a woman's, with glowing skin and deep eyes. They seemed to wear eyeliner, some of them. It made her feel nervous when Brother had knelt beside her, trying to teach her how to pray. Now she could feel him looking at her in the sari, approving of her effort.

He moved to the head of the procession, bowed to Althea. "Madame," he said, "will you join in celebration?" She stepped off the verandah. As she put her hand on his forearm, like a bride, she felt the sari's skirt begin to slip down. Clamping it with her left elbow, she strode into the mass of beggars. They smelled like rotten honey.

"Very graceful," Brother approved. "Sari is a woman's most adorning garment. Are you in mourning for your husband?"

"What do you mean?"

"White is for widows," he said.

"Where I come from, white is for brides."

"Ah," he said, and suddenly let go of her arm.

They walked into the dark, among the soft rolled trunks of the banana trees. All around them the rattling of the drums, the keening of the people. Brother Jesūnandā, whom she'd told about her sunset exercises, asked her laughing if she'd prayed to her husband again today. He joked that he was going to describe her pagan devotions to his nuns as an example they should not follow. Teasing, but he meant it, Althea knew. Brother Jesūnandā had told her there was a grace available for the asking if you asked the right Person in the right Way. All she had to do was try it, try it even once. Althea had refused. Give it to me without asking, she'd told him, after that I'll do anything you want.

14

Cheef! The bus stopped, let its breath out, right in front of the clinic. Before Maggie could start to get down, the neighbors' dogs raced up and started skirling in the road. *Auc, auc, auc, auc, auc,* they barked, gulping air as a substitute for raw flesh.

She kicked her foot out the bus door to see if Bobby or Bestia or Chocolatín would clamp fangs on her sneaker. Somewhere in the mists of history, a Doberman had passed through Piedras, and today its mutts were especially fierce and frightening. Behind her, the driver's assistant raised his arm and yelled *"Fuera!"* The dogs scattered, hunching backwards, growling and lifting their upper lips.

Maggie bent down and pretended to grab a rock from the bus' metal step. The beasts receded long enough for her to get off and avail herself of a genuine stone. Only after the bus had left did they start wagging their tails and smirking, dishonestly, as if apologizing for not having recognized her at first.

A neighbor's skinny yellow bitch ran up and sniffed her jeans hems, thoroughly and delicately, seeming to approve of all Maggie's adventures.

It was eight P.M. There were clouds over the moon. The clinic's lights were on, the generator beating like a heart. Maggie felt like the protagonist of a Central European fairy tale, arriving home after years lost in a forest. Missing was the high-piled snow for buttery squares of light to fall on. The clinic was the first light for miles: starting above Piedras Baja, all the houses and hovels had hunkered invisibly along the road. *Corte de la luz.* The power was out; it had given her a chill.

The clinic was locked and chained from the outside. Carson must have turned the generator on for her and gone out walking, as he and Maggie often did on power-cut nights. They'd gaze at the stars spilled across the sky like cottage cheese. Passing other houses, they'd glimpse a candle through a shutter's crack or hear intimate murmurs — a hovel might salute them in a human voice. Mostly, though, Piedrasinos went to sleep at sunset when the lights were cut, as they'd always done before the hydroelectric plant.

Maggie could not read the combination lock. She wished the bus had stayed, to shine its headlights on the numbers, but the driver was long gone, running through the first eight notes of the *Bridge on the River Kwai* theme on his electric horn. He roared up the river flats, imperiling an audible pack of racing, barking dogs. The flats were a stretch of exhilaration for drivers after the terrors of the mountain road. His joy would end in three kilometers, where the road turned uphill to wind even more tortuously to the El Mirador fork, past Piedad, to end at La Tormentosa, the last place.

The headlights flickered epileptically entering the riverside trees, then stopped at the center of town, where they stayed fixed longer than usual. The driver must be getting refreshments before going up, leaving his lights on to illuminate the darkened store.

At last the lock loosened and fell open in her hand. She pushed the door open and walked into the lit room, receiving a shock like cold deep water. Why had the shelves been cleared? Why was the refrigerator gone? Had those things ever existed?

She stared, but the objects would not appear. Had Carson moved up to the mine already? Had he sold the fridge, finally admitting it was useless? Did he know Maggie had betrayed him deep within her mind? Had he returned to the United States? There was no note on the counter. She said his name once, quietly. "Carson?" The rooms absorbed the sound, gave nothing back. In the hall beside the bedroom door, she could see his white doctor's coat hanging on its nail, a horrifying bit of normalcy. How often had she imagined, for her own amusement, that some apparently innocent transition was really the first scene of a horror movie? She blinked hard, as if a readjustment of focus would bring back the right view.

He must be dead in the bedroom, lying on the bed with his throat cut. Bandits! If she called his name once more, they'd jump out and kill her too.

She fled up the road toward the village, evil breathing at her back.

Liliana was right, Piedras was dangerous. There was nowhere to escape to, no one to call for help. The police post was hours uphill, and where was Carson? After two hundred yards she stopped, panting. No one had followed but the night, which now asked for recognition, pressing upon her its gentle, natural stillness, its silence emphasizing the river noise. The road was luminous under the moon. Above her were two horizons, the canyon rims, two softly jagged lines that seemed to be spreading slowly apart because of how the wind was moving the clouds. The clouds were battleship gray, and the moon glinted behind them, yellow as a hepatic eyeball, its golden light dispersed. The mountains were black velvet, much darker than the sky. She felt uncertain that she'd actually come from beyond the top of the right-hand horizon just that very day, and from a city. Believing this was as difficult as believing that the refrigerator and Carson and the medicines were all gone.

They had to be somewhere. Nothing was ever missing, Maggie thought, things merely got displaced to where you couldn't find them.

She continued walking toward the town. As she got closer, the river seemed to bring a faint human roar, barely distinguishable above the water's noise. A light, woman's voice rose skipping over the rapids: inarticulate, clear tones, next a laugh, or a wail. A bigger party than usual at the general store? Most nights there was at least a dogfight happening, a couple of guys in chairs drinking beer and little boys kicking the dogs to keep them going. Maybe the refrigerator was being auctioned off.

She walked steadily, not looking back, resolved not even to think of whatever might be following. At the road's bend, the split boulder looked big as the moon, crashed onto the ground.

A crowd had gathered. The bus was still parked where it had stopped, askew and blocking most of the road, its headlights shining into the door of the *tienda*. The bus was empty, and in a small flash of inadequacy Maggie realized she might not recognize its driver or any passengers in this crowd and poor light.

Dozens of people stood on the packed earth outside the store. No one spoke above a murmur, but everybody was talking. At the edge of the crowd was Vicente, conferring with a friend, heads together, both of them glancing, rather furtively, in and out of the circle of their conversation. She smiled and began working her way toward them to ask what was going on, but Vicente discreetly shook his head, barely a tremor, just in time for Maggie to change direction, staging a mistaken recognition of a woman ten feet to Vicente's right.

The woman pushed her lips toward the store, indicating that whatever had happened was inside. El Doctor Calzón? In there, the woman said. Like a zombie, Maggie turned away and let herself be pulled toward the heart of the drama.

No one stopped her. Men and women were bunched around the door, peering in, yet leaving a corridor for the headlight beams. First she walked right up the middle and stood trying to see in, until a couple of men pulled her aside to remove her shadow. A woman shifted to let her by. She slunk in and stood against the wall, her spine pressed against the sharp edge of a shelf.

A man lay on his back on the floor, his face in shadow. A blanket covered his body. He was thin and his shoe bottoms pointed toward the door. The leather was white with scuffing, and there was a worn knothole at the ball of his right sole.

Maggie's husband was crouching next to this man, holding his hand. Carson's beard was long and sad; his fine bangs fell past his forehead.

Before they had gotten involved, but after they'd noticed each other, she'd watched him take another woman's pulse at an academic party. He'd been flirting with a lecturer's Venezuelan wife about her new exercise program. I can tell you, Carson had said, whether it is working. He'd taken her wrist, seeming to listen so carefully to the woman's body that he could have heard her heart, not just beating but speaking all its secrets. The lecturer's wife had felt this. She'd been suspended inside Carson's concentration for a full half minute, until he raised his head and announced that her heart was beating slowly, less than once per second, and that slow was good. Then they both had laughed. Maggie, stricken with jealousy, had wanted to offer her own wrist, ask Carson to touch her with that same deliberation, fingers bruising her thinnest skin. She'd wanted her blood to drum against him from the inside. But back then, Larry had been watching.

Nor had Carson ever taken Maggie's pulse, though he'd allowed her, plenty of times, to measure his, for the sake of training. His heart beat exactly sixty times per minute.

Tonight he was not counting beats. He was merely holding this man's hand, looking into his face, Carson's body curled and reflective, as if absorbing the other's pain into himself.

She walked up and stood next to him. "Hey, love," said Carson, falsely casual.

She crouched beside him, touched his thigh with her fingertips. "What's going on? Anything I can do?"

"No. Shht, quiet." The crow's feet at the corners of his eyes were deeper than usual.

She followed his attention to the man on the floor. Both legs were squirming, feet fluttering like a minnow's fins. His cheeks were shiny with sweat or grease, and he was muttering vehemently, occasionally saying a bad word. *Puta, carajo.* As Maggie got closer, she saw his face and knew him. Nasir Dabdoub, the storekeeper. His eyes rolled around, resting on one face after another.

Carson's jaw hung slightly open in fatigue or fear.

"Should we take him to the hospital?" Maggie said.

"You're joking."

"There's the bus outside," she said. "We could turn it around."

"He'd be gone before the bridge."

Maggie absorbed this information. Gone meant dead. "People will see we tried." What a thing to say in front of everyone, even though she knew they wouldn't understand a word.

"They know he's dying. Right now the guy is calm. If we move him, he'll suffer worse."

"There's really nothing we can do?"

"Nope. They must have pierced his liver. And you, how are you?" Carson turned his head and looked at her at last.

How am I, she wondered. "Fine. I gave your water to a lab." Although grateful to him for asking, she stared back at him hoping to elicit some deeper softness or recognition. "And you?" she asked.

"I sat alone until they came to get me." Now he leaned across and whispered into her ear. "These wounds are really strange." He pulled up the blanket and Maggie hunkered aside so the light could fall on their patient. Several round bruises in the soft, pale belly flesh, the size of the smallest coin. Nasir's belly had a line of hairs that would no longer be of any use to anyone, even as decoration. "Six stab wounds. They used a long weapon like a needle."

She bent down and saw that the bruises were actually holes, black at the center. Nasir's thin flanks were turning bluish under his skin's pale yellow.

Carson indicated the length of the needle, half his forearm. "It's the bandits' specialty. From the coast, if I heard correctly. No blood spills outside, but death from internal hemorrhage." He pulled down Nasir's shirt again and gently replaced the blanket.

"*Señora,*" the wounded man said, squirming. His arms and legs hadn't stopped moving. "*Me duele, Señora.*" It hurts me.

Maggie was surprised that Nasir had seen her.

"*No se preocupe.*" Don't worry. She had no right to say this. She laid one hand across his sweating forehead, but her palm must not have been comforting, or else Nasir just couldn't keep his head still. He rolled it from side to side and Maggie quickly took her hand off again. He didn't stop shaking his head now, like a child in a tantrum of refusal.

A froth the color of strawberry ice cream came up between his lips. Pulmonary, she wanted to say to Carson, but didn't because the walls of the room had begun to press together. Everything shrank to a small, flat, round area. Men's and women's faces receded around the edges. "Just a second." She swooped for the door, got halfway through, pressed her forehead against the dirty painted cement of its jamb. Her mouth filled with liquid of which she allowed a little to drop out. Saliva was remarkably elastic, she thought, as the drops turned into a stream that extended past her chest before it broke off. Please let me not vomit, she thought. She tried looking up at the sky, but the stars seemed to vibrate in position. How nice air was! Like champagne. Cool, with a little moisture and the smells of things that grew by the river. Across from the store was a stone retaining wall. From its top grew the forty-foot papaya tree that Nasir had told her sprouted from a rind he threw away five years ago.

A few deep breaths. She felt better, until Nasir's liver-colored dog started sniffing around the little spot she'd drooled upon the ground. The crowd shouted *"Fuera!"* A rock the size of a bun hit the dog's ribs. A meaty thud. The dog cringed, whirled, and trotted rapidly away, holding itself in a crouched position.

"Está bien?" The people in the yard asked her, or maybe they meant Nasir. Same verb.

"No sé," she said, I don't know.

A woman offered an opinion. There were murmurs of assent.

Vicente appeared, walking out of the crowd. He put one hand on her shoulder and spoke in English. "Nasir, he dies. Go inside, okay?"

"Okay."

They went inside, Vicente behind Maggie. He pushed without touching her, blocking her retreat, as he had pushed Luz María — three days ago? — into the clinic. Maggie could feel a bouncy, physical aura coming out of his chest.

Someone had knocked over a large sack of dried macaroni which crunched underfoot. Nasir's store was just as full of goods as ever. Doña Albita would have to take over the business. Would she sell all of it piece by piece, then leave? Or would she stay in Piedras? When a person died, a whirlwind suddenly stopped and millions of objects fell to the ground. Maggie thought of her grandmother. If and when Julia managed to ship Althea off to some Shady Hill or Green Meadow, she was also capable of inviting a charity to drop by with a moving van.

I want to leave here, Maggie thought with urgency.

Carson was still kneeling by Nasir, but his eyes looked for Maggie now. He registered Vicente standing beside her with a faint look of questioning or displeasure, the supercilious twitch at the left corner of his mouth that reminded Maggie a little of her father, Calvin. Nasir's eyes were closed but his lips and tongue were savoring the pink gummy froth. Eating himself, Maggie thought with repulsion. Carson got to his feet as the two of them approached, and Vicente stepped back quickly into the shadow, as if he preferred Carson to strike Maggie instead of him. Yet from there he greeted Carson, offering his hand. *"Buenas noches."*

"Who's this?" Carson said in a peremptory tone.

"Vicente Quispe Cruz," Maggie said. "He brought Lady Maggy."

"Ah," said Carson, "you are the *papá* of Lady Maggy."

Vicente didn't correct the imputation of fatherhood, Maggie noticed, he just nodded and shook Carson's hand. But he wouldn't have anyway, not now. The sight of Nasir's sweating face made her mind feel like raw egg thrown against a wall, sliding down.

She said, "Can't we put him on the bus? Really, are we sure? We can't just let him die here! Let's take him to the clinic at least." Belatedly she recalled there was nothing left at the clinic to save anybody with.

Carson said, "Please don't get hysterical."

She stamped her foot. "I'm not! If we can't do anything, then maybe we should leave. He's not our relative. I've never watched a person die before."

"Calm down. We ain't going nowhere." Carson squatted down again at Nasir's shoulder.

She smoothed her T-shirt, squatted next to Carson with one hand on his thigh for balance. Vicente stood dark and stiff above them, like a best man.

Be with him, Maggie told herself. Think how he must feel. Nasir started uttering awful, strangling groans. A louder murmur went through the crowd, and people started jamming into the doorway. The ones already inside shuffled closer, pushed from behind, some almost falling. Vicente began to herd them back, the way Maggie's father did at golf tournaments, raising his arms and walking forward, calling quietly for silence, silence.

Maggie appealed to a woman standing above her. *"Hay sacerdote?"* Is there a priest? The woman shook her head.

"Hermano," said Vicente, flicking an imaginary drop onto Nasir's forehead. Brother.

Nasir opened his eyes as if the drop had been cold.

"Te queremos," Vicente declared. We love you.

The shopkeeper struggled a bit, noticed Vicente, and called for him by name. *"Aquí, papito,"* Vicente said. Nasir started trying to sit up, and Carson and Vicente both put their arms behind his shoulders to support him. The shopkeeper's lips moved and Vicente leaned toward his face to hear whatever he was saying. Nasir squeezed his eyes shut and muttered, muttered on. His voice was full of liquid rolling in the back of his nose and throat. He seemed to be telling what had happened, and Vicente kept saying he understood. *"Sí, sí, ya, papá, ya, sí, papito, entiendo."*

He gently passed Nasir onto Carson's arms. Carson nodded, taking the weight of Nasir, who was still breathing.

Vicente stood up and asked the room who else had seen the robbery. He said three names, which Maggie immediately forgot. Everyone stared at the floor. Some people were moving their heads vaguely, in distress not to be able to say definitely yes or no. Vicente yelled *"Sí?"* One fat man with a dimpled face said *"No,"* sarcastically, under his breath. There was a murmur of dissent. Vicente repeated the names with more certitude, shaking his head at people's fear and stupidity. Still no one spoke.

"No pue' ser," the shopkeeper mumbled. It can't be. His breathing began to make a loud sucking bubbling sound, so Carson laid him down. A carnation of froth grew from his lips. Now his breath turned into a retching metallic clangor, like parts falling off the bottom of a moving car. Men and women pressed in closer.

"Aire!" Carson cried, but they all ignored him. Nasir's neck started to swell. Carson said, "Pneumothorax," and ripped the shirt from his neck. They all saw more bruised holes on his chest, just in front of his right arm, inside the shoulder joint.

"Verduguillo," Vicente said. The name of the knife, the little executioner.

"I never saw these." Carson bit off chunks of adhesive tape to seal them. "You should never have sat up," he shouted in English at Nasir, who was resisting being laid down again, craning his neck to see new bandages, new wounds.

"Ay, es mi pulmón," it is my lung, Nasir said, having understood at last. He relaxed and lay back, his stare fixed loosely on the ceiling. Maggie would always remember seeing a person disappear without disappearing. *"Aay Diosito. Diosito míío,"* a woman wailed over and over. Doña Albita had been standing in the dark, behind the glass counter. Now she came out to kneel at Nasir's side. Maggie stood up to leave space for her.

"*Puta mierda*," Carson said richly under his breath. He recited all his Spanish swear words. "*Coño, carajo, puta, pendejo, mierda.*"

"Stop that," Maggie said. She squeezed his shoulder and he stopped.

Liliana was wrong, Maggie thought. He does know I exist.

Doña Albita sat down on the floor, placed her husband's head in her lap. Everyone stepped back, but stayed in range, watching as she bent over her husband's face, stroking and tucking his hair behind both ears. She told him to take care. It had impressed Maggie since the beginning how Peruvians weren't very demonstrative in public.

Outside, the road was the same as usual. The air was soft and the mango trees a positive blackness against the bright cloudy sky. The river roared on and on. How could there be so much water in the world to keep the rivers flowing day and night?

Carson walked in his own wheel rut, a yard to Maggie's right. Without any preamble he started telling what he'd heard and understood. Three bandits had come down from a place called Meado de Vaca ("cow piss"), on the eastern edge of the *puna*. It wasn't clear whether they were residents or fugitives hiding out there. People seemed to know who they were.

Why would anyone choose Meado de Vaca, Maggie wondered. Eight hours before, on the bus, she'd passed through it again: two dozen hovels scattered around a forty-foot mud puddle in which pantless babies stood thigh-deep. The only grace of the town was the humor of its name, inspired by that central wallow of murky water. Generally it resembled an ogre's den where drying sheepskins rattled stiffly in the wind. Bones and garbage littered the ground. The shacks were piles of sticks and stones, kept low because of the incessant wind and caulked with turfy clods — all was blackened by age, wood smoke, and poverty. Men leaned in the doorways, scowling, never waving at the bus. Women turned their backs and ran, throwing stones to scare herds of stunted, spaniel-sized goats and sheep.

When the three men had come into Nasir's, he'd served them beer and even turned on his old World Cup video, taped by his brother from Cajamarca TV. They'd drunk steadily all afternoon. At sunset he'd finally asked them for a payment, and the men had said *sí, sí, claro, seguro,* they'd pay with Nasir's own cash and gold. He'd known he was lost. They'd stood up, drawing their needle knives. One got behind him and the other two grabbed his arms and pushed him into the storeroom, where they forced him to dig up the sack of nuggets he kept buried in the dirt floor, about two hundred grams of gold. Everyone knew it was there.

"How much is that worth?" Maggie wanted to know, but Carson didn't have the answer.

Next they went out front to take the cash. Nasir offered to unlock the wooden box, hoping to grab his pistol from under the counter, but they'd sucker-punched him instead, smashed the box, and then given him a few jabs with the *verduguillo,* as many as pleased each one. Doña Albita had watched it all from the crack of the kitchen door. While they'd been in the storeroom digging up the floor, she'd sent the shave-head boy for help, but he'd only run away in fear.

Carson fell silent and Maggie knew he was entering the rest of the story as it reeled through his mind, the part that included himself. His self-blame for not noticing the chest wounds earlier. They were just walking past the boulder. Her belly tightened, imagining the sensation of the *verduguillo* going in. She had her own selfishness, feeling terrible for having been exempted from dying on the floor. Unworthily, it had come to her that she could have borne Nasir's death better than Nasir, because she would have known it was not her true destiny. She could have had some other end, whereas Nasir might have suffered from some final, bitter thoughts about what it meant to have been born in Damascus only to come down to this ignominious dying on the floor.

Give the man credit, she told herself. Credit was all she had to give to him, or rather to his memory. Her own death would be just as intimate and limiting.

"He might have been saved in a big-city emergency room," Carson said.

"Not even," Maggie said. Surely there had been no such murders while Comandante Oquendo had ruled this valley. All bandits would have had to register with Fortunata right away. She found this idea reassuring, dampening Liliana's alarums. Even if Vicente had less power now, he was on her side and Carson's.

Out on this part of the road, the river took a bend and the sky was bigger. The wind had cleared the sky somewhat, so that only half of it was now covered with clouds, the half that included the moon. The other half was perfectly clear and still had a lot of stars. The road was lit a dull pinkish gray.

Carson's solid shadow was moving up the road, getting ahead. Maggie quickened her pace. She wanted to grab his hand, but in their year and a half together she'd learned, not to respect his wish to be left alone, but to wait until he looked ready to be touched. Defeat made the risk not worth taking. Staring up at the mountains, she tried to find their friendliness again, something to cling to that wasn't him.

The clinic door was still ajar as she had left it, the transparent bulbs still glaring hellishly in their sockets.

Carson said, "What the hay?" He turned to her. "You left this open?" In Maggie's head was a sound like a fist on piano keys. "I told you," she said. "I told you. I tried to tell you. In the store." Had she? She followed him past the bare shelves and counter, talking all the way. "The chain was locked when I came back. I thought you'd gone out and left the lights on for me. The fridge was gone, I swear! I ran out because I was scared they'd be hiding in the kitchen or the bedroom." She felt like a liar. Now that she was with Carson, it was obvious that the clinic was sterile, empty.

"You must have left it open. No one knows our combination and there is no other door."

But there *was* another door — the realization dawned on both of them at once. They walked swiftly into the kitchen, where everything was undisturbed except for the back door, open wide and unresisting on the night, the river's roar. Carson found a key still stuck in the outside lock. "Well, now at least we have a key," Maggie said. Foolishly, they hadn't asked Don Zoilo to bar the door. They'd thought of it, just as they'd wondered how to chain down the refrigerator. Carson cursed under his breath. "Those punks, those rotten kids next door."

"Don't jump to conclusions."

The bedroom was a tornado's aftermath. The burglars had slid aside the mattress, thrown all the clothes and bedding onto the floor, and kicked in the bottom of the *armario* looking for a secret compartment. "They took my hiking boots," said Carson. Luckily, when the burglars had torn the mosquito net from its hook, they'd tossed it onto the very floorboard where Carson's pistol and shotgun lay hidden. He stomped on one end to lift the other, took out his weapons, and laid them on the bed. "Don't," Maggie said, but he ignored her.

Then he stood on the bed frame to shove his hand between the roof sections. The valuables were still there, duct-taped inside a plastic bag. Carson pulled the package open, strewed traveler's checks, money, credit cards, passport, plane ticket across the mattress. "Your stuff's missing," he cried, then they both remembered that Maggie's papers were zipped inside her jacket; she'd needed them for Cajamarca. She tossed hers on top of Carson's, feeling simultaneous grief and elation to see the powers of flight that defined them in this place. "Thank God," she whispered.

"Yeah, thank God they are so dumb." What could they want with a refrigerator?

Tonight Carson looked old, standing in the middle of the room, the skin raw and wrinkled around his eyes. Maggie wished he'd shave his beard, so she could see unscathed flesh on his cheeks or upper lip. Clorinda's idea that he looked like a conquistador was certainly important. Conquistadores were killers. Who wanted to be healed by a killer?

Carson kicked the chair upright, sat down on it to flatten and retape their valuables. Meanwhile, Maggie fixed the bed. The sheets were clean enough, despite being on the floor. Good thing she'd mopped before going to Cajamarca. "Who had our key?"

"Not Fortunata," Carson declared.

Fortunata was just the person Maggie had been suspecting. "So why wasn't she at the store with everybody else?"

"She wasn't?"

"I didn't see her." Absence from a commotion was unlike their cook. She'd have found her way to Maggie in the crowd. A mad, disagreeable conviction swelled up in Maggie that this theft was Carson's fault, one way or another. She watched him poisonously as he stood on the bed, pushed their valuables back between the corrugated sections, then stepped down. When he knelt to retie his sneakers, she knew he'd go back outside. "I'm coming," she announced.

"Anybody else would have locked the door behind them when you came to find me," Carson said.

"I told you, everything that's gone was gone already."

"I'm going out! You're staying in! Isn't it obvious! We can't both go out!" Carson stalked from the room.

"Obvious? Don't leave me here alone!" This was ridiculous. Awful. Carson kept on walking. The idea of being here by herself, obligated in some way to clean up, made Maggie feel clawing, desperate refusal. She twisted past Carson in the hall, stood in the clinic doorway so he could not get by her. He feinted left once but she matched him, then he raised his palms and took a quick step forward, pushing Maggie backwards so she tripped and fell onto the cement. "Hey!" she said from the floor. "That's not okay."

"You asked for it," said Carson, stepping around her to the stool where he had left his satchel.

Maggie's cheeks and forehead throbbed hotly. She picked herself up and jumped in front of him again. "You're not going without me."

"*Fuck,*" Carson screamed, and shoved both her shoulders with his fingers, trying to knock her down again, but she ducked and rushed him, grabbed him around the waist with both arms. At this he went limp. She refused to let go of him, though she could feel his rage and disgust. She knew he was staring blankly over her head, toward the door. "Say you're sorry for pushing me down," she said, feeling quite unworthy of any apology.

"Let go of me," he said. "I got to go. Got to go back downtown. The police are coming. They want my report. I'm the doctor."

"You have time to say you're sorry, *Doctor.*"

"Okay, *sorry.* Now will you let go of me?"

She did, and he stood staring at her. He said, "Anything else? Otherwise, I'm going."

"Are you going to go start accusing people? There are murderers out there, don't forget. Be careful. You never know who they are."

Carson's face was lurid, shadowed. "Don't lecture me."

"I want you to talk to Vicente first. He's our friend. He knows who did it."

Carson sneered, "He knows? Is he going to solve all our problems?"

"Yes," Maggie said.

"He's going to bring Nasir back to life, find our refrigerator, clean the lake, and get profit sharing from the mine?"

"Yes, yes, he is," shouted Maggie.

Carson began to leave the room, but after two steps he turned and said, "When did you see him?"

"Two days ago, in Cajamarca."

"He's following you around?" He came back to her, put his hands on her shoulders, pushed her all the way down the hall until he'd sat her on the bed. "I hope you told Klaus Wechsler about this guy. I don't like the smell of him at all. You get some rest. You've been on the bus all day. I'm just going to go up to town. I'll talk to Vicente if that's what you want. But I won't believe a word he says. Now if you'll excuse me, the Guardia Civil is coming down from the checkpoint and they need my report. It could take a couple hours. Look, I won't go off the main road, I promise. I'll just walk up and back. In between I'll be at Nasir's. Sorry I pushed you. But I am also very, very angry."

"It's okay." Maggie's brain cleared for a moment and she knew what she must ask. "Don't mention Vicente to the cops?"

Carson swore, regretting having come to this hole, this armpit, Piedras.

"I'll wait here for you," Maggie promised. "What if they come back?"

Carson threw himself face-down across the bed to put the shotgun back into its hiding place; then, as he stood up, he pulled the pistol across with him. "On second thought," he said.

"Don't take the gun," Maggie said.

"It's only a pistol." Carson shoved it into his belt and pulled his shirt over it, then zipped his jacket partway from the bottom. The pistol was invisible.

"Carson, please!" Maggie didn't know what she was pleading for. She stood up and hovered behind him, rubbing her hands nervously on her ribs. "If you come back after the lights go out, how will you know it's me? How will I know it's you?"

"Same as any other night," said Carson, smiling now. On second thought, he told her to keep the shotgun handy. Where there was one extra key, there might be two. "Promise you won't kill me, and I won't kill you." He was cheering up. He made her get out the gun and hold it along with him, all of their four hands on it. He turned its nose away from both of them. "Rule Number One of the Gun. Never point it at anyone you don't intend to kill." Gently he took his hands away. Its barrel drooped toward the floor, ten times heavier than Maggie could imagine. "Guess you need a little lesson."

They sat side by side on the bed, and as he showed her the shell and pump and trigger, the crude but foolproof operation, Maggie realized she had entered Carson's reality at last. Here, there were consequences that mattered and that lasted. Irreversible, tragic time. A gun was like a baby, she thought. It allowed no turning back. She understood why Carson considered guns as the solution for certain types of problems. This shotgun could be very effective.

"Why don't you try to get some sleep," he said.

Maggie laughed through her nose at this.

"Nothing's going to happen, so why not?"

"Wait just a second." She pulled the gun toward her, feeling its weight, heavy as the heart of a white dwarf star, and slid down under the covers. "Let me just pretend." She touched the wooden stock, whose smoothness almost made her fall asleep, and put her fingers on the trigger. Carson was telling her to try. She forced her eyes open to aim the gun at the door.

"Move your foot, for God's sake! No, just shoot right through the blanket."

"I don't want to ruin it." The blanket was her favorite thing in the house, a synthetic Chinese pile job, brown, depicting tigers stalking in tall grass.

When she was dead, for her there would exist no blanket, Carson told her. Now he had to go. She should chain the front door from inside. He'd use the back door, now that he had a key. He'd call her name outside until he heard her answer, and only then come in. If anyone showed up without announcing himself, that was what the gun was for.

Carson carried the pistol as they walked all around the house, locking the front door and checking the window bolts, even lifting the lid of the Jewel of Piedras. Maggie felt glad to have a witness to the fact that the house was empty. Otherwise she might go back on her own perceptions, wondering whether she'd seen something and someone where she'd seen nothing and no one. This was a confusing night in general.

The air sealed inside the house began to throb. Carson rehung the mosquito net and let it float down around her. Blurry through its yellow haze, he promised once more nothing would happen. She wished he could explain to her again (had he ever?) why she had to stay here, but she didn't ask. "Vicente's wearing his white cowboy hat tonight," she reminded him.

At the door of the bedroom Carson looked sardonic, attractive. "Want me to turn off the light?"

"No thanks."

Seconds later, she heard the back door click. "Okay, bye!" Carson yelled from outside. "Can you hear me?"

"*Yes!*"

"*Okay!*"

A lock was not a limit, nor could stony limits hold love out, Maggie muttered as she settled back on a high pile of pillows. She laid the gun on the side of the bed where Carson usually slept. It was almost heavy enough to simulate his weight.

He loved her after all, she thought. He wanted to protect her. This idea was powerful enough to make her get up and fold all of Carson's clothes and put them back in the *armario* — a gift to him, which he would not appreciate. Then she lay down again. Sleep, sleep, she thought, but her mind would not sink. It was too hot. She threw off the blanket but then felt exposed. So she got up, turned off the light, returned to bed, repeating aloud his promise: "Nothing's going to happen." Her voice traveled from wall to wall, scary in the dark. A bandit could come in, turn on the light, and see her. There were voices inside her head, besides her own and Carson's: Liliana's, Julia's, and Althea's. Had Althea ever learned to shoot? She had the gaze for it, blue-gray eyes that were scarily steady.

It was the gun that kept Maggie from sleeping. If she trusted Carson, nothing was going to happen, so she didn't need to sleep with a shotgun, right? What if she rolled over on it and blew her own head off? She clicked the safety back on, dropped the gun into its slot between bed and wall. Her fingers came up covered with sticky cobwebs which she wiped on the bed leg, glad that the darkness hid the egg sacs and sucked-dry fly bodies that accumulated so quickly here. Spiders were friends, she reminded herself, and good luck; they ate mosquitoes, prevented malaria. She shoved the blanket below her feet, tucked her T-shirt around her thighs, and lay waiting in the heat for sleep with her hands folded on her breastbone.

No air moved. She rolled onto her right side. Sweating, covered with sweat, she snaked her upper body out from under the netting and lit a mosquito coil from the box they kept under Carson's side of the bed. Coils were for nights of love, when the mosquito net was in danger of being damaged or pulled from its hook. The smoke was pesticidal but it reminded her a little of sandalwood, and by now it had developed erotic associations. As soon as the room was sufficiently toxic she stood up, twisted and knotted the mosquito net, and stabbed it onto the ceiling hook.

She lay down again. Nothing was left to rearrange. Why hadn't she insisted on going out? Carson's Spanish had improved, but he still missed half of what was said.

She began to hear the river rapid. The dangerous, haunted river, full of whirlpools, currents, drownings, secrets. The river that drew you back if you drank it. Its sound got louder and louder as the burning red tip of the *espiral* moved slowly, circling inward.

A brushing noise. She thought she heard it. Yes, there it was. Again. Someone sneaking into the house, trying to be quiet, swishing his feet. Barefoot. Soft cold skin on the clinic floor: she could almost feel it on her own soles. Or maybe she'd started falling asleep and the sound of movement was part of another dream.

She'd been trying to ignore the sound for quite a while now.

Then came a sound like a voice, not Carson's lovely deep rumble, but higher, between a whisper and a squeak, a woman or a child. There had been women and children in the Shining Path, Maggie had read about them. She held her breath and wished her thudding heart would stop interfering. The sound stopped abruptly.

She let her arm hang down between bed and wall, fingers touching the gun. A bullet could hit her in the back right now. At this thought, her shoulder blades snapped shut. She quickly hauled up the gun, pulled it under the blanket, thinking she'd made too much noise. But she couldn't stop yet. She set the gun down on her belly and fumbled for the safety, gripped the grip, rested the barrel on her knee, and moved her foot aside. In that direction was the door, at that height was a person's head.

Go ahead, she thought, make my day.

Ten eons passed in uncreated silence before she dared relax her leg, which was slick with sweat, getting stiff. She could move a tiny bit: better for an intruder to think she was shifting in sleep than being unnaturally quiet.

Why had they not sold the refrigerator long ago? How had she let herself get locked into this house? The silence went on and on, deepening, as if she were walking down and down into a swamp whose bottom never leveled off. She grasped her crotch for security, the hard, immutable pubic bone. Holding this in one hand, she slid the gun off her slick belly altogether, sat up, touched her bare feet on the gritty floor; then grabbed the gun again. Clamping it under her arm, she stood up, knees bent and shaking. No sense leaving it behind, or someone would find a way to get around her, grab it, bring a foolish end to her life.

The mosquito spiral had burnt out. There was no light whatsoever in the room. On the way to the door she kicked her own shoe by mistake. The rustling sounds began again. Thieves, startled, or conferring, going through the remaining medicines in the clinic — looking for opiates? How had they gotten inside this time? Maggie must have slept for a second and not heard the snick of the back door lock. Had they been watching outside, waiting for her to be alone, to fall asleep? Vicente had surprised her in the plaza of Cajamarca. Was he waiting for her once more, in the darkness of her own house, to kill her? Her belly flickered.

She crept down the hallway, guided by her fingers against the wall, the gun dragging at her arm. Her ears like a bat's tried to judge the origin of a noise that wasn't there.

At least she wouldn't die in bed, she thought.

A crash came from the kitchen. Maggie ran to the doorway and stood the way Carson said, with her legs apart. She pulled the trigger nervously, once, but it didn't move. Harder, she thought, both fingers, squeeze. She closed her eyes, pulled as hard as she could.

At the last second she remembered the stove's fuel and jerked the barrel up.

Blast of noise — she'd never known how loud a gun could be, or how it would swerve and kick her. "Ow!" she shouted, and had the stupid thought that now she had spoken she could be aimed at, killed.

The kitchen was empty.

Empty of life, anyway. A corpse was the definition of stillness. If she'd killed a person, she didn't want to see the body. It was certainly a man's. She could imagine herself walking out into the road and begging the first person she met to please remove a *cadáver* from her kitchen. Yet she could not walk out; she was still locked in. Locked in here with whatever she had done. Carson, save me, she thought. She said "Hey?" but there was no answer. She switched on the light which fizzed loudly and went out. It did this often. Nasir had promised to renew the wiring. Now he never would. She stood for half a minute before taking the few steps back toward the clinic to get the flashlight from its predictable nail. In its beam she walked the hallway like the axis of a drowned submarine. There was the kitchen crime: garbage can on its side, the day's food scraps strewn across the floor. Rats. They came in through the sink drain. Fortunata failed to burn the garbage every night. Carson had blocked the drain hole outside with steel wool and flattened cans, but rats with strong teeth and muscular legs pushed and chewed through every barrier.

Maggie was glad she hadn't killed anything, even a rat.

She swept the beam around the room and saw where the blast had hit the wall. There was a foot-wide, brown conchoidal fracture. The hole looked deep enough that with only a little digging she could surely have pushed the tip of her finger through to the outside. No holes in the roof, luckily, no ricochet. Lucky: she could have been blinded or killed. Shaking, she put the safety back on. How could she stay in this house now?

In the bedroom, she put on her jeans with no underwear and tucked in the huge faded T-shirt she used for a nightgown. A boxing-match promotion, it had been given to her in a bar one afternoon. She remembered vividly the day she'd gotten it, sitting on a stool at the Shamrock, drinking beers with Michelle Savitsky.

15

THE CLOUDS had disappeared. Everything was bathed in moonlight the color of mercury. A perfect night for a manhunt. The only invisible things were the blackish-purple flowers on the jimsonweed beside the road, so close to the color of midnight that she could barely see them even in daytime.

All three of the neighbors' dogs were sleeping in the flower bed's softer, turned dirt. No wonder Maggie's flowers always died. The dogs looked like chiseled, oval stones, moonlight gleaming on their tight small bodies. Bobby, the biggest, opened one eye, then closed it again, curling himself more tightly, nose to tail. The river roared on, on, on. She walked onto the road, her steps crunching. She hoped that the big chain on the outside bolt would be a sufficient sign to Carson that she'd gone out. If she didn't leave the road, she was sure to meet him.

Far ahead, the line of eucalyptus above Nasir's retaining wall fluttered silver in the light. Maggie recalled Nasir's one tale of moral self-doubt, how he'd stolen the seedlings from the government and they'd ruined the soil of that field. Now from under the trees a small pumping shadow emerged, running in her direction. A person, a man, but not Carson. She panicked — whoever this was, he must not see her. She ran thirty feet back to the door she never should have opened. Locked, locked! She fumbled with the numbers, tumblers, almost visible, not quite, cylinders and fingers the same ash gray. She slammed herself inside, bolted the door, and stood aside, thinking of Carson's shotgun far off in the bedroom.

"Doña Maggie?" The warm, thin voice, by now she knew it well. *"Soy Vicente. Estás bien?"*

Her back flat against the wall, she said his name. Yes, she was all right. Again she slid the bolt and went out. Foolish, Liliana would say.

No hat, after all, but she should have recognized his silhouette, compact as a boy's. From up close she hadn't known how familiar the aura of his body already was to her, its power and weight far out of proportion to its size. This was why Quechuas called themselves Runakuna, stone people, because of their density, she thought.

"Qué te pasó?" Vicente said. What happened to you? He took both her hands, saying he'd heard gunshots, *tiros,* and had rushed here all the way from town. Was she okay?

Just one *tiro,* Maggie told him, at a rat that wasn't there. She wanted to fall into his arms, yet the touch of his hands was simultaneously disturbing, too intimate. At her first move of withdrawal he pulled his hands back nervously, as if she'd been going to slap their backs.

They sat next to each other on the stone wall, facing the road. One by one, the dogs stood up and trotted down off the road, as if offended by human self-consciousness.

The dark mass of scrub on the other side sucked up the night's luminosity so completely that it seemed to be watching them.

Vicente teased her that, indoors, it was considered more polite to attack rats with a broom. What had her mother taught her?

"Let's not begin with what my mother thinks," Maggie said.

"You can tranquilize yourself," Vicente said. "The bandits are far away." They'd chosen the full moon to run all night. Nor would they stop at dawn. Two hundred grams of gold was no burden, and coca gave them strength. In three days they could be anywhere. He began peeling an orange from Nasir's grove, where several trees overhung the road. *"Quieres?"*

She took half. "Did you see Carson?"

"Yes. I promised him I'd find your refrigerator." It had to be very near, hidden under a bush or a pile of straw, waiting for the right truck driver to pass by. Piedrasinos had stolen it, taking advantage of Carson's absence and the commotion in town.

"Poor Nasir." Maggie bit her orange half and saliva rushed painfully into her mouth. The fruit was juicy, but too sour.

"He is at peace," said Vicente, "leaving us with all the problems." Nasir was laid out now, in the back room of his store, with candles at his head and feet. Most of Piedras was in with him, except Carson, who sat in the restaurant drinking *gaseosas* with the Guardia Civil.

"I asked him not to mention you," said Maggie, answering Vicente's tone of blame.

"So he said."

"Anything else I should know?"

"I asked your husband not to file a *denuncia* of the robbery. They'd start the investigation by beating Fortunata. Who knows where it will end." Tomorrow, Vicente repeated, he and his friends would find the stolen objects. The loot could not be far away. He already suspected who had stolen it.

Maggie could well imagine what Vicente's gag order had sounded like to Carson. "So who did it? Who had our key?"

"You will laugh."

"Not Fortunata, I hope." The cook had often proposed putting the refrigerator to use, to store cold drinks for sale to passing traffic. Customers who didn't feel well could ask to be examined by the *Doctor*.

"No, no. You are paying her too well." And Vicente recited a proverb about appreciating the teat one is given to suck upon. Fortunata was among the few who did.

"Did Carson agree not to file charges?"

"*Quizás,*" said Vicente. Maybe. He couldn't tell.

"I'll talk to him myself." Maggie slid down from the wall.

Vicente said he'd walk her to the store, but excuse himself before coming in sight of the door. He must not let the police see him, especially tonight.

As they walked up the road together, Maggie felt safety on her left side where he was, but also on the right and at the bottom of her belly, because Vicente was there. A radio seemed far from necessary. Liliana was afraid of remote places, that was clear. As Maggie relaxed, a plan formed in her mind. She'd go to Cajamarca, promise Julia ten days at Christmas. Even that was a concession. Carson's idea was not to leave Peru until the end of their first year of work. They'd arranged a week off in January, with a government-service nurse filling in, but January was summer and they'd planned to visit the Pacific beaches.

She almost didn't want to look at Vicente, then did, after all. He'd gotten a haircut in Cajamarca from some incompetent barber who'd left him looking like an eighth-grader, with a cowlick that made his half-inch bangs grow straight up from his forehead. His profile was completely Indian, though, his cheekbones cruel and sentimental as a tourist carving.

They stopped at Nasir's grove to pull two more fruits from the lowest branch. The Incas would have executed them for stealing, but they agreed that in this case the owner would not mind. "So you have a gun?" Vicente said.

"My husband has two," Maggie told him.

"Good," he said. "Very good." She waited for more, the reason for all this goodness, but Vicente didn't say it.

She walked into the store knowing he watched her from the outer darkness. At the center of the room, under the bare light bulb, Carson and the two policemen sat like actors in a play. Even Maggie knew they should never sit so in the light, not on a night like this. Anyone could shoot them from outside and run off without being seen.

Someone had thrown buckets of water across the places where Nasir had bled. The brick-colored rinse had flooded out the front door, off the step, and into the packed dirt outside, which had sucked it up. Maggie wondered whether the clinic floor had ever been bathed in blood. The three men waved at her curtly without welcome, so she walked past them to the glass counter where the boy helper had fallen asleep, his head on his crossed arms. When had he returned? Why had Albita permitted him to stay? He was not her son; she'd bought him from a family uphill, to replace her boy who'd drowned.

Coin-sized bald spots gleamed in his buzz cut. Ringworm — it must have been the reason they'd shaved him in the first place. When he lifted his head, she bought from him a yellow Inka Kola and her favorite soft, sweet yeast bread, covered with large grains of sugar. Flies walked on these all day but they'd never yet made her ill. She gobbled the roll in three bites, paid for another, and walked with it over to the table.

"*Buenas noches.*" She pulled up a chair. "*Permiso?*" The two policemen accepted before Carson could demur. "*Sí, claro, buenas noches, Señora,*" they said. One was young, with a tender Indian face. The other, slightly older, had enough Spanish blood that he should have shaved four times a day, to prevent grizzle, which of course he didn't. This older man's face had a hooded, shut-down look around the eyes, and Maggie judged him best avoided.

Carson put his hand on her thigh while she explained, in Spanish, that she'd been frightened, all alone, on such a night, and had decided to come here. At the end she said to Carson, in English, "Can we talk for one second?"

"I'm finishing the medical report." He pointed out the coat of arms of Peru atop the official report pages, long pulpy sheets filled with the older man's handwriting, dense, florid, and full of interlocking curlicues. Glancing at it, Maggie deciphered the word "*desventura,*" misadventure.

"Please," she insisted. "It's really important." She excused them both from the policemen. They turned their chairs away and she leaned on Carson's shoulder, whispering into the whorl of his left ear, "Ease-play, on't-day omplain-kay about-yay the idge-fray."

Carson pushed her back from him. "They say it's a civil *denuncia* and can't be filed till Monday. I think they want a payoff. So on't-day orry-way, ove-lay. I'm sorry you got scared. Want to hang out here till I'm done?"

Just then the older cop cleared his throat.

"Go pay your respects," Carson said. "Catch you later."

Behind the counter, to the left of the kitchen door, the storeroom was full of gently shifting yellow light and murmuring sounds. Maggie excused herself with meek propriety and went to see.

Nasir was laid out under a blanket, on a wide bier made of wooden crates. At each corner was a thick, flat river stone with half a dozen candles on it, melting into pools, radiating the guttering golden light that had defeated the glare from the ceiling's single bulb. The room smelled of kerosene from several lanterns that also had been placed on top of sacks and boxes. A surprising number of people sat on chairs or stood against the wall. The atmosphere was hushed, charged. Men gripped unlabeled bottles of cloudy, bluish cane liquor; their faces were already greasy with sorrow and drink. Doña Albita shared a chair with another woman, shoulder to shoulder, leaning on each other. In a little while she noticed Maggie standing in the door, and she waved, inviting her to come in, sit down. When Maggie hesitated, Doña Albita waved more insistently, then got up and came toward Maggie. Her face was soaked and shattered, large tears rolling down her finely wrinkled cheeks. No, no, Maggie wanted to say, don't take care of me, but instead she gave both hands to Doña Albita, the same hands she'd given to Vicente half an hour before, and offered whatever lame consolations came into her head until Albita collapsed against her, sobbing, *"Era tan bueno,"* he was so good. Maggie helped her to sit down again. Albita crunched her black shawl against her face, and her friend put both arms around her shoulders.

Someone gave Maggie a glass of cane liquor and she took it, raised it toward the dead man as she saw others do, and drank it all at once. She went to lean against the wall on the women's side of the room. Women refilled her glass, touched her shoulders. She thought of Liliana saying, "We women need each other." These women embraced her in their presence. Perhaps the way they stood tightly at her sides, accepting her, was part of Vicente's effect upon her life. They explained that this *velorio* would last two days and then would come the burial. Maggie thought that if she had not been married to Carson, she might have stood there that whole time.

She was about to ask for Fortunata when all at once she heard chairs scraping and the policemen's voices gruffly bidding goodbye. *"Hasta mañana,"* she whispered to the women. On the way out she paused at Nasir's feet and crossed herself, hoping to be understood by something, someone. Anything, anyone.

Carson put his arm around the small of her back and they walked out into the night together. Facing the same stretch of road, it seemed to Maggie that she'd walked it a thousand times today. Carson scolded her a little, saying she'd make a bad detective. She should be more suspicious of Vicente's offer to bring the refrigerator back. Was Maggie becoming his mouthpiece? They argued about Vicente all the way home, and even, for a while, in bed afterward, until Carson announced self-righteously that he had to get some sleep, rolled on his side, and promptly began snoring. Maggie lay awake talking to him out loud, hoping to disturb his rest, but also regretting the many other loving and important things she could have told him.

❖

Eleven A.M. The clinic was stale, sealed, hot as the inside of a clay bread oven. Still Carson slept, the sharp wing of his shoulder blade turned toward Maggie. She crawled up his damp back wondering if she really wanted to make love or whether she was trying to acquire concessions, forgiveness, reassurance. Yes, she decided when Carson curled miserably away, muttering that he wanted to be left alone for half an hour.

She got up, put on her ragged kimono, and stood over him insisting that she had many more things to tell him. Walking into the kitchen, she was glad to see her bullet hole first and by herself. Not as bad as it had seemed last night: it had ruined a lot of Carson's plaster, but the hole was hardly wider than her two spread palms and fingers. She felt almost proud of it. A few handfuls of mud would fill it in; Fortunata must know how.

She sat on the small, hard chair waiting for the water to boil, feeling too rough and weary to bustle around the clinic flinging windows open and assessing damages and loss. From where she sat she could see the heavy cable securing the front door's inside bolts. Was the empty clinic waiting for the smell of an alcohol swab and the voice of a patient enumerating his complaints, as other rooms in other houses waited for the rattle of plates and children's laughter? Perhaps this building would prefer for a peasant family to come and live in it instead.

She lifted the kettle's lid. Bubbles the size of seed pearls clung to its bottom, detaching themselves slowly, one by one. The surface was just beginning to rumple when the raw electrocuting sound of the front door buzzer sounded, like an alarm inside a prison. She ran down the hall to wake up Carson, but he already had his pants on and was raking a comb through his hair, ducking before the mirror. "I got it," he said. She dressed quickly, pulling on her filthy jeans, stiff from last night and yesterday, and the day before, and the day before that.

It was neither Vicente nor the cook but a woman and a child. Four-year-old Wilmer's face was swollen and miserable. Obligingly he coughed his wet, rattling cough, then lost control of it. His mother said many people had fallen ill from the cold last Tuesday night, a night Maggie and Carson remembered as slightly cooler, almost tolerable. Carson sat Wilmer on the table, made him say "Ah," and questioned the mother in Spanish that was halting but so competent that Maggie intervened only twice before she smelled the kettle burning dry. On her return, Carson was unlocking the aluminum trunk to offer aspirin, and advice about boiled liquids in quantity. Their lack of patients had a silver lining: the reserve stock of medications was intact.

"Upper respiratory infection (viral)," Maggie noted in the log.

"Tienen bultos afuera," the mother said, you have packages outside. There sat two black fiberglass sacks of the kind used for harvesting potatoes. One held the refrigerator and the other the medicines, all jumbled and dirty and with only the cough syrup missing. Carson said he felt sorry for anyone who'd drunk all ten bottles, especially since the syrup was not opiated. They dragged the sacks by the necks indoors, threw away the ruined vaccines and snake antidote, and shoved the refrigerator under the counter.

"What was it you had to say to me?" Carson wanted to know.

Maggie invited him into the kitchen. She apologized for the hole, explained how Liliana and the rats had scared her. In the clear light of morning she felt much more sanguine, only a little hung over emotionally. After she'd finished telling him everything (leaving out only her attraction to Vicente, which was distracting and irrelevant, even to herself), Carson declared this was one of those times when you began to wonder.

"Wonder what?" Maggie asked.

"Whether you should leave a place," he said.

At this moment Fortunata rang the buzzer, having come to announce that they were expected at Nasir's. *"Array!"* What happened! She'd been kept home all last night by her five-year-old, who had Wilmer's flu. He'd coughed to the point of throwing up. "Why didn't you bring him?" Maggie asked, hurt, despite knowing that last night she could easily have gunned them down. Oh, only a cold, said Fortunata; her child was strong and would get better by himself. Carson, who had never cared whether Fortunata brought her children to visit the clinic or not, rummaged out some aspirin from the filthy sack. "Don't worry," the cook said, pocketing the pills. "You'll see, Vicente will occupy himself with your *problema*."

They locked the clinic and walked to the wake together. Mourning had resumed, or never stopped; the road was blocked by staggering, drunken men and women. Doña Albita had opened the blue fifty-gallon drums of *cañazo* in the storeroom and was siphoning them out without charge into any empty bottle, even waiting mouths. This liquor was made in Piedras Baja, at a farm where a donkey ceaselessly turned a wheel that crushed the cane, and the resulting juice spilled into a drum set over a fire, evaporating into a system of car radiators. The resulting brew combined the oiliness of kerosene, the smell of an electrical fire, and pubic funk. It delivered a numbing occipital blow.

Cries of welcome and embraces. They were pulled inside the store. "Doctor Calzón! Seño-o-ora!" Maggie drank two quick tumblers ceremonially offered on a tray. Immediately she felt sharp wires being threaded through her eyeballs and down across her cheekbones, to be tightened later. Yet it was impossible to avoid drinking more. She and Carson were led into the storeroom, seated side by side among the Piedrasinos, to toast with them the memory and to revere the mortal remains of he who in life was Don Nasir Salim Dabdoub Ahmed. Everyone was smoking cigarettes. The shave-head boy went around glumly refilling every empty glass. Nasir's mouth had tightened, as if he felt shy at finding himself the center of attention. It amazed Maggie that he could be present, still so recognizable, yet unable to sit up.

At three-thirty, Carson and Maggie tried and failed to count their doses of *cañazo,* and beer, and white rum, and bad whiskey mixed with Coca-Cola. Maggie's armpits and temples oozed yellow sweat. Conversations all blurred into one, girls whispering they needed birth control. Maggie had to tell them Catholic Charities forbade the clinic to dispense it, but that there were pharmacies in the city, and down here many women, including Doña Ema, knew how to care for themselves with cost-free herbs. Speaking of Ema, where was she? At home, ashamed, Maggie learned. Her husband had left her again, disclaiming the child, saying it belonged either to a truck driver or to Jesus, not him.

Maggie excused herself to pee. As she stumbled across the dry stones of the river flats, a white orb of blistering sunlight erased all corners of her recent memory. The present, visible world was thin and horribly precise, as if compressed between two lenses. Barely making it to a clump of bushes, she splattered her dusty sneakers. It felt grand to be alone and thoughtless, with tomorrow's headache all there was to dread. She peered across the wavering expanse of sand toward Doña Ema's, considering setting forth to see how Ema was. Unprofessional to show up drunk. Carson would worry. Besides, the riverbank was disheartening, seeming so vast as to require three days and a camel to arrive. When she headed back in, the earth rose up once toward her, and as she fell to her knees, she saw a small black snake, its tail vanishing among the roots of a thorn bush. Funny, she thought, Fortunata said there were no snakes in Piedras.

Each time she and Carson tried to leave, drunken people hauled them back by the elbows with dislocating force, plunking them into their chairs, where they ended up accepting more *cañazo*. The floor was slick; wet lips loomed and disappeared. Doña Albita leaned sharply sideways in her chair, dressed all in black and crying with abandon. When Maggie and Carson went to pay respects, Albita sank her voice to a conspiratorial whisper and asked Carson to help carry Don Nasir to his grave in the cemetery south of town. The procession would occur tomorrow.

"How do you say 'remind me'?" Carson said. When Maggie translated, Doña Albita raised both feet from the floor in laughter, nearly falling over in two directions. *"No me olvidaré,"* she said, patting Carson's arm, I won't forget. Then, herself reminded, she began to weep again.

That night, having somehow arrived at home, the last thing Maggie saw was the blurred, ghostly ring of a chamber pot, which had mysteriously appeared under the bed for her to throw up into. The following day, the gringos awoke in such a state of wretchedness that when Fortunata came around, cajoling them to return, prescribing more drink as the only cure, they obeyed, willy-nilly.

Most mourners seemed never to have left. On the store steps, two men slept where they had fallen. Maggie and Carson stepped over them. When they walked into the storeroom there was a general guffaw as everyone recalled last night, when Maggie had tried to help the men who'd carried her home, moving her little feet in the air, like this! They twiddled their fingers. Fortunately today the *cañazo* was running low and toasts were made in beer. At midday Fortunata organized the slaughter and roasting of a calf, a pig, and twenty chickens. By midafternoon, Maggie felt she'd hit her stride, but it was already time for the burial.

Don Zoilo, the carpenter, brought the coffin he had built and painted black with a shaky silver cross and Nasir's full name in capitals. Everyone filed outside and stood under the trees. No band was available to play sad boleros of the cavalry, thus the hammering of the coffin nails resounded from the back room, each blow accompanied by shrieks of refusal from Doña Albita that sounded like the same nails being pulled out.

Due to the inebriate state of the pallbearers and mourners, the procession to the walled cemetery was solemn and disorderly, Doña Albita stumbling along half carried by four of her largest women friends who were barely more competent at walking. Ahead of her the coffin tipped and lurched as if Nasir were fighting to get out. Stops were called where the coffin must be put down lest it fall onto the road and God forbid break open. Carson, alone among the pallbearers, did not weep or stagger. Pale and cadaverous with drink, he walked as if following the edge of a ruler until he was told to stop.

When at last the coffin was lowered by ropes into the grave, one man fell to his knees and began tilting slowly into emptiness, and would have fallen in had Carson not grabbed the tail of his jacket. Its vents ripped as the man regained a sitting position at ground level. He began to weep and blubber. Another man pulled Carson to the head of the grave and asked him to make Nasir's last oration, since he was the most superior person present.

All the men removed their hats. Carson's face looked clammy as he stood atop the pile of dirt. "I'm not superior," he slurred in English. "I'm your doctor, Don Calzón."

"Go on," Maggie said. "I'll help." She climbed a little way up the dirt pile.

"Ladies and gentlemen," Carson said, still in English, "I don't know what to say."

"Mention Syria," Maggie whispered, for Carson had been there. But he just stared fixedly over the black heads of the crowd.

"*Señoras y Señores.*" Maggie translated, inspired. "My husband says, 'I am a doctor, and my job is to postpone the ultimate finality, which you see and contemplate before you.'"

"Amen," someone said.

Carson gave her a startled, oddly happy look. "Tell them I'm the last person who should ever be standing here," he went on. "I feel I should have saved this man. He was my best friend here, I guess."

"My husband wishes he could have saved this man, his friend and ours," and Maggie extolled Nasir's virtues for a while. "But all doctors fail, all worldly means are finite. What comes beyond will prove the grace of our futility."

"Amen," said the whole crowd. The first shovelful of dirt fell on the coffin. Doña Albita screamed. Who would take care of her now?

In the week after the funeral, they treated someone every day. More colds; a woman with malaria, which she called tertian fever; a teenage boy with Down's syndrome who had begun to masturbate in public (a Pentecostal exorcism had only made him worse); a farmer who'd walked nine hours to reach the clinic after a neighbor had tried to extract one of his molars with pliers (Carson gave him a shot for pain, and then cash for bus fare and a Cajamarca dentist). And two miscarriages, and a baby born dead. Doña Ema never appeared, but she was all right, still pregnant, Fortunata said. Maggie didn't mention her to Carson, lest he say Ema deserved to be abandoned.

His experience orating on the dirt pile was hard to describe in words, Carson said, but it had made him want to stay in Piedras. He had to help these people, now that they'd offered him their trust. Three infant mortalities could be normal, but he was more and more convinced there was a problem in the river. Lady Maggy hadn't returned for her checkup, but her troubles seemed clear. Even the teenager's Down's syndrome might be traced to maternal toxicity. He'd go up to the mine and start that clinic, as its director, Ignacio García, had invited him to do. How long ago, only a week? Ignacio was unlikely to act against his own employers. Nonetheless, Carson could sound him out, look around. He fumed that they had no money for hair analysis, and that the water test was so slow and so expensive. The Cajamarca lab had sent the sample down to Lima, telling Maggie to come back in a month or so.

Vicente dropped in at four o'clock on an afternoon that was beginning to seem slow. Carson and Maggie were sitting in the kitchen telling Fortunata how fickle they felt, to be relieved on a day when nothing bad had happened. When next the buzzer rang, they laughed with ironic pride, until they saw it was Vicente. He'd stepped inside and was holding his white hat, blinking in the sudden shade. "*Hola,* Vicente," Maggie said excitedly from the hallway. "Carson, Vicente! Vicente, Carson!"

"We've met before," Carson said.

They retired to the kitchen, where Fortunata clucked like a hen, as flustered as the first time the Comandante had appeared.

"*Por favor,* Fortunata," Vicente said, motioning her out of the room.

Had the young men who robbed the clinic presented an apology, he wanted to know.

No, said Carson and Maggie at once. They hadn't forgiven the theft, but its memory was fading. They'd changed the back door lock, and Don Zoilo had added a bar. The refrigerator sat inert inside its sack, awaiting the next government yellow-fever vaccination campaign. "My boots are still missing," complained Carson. He asked Vicente, "*Quién fue?*" Who was it? Maggie added, more seriously, that despite getting most of their stuff back, they feared being robbed again.

Vicente looked grave. That was the problem. Even if restitution was imperfect, it must include an apology, or the community remained in jeopardy.

Impatient now, Carson asked, "*Quién?*" Maggie wished he'd thank Vicente instead.

"*Sus vecinos,*" Vicente answered, your neighbors. He twitched his lips and chin upriver. Boris and Limbert, the sons of Doña Ema.

"Big surprise," said Carson.

"You promised me I'd laugh," said Maggie to Vicente.

"They were sleeping with the nurses," Vicente told her. "That's why they had the back door key. Boris was twelve when he started. Limbert ten, I think."

"You owe us a fuller explanation," Carson persisted.

"*Bien,*" said Vicente. He'd start from the beginning, if that was all right.

16

THE KETTLE BOILED, but the gringos sat listening to its breath like a congested lung. Carson gripped his knees and glared at them like a rheumatic old man. Maggie glanced nervously back and forth from him to Vicente, who had talked for nearly an hour, addressing much of his speech to Carson. Now he caught Maggie's eyes and held them in a deep, burning stare. It pulled a flash from her core, which she would rather he hadn't seen. Yet she didn't dare look away, after all he had said.

"Water's boiling," Carson announced. Maggie pretended not to hear his words as a command, one of her recent tricks. Soon Carson sighed, got up, and made the coffee himself.

She could see so clearly the hovel where Vicente had been born, with its unglazed windows and walls of rough brown adobe bricks — all because of how he'd said it: "I first saw light in a hut with a packed dirt floor." In the rhythmic, slightly antiquated Spanish of the mountains she had felt his inevitability, as if she had known his story always.

He'd been born into chattel slavery, his parents *peones* on a small hacienda in the southern part of the country. Freed by the agrarian reform, but unable to subsist on their granted plot, they'd walked to the city of Cuzco. There Vicente's father had been blinded, welding without a mask. Afterward he could only drink and sit in the sun of the courtyard. Everyone else worked: mother and younger sister knitting sweaters for tourists, Vicente shining shoes, his two brothers carrying loads, and Alida, his older sister, attending the counter in an electrical shop. Father attacked mother on nights when he was drunk, dragging her out of bed by the hair, once even managing to break her forearm in a door. Yet she refused to leave him, knowing that without her, he could not survive. She asked her sons to protect her as best they could, and to understand that their father's rage was directed at his sufferings and degradation, not at her. She was a saintly woman; she insisted on education for her children.

At the university Vicente had studied archaeology. If he'd written a thesis, his topic would have been Inca administration, which he still considered the most enlightened social system ever devised. He'd also played *charango* in a student ensemble, traveling all over Peru trying to revive traditions among families like his own, displaced peasants in city slums. One by one, friends in the group began to disappear; slowly the others learned they'd been arrested on suspicion of inciting the populace under cover of flutes and drums. If it is true that pride is dangerous, it was also likely that Sendero was recruiting quietly among the spectators, but it was also incontrovertible that none of the musicians was a member of anything more radical than the band itself.

On that inevitable day when the secret police arrived at the university, Vicente had managed to escape down a side alley. Leaping a wall, he'd watched two lovers, a boy and a girl, blown to a pulp against the wall just opposite. He'd taken refuge at an uncle's, never returning to the university, visiting his family only late at night. Yet he hadn't wanted to leave Cuzco, for fear of what might happen to his mother. That was when he'd begun to use the name Oquendo, naming himself after a revolutionary poet.

He'd lived in this manner for several months, until his sister Alida was raped by a rich man's son, and next by the police to whom she'd dared to report the crime. Out of shame she'd run away to Lima, to make her life in the streets. It had been in search of justice for Alida that Vicente had first contacted the Sendero Luminoso.

Sendero had arranged for the guilty parties to meet with certain accidents, and then had demanded of Vicente certain acts of loyalty as repayment, which he'd found himself unwilling to perform. He'd fled Cuzco in the back of a beer truck, crouching in a small cavity amongst the plastic cases. After searching fruitlessly for Alida in the *pueblos jóvenes* of Lima, he'd joined the newly formed Black Rainbow Movement, which sent him north into the highlands. At first he'd mostly scribbled on walls and sat around in *chicherías* trying to raise peasants' consciousness. Slowly, as the guerrilla war guaranteed the isolation of rural villages, he and his group had recognized the need for autonomous local governments. It was the perfect opportunity; Piedras had been the fourth village to accept them.

He was candid about the airstrip, and how its enormous profits had slowly destroyed the Black Rainbow in spasms of greed, corruption, and egoism. Even up to now, the so-called Golden Age of Piedras had left behind its scars: the insoluble dissatisfaction of some people, weak characters Vicente thought, who for a short time had lived as they believed the outside world had always lived at their expense, on wealth obtained without sweat. He'd tried to teach them that their minds were diseased, destructive, unnatural, feverish, and monstrous, no different from the conquistadores'. But these minds had already changed, become unable to listen. With the airstrip defunct, they were tortured by the shadow of the mine, La Tormentosa. People found it unbearable to watch Canadians extracting tons of gold from their own mountain, letting not a grain fall to the valley's bottom. Nasir had been murdered by three such malcontents, former Rainbow members. The gold they'd stolen had amounted to a couple of thousand dollars. A tenth of what Maggie had suspected, yet, as Vicente said, it was enough to prevent them from ever returning, as long as they had the good sense to invest in a minibus and set it running on some route in Lima, or Trujillo.

As for the matter at hand, the theft of the clinic's refrigerator, Doña Ema's sons had similar bad ideas, gleaned mostly from the television and the example of their wretched parents. Ema's husband had abandoned her yet again, claiming the miracle baby was not his. People said she was lucky to be rid of the man. He'd been unbalanced ever since his army service. People were afraid of him, and of his boys. Yet Vicente believed that the boys' hearts might not yet be fully hardened. They were frustrated young men, thwarted by lack of opportunities in Piedras.

"Can't you invite the mine to use your old airstrip?" The idea had come to Maggie in a flash. Her voice faded as she heard herself expounding yet another infantile scheme.

The mine was building its own airstrip, Carson said to her.

"I know!" said Maggie bullishly. "Wouldn't they like to save that money?"

Vicente said, "For various reasons, the old airstrip is not safe."

Carson spoke to Vicente directly now, in his broken Spanish. You couldn't stop progress. He didn't think Vicente wanted to. "How do you say, 'You want a piece of the action'? He's a fool if he doesn't." Carson drank his coffee black. Now, with the bottom half of his face hidden by the enamel mug, Maggie saw his eyes narrowing mistrustfully as he observed Vicente's efforts to shake condensed milk down from the bottom of the can, where it would be clinging like a half inch of library paste. She decided not to fetch the can opener, even if it meant going without milk herself.

Vicente smiled wryly, set the can aside, and declaimed the old saying that Peru was a beggar sitting on a throne of gold. In this much he agreed with the malcontents, that it was hard to watch one's possibilities being trucked away to Canada. The mine should hire local workers, help pay for a school. Unfortunately, there was no one in the Rosario capable of negotiating such concessions.

"Don't look at me," said Carson. He asked Maggie to explain that miners were hardly better than slaves, and that under current policies, designed to encourage foreign investments, no one in the universe could ever persuade the corporation to dilute its profits. In Carson's opinion Piedras would be better off without the mine, period. Lately, he'd been making a list of crops they saw on walks: mangoes, oranges, limes, several kinds of papayas, sugar cane, peppers, squash, tomatoes, peas, beans, tree tomatoes, and the huge green striated melon that was trained to grow on roofs or hang from trellises, and from which a refreshing drink was made.

Vicente must think Carson was baiting him, avoiding him — and he was. Yet Maggie knew that her husband was also sincere. He hated technology. In the shower he sang of pickin' pawpaws in de pawpaw patch.

In her mind Larry said again, "You can't say the cat is gray. You have to ask the cat." Asking the cat wasn't enough. Who knew what answer the animal might be inclined to give on a particular day, or how its eyes were built.

She gripped her mug with both hands as hard as possible, palm prints melting flat against the hot enamel, and listened to her husband and Vicente talking. With the moral clarity of a four-year-old child, she saw how they deceived each other on the surface, circling like two dogs unconscious that their interests were identical. She wanted each of them to see that the fire inside the other was the same. She'd brought them to this table; now it was essential to make them understand how close they were to one another.

Julia had always told her that she lacked common sense.

Carson shifted his chair heavily and said, "I'm sorry, Vicente. You're going to have to work this out for yourselves down here. Maggie and I aren't development experts. We're health workers."

She hurried to translate.

Vicente pursed his lips. "You are our crazy gringos. You have returned our lost hopes to us. Even one small ray of light is an enormous change. Little by little, we have to believe, our hopes will become reality."

"Little by little!" Maggie cried. "Can't we make something happen? My husband's starting a clinic at the mine. Weren't you planning to talk to the director, Carson?" Turning to him, she said in English, "Weren't we training an assistant?"

"Maggie!" Carson said.

"You know how I feel."

Carson's long, pale fingers were splayed flat across the dark tabletop. He said, "On't-day elieve-bay everything you ear-hay. Want to be careful here."

Vicente gave Maggie an alert look, but she didn't translate. She remembered his three words of English on the night of Nasir's death. He'd understood enough, and Carson had meant him to. At the moment she disliked both of them.

Vicente said, in a ministerial tone, "Señora Maggie, your husband is right. See what happened here this week. When killing begins, misery only grows. Meanwhile, a small positive step can bring great joy. Health is the greatest wealth. I constantly say to our people, no matter how far we have fallen, there is only one thing to do. We must lift ourselves up and go forward, *salir adelante,* toward the positive. So my mother used to say. I only repeat her words."

"That's really true," Carson said without irony. *"Muy verdado."*

Which was more dangerous, Maggie wondered, loving an idea or loving a person? Or loving a person who loved an idea?

"Speaking of stealing," Vicente said. "What time is it?"

It was four-thirty by Carson's watch.

"We cannot let this day pass," said Vicente. "We have prepared a community meeting. It would be important for both of you to attend." Don Sixto, an old friend, was waiting at the store in town, ready to call forth the Piedrasinos. "*Vamos?*"

Carson and Maggie looked at each other, shrugged. "We don't need a public scene," Maggie said.

"You must understand, the apology is not only for you. It is for everyone. You will help us to heal our community trust." The boys had terrorized Piedras for years. As children they'd cut off dogs' tails with machetes. They lurked on hidden paths to grab the breasts and crotches of young girls. They stole chickens, and ate them, when the owners went to Cajamarca. Last October, during the feast of Piedras's patron saint, they'd entered unguarded houses to steal radios, money, and jewels. Only yesterday a case of beer had vanished from Doña Albita's. Who else would take advantage of a new widow? Now, on top of her sorrow, Doña Albita would have to pay for the plastic case and twelve glass bottles.

October's fiesta thefts had been denounced to the police. The boys and their mother had spent an hour in the police checkpoint, high on the other side of the canyon, but the matter had slid away, evidently lubricated with some donation. No items were recovered. They'd all been sold to miners and truck drivers on the road above Piedras. "But their mother is the cause," Vicente concluded.

"No kidding," Carson said. Taking pleasure in his outrage, he told Vicente about his long-standing water feud with Doña Ema. Some mornings he still had to march out with his shovel. On top of that, whenever Carson left the house, she and her boys had the gall to show up and eat the gringos' food.

Was this all true? Vicente wanted to know.

It was, admitted Maggie.

"*Desgraciados,*" Vicente said, so bitterly convinced that Maggie regretted her assent. She tried to explain that the boys were not all bad. They made her laugh; they'd taught her the steps of the *huayno*. As for the lunches, she'd invited them, keeping tabs on Doña Ema's pregnancy.

Vicente ignored her babbling. Time to go, he said. Maggie should summon Fortunata.

It was with relief that she went behind the house and found the cook, sitting on her tiny wooden bench, shelling beans into the dishpan, humming, facing the river, not watching her own hands. Though Maggie apologized for interrupting, Fortunata stood up immediately, setting the *palangana* on the ground. Of course she wanted to come. Those boys had stolen her husband's watch right off his wrist, one night when he was drunk.

Don Sixto was a very short, potbellied, bowlegged farmer. Under the Black Rainbow, he'd been chief justice officer. With him was a younger man, also from El Mirador, who had thick curly hair and had lost his middle incisors. They'd drunk liters of beer while they waited in the store. Four tall brown bottles were grouped on the table. Their mules, a dark bay and a buckskin, were tied up in the shade outside.

Don Sixto wore a taupe windbreaker, a plaid shirt, and very clean, deeply cuffed blue jeans over his dusty boots. He looked a little more prosperous than the others. In another life he would have been a businessman, a burgher, a man of substance, Maggie thought, until with a jolt of recognition she realized he was exactly that. How flawed her upbringing had been! Behind a gate, under her mother's influence, she'd been imbued with subtly disrespectful assumptions. Now she was in the real Peru. What did people think of her? At least she recognized Vicente as an equal.

Don Sixto stood up when he saw Maggie, Carson, Vicente, and Fortunata. Introducing himself to the two gringos, he added, after his name, "At your service." The young man's name was Marco Antonio, and he would come along with their party. Maggie made a point of shaking Marco Antonio's hand; his breath smelled of his rotting teeth.

As plans and formalities proceeded, she couldn't take her eyes off Don Sixto's nose: its tip went down so far that his nostril openings were vertical. Six or seven hairs grew into them from his upper lip. This feature made him appear capable of evil, though Maggie told herself it wasn't fair to physiognomize. Otherwise, his face had the tight, magical sheen of certain older Peruvians who knew the limits of their lives, what was a man, what was a woman, and what was God. Such people seemed charmed, and held in security, by this knowledge.

Combined with a capacity for evil, Maggie thought, emotional security was bad, not good.

He put on his straw hat, darkened to gold with age, with permanent sweat stains around the headband. *"Vamos,"* he said.

Doña Albita came out, but she didn't charge for the beers. She said, *"Regalo,"* gift, and wished them luck in their errand to confront the youthful *desgraciados.*

They walked outside, into the arena of packed dirt, waiting while Marco Antonio untied a large wooden drum from the back of his mule's saddle. Don Sixto knew the way to Doña Ema's house; he'd been there two days ago. Why, Maggie wondered, feeling caught up in forces she did not understand. Yet this was just the inclusion they'd been waiting for. They were part of the community. She reached for her husband's hand. Carson was asking what would go on at Doña Ema's, overriding Fortunata's eager assurances that now they'd see, now they'd participate, this was how it all had been under the Rainbow.

"We present the case," Don Sixto said, speaking slowly and with ponderous hand gestures, presumably to help Carson understand him. "We adjudicate a penalty."

"And if they are not home?"

"But yes, they are."

Marco Antonio went ahead, striding at an alarming speed up the stone stairway and along the steep, narrow dirt paths, beating the drum with rapid, full strokes of his arm. Maggie and Carson were last in line, as conspicuous as newlyweds or the sponsors of a feast, until people began to emerge from doorways and run down from smaller paths to add themselves behind. Skinny dogs skedaddled or barked, children watched from doorways. More and more people joined the crowd. Eventually Maggie was followed by at least half of Piedras. She recognized faces from the wake at Doña Albita's.

At the highest point, just as the procession turned downhill, Ofelia came skipping down. She was squeezing a very young brown puppy. Shifting it into the crook of one arm, she slipped her free hand into

Maggie's, and turned her calf to show the pig's bite, now a deep, ugly blue scar. It hadn't affected her light step, even at this pace, which was keeping Maggie at the edge of her breath.

Where was everybody going, Ofelia wanted to know.

They stopped at the side of the path, and while Carson knelt to examine Ofelia's leg, Maggie explained about the robbery. Ofelia's eyes grew round. She'd heard the boys took a bunch of drugs, then vomited all night. She would have liked to come along and see the justice, but this puppy needed its mother. She swung the hapless creature by its front legs for Maggie to admire its fat pink belly. A bad way to hold a puppy, Maggie admonished her, feeling unnecessarily stern. Anyway it didn't matter, as her advice had no effect.

"*Estás bien,*" Carson said.

"*Ya sé,*" Ofelia chirped, I know. This dog was a female and her name was Flor de Papa, Potato Flower. The name of a song. She slung it over her shoulder and ran off singing in a thin voice, copied from the falsetto of female *huayno* stars: "*La flor de papa, la flor de papa!*" She was almost of an age to be fondled by one of those twerps, Maggie thought, hurrying to catch up with the others.

Dusk was falling as they crossed the river road. Doña Ema's house was already guarded by a half-dozen able-bodied men. The house looked smaller, scabby; all of the melons had been harvested from its roof. For once Maggie did not want to enter, nor did she fantasize a different existence for herself inside, full of smoky warmth, roly-poly babies crawling all over the floor, and visits to the river where she might glimpse the pale sexual ghosts in their secret world below the waters. Instead, she heard Liliana's voice in her head, asking how people could live in such a place. This was just the kind of dwelling described in rural health manuals, where Chagas beetles dropped from the thatch, bit you, and infected you with a microorganism that produced few symptoms until your heart failed three years later. She poked Carson, intending to ask him the insect's elevation range, but the crowd was swelling forward.

The bottom half of Doña Ema's door was blocked by a grubby sheet of plywood. Don Sixto slid this aside and ducked into the front room, motioning the rest to follow. He must have found a switch, for suddenly the room was lit by one bare and searing bulb. It was empty of furniture. Guinea pigs cheeped under a pile of black potato sacks.

The dirt floor was littered with potato peels, corn husks, and the guinea pigs' tiny poops and urine stains. One wall bore a faded, torn, dusty poster of an Argentine rock star with a shoulder-length perm, aggressively wielding his microphone. Where had the boys gotten this, Maggie wondered. She felt sorry for them.

Quickly the room filled with so many people that Maggie thought its walls might burst. She was mashed in amongst bony bodies, fat bodies, male and female bodies smelling raw or oily, smoky, drenched in hair oil, flesh different from her own. She wanted to lose herself and Carson in the crowd, but its mass kept jostling, opening toward the front, pressing from the back, as if digesting the two of them toward a designated place in the front of the room.

"Ema!" Don Sixto called in a loud voice.

The door's fringe rustled. Maggie craned her neck to see Ema half tangled in the plastic strands, wearing a baggy dress. Her eyes were always small, but this evening they looked like gun slits in a bunker. Bruises, Maggie recognized, healing but still puffy, yellow-green. No wonder she hadn't wanted to show herself at Nasir's funeral. *"Hé?"* She tilted her chin back, crossed her arms over her chest.

"But this woman has been beaten," Carson announced. "Doña Ema, are you all right?"

"Qué te importa," what do you care, Doña Ema answered. *"Estoy divinamente bien."* She was divinely well.

"She's accustomed," someone whispered.

"Your sons," Don Sixto commanded.

Brazenly, she lied that they'd gone uphill to get her donkeys.

"Veremos," said Don Sixto. We'll see. "You know why we have come."

Doña Ema looked at the group, at Fortunata, at Maggie and Carson. She nodded.

"Say the reason," Vicente ordered her.

Looking at the floor, Doña Ema muttered that it was because her sons had stolen the refrigerator of the gringos and then they had returned it.

Standing in the poverty of her rooms, Maggie understood that Doña Ema could not get her sons to work at all. They did not want to be *campesinos* — and why should they, Maggie thought, when the world above the canyon was so large and so luxurious, in their imaginations one great Hollywood, New York, and Buenos Aires. Alas, they could not leave their mother, especially now that she was alone again and pregnant. Since they would not work, Ema must live from whatever they stole, and they were too young and dumb and spoiled to rely upon. This time, they'd gotten her into real trouble. Or was it Maggie who was truly most responsible? She should never have given Ema that advice on getting pregnant.

Don Sixto faced the crowd and spoke in the voice of the archangel Michael, surely audible throughout the house and yard. "Because they stole! Not because they returned. They only returned because we fished them out. And how did we fish them out? Why is this the first house I decided to investigate? Why, if there is robbery, even during a saint's festival or a funeral, is it here that lost objects come to rest? Why is it a good idea to inquire of Doña Ema and her sons? Because you three have no shame! No respect for your neighbor, nor women, even animals. Everyone knows it, even the authorities who by their own corruption permit you to continue hardening your hearts. When the ex-Comandante and I came to you, we asked only for the return of the stolen objects and an apology to the North American doctors. No punishment. Yet you did not complete your charge. Do you not agree that where there is no shame, no repentance, no learning, no regret, then punishment must come? Only then, the criminal feels in the flesh the wrongness of his acts and decides not to repeat them." Don Sixto concluded by turning sideways, opening his windbreaker and showing something to Doña Ema. "Bring your sons!"

"What is that?" Maggie whispered to Fortunata, fearing the worst.

"He carries a whip," Fortunata whispered back. "*Chicote.*" The crowd in the room murmured in a way that made Maggie glad she had not stolen anything in Piedras.

"*Silencio!*" cried Don Sixto.

Marco Antonio came in and reported that no one had seen the boys leaving the house.

"*Ya, ya,*" said Doña Ema, and ducked under the curtain into the next room. In two seconds the boys appeared. They wore jeans and tattered sneakers. The older one, Boris, had a baseball cap turned backwards.

A thin, white-haired man standing next to Maggie shouted, "They stole the silver frame from my wife's portrait." And he made a ripping motion with his hands to show how they'd left the image of the departed one.

The two boys stared at the floor while the assembly pushed forward, shouting accusations, until Don Sixto cried for order. He made the boys stand against the wall where everyone could see them, and in flowery language listed the particulars of the theft. "Doctor Calzón, testify, say to them what you have to say."

Carson half turned toward the crowd and said, in his own bad Spanish, that medicine was property of the sick. The boys could have killed someone.

The boys' expressions remained studiously blank. Obviously they'd learned the power of not caring, or of seeming not to.

"What do the people think?" Don Sixto cried.

"It is as he has said," an old woman cried out. "To steal medicines is grave."

There were murmurs of assent.

"What does the Señora Doctora have to say to these boys and to their mother?"

Maggie turned to the crowd. Her tongue felt like a large, dry towel.

"Go on," Don Sixto said.

She took a breath, but found no word behind it. She stared at Doña Ema, silently begging for her pity and her understanding, but Don Sixto was glaring at her, and so, weakly, she began, "My husband . . . My husband and I . . . now . . ." The boys had been right to steal the refrigerator, she thought. It was an expensive, useless item.

Doña Ema stared back, menacingly, out of her battered face. She said, "What do you care, gringa? When you go home you will have refrigerators and cars to your liking. No one goes to your whorish clinic anyway. We know your injections and your pills are poison, poison for our children. I will never bring my child to you. Your clinic is accursed. After visiting you the babies grow thin and sick, they will not eat, they have diarrhea until finally they die. My grandmother told me about the Pishtaco, and I never believed he was anything more than a ghost until today, when I see him standing in front of me. Not one but two Pishtacos, male and female! Ask yourselves why this woman has no child!"

She had struck a chord. The crowd receded toward the door, forcing several people to step backwards, over the threshold and out. Then they all surged forward again.

"Order, order," shouted Don Sixto.

Carson lifted his eyebrows at Maggie. He raised his hand. Don Sixto nodded to him, and Carson began to speak, in his most warm and calming voice, asking Maggie to translate. He wanted Doña Ema to tell him whether children had also been sicker when the nurses were in Piedras.

"Yes!" Doña Ema said belligerently. *"No ve?"* Don't you see?

And were they sicker again now? And better in between? Had it been better when there were no outside doctors? This much Carson wanted to know.

"Yes!" Doña Ema said, looking ready to choke with anger and confused joy.

"And was not the mine closed during that same time? More or less?"

Doña Ema didn't answer.

"Yes," someone in the crowd said.

"This is important, thank you," Carson said. If kids were getting sick, he asked people please to bring them in. A child might have a diarrhea that was curable, a simple matter of boiling water and maybe giving pills, or there might be poisons flowing from the mine. "I've sent a sample of our water to be analyzed. Soon I will know for sure." Carson cleared his throat, swallowed, and went on. If what Doña Ema said was true, and children were sick and dying, why had he seen none of them? Even Boris and Limbert listened as he explained how he'd worked for twenty years in wars and refugee camps and in places where poverty was so dire that nobody picked up the corpses of beggars who died in the night. He hadn't cured all patients, nor saved Nasir, but it had been his privilege to help many of those who came to him. "If you think I'm a murderer, if that's what you all really want to think down here, you're welcome to your opinion. I'm fed up with feeling like a suspect. If you all aren't interested in what my wife and I are here to offer, then we'll leave. Tell this bitch Doña Ema that ruining her party is the last thing we want to do."

Rolling down the groove of translation, Maggie forgot to tone down the last sentence; it brought a gale of laughter from the back. Carson shoved his hands in his pockets and stared defiantly at Maggie. She moved closer to him, but didn't dare take his hand.

The crowd was muttering. Though Vicente was looking at Carson, he loudly called for order and a return to the original proceedings. This was not the gringos' trial. Did the boys want to say words in their own defense? Did the mother?

"Liars, thieves, speak of what you have done," cried voices from the crowd.

"Poisons, toxins, all are being poisoned," other voices said, until Don Sixto roared for silence. Anyone wishing to add his voice? Did the accused protest their innocence? Did all three admit guilt? Did they admit guilt?

Limbert mumbled yes and he was sorry. The older boy and his mother nodded mute agreement.

"*Gracias,*" Maggie said.

A shyness seemed to cast its shadow now across the crowd. Maggie caught Vicente's eye, hoping he'd step forward, acknowledge the apology, and sift all these issues into some grand concluding argument. Having heard his powers of rhetoric, she believed he could do that in his sleep. Instead, he just grinned at her wackily. After a longish pause, full of rustling and whispering, one man at the back of the room called for *castigo,* punishment. The apology had come too late. What penalty might return these boys to a good path? As a mother, Doña Ema was at fault, even more than the boys.

"*Chicote!*" the crowd insisted.

"The whip!"

"The whip!"

"Ho, doggies," Carson said to Maggie.

Don Sixto uncoiled the whip he'd been carrying inside his jacket, a four-foot bullwhip of round-braided rawhide, with a broomstick handle and a spray of knots at its business end. Shaking this at the whole crowd, he announced that the community had spoken. The proceedings would move outside.

Someone brought a bench and set it parallel to the river. The boys took their shirts off and sat down gripping its edge, facing away from the crowd. Doña Ema retired around the corner of the house and came back holding her cardigan sweater over her breasts. Her right arm bore the marks of her husband's grip, where he'd held on while striking at her face. People muttered as they saw her. Maggie looked carefully below the sweater, making sure there were no more bruises, that the husband had not kicked her in the belly.

Don Sixto commanded the boys to stand at the garden fence. "*Pantalones*," he reminded them. Maggie could feel the crowd, implacable behind her as the boys lowered their jeans to the knees. Below the waist their bodies were pale, their buttocks so smooth and sculpted they seemed to require the pain, the scars. The light was all but gone; their flesh looked ashy gray. It was not cold, but Maggie was sure the boys felt cold — she was shivering herself, her whole skin tight with its own intactness. Vicente came to stand next to her and Carson. In a low voice he explained that this was how *peones* were punished by their overseers in the days of the hacienda.

"Why do you do think it's good?" Carson asked.

"Can't we leave Doña Ema out of this?" asked Maggie.

No, people thought twice after receiving humiliation. Whipping was mild. In other villages, if there were incorrigible persons, thieves, rapists, murderers, and the people could not live with them, and the police did not help, then miscreants were hanged, stoned, beaten to death, or even burned alive. Two years ago, across the canyon, the people had burned a witch inside her own house. Vicente pointed upward.

"A wealthy widow with land, but no children," Maggie guessed.

He nodded, surprised. "How did you know?"

"Please." She swerved back to her former theme, asking him to forgive, postpone Doña Ema's punishment. Hadn't she suffered enough?

"It is she who sends them," said Vicente.

"I'm not doing it," Carson announced, as Don Sixto asked for those who had been harmed to step forward. But Vicente nudged Carson and Maggie into a group of ten people: men, women, Fortunata, and a girl of fourteen. Don Sixto handed the whip to the first man. "*Dale*," he said. Give it to them. Doña Ema began to weep and beg in a high screaming voice. The man holding the whip laughed at her. He had a hard but pleasant face. He shook the whip short and sharp, stepped close to the boys, and lashed each of them on the buttocks with the full force of his arm, forehand, backhand. "For what you did, *sucios,* to Merceditas." Both boys yelped. On their buttocks the welts came up rosy bright. Then he stood behind Doña Ema, his face working. He called her a shameless one, but he would hurt her less, because her husband had begun her punishment. At his blow Doña Ema gave a shriek followed by a series of loud, insincere, but frightened cries.

Next was the man whose dead wife's portrait had been torn. He struck Ema lightly, saying his wife had been her friend. To the boys he said, "Learn to respect," and hit each one with a full backswing on the buttocks, then overhand across the shoulders. Limbert fell down crying in the dirt. Boris bent down to pull his brother up, and spoke to him through gritted teeth. Still on the ground, Limbert glanced fearfully back at the crowd. His face looked swollen, damaged from the inside. He got up, awkwardly hitching his pants, and the boys stood arm in arm, leaning on each other. Drops and smears of blood streaked their backsides and shoulders.

Carson touched Don Sixto's arm. "Hey, enough," but Don Sixto ignored him. The third man stepped up briskly and dealt a mighty lash to Doña Ema, so that the skin across her midback split open on a diagonal and she fell sideways onto the bench, crying unfeignedly and with all her might. The man explained, "Because with you no one can live in peace." Then he tapped each of the boys, saying, "Don't steal!" Someone cried, "Harder! Like that they'll never learn."

The whip came to Carson, but Carson refused it, taking Maggie's arm instead. "Come on, Maggie. They can finish this without us." Maggie was afraid to leave. She whispered: Carson should acknowledge Limbert's apology, call Doña Ema to the clinic. Anxiously, she repeated the same to Vicente, who bowed slightly and formally announced their departure. The Doctores were going home, having decided that as physicians their job was to cure pain, not to cause it. He ordered Doña Ema and her boys, and everyone else, to observe the Christian compassion shown by these very people who had been uncaringly harmed by the criminal family. "May shame penetrate your souls more deeply than the strongest physical blow, and may you decide to reform."

"*No más daño,*" said Carson, no more damage. Then he laughed and added, "*No más* water stealing, either!"

The boys turned to look at him, their soft mouths slack with pain and disbelief. Maggie felt they were her own sons, whom she'd fed so many times. What would happen to them now?

Walking away, she could hear the crowd arguing loudly about whether to continue the *castigo.* Her scalp shrank, her back tingled, lashed by eyes and opinions.

"Fortunata's going to be disappointed," Carson predicted. Wrongly, for as he spoke, the rhythm of roar, then blows, then cries began again. They stopped to listen, and decided from the interplay of sounds that Ema had been exempted.

It was fully dark now. At the river terraces' first steep upward tilt they shuffled, hoping not to catch their toes under a root or miss a sudden undulation of the ground. Carson went first, asking which way they'd come. "Keep heading uphill," Maggie reminded him.

They soon lost the trail, eventually thrashing out onto the road's knee-deep ridge of dust and gravel. The pale road held reflected starlight, moonlight; they could walk on it without a struggle. Maggie pulled up even with Carson and confessed how ashamed she'd felt, facing Doña Ema. Worse, she would have whipped the boys. Not that she'd wanted to, but she would have been afraid not to. "Thanks for getting me out of there."

"Hey, we learned a lot," said Carson. "Now we hardly need the water test."

His face was invisible in the darkness. His head, with the outline of his straw hat, was darker than the sky behind. It was like talking to a photographic negative. "If a totally justified war broke out," Maggie asked him, "would you kill?"

"But of course," he said, "wouldn't you?"

17

WHEN MAGGIE opened the clinic door the next morning, a dozen people were waiting outside: Vicente, Luz María with Lady Maggy slung in a shawl on her back, Don Sixto and Marco Antonio, Fortunata, and a delegation of mostly women, several of whom were pregnant. They'd come to talk with el Señor Doctor about the poisons in the water.

"Why didn't you ring the *timbre?*" Maggie chided them, trying to overcome a creepy feeling as she invited them inside. How long had they been sitting there?

Everyone seemed preoccupied, though, subtly agitated. Maggie felt it too — a light, suspended horror in the air. The recent past had begun to seem a fixed, phantasmagorical background, or some long tunnel they'd all come walking down together. She could hardly remember how she'd felt in Cajamarca, much less at any previous time. Her heart began to pound when she saw that one of the women carried a broomstick wrapped in red satin. It had to be the Black Rainbow's banner. To Maggie's relief, she propped it in a corner by the front door.

This must be what it felt like, she thought, when Althea got dragged into the current of the river.

At Fortunata's suggestion, the men carried all the kitchen furniture into the clinic room to hold the *conferencia*. Carson sat at one end of the table, Vicente at the other; Maggie at Carson's right hand. Fortunata and Don Sixto took the remaining chairs, until Maggie gave hers up for Luz María and Lady Maggy.

Facing backwards over her mother's shoulder, Maggie's namesake consisted mainly of an amazing new thatch of black, shiny hair. How was she, Maggie whispered, ducking to have a look. "She's beautiful!" she lied. Lady Maggy's expression was thin and sour, and she had bruiselike crescents under her eyes. When Maggie cooed and twiddled her fingers, the baby's pupils slid up toward the ceiling. Soon Luz María slung her around to the front. Maggie tried to tell herself that Lady Maggy was just a lumpish infant, and that Luz was feeling shy at being separated from the rest of the women, who stood together by the examining table, rustling and whispering like schoolgirls. But she knew better.

She wished she weren't so repelled by this poor child. How much worse it must have been to be Althea, she admonished herself, helplessly watching her own son's life dripping out of his anus. She forced herself to caress Lady Maggy's hair before standing back among the women.

"We think we are being poisoned," Vicente announced. Several of the women cried out in agreement. Fortunata and Don Sixto were ready to march up to the mine. By tomorrow, they could get the whole valley to participate. Marco Antonio thought it better to wait and try to coordinate a strike by the miners' union. A strike! No, one woman said, the miners would never agree. Several arguments broke out at once; the women lost their shyness and approached the table as a group. The marchers must carry weapons to defend themselves against the army guards, said Don Sixto. *Escopetas, porras, pistolas, machetes, piedras.* Shotguns, clubs, pistols, machetes, stones. No, said Vicente, they'd go in peace, bearing a white flag. Only women should go, women and children. But women were sure to be ignored — no, women and children would be shot at, just the same as men . . . "*Momento, momentito. Calma, por favor,*" said Carson. The hubbub did not diminish, so he stood up.

"The Doctor speaks," Vicente said. "Let us listen."

This was the real beginning, Maggie thought, as Carson spoke into the hush, saying it was not yet time for a confrontation. The valley must make a concerted, reasonable plan, not just form a mob and rush uphill. Soon they'd have the laboratory analysis.

"They won't care about the analysis," argued the woman who had brought the flag. "They'll only make another, proving that the water is clean."

Carson was a step ahead of her. "Right, Señora, *correcto*." This was why it was important to prove that people's health was being affected. "We don't know that yet, *cierto?*"

"What about my daughter," said Luz María.

"We aren't sure," Carson placated her.

"*Marcharemos*," Don Sixto simultaneously said, we will march.

"Let us listen to the Doctor," said Vicente. "In any case, we never rush to battle unprepared."

Waiting for the water test would not be a waste of time, Carson said, if the clinic registered all medical problems that seemed to come from water. Hair samples would be taken for analysis. Scientific data would be their most powerful weapon against the mine's inevitable resistance.

There was a murmur and a shifting of chairs. "They are not witches," Vicente said. "I give my word. When they will cut your hair, it is for a good purpose."

Maggie looked around the table, around the room, and saw the faces the color of saddle leather, and on them a charred stillness that was the ancient mask of distrust. Carson kept on talking. Health was the first priority. Pregnant women and young children must not drink from the river or the lake, but fetch their water from streams and waterfalls, until further notice.

Health was the first priority, one of the pregnant women slowly admitted.

They agreed to wait, to hold another meeting once the lab results were in. Meanwhile, the clinic would inspect the population. Half the week, they'd work in Piedras; then Carson, Vicente, and Maggie would visit nearby villages and set up temporary *consultorios* in the plazas. Not only mothers and children but all sick people must come, since, as Carson reminded everyone, a person might not know the real reason for his problems, and every illness deserved attention, no matter what its cause. On Saturday, Carson would travel to the mine. Marco Antonio would go up separately, speak to the miners' union representative.

The women would spread word.

"*Prepárense*," Vicente teased Carson and Maggie. Prepare yourselves. He left with the others, but promised to be back early tomorrow morning. Maggie was glad to see the Black Rainbow's banner still reposing in the corner. She didn't mention it to Carson, though; instead, she helped him move the chairs and table back into the kitchen, and they sat down to eat fruit salad, tea, and rolls with jelly, the breakfast they had missed.

"Look how he invites himself onto clinic staff," Carson grumbled.

"Obviously we need him," Maggie replied. "I thought we'd decided that already." When Vicente had entered the room this morning, she'd felt it again, the unfabricated resonance between them. She wondered if he felt it too, or whether it was some quasi-romantic delusion of hers. He was the only person she'd met in Piedras with whom she felt the possibility of a natural, deep friendship. Fortunata was her friend, of course, but Fortunata was from another planet, a different type of friend.

"He needs us more," said Carson. "He needs this crisis." Carson was resigned to working with Vicente, but he wanted Maggie to know that he didn't believe a word of that life story. Vicente must have plagiarized it from one of those adult comic books Maggie loved so much. She tried to convince her husband that guerrilla war was essentially a melodrama, but this was not what Carson meant.

"He's a pathetic schmo," Carson said. "The Inca empire — give me a break!" People might love him, but they wanted four wheel drive and MTV, not Inca jobs breaking rocks or weaving llama hair.

"I would have thought you'd be more worried that he's dangerous," Maggie said. What an odd way to defend someone, she thought. "You know, like Klaus and Liliana said."

"It's possible." Carson shrugged. "But I did talk to the police about him. They know he's here, they simply can't be bothered to arrest him. El Mirador is too remote. They don't like walking. Vicente's a smart guy. He knows all that. He says it himself — drug money was the only reason his empire worked. If his Colombians are never coming back? Training him, leaving him in place here? Best thing that could ever happen."

"That's probably right."

"He's not a bad guy," Carson said now. "He's smart, and he cares, and he's got the charisma to pull things off. I'll definitely recommend him to Catholic Charities."

Don't minimize him, Maggie thought, he's one of us. She looked at Carson's long, thin thighs in black and rusty jeans as he sat relaxing in the wooden chair, looked at his sunburnt forehead, which seemed to have gotten loftier since she'd known him, and she tried to feel reassured. Last night, he'd spun out all kinds of plans, elaborations and contingencies, bringing Greenpeace into the struggle, even flying Vicente, the grass-roots leader, to New York — too bad Vicente didn't wear feathers or he could end up addressing the UN. Carson had sounded like a little boy working out an elaborate fantasy, but when Maggie had asked herself, Why not? she'd realized she had no right to predict his failure.

All of Carson's decisions and opinions, his calibrated judgments and perceptions — when and how had he fit them all together? Usually it amazed and delighted her when he exposed his inner world to her, yet for some reason, lately he was giving her a chill. What was she afraid of? That these two men would unite their purposes and leave her behind, alone in her confusion?

She said to Carson, hiding an unjustified desperation, "You know, you remind me of my grandpa Johnny Baines. On the surface you both act like you're so logical, but when he finally figured out how to predict earthquakes, it was in a dream he had or something." Carson had heard the story before, but she made him listen to it again. Six months before he'd died, Johnny Baines had handed an envelope to an assistant containing the projected dates and locations of four earthquakes in Japan, the Ryukyus, Chile, and California. Every one had come to pass, prompting a great posthumous scramble through Johnny's notebooks. His figures hadn't added up, and probably never would, though boxes of notebooks, their pages dense with notations, still sat stacked in Althea's Cambridge basement, awaiting a genius of the future.

"Sure, of course," Carson said. "I know how he did it, more or less."

"How do you mean?" Maggie was pleased, relieved that he'd responded.

"It ate at him day and night." Her husband pulled a pious face, mocking his own sincerity. "Not just his own kid, you know. Unnecessary death in general. You go to bed with it at night, and you wake up with it in the morning. Your granddad barely even knew how he'd processed all the information, but he was working on it all the time."

"You're like him," Maggie said. "Some might use the word 'obsessed.'"

"Yeah, well," said Carson. "Craziness makes the world go round."

"Doctor Underwear!" she teased him. To her surprise, it seemed she'd made him happy for a minute.

Encouraged, she followed him into the clinic, worrying aloud that Vicente and Don Sixto might blow the mine sky-high. No way, Carson reassured her. They'd never bite the hand they hoped, one day, would feed them.

"You don't think he's using us?"

"Of course he is. That's what we're here for. We'll use him, too."

That sounded ugly to Maggie. "For what?"

Vicente was the only person who could make sure that people didn't drink the river water, said Carson with sudden, gloomy certitude. Abstinence was the only way to keep the heavy metals out of people's bodies. No water plant ever would be built, or not for a dozen years. By then, Carson hoped, he and Maggie would be long gone.

"Don't say that," Maggie told him, unable to bear the thought of leaving Piedras.

"You're right," said Carson, misunderstanding her. "*Yo soy macho.* I really want to win."

That night, after a dinner of fried beef and onions, they lit an *espiral* and two candles, and after the room was full of smoke they pulled up the yellow mosquito net and made love. About halfway through, Maggie saw Carson's left eye above her face, glinting into the dark. His chin was straining forward. From this odd perspective his eye was just a slit of pure dark pupil, glinting watery and dry at once. She felt as if she had just come out from behind the shoulder of the moon to witness all the stars, and everything; but she was out in space, with nothing around to hold her.

Afterward they lay together for longer than usual, not minding the heat. Carson left his arm lazily around her, and she traced the outlines of its muscles. Their whole sides were touching. In this heat, his naked skin made her feel pleasantly feverish. She said what a strange, far place this was to come to get to know each other.

Carson tightened his arm and said, "Aw . . . babe!" as if she had surprised him. But he seemed distracted, too, a little; she was glad they'd had that long conversation earlier, because it helped her to imagine what was going on inside him now.

He dropped off to sleep. Maggie lay awake a long time, worrying about Doña Ema, Lady Maggy, and all the misery that had been summoned for tomorrow. It was nearly four A.M. when she crept out into the clinic room and unfurled the banner. It had sequined insets and close-set silver stitching that glinted in her flashlight's beam. Crystal blood dripped from Atahualpa's severed neck — she rerolled the flag around its broomstick, wondering whether she was really ready for what these people knew was needed.

Forty people had lined up by eight, and forty more by nine. Vicente told them all to wait while the clinic prepared itself. An impromptu soccer game got started in the road; a woman brought a pail of peach tea and began to sell it by the glass. On Vicente's orders, benches appeared, planks on beer cases against the outside walls, with several more inside. People stood around discussing Carson's mural; he was delighted. Maggie took the top sheet off the bed and strung it up to allow for private examinations. Carson explained triage to Fortunata, who'd be standing at the door.

Just before they started seeing patients, Carson took Vicente aside, and the two of them spoke conspiratorially, looking at the floor, as Vicente and his friend had done on the night Nasir was killed. Maggie, setting up the ledger, watched them from the corner of her eye. She felt possessive, envious. To combat these unworthy feelings, she used unworthy tactics, reminding herself of belittling comments Carson had made about Vicente.

Soon it was clear what they'd planned, for Vicente told Fortunata to go out front and send everybody home until tomorrow, except *agudos, moribundos,* and mothers with babies and children.

No one was very ill, so they took the youngest babies first. Vicente held each infant while Carson, grim and focused, touched the soles of its feet with the tip of a ballpoint pen, glancing at its face and nodding encouragingly, as though the infant were answering difficult questions. Maggie wrote down each baby's name and date of birth, then Carson's evaluation. Listless or alert. Dehydrated. Parasites?

Underweight, overweight, average. Malnourished. Robust, healthy, pale. Lastly, Vicente clipped a strand of each child's hair, which Maggie sealed into an envelope against the day when they'd have lots of money to analyze these samples. Only a few mothers refused this dangerous service, which could have led to their babies' death by sorcery.

Some of the mothers' mouths hung open, like the babies', but for different reasons. Each hour Maggie instructed them, in groups, to get their water from the hillside streams and boil it. She handed out packets of rehydration salts; since there were no baby bottles here, mothers must feed their youngest from their own lips, like birds. She warned them that the water would taste of salt, but that it was good and healing. Some mothers of healthy babies looked jealous, as if the shiny packets were talismans or presents, so she gave away some extras.

Two infants seemed to have the same vague gaze and twitchy, listless limbs as Lady Maggy. Children aged four, ten, and fourteen had suffered cognitive impairments, and there were many instances of a creeping rash that spread, turned scaly, and never went away. Two underpigmentations of the skin, and seventeen tales of stillbirth, early death, spontaneous abortion, and monstrous deformities, all of which Maggie recorded as "unconfirmed verbal reports," with approximate dates.

Fortunata's voice rang with gladness as she stood in the door calling the names of the next three women who could move to the indoor benches. She kept officious order, shoving patients back into line, pulling them forward by the upper arm if they seemed in need of attention. Maggie teased her that she needed a whip like Don Sixto's. Numerous people were curious about the rushing-water toilet, and Fortunata sent them around the back where a nephew charged them ten centavos each to use it. When Vicente noticed the flow of traffic up and down the hall, he put a stop to the enterprise.

Communication was complicated, babies squalling and squirming, Maggie taking notes and simultaneously translating in two directions, Vicente whispering apt-pupil questions in her ear to be relayed to Carson. "He says to ask what hour of night he usually cries" or "We use a plant to cure cystitis." Carson said Vicente would be a great health worker one day; all he needed was experience. In the past, when he'd told Maggie the same things, she'd felt both flattered and diminished. Watching the same scene from the outside, she recognized what had demeaned her: Carson's implicit belief that medical knowledge was the most important in the world, and that anyone who learned it was thereby fundamentally improved. Vicente was not to be defined by this, she saw. He received Carson's praises with a silvery smile, which only caused Carson to insist further, Vicente to be even more polite. Maggie felt secretly delighted by their battle.

The next day's patients were mostly men, who mostly said they were not sick but had come to the clinic in response to a summons from Comandante Oquendo. After Vicente prompted and explained, each one yielded up his list of maladies. Malaria, asthma, badly mended bones. Maggie could hardly bear to inscribe their conditions in the ledger, since most were incurable, at least on Piedras's terms, and Carson could only offer the advice to return to a strategy of endurance. This felt wrong, for each man's confession had seemed to weaken him; each had uttered a hope of cure, however secretive and humble. What was the purpose of arousing hope just to dash it, Maggie wondered. What would be the end result of this campaign? Writing down their names — Fausto, Sandalio, Nemesio, Pámfilo, Porfirio, Xenón — she felt she was enrolling martyrs for the future peasant uprising.

They did find a bunch more skin conditions and gastrointestinal problems — and two cancers, so Carson began to say the incidence was high.

Today he'd decided to communicate directly with his patients. The interviews were more laborious but less confusing, since only one person tended to be talking at a time. Now when he explained things, or needed a missing word, he looked to Vicente, not to Maggie, and so did the patients. He admonished Vicente to take notes and study them each night. "Do you read English?"

Vicente shook his head.

"That will make it harder, at least for the short term."

He'd been considering giving Vicente all of the study materials, Maggie saw. She'd been replaced: she was no longer Carson's assistant, now merely a scribe, a secretary. From inside a silence that at first was crystalline, then corrosive, she reminded herself that this was what she'd wanted, this was what she'd planned, for these two men to work together and connect. Yet whenever Carson turned to her and said, "Got that?" she had to roll her eyes and blink, to hold back the tears of rage.

Late in the afternoon, Vicente overrode one of Carson's diagnoses. "That man has *susto*. Or else he is bewitched. Don't you think so, Doctora?" He turned to Maggie, who had given up expecting to be talked to. She got flustered, said she didn't know. She saw Vicente's eyes flicker, watching her swim up out of the dark tunnel where she'd been lost, or hiding. "Maybe so," she said. Encouraged, the man told his story about fighting with his neighbor over a land boundary, then the next day he'd tripped and fallen from a high place. After that, he'd gradually lost the power of speech, until now he could only whisper. He had several other enemies.

He should go to a shaman, Vicente recommended; the *brujo* of Meado de Vaca was powerful in placing and removing curses.

"Sounds good," Maggie said, "as long as we find nothing else wrong with him, right Carson?" She whispered to her husband that the man must feel guilty about cursing his neighbor. Maybe witchcraft was like therapy, and would undo the problem.

Carson shrugged. "He could have the big C. He smokes." Only tests would show it. For now, he could try the shaman, and return in a week if magic failed.

"*Cáncer*," Maggie translated for Vicente after the man had left. She was ashamed of her flippancy.

"*Susto*," Vicente insisted, fright. This patient lived near a friend of his, who reported that the man's nightmares and orgasms woke the neighborhood.

"*Susto*," Maggie wrote. *Susto* was a common supernatural ailment, which Fortunata had explained but Maggie had not completely understood. She assumed that the term covered a range of ills — worms, hypothermia, psychosis. Speech was affected. Those afflicted turned pale and sweated; sometimes they died.

For the rest of the afternoon, Vicente made sure to ask Maggie's opinion, even when Carson bridled at the unnecessary delays. Soon she felt herself on solid ground again, safely rescued from the pit into which she'd been descending. Vicente's childhood predisposed him, she thought with some gratification, to be upset at how casually a man could treat his wife.

His sensitivity was surprising. Just from the side of his face, Maggie could tell the quickness of his understanding. She began to watch for what he was observing. The lines in the face of a woman who had trouble sleeping, the hooflike feet of Piedras's poorest man. Often, when she was struck by the humble nobility of a person who'd endured a round of sorrows, Vicente turned and looked at her. Several times too she had the weird sensation that she could hear his mind saying things to her in English.

It was after dark when Doña Ema hobbled in, supporting herself on a stick of driftwood. Carson greeted her with gravity and kindness, helping her into a chair. He put gauze and an enormous bandage on her split back, and advised her to bathe her fading bruises in water boiled and cooled. He soothed her, saying her injuries weren't serious, no broken bones, no apparent damage to the coming child. Then he asked about her husband, but Ema didn't want to speak of him.

Vicente warned, "Far away, he'll be, if he knows we have our justice again."

"Do you feel safe at home?" Carson asked, with a quelling glance at Vicente.

"I have my sons," Doña Ema said. As if in answer to Maggie's unspoken thoughts, she added, "They're always with me now."

"How are they feeling?" Maggie asked. Rumor had it the boys had been beaten severely.

"They are very strong."

After Ema left, Carson said to Vicente, "You should never have threatened her husband." Abuse cases were *delicado,* requiring a confessional's secrecy; only the victim could call for leaks to outside authority. Ema had been right not to reveal where her husband was. Who knew what he'd do to her next? "In this clinic, Vicente, you are my assistant. You are no longer Comandante Oquendo. *Comprende?*"

Vicente grunted.

Carson looked at him, and as if giving in to a temptation, sniffed, "I never liked that woman, but I never felt the need to beat her."

But what Vicente did, he had to do, Maggie thought.

A few seconds later Vicente said to Carson, "I am ready to do whatever is correct, Doctor. Thank you for explaining your *criterios.*"

In this, Carson seemed to hear an intent that pleased him. Maggie heard another.

At dinner, she told Carson that the dates she had recorded, when babies had died or been born with problems, so far seemed to correspond with the dates of operation of the mine. She showed him the graph she had begun to make. "Excellent," he said.

Carson admitted he was glad to feel the urgency again; he hadn't felt it since treating wounded soldiers in Angola. He thanked Maggie for rescuing him from Harvard. Today he'd realized something important. He loved his work. Loved to fight against the odds. Loved it when you saw that all moral issues were based on the finality of human pain. That finality was horrible, but to fight against it made him feel alive, even though he knew in the end that he could never really win. If it was okay for Maggie to hear this, part of the problem had been the death of his long-time lover, Maxine. He'd mistaken grief for a more general despair, but that was over now. Had he stayed at Harvard, futility would have become his middle name, his permanent condition. He'd even begun to appreciate Vicente. "You foresaw how this could work," he said to her. "I'm glad you kept pushing." His speech on Nasir's grave had been the turning point. Public relations wasn't always insincerity. It could be the art of causing better things to happen.

"Next time, listen to me sooner," Maggie told him, wondering why she felt farther away from Carson than ever before. Yet she was unable to say anything to bring him closer, as if she were trapped in another dimension from which communication was impossible.

He agreed. They went to bed, exhausted.

❖

El Hoyo was no paradise, though it had a plaza, two cross streets, and a few acacia trees planted in crumbling cement tubs. The place looked as though it had been hit by a neutron bomb. Its plaza was empty, its fountain dry, and the bust of Admiral Grau stared emptily back toward 1928 when it had been set atop its pillar. Most houses were shuttered and padlocked. Vicente said the people must be out working in their high potato fields.

They ambled past the municipality, whose several colors of paint were peeling down to the brown adobe bricks beneath, and stopped at a little store, where Carson bought Cokes for all three of them from a young, thickset man of about twenty, whom Vicente curtly ordered to set up the medical table, over there, under the trees.

They sat on an unpainted wooden bench and stretched out their legs while the young man did Vicente's bidding. A passel of runny-nose kids appeared, peeking from corners, and Maggie took a handful of candies from a jar, placing a coin on the counter in exchange. The kids raced up to grab, then ran away to eat, like wild animals.

Carson cleared his throat, but apparently decided not to criticize her. His policy was never to hand out candy or money to children, so as not to encourage cavities and begging. But Maggie could see that Vicente approved, so she continued, managing to coax a little girl of four or so out from behind a stack of wooden soft-drink cases.

She wore grubby knit leggings and had a ponytail sticking up from the top of her head, held by an elastic band with two transparent plastic balls on it. When Maggie had been her age, in Mexico, the maid had combed her hair this way; she suddenly remembered how she'd thought it very glamorous. With all naturalness, the child climbed into Vicente's lap and sat there sucking fiercely on the sweet. Vicente learned her name, Guisella. "A ballerina's name," Maggie said to her, wondering if this Guisella had ever heard of ballerinas. She reached out and gently bounced her palm on the little girl's top-knot, causing her to hide her sticky face in Vicente's T-shirt.

Carson observed that obviously this kid had not seen many gringos.

"She's scared," Vicente agreed. He put his face down near the girl's cheek and whispered, "Don't be scared of the Señora, she's going to give you another candy." So Maggie did. Over the top of the child's head, Vicente gazed at Maggie and asked why she had no children.

Carson had turned on his seat to watch the young man setting up the medical table, spreading the white cloth, pinning on the red paper cross. He gestured for the table to be moved left, then back, into the shade of a palmetto. He acted as if he hadn't heard a word Vicente had said. Taking him as her example, Maggie did the same.

"Don't you like them?" Vicente persisted.

"*Me encantan,*" they enchant me. It was the obligatory answer. The question was obligatory, too — for her. Why not for Carson? Still, Vicente's questioning had reached her. Maybe it was personal this time.

"Why don't you have any, then?"

Carson turned and said with irritation, "If we had a child, we would not be here." Then he stood up and walked toward the table.

"That's not true," said Maggie to Vicente, behind Carson's back. Too late, she realized how disloyal this had sounded. All she'd meant, or thought she'd meant, was not to insult Peru as a location for child-rearing. She backtracked, explaining that she and her husband wanted to take care of children who had already been born.

Vicente said, "Which one of us is the one who is too many?" He lifted Guisella from his knees and tried to set her on Maggie's lap, but the child had reached her limit. She shrieked and slipped down, and ran off along the wide dirt path, shrieking again and again. The other children, who'd been watching, all started running away and shrieking in imitation, making a game of being terrified of the strangers, then forgetting it was a game. Abruptly Guisella tripped, fell down, and, struggling to her feet, stood weeping until her big sister came back and swung her awkwardly piggyback. The big sister stumbled on behind the others, calling "Wait! Wait!"

Seeing Maggie's stricken face, Vicente said, "They're only children."

Satisfied with the table, Carson returned and said, "Let's get started."

"Go and bring the mayor," Vicente said to the young man.

The mayor was out of town, the young man said, smiling apologetically.

"When he returns, you will tell him everything we said about the water." Vicente turned to Maggie and Carson, audibly remarking that this young man was lying.

"We don't want problems," the young man mumbled.

"Children are afraid of you, adults of me." Vicente laughed. To the young man he said, "Why didn't you lie at the beginning rather than waste our time!"

They still had enough daylight to walk downhill to Pullo, where the earth was red, and so the mud-brick houses were the same color. Each house had a red wall around it, with small bluish aloe plants growing on top, the plants coated with brick-colored dust. Two patients came, one young man with a cold and a lady complaining of arthritis, then a man leaning on his brother's shoulder, the same brother who had sliced off most of his calf muscle with a machete as they were clearing a field together. A fourteen-year-old girl appeared saying she'd had a miscarriage, a mother whose two-year-old child was deaf. Maggie handed out a dozen rehydration packets.

Lastly, a young woman came to lead them, with apologies, into the stifling darkness of a house where her great-grandmother lay on a bed, in a nest of rags, her eyes squinched shut. Althea, Maggie thought. She was a hundred and ten, according to the great-grand-daughter, and her face was covered with innumerable wrinkles that began at her toothless mouth, like a bag with a knot in it. Her great-granddaughter bent down and shouted in her ear, but she did not stir.

Carson burrowed among the coverings for an arm and pulled it out, releasing a thick, greasy reek. It looked like a mummy's arm already. He held its wrist tenderly for a minute. Maggie imagined how his mind swam down the threadlike veins. Stealing a glance at Vicente, Maggie saw him watching Carson with a curious, almost disgusted expression.

It had been days since she'd remembered Julia's threats. She should have gone to Boston right away. Now it was too late. She was involved, responsible; she had to stay in this valley until the water analysis arrived. It was unfair, she knew, to be upset with Carson for not wanting to help her grandmother; but it was also true that he'd never do this for Althea.

Carson set the skinny yellow arm down gently and tucked it under the blankets where it had been before. The woman's face scrunched tighter. Her great-granddaughter said sadly, "She doesn't eat. Is there nothing I can do?"

Carson shook his head. "Keep her clean and warm."

"You can whisper in her ear." Maggie couldn't bear to have nothing to offer. "Tell her that you love her and that everything is all right." At the divinity school, the halls had fairly murmured with lore on Death and Dying. The dying were thought to want permission to die; they were thought to be confused. This old lady seemed the reverse to Maggie: determined, trying to leave this world. Forgiveness might release her. The great-granddaughter nodded, so Maggie went recklessly on. "If you like, tell her to look up and see the light of Heaven, full of angels who love her, ready to take care of her."

Yes, the great-granddaughter said eagerly.

They emerged blinking into the light.

"The New Age comes to the Rosario," Carson observed.

"Go and fuck yourself," Maggie said, her attempt at a light tone failing. Carson scowled at her. He often chided her for using strong language.

At the first curve of the trail, Vicente hung back to tell Maggie he had found it very pretty, what she'd said. He touched her on the shoulder and Maggie felt the jolt travel through her body, into the ground. What a sucker I am for a crumb of attention, she thought.

When they had walked fifty yards, the young woman came running after them to tell Carson that her great-grandmother had smiled and said yes, then fallen asleep. And that no one had wanted to speak of this, but two monstrous babies had been born in town this year, one with a tufted tail and the other without skin on its belly, its organs hanging out. Both had died unbaptized. While Carson took notes, Vicente whispered to Maggie, "*Ves*, all people need is a little *cariño*. She took confidence in us because of you. You are like us. You understand."

Cutting straight down a switchback, they barely managed to catch the bus downhill. All seats were full except the last long bench. Maggie was grateful that the scary window view was blocked from both sides, but squashed between Vicente and Carson, she was excruciatingly conscious of them both. She adopted a neutral policy: when either of their bodies bounced against hers, she did not withdraw, but she did not encourage contact, either.

❖

Cachabambita was south of Pullo, close to the bank, on the far side of the river. It had a new mayor, a son of the village who'd been successful on the coast. He wore thin orange shoes and a dark, tasteful plaid shirt. He came out beaming to shake hands and greet the North American doctors, of whom he'd heard so many, many good things. Peru was a disgrace, he said, nothing functioned here. He guaranteed to publicize to all of his citizens not to drink the river water. And yes, if any monsters or idiots were born, he would send down the child if possible, and if not, a sample of its hair and its mother's hair. In Cachabambita, many babies died or were unwell. As he went on explaining how all this was the misery of Peru, how Peru was a beggar sitting on a throne of gold, Maggie saw the impatience on Carson's face, and hoped that the mayor would not notice it.

Four mothers soon appeared, along with various *curiosos* who tried to gawk at the examinations. Vicente shooed them away. Carson pantomimed simple procedures while Vicente added words. Maggie stood outside the privacy screen made of flour sacks, fending off the mayor, who wanted to practice English: "Doo, joo, light, Peru?" He asked whether the clinic could offer jobs; Maggie lamented that Vicente was their only assistant.

"*Asistente?*" the mayor said, sneering, as if he'd never heard the word. He turned to Vicente, asking if this could be true.

"*Sí, porqué no,*" said Vicente musically. Yes, why not? He gazed at the mayor until the mayor glanced away.

A small group crossed the plaza herding a girl of twenty. She was very pregnant, and naked below the waist. Her slender body was black. As she got closer, Maggie saw the darkness was just dirt. Her bare feet were crusted and cracked. Her name was La Lula, the people said. She was an example of a retarded person.

"One for the records," Carson said. He told Vicente that in India such people were considered holy. Vicente elaborated for the crowd, saying that the Señor Doctor was glad that this town took such good care of a poor *opa,* for it was a holy duty.

"Oh, very well we have taken care of her," observed a male voice from the back of the crowd.

Carson confirmed what everyone could see: La Lula was seven months pregnant. No use asking who the father was, Vicente murmured. Who were La Lula's parents? he asked loudly. Dead, said the voice of the crowd. Who will take care of her child? Vicente asked. Give it to the gringos, said the same mean man's voice from behind the rest.

Carson announced that La Lula's child would probably be normal, but that she might need help to care for it. Find a mother for the creature, Vicente commanded the crowd. An aunt. A cousin, someone who wants a *criadito,* a child to raise. Otherwise, this *opa* could let the baby die.

No one answered for a while. Then the mean voice said, "Look who repeats the commandments of the gringos!"

"Who speaks!" Vicente cried, but no one answered. "Who?" The crowd shuffled and withdrew slightly. "Cowards," said Vicente. "Those who love life will listen well. The rest of you may kill your children, or slowly die of poison."

La Lula giggled lewdly, swiveling her belly from side to side.

If she enjoyed sex as much as it seemed, surely she could let an infant find her nipple, Maggie thought. Vicente was telling La Lula that if strong pains came in her belly, she should call out loudly and run to any friendly person for help. La Lula just laughed and looked at the sky. Unlike most people around here, she had beautiful white teeth.

Maggie asked quietly whether La Lula would miss the baby if it was taken from her.

"She will forget," Vicente said. "Why, would you like to have it?" His voice was tender; seeing Maggie's mistrust, he quoted her words on caring for children who were already born.

"People would say the gringa came and stole it," said Maggie bitterly.

"*Verdad,* Señora. Anyway, I think you'd prefer to have your own."

"Guess I'd better not get pregnant," Maggie said that night. She and Carson were lying side by side in bed, staring at the ceiling, their bodies so stiff with exhaustion that neither of them had wanted to get up and turn off the light.

Carson pulled himself up on one elbow. "Have you been worrying about it?"

"Yes, but I'm not late or anything," she said. She could feel his gaze honing the outline of her profile, but could not turn to him, not even to his tenderness. She should have shared this part of herself with him long ago — after all, he was her husband, the most relevant person. Still, she could not muster the courage to tell him what she was thinking of.

She was thinking of a hibiscus flower in her belly. Of the young women she'd seen all over Peru, carrying babies in bright blankets on their backs, as if they were no burden. Of how children gathered around everyone's knees as people sat relaxing in front of their houses. Of the older kids who played and ran in packs through the villages, supervised by any adult who was nearby. Of the way people said that children are the love inside the home. She could almost feel an infant lying between her breasts. It would fit between her navel and her collarbone. It would weigh her heart down nicely.

Meanwhile, soundless weeping surrounded Lady Maggy and all the children on the clinic's list. There were dozens of cases now. Maggie's wishes were not reasonable.

"You didn't fall for Vicente's guilt trip," Carson mused, lying down again.

"What guilt trip?" Though Maggie knew quite well.

"You remember, in El Hoyo." Carson's finger touched the top of Maggie's ear as he recited, in a mocking voice, Vicente's question. He also reminded Maggie of the cruel insults Doña Ema had offered that night. "Such a primitive mentality. Women are wombs on legs, and if you don't have kids you're worthless. I wish I could protect you." Maggie thanked him. "I'm not sure I really need you to," she said, trying to begin the other conversation. She thought she'd spoken gently, but Carson sighed hard. "Okay, I won't." He got up, turned off the light, and lay back down.

"I hope it'll eventually go away," she told him in the dark. "Honey?"

Carson said firmly, "Me too. Good night, dear."

She lay there blaming Vicente for putting the idea of a child into her mind again.

Carson took the next day's bus up to the mine, saying he might return that night, more likely Sunday. Maggie pleaded to go. She could chat with miners' wives about simple sanitation, or translate the sub-tleties of Carson's meeting with Ignacio.

"Man the clinic," Carson said. "I need to talk *mano a mano*. You'd hate the road, anyway." He paid Vicente, told him to take two days off. After being in Piedras all week, he must want to check on his house upriver. Monday, they'd resume the schedule.

Vicente nodded in a slow, pondering way, then Maggie saw him turn left outside the clinic door. He walked north, not toward El Mirador at all, but toward the bridge and Piedras Baja.

18

IN THE CONVENT CHAPEL, qualities became things. Purity was the white smock all saints wore as an undergarment. Admonition a pointing finger. Fearlessness was eyes raised Heavenward while arrows pierced the chest. Althea felt closest to a little yellow dog who leapt up to lick a sore on Lazarus's thigh. Hunger, she thought, or love? Love that doesn't care about dirt and germs. Like the love that the priest, Brother Jesūnandā, shows, washing the feet of the poor. Or like my own curiosity and hunger? A mind without pride.

She had taken to sitting in the chapel through the afternoons of the monsoon, feeling protected by the curtains of rain. Outside, huge drops splashed in liquid mud, forming saucer-sized indentations. Ripping the leaves and flowers, then joining a myriad of other drops all rushing down into the deep gutters. When a gust of wind blew, rain sprayed in through the church windows even though the verandah was six feet wide. Althea sat near the center aisle to avoid getting soaked.

One day Brother Jesūnandā came in, wet, his hair in a row of Roman-soldier curlicues across his forehead, his peach gauze gown stained pumpkin by the rain. Althea had the impression that he was seeking a moment of solitude, but he recovered from his surprise at seeing her by reverting to his function as priest. He asked in a tone of superior comprehension whether she'd been praying. She said no, she had not; she already had everything she needed in life. He said: Prayer is not just a list of wants. At its best it is a celebration and an offering. Open yourself, open your heart, be with God. Then your prayer will always be satisfied. And your life will change. You will see that God is in you — eventually, that you are God.

Althea turned her face toward him, daring him to see what was in it.

❖

Her mind had been unpleasantly at work since soon after she arrived at the convent, seething and working and worrying, calling up the loss of her son — not that she ever forgot about Christopher, not for an hour.

Johnny's earthquake kept the bad memories alive. Or rather, thinking of Johnny in an earthquake. What if he died, too?

She'd begun by wondering in good wifely fashion how and where he was. Whether something would be shaken loose in him when he saw the mountains falling. Then she'd understood that she'd sent Johnny to Mongolia not for his own benefit, as she'd expressed to him, but because she wanted him to be broken in spirit, as she had been broken. She wanted him to see the face of death. A thing it was not within her rights or her powers to show to anyone. Instead, it seemed likely that Johnny might experience the earthquake as the most important thing in life. This idea filled her with helpless rage.

Then what if Johnny died?

She reminded herself of a man she'd seen in a late stage of rabies, tied to his bed by villagers. They'd brought Althea to him in hopes that she might help. The man spoke English; he'd been the local schoolmaster. His mouth working, he told her he was desperate to be untied in order to bite her. He wanted to bite everyone.

Christopher's death had taken her into the unimaginable, some dark stratosphere where she could not remember time, how many days her son's illness lasted. She'd sat next to him all day, all night, urging him to drink, drink, the same river water that had infected him, all there was, strained through several handkerchiefs. He refused to swallow. At first he whined, closed his lips, and turned away. Later he let the water dribble out. His skin shriveled on his bones. On the day when her houseboy returned with a load of firewood tied to his back, for boiling, it was too late.

He lay dead for two days in his crib. Then on the stone floor of a local ruin with other dead. Looking less and less like himself while Althea harangued the carpenter and warded off the priest.

When Johnny had returned, she saw him from an immense distance, thinking, You, you who know nothing, how can you imagine that you are actually taking charge? This distance had remained between them ever afterward. Johnny seemed to walk through the world in a caul of innocence, which Althea alternately saw as fortunate and evil, which she envied and despised. And now, like a snake, a horrid witch behind a curtain, she had seen her chance to strike, to spread her suffering to him.

❖

"If you desire it," Brother Jesūnandā said, "I will hear your confession. Perhaps you need to cleanse your heart, empty it, before it can open properly."

"I'm not a Catholic," Althea said. "As I understand it, you'd have to baptize me first."

"The rain is sufficient baptism in my religion," Brother Jesūnandā said. "I wonder whether you can consider it so."

"I'm thinking about my husband," Althea said. "And my son."

"You have a son?"

"I have a son who died."

"There can be no worse pain."

"How would you know?" she whispered. She felt entitled to ferocity now, and with this stranger. This man in a skirt who did not want to be a person like the rest. "You don't have any children."

"Oh," said the priest, "but I do have. Many children. Many are alive, but every one was taken from me."

"Explain yourself," she said. "If you don't mind."

"Oh, no," he said. "I'm sorry." Althea told him what she knew. He'd been born in Assam. He'd been a Hindu priest. In Calcutta, Assam was known as a place of magic and astrologers. The British ladies invited Assamese priests for parties, for divinations. There were rumors of a temple devoted to women's private parts. Women who could not have children went there, and strange ceremonies were performed. The planets were made to align, and then they conceived. Althea giggled despite herself. "Can it be real?"

"What if those wives were the ones who had infertile husbands?" Brother Jesūnandā said.

"I thought that was all gossip," Althea said. She would have laughed at the idea, only Brother Jesūnandā's face looked sad, or at least serious: wanting her to understand and, above all, not to laugh at his religion.

"Yes," he said. "God gave them all children through me. At first I liked it. My flesh was always weak. Later I changed, and I could not stand giving myself again and again to that . . . loss, that nothingness. We gave the ladies a drink to erase all specific memory of how the God had come to them. I should have had that too. Except for one, most would not know me in the street. But I recognized all, all."

Althea was pierced by envy of the one woman who remembered him.

She said, "And so why didn't you just become an ordinary man? A father?"

"I *am* a father," he said, "in the Catholic way now. People have expected me to be a priest since I was four years old. Anywhere in India, they will find me." He pinched up the chest of his robe. "Maybe I am too cowardly to live without this."

"I am wondering," Althea said, "whether I want my husband to be dead. For a year, since our child died, I have hardly made love with him. Only when I force myself, and then he knows. I tell him it is sadness, but now I think it is hatred that prevents me. I feel he does not deserve any happiness. I feel that all his happiness is at my cost."

"You have come to the right temple," Brother Jesūnandā said. "Look at her face" — he nodded toward the Virgin — "ask for your sickness to be removed."

"I have. I am."

"She had other children after Jesus," Brother Jesūnandā said lightly.

The chapel was full of flowers and candles. The procession knelt and prayed and sang in front of it. Althea felt like a child, dazzled by images and colors. She'd never become part of a parade before; her heart, her bones, her skin, were jumping to the rhythm of the drums. She let her voice rise and waver in approximation of the melody, not caring how she failed. Next to her a beggar woman wept, her face turned up, tears running down her flat wrinkled cheeks. Althea thought, Maybe I understand what she understands, the loss of barriers inside.

She left her shoes behind, in front of the church. And moved onward, stepping on the sari, pulling it down. She recovered it, gripping the white cotton between one elbow and her ribs.

They went on toward town, past the cow barn's long roof and the red, hoof-trampled mud of the corral. The drummers stopped while Brother Jesūnandā blessed the great mild Zebu where they crouched now in utter darkness. Stepping aside, out of the torchlight, Althea finally managed to shove a bigger hank of her sari beneath the waist belt. Now it hung crooked but secure.

Next, by the gate, they stood silently before the cottage where the French priest was dying, tended by Indian sisters. Brother Jesūnandā came from the front of the crowd to find Althea, led her to the window to look in. Usually the cottage was off limits. "Look, he is in Heaven already." The window lit by lanterns was a stage. Inside, the old father lay gasping, an edge of warm light along the ridge of his enormous Gallic beak. Women bending over him, touching him, their brown round faces framed in white. With a slight shock she recognized the scene, her first dream ever to come true.

The procession went out onto the high riverbank. No longer a green bend clotted with washermen, the Kavita was filling up with violet steam like a magician's prelude. They walked through the soft sand under coconut palms. The sand was still warm from the day.

Brother Jesūnandā came up from behind her. "Someone might have thought these were an offering," he whispered. His mouth at her ear, his breath smelled of wine. How could that be? "To themselves." He pushed the sandals into her hand. "Put them on," he commanded.

"They *were* an offering," Althea said.

"You'll get worms. You'll cut your feet in town. You are not one of us, your feet are soft. Put them on."

"All right," Althea said, throwing them down in front of herself. Flap, flap.

She had learned she was a member of the Untouchable caste; her own servants wouldn't eat food her shadow had fallen upon; yet

Brother Jesūnandā had carried her sandals. He had done that for her, she thought, a thing as horrifying for him as washing beggars' feet.

The last red bubble of sun was gulped under the horizon. The sky went black. Town was full of thousands of people shouting and writhing. The Indigents' Procession funneled into the main street behind an enormous image of a black-haired goddess carried on men's shoulders. An elephant stood at the side of the road, handing out glasses of milk with its trunk. It swung each glass into a bucket, lifted it dripping, in relaxed rhythm. "Take one," Brother Jesūnandā said. "It is the essence of the festival."

The milk was sour, thick, and sugared, with a musky green-brown undertaste. "What is it?"

"*Bhang lassi*. A gateway to God."

It went down all in one piece, like saliva. She thought she'd vomit, but didn't.

"Don't leave me," Althea said as the crowd pressed against her, nearly lifting her off her feet. She began melting into the stream of endless life, color and stink and noise. Someone threw a handful of colored powder on her, staining her sari purple and red and yellow. It will never come out, she thought. The priest's strong fingers gripped her forearm, saving her from a whirlpool. They swam together through the gates of the white temple that had always stood at the end of the road. Althea had never been inside — it was barred to non-Hindus. "Don't worry," Brother said, reading her thoughts, "I am with you. And you with me. Remember only that." The domes lit by the moon looked like vertical bunches of bones. There were bonfires inside, and a maddening sound of hundreds of bells all ringing at once.

19

MAGGIE STOOD holding the sides of the clinic door with her two hands, letting air reach her armpits and ribs. Tears welling around the edges of her eyes were only slightly cooling. She stared fruitlessly up the road, raging at its emptiness and at her own need to stand and stare. Carson would come back on tonight's bus, or with Cantinflas, unpredictably. She knew all this; she'd agreed to it; yet she desperately needed to talk to Carson. Why was she always home when Carson left, but he was never here when urgent summons came for Maggie? Why did she stand here so loyally, when he never asked permission before enacting his own plans?

Yesterday, a garbled message had come across Radio Horizonte, summoning a person who might have been Maggie to contact friends who might have been the Wechslers. Fortunata had already given her opinion: Maggie should have gone to Cajamarca on yesterday's bus. Her grandmother was dying, or about to be locked up in an asylum. Fortunata was in the kitchen, having come in on a Sunday, unable to resist being the first to know what Maggie decided to do. Maggie was avoiding her. They'd exhausted all discussion yesterday, Maggie's point being not to abandon the clinic while Carson was still away, unless there was an emergency, in which case the radio message would surely be repeated. In hopes of that, today Fortunata had left the radio on full blast. The message had not been read out all morning, but now Fortunata claimed that Sunday's announcer was usually hung over. Furthermore, once should have been enough — Maggie was not a child! Maggie was sick of Fortunata's arguments.

The cook's interest had a prurient quality, yet she gave far more importance to Maggie and her doings than Carson ever had. Truly, she'd remarked today, why was Maggie so dependent on her man? "As a woman, better to make him run after you!" Maggie, sick at heart, had been unable to voice an answer. *"Ay, Señora,"* Fortunata had said ruefully, *"me preocupas,"* you worry me.

Despite the cook's busy presence, the house felt empty without Carson, without patients. A continuity had been broken, leaving the stasis of this blistering day, not a shadow anywhere.

Maggie needed to make a decision — perhaps she had, in being unable to push off from such a vacuum. She felt paralyzed. It was too hot to do anything, even to read her Russian novel. She was trapped here with her mind, her stupid thoughts which she was unable to replace with any others. Last night, she'd prayed for Carson's return, offering up in exchange all of her selfishness, all her grating imperfections, particularly those which arose in his proximity. Today she was furious with him, and with herself. How, she asked herself for the thousandth time, had she let him become so important? Why didn't she just take off? Yesterday's bus was long gone, but she could be packing her small bag right now. She could even hear him telling her, "Go on ahead and go! What makes you think I'd mind?"

Come back, she thought. You don't know how much I need you.

The ocher heat stank on the dead and useless road. Nothing moved until, just as Maggie turned to go back inside, a bull's blood bird flicked in and out of the branches of a nearby thorn bush. It flew across the road and hid in the bushes there. A sign, she hoped. Between thorny moments, willed acts, and forced decisions, vivid life made a flashing appearance.

Yesterday, Luz María had come to invite her to lunch at Piedras Baja, saying that her mother had made a giant pot of *ají de gallina* — even enough for Fortunata! — this after Vicente had asked her to consider Maggie's lot, how lonely she must feel and scared without her *esposo*. Maggie had been unable to suppress her elation — not only to be invited with such tenderness, nor to be distracted and fed things Carson wasn't, nor even that it would be her first meal at anybody's house in Piedras, but also (mostly) at the summons from Vicente, a call she felt inside her bones. She'd tried to explain to Luz María the expression in English, "Wild horses couldn't keep me away," but Luz María had only smirked and shrugged. Just as well.

Ten people had sat at tables in Luz María's courtyard, with the radio playing its staticky haunting music, and the dogs and chickens underfoot, and the pig smell. They'd eaten and drunk beer all afternoon, Vicente sitting next to Maggie, and Luz at the far end of the table. Lady Maggy had lain at Luz's feet in a battered cardboard box, swaddled in crocheted blankets despite the heat. She seemed to be staring at her own fingers, focusing at last. Whatever she became, it was clear that Luz would never abandon her.

For the first half hour, Maggie had found herself compulsively bringing Carson into the conversation, repeating his remarks and divulging his ideas, but it was soon made clear that no one wished to dwell upon the valley's fears and dangers, not today. Luz's uncle Zenobio, a burly man wearing a teal-green, counterfeit "Denver Coyotes" baseball cap, announced that in two weeks he was sponsoring a festival for John the Baptist, the saint he kept in his house. That was the holy feast of Saint John's Beheading, and they'd already entered a period of *promesas*, atonements, and self-examination. "Would we give our life for *devoción?*" Uncle Zenobio hoped so. He invited Maggie and her *esposo* to his party on that night, here at the hacienda.

Maggie was embarrassed not to have recognized Saint John in his brown, off-the-shoulder robe; she'd always liked the idea of him, living out in the wilderness, eating bugs and honey. She told Uncle Zenobio that her grandmother had been a devotee of this saint, which led to the story of how her grandparents had washed up at Piedras, and of the conception and tragic death of Maggie's uncle. Uncle Zenobio was very excited to hear of Maggie's connection. He told of the many miracles Saint John had performed, of punishments he'd meted out, once pushing into the river a vanload of people who'd come to his festival just to get drunk. All agreed that Maggie belonged in this valley as much as anyone. "You shall dance with us, Señora!" Uncle Zenobio paid for a brass band to come from Cajamarca. Saint John made a tour of town, on the shoulders of his devotees, before returning to stand all night before the church, watching people dance and celebrate him, all at Zenobio's expense. When the procession passed the clinic's door, Maggie and Carson must come out and join it. Uncle Zenobio's great lament was that no priest could be persuaded to make the trip to town to say a Mass that day, not since Don Héctor's death. The new priest didn't approve of dancing, and he overcharged. "Extortionist," Uncle Zenobio grumbled. "All he cares about is money."

Rolling on a wave of convivial condemnation, Maggie had announced that thing she'd never said aloud before, that her mother, Althea's second child, was the daughter of a priest. (It would never get back to Julia, she was sure.) As she spoke, it sounded true, and her audience immediately confirmed it. When you lose a child, you urgently must make another one, reflected Luz María. Priests had lots of children, Fortunata said. They were no different from other men — no, worse, said Luz; most men were willing to give their child a name, if nothing more. Only Vicente noticed how noble it was of Maggie's grandfather to take Julia as his own.

Held within these people's understanding, their amused, wide tolerance, Maggie had felt a missing piece of her soul flying back to live inside her. She wished Julia could be here, or at least the tormented part of Julia's spirit — yes, it would need to be disembodied from the rest of her. Perhaps that tormented part is simply me, Maggie thought. Perhaps I was sent out into this world to resolve my mother's sadness.

Luz María said, "Huascarán fell upon Huaraz again four years ago. My mother heard it on the radio. Many dead. It would be good to predict the seismic movements."

Vicente laughed, and said her name reproachfully: "Luz María!"

"If you can predict a thing, you can avoid it," Luz María insisted.

"One never knows," said Vicente. "Where there has been one earthquake there can always be another, *eso sí*, but defining the moment is another matter."

"You cannot predict an earthquake" was Uncle Zenobio's opinion. "But I am in accord with the Huarasinos. Here in the Rosario we have had *temblores*, but if we moved Piedras, where would it go? Higher on the mountain, there is no flat ground. The *puna* has sufficient towns."

Luz María said furiously, "Our earthquakes here are not so large."

Fortunata said that always before an earthquake, an old woman came to every house asking for food and water. If you helped her, she placed a secret mark so that the house was spared, but people who turned her away felt the brunt of the disaster. This woman was very ugly and old, and she usually had a little dog with her. She was the earth goddess, Pachamama.

"The saints protect us," pious Zenobio corrected her, "if we have faith." Turning to Maggie, he said, "Pachamama, giant boas, talking rocks — all that is superstition."

"What color dog?" Luz María wanted to be sure to recognize the goddess.

Fortunata gave her a disgusted look. "What does it matter? A small dog."

"The ancient ones lived higher up the mountain," said Vicente to Maggie. "I've seen their ruins, from before the Incas." Piedras was an ancestral location, surely because of its river crossing. Someday he'd show Maggie the ruins, if she wished.

Maggie did wish, of course. Though as a proper wife she made sure to mention inviting Carson, she was certain he'd be uninterested. So far, he'd refused to see the dwarf's cave and Maggie's swimming place.

"The river cuts and cuts," Luz María observed. "We are moving downward."

"That's geology!" Maggie happily declared. She would have liked this conversation, both intimate and desultory, to go on forever. She was about to tell Luz María, of whom she was no longer jealous, that it had taken the scientific world hundreds of years to see the point that Luz, untutored, had just made.

Suddenly no one was talking; Vicente fiddled with the radio knobs. *Reeew, reeeowr.* "*Algo para tí,*" something for you. He turned up the volume to an unbearable pitch, then down again. "*Shh, shh, Señora,*" Luz María said, "*los anuncios.*" She nodded at Maggie, wide-eyed. On the radio, an engine roared, and then there was an echoing reverberation of wind. This was the sound logo of Radio Espacial, Space Radio, intended to imitate a flying saucer taking off.

"*Ay, sí,*" said Maggie, pulling up her chair. Often she and Fortunata listened to these announcements; it was one of their amusements. The *locutor* machine-gunned from under his thyroid: *For the district of Machipampa. Whoever has harvested bananas! Place them by the side of the road for pickup! Branches must be clean, uniform, and free of spiders.* And he rang a bell: *bing!*

Machipampa was halfway to Ecuador, Vicente explained to Maggie.

Miss Fanny Morales, Fanny Morales, please call your mother at once. Anyone knowing the whereabouts of Fanny Morales and her minor son, Isidro, please present this information to your radio station, Radio Espacial. Bing!

"What happened to Fanny?" Maggie wondered. Completing the stories was part of listening.

"*Se escapó,*" said Fortunata, stating the obvious.

"Her husband is in my mother's family," Luz María said. "She's a whore."

Fortunata gave Maggie a look. Meanwhile, the radio told everyone not to believe that Jesús Briceño Condori had been in jail for four years. No, Jesús was returning from a trip, and his mother could expect him home tomorrow, on the bus.

Another roar and whoosh, and the announcer's voice began to skirl as if announcing lottery prizes. *Now we have news for a stranger. For the German nurse in the valley of the Rosario River, your friends in Cajamarca ask you to contact them. I repeat: the nurse from Germany, contact your friends in Cajamarca without delay.*

Now everyone talked at once. "That's you," Fortunata said somberly. "Someone in your family has died."

"No," Maggie said. "I'm not German, and I'm not a nurse."

Vicente said, grinning, "They say you are German because you are blond."

"Blond, yes, and tall, like a German, that's why," Luz María said excitedly.

"In my country, they say my hair is brown."

Yes, said Vicente impishly, but didn't she see that, from the point of view of black, it was yellow?

Fortunata said, "The radio makes mistakes, but still, it is you."

Maggie was definitely the person. Radio Espacial had begun passing the message last night. At first the announcer had named the clinic of Piedras. He could write, but he could not read, so he spoke from memory. His messages evolved throughout the day; one learned to interpret. "There is no other nurse in the Rosario, you see?" insisted Luz María.

What time last night, Fortunata wanted to know. Why had Luz María and Vicente not run immediately to the clinic? No one answered, and Fortunata settled back in her chair and crossed her arms, having proven a long-standing point.

Bewildered, Maggie said, "How does the radio know I'm here?"

"You are the *gringa famosa*," Luz María's mother declared.

"You have friends in Cajamarca, no? They placed the announcement," said Vicente.

Klaus and Liliana: of course, after twenty years they knew the tricks of rural communication. They were trying to get her out of Piedras, was Maggie's first thought. Their grapevine must have said something about Carson's toxic-waste campaign.

"Wechsler, Wechsler," Vicente ruminated. "This is faster than sending his driver. But! If this was a true emergency, sending the driver is more sure. I say it is serious, important, but not a matter of life and death."

Maggie felt cornered, as if the sky had emitted some bright beam upon her. I'm not going anywhere, she thought as the transistor continued down its urgent list. *Anyone who sees a four-wheel-drive Jeep with a tire on its back, color brown, belonging to the Ministry of Education, please report its location to the office in Cajamarca. Bing!*

"That Jeep. Its driver has relatives in Olluco," remarked Uncle Zenobio. "He always goes."

Fortunata again scolded Luz María. "You should have run to us last night, when you first heard this." She slammed her palm flat on the table. "*Ve, Señora, escucha*. You must go! Someone is dying, or is dead, or is in grave condition. If your mother wants to say her last words to you, then what?"

"My mother is in perfect health," Maggie said.

"*Tiene que ser*," Fortunata said, it must be. She recited for everyone the story of Julia's evil plans for Althea, including a full description, first given to her by Maggie, of the horrors of U.S. nursing homes, where old people were given tranquilizer shots and strapped, drooling, into wheelchairs in front of televisions. "Your mother has interned your grandmother in one of those asylums. You are the only one who can rescue your *abuelita*."

"The radio would mention health, and family," Maggie repeated. "'Call your mother,' something like that!"

"They did not want to frighten you," said Luz María's mother.

"You should at least call home," Luz María agreed in her small voice. "Call your families."

"What will Carson say when he returns and doesn't find me?"

"We will explain," said Luz María.

"You cannot explain well enough," Maggie said.

The Peruvians all laughed.

What if a baby got pneumonia again? What if someone else got sick? Maggie's family could get doctors, but not the Piedrasinos. Carson had left her in charge of the clinic, and the clinic was all that stood between life and death for Piedras. She must wait until he returned, she told them. Anyway, they were both going to Cajamarca soon. How could she go to the United States before the water test came back? She indicated Lady Maggy. "For her sake, I'm not going," she said. *"Punto final."* Period.

Luz María fell silent, but Fortunata continued chipping away at Maggie's objections. Vicente was now the assistant. The clinic was not alone. Carson would return tonight: he and Maggie could kiss in the bus's door as Carson got off and Maggie climbed on. How could it be Maggie's fault if someone died in Piedras? Even the best of doctors never really stood in the way of death itself. Proof was that doctors died, and the residents of the powerful United States. The worst would be if her grandmother passed away and Maggie had not spoken with her.

"She's not dying," Maggie said. "I spoke with her a week ago. She told me not to come."

"We know nothing," Vicente said. "Only that Klaus Wechsler always has a reason for what he does."

Vicente had walked her home. The story of Althea had bemused him. How strange for Maggie to imagine her grandmother inside these very canyon walls! To wonder whether an ancestor had walked right here, or here, must be like trying to palpate the body of a ghost, or see the other world. "You must resemble her, no?" Then at the clinic door he'd said, "Lock this well. Your husband should not leave you here alone."

❖

Today, Sunday, Maggie had awakened feeling as if the floor were dissolving under her. Possibilities, all dire, spread in every direction. By noon, she'd tied herself in a thousand knots, and now it was three. Though the blasting heat was not yet fading, it was no longer fueled and growing. High time to dismiss Fortunata and quit gaping in this doorway, driving herself insane. She could use the river on her skin, to cool her off. A cool skin might bring a coolness toward everything.

She walked into the bedroom, put on her black panties and a sports bra under a shirt and jeans. Moving through the house, she couldn't stop being amazed at the silence that was swallowing and engulfing everything. It was loud, like the sound of electricity passing through wires overhead. She stood in the door of the kitchen telling Fortunata she was going for a swim, on this side of the river, just above the bridge, at the trail that forked downhill, just past the stony field where that dwarf's hole was. She'd be home in two hours. If not, Fortunata should please send Vicente or Don Sixto out to find her.

"I'll tell Vicente to go look for you right away," Fortunata said, smiling.

"Please don't!"

"The river is not safe."

"I never go in past my knees, as you've advised me, Fortunata. For safety's sake, I think someone should know where I am."

"You need to be rescued *before* getting in."

Maggie walked up the road, enjoying how the dust puffed in and out between her toes. Soon it would be washed off.

Clambering down two enormous boulders, she dropped onto the small beach she had discovered. It was only ten yards long, bounded by two rock falls and the driftwood nest. She had never seen a footprint here besides her own. The bank had eroded further since last time; now it was a cliff in miniature, with sand turreted in layers where it had been laid down damp, had dried and hardened, and been cut by water as the river bend ate away the land.

She sat on a rock at the top and took off her sandals, then slid down the sand cliff leaving two wide round tracks of bare heels. The sand was brownish gray and warm. She walked across it to the sharp nest of driftwood that was her fortress. Stones had caught in the forks and roots of broken trees whose shapes lacked only a bit of a carver's alteration to become frozen representations of souls screaming in Hell. One particular root was so vivid that she only had to glance at it to see the stiff faces and writhing limbs. A bearded face stared at her, trying to exclaim that it was proof that souls were trapped in matter. Just so, the vastness of the canyon seemed to indicate that the world was beyond comprehension.

She undressed to her black underwear, exposing her pale limbs and waist to the sky's shock. Folding jeans and T-shirt into a neat, soft square, she laid them on a barkless driftwood limb.

I am a child, she thought. Only my grandmother knows where I am, and how I am, and who.

She eased into the chilly gray-green water just below the boulder, gasping, inch by inch. The water sucked at her calves, leaving holes behind them. The river roared past, just a few feet beyond this cove which was not completely sheltered. Holding on to a thick, jammed branch, Maggie lowered herself to lie flat in the water. Floating, she held tight while the current pulled at her arm sockets. Her fingers stiffened, burning against the branch. If she let go, she would be swept away and killed. Impaled or crushed, chewed up, spat out by the hydroplant's gates.

She knew how her skin would feel after this, immaculate, tightened. She hung her face into the water. Exhilaration made her breath short. Not only fear, but a near faint of delight. The muscles of her ribs clenched, cold. The crease under her buttocks tingled, the backs of her legs ached with joy. Carefully, one hand at a time, she moved her grip onto a lower branch where she could straighten her arms, let her whole head go under. She raised her face, gasped, and dropped it into the water, kept it down, opening her eyes to the opaque water, flat as paint. Slowly, dimly, rocks appeared, like giant eggs a foot below. The current blurred everything. The palpitation of her own body roared in her ears, indistinguishable from the river, river, river.

The water hammered at the seam of her skull and rippled bubbling down her skin.

She pulled herself against the current and, hand over hand, got out, a tree frog climbing, wet and mostly naked, up the driftwood branches.

The desert canyon walls were hot, white. Across the river was a cliff, like a step two hundred yards from shore, made entirely of compacted oyster shells. The air was still, dry, vaguely misty, and the sky unclear, a pearly gray-blue. High above the front of this cliff, on an updraft, a hawk soared in stillness. The dry sand smelled of lime peels; her soles fried; she had to run from water to shade and back again. She felt ten years old, alone; for this part of the day she had lost her skin. She was nothing but eyes.

Hours in the river, by the river. Drinking the water, lying in the pee-warm margin. Sitting in the shade. All day in the river, the water brown, her underwear crotch growing heavy with sand the color of lead. This was Peru. It was also nowhere. She gathered colored rocks into a pile, found some animal's shoulder bone. Watched the old birds soaring. Felt her face burn. One day she hoped to find her own ruin or her own piece of ancient pottery, even a gleaming golden grain amidst the sand, but today she was too young for that.

How long had she been there when Vicente came, wavering out of heat and light, toward her? She felt the interruption, looked up, and there he was, a black spider silhouetted against the glittering air above her. He stood on the same bank, fifty yards uphill, on the wrong trail.

"*Hola,*" he said, swooping down to sit beside her. She hunched away from him like the child she was. His voice quietly roared her name, "Maggie!" No one else pronounced her name like this, tentative and resonant, like a bell never struck before.

Vicente, dark Vicente. She stared at the web of his thumb, the line where brown outer skin met pink inner skin. "*Hola,*" she finally said.

He told her she was stupid to swim alone; she could easily drown. "You try," she told him, and showed him where to hold on.

"I know a better place," he said. He led her under the bushes, where the stream ran out from under the waterfall, still and cool. In the shade of the cliff they clambered up slippery spray-wet rocks to where a column of icy water fell and fell and fell through a cylinder of wet black stone. The air in here was wintry, damp. He stripped off his clothes and stepped under the waterfall shouting. She watched him closely, the water an exploding star above his head, sluicing down his burnished chest and dripping through the black nest of pubic hair, off the tip of his penis. His eyes were squinting shut. Next it was her turn. The water shattered her. It was unbearable, cold, absolute zero, the opposite of all the experiences she'd had since coming to Piedras, since leaving Larry, since learning she must learn to be alone. It was powerful enough to erase everything and bring her back to innocence.

Nearby the sand was warm and dry and soft. Where no one could see, they lay down together, panting. The bull's blood bird chirped invisibly.

Maggie felt as if she had already kissed Vicente, under the waterfall and many times before that. Nights, unknowing, ever since her sexy dream in Cajamarca. Of course she had been leading herself toward this since the first time she'd talked to Fortunata, luring him to her. Why had she not felt the convergence as inevitable before yesterday? The smell of his mouth had been familiar from her adolescence.

He'd dressed again for warmth. Now she unbuttoned his shirt, one by one. His chest was heaving as if he were waiting for her to stab him. There were drops on his neck, which she dried with her tongue. He placed his shirt under her hips. He put one warm palm under her black bra and pressed her nipple between two fingers. Teasingly, with the forefinger of his other hand, he questioned the band of her panties. She nodded. Her fingers were in his mouth, and his brown throat tasted like water on her tongue, as his fingers went inside her. She couldn't wait for him to get inside more truly. "Desire for union," Vicente explained, pressing back as she pressed against him. She laughed at his earnestness.

When they had finished, they looked at each other and began again. My fault, said Maggie to herself, with Vicente inside her again. She couldn't imagine wanting anything more just then, no matter what the cost. Or even because of the cost.

Afterward, Maggie ran her hand over his thick, short hair. It felt just as she'd imagined, peltlike. She gazed into his face, which could never again return to being unfamiliar, then she lay beside him, and they stared up at the white sky together without saying anything. After a while he kissed her hair, saying he wanted to keep them safe by arriving separately in Piedras. "You're tired," he said. "Don't get back in the water by yourself."

❖

In the water again, she held her peeled branch. Cold roar in her ears, goose bumps on her skin. One last dip, she thought, chilled. To cleanse myself. To erase what I have done.

She decided to try floating head-down, to let her hair swing into the current and the water wash between her legs. The branch was smooth and low. It was troublesome to hook her knees properly over one branch, shins under another, but at last she did it, safely. Her hair turned to seaweed and got longer. Her skin sloughed off, dissolving into the river.

Hands gripped her knees. They were hard hands, strong. She gasped and swallowed water. Someone to kill me, she thought, trying to lift her neck, open her eyes to see who. Vicente. Vicente! His face hung close. "Wait!" he said, but she'd already kicked him with her knee. As her eyes and mouth rose from the water again she saw him lurching forward, holding his nose with one hand full of a gob of blackish blood. His other hand still reached for her. Sorry, she cried, swallowing water because her head was under. Her two knees slid off the branch, and with a long scrape down her thigh the current took hold of her and pulled her down. She tried to push her feet toward the bottom, but could not find a thing below the surface except the rush of water and more water, going up her nose, into her mouth. Her eyes saw one flat plane, so she closed them.

Swept out past the edge of the big boulder, she entered the main current and was rolled onto her back. Gasping, her face came out in one long scream toward the sky. What an idiot I am, she thought. I'm going to die. I've killed myself. Her head went under and her eyes opened in the stinging, foamy yellow water. She was spun over and over. Coughing, flailing both feet, arching her back and hooking her free arm overhead, she scraped her forearm on something sharp.

Grabbing it, she felt it yielding, sinking as she tried to buoy herself. It was a dead tree, green or waterlogged, floating in the current as fast as she was. Now it crashed against her shoulders, knocked and pushed her, crowding from behind, trying to grab her in its sharp stabbing twigs and push her under. She lost all hope as she and the tree were entangled, arm in arms. They bashed quickly over a big stone, which freed her from the dead and clutching branches.

Remembering advice she'd read or heard, she maneuvered her feet downstream, sticking them out above the water, and was swept with terrifying speed past several large rocks. She was a boat now, her back scraped raw. Below her heels, she could see the next narrow gap between two yellow walls of cliff. The roar of the river got even louder. That was where she would die, where the water leapt down in figure eights between enormous rocks. Again she shrieked, but of course there was no answer except for the noise of the river. She was dead. She would have to forget Vicente, Carson, her mother, everyone. They'd have to forget whoever she had been.

The water went deep here, relatively smooth, though she could feel it swirling hard under her. Her face rode above the rippling waves. She spat. Time returned, grew long.

There was a wider spot ahead, no rocks, and the water became shallower. The roar of the river was high-pitched, almost optimistic. Unthinkingly, she flipped onto her side and belly and pulled for shore so convulsively she might have torn out of her skin.

The opposite bank rose under her, hit her chest. Here was a beach of black mud and smooth, egg-sized cobbles, with bushes growing out of it. The edge was slimy. She lay on her stomach, hyperventilating. The current was delicate here at the edge, a mere ripple in transparent water half an inch deep.

Her legs wouldn't hold her at first. Eventually she stood up and splashed the black silt off her body, more or less, then walked gingerly across the stones. Standing up was strange, since gravity made her heavy again. Her cold wet feet were too soft for these rocks. How could she have left her shoes behind?

She was the only person on earth, ripped out and cold inside, as if an element of her soul had been removed.

She hobbled far enough onto the wide beach so that she could be sure no arm of water could reach out and grab her. There were long driftwood sticks jammed between the bigger rocks, and a rack of cows' ribs half embedded in the sand and stones — the animal must have died in a flood. Years ago or last year? I am out of time, Maggie thought, here with Althea's cow.

Everything was hard and glaring white. Except for the lack of any other living soul, there was no visible evidence that she was not simply relaxing on a beach. She could have been in Costa Rica, Carolina, India, anywhere. She sat down again on a hot rock, printing it with her wet underwear. It nearly steamed. What a fool I am, she thought. Tempting fate was asking to be proved wrong. Now I'll have to walk back to Piedras, as naked as that retarded girl, La Lula.

She sat catatonically watching the too bright blood braided with water, running down through the short light hairs, lighter than the skin on top of her thigh. Best not to waste all that blood. Who knew when she'd be fed again? She put down her face and licked her thigh. It tasted like salt and rusty bucket.

This was a huge flat sandbar covered with stones and ringed with buzzing bright green thorn bushes. At the downstream end there seemed to be a small creek or river running flat below another stringy waterfall. I lost that boy, she heard her grandmother saying. She had no desire to investigate.

The bull's blood bird tweeted red in the bush.

As Maggie's reasoning powers returned, she understood that she could not be very far downstream from the bridge. She hadn't even reached the second set of cliffs. She was on the Piedras Baja side, the Cajamarca side, the side of civilization. Ha! This stone beach seemed a place where she could easily fry to death before anyone came walking along. Perhaps she should hobble to its southern edge and start looking for a trail into the shrubbery. Trails were everywhere: people went all over with sheep, with goats, with fishing poles, and sometimes, like herself, for other reasons.

She thought she'd seen Vicente falling into the water too. She hoped he was dead, even though it would be her fault. Fortunata had known it — known Maggie had wanted him to find her.

Carson returned at ten o'clock that night, banging on the door like a policeman come to arrest her. Maggie had fallen asleep with the shotgun in her bed. She yelled that she was coming, put the safety on, and slid the gun into its place under the bed.

She ran to the door, pulling him in.

"What's this?" Carson said, pleased. She rubbed against him, refused to let him take a shower. "Get on top of me," she said, "hurry."

"Did you miss me or something?" Carson asked. "I'm going to the mine more often!"

In a voice muffled by Carson's weight, she told how she'd almost died. "The worst was thinking I'd lost you." I did lose you, she thought, trying to embrace him again.

"Why did you go swimming!" Carson sat up.

"I was only in knee-deep. I slipped."

He had to inspect her wounds. She showed him the cuts, scrapes, and bruises, which were beginning to be sore. These marks must be Vicente's thumbs, from when he'd tried to grab her thighs and save her; they were camouflaged amidst many others. Just this once and never again she'd lie, she told herself, so as never again to lie to Carson. "I'm sorry," she said. He pinned her arms to the bed and kissed her. "Please, oh please," she said. He smelled sweaty, but not so strong that she couldn't make up her mind to enjoy it. Camembert and yeast. She asked him to hold her down, so that she could barely move, while he put his penis inside her. Carson was bigger, heavier than Vicente. For almost two years now she had all but forgotten the possibility that he was different from other men, that there could be anyone different. Tonight she had to drive the notion of Vicente out of her head, the sensations of his dense, narrow body writhing on top of her, muscles hard as a snake's. Luckily, she'd only made love with him twice, or there might have been some clue, some new, strange movement adjusted to that different body.

She concentrated, hard, on Carson, on his strong bony chest, the tuft of hair between his breasts. The hairs around his nipples, growing inward like a passion flower. How could he not know? With Vicente she'd come skittering, like a strong breeze across water, then dropped into some vast dark openness where she could feel him trying to reach her. With Carson, because she was a bit distracted, having lost the right to take what she needed from him, he came before her.

"May I?" she said, looking up at him. It was a life-and-death matter to come — not to be left behind, alone, like a whale suffocating on a beach.

"Sure, honey."

This orgasm slammed through her like hitting a boulder in the current. La Lula, she thought, I'm La Lula. I'll come for anyone.

There Carson was: he'd reappeared beside her in three dimensions, pale and moist, as if he'd just been baked for her. She knew he was willing to stay.

He got up to wash but she lay there, his sperm itchy and alive on her thigh. She hadn't used her diaphragm for either man. That was stupid, she now realized. One would not erase the other. The situation was recrystallizing around all three of them like cyanide in a test tube. Someone could be killed if we aren't careful, Maggie thought, feeling distantly the shotgun, heavy in its lair beneath her side of the bed. If Carson found out, she couldn't tell how he'd react, and there didn't seem any safe way of testing in advance. Do I love him, she wondered.

When she heard him leaving the bathroom, she forced herself not to think about anything except what was in front of her. She stared at his long, pale, dark-haired body until he said to stop it — she looked as though she were looking at the last thing in the world. "Don't turn off the light," she said. "I have to tell you what else happened yesterday, while you were gone." They lay with one finger interlaced, watching the long-legged mosquitoes softly bouncing against the yellow netting and probing its holes with their hairlike proboscises, while Maggie told about the radio announcement. Again she lied, by omission, but she decided it was part of the same, first lie, the lie she'd tell just once, once so that never again.

About the radio, Maggie did agree with Fortunata: Althea must need her. For some reason, she could not voice this fear to Carson. She felt that her tongue was being controlled by someone else, hearing herself explain that the way the radio message had been phrased, it sounded like Liliana was calling in the chips. Liar, liar, boomed voices in her head; these softened when Carson announced that he had an important fact to add, a fact Maggie could not have known, which added support to the Liliana theory. At the mine, Ignacio had turned on Carson, had accused him of getting embroiled with seditious peasants, enemies of the state. He'd threatened to call the dreaded investigative police if Carson persisted in criticizing the mine's effluent water, which was pure. Furthermore, to seal this line of conjecture, the mine director possessed a radio telephone, a direct line to the police in Cajamarca. It made sense to think that Ignacio had called the police, and that Liliana and Klaus had found out somehow and were worried, trying to warn them.

Yes, Ignacio, whom Carson had liked so well at first, had been vehemently unreceptive. He'd forced Carson to promise never to mention toxic waste again, on pain of being barred from the property of the mine and possibly expelled from Peru. According to Ignacio, all effluents were processed through a Canadian machine. The trout had died years ago, fished out. Infant mortality was fifty percent already. There was malnutrition; pregnant women drank as much alcohol as men. These peasants wanted free money. Innocent Carson had fallen into their hands. The mine had been in operation half a century — did Carson notice Piedras full of grown-up idiots?

Maggie laughed, imagining the mine director's face when Carson had raised his eyebrows and murmured, "*Quizás*, don't you?" They'd been drinking whiskies. After this, Carson had dropped the subject, and a semblance of friendship had returned.

"Sly, sly," she said, pushing his near nipple down inside its aureole. "What about me, should I go to Boston?"

Carson said to go wherever her heart told her to be. The water test would be ready soon. If she was willing to wait, they could go up together. She licked her finger and blew on it so that his nipple would stand up. "Heart says stay." Did it? It was going like a jackhammer. She lay her palm flat on Carson's ribs, felt them moving lightly as he breathed, felt also a faint thudding from inside.

Carson's chest, where it rose pale and heroic, had the shape of the side of a white tulip. What a good man he was. She knew she must protect him, so he could do what he had come to do. She'd wanted to feel the normal gratitude after sex; she hadn't bargained on this magnified adoration. Was it love or guilt? Did she love Carson truly, truly? How ever could she tell, now that she'd fractured their relationship? She felt he had forgiven her without knowing what she'd done. He was someone to live up to. He must never find out. Tomorrow she would tell Vicente that what had happened was an accident. She couldn't leave Piedras before doing that — cutting it off.

Carson was glad she'd decided to stay. He needed her, he didn't know what he'd do without her, especially now with all this horror going on.

"Maybe the mine director's right," Maggie said. "None of this is really happening."

"Yes it is," Carson said.

20

ALTHEA REMEMBERED Mongolia as the pink liver between yellow China and the green USSR. It wasn't hard to fill it with Johnny's images of barrenness, vodka, and clouds of dust. Nor the roar of mountains falling, a sound she knew herself.

Johnny had come back dirty, changed, like a war veteran, with a layer of unhealthy fat, a beard, and a new tin suitcase full of a smelly long coat and forty pounds of scholarly papers in languages and alphabets he didn't know how to read. These papers were given to him in Moscow, where he'd spent three weeks on his way back.

He told her he had made one lifelong friend he'd never see again, and that he could now feel the earth's tensions through the soles of his feet, although not in a "rigorously quantifiable" way. He had intuitions, he said.

Althea was changed too, but Johnny hadn't noticed and she hadn't talked about it.

Turning from the window, she saw the corners of her room filling up with liquid darkness. On the still-lit wall behind her was a maroon scarecrow shadow moving its skinny arms. She could make it dance, since it was she. A mad puppet tangling herself in the shadow of the folding wooden screen she'd bought after the procession. Sandalwood lacework: vines, birds, flowers, and buxom wasp-waisted Hindu nymphs stroking meek deers' necks, the necks interlaced, forming hearts. It took up half the living room, but Johnny had not noticed it. She would not tell him, then, how she'd commissioned it from a young artist, a tubercular man with a wife and six children, one blind eye, and the face of a saint.

Before Johnny left, two hundred yards was the distance from home at which she had begun to feel afraid. But to find this artist, she'd left the convent, walked between mud walls, across threshing floors, through shared courtyards where women and children stared at her and then ran into their lightless hovels. Ever since the night of the procession, she felt she had a right to enter any temple, any sanctum.

She was accustomed to not telling Johnny things. His absence always ended at the moment of his arrival, so the events and adjustments that had absorbed her while he was gone disappeared suddenly, as if they hadn't come to pass. There was never enough time before he went away again to tell Johnny everything that happened while he'd been gone the time before. He was not interested in the mundane things that fascinated Althea: piebald and skewbald rats, the cobra behind the water jar, or the milk seller's brass bucket. She had always believed that she could not fully rejoice in those or any other of the details of life unless shared with another human being whom she could imagine interested. So she seduced her friends, in letters, working hard not to bore or frighten them.

Now she had discovered her capacity to swallow words altogether. It took the same force as for the earth to twitch the Meghā road aside from its destination, or to lift a flat stream into waterfalls. She would never in her life tell anyone about the procession, or Brother Jesūnandā.

One more month and she would know beyond a doubt.

Inside the lit dining room, Mother Superior's habit fell in unimpeded folds, her ramrod spine refusing the chair's support. Brother Jesūnandā leaned toward her, facing Althea without seeing her, following Mother's conversation with interest and respect. Across from Brother, two empty chairs waited for Johnny and Althea to sit down.

"Tonight we have a ready-made topic," Brother Jesūnandā said in his fluting English. "Mr. Baines must tell us of the earthquake."

Johnny began from vastly far away, repeating what he'd told Althea on their first date back in Texas, a lecture she'd found seductive. Geologic time, stones' time, both speeded up and infinitesimally slow. Continents bulged like margarine, sea bottom rose into the sky, becoming the storehouse of ice. Continental drift. Stating the obvious, how Africa's hunched back should nestle against Latin America's breast and knees like lovers, or a mother sleeping with her sick child. In seventy thousand million years, they'd see India shoved under Russia, Italy under Europe. San Francisco, an icy isle where puffins bred.

Kangra 1905, Assam 1897, the Allah Bund. There was suddenness, too, in geology. Some earthquakes destroyed everything human; those were what Johnny studied. Earthquakes killed twenty thousand people at a time, raised and lowered the foothills five, ten, twenty feet. He'd measured all of India's quakes. He'd studied the faults of South America. Chile. Peru, where the mountain ate his and Althea's child.

"To us it's a catastrophe when the earth gapes open and what we stand on turns to jelly, but to the geologic god — if you will, Sister, Brother — and to even vaster gods whose time is to geology's as geology's is to ours — these are only foldings and unfoldings. Ocean bottom turns to a desert and the deserts are replaced by rivers are replaced by coral seas. Forms of life appear and disappear. Do the mountains suffer? No."

Johnny lifted his glass of wine and drank, and Althea knew he had forgiven the earth.

Brother Jesūnandā toasted Johnny's god, but he gave Althea nothing.

The next Sunday she told Johnny she had gotten into the habit of confession. In the chapel she stood in line behind a hundred skinny women in red saris, waiting for Brother Jesūnandā. They carried baskets of flowers and food which they'd leave outside the confession box.

Why did I not see that nothing has changed for him, she thought. These must be the infertile wives, and one unfaithful one.

She knelt at the curtain. British fabric, ugly, nubbled. Father, she said.

Yes? His voice.

Good, since it would not be a confession for any other priest, she thought wryly.

I will leave my husband for you, she said.

But I will not leave my temple for you, he said.

But it's your child, I am sure of it.

She thought she heard him gasp. Are you sure? How do you know? How do you know it is mine? Did you not follow my advice?

Of course I did, Althea said, I slept with my husband right away. Only to buy time, so I could think. With you I knew I had conceived, the very next morning. It was like a miracle. I felt so happy. It's you I love. I have come back to life. My husband hardly knows me, he never knew me, he doesn't care to know me. But you . . .

Silence.

I'll know when it is born whose child it is. And then —

Every child is God's child, Brother Jesūnandā said. I am . . . sorry, but I cannot intervene. What would I do in the United States? I'd die. You cannot make me into your creature, memsahib. Your servant. I have served you as I could already.

How can you think I'd want you to be my creature. I thought we would live here, together.

I have already told you I cannot be anything but a priest in India. And you would not survive here, with a child, alone. Where would you get money? India will eat you alive. Then there is nothing between us. Take the child, he is good for you. My gift.

She, Althea said. Maybe.

She. He. Be brave. And remember, we are in public here. There are others in the line behind you, waiting to confess.

A Hindu demoness to whom water looked like fire and fire like water — to whom evil presented itself as right and generous. A being with four fangs and naked breasts, suckling a healthy girl child, born with astonishing amounts of black hair.

"My great-grandmother was a full-blood Cherokee," Johnny Baines decided aloud. "Once you have it in you, you never know when it might pop out."

21

MAGGIE'S SOUL had been haunted by deficits, shadows, and unknown things far more than by the facts that everyone knew and accepted. Secrets and absences could control a person's life. They'd pulled her here, to Piedras. She'd believed that when the secrets got explained, the hole in her soul would be filled in. And so, without quite acknowledging it, over the past few months she'd forged a chain of events and adopted it as her own history. Nights when she couldn't sleep, or during hours spent idly staring at the river, faint memories had fit into uncomfortable suspicions. Eventually her speculations had begun to pull her forward like the river, into a vivid trance of moving pictures and experiences. She knew what Althea had thought and felt, what Althea had done and chosen. Deciding upon, or learning, her grandmother's story had seemed like walking down paths inside herself, first this one and then that one, finding logic at each turning. Her evidence was scanty, pieced together, still leaving room for the interpretation Julia would have given: Althea was a perverse fabricator, teasing, or hiding something. Still, the logic by which Julia was Brother Jesūnandā's daughter had come to seem inevitable. The idea resonated, filled a gap. Julia's tall, stalking posture often reminded people of women who carried water jars. Oddly, though, the corollary — that if Julia was an Indian's child, then Maggie was an Indian's grandchild — felt unimportant, except as a logical consequence of that chain of brain-racking she could now abandon. Now that she'd completed it, she hardly cared whether her story was strictly true.

She'd come home; she knew it. Whether by accident or fate, or as the result of her puny thinking and worrying and analyzing and deciding, Piedras was inside her, full of magic, the canyon's sides her bones. Here, each day's noon could last for hours. She would have expected to relax now, to sit with other people, half tipsy and replete, in the shade of the mango trees, forever. Of course, she should have known better. As soon as she'd told herself Althea's story, the river had dragged her off, into deeper gaps and holes, whirlpools to pull her under. At the bottom she'd met a wet and dripping man. Maggie's weirdest notion, which she would never have admitted to anyone, was that Vicente had been sent to her as a kind of emissary, proving the truth of what she had discovered. To harbor such convictions gave her dread. It wasn't rational. It had to do with the way she felt in his presence.

That day she'd almost drowned, he'd found her again on the other side. He'd crossed the bridge, come running. Her clothes were in his hand, hanging there like an excuse. He'd tried to embrace her, putting both arms around her from the front. She'd pushed him away. "You almost killed me," she'd said. "No, no," he said. "No." They'd stared at each other, wet, both shaking, shaking with cold. Then ear to ear, and crotch to crotch, their bodies had locked onto one another. She'd let herself feel protected in his arms, though he had not saved her. She'd thought about where his soul had formed, in the underworld where Atahualpa waited for deliverance, where her uncle Christopher lived, and her grandfather Johnny, and Domingo the lost raftsman. Her own soul had come back from there, from the black tunnel where the river had tried to take her. Now she was reborn, alive, raw, on the surface of the world, with Vicente saying he was glad.

He'd asked if she'd be happy, no matter what happened now. "Yes," she said quickly, to cover a no that was roaring up inside her, louder than the water, but no was the answer to a completely different question.

For if she let Vicente reach her (and she seemed to have little choice in the matter, since most of what he said and did seemed to reach her automatically), the danger and requirement was losing Carson. She could foresee where the river wanted to drag her next. Vicente would give her a child. Perhaps he had already, even indirectly, by throwing her off balance, unprotected, into Carson's arms.

Where she must stay, because of the poison in the water, because of the crisis in the valley, because of the vows she'd made.

It helped that Vicente did not show up at the clinic for three days. Plenty of patients came, five or six a day. Carson muttered that they hardly needed an unreliable Peruvian assistant. Typical! Vicente had just been paid; he must be off squandering, drinking, visiting the city; he'd be back when the money ran out. Maggie tried to adapt Carson's mean interpretations to her own lover's feelings, abandonment, humiliation — but she couldn't bring herself to see Vicente as a typical macho, now boasting of his exploit in some Cajamarca bar. She did lecture herself that if Vicente meant to convey that he regretted and denied what they had done together, it was only fair and she should take it calmly, since it was the same message she'd been planning to give to him.

Self-lecturing didn't work. She was dying to see Vicente and couldn't bear his absence. The best she could do was to keep burying her fingernails in the wooden frame of the clinic's front door, to stop herself from flying out to search for him, falling on the ground at his feet, begging for a crumb, an explanation.

She forced herself to make love with Carson, hoping that the motions of their bodies would erase this chaos of unendurable emotions, dissipate the implacable chill that had begun to rise inside her, turning her away from him. Again, she left out her diaphragm — to do away with a barrier, to tempt fate to bind them irrevocably together. Meeting her husband's eyes, she silently begged him to notice how she was feeling, as if she were stuck in the small end of a telescope. If he'd only notice, and ask her if anything was wrong, she could have answered no. But Carson didn't.

I can't let this happen, she thought. It's up to me to save us. She lay awake half the night wondering, planning what to say. It was ethical not to mention Vicente, as long as he was only a catalyst for deepening her bond with Carson. She could no longer hold back, though;

there was no time. She could already be pregnant. Madly, she liked the idea.

"What if I wanted a baby?" she asked Carson at breakfast.

"Is that a real question? 'What if?'"

"Yeah. What if?" His sperm was leaking out of her, onto the chair. It would serve you right, she thought, if some of it has swum the other way.

"Well, I don't know! Funny way to put it, don't you think?"

"What if I was really asking?"

Carson looked at her, grimacing. "Mm. Then I guess it would be a problem. We can talk about it if you want, but you know how I feel about it, right?"

Gulping, she said, "Tell me again?"

"That it would be irresponsible of me to bring a person into the world whose existence I don't believe in. I don't think it would be good for that person. You understand."

"I do." Maggie considered a possible child in her belly. Don't listen to him, she told it.

"So if you wanted a child, as you say, I wouldn't know what I could do for you. When we got married, you agreed you didn't want kids."

"I know."

"Do you want a divorce?"

She shook her head. Carson shrugged. "Sorry," he said, and touched her leg briefly before going back to eating his eggs. She watched him finish. "I don't know what I can do," he said, getting up with his plate. He stood over her. "All right?"

"Yeah, well, I guess," she said. Why had she bothered? This was the conversation she'd expected to have. But why couldn't Carson examine himself for a change? He seemed to think his principles were made of something better than mere human feelings. "Sorry," she muttered. "It kind of occurred to me." No, that was a retraction. "Strongly! I've felt it since the third day we were here. Otherwise I wouldn't bring it up." She fumed on in thought: Can't you see I'm trying to save us? This isn't just about a baby. I'm begging you, but you can't see that, and that's a worse *problema*.

"Right, okay." Carson stood waiting to be dismissed. She turned to finish her breakfast, wishing he'd go away on his own. "What's eating you?" he said, not having left. "Why do you have to bring this up right now? Your timing sucks, I can tell you."

"I know how it sounds," she was able to say, "but what if I can't help it? Asking a question doesn't mean I need to have a baby right this second!" He was right about her timing. If she was already pregnant, she'd just given him reason to think she'd tricked him into it. What if he said yes? What if he said yes, and she was pregnant, and then the baby turned out to be Vicente's? This was not an entertaining irony to be stuck in. For the first time, she regretted adopting Althea's precedent so wholeheartedly.

She needn't have worried about Carson's ever agreeing. "Jeez," he said. "You're so unhappy and pissed off. Are you getting enough sleep? I'm sorry, dear, I know you're under stress. We all are. Things are kind of stressful around here right now."

She jerked her shoulder away from his touch. "Try considering that what's bothering me might actually be the thing I *say* is bothering me!" She glared at him until he shrugged and went away. Then she put her head down on the table and cried, too disgusted with herself, and him, even to wish he'd notice.

That day one of the new mothers came in, wondering if a second child, a twin, was stuck inside her. Placing her hand under his on Doña Justita's soft yellow belly, Carson asked Maggie to palpate. Hernia or tumor? It didn't move. "The second," Maggie whispered. Carson's lips were pale and tight as he wrote out a chit, telling the woman she must give this to the health officer in Cajamarca as soon as possible, an authorization for x-rays and treatments, paid for by the government. Doña Justita looked at it askance and hid it in her bosom. Would she go? If she did, would she get any kind of help?

So this was the enemy, and this was how it hid itself, and showed itself. I'd do anything for you, Doña Justita, Maggie thought, ashamed, for there was nothing. Surreptitiously, she pressed her own belly, finding nothing there either.

When Vicente came in the next morning, Maggie barely recognized him, back in his disguise as an unrelated person. As he explained how his neighbor in El Mirador had begged for help with an overripe tomato harvest, Maggie traced the faint bruises under both his eyes, knowing they weren't from sleeplessness or a hangover, as Carson was joking. "You must be kidding, Vicente. Tell me how you got those." His arms had given way as he was trying to pitch a full to-mato crate up onto the truck, Vicente lied. Maggie could barely breathe, recalling how she'd given the shiners to him herself. He'd probably waited for them to fade a bit before returning to work.

After that, all he had to do was ask how Maggie felt after nearly drowning. He'd heard the story yesterday. Was it true? Was she all right? "I think I'll never be the same," she said, hearing her own voice falter, Carson behind her saying, exasperatedly, "Ffft!"

She waited several minutes and then, holding all her dignity, walked outside and hid in Carson's outhouse. Sitting on the toilet's closed lid, she cried for everything she'd lost, everything she could not modify in herself. Her feelings were as intractable as mountains; she'd lost all capacity to crush them. When she emerged, Vicente was waiting for her on the path.

"I refuse to make you suffer," he began.

"It's not you," she told him. "I wish we could run away from here."

"We can't, Señora. We have this work to do."

Twice each day she waited in the kitchen for the radio message to be repeated. If it was, she'd vowed to obey it and go immediately to Cajamarca. But the summons never came again. Although its absence was a silent accusation, without it she could find no reason, no excuse to leave.

She met Vicente in a deserted herder's hut far up the canyon's side. They spent hours together, naked, glorying. These were the golden days of August, when wheat fields clung to the middle folds of the vast, black, bald-topped mountains like square gold sequins. The sky was dry and blue and brilliant, and the air so clear, so sharp and warm and slicing, that it became once and for all self-evident to Maggie that there is no division between sky and air, that the heavens always touch the ground.

She had sufficient time to examine Vicente's face, every inch of his skin. The slatted muscles of his thighs. His purple nipples. He was perfect, the perfect color, she told him, setting their forearms next to each other. No, she was — white was, he replied. Maggie was outraged. No! But Vicente rejected her perception that her skin was now sunburnt, a shade equivalent to his. At last he admitted that no skin was white, not even hers. *Perdón,* sorry, he said — then what about a sky just before sunset, during the rains? I'll call you that. As he spoke, he caressed the hollow where her inner thigh met her body, where the skin was a color that Maggie could not see. In the end they agreed: not enough colors had been invented.

Usually they made love, but sometimes instead they'd lie side by side gazing up at the burning, cloudless sky, one leg thrown over the other's, while Vicente told stories of the rain forest where he'd once heard the cry of a bird, or Maggie joked about how postmodernism had driven her out of the United States. She even asked him what would happen if they conceived a baby. His mouth came down, a hairsbreadth from her lips. "I want everything with you." They kissed, for they had nothing left to say.

After spending time with him, Maggie often felt unbalanced by happiness. On her way down the mountain, she'd stop and contemplate the poisoned river, gaze across at the hamlets they'd visited as a medical team before returning home. Nevertheless, Fortunata noticed a change in her demeanor, and hinted around until Maggie paid her a little extra from her own salary to ensure the cook's discretion.

Meanwhile, she continued to make love with Carson. Although she'd decided that he'd never had any idea what went on inside her, nor any desire to find out, she hadn't gotten over needing him to trust her and to stay the way he was. Even if she loved Vicente more, could she really survive as a fugitive's wife? How much did she love Peru?

She'd have found it amazing that she didn't explode, except that her contradictions and betrayals were eclipsed by the evil that flowed down the valley, and by the urgency of fighting against it. They all three felt it, insidious and massive, blocking out the future just as the canyon walls blocked the sight of the outer world. Each day, they worked together gathering evidence that, indeed, they, like all the other people of the Rosario, were being poisoned, slowly dying. They tried to drink nothing but beer and Coca-Cola, but it was hard to avoid the river water altogether. Sitting around Albita's store, drinking until late each night, they named themselves as comrades in arms. Sometimes Maggie even imagined Carson already knew everything, and didn't mind.

Carson and Vicente did the examinations and Maggie kept the

books, her neat graphs and columns belying the horror of the mounting evidence. Tumors, rashes, white patches on the skin, babies with palsied, listless limbs. Almost as comic relief, Doña Ema showed up every other day, reporting one small pain after another. She was growing larger. Carson repeated to her each time that the miracle baby was healthy, but clearly Ema was lonely, and also she worried about her husband, who was said to be wandering in the hills, drunk, half out of his mind, uttering threats against her and everyone.

"*Mañana,* when Carson travels to the mine," Vicente said on Friday, "you should accompany him, Señora. I had the idea to go by myself to visit more of the high villages. I won't ask to see the sick. I'll talk to the women, play with their children, and tell them our perspective about sanitation, birth control, and especially water, as we have been doing."

Maggie despised Carson's look, bored and superior, as he told Vicente that he was not yet authorized to represent the clinic. "None of us should leave," she interrupted. "Sunday is Saint John's Beheading, so tomorrow is the procession, *verdad?*"

"How did I forget!" Vicente cried. "No one will be anywhere. They will all be here."

"What about the miners?" Carson asked.

"Many will come," said Vicente.

"They won't shut down La Tormentosa, not for this," Carson predicted.

"Shouldn't we join the festival? We're invited," said Maggie, explaining to Carson about Uncle Zenobio's relationship with the statue, arguing how good it would be to participate in this community event. Things had been getting so depressing. Personally, though she didn't say it, she was eager to do whatever was required to get Saint John's attention. Even if the stories about him were pure superstition, surely it was harmless, worth the gamble to join his festival? Fortunata said dancing was a *promesa* to which Saint John always responded. Carson argued it was wicked to rely on magic, for it cut you off from real solutions.

But what if there were no solutions? And who could prove the stories wrong? Maggie had always begged the sky for aid when she was desperate. She'd even constructed a rationale for the practice: admitting you were at wits' end could open you to new possibilities beyond the tendentious, habitual strategies that hadn't worked or had caused your problems in the first place. She knew, partly from Althea's story, that the sky didn't always send help at the time or in the way one wished. Yet she wanted to prove that she was ready for the truth; in any case, she was unwilling to give up the idea of setting invisible forces in motion. Maybe, before the test results came in, everything could be rectified — the lab sheets rendered blank, the water clean and harmless.

Carson said he'd sleep on it. Just now he wanted Vicente and Maggie to know they'd done good work today, but that they all had a long way to go, and it was late.

"But you both should dance," urged Vicente, refusing to be dismissed. "Stay here, Don Calzón! People fight at festivals. Sometimes people die. We have a saying, *Que no es fiesta sin muertito.*" It's no fiesta without a little death.

Uncle Zenobio could rustle up costumes for both gringos. He owned two minibuses and a truck, which he hoped to prevent from crashing. Worry made him a great sponsor, never counting costs as he laid out cash for food and drink and music. Each year he rented piles of costumes in Cajamarca and brought them down in his buses, along with the brass band and a DJ.

"I can't dance," Carson said.

"Don't worry!" At a small festival like this it didn't matter. This wasn't even the main festival of Piedras, just Zenobio's idiosyncrasy. There were no more than two groups, the Incas and the devils, plus a few independent dancers disguised as spirit bears. Vicente had been asked to be the Inca emperor, but that required riding on a litter without a mask, and the police were always present. So he'd joined the devils instead, who cavorted by the dozen, unrecognizable in tin masks. Carson should join the Incas, though. They reenacted the Conquest, and with Carson's dark beard he'd make the perfect Spanish priest. As priest, he'd only have to walk along brandishing a crucifix, making faces as if he wanted to convert everyone from paganism. It was a comic part, fun. The priest wore no mask either, which for Carson was an advantage, allowing him to be recognized as Doctor. Maggie wouldn't fit into the Incas, but there was always room among the female devils. With her height and long legs, she'd look best as Satan's wife, the temptress who appears once a year in the upper world to tell everybody's secret sins. "Sounds about right," said Carson. Luz María also danced as Satan's wife; Luz would love to have a partner and could show Maggie the steps. It would bring prestige to Uncle Zenobio, since at large fiestas Satan had two wives or more.

Devils' steps were simple, as Vicente demonstrated. "Left, left, see?" He pranced in a triangle, swiveling his elbows, then he stopped, stood panting in the middle of the floor.

"Nice," Carson said. "I'm sure the fiesta's very nice. But I'm anxious to get up to the mine again." He'd wasted his last visit arguing with Ignacio. Now he'd like to run a clinic, quietly checking whether he could enlist any miners in the water campaign. "My question is, can I trust the two of you alone with whatever's likely to go on down here." This sent a shiver up Maggie's inner thighs.

"*Tengo miedo*," I'm scared, she said. "Aren't we more likely to get the emergency?"

"Nah," Carson said. "Mines have accidents. I'd say the chances are about the same. You did fine when I left you here before. Now you've got more training."

"Go up on Monday, Doctor, Monday!" Vicente cried. "We'll introduce you to miners at the fiesta, where you can speak together openly. Monday Piedras will be dead, worse than a Sunday, while the mine will be working at full strength."

That convinced Carson. He'd even play the priest.

Cacophony of flutes and drums, trumpets and tubas. First came Uncle Zenobio and his wife, solemnly dressed and carrying a China baby dressed in lace — our Savior. Behind them, on his two-ton litter, the saint swayed oceanically, majestically, slowly borne along on the shoulders of three dozen sweating, stumbling men in dark coats and shiny ties. From the back, where Maggie was, Saint John's brown plaster hair was barely visible above the mass of dancers.

Close behind Saint John, the Inca king was also borne along, more precariously, on a foil-wrapped wooden chair with raw construction planks thrust between its legs. Still, the Inca was able to hold his face in an expression dour and noble, worthy of his queen, who rode behind him, wearing lots of red lipstick and sitting delicately cross-legged on what seemed to be a ladder, draped with a blanket, carried parallel to the ground. Behind the royal pair paced warriors playing drums and panpipes in an eerie, primordial clash that seemed just about to form itself into a melody but never did. Then came the virgins of the sun, average age twelve, wearing short shifts and rubber-tire sandals with ribbons cross-tied up their calves. Behind the virgins marched conquistadores in helmets. Among them, Carson, in gray priest's robes, hammed it up, leering and enjoying the laughter of the crowd. Sashaying all around, darting in and out, were the spirit bears, adolescent boys in union suits who didn't look like bears at all. They wore white knitted ski masks with red knitted lips, teased everyone in falsetto voices, and battled one another with limp whips of braided yarn. There was a condor, too, dancing on tiptoe, waving ratty wings. With a black plastic bag loosely veiling his human nose and mouth, only his eyes were visible. He wore a mirror on his forehead, and a crown of parrot feathers topped by a rubber chicken's head, spray painted black and red to make it into a condor.

The devil group was last. First danced the kings of Hell, eight feet tall in enormous masks covered with snakes and dragons: Lucifer, Beelzebub with matted whiskers growing out of his whole face, and a big fat Satan with bloodshot eyes the size of grapefruits. Then came half a dozen little female devils, the same size as the virgins of the sun, and after them, Satan's two wild, magnificent wives, shaking horse-hair wigs dyed orange. Next was the brass band, playing the devil's tarantella, and last of all a hellish, roaring squad of ordinary fiends barely held in check by the archangel, Michael, who blew a whistle to control them.

Maggie's consciousness had shrunk. As Satan's wife, mostly she was hearing herself panting inside her mask, which had sagged and slipped under the weight of an enormous plaster snake growing out of its forehead, so that she couldn't see out the eye holes. Doggedly, she tried to prance along, tilting hips and head with the nasty coquettishness Luz María had demonstrated earlier. Maggie kept lifting the little pointed red boots that felt like genuine cloven hooves forced over her feet. Fortunately the bass drum had become the power that lifted and lifted her knees, allowing her to continue the ragged struggle of her breath and almost forget that each time she picked up her right foot, the ball of it would soon slam down again onto one small sharp nail she'd hammered up through the sole of the rented boot by dancing on the stones. The insole was slick with moisture. Not sweat, since her left boot was quite dry.

The dance was endless. From time to time a whistle blew to change the step, and Maggie would raise her chin and try to glimpse, through the mask's fanged mouth, what Luz María was doing. Twirling, okay, great. She let herself go, flying in a satisfying circle whose end was unpredictable — she'd nearly fallen twice already, once when her high heel had slipped alongside a rock, once when her ankle had collapsed on landing. But she'd forgotten those shocks, for now she was in the air again, twirling in reverse, flying counterclockwise and landing on her good foot, for this one step's duration facing backwards with the mask bouncing up into place, momentarily awarding a clear sight of the band behind her, the bass drummer's feet leaving the ground as he whacked the white leather circle once again with all his might.

She couldn't see Carson or Vicente, though she could sometimes hear the devils, roaring and guffawing from behind the band.

The procession was supposed to start at noon from Luz María's, but the band was late, so it was three o'clock before Saint John came out of his glass case. Leaving Piedras Baja, the procession lurched across the bridge, attained its rhythm at the clinic, passed the tomato fields and Doña Albita's store, then went out of town as far as the cemetery before turning around to go all the way back, across the bridge, to stop at last in front of the church, where the dancers removed their masks. The saint was set high on a pedestal, and a light was adjusted to shine on him. The band set down their instruments, white tubas in a row like snails uncurling, and began to drink beer as fast as possible, as was the musicians' due.

Uncle Zenobio hooked up the sound system. Huge speakers began to blast cheap *chicha*, disco versions of Andean songs. As the DJ began to flatter everybody, the girl devils who'd danced in front of Maggie prevented her from finding Carson or looking inside the church, whose door was open for a change. No, they grabbed her arms and made her sit down with them to drink toasts and recover. Maggie offered no resistance. She huddled next to Luz, leaning on her shoulder to remove her right boot and show everyone her blood-soaked sock. While the devil girls gasped, Luz fixed the nail somehow, pounding awkwardly at it with a rock, and returned the boot to Maggie with the advice to put it on and forget it until later. Uncle Zenobio came around, and a waiter with a tray, cajoling everyone to drink a shot of liquor. The young male devils postured at a distance, magnificent in their capes and sequined breastplates, but Maggie couldn't find Vicente among them.

After a while it got dark and people began to dance. Maggie cavorted with the devils, then slowly moved into the heart of the crowd, where Carson was jiving with the Inca queen, holding up his priest's robe in one hand. He waved for Maggie to join them, but was prevented by Fortunata's violent embrace. Fortunata was not in costume but clearly had been enjoying the parade. Entirely drunk, she kissed Maggie wetly and babbled out her love. Maggie danced with her, holding hands, and then tried to slip away, but Fortunata screamed no! no! and held on to Maggie's thumbs, which would have broken had not Maggie kept on dancing, dancing, dancing.

Then it came, the pull on Maggie's arm. It was Vicente. "Dead," he whispered. "Who?" "Just died, you have to come." "Who?" Maggie, disbelieving, allowed herself to be pulled along, out of the dancing and into the dark. "Who?" she asked again where it was quiet enough to hear.

"Lady Maggy."

"No!" They ran along the paths, in the dark, Vicente's sequins catching bits of light from the party behind them. Although it was pitch black under the mango trees, Maggie felt they were encased in a ball of invisible radiance, which didn't help her see but swept her forward, preventing her from falling.

"How did it happen?"

"I don't know. She fell on her head or something."

"Where's Carson?"

"Already there."

"She can't be dead! Who was with her?"

"No sé. Luz María's little brother came and said."

They slowed to a walk, having reached the path that led to Luz's.

"Has anyone told Luz?" Maggie asked, but Vicente didn't know. They passed rapidly through the darkened room where the saint's glass box stood empty. Vicente led Maggie across the courtyard, ducking into a narrow corridor half blocked with rags and mops and boxes, then into the small cement room where Luz lived. It was barely high enough to stand up straight, barely wide enough for the bed Luz had shared with Lady Maggy. The walls were a dirty pink. Piles of clothing rose at the foot of the bed. Maggie noticed a scrap of printed cotton pinned under the foot of Luz's treadle sewing machine.

Carson, still dressed in priest's robes, was sitting on the bed next to the baby, whom Maggie instantly recognized as dead. Not even a small child could mistake it. Lady Maggy was wrapped in a fat ball of blankets with only her face showing. Though her dark eyes were both open, shining slightly, her body was stiller than still, her tiny mouth stiffly gaping, her copper skin already shading toward a subtly lurid verdigris. Luz María's mother stood helplessly aside. "What happened?" Maggie whispered. Carson said it sounded like a seizure.

"The earth has eaten her," pronounced Fortunata, bustling past everyone to take the child in her arms as if it were alive. Carson had to stand up abruptly to make space on the bed. Fortunata began trying to close Lady Maggy's staring eyes, but they wouldn't shut. "Go and find a long white cloth to tie her jaw," she ordered Luz's mother. "It's stiffening already." Luz's mother disappeared, relieved to have a duty.

"Right," said Carson.

At this point Luz María came in, stumbling, on the arms of two of her sister devils. She reeked of alcohol. Her costume, black and gold, encrusted in jewels and luscious dragons, filled the room with its dreadful luxury. Fortunata offered the child but Luz shrieked once and collapsed to her knees, onto the bed, on Fortunata's lap, and pressed her face to her child's, murmuring, "What now, what next, *princesa?*" Fortunata stroked Luz's long black hair.

Maggie turned away, weeping at last.

"Let's go find a coffin," Vicente said to Maggie. "Good," said Carson, overhearing. Maggie asked whether he needed anything from the clinic, but he didn't. He'd stay to help Luz and her mother wash the little body. Later they'd interview the mother, to try to get more details. "It doesn't matter a whole lot," Carson whispered in English. Their eyes all met, agreeing.

Maggie and Vicente went to find the carpenter, Don Zoilo. He wasn't at the party. Someone said he'd stayed home, for he had joined the Evangelicals. On the road, Maggie's horrid boots required her to continue prancing as if across hot coals. Since there was no real rush anymore, they stopped at the clinic to get her sneakers, and a flashlight, and money to pay Don Zoilo. Clearly it was good that Lady Maggy would not have to grow up to be an adult, but whenever Maggie recalled the sight of Luz in her costume, hunching over her child, it was as if she'd seen the inevitable, cruel denial of everyone's most tender hopes. She came out of the bedroom weeping.

"May I?" Vicente asked, touching her shoulder. She nodded. He took her in his arms, gently, but she rushed at him, their devils' breastplates clashing. *"Tú eres tan bella, no aguanto,"* Vicente said, you are so beautiful, I can't bear it. He kissed her hair. Then Maggie raised her mouth and kissed him back, until the child's dead face appeared and she broke away.

They walked uphill to find Don Zoilo. On the darker parts of the path, where Vicente wanted to take her arm, she refused his help. I'm lost, she thought.

The carpenter, awakened from sleep, showed them one tiny white coffin which he refused to sell, for he predicted lugubriously that Lady Maggy would have grown to the size of a four-year-old in death. He hauled on his jacket and went down with them, to measure.

Thus began a phantasmagoria in black and gold that continued for days, so that for the rest of Maggie's life, her mind would turn inside out each time she recalled it. On returning to Piedras Baja with Don Zoilo, Maggie and Vicente learned that the fiesta had produced not one *muertito* but two: a young man had dived off the center pylon of the river bridge, having bet a glass of rum that he was strong enough to swim to shore. This time, no rotting pig had saved his life. He'd hit his head on a rock and had been dragged into the current, his body never to be found.

The next day, Sunday, the actual day of Saint John's Beheading, Carson had been unable to contain his need to go back up to the mine and work, work against the causes of such misery. He got on the bus, deaf to Maggie's pleas that he remain below, if only until Monday morning, as he'd planned, to sit in vigil with the rest of Piedras in the room with Lady Maggy's body, and the saint, and a cross of purple flowers representing the dead youth.

"The earth has eaten both of them," Fortunata repeated cheerily. "For next year's festival, we must produce more." She cackled. "I'm old, but what about you, Doña Maggie?" She poked Maggie in the side; Maggie recoiled. "You, then, Zenobio! With that belly, when are you going to pop?"

Safely locked in his glass box, the saint stared upward, as if denying he'd had anything to do with any of this.

"It's the water," Maggie said to Fortunata. "The earth is angry, you could say."

Fortunata whispered, "No, it's Luz María's own fault! She disrespected." Under the Black Rainbow, Luz had moved the saint into a storeroom. She'd been only twenty, young and full of revolutionary fervor, angry with the saint for allowing the poor to be poor and the rich to be rich. Uncle Zenobio had rescued Saint John, locking him into that case. He'd had it made, and it was very expensive, bulletproof glass. Too late, though, for Luz María.

Maggie no longer knew how to placate the saint. That night, and again on Monday, she betrayed her husband in his own bed. She could not help herself. She dragged her lips lightly across Vicente's taut brown chest, down his belly, all the way to his ankles, celebrating the fact that she always knew it was him, him, present in every inch of himself, until he forced her to lie still and listen to his tongue. Their bodies twisted together like two boas. Afterward, when Maggie got up to bring him a glass of water, walking past the clinic door she felt as if a cold breath had blown on her, telling her she was already dead. Back in bed, she told Vicente she was terrified, she didn't know of what exactly, though she could begin to try to make a list. Vicente told her to still her thoughts, and remember that faith and affection, *fe y cariño*, could protect a person anywhere. So his mother had taught him.

She looked at him, and saw her closest relative, and almost allowed herself to imagine having a future with Vicente. She hated the idea of leaving Carson. Leaving Larry had been enough, too much, already; yet if she didn't correct her life herself, she knew by now that the saint or the river or the earth would eventually correct it for her.

We can't do anything yet, Vicente told her. She agreed.

Carson came home Tuesday, carrying the body of an infant who had been born without a brain. He rode down on the bus with a grim delegation: four men and one woman, the woman bearing the wrapped body of her newborn, which she'd saved unburied for Carson to see. She lived in one of the hovels up by the intersection where the mine's road started. Because her husband was a road worker, on the mine's payroll, the miners had heard of the death and fit it together with information that had been seeping in toward them from various directions, including a message from union headquarters in Ayacucho. They'd been waiting for Carson. Tonight, they called a meeting with him and Vicente. Carson said he'd take advantage of the occasion to offer a progress report, so Vicente hurried off to El Mirador to fetch Marco Antonio, Don Sixto, and the women's delegation.

The corpse was starting to stink. Carson photographed it as it lay on the medical table in the clinic, practically faceless, its head caved in like a soft doll's. Maggie volunteered again to fetch Don Zoilo. Trudging uphill, her thighs still sore from dancing, she realized she'd be spending the rest of this week's salary on another coffin. What was she supposed to understand by this? She was right to wonder, for what had begun to happen was barely under way.

22

MAGGIE AND ALTHEA were alone in Althea's bedroom, in the house on Ash Street. The day nurse was reading last April's *Glamour* in the sunroom at the end of the hall, where Althea kept her dead husband's fossil collection. Julia had just called to say that she and Calvin were safe, home in Connecticut; she thanked Maggie for taking over. It showed that Maggie cared, but Julia still couldn't understand the two-week delay in coming. How could Maggie have ignored the radio summons? She was lucky Althea hadn't died.

Returning after a fervid ten-minute wrangle with her mother, every phrase of which had been repeated dozens of times in the past few days, Maggie saw that Althea had fallen asleep, her torso stiffly tilted across all the pillows of her bed. She couldn't help finding the family resemblances around Althea's mouth and eyes.

She sat down in the straight chair by Althea's bed, resolved to banish Julia from her mind. With parents gone, she could release herself into her own luxuriant, full-blown worries. Was her period due, or overdue? How long since she'd burned her last bloody pads on the rocks behind the clinic? And what was happening in the valley now? Each night when she and Althea and her parents had watched the TV news together, Maggie had half expected to see someone she knew, standing at the head of a crowd of miners. For the night before she'd left Peru, Klaus and Carson and Vicente had scheduled a demonstration at La Tormentosa. If it had taken place last Saturday, as planned, then U.S. television had failed to cover it. That was good, since a strike at La Tormentosa would be worldwide news only if the army started shooting. Even then, Maggie reasoned, they'd have to kill at least twelve people to merit the coverage.

Now that her parents were gone, she must call Liliana.

As if she could hear the high whine of Maggie's anxiety, Althea woke up. Her neck strained, her gray eyes shifted, blinked, then fixed on Maggie. "Get me a drink," she commanded. "A martini. A Pisco sour. Jackal urine. I don't care."

Maggie said, "You know they don't let you drink on painkillers. Would you like some orange juice?"

"No!"

"Water, then?" Maggie lifted the half-full pitcher on her grandmother's night table.

Althea's chin pulled up toward her nose.

Maggie stood, emptied the pitcher into a potted dracaena. "It was getting old," she said in self-justification, and sat down again.

"Old," Althea said. She pronounced it "ow-wuld." It was an accusation.

"Julia called," Maggie reported. "She got home fine, and she'll be back to see you next week."

"Well, Ah won't be here to see Julia," Althea said.

Maggie sighed. "Grandma, please don't talk like that." She sounded just like Fortunata, who often said the same to Maggie. Here's where I got my shocking tongue, she thought.

"Talk like what? I may be unavailable."

"I'm so sorry I didn't come sooner."

"Why? I told you not to!"

Deep in the basement, metal clunked and the heating came on, forcing hot air through the floor grates. The Rosario's rapid, running behind the clinic, made exactly the same sound.

In the wee hours of last Wednesday it had rained, a scatter like pebbles on the corrugated roof followed by a blasting, vicious roar. Maggie and Carson sat up terrified. "Landslide," Maggie guessed. Then she felt a drip coming through the mosquito net, and both of them smelled the rain.

The noise on the roof was unabating. The sky seemed to wish them harm. Drips began immediately, all over the house. The *chorro* onto their blanket was strong enough that they had to move the bed, thus losing the mosquito net. Luckily the mosquitoes were stunned and sluggish, barely able to maneuver through the thickened air, so they were easy to kill.

At six A.M. Carson got up to look out the door on a gray and limited world. Rain fell in a thick fringe from the edge of the roof. Water rushed in two directions, both up and down the road. The thorn bushes looked green as a jungle. Again Maggie's zinnias had been pounded flat; the flower bed was calf-deep in muddy water. This rain deserved a bigger reputation. It was ten times worse than the famous monsoons of Asia, Carson said, bringing coffee in bed to Maggie, who drank it wishing rain really could shut off the world.

All day Wednesday it had poured. No bus came by, nor did Fortunata appear, nor Vicente, nor the miners' delegation. No one. Maggie was glad, glad.

Just before sunset, when the downpour had stopped and a fragile golden light fell between the mountains, Luz María had arrived lugging a bucket covered with an enamel plate. She lifted the plate, which ran with condensation from a bean drink she had made, pink and white in color, shot full of liquor and sugar. She asked permission to warm it on the stove, right in the bucket. She wanted to ask Carson and Maggie to be the godparents of her next child. They'd been so good to Lady Maggy.

Maggie refrained from asking where, when, and from whom Luz expected to get this next baby. She and Carson drank cups of bean liquor while Luz María laid out her offer: a permanent free room in her mother's house, and a feast, one of her mother's suckling pigs. Or a chicken, even a calf. "What food do you like best?"

Carson grimaced.

"Should we do it?" Maggie asked him in English. She felt halfway responsible for Lady Maggy's fate, having demurred on becoming her godmother. Unbaptized children were unprotected, she'd learned from Fortunata.

"*Absolutamente no!*" Carson forbade Luz to have another baby. Luz, cowlike, asked him why, and he snapped out at her. As long as the river was contaminated, she risked having another one like Lady

Maggy. At this, Luz began to cry, and so did Maggie. "Sorry," Carson said, twisting in his chair. "Tell me how else I could have said it."

Next, Vicente had arrived at the front door, wrapped in a shower curtain and wearing rubber boots. His hair was dripping down his forehead. Luz María greeted him eagerly but he talked right past her, to Maggie. "Your German friends are stuck up on the mountain."

"Who? What? Did you hear it on the radio?"

"No, you can see their Jeep from here."

"He knows their Jeep," Maggie said quietly to Carson.

They all went outside and Vicente pointed up the mountain. The Jeep was stuck where a stream came out, he said. Halfway up, next to that pale road cut, did they see it?

Luz María did. The car was black and looked like a *camioneta,* a small truck. When Carson and Maggie still couldn't find it, she consoled them saying it was tinier than a stinging ant. "Follow the line of the road," she said, sweeping her forefinger.

"People are helping," Vicente said. "A dozen."

Carson went for his binoculars. With them, they could see the scene: Klaus and Liliana and their driver — Suárez? Sánchez? by now they'd forgotten his name — standing around while farmers pried at the Jeep's back wheels with long poles. "*Barretas.*" Carson had recognized the implements. "*Barretas,*" Vicente affirmed, without binoculars.

"My grandmother is dead," Maggie had said, going inside to pack her bag. Her hands shook as she smoothed out the creases in her good black skirt.

❖

Althea had broken her right hip, driving her blue Ford forty miles an hour through an intersection. Braking, skidding, she'd collided with the side of an elephantine white recycling truck. She claimed its driver had backed out of a store parking lot without looking. The truck driver, along with his helper and everyone else in the world, knew that Althea's license should have been revoked long ago. For years she'd been carving her half of the road out of the middle, but no amount of reasoning or pleading could stop her from taking the car out whenever she felt like it.

She would never do it again.

Elevated mortality rate, the doctor said, within the year. Julia had already invited a minister to drop by, some old chum of Lester's. Althea hated churches; still, Julia believed that a minister should meet her before he composed her eulogy. No one knew quite how to announce the visit, scheduled for next week. Even Lester had suggested a white lie, that the minister was a history buff interested in Johnny's mapping of the Burma Road. No one was sure Althea would be fooled, but only Maggie had argued for full disclosure.

"Warn him," Julia said, "to check all facts with me." Half the time Julia argued that Althea had always been like this and it was only now that others noticed; the other half she expostulated with her: "Mother, please, get hold of yourself!"

Althea had become a notoriously bad patient. Outraged to find herself in a nursing home, she had pressured Julia and the doctors into releasing her only four days after hip surgery. Here at home she had nurses day and night, and a physical therapist who came three times a week to force her to put weight on the leg. She was cordial enough to her family, but beastly to the staff. One of the day nurses joked that she was going to write a book about Althea. Her demands to be dressed in tennis whites or evening clothes for the visits of the physical therapist. Her complaints of abuse, including accusations that the caretakers were stealing painkillers in order to drug their children for perverted sex. "Such a character," they had begun to say of her.

All her life, Althea had seemed a rather shy woman, a plain dresser, stubbornly subdued: a use of stubbornness that Maggie disapproved of, Maggie who had always wanted better examples from her family than she'd received. Whatever was happening to her grandmother now, it seemed too late for grand reconciliations and gifts, any family scene illuminating the surrounding darkness. Althea was slipping into senility, or a kind of grand uncaring, as blithe as it was sinister. Yesterday she was ranting about white slavers surrounding the house, ready to kidnap her and cart her off to the Casbah. Julia had kept correcting her: "Motherr!"

Maggie was glad Julia had left. Lurid sex fantasies could keep a person alive, she believed. Something was needed to combat this sickroom architecture. The walker's chrome bones, the blue kidney pan, the toilet on its frame, a tray holding a half-gnawed chop. Things utterly out of whack with all the other objects that had furnished her grandmother's life, things of stone, wood, wool, straw, leather, clay.

❖

The Jeep had surged up to the clinic door just after midnight. Klaus stepped out, announcing he'd brought the results of the water test and urgent information. Maggie and Carson ushered Klaus, Liliana, and the driver straight into the kitchen, where they'd set out a simple meal, roasted potatoes with oregano, cheese, and hot peppers. They'd had hours to prepare this food, watching the Jeep's slow zigzag down the canyon's far wall, halogen headlights stabbing the darkness.

"Mmm! I am starving!" Liliana sat down, spreading her thighs slightly to get closer to her plate. Maggie felt a great affection: somehow, in the weeks apart, she and Liliana had become closer friends. "But Maggiecita, why don't you come when I called for you by radio?" Maggie explained how confusing the message had been. Liliana interrupted, "You knew it was for you. Your grandmother again went in the hospital. Now she has come out, but your mami says she is not good in health, and she might die. I think you have to go. I myself think so, and so I am having trouble finding any more excuses for your mami." At that, Carson put in gallantly that Maggie had been on the point of going, but since the message had not conveyed a clear emergency, she'd chosen to stay with the water campaign. Apologetically, Maggie asked Liliana why she hadn't repeated the message, if it was so urgent. "But we did. We told him, repeat it all the week!"

"Speaking of the water," Klaus began, "I've been hearing things about you, Carson. Where is our friend Vicente Quispe Cruz? You and I and he must talk."

Liliana made faces at Maggie to indicate she'd explain more later.

❖

As for Maggie, if she was pregnant, no fantasy could stop the baby from growing bigger and eventually coming out. How did so many women survive this terrifying process? She supposed they tried to lean on their men, to help them feel less scared. Maggie thought of Vicente, and as usual felt a little better. Except, except, except. And besides. Maybe, because of the water, she ought to stay in Cambridge. That was safest, yet she could hardly bear to consider it.

"I'll make coffee," she suggested now.

Althea's windy whisper gathered steam, became a voice that rose above the sounds of the heating system. "I'd never get to sleep. Sun's over the yardarm. Time to name your poison. Ah. Poison. That's what I really want. An asp." In her dry mouth the pointed tongue clicked, protruded.

"I'm sorry, Grandma." She reached for her grandmother's knuckly hand. "Wish I could bring you what you want."

"Ya cain't." Althea jerked the hand back, slithered it under the mess of sheets, crumpled towels, newspapers, detritus that littered the bed. "Leave me alone. I got to prepare to meet my goddamn Maker."

"You're not dying."

"Oh, shut up. Of course I am. This is the end. Look." Althea tossed back the top half of the blanket, opened both legs so that the knees fell sideways, exposing her inner thighs. The left thigh was silver-skinned, a fine fresh salmon; the right one looked small and dead, with banana bruises around the knee. An edge of gauze dressing peeked out below the Christlike diaper taped across Althea's belly.

She was wearing Johnny's socks and pajama top, ten years after his death. One sock had a hole in the toe. The shirt was faded black-watch flannel, missing one button, another fastened wrong. Half of Althea's chest was visible. Like her left leg, the inside edge of her breast looked young and shapely, almost girlish.

"It's freezing in here." Maggie leaned forward to get the blanket off the floor. The thermostat was set at sixty-two, still Althea's maximum.

"I'm not cold," Althea said. "I want you to look at my laigs."

"I see." Maggie did see: humiliation, finality, and the lack of any reason for this and any other human damage. "And I'm very sorry."

"Good," said Althea, almost gently. "I kept them out of the sun for nothing all these years. You, you're young. Might as well give up now. Make it easy on yourself. The only good thing about old age is that nobody cares, including you."

"You had Johnny," Maggie suggested. "You had my mom. Doesn't it give you satisfaction to look back on all that?" Drat. What business did she have cajoling Althea to appreciate things she had already lost?

"Everything is a mistake," said Althea extravagantly. "Johnny was useless when I lost my firstborn. I had hopes for Julia, but you see what she came to. Trying to see her face in the dinnerware. And that husband she adores, that Calvin. God! He's rigid as a plank. If my daughter had any gumption, she'd have an affair."

"Julia's my mother," Maggie said. "Calvin's my father. Those are my parents." Did Althea really regret her life?

"Sorry," said Althea. "I thought you'd agree with me."

"Do you approve of affairs, in general, Grandma?" How nice it would be to confide in her grandmother about Vicente. Althea might sympathize. Might blab to Julia, too. Obviously she was no longer into suppression. Julia could easily be persuaded to disbelieve her, but Maggie never wanted to side with her mother in questioning Althea's sanity.

"Trying to avoid mistakes is the worst mistake of all," Althea pronounced.

"I've been wanting to know whether you had any advice for me. Anything you feel great about, or that you still regret." Maggie should try to find out what a person did when her mistakes all fell on her at once.

Her grandmother's mouth worked. "Famous last words, eh?" she said. "You're my favorite offspring, you know. I certainly want you to know that, now that we're alone."

"Why thank you," Maggie said.

"You do take after me," Althea reflected. "You've got my high forehead. I see you running all over the world. That's good. Opening new roads. Your big sister, she's more cautious, like your mother. Your mother's always been a frightened person, deep down."

"I know the reason, Grandma."

Althea pulled the covers up to her chin and glared at Maggie, who had a fleeting impulse to say, Grandma, what big eyes you have!

"You know what I'm talking about, Grandma, don't you?"

"Don't you have any better things to worry about?"

"Yes, Grandma, actually, but . . ."

"You think I'm going to die," Althea said. "That's fine. Let's talk about Julia, then. I could have loved her so much more if she weren't so afraid to be a nigger. Afraid to be herself. Every day she wishes her face weren't so round." This was probably true. Julia had often praised Maggie as a child, saying what a pretty heart-shaped face she had.

Althea slid down flat in the bed, still holding the sheet up to her chin. She squeezed her eyes shut.

"Sssh!" Maggie said. The nurse, in a room fifteen feet away, was black Vietnamese. "*Please* don't use racist terms."

"Nigger-nigger-nigger. It's a good old-fashioned word." But Althea was whispering.

"Stop it, Grandma! I don't care how old you are."

"You'll never know what it's like when your children reject you. She didn't have to be, you know. She didn't have to exist. *I* made her!"

"If I didn't exist, I wouldn't care," said Maggie.

"I'm glad you're here. I've said so many times. But you don't know what you're talking about." Althea's eyes closed tightly, preventing Maggie's answer.

"What if I do know?" Maggie said. "What if I've figured out about your priest!"

Althea's eyes opened, glaring under her frowzy, worn-out permanent. Her legs, her fingers struggled amongst the bedclothes. Maggie felt sorry for disturbing her.

"Julia hates it, but I don't." Maggie repeated Julia's parting instructions from this morning: not to believe a word Althea said. Julia had told an elaborate story, saying Althea had been accused of adultery by the British community, an affair with a minister or a doctor. Now that she was senile, the story had popped out of a wrinkle in her brain, and Althea was repeating it as true, perhaps a wish fulfillment. If she mentioned any affairs, Julia wanted everyone to know they hadn't happened. "She'd rather think you're crazy, Grandma."

"But you believe in me." Althea's face became so sly, so smirky-shifty, that Maggie couldn't keep from grinning. "I slept with the priest and she's a Hindu child. So if I told you that, you would believe me, even though you're not supposed to?"

"Yes," said Maggie. "It must be true! Please tell me!" She'd convinced herself that the factual truth didn't ultimately matter, but now it ultimately did.

"I sure did pay," Althea said. "I wish I could talk to him again."

"I could go to India. Try to contact him for you." Maggie put her hand on Althea's wrist, hoping she'd never be old and yearning for a lost Vicente. "What town was it again?"

Althea made a wry face and said Brother Jesūnandā could not be alive. Her voice was soft. Althea could tell when people weren't alive. Don Héctor, too, had died. "You and I, chased all over the world by the same old devil." Here she paused and looked up at Maggie soulfully. "What about you, young lady? Is there anything you would like me to know?"

"Grandma, I'm in a situation that I think you'd understand."

"Uh-oh. I better leave you my house."

"No, Grandma," Maggie said, flustered.

"Dear, I mean that. Sell it if you want. You'll need it more than anyone, I reckon. There, that's my last will and testament. Bring my lawyer," she called past Maggie's shoulder. "I got to change mah will."

Turning, Maggie saw the day nurse, who had come to the bedroom door with her bag of things to wave goodbye.

"You!" Althea cried. "Can't you hear me? Too much hair over your ears? Get a haircut!"

The nurse was a tall, glamorous young woman with a flipped, straightened, Barbie-doll perm. She rolled her eyes theatrically at Maggie, and said, as if Althea did not exist, "Olena is going to be twenty minutes late. Mind if I leave?"

"Fine. Thanks. Bye," said Maggie. Althea sat up, quietly elated.

The woman disappeared from sight. Maggie could not remember her name. These nurses cost hundreds of dollars a day, and no one could prevail against their slackness.

No matter where in the world you were sick, you needed family to take care of you and feed you properly. If Maggie was pregnant, she should keep this child, for purely selfish reasons. "I'll get you something to drink." She took the pitcher off the bedside table.

"After all, I don't have to drive anywhere," Althea said hopefully.

Maggie had forgotten about the martinis, the jackal urine. She'd been planning to bring water only. The conversation had put her in a strange mood. She wanted to forget everything, and simultaneously to celebrate. I'm a Hindu child, she thought, running wild.

Althea's constitution was still powerful. It wouldn't kill her to have a drink. Probably just soothe her a little, make her even more truthful and amusing. Maggie went down the basement steps, found a bottle of Clos de Vougeot. It was a 1966, and Calvin would miss it, but it was one of the few names she recognized. When she came back up with the open bottle and two tumblers on a tray, her grandmother was staring out the window. White, late light slanted in through the shredded damask curtains.

They held their glasses to the light. "Ruby, pink, brown," said Maggie.

"Black, gold, and purple," Althea said.

They drank together in silence, one glass. "To the truth," said Maggie as she poured the second. "The Godawful truth," said Althea. They sipped again, Maggie thinking it should be her own last drink for some time, if she actually was pregnant.

"I see Johnny's face before me," Althea said sadly. "I hope you will stay with me for the rest of your life. I mean my life. He did. That would be the happiest day. Already is. It won't be long now. I haven't told them, but it's hurting me to breathe. The only good thing about old age is nobody cares about you anymore. So you can say and do as you please. That's the ticket. You'll all find out. You'll all forgive me one day."

"Don't be saying last words, Grandma."

"Oh, but you asked me and now I want to do it. Let's see. You were asking for advice? Aren't I the wrong person?"

"Tell me once and for all if it's true."

"I promised Johnny I would never say, as long as I lived."

"I won't tell Julia or anyone else, I swear, Grandma. Please!"

"Well, I'm half dead." Althea slurped at her glass. Then she nodded, eyes beaming at Maggie. Her lips were pressed tight. "Mm-hmm, mm-hmm," she said.

So here it was. Maggie no longer needed to prove her mother wrong. Now what? "You loved Johnny, too, or did you?"

"Of course, dear. He was good. My Johnny. He adored me. I didn't deserve him. I couldn't ever leave him."

"I find that relevant," Maggie told her. "Anything else I ought to know?" She was still afraid to ask if Althea wished she'd done things differently. All in all, it didn't seem so.

The front door opened, letting in the wet, ripping sound of tires on the street. Boots stamped at the entry. Althea's knees began to tremble, her heels fluttered against the mattress. "What's that?" It was a stage whisper.

"It's just Olena," Maggie said. She pulled the blanket over her grandmother's legs. "Don't worry." But the legs still shook.

"Olena?"

"That night nurse. The one who gives massage."

"Oh yes, the fatty. Olena. Brand of margarine. What kind of a name is that?"

Maggie put one hand on Althea's jacking knee. "It's Russian. She gave it to herself. Are you all right?" She squeezed the kneecap, hoping to warm it into submission.

"I can't remember if I like her. Some of these gals, I think they're coming to drag me straight to hell."

"She's okay. I guess."

"Olena. Petroleum product," Althea said. Her leg relaxed, then quivered again as soon as Maggie lifted her hand.

"It's her grandmother's name, Grandma." Sometime last week, Olena had had to be reimbursed for a bag of groceries, and had asked Calvin to write the check to "Susan Petkoff." She should change her last name next, the Goodwins all had said. "She wanted to honor her female ancestors. She told Calvin she'd had five names in this life, if her marriages all counted."

"Ha. Well, that's better. I've had dozens of men myself," Althea cackled.

"Priest and who else?" Maggie didn't think so.

"Never mention him to Julia. Swear!"

"Grandma, I swore already! Quick, take a glug of this mouthwash." She grabbed the wine bottle and ran on tiptoe toward the upstairs bathroom. Passing the stairs, she could see the back hem of Olena's denim skirt bobbing as Olena replaced her snow boots with apostolic sandals. She looked familiar, as if she might have worked at Harvard. Maggie bit off a dab of toothpaste and stashed the Clos de Vougeot under the sink behind some dried-up sponges, where it took on the appearance of a poison. Four inches left, ten dollars' worth, and she hadn't focused on its nuances, which she might need to describe to Calvin, should he notice the theft.

Olena was lumbering up the stairs. She was over fifty, but with her fine transparent skin, round red cheeks, and unworried forehead, she looked miraculously preserved, until her smile revealed small brownish teeth.

"Hello!" Olena said. "It's snowing out! The sidewalks are terrible! How's everything in here? So nice and cozy!"

"No it's not," Maggie told her. "It's freezing in here."

Althea called from her bedroom in a parrot's querulous, lost voice. "Hello?"

"Olena's here!" said Maggie. And to Olena, "Everything's fine, though she was feeling anxious a minute ago. Thanks for coming."

Together they walked into the bedroom and saw Althea, a murky shape, struggling to raise herself. The room seemed much darker than when Maggie had left it.

"What do you two want?" Althea said.

"Hello, it's me, Mrs. Baines!" Olena said, brushing past Maggie. "Sorry I'm so late. Were you sleeping? Why are you lying here in the dark?"

She clicked on the bedside lamp, fixed pillows, ran her hand under the blanket. "Your feet are blocks of ice. Would you like some water? How is Mrs. Baines today?"

"Fine. And yes, and no, and please, and thank you," Althea said. "Mrs. Baines is very well, just living the life of Riley." She cleared her throat and glared around the room.

Olena laughed. "We're feisty today."

Althea settled back against the pillows and assumed an expression verging on meekness. "You'll give me my rub?"

"Certainly."

"I've got pins and needles in both feet. And I'm feeling very nervous. I get the heebie-jeebs lying on my back all day. But you'll fix that. Won't you? You'll make me relax?" Althea was breathing through her mouth, panting almost. She had bright red, allergic-looking blotches on her cheeks. Maggie regretted giving her the wine. It seemed to have increased Althea's frailty, so her tough talk no longer seemed the sign of a strong mind but rather of a cornered desperation. Maybe this was an effect, on Maggie, of Olena's presence. "Certainly," Olena said. "Have you taken your anticoagulant?"

"I've had nothing but pills since dawn."

Maggie leaned on the doorjamb, not volunteering to refill the empty water pitcher Olena set at her elbow, on top of the chest of drawers. Instead, she watched her grandmother blinking with heron-like dignity while the nurse refolded the newspaper, closed the curtains, stacked the lunch tray with an assortment of dirty dishes and debris.

"How about rolling onto your stomach." Olena pumped a dab of cream into her palm.

"Scram," Althea said. "Vamoose."

"Excuse me?"

"Get out! I thought of one last word to tell my granddaughter."

"Oh, yes ma'am, very well." Olena huffily left the room.

"Look in that top drawer," Althea said. "No, the other one. Maybe it's in the closet." Rummaging under Althea's direction, Maggie at last found a pair of paisley ankle socks, knotted together. Inside was a ring of coarse yellow gold, with a magenta cabochon stone set into it. "Your Burmese ruby," Maggie said. "You took it out of the sugar bowl."

"I was afraid someone might eat it. That's for you, dear. I'm glad I could remember where it was."

"Thank you, Grandma."

"Don't say thank you till you know what you are getting," Althea said. "That's the only thing he ever gave me. Does it fit?"

"On my middle finger," Maggie said, holding up her hand.

"Very nice. See, that was his, from when he was the Hindu kind of priest. This way, you won't ever have to wonder whether I was senile at the end and just told you any old thing." Althea smiled with satisfaction. Her pale eyes softened. "Everybody always thought Johnny gave it to me. It was my souvenir of him, as Julia didn't turn out to be."

"We know why Julia decided to be that way, though, Grandma."

"Oh yes, we do indeed. I should have been nicer to her. I wish I could have, but I couldn't help myself, you see."

Maggie made a silent resolve to convey Althea's regrets to Julia, somehow.

"It wasn't my fault, was it, if I loved him so? Some things you never get over. You understand that. I know you do. You said so."

Maggie agreed, though it seemed to her she'd told Althea something slightly different. "Grandma, I am really, really, really glad I came to see you." She squeezed Althea's hand, and then bent down and kissed her.

"Thank you, dear. You've saved my life. I feel perfect."

Snow was falling slowly past the tall windows. This year's first snow had come unusually early. Big flat flakes like shreds of ash. Some were traveling upward. Inside and out, all distinctions were vanishing into a pewter-colored flatness.

"Isn't the snow so nice and peaceful?" Althea said. "Maybe I'll have my massage."

23

"YOU SHOULD HAVE called her 'Your hand-maiden,'" Julia said. "Don't you remember, I *asked* you just to read the service straight from the Book of Common Prayer."

The air around her head was cubist, shattered.

The minister had just introduced Althea to God as "Your beloved servant." He said, "I'm sorry. Of course I remember."

Julia, Maggie, and Maggie's sister, Sonia, stood just inside the church exit, hair all blue under a blue emergency light. Why did they keep this church so dim?

With them were Lester Weeks, Althea's boyfriend, and the minister, Stoddard MacLean, who had just performed Althea's funeral. He was twenty-eight, the nephew of one of Lester's old friends, fresh out of Harvard Divinity School. Maggie had joked with him about how, at Harvard, Jesus was equivalent to Santa Claus and the Easter Bunny. She'd refrained from asking after Larry or any other possible mutual acquaintances. So far she'd called only one friend in Cambridge. No one else knew she was here.

Stoddard apologized again.

They all had on their overcoats, waiting for Calvin to come out of the office where he was giving his address for billing. It was typical of her family, Maggie thought, to end up in arrangements that felt trumped up, and lonely. She could explain it now: it was because they were secretly foreigners. Even Calvin had been happiest in Colombia. Sonia and her husband had gotten married in a white church they'd seen in a travel article about Vermont — Alexandre was an architect and had admired it. Johnny Baines had rested in Cambridge Cemetery for ten years, but this afternoon would be the first time his family had ever visited him as a group. And now this morning, within yards of her grandmother's coffin, Maggie Goodwin had tested herself for pregnancy in the church bathroom, so she could anonymously dispose of the box and dipstick.

A pink haze had formed instantly on the white blotting paper.

There were no false positives, she'd learned. Still, she'd tested herself again, and again had seen the double bars. "Whee!" she'd squealed, pressing her forehead against the toilet stall's cold marble wall, the color of canned dog food. She'd begun to feel her body pullulating inside, rich as soil or soup. Her knees went weak. "Oh, God."

Arsenic, lead, mercury, and cadmium. Klaus and Liliana had brought down the lab report with them last Wednesday, results that were equally positive. She'd drunk the river for eight months. Was it her moral duty now to stay in Cambridge? Would new, clean water wash out all the old?

A library book lay hidden under her bed at Althea's. Unfortunately it was for laypeople, lacking detail, and, in this country of safety, mercury was the only metal mentioned. Mercury was bad enough. In gray, square photos she'd seen the child without a brain who was buried now in Piedras. Stump arms, fused fingers, eyes without pupils, bodies like cloud formations. Fortunata would have warned her not to look at such pictures, lest they affect her baby. Maggie understood why. She was Julia's daughter, after all, letting herself be carried away by the worst imaginings. She must fix her mind upon the dozens of perfect babies born in Piedras, despite the water, despite everything.

Tomorrow she'd make a doctor's appointment and mail off a lock of her hair. She'd already talked to a lab in California. The hair test took three weeks and cost two hundred eighty dollars, causing her to wonder why she'd snipped off so many black *mechas* and sealed them into envelopes. Relics, she decided, to be analyzed a thousand years from now.

Two nights ago, Althea's doctor had insisted, repeated, that Maggie had not murdered her own grandmother by plying her with wine.

Althea's cause of death had been a pulmonary embolism. A blood clot had traveled from the leg into her lungs — even her nervousness had been a symptom. Carson would have seen it coming, but Carson was not here. Just now, Carson was only one of numerous impossibilities.

Why did distance limit physical sight? Why couldn't people hear each other's thoughts?

The baby inside her was ten million times the size it had been.

The plan was to follow Althea's hearse to the cemetery in two cars. The rest of the mourners, a dozen or so people including Olena and another nurse, had already gone home. Too cold for graveside speeches in this unseasonable year. People were proclaiming a new ice age. Last night, they'd heard, the frozen topsoil had had to be opened with a jackhammer.

Althea's coffin stood by on its wheeled cart. Hermetic, made of streamlined steel with a shimmering pale gray finish, it reminded Maggie of a small, new Mercedes-Benz. Impossible to imagine Althea's body inside it, nor anyone else's.

This chapel by the river was the saddest room Maggie had ever occupied. It smelled of myrrh and burnt matchheads, and there were no flowers anywhere, only an arrangement of dried bittersweet, raw material for a crown of thorns. Darkness wept from the unadorned stone walls, pressing in on everyone. The tiny Jesus on the altar looked emaciated after his long winter without food, water, and sufficient light. Maggie missed the Andes, where saints were so dangerous they had to be boxed in bulletproof glass, and where even the poorest village chapel was as full as possible of gold, dusty velvet, sky-blue paint, and plastic flowers. Down there, it was easier to believe in a higher world, or at least to feel sure that someone else believed. Just think what a nice plaster Virgin could do for this place, she thought, a nice pregnant Virgin in an Empire-waisted nightgown.

Julia dabbed at her eyes with a handkerchief, smudging her mascara worse than before. She looked as though she'd suffered a basal skull fracture. "Your eulogy," she said to Stoddard. "It was full of mistakes, too. Errors of fact as well as of tone."

Maggie leaned against the holy water font, rubbing her forefinger along its nubby granite lip, feldspar and diorite crystals smoothed by human touch. There was no water in it, just a stain of damp that tempted her to lay her tongue down on it. If there's a Heaven, let it help us now, she thought. For if you'd listened in a certain way, Stoddard had suggested that Althea had been an unfaithful wife and Johnny had been insane; and worst of all that Julia — he'd said this directly — was vain and spoiled. He hadn't mentioned Calvin at all, not that Maggie could remember.

Stoddard asked what his mistakes had been. He'd tried to make the eulogy true to life.

"Nothing is true to life if it isn't true to facts." Julia sniffed, put her handkerchief inside her coat's left sleeve. "Wing walking, for instance. My mother never did that."

"Sorry," Stoddard said again. "I thought Lester said she had." He'd begun the eulogy with the image of Althea walking out onto the wing of a DC3 as it flew over Angel Falls in Venezuela.

Lester piped up, saying he remembered the night Althea had told him this story at the Harvest restaurant, comparing the wing to a silver sidewalk. The wing's stability had impressed him deeply: it had become Lester's private emblem for Althea's bravery as well as the needlessness of certain fears, such as the fear of death. Stoddard had used it that way.

"I liked it," Maggie said. When Stoddard had invited the congregation to imagine Althea alive, held in space by some invisible, unexpectedly solid thing, she'd seen her grandmother vividly as a much younger woman, placing her feet carefully along the flattest part of the wing, staring at the toes of her sneakers to avoid the suck of space. Wind in her hair. Dark green jungle unrolling not so far below.

And now, on this cold afternoon in Cambridge, she could see Althea just as clearly, leaning forward across the restaurant table, her long pale hair pulled untidily back. "The wind was so cold on my laigs. My Panama hat blew off and I didn't *dare* look where it went."

Lies?

Althea's pale, gunmetal coffin shook with silence.

Maggie touched the priest's ruby ring in her pocket to remind herself of what was true. Its gold was oddly hot. Warmer, it seemed, than flesh, it reminded her of Vicente.

Her mind flew off to find a place where the two of them could live together with their child. If not El Mirador, Bolivia, halfway to the sky.

Vicente would finish his studies at the university while Maggie got a job in the U.S. embassy's public health programs. Their child, Vicente's child, would be a boy. He'd walk precociously. He'd have opinions. Perhaps he would grow up to be an artist, because of the many worlds he'd had to inhabit. In all of them he'd feel at home, knowing himself to be both of his parents' hearts' desire and light. She saw black, snapping eyes, and the humor in his face.

Their home would be small, dignified, with tile floors and shabby colonial balconies. At first, Maggie might find an Aymara nanny, a strong-minded woman, one incisor rimmed with gold. Not that Maggie didn't want to pamper her own baby — a child should have as many mothers as possible, one extra at the very least, as Maggie had had, to open all the chambers of its heart. Of course, the nanny would bring her own children to the house. They'd all go to the plaza together, speaking a mix of languages. Feeding pigeons, watching her son run around on fat, sturdy legs, Maggie would know she needed nothing more. Then, in the evenings, she saw how it would be when Vicente came back from his classes. Lamplight. The clean lines of his jaw, the joyous power of his arms as he swept their child off the ground. He'd meet Maggie's eyes and kiss her lightly over their son's dark head. "Let's make another," he'd say.

Or they might also go and live in France . . .

"You may love that story," Julia was saying, "but Mary Lou Kaminsky did that. She was a friend of Althea and Johnny's. She was married to a cargo pilot, Frank Kaminsky. Mary Lou was quite the daredevil. She used to parachute, too."

"Didn't we meet her in Colombia?" said Sonia. Sonia was famous for her memory. "She wore a Panama hat and pedal pushers. She had a big white poodle. She smoked a Cuban cigar with Daddy."

"That's right," Julia said. "That's Mary Lou to a T."

"They were friends," Maggie said. "Why couldn't they all have gone out together in Frank's plane, even just once?"

"My mother was a compulsive liar, that's why," Julia declared. "There, I've said it. I shouldn't blame you, Stoddard. 'Handmaiden,' though, I really did want that word. She was a biblical wife. I won't say it was her only virtue, but it was one of her main ones."

The Bible contained many kinds of wives, Maggie thought, and you're as big a liar, Julia, as your mother ever was.

"Well, well, well, now, many things get lost in the translation," Lester interjected, rubbing his hands together.

Lester had turned out to be just as Maggie had imagined, with cheerful, tight red cheeks. Today he wore a black karakul hat and rubber overshoes, and stood blinking hard, as if he were making an earnest effort to understand the conversation. Perhaps he was a little deaf.

"I truly didn't mean to insult anyone," Stoddard said. "Least of all your grandma." His hands were clasped in front of his crotch, a sure sign of fear in a man, according to Carson.

"Who told you Sonia and Alexandre met in a singles column?" Julia said. She snapped and unsnapped the clasp of her purse.

Sonia said, "Mom, that's no big secret."

Do you love the world or don't you, Maggie thought. That was the only question. Yes was the only answer. It hummed and resonated inside her body, echoing Vicente's favorite saying: With faith and affection a person could walk into a lion's mouth.

What if the baby was Carson's?

She saw herself, five years from now, making graphs for Carson in his new clinic in South India. Nurses, doctors running around asking him for direction. Or asking Maggie, for she was second in command. She wore a white sari; her hair was longer, beautiful. Their child was tall and slender and intelligent — Carson was proud of it. Local people had learned to love Maggie and respect her, for they knew whose granddaughter she was. In the evenings, out under a banyan tree, she gave literacy classes, in English, to local ladies. She was fluent in Hindi and Telugu.

It would build her character, to live in the lion's mouth. She'd become as strong as Carson. Carson would continue exactly as he was. Over time, his trust in her might soften him a bit. He'd make an admirable father, once his duty was clear. He'd fall in love with his child, and remark that it had his eyes, his chin. They'd have a noble life, all three.

Would Carson be as noble as Johnny Baines? If she told him the child was half Peruvian, half poor, already alive for him to care for?

"I loved Althea," Lester announced. "She made you all sound like such a wonderful, lively group of people. I had no idea you'd be upset."

"Stoddard never actually talked to Grandma, did you?" Maggie said, belatedly realizing she was shifting all guilt onto Lester.

"Never met her," Stoddard said, testily now. "I'll try to do better at the cemetery, unless you prefer me not to go?" Nobody moved. "Stay, we want you," Maggie said, feeling sorry for him.

Stoddard waited a few more wounded instants. "Okay then. See you there."

"We should have used the regular minister," Julia said when he had gone. "Not him."

Lester lifted his hands defensively, then lowered them again. His tie was Armani, Maggie recognized, a chunk of disused cultural information floating back into her consciousness. Gray blobs on a red ground, edged with electric-blue fluorescence, like dyed cells under a microscope. Notochord, egg yolk, Maggie saw, furiously budding cells.

I'll have twins, she thought, one for each father, like a dog bitch. Spend the rest of my life lying sideways, giving suck, letting them crawl all over me. I don't care where I live.

Two men in orangey tweed jackets and rubber-soled loafers came to roll the coffin out the door. "Stay in where it's warm," one of them said. "We're just putting her in the car."

The wooden door sighed shut, hesitating on a final puff of air. When it had closed, Julia said, "I only wish we hadn't argued in front of my mother's coffin."

"Oh, Mom! It's natural to be upset," Sonia told her.

"Thank you," Julia said. She licked a corner of her handkerchief and wiped carefully under her lower lashes, managing to clean off the last smears of mascara. She put her handkerchief over her mouth, then bit her knuckles through it. Julia *was* vain: she'd had her teeth recapped five times. Carson cited this so often, even Maggie leapt to her defense: "The new polymers were better!" It might be nice to get away from Carson's rigid judgments.

"Ready?" Calvin reappeared at last, walking briskly. "Hey, hey, what's all this?"

"Mom's sad, and she was upset with the eulogy," Maggie said. And ha, guess what, I'm pregnant! Would she ever tell her family? She laughed inwardly, recognizing her own lack of foresight. Obviously, the entire world would find out eventually, not simply that she was pregnant, but that some man or other had gotten inside her. Procreation was sickeningly public. She'd be huge.

"I have a few points I might like to mention, too," Calvin said.

"No, oh dear, enough, poor Mother," said Julia, starting to laugh and cry at once.

Maggie and Sonia surrounded Julia with hugs. Maggie felt her belly against her mother's hip. Amazing to think that Julia had given birth. So many ordinary women had endured that raw, bloody, screaming event and they were still walking around looking ordinary. Not just women endured it, she thought. All human beings hung upside down and weightless in the dark until crushed and ejected. This was a revolutionary view of things. How did anyone forget? Forgetting was as amazing as remembering. "I love you, Mom," she heard herself say.

Calvin, who'd stood aside, now cleared his throat. "They wanted to charge me for their priest, even though he didn't speak. I refused. Shall we go?"

"That's ridiculous." Julia straightened, put her fingers through the crook of Calvin's elbow. They filed out the door and down the wide stone steps. The steps and walkway had been shoveled, but the wheelchair ramp had not. It bore black, parallel tire tracks, the marks of Althea's progress.

At the grave there was a pile of dirt under canvas, a ring of rhododendrons and hemlocks. Johnny and Althea were to share a red granite headstone, but Althea's name had not yet been incised on it. Snow had blown against the roots of the trees. The cold ground ached up through Maggie's shoes. Maggie remembered the day, ten years ago, when Johnny Baines had died. She had still been married to Larry, unable to imagine what would be happening today.

Two cemetery employees in thick coveralls were standing beside the trees. They took over from the men in tweeds, setting the coffin inside a square arrangement of pipes. After fiddling with straps and ratchets, the gravediggers looked questioningly at Calvin, who nodded. They flicked a switch and a humming motor lowered Althea into the ground. Stoddard said, "Moment of silence?"

While they stood with heads bowed, Maggie peeked at Calvin and Julia. They were holding hands. Once she'd met a Spanish man who'd told her humans mate for life, like swans. It didn't matter how long the relationship lasted, whether it was with a man or a woman, or whether it worked out. You could see at the corners of a person's eyes whether it had happened yet. Carson, she thought, had been most truly mated with Maxine. Nonetheless, she saw him dying of her cruelty, a bewitched swan prince at her castle's locked gate. If only she weren't pregnant, she could go, kiss him, and push everything back to the way it should have been. But no. Irreversibility was the first of a mother's lessons. So much for my experiment in happiness, she thought — it wasn't over, but it had taken its own uncontrollable course.

She'd have to stay in Cambridge until the baby was born and she could see whose it was. Nine — eight — months was a long time, but Carson and Vicente had plenty to keep them busy down in Piedras. They didn't even know Althea was dead. There was a difference between telling lies and living them: one was permissible in order to prevent the other, she decided.

When the coffin was down, Julia walked over to the pile of dirt and pulled off a corner of its canvas sheet. The sandy soil had already frozen. She clawed up a small handful in her glove and threw it onto her mother's coffin, where it fell with a sound like sleet on a window.

One of the men in tweeds held out the shovel timidly. "Any of you like to use this?"

"Althea didn't approve of burial," Lester remarked. "She told me she'd like to be fed to vultures, or burnt up in the crater of a volcano."

Calvin said, "None of that was in her will."

Lester said, "Her kind of person would forget to stipulate."

Julia shrugged and began walking back toward the cars. Calvin followed her, trotting to catch up, putting his hand under her elbow. The gravediggers picked up their shovels and looked questioningly at Stoddard, who said, "Okay." Lester, Maggie, Sonia, and Stoddard stayed for a few minutes to keep the men from feeling lonely in their work.

Back at the house, there were holes in the air. Althea's portraits were all changing, the highlights receding from her pupils. Carson had begun to recede from Maggie, too. She glanced at the Russian novel she'd insisted on bringing, a book that was connected to him. Sure enough, it had shriveled slightly on the nightstand.

"Liliana? It's me, Maggie," she whispered into Althea's bedroom telephone.

"*Quién es? Más fuerte! No se escucha!*" Who is it? Louder! I can't hear!

"*Maggie!*"

"Maggie! Are you coming back? Things are crazy here. We need you!"

Maggie sat down on the edge of Althea's bed, where her grandmother had died two days ago. She closed her free ear with a finger while Liliana told everything into the other. Three hundred people had marched upon the mine last Saturday, bearing white flags. Doña Ema's abusive husband had been found beaten to death by the river. People said his sons had done it.

❖

She walked down the stairs gingerly, a ghost already absent. Her family had all changed clothes and reassembled in the living room, where Lester had lit a fire. She missed them in advance, their safe, familiar clamor and the silly poses she'd so diligently uprooted from herself. Julia and Sonia sat side by side on the couch, crossing their ankles in the same ladylike way. Calvin was jocosely opening another Bordeaux from Althea's cellar. Most of the best bottles were missing, Lester confessed, because he and Althea had drunk them.

"A toast," Lester proposed. "To *her.*" The way he spoke of Althea made Maggie glad, even for herself. For everyone. She toasted, then established herself in the wing chair.

Sonia addressed Lester. "When he invited her presence to remain with us?"

Lester nodded yes, yes, yes.

"I felt her," Sonia went on. "I really felt her, hovering. Am I crazy? What do you think that means?"

"Death is not the end," said Julia.

Swaths of darkness were beginning to fall across Althea's living room. The streetlights were being turned on, sector by sector, from some central switch. The bulb in front of the house went on, off, then quickly on again. "What's that!" Sonia said. "Did anybody see that?" No one responded. By the fire, Calvin and Lester braced their legs and swirled their wine. Maggie stared at the Persian rug they stood on, trying to decide whether the shapes in it were animals or plants.

Calvin cleared his throat and announced that Althea's will was to be read soon. He hadn't spoken to her lawyer since Johnny's death, nor had Althea, probably, but his recollection was that the estate went entirely to Julia. The house was the greatest asset; she'd probably sell.

"I love this house. Rent it to us, Mom?" Sonia fantasized.

Maggie had to get back to Piedras. Last Saturday's demonstration had succeeded, according to Liliana. Three mine company vice presidents were flying down from Canada the day after tomorrow, responding to concerns about the water. Though the mine had expressed some predictable objections, it appeared that the Rosario's clean water campaign was going to be shockingly painless.

Maggie would still send off her hair sample tomorrow, but she'd get her checkups in Cajamarca, where Liliana would know the competent physicians. Her pregnancy wouldn't show for a while, and by then she'd know what to do. She hadn't mentioned it to Liliana, but somehow, talking on the phone with her, Maggie had realized that she'd been considering her options backwards. Vicente, not Carson, was the man who might be willing to raise a child that was his in spirit, if not in flesh. At that lunch with Uncle Zenobio, he'd praised Johnny for adopting Julia. Meanwhile, Carson would have trouble taking on even his own kid.

She had to talk to Vicente as soon as possible. Vicente, before anyone else.

Calvin said to Julia, "The graveside prayer was all right, wasn't it, honey?"

"Yes, but again he made my mother sound like a different kind of woman from what she was."

When Althea's grave was being closed, Stoddard had dared to make one more remark. "Althea Baines was a woman remarkable not only for her unique life history, but for the depth of her loving self-sacrifice on behalf of her husband and her daughter." It was true, all sad and true. Maggie remembered how Althea had said, "I paid." She thought she'd finished telling herself Althea's story, but it kept continuing, and continuing to change. She'd pay, herself, as well. In the end you gave back everything, even the body you'd been issued. So you had to make the meantime count. Althea had been saying that, too, on her last day.

Tomorrow would be simple, anyway. Hair sample, plane reservation, farewells. She'd regret withdrawing her offer to help Julia deal with Althea's possessions. Depending on how things worked out, maybe she could return in a few weeks.

Lester said, "Why don't you tell us a little about her, then, in your own words, Julia?"

Maggie slid down to lean her head on the back of the sofa, stretch out her legs, and gaze for what might be the last time at Althea's dado molding. She was inclined to sit in a new way, with her womb protruding. I should be the one to speak, she thought, haul out the ruby ring, make sure Althea's priest is not forgotten.

Julia sighed. "I'm so upset. I don't know where I'd start."

Maggie said to the ceiling, "You know something? That afternoon when I was with her, just before she died, Mom? Grandma said she'd been too hard on you. She loved you, but she wished she'd been able to show you better." She dropped her chin in order to stare at Julia's face, her thin, straight nose and dark eyes, features she'd seen in some issue of *National Geographic*, features that, slightly blurred, gazed back at Maggie from every mirror.

Julia replied, with a lively resentment, "Fortunately, your grandfather made up for her neglect. Daddy gave me all the love I ever needed."

"Even though he so often went away," Lester mused, swirling the red wine in his glass. "Althea often spoke to me about how anguishing her husband's absence was. Yet he made his daughter feel beloved. That's wonderful, Julia."

"Grandma took you places, didn't she, Mom?" said Sonia. "When Grandpa went away?"

Yes, when Johnny went away, Althea had taken Julia on walks, even on trains, away for days at a time. Julia had found some of the trips quite frightening. They'd gone to the Juggernaut temple, seen people burning by the Ganges.

Althea would have met her lover on those outings, Maggie thought. Not would have, did. She did, I did, we both did. Julia had been introduced to Brother Jesūnandā, and she'd hated him all the more because Johnny Baines had not been there.

Julia was recanting. "I'm sorry, Maggie, I should have acknowl- edged what you just said. It was very important. It's been hard to be Althea's daughter, as you all may know. Keep in mind how the death of my older brother rendered her unbalanced. Why else do you think Johnny interned her in a convent? I believe she never recovered. I must always have reminded her of losing her first child. She loved me, of course, but I knew from very early on that for some reason I made her upset. When she looked at me she'd get tears in her eyes. Sometimes she'd burst out crying. Can you imagine? I've had to work to understand her, and forgive. We all lose things in life." Julia's own eyes filled with tears, and she wailed a bit. "Oh, God!"

Maggie decided not to bring up Brother Jesūnandā after all, not now. Some other year, she'd do it, at some other gathering by fire-light, when everyone was together and Maggie was explaining how she'd come to conceive this son, this daughter. She could feel the child's small, warm, surprisingly heavy body leaning against her thigh. This time it was a girl, dressed in long wool stockings, a jumper and beret. Perhaps she had no father, and Maggie had raised her all alone. How long would it take the family to accept this? Ten years, four, eight? Lately, Maggie had grown accustomed to predicting conversations, good and bad. Looking at her father's face, her mother's, even her sister Sonia's, she saw how their expressions would alter when she insisted on Althea's story, and knew it was better not to start discussing her current life with them. "Don't have this child," they'd say. Yes, another reason to get out of here as soon as possible.

24

MAGGIE PEERED at the poster, wondering when Carson had taken Lady Maggy's picture. Who else in Piedras owned a camera? The baby's pinched, bleary face had been blown up and plastered all over Cajamarca, starting on the airport road, where it had surely been intended to greet the motorcade of mine vice presidents as they arrived from Canada. *Asesinos!* the caption screamed over and over, around the rim of the plaza fountain, beside the door of the fancy white hotel, all down the nunnery's long wall. *Killers!* Maggie had seen the same tiny face, on the front page of the Lima paper, floating here and there above a crowd of demonstrators. She hadn't recognized it until now. Poor little hero, didn't want to be, she thought, touching the gray and grainy, crinkled cheek, which had returned to the same cement color as on the day she'd first met Lady Maggy, the day Lady Maggy had had pneumonia, the day the past had begun to roar, unstoppably, into the future.

Maggie hoped that Luz María was burning now with some kind of avenging, redemptive fire. Where was Luz? Where was Vicente, where was anyone? Alone in the deserted plaza, Maggie could feel their presences emanating from all of these poster-plastered walls. Vicente. Carson. Fortunata. Luz. Were they in danger? The Lima paper hadn't mentioned injuries or deaths, nor the names of anyone she knew, nor any relevant locations other than the province of Tocuyo, which contained the lake and the mine but was to Maggie an unfamiliar geographic designation.

By now it was likely that Calvin had heard of the Peruvian mine strike, so she was glad to be able to hope that his *Wall Street Journal* hadn't printed a map, or anything else he and Julia could associate with Maggie. This morning, the strike had gone nationwide. All mines in Cerro de Pasco, La Oroya, Huancavelica, and Huancayo had declared a four-day stoppage. The miners had been joined by truckers, university students, ecological groups, and two or three political parties. The list of complaints was long against the government's privatizations and its shortsighted, pro-foreign, anti-national, slavish, uncontrolled, corrupt extractive policies. So far the president was maintaining his usual stance of dictatorial imperturbability and had issued no statement. The problem had not attained significance; he was used to being criticized; he'd increase police visibility for a while as a reminder of what could be expected if his mood was further challenged.

It was dusk in Cajamarca, a clear lavender sky with bats flitting around the cathedral. On the ground only a few dogs trotted about their business in a city so still, it gave Maggie the sensation that her ears were plugged or her head was underwater. An unmanned tank squatted at the plaza's higher end, its cannon pointing straight into the topiary garden, threatening to blast the features off the cedar Inca's face. Looking into the black O of the cannon's mouth, Maggie wondered whether there would be a bus tomorrow morning down to the canyon.

She'd taken one day too long to return, hopping the first available flights down the west coast of Mexico and Costa Rica, and catching the last seat on today's eight-passenger prop, Lima to Cajamarca. Half the passengers had worn military uniforms. She'd sat across the foot-wide aisle from the scariest one, a pudgy man in tiger camouflage and sunglasses, a torturer or an anti-terrorism expert for sure. Yet he'd insisted on talking in English to Maggie, telling all about his years at Indiana University. She'd felt obliged to answer, second-guessing at normality while wondering whether he was applying imperceptible interrogation techniques to her. His name was Juan Carlos Yáñez. He had a wife and three kids in Lima. Maggie asked their ages, repulsed by the temptation to announce her own impending motherhood. He said nothing of the mine strike until she felt compelled to broach the subject, asking in her most girlish manner whether it was the reason for his trip. He'd replied apologetically, "This is the disorder of my country."

Yesterday, predictably, the Canadian vice presidents had not come. Two hours late, they'd faxed an apology and a revised arrival date, but the waiting crowd of one hundred fifty people had not been satisfied. They'd burned an effigy of Scrooge McDuck in the airport parking lot and smashed a dozen windshields. Today Cajamarca's normally barren airport lobby was full of soldiers in black bullet-proof vests, and two bomb-squad armored cars sat splayed in the vacant parking lot. Juan Carlos Yáñez remarked that the Canadian delegation had decided not to come at all, citing personal safety as the reason.

Her heart raced, walking out to the taxi line without the slightest trouble, shaking hands with the torturer, and wishing each other good luck. Juan Carlos Yáñez hadn't batted an eye when she'd told him she was a health worker on vacation, meeting her husband in the historic city of Cajamarca. Now he wished her a pleasant trip. "This is nothing," he reassured her. "It will — how do you say — blow out? blow away? I forgot. Which is the opposite of blowing up?"

"Blow over?"

"Yes, over, blow over! This will blow over in a couple of days," he promised. "Enjoy. Until we meet again."

Enjoy? She'd always hated that expression. She was glad he didn't offer to share a cab to town.

She'd had herself dropped off in the plaza, taking a two-block detour when she saw the bottom of the Wechslers' street was also stuffed with military vehicles, all parked facing downhill at the plaza, leaving no room to squeeze between the stone foundations and armor plate. Tanks, paddy wagons, canvas-covered personnel trucks. The police station was on the next, uphill corner. On previous visits she'd enjoyed the frisson of walking past it, smiling at the impassive twenty-year-old guards inside their boxes and wondering why the wall of flabby, bullet-ripped sandbags had never been removed. She'd played a mental game with the ancient Black Maria that stood perpetually at the door, transforming it into a sinister barouche, ready to whisk the vampire police chief to his next dark opera. Scarred with bullets and deep gouges, its windows dull with age and disaster under heavy, kinked steel mesh, the Black Maria was no longer a monument, a message, a symbol, a reminder. It was ready for action, ready to eat someone.

✤

She pressed the Wechslers' buzzer and stood waiting to hear Clorinda's flip-flops on cement. Instead there came a clopping of hard heels, and an unfamiliar pair of black eyes peered out through the peephole of the gate. Maggie rapidly explained that she was a friend. *"Soy amiga de los Señores, Klaus y Liliana Wechsler."* Wordlessly, the peephole closed and the heels again receded.

"Liliana!" Maggie yelled, thinking she heard her friend's intonations from the far end of the driveway.

"Shh, shh," Liliana said, opening the screeching gate. "Come inside."

They walked to the back patio, where Klaus sat at his computer, as usual. "Ay yay yay," he said when he saw Maggie. No, her parents hadn't called, not yet.

✤

She knew how lucky it was to have Klaus Wechsler's friendship. Two weeks ago, when Julia had called for Maggie to fly north, he'd decided to go down with Liliana and give Maggie and Carson a piece of his mind. He'd been watching them head for trouble long enough.

Give up the water project, was Klaus's heartfelt advice. It was futile, dangerous. Failing that, he'd passionately insisted that Carson, Maggie, and Vicente remain in the background, if not for their own safety, then to avoid political taints and accusations that would undermine their cause. This had been an artful argument, convincing not only Vicente and Carson, but even Don Sixto and other hardcore committee members.

Klaus had some odd power to predict the future, Maggie thought. He was the only reason why she'd been able to circulate through Cajamarca freely, why Carson and Vicente had not been immediately arrested after the march at La Tormentosa. Following Klaus's advice, the demonstration had been led by Don Sixto, Marco Antonio, and Luz María. They were the water campaign's local organizers, known to be working with the miners' union. Klaus's thinking had been confirmed when Ignacio García had stepped out of his office to sneer at the assembled crowd, "Where is your leader, that Communist gringo doctor?" Don Sixto's answering indigenous roar had driven Carson out of Ignacio's head, temporarily at least. Carson's name had never reached the authorities, but arrest warrants had been issued for Marco Antonio and a couple of union members. Five miners were in jail, including one who'd been caught stealing dynamite. They weren't in a normal jail, but an informal and illegal pokey behind the mine's army barracks. Their legs were in irons, Klaus said. He'd found a lawyer for them, but it was difficult to get a person out of jail who wasn't officially in. No charges had been filed, and the mine had powerful friends. "The more you learn about how things work here, the more you want to weep," Klaus said. He was considering moving back to Germany, at last giving in to Liliana's dearest dream.

An old Kreuzberg radical, Klaus had worked with Vicente and the Black Rainbow for years, coordinating their airstrip and advising them in dealings with the Shining Path, the Peruvian army, and the Colombians. When the new president was elected, Klaus had advised Vicente to write his recanting letter. Klaus himself had never been known as a rebel sympathizer, so when he'd offered to keep tabs on *campesino* organizations, the new government had embraced him eagerly. He'd even been able to keep a small and sanctioned finger in the cocaine business.

One faction of ex–Black Rainbows still considered Klaus a friend, and fed him information about other groups and factions. Earlier this year, they'd hatched a new project together, Klaus serving as banker for periodic deposits of gold dust Vicente was collecting from his remaining loyalists. The Rainbow intended to use the gold as capital for small loans. Klaus had successfully limited himself to an advisory role up to the day Vicente came to Cajamarca with a sack of unrefined gold dust, begging Klaus to store it. It was leading to envy and infighting among the Rainbows, like in the bad old days of the cocaine business. "He came too late," Klaus said. "Some guy got killed."

"Nasir!" Maggie cried, remembering the day Vicente had met her in the plaza; but Klaus didn't care to hear her piece together the sequence of events. She let him go on. After Nasir's murder, Klaus had suggested setting up a corporation in whose name the gold could be assayed, refined, sold, and deposited in a bank; but the Rainbow was unable to elect any of its members to act as the gold's official owners. Vicente was the only one they trusted, but his name couldn't appear on any paper. Were Vicente suddenly to become rich, suddenly it would become worthwhile for the police to imprison him and confiscate his assets. The Rainbow's gold would be absorbed into the bricks of some police chief's swankienda, newly constructed in a fancy Lima neighborhood.

On Maggie's last visit, just before she'd gone to the United States, Klaus and Liliana had shown her what twenty thousand dollars' worth of gold dust looked like. One inch of sand — black, because the ore was mostly silver — lying on the floor of a terrarium. Liliana had scattered sticks and an empty saucer on it to substantiate the claim that her son's pet lizard had once lived there.

Tonight, Klaus told Maggie he'd driven down the canyon twice since she'd last seen him. Knowing the new government's thuggish mentality, he'd begged permission to sell off all the hoarded dust and use the money to buy water filters. Gold dust was unlimited, diffusing slowly downstream in the river water. A sluice system could be built, and within a year the Black Rainbow could collect enough money to donate a small ceramic filter to each family in the valley. Eventually, Piedras could build its own purifying plant.

Both Carson and Vicente had rejected such weak half-measures. Twenty grand? That was a hundredth of what was needed. Why should the people pay to repair the mine's callous and murderous negligence? No, the mine must halt its toxic contributions. It must share its profits, too.

Once upon a time, Klaus said, Vicente had been amenable to reason. Under the influence of Maggie's husband, he'd become a lot more stubborn lately. Carson seemed to think he was personally immune to danger, besides being oblivious to the danger he might bring to others.

"It's my fault," Maggie told him. "I brought the Black Rainbow to the clinic."

Klaus could not agree. He'd recognized Carson's type the day he'd met him. The Black Rainbow would have come to him eventually. "I have no idea what those two are doing right now," he said. "Carson didn't once come up to Cajamarca. Ignacio García, he was at the airport. As soon as he knows his bosses aren't flying in, he takes off in his truck. Smart. Only he should have run in the other direction."

"I could have hitched a ride with him," Maggie joked.

"García is disgusting," Klaus said. "A little son of his father. His father is General Federico García Mesa. A man you never want to meet."

"He hates his father, I bet," said Maggie. Even at a distance, Ignacio had always seemed to her a tortured character, charming, immoral, and self-hating. Sleazeball was Carson's word.

"You sound like my wife," Klaus said. "Liliana would find the reason to forgive a snake for biting her."

During the initial demonstration at the mine, Ignacio had ordered the army platoon to put down their guns. He'd been soothing, conciliatory, offering 100 percent sympathy and support. His bosses would be ready to cooperate, but only if real proof of danger and damage was being offered. Surely the Piedrasinos understood that a single sample of lake water was insufficient, not to say irrelevant, misleading? Cyanide was biodegradable. The lake toxins were most likely the *campesinos'* fault, runoff from their farms around its shore: ash from burning off the corn stems, fertilizer, pesticides. Water got purified, anyway, oxygenated as it ran over rocks, downhill. Many samples must be taken, a thorough study begun. Why only the lake — why had the river not been tested before declaring such a crisis? Why had the Piedrasinos not begun by cooperating instead of being so antagonistic? As for the clinic's data on local health problems, the Canadian company would be happy to run the numbers through their own computers. They had several full-time staff working just on ecology. It was not too late to arouse a spirit of harmony.

Klaus laughed. "We had a hard time, after that speech, to unconvince Don Sixto from setting off a ton of dynamite."

"I have to get back down there," Maggie said.

"I don't advise that."

"Oh, come on, Klaus. What would you do if you were me?"

"You won't see me returning. If I were you? I'd leave the country. *I* might, like I said."

"*You* should, Klaus. You're burned out. I'm going, though. To Piedras, I mean."

"Maybe you'll have better luck with Carson than I did. Somehow I doubt it."

"Me too," Maggie said.

❖

"How horrible is everything! I am sure you should not go back," Liliana said. "I *hate* that poster. Now you say it was your same baby, that baby that you saved!"

"I am sure I should," said Maggie. "I just found out I'm pregnant." She begged Liliana to keep the news to herself, and especially not tell Klaus for a few days. Carson had to be the first man to know. "Look, I bought this water filter. I'll be safe. I'll only drink from this."

What an amazing justification her expectant state provided! Liliana understood the decision immediately, risky as it was. If she told Liliana the whole story, Maggie thought, Liliana would still agree with her. This conjecture gave her so much strength that she decided not to test it.

❖

Incongruously, there was no security at the bus station. Perhaps dawn was too early for soldiers. Here, to Maggie's relief, the ordinary world continued. The same women selling steaming coffee from tin kettles, and cheese bread, and soda pop to travelers; and their same grubby kids playing with the same bottle caps. When the bus got under way, the pale sun slanted flat across from the edge of the altiplano, making the dewy fields look frosted.

Maggie had never felt as determined. If she could have flown out the bus window, leapt off the ledge called the Devil's Balcony, landed in the river, and swum upstream to the clinic, she'd have done it. Instead, she itched, sweating in her seat while the bus made its jolting progress. Hurry, she silently urged the driver. Downshift, forget the brakes.

I'm taking you to meet your father, she told her child.

❖

The clinic's door was open, Carson's painted plywood tent sign standing bravely in the road. She and Carson had joked about one possible translation: SANITARY POST. GRATUITOUS ATTENTION. Her husband wasn't there, however. Only Fortunata answered Maggie's call. She came out from the kitchen, wiping her hands on her skirt, and gave Maggie a giant hug. "I knew you were coming. I waited for you. Terrible things are everywhere. Your husband is at Doña Ema's. He left half an hour ago."

"Vicente? Have you seen him?"

"Yes, *mi amor*, Vicente is there also. Together, your two loves. They have a guest, *un invitado*. Run! They may all leave soon. Go by the river, not the road."

Doña Ema, too, flung her arms around Maggie, squeezed her, and whispered yes, yes, it was all true. Her evil husband was dead, and the miracle child was still inside her. Because of it, Saint John had saved her life. "He kicks already! Feel." The fetus's heels rumbled distantly under Maggie's palm while Ema explained that her husband was buried in an unmarked grave, reported drowned, God have mercy on him. Ema crossed herself. And Vicente, el Señor Doctor, and the mine director were all together, in the pigs' house behind her garden. "With my two sons."

The shed was overgrown with squash vines, half collapsed. Ema led Maggie around behind it, hissed a signal, and then pushed her through a rank, hairy wall of leaves. Inside, it was stifling hot, with an ammoniac smell. Bars and triangles of light came through the cane walls, landing on the faces of six men, all of whom looked like prisoners at first, POWs in a Japanese camp. Maggie discerned Carson, squatting on river rock. "Hi," she said to him. "How's it going?"

"I didn't want you here," he warned her.

"I'm here anyway," she said. Turning to everyone else, she greeted them in Spanish. Only Vicente answered. *"Qué tal tu viaje?"* How was your trip?

"Good. Well, my *abuela* died."

"Pésame," the men murmured in condolence.

"Klaus told me," Carson said.

Vicente went on talking to Maggie. "We have a prisoner. I present to you Ignacio García, director of La Tormentosa."

She bent down to shake Ignacio's hand, for he was sitting on the ground, his ankle closely chained to a wooden stake. "Glad to meet you. My husband told me about you."

"*Encantado,*" Ignacio replied sarcastically. He had a coarse, rather pleasant face. His chin was covered with curly stubble.

Don Sixto sat above him on a stool with Carson's shotgun across his knees. He grunted for Maggie to leave his line of fire.

"*Disculpe,*" she apologized, backing into the only place left to sit, against the wall between Boris and Limbert. Shifting aside, Boris said to her politely, "Welcome back, Señora." He expected her to understand him, why he was here. She nodded and squeezed Boris's young, hard-muscled arm. Again, she remembered being pregnant.

Settling her hips between the boys', she stared at Vicente, absorbing him. A thin line of light curved down his cinnamon cheek. His smile was as quick and wry and bright as usual. "We were *planificando,*" he explained.

"*Sigan,* go ahead. I don't want to interrupt."

"What news have you heard outside?" he asked her.

The intensity of his gaze made her feel faint. How could anyone not notice? "Today a nationwide miners' strike began," Maggie intoned, "paralyzing extractions and costing millions of dollars in foreign exchange. Cajamarca is full of tanks and soldiers. *Pues,* everything is quiet. There was going to be a vigil in the plaza tonight, but now it has been canceled. Three-day curfew for the duration of the strike. What else. Oh, the Canadian delegation won't come, I heard. The president is ignoring us, so they'll probably do the same."

Ignacio groaned.

"Everything is not quiet," Carson told Maggie. "Not at all. What time did you leave the Wechslers' this morning?"

"Five. There was nothing on the radio. When did you, um, capture Ignacio?"

"This is his second day with us." He'd been racing back from the airport. Just above the El Mirador turnoff, Cantinflas had found the road blocked by a row of large stones. Several men emerged from the roadside bushes and invited themselves into the front seat. When they asked Cantinflas to drive back downhill to Piedras, he did not resist. Cantinflas was friendly toward the Rainbow, especially with a pistol at his head.

They hid Ignacio at Doña Ema's. The people had wanted to shoot him on the spot, as revenge for the killings at La Tormentosa, but Vicente had stopped them.

"What killings? Maggie said. "The newspaper said there hadn't been any!"

Two nights ago at the mine, a mass of Rosarinos, mine workers, and their wives and children had assembled in silence on the muddy soccer field, waiting for the Canadian delegation. They carried protest signs, but also wreaths of welcome.

Hours passed. As night began to fall, the news had come: no plane had landed.

Who threw a rock? Was a rock thrown?

One nervous conscript fired into the crowd. Panic among the miners: they leapt forward to throw their children to the ground. The soldiers, fearing attack, opened fire, killing two miners, one ten-year-old boy, and one woman; and wounding six people, including children ages six, ten, and fifteen. Many of the soldiers wept when they saw the bodies left behind on the field. They said they'd tried to aim high, and it must have been true. Otherwise, there could have been ten times as many dead.

"That wasn't in any news," Maggie repeated dumbly.

"Are you surprised?" Vicente asked her. "Luz María was standing in the front line, but *por suerte* she is all right."

"You should have let me drive on," Ignacio said. "I would have forbidden them to fire."

"*Silencio,*" Don Sixto growled.

"He was barely leaving the airport when it happened," Boris whispered to Maggie.

Again Vicente called on el Señor Doctor to speak his judgment. "*Continuamos?*"

"Free me!" Ignacio pleaded. "No one cares about me as a hostage."

Everyone ignored him.

"If they kill Ignacio, they'll all eventually get killed, I'm telling them," Carson said to Maggie. "Vicente agrees with me, but we're kind of a minority. Why don't you translate?" He predicted that the army would be called out. The air force, even. The murder of a mine official would mean that terrorism had revived. Could a handful of canyon folk and miners stand up against the national armed forces?

The question was whether they should let Ignacio go free, in which case he promised not to prosecute them and to do his best for the water cleanup. In the end, cooperation with the mining company was the only answer. Anyone harboring fantasies that the Piedrasinos might run the mine themselves should recognize the impossibility of this and drop their foolishness right now.

"*Mentiras,*" lies, Don Sixto declared. "He will do none of that."

There was always kidnapping, then, Carson went on reasonably. Kidnapping offered leverage and minimized the potential loss of life. They had the candidate right here. There would be no further need for suicidal demonstrations. In English he said to Maggie, "Safest thing for this guy. Out there they want to lynch him."

"I am trying to explain," Ignacio pleaded. "They will never ransom me, they told me this. It's the anti-terrorism policy. Not even a negotiation. Believe me! I should have had this tattooed on my arm!"

"We will kill you, then," Don Sixto said, shifting the long gun on his knees.

"He's a general's son," Maggie contributed. "How can he be as unimportant as he says?"

Don Sixto nodded, agreeing for once with Maggie.

"You don't know my father," Ignacio said. "The world's hardest man. That policy is his. *Because* I am his son, he will not make any exception."

Carson ruminated for a moment. "What if we had two hostages? Him and a North American doctor? I volunteer." Carson offered himself on the condition that the Rainbows must not kill Ignacio. Killing hostages was a bad idea; besides, Ignacio and Carson had been friends, if only for one evening. In return for his life, the director must swear not to try to escape, and if caught, to testify to his captors' kindnesses. He was not to be tortured psychologically. His total suffering would be not much greater than anyone else's.

"Thank you," Ignacio said. "I swear, on my mother's grave!"

"Carson keeps his pistol," Vicente quickly said. "Carson is not really a hostage."

"Right," Carson said. "I'll just make this event more visible, and maybe stop the army from killing all you guys."

Don Sixto protested. How could they prove they meant business unless they were willing to carry out a threat?

"Kill me, if you really have to do someone in, Sixto," Carson said. "Of course, I hope you would restrain yourself." He went on. No one had to be the wiser that the Rainbow's threats were empty. They'd benefit from the bad reputation of other guerrilla groups, especially Sendero. All the Canadian company had to do was fund a bank account. Klaus Wechsler could confirm the deposit. It wasn't as if they were asking for assassins to be freed. Their demands were reasonable. Public opinion would be on their side, as long as the hostages were gently treated.

"We must ask for more than money," Vicente added. "A school. Jobs."

"They can put money in, take it out the next day," Don Sixto reasoned. "They can let us rot without an answer. If they hire us to be miners, they will let the *socavones* fall in on us."

"Not if all the newspapers have heard about us," Carson told him. The miners' union was already faxing Lady Maggy's face all over the world. Once the kidnapping party had had time to escape, the Rainbow would issue another statement and a list of demands.

Boris spoke up now. The worst was if the army found them. They were so incompetent, so cruel. The army would kill them all, including the hostages.

"If it's an American," Vicente said bitterly, "they'll try to shoot around him."

"*Tal vez,*" perhaps, Ignacio said heavily. He recognized the realities described. If he had to stay a captive, he was as eager to run, and keep on running, as anyone. They should leave as soon as possible, but where would they go?

"We are from this zone," Don Sixto said with finality. "When we want to hide ourselves, not even the devil can find us."

"Shall we vote?" Vicente said.

The vote was unanimous, Maggie abstaining. The party would leave in one hour, heading first for El Mirador.

"One second," Carson said. Whether the Canadian company answered their demands in sixty days or not, he asked the Rainbows to promise to let the mine director go at the end of that time. He'd stay on as a substitute himself, depending on what had gone down.

"Too much," Vicente told him. "We will make that decision in its own time."

❖

Sneaking back along the riverbank, Carson told Maggie his new nickname. The Rainbows called him el Che, because Che Guevara had been a doctor too. With one difference: the real Che had never minded shooting people in the head, and el Che Gringo would rather die himself than permit such actions.

Was he a leader, a martyr, a hostage, the doctor of an expedition? He delighted in this confusion. He complained to Maggie, in jest, that she'd succeeded all too well in her efforts to change his life. "My career has developed into this P.R. stunt. What do you think, now I'm an American hostage! I'll be famous all over the world."

"I'm going to be a hostage too," Maggie said. "You can't leave me behind."

As Carson's mouth was opening, before he could form an answer, she quickly shouted, "I mean it. I'll turn you all in!"

"You're strong. I guess I don't see why not." Carson had always trusted her. "There could be some advantages. Let's see what Vicente says."

They shoved raincoats into their backpacks, grabbed all the dry noodles from the kitchen. Fortunata wept when they told her of their plans. "You will all die," she told Maggie.

"Pray for me," Maggie said.

Carson got the pistol out. "I want one too. The shotgun," Maggie said, dancing on her toes behind him. Carson understood her feelings, but reminded her that he'd loaned his shotgun to Don Sixto. It was going to be impossible to get it back, since Don Sixto was handing down his ancient bolt-action rifle to Boris. "You don't need the weight," Carson said. "When these guys run, we'll both be lucky to keep up. Anyway, you've never practiced. You'll have to trust in me. Are you ready to die with me, darling?"

"No," Maggie told him rudely. Then, "I'm sorry. I can't say yes to that question. I'm no martyr. I wasn't brought up Catholic like you."

"You're right," Carson said. "This is a pro-life mission. We've got God and the Pachamama on our side."

Maggie knew that the fetus was still in communication with its deepest origins. Love, the love of life. Yet as she and Carson walked out into the white glare of sun and dust, she felt the earth pulling down on her belly, pulling her toward itself. There was another way of understanding what Vicente and his mother always said, that with love you could go anywhere. You could even let yourself disappear, back into the belly of the earth.

Vicente rummaged through Maggie's pack and threw out the ceramic water filter. "Too heavy. In the forest the water is pure."

25

THE BLACK RAINBOW had an established escape loop that led into the forest, then from cabin to cabin to cabin. If the rains held off, in twenty days they'd come out in another *departamento* where no one would expect them to be. They could hide, a day's walk from the town of Mollepata, where they had friends. These friends had proven their loyalty in the old days of cocaine paste and the landings of the small, green-striped planes. Boris and Limbert could saunter into town, listen to the radio, evaluate rumors, buy food. The friends still had one plane that could be made to fly, and was big enough to carry six people to Bolivia. One seat would be empty, since Boris and Limbert could go home on a bus. They were still boys. No photograph existed of either of them.

Seven people — Vicente, Carson, Maggie, Boris, Limbert, Don Sixto, and their prisoner, Ignacio — all ran eastward, in the unthinkable direction. It was a fox's strategy, designed by Don Sixto, to escape into the mouth of danger, toward the mine and then into the forest which everyone believed to be impassable, uninhabited, a place of death.

They stopped in El Mirador long enough to write a press release and send it back to Klaus. Not by bus, not by road at all, but by trails, a messenger on foot. Next, on borrowed mules, they rode up toward the mine. Just before the crest of the mountains they stopped climbing, turned onto an Inca highway that led south, behind the mine, then east to a yellow-green pass called Abra Vaivén. Here the stones of the highway dispersed, and the land became too rough for animals.

Vicente untied the mine director's hands. "Lean down," he said, and Ignacio inclined his head for the blindfold to be loosened, and looked sharply around himself, as if recognizing the landmarks of the last moments of his life. Dismounting, he shook out his legs and stretched his body in a kind of satisfaction. "I know where I am," he said, and laughed a little. "On that pass above the Río Yatiri. *Correcto?*"

"How do you know that?" Don Sixto growled, unloading Carson's shotgun from the buckskin mule mare.

"I know well. I know also that no one will find us, *jamás,* if down there is where we're going," the mine director said. He'd once walked half a day's distance below this, as far as the lagoon, hunting deer and foxes. His men had refused to camp at the lagoon, the source of the accursed Río Yatiri. They'd lied, saying there were no trails onward. Ignacio had not forced them, knowing they were terrified of the unearthly rainbows and lightning bolts that had protected these valleys ever since the Incas had dumped their treasures here.

"There are trails," Don Sixto told him. "We hide the entrances."

"*Claro,*" Ignacio said.

"We enforce the ancient prohibitions," Vicente added, "but even without our help, all strangers who go in there die." In the forest a man could step on a patch of ground, and it would not be ground but matted creepers. These would part, and he'd fall into a vacuum of a thousand feet. A man could approach a cabin and be greeted with a bullet. He could become lost, and no one could retrace his steps, for even if he'd cut his trail the plants grew back within days.

Each person received part of a mule's load. Maggie's was lightest, five kilos each of rice and sugar. She'd brought no toilet paper, no toothbrush, no change of clothes.

An old Black Rainbow member led the mules away, disappearing one by one into the white fog. At the pass's open top, Don Sixto ran back and forth like a beagle sniffing for the downward path. At last he led them around an outcrop, down through a valley of sharp white stones and ledges that became cliffs. The grass was an acid yellow, covered with dew.

Hard travel, down the fields of wet grass, knee high, shoulder high, with tips sharp and transparent as spun glass. As soon as night fell, they rolled themselves in sheets of plastic to lie shivering, awake. At three A.M. they moved on; by dawn they'd left the black lagoon behind. Maggie saw why Ignacio's guides had been afraid of it, expressionless as Lady Maggy's eyes.

Down the back of another pass they tumbled, then the length of two more grassy valleys. Boris, Doña Ema's older boy, walked last, behind Maggie. He seemed happy in the wilderness, though he said he'd never been so far out before. He loped easily along, occasionally brushing the muzzle of Don Sixto's old gun over the tips of the tufted grass, letting himself fall behind at the pace of Maggie's struggles. For a time she amused them both with shocking tales about the United States, where even the poorest young men wore sneakers that cost a hundred dollars, and winter snows were so deep that cars had to be dug out with shovels, and you could furnish an apartment entirely by scavenging from the sidewalks on days when garbage was collected. Boris had seen such things on *la tele,* but he'd believed most of TV to be a fairy tale. As they began to discuss what was real, what was needed in life, and what was not, Comandante Oquendo entered the conversation. From the way Boris spoke his name, Maggie could tell that Boris loved him almost as much as she did. Hearing Boris go on about him gave her a secret fuel.

Meanwhile, though, her pack straps cut at her shoulders, the burden swinging her off balance. She peered at the roots of grass tufts, where deep limestone holes lurked, some big enough to swallow a mule, others small enough to take hold of Maggie's boot. How could the men stride ahead so quickly? Just as she was thinking this, Boris said, "Don't worry so much, Señora." His encouragements only confirmed her awkwardness.

Soon, they'd lagged so far behind the others that she persuaded the boy to go past her. He loped on by, and she saw how ashamed he'd felt to keep pace with a woman's weakness. It was a relief to let them all go on. She pretended she didn't know them, that she was wandering through this mist by herself.

Invisible ahead was everything, including the moment when she'd be able to see Vicente alone. We must have faith, she told the child inside her, even if we can't see why.

She came on the men abruptly as they rested, sprawled on a clutter of stones. When they'd reached the wall of green they'd stopped. The trail was a hole into the thicket, low, as if tunneled by small animals. Maggie stood at the edge of the group, her knees wavering with fatigue. The grass was wet and there were no stones left to sit on. Vicente and Carson sat together on a large, flat rock, sharing a bag of coca leaves, the peasants' endurance drug. She wanted to shove in between them, beg for a pinch of what they had.

Don Sixto noticed her and got slowly to his feet. "*Ya,*" he said. They had to reach the confluence before dark.

"*Estás bien?*" Vicente asked her. She nodded yes. Her mouth tasted of zinc, and her breath had not stopped roaring in her ears. She would not have thought she could run all day at this altitude, but she was doing it. She prayed that the fetus was not getting overheated. No chance to ask Carson, nor consult a pregnancy manual, nor ask for extra rest.

Boris and Limbert pulled out their machetes, since as Don Sixto said, this trail had not been refreshed in several months. She could see the scars where branches had been cut last year and the year before. The gray, cut ends were sharp as killing stakes. To avoid detection, for the first few yards they'd make no fresh cuts. After they'd all gone through, Don Sixto would stay behind to pull bushes across, to close the door behind them.

Now they were in the forest, where it was dim evening all the time. A drizzle began immediately, pattering and dripping from the leaves. Don Sixto barreled past, almost knocking Maggie down, and not apologizing. He disapproved of her presence and had said so more than once. She didn't care. Here she needed her hands as well as her feet to clamber up and down the knife-edge ridges as the trail struggled to stay out of the slicing chasm of the Río Yatiri, which could be heard but not seen. Where the hillsides flattened there was still no mercy, for the party waded through mud lagoons strung with prickling vines for handholds. There were steep, raw, red landslides, vertical swamps, networks of roots slippery black above the surface of rotting waters. Maggie tripped, grabbed ant-covered branches, fell down dozens of times. Once, deceived by a solid, floating carpet of bright green shamrocks, she stepped into a neck-deep pool of chilly mud the texture of diarrhea.

For love, she chanted in her mind, for love I'm doing all this. The words whirled and slipped, turned meaningless, until she realized that the only reason not to turn back was that she couldn't face the journey in reverse. The treacherous valleys, the rocks scattered like teeth, the accursed lagoon. Forward was preferable, even if it was worse.

At least this country justified the Rainbows' claims that they would never be followed, and if followed, never caught.

She got used to seeing the men only when they rested, practically falling over them in the clearings where they sat, crowded together. Everyone was more relaxed now, knowing the mine director could never escape. Don Sixto never even waited for her to sit down before stubbing out his cigarette and saying, "*Ya, seguimos.*"

He had no mercy for her, for anyone. This was his nature.

The full name on his birth certificate was Sixto Bastardo, his surname chosen by the priest to punish his mother for not being married to any of her children's fathers. Maggie was still a little shocked, still slowly absorbing the mores of this Catholic country which now seemed to her insanely cruel, deluded. At last she'd found a limit to her cultural tolerance, here where so many children were abandoned by their fathers, and the fathers were hardly blamed for turning their women into fools and whores, their children into bastards. That was what a man was, a beast who needed sex. Knowing and agreeing what he was, a woman should be loyal to him, and desire to be a mother to his children, proving her good heart. Better a whore than a frozen hag — and then all the little boys and girls grew up and did it over again.

Everyone except Vicente, Maggie thought, fighting off her own dread, which roared inside her, loudly articulated in her parents' voices and vocabulary. Since she hadn't stayed to listen, she told herself, she could ignore them now. She'd known Vicente in her soul, as deeply as she'd ever known anyone or anything. If she was wrong, and he was not true, she might as well be dead.

Besides, he'd promised. She'd felt embarrassed at the time, as if she were dishonoring them both. Now she was glad she'd asked him about a baby. "I want everything with you." He'd said that, and that should be enough. She had to trust him, and stop thinking about it.

He'd hidden in this forest for weeks, when he'd been a fugitive. Back on that hillside above Piedras, he'd loved telling her about it. She put one foot in front of the other, now, to the tune of his resonant voice, swinging through his favorite words: "*La selva verdenegra, donde no hay nada.*" The black-green forest, where there is nothing. He'd talked about the scarves of mist, garlanding the trees; about how ferns and red-tipped bromeliads grew up from the tops of branches, trees upon trees. Of the flights of toucanets bursting from the trees to fly across a clearing or a river. Of the buried bones, buried stones under this world of tangled green. And the cliffs, covered with red glyphs of condors, suns, and pumas. The hidden settlers' cabins, unknown by any law. The settlers, poor, illiterate, walled off from the world by trees, and fear, and superstition; and by the crimes they had committed on the coast. By old and new prohibitions, and by the harshness of this wet, terrifying land. And by rain, during the long season that was to begin soon.

"That forest is the most beautiful place in the world," Vicente had said. "I wish I could take you there."

They arrived at the cabin just as darkness was rising from the ground to meet the darkness lowering from the sky. Don Sixto dropped his pack, whistled sharply twice, and walked forward into the log-jammed clearing. He pushed his palm back at them, reminding the rest of the party to stay hidden. Strangers would be shot, but Don Sixto's niece Marisol lived here with her husband and children, and her husband's older brother's family.

"Here I stayed," Vicente said, describing with affection the small Inca ruin over the crest of the hill, and Marisol's breakfasts of corn fried with pork rinds. Maggie and the boys shouldered forward in order to see out the trail's mouth.

The air in the clearing was green, jellied with moisture. Two hundred yards away was the cabin, small, black, and wet-looking. Its corrugated roof glinted dully. Beyond it, the ground sloped down toward a stream whose far bank was a vertical mountain wall.

Carson remarked that this cabin was just like what his and Maggie's ancestors must have built, arriving in the New World. In a couple hundred years, he predicted, a shopping mall would occupy this spot.

For now, Maggie thought, the balance between the forest and the people seemed uncertain. All around the cabin, trees had been felled haphazardly and lay rotting in a maze of stumps and treacherous crossed boughs. Was it a trap, a device to keep people away? No, Vicente said, the trees had been slashed down ten years ago, when the settlers had first arrived, but because of the rain and fog, and the settlers' inexperience, the wood had never dried enough to burn successfully. By now the two blended and extended families who lived here had cleared more fields on the other side of a ridge, where it was sunnier. Each morning the men and boys walked over there to work.

These limestone mountainsides, cut by torrential streams and rivers, were so nearly vertical that this confluence was the only place within three days' walk, in any direction, where it was marginally possible to farm or build. Therefore it had this Inca ruin; therefore the settlers, too, had chosen it. The Incas had known where to live and how to walk in the mountains. All that was necessary was to find and follow their traces. This confluence had also been a junction of Inca highways. The Río Yatiri's had been small, and its stones had long ago sunk into the swamps. Tomorrow, if the fog cleared, they'd see across the valley the great north-south trunk road that had linked Cuzco to Quito. When they reached it, in two days' time, they could really run. The Black Rainbow always used Inca trails to escape.

This valley had lain uninhabited for centuries, Boris mused. "Ten years ago, two families arrived. Tonight, seven guests. Who knows about tomorrow?"

Don Sixto's whistle came, and then the man himself, swinging leg by leg over the felled trunks. He was accompanied by Roosevelt, his niece's husband, a lanky, humorous man who was wanted for his involvement in the drug trade. Roosevelt had a long, unshaven chin and a scraggly smile, which somehow reassured Maggie that this errand might still turn out all right.

Roosevelt and his older brother, Wilson, had built this cabin by hand. It had no chimney, no real walls, just logs with spaces between them for smoke to escape. Its fence was of cedar logs, as wide in diameter as Maggie was tall, with brambles laid all along the top, except at certain entrances, to keep out jaguars. The logs had machete-cut handholds and footholds. Roosevelt put his toes in the lowest and sprang over. One by one, the men imitated him.

Standing momentarily atop the gigantic log, Maggie understood Vicente's feelings about this forest. It formed a circular wall around them all, elaborate, ornate, complete, pressing inward until she hovered in a timeless transparency. No need for human fears.

Outside this silent clearing the world was making a tremendous noise about her. Her parents had surely heard it, as Maggie would have, if she'd been anywhere other than here. Four days ago, half jokingly, she'd told a friend in Cambridge to send the army into Piedras if he didn't hear from her. She prayed he'd forgotten. How could she have made such a disastrous remark, not specifying which army?

They crossed the yard, an ocean of churned purplish mud, with puddles in tracks, littered corn husks and shreds of plastic, and a broken rubber boot — reeking, rotten mud full of the green, white, brown, yellow, curled and piled, fresh and dissolving excretions of babies, turkeys, pigs, and chickens. Passing the door of the ground floor, they greeted an indeterminate number of adults and children who sat in the dark around a fire that must have been burning all the time. Its smoke was why the cabin's logs were black — smoke would protect the wood from bugs and moisture, too. Deciding on these links reminded Maggie of her first day in Piedras, the joy she'd felt burning garbage by the river, figuring out how things fit together, leaving room for her among them. How had that day led to this one?

"You will sleep there." Roosevelt pointed upward. *"Allí." Ay* was the sound he made. Vicente led the way up a notched log to an attic where corncobs and strips of pork fat cured in the smoke rising through the floor cracks. There was barely room for everyone, since half the attic was full of a mountain of corn ears. On top of the pile was a three-fourths-life-sized bundle, like an enormous ball of white cotton string. *"La momia,"* Vicente whispered. The families had robbed it from a tomb. Maggie imagined it inside, brownish orange like a peach dried hard, with shriveled skin and empty eye sockets staring out at her with x-ray vision. Vicente explained that the settlers were afraid to unwrap it, even to check for golden ornaments.

Rather, they prayed to it as if it were a saint. "*La carne,* flesh, is more powerful than plaster." Vicente laughed, glancing at Maggie. "Besides, it is their own ancestor, not imported from Rome or Spain."

"Let's ask it to curse the trail behind us," Maggie offered.

All at once, on the roof, the rain became a cascade of nails. "Just in time," Don Sixto said. They'd planned to spend one night in this cabin, then move on. Now he predicted this rain would last all night and into the morning. If it did, he and Vicente agreed they could stay one extra day. Tonight, the party was exhausted. They needed rest, food, and sleep. If anyone was following, the rain would stop them too. On the third day, rain or shine, the fugitives would set forth in predawn darkness, moving farther into the forest.

The image of Juan Carlos Yáñez swam into Maggie's head, pudgy in tiger fatigues. He would be stopped by rain, she hoped. The trace of his handshake still itched upon her palm.

While the men dumped their packs in one corner, Maggie kicked aside some scattered corncobs and spread her old red sleeping bag next to the outer wall. "*Al sobre,*" Boris quipped. Into the envelope. Her thighs were quivering, spent; she could barely flex them to crawl in. Turning onto her side, she peered out between the logs. From here you could see the Inca ruin. A few listless cows grazed inside and around it. They'd been brought in by another route, along the Inca highway.

The men went down the ladder and outside. Maggie closed her eyes and thought she could feel her uterus crawling up into her abdominal cavity, as the medical books had said it would do that week. What if her child did turn out like Lady Maggy? If Maggie were in the States, they'd look at the fetus on a TV screen, probe her body with gleaming instruments. Here, Fortunata would scan Maggie's past for possible infractions against saints, stones, the secret nature of all things. Ema, Fortunata, pray for me.

Women's prayers were not enough, Maggie thought. Her body was filled with the madness of pregnancy, bliss and a complicated insanity. She was a blooming red rose surrounded by parchment skin. Inside her were two hearts, both beautiful, alive. Both needed Vicente desperately.

Distant laughter woke her. The men were bathing in the Río Yatiri, taking advantage of a break in the clouds. She spied them through the logs' crack, shining, naked, and cavorting like schoolboys, not bothering to hide themselves. The sun on them was lurid as the light from an atomic bomb.

She must have dozed off again, for here was Carson, cajoling her. "Come down, hon, come on." Food was a priority; she recognized this. She crept down the ladder and ducked into the darkness of the main cabin where a woman her own age perched by the fire on a split log. This must be Marisol. They greeted each other cautiously, members of different human categories.

All the men were there already, sitting on logs and eating. The mine director nodded at Maggie. The rope binding his wrists had been loosened to let him hold a spoon.

The older settler wife offered Maggie a log stool with a folded blanket cushion. The woman took Limbert's bowl, flung the dregs outside, and refilled it with soup for Maggie. Ribs, thin as a chicken's, and a whole yam stuck up from a broth as dark, rich, and delicious as if it had been stewed with dried porcini, truffle oil, and wine. Maggie tore at the thick muscle inside the rib cage. "What kind of meat is this?"

Vicente pointed at a cut-off scaly hind foot hanging over the fire and described a rodent, nocturnal, with a spiked tail. It ate the settlers' corn; that was why its meat was rich, but also why it had had to die. He glanced at Marisol, who reached up and handed the claws to Maggie. Smoked, they would last forever. "*Talismán*," Vicente said. She closed her fingers over the foot, whose narrow bones fit into the crook of her palm. Her belly pulsed with gratitude for Vicente's helpfulness, his curiosity, his gentle explanations. If she had it to do over again with him, she would. Had she ever doubted it? She hoped his child would look exactly like him.

She remembered to thank Marisol, who smiled shyly back at her. Now she looked over at Carson, cocooned in his own buzzing oblivion, elbows on his knees. His eyes looked red and weary. She'd have liked to slap him. She'd do anything to save him. "Ever hear of an animal with three toes?" She dangled the foot before him. "Besides a sloth?"

"Soon all wild animals will be extinct," Carson predicted.

Maggie's chest ached to hear his sad, didactic tone. She wished he'd shaved off his beard. It came to her that she'd never see the naked chin beneath it.

After eating, she excused herself. Outside, the rain spat down from a dim, roiling sky. Her clothes were still damp, but she had better pee before going to bed. She crawled over the logs at the back of the farmyard, climbed past the brow of a hill. This rank grass hardly needed her pregnant hormones. Beneath it, she recognized the softened edges of Inca terracing, forming an amphitheater behind the cabin.

She wished Vicente would come out and find her, but she knew he wouldn't, yet. She'd seen him watching her, offhandedly registering her departure. By the set of his head as he'd turned back to the conversation, he'd told her he would not follow.

Here in a small pit in the grass she squatted and pulled down her pants. No one could see her here, not even the sky, which was hidden from itself by a thick cottony layer. She imagined orange muzzle flashes, burping out from the edge of the forest.

Unseen, unknown, she peed on rags and bones scattered and half buried in the grass.

Clambering back over the log wall, she accidentally rested one hand squarely on a large, cold mound of turkey shit. It was green, of a surprising integrity and diameter. Though she tried to wipe it off on the log, her pants, finally the edge of the cabin, she could not. Tears sprang to her eyes. She felt marked, culpable. She was a bit too shaky, that was clear.

Everyone else was still inside, eating soup and talking. She must rest, for the child's sake. Her kneecaps were so sore underneath that she could barely climb the notched log ladder. The corn attic's ceiling was too low to stand straight, so she pitched herself across the floor, zipped herself as fast as possible into her sleeping bag, needing its protective halo of goose down, its comforting stale smell. Wrapped in it, she lay listening to the men guffawing downstairs. Everyone was liking the mine director. He'd insisted on carrying the bottle of whiskey from his pickup truck. Bad whiskey, made in Peru, but still. Tonight, judging from the hilarity below, they would polish it off.

Boris came up, saying he did not drink. She was glad. He posted himself in the doorway, leaning against one jamb and hanging his feet outside, over the log ends. He stared back at the trail on which they'd come, his shoulder a gray cutout against the darkening sky.

"Why do stars fall, Doctora?" he asked Maggie. He'd heard that everyone had his or her own star, which fell just before that person was to die. Was this true or just a superstition?

She liked Boris. Sometime yesterday she'd decided that he bore a resemblance to the young Cassius Clay. When had he changed from Boris the delinquent into this sensitive, thinking young man? Horrifying as it was to consider, maybe his father's death had been necessary to free him.

Now she tried to explain to Boris the enormity of the universe as described by science. Stars didn't fall, nor belong to anyone. Everything was vaster than a person could imagine. She would have liked to adopt Boris, or send him off to a university, but he didn't agree with her ideas. When she was done, he told her it was hard to believe that a falling star could be a random piece of dust, not aimed at anything. This contradicted his observations when, in the pallor of many mornings, he'd seen a star lose hold and come streaking down. "Not today," he made sure to say.

They both fell silent, Maggie wishing she hadn't claimed to know the reasons for things. It was too late to retract her explanation, but she took comfort, knowing that in their different ways she and Boris were thinking the same sad thoughts.

Past his shoulder's shadow was the darker gray of the fog. Somewhere inside that fog was the trail they'd come down. Though Boris was watching for police, tonight there was no chance of being reached, now that mist was darkening the trail. Even for Don Sixto, that trail would be impassable in darkness. Tomorrow, the fear could start again, no earlier than noon.

Onward from this cabin, the boy now told her, the trail wound southeast along a terrible hillside, far above the Río Huacatinti. Except for the ease of falling, once they'd left this clearing the danger was behind them. No soldiers or police could come from ahead, for it took three weeks to get in from the other side. There was a second trail leading to this cabin, starting from where the Inca highway passed a little town farther north, but as soon as the kidnapping party had moved onward, a warning could be sent if soldiers appeared. Every settler family had many children, so one would not be missed. Anyone above the age of seven was familiar with the forest, able to hide and run faster than any soldier, old enough to be trusted with a message. Even a five-year-old settler child could run in an hour a distance that took outsiders half a day. No army unit could ever traverse this forest secretly. Anywhere beyond this cabin, a settlers' ambush could kill the first patrol.

Don Sixto's head appeared at the top of the ladder. Then Ignacio's, then Limbert's. Ignacio giggled drunkenly as they tied him, leg and wrist, to the logs of one wall. Boris, Don Sixto, and Limbert would share a blanket, sleeping jammed together at the doorway. Carson flung his sleeping bag between Limbert and Maggie, and said, "Move over." Tipsy, he stumbled on Limbert's feet, then zipped the bag up over his head. "G'night," he said from inside.

Vicente loomed over them and said, "I must guard the outer wall. Move over."

Maggie closed her eyes, which were filling with tears of gratitude, and rolled sideways, making room. Vicente settled himself between her and the wall. Pretending to be a good wife, in case anyone was noticing, she turned toward Carson and pressed her nose against his sleeping bag. His arm was like cement. Now she felt Vicente turning too, quietly pressing his chest against her back, his loins against her buttocks. She pressed back, felt his penis harden. She came two seconds later, quietly, ecstatically, breathing through her open mouth.

She knew Vicente knew. Surely Carson hadn't noticed. She felt sorry for Ignacio, chained alone while the other six lay touching one another. Limbert fell asleep first, snoring a little. The sound of everyone else's listening to him, wishing for the boy's protection, was a kind of buzz in the room, softening and deepening the heavy, stiff noise of the rain.

They slept into the morning. As the men began to stir, Maggie struggled, unable to open her eyes or bring herself to the surface. For one long moment she couldn't tell which man was which.

Even under this galvanized roof, Maggie wondered how corn ever dried here. All night and into the morning it rained, and this was considered the tail end of the dry season. In the cabin the air was swollen, full of humidity that condensed, coating every solid object, greasing skin. Roosevelt laughed at Maggie's complaints. This was not rain! It was only a sign of rain. When it proposed to rain, it would rain in earnest. The true rains were coming soon, in a few days or weeks, and then everyone would be trapped, unable to cross the raging streams. All trails would be drowned, waist-deep. The mountainsides would collapse under their own weight, leaving bare cliffs like teeth exposed in the greenery.

They ate corn kernels fried with pork rinds. At ten the clouds suddenly parted, and shafts of sun strafed the clearing. More dark clouds were pressing from the west, though, so departure remained unwise. Tomorrow without fail. No one was looking forward to it.

The sun was Maggie's chance to get out of the cabin. She told the men she wanted a bath, as they'd had yesterday. She would go down to the river.

"You could be seen from the high trail," Don Sixto told her.

The high trail, the Inca highway, was a hairline in the trees, miles across the valley, but Maggie remembered how easily Luz and Vicente had spotted Liliana's black Jeep. She promised to take a circuitous path, hiding herself among the rocks, and then bathe in the north-south stream instead of the Yatiri. "I deeply need a bath," she said, hoping to scare Don Sixto a little with the specter of female filth.

"Believe her, Sixto." Carson raised his eyebrows at her.

"*Lo autorizo*," said Vicente nonchalantly.

Silence under the loud roar from the purest stream water falling over limestone.

Maggie's legs were so sore she could hardly slither down the bank. Behind a huge log she'd found her own still place, a pool where the mountain stream wouldn't carry her off or crush her, and where the people in the cabin could not see her, nor anyone who might be looking with binoculars. The log had fallen sideways; its diameter was as tall as an ordinary house. It held up an even more enormous, tilting slab of rock, hiding her completely except from the eyeless cliff face directly across the stream.

Even so, she bathed modestly, in a T-shirt and underwear, luxuriating for one instant in the frigid water combing down over the rocks, already filtered through mats of moss, from trees and slopes and rocks no human being had ever seen. Looking at her belly, she thought how deceptive were appearances, for it was as flat as ever.

She had not said anything to anyone. She had not had a moment of privacy with anyone, let alone Vicente. Carson, preoccupied, had not touched her, hadn't noticed her hot, hard breasts.

Her white legs were like grubs underwater, her toenails rimmed with mud. With the water so cold, the rocks of the streambed hurt her feet. Looking back, she could see the cabin's smoke falling to the ground in the thick, wet air. The trail they'd all walked in on was invisible in fog.

She'd loved Vicente's stories about this homestead. The place where he'd slept in a ruin, where he'd heard the sweet whistle of the bird and had known that the earth was a seamless, living presence. He'd never been the same since. So he'd told her during their sun-blasted afternoons at the shepherd's hut. It was the same for Maggie: ever since arriving here, she'd felt the forest invading her, dissolving her ever more deeply into itself, herself, Vicente.

Vicente's bird was supernatural, surely. Since entering this forest, not a single bird had spoken. Everything felt suppressed and stifled by the fog. Perhaps even the birds knew enough to be afraid, to still their songs right now.

Waiting for him beside the stream, she knew he was bound to come to her. She and Vicente were one, not only in flesh. He would come out to her, and honor all his promises.

She pressed her mind against him. Now, come out to me, come now. She looked up, hearing his footsteps swishing in the rank, wet grass above the bank.

He was there, above her, sliding down to be beside her, just as he'd done on their first day together, by another river. She wanted to embrace him, but a curious, resonant shyness hovered between them, as if their magnetic poles had been reversed. She stood up, instead, to greet him. He'd come with his pistol. She could see it hanging inside his canvas jacket.

"I'm pregnant," she told him right away.

His head snapped back. *"Estás segura?"* Are you sure?

"Yes. It's yours."

"Are you sure?"

"I took a test."

He looked sideways at the ground. He lifted his hand toward her shoulder, and let it fall again. There were tears in his black eyes. He made a small sound, *Mmh,* then said, "Our life has changed."

"I'm prepared to leave Carson," she told him.

He laughed. "But am I?"

The enormous, tilted rock sank a little lower over both their heads.

"Coward," she said, and he turned his back on her.

Looking up, over the edge of the bank, she could see the tips of the messy forest trees and the smoke from the cabin spreading a little before being pressed down toward the earth. There was the trail into which they would fling themselves tomorrow. It started as a log across the stream, rose from the bank as a swath of cow-trampled mud leading to another ragged hole in the vegetation on the opposite bank. The door to the elf world, the door of no return.

Vicente shoved the toes of his rubber boots under the gravel of the stream, releasing a cough of reddish silt into the water. "Don't you see where we are? You're crazy, a crazy gringa. Why did you come here to tell me a thing like this?"

"I thought you'd want to know." Maggie swayed on her feet beside him. They were two separate columns of flesh and thought, the space between them glowing, frigid, ionized.

Vicente kicked the silt again. Yes, *claro,* he did want to know. "But why didn't you tell me before we left? You understand why we are here? That we cannot stop?"

"Yes. That's why I came." She could have listed a thousand reasons why she was standing beside Vicente, beginning with rain, wind, and sun. "When was I supposed to tell you? In front of everyone?"

"You are *en estado,* you cannot continue," Vicente announced.

"Why?"

"With child?" he said. "You want both to die? Forgive me, but how do you know it is ours?"

Based on feeling, mutual feeling and knowing, based on promises and intentions. "We wanted it, remember? You said! *Pues,* after that I stopped protecting myself."

"I never thought a *gringa* would maneuver in such a way." He turned his back on her and crossed his arms, and from that position he said No. No, no, no and no. That was it. *Ya.* He had decided. Maggie was not thinking clearly.

"Maneuver! How dare you use that word!"

"Did you not make love with your husband?"

"Yes, but . . ."

There was a need for cruelty now, he said, still turned away from her. Delay was death, so he had no time to sit pondering this and that alternative. If she did not leave voluntarily, he would drive her away like one who throws stones at a dog to make it return home. How could she stay here? She needed other tests. She'd been drinking the same water as all the girls of Piedras, no? What if something was wrong with the baby?

"I sent my hair off in the mail. Look, I'll go out, I'll wait for you in town."

Some town full of police? She'd bait their trap. "*No gracias.*"

"Then I'm staying. I don't care if we all die. I'm staying."

No. He was the father of Lady Maggy. He had a woman in El Mirador, another in Cajamarca — and that one also had a child of his. Two in fact. His destiny as a guerrilla had made it impossible to marry. Now destiny had caught him again. He was beginning to understand his life. He'd die in prison, or from a bullet, and so he must say the same to Maggie now as he'd said to all the others. You must understand me, I cannot be a father, I have a greater destiny.

She heard him breathing, hard, through his nose. "You lie," she said, experimentally. Sounding just like a woman to herself, she told him she hated his destiny. She didn't believe him when he spoke about his destiny. Destiny did not exist in advance. Destiny was adopted by each person. It was a series of decisions. Vicente did not answer, so she went on experimenting. "You're lying. I know you want to live. You want to be with me. I want to be with you. We could live here, in the forest." She liked the idea, but still he didn't answer. "Or somewhere else, like France, the United States, Bolivia. We could hide in Bolivia, or anywhere, anywhere you want to go. I love you."

"Bolivia!" Vicente sneered. Their destinies had parted. She could not stay with the fugitives, and that was all. She must return home to the United States.

"Don't insult me. Home? My home is not the United States."

"Well, then, where is it?"

"In you," she whispered. "I'm so sorry I was married." She might have fallen had he not caught her. Into his ear she murmured crazy things, begging him to let her wait for him in Cajamarca, at Liliana and Klaus's.

"*Loca*, I never believed that you were married," he said, kissing her neck. "Never, *jamás*. Why are you trembling?"

She was, her thighs and jawbone shivering uncontrollably, though not from cold.

Even Vicente's strength was not enough to resist the earth's whole gravity, which was pulling Maggie to the ground. He sank down with her. "*Perdón*," he said. The hollow in his throat was golden, throbbing.

"Hey, asshole!" Carson's voice.

Vicente slid his arm out from under Maggie's shoulders.

Carson stood up on the bank, his legs and arms jerking. "Hey! Asshole!" He had the flat gray pistol in his hand. Maggie tried to rise, thinking to run up the bank and stop him from shooting Vicente, but Vicente pressed her to the ground behind him.

Carson said, "What are you doing with my wife?"

He doesn't care to know what I am doing, Maggie thought, the last strand of her love for Carson breaking.

"Don't move," Vicente told her. He stood up slowly, addressing Carson. "Would you like to shoot me? Go ahead and shoot me, gringo. You don't care. *Claro*, the sound will bring the police directly to us."

"I want to kill you," said Carson, and he pulled the top half of the gun back, to cock it. After the first shot, Maggie knew, he'd have nine more in succession. "Carson!" she cried. "Don't!" This only caused him to pull the trigger prematurely, shooting up into the cliff's face. The shot reverberated everywhere, circling the valley, rolling up to the clouds and back again, like a flock of birds. A fistful of shattered limestone sifted down into the water.

"*Estamos fritos*," Vicente said.

"Shit," said Carson. "Shit, goddamit, *mierda!*"

"You guys had better leave," she told them.

❖

No longer bothering to hide herself, Maggie wandered back toward the cabin alone. The two men had run ahead, to begin the urgent process of departure. Halfway across the field of slaughtered, rotting trees, she traipsed into the ruin. Its ceiling had fallen, but three of its walls were intact, six feet high with the regularly spaced keyhole openings that marked it as an Inca structure. Some openings were windows, others had been closed with narrow stones to form handy storage niches. The keyhole design resisted earthquakes. So Johnny Baines had told her, and Vicente too.

Why had the settlers not restored this building, Maggie wondered, far lovelier and more permanent than their log cabin. Maybe they'd been afraid. They called all previous inhabitants *gentiles,* which seemed to indicate something demonic, like "unchristians."

Tumbled cubical stones lay scattered and half buried in the thick grass. All the walls were softened by purple moss and garish lichen. A few cows grazed the ruins, boxed in by the fallen trees. Here was a reddish plant with three-sided stems; there a strawberry with one wee, rotting fruit. Herbs used to treat stomachaches and headaches, planted by the *gentiles,* the settler women had said last night.

Maggie pawed the grass, searching for *ruda.* There was none. It must grow in drier, sunnier places. *Ruda,* blue-green and stinky. It had brought a costly happiness to Doña Ema. Months ago, Fortunata had given Maggie a cutting from her garden, and Maggie had planted it in front of the clinic, to attract business. Just before leaving on this expedition, she'd noticed it thriving. She'd considered, and then forsworn, bringing a tuft of it in her backpack, hidden from the men, to be boiled in milk just in case she needed not to have this baby. Little had she known how difficult it would become to find fire, or milk, or enough privacy for boiling any potion. She wondered if chewing *ruda* raw would work, or if the herb had worked at all, ever. Not knowing the dosage, she could have guaranteed herself a monster.

She'd come this far in order to lose that option, had she not? She just hadn't anticipated how completely everything else would fall away.

26

PAIN, as she hurled herself at boulders the color of a ginger cat, over fallen logs, up mudbanks and rock ledges slick with rain, with water running off them. Some ledges were tall and overhanging, so she had to kick her legs and belly up over. Muscles screamed in her thighs, chest, stomach, ribs, and arms. Her hair hung in her face, and the rain ran into her mouth salted by the sweat trickling out of her hair and down her forehead. There were tears, too, but she was almost too wet to know it.

Boris was behind her, pushing. As if with a whip he lashed her on and on. He was in a rage, obviously. She knew how he must be feeling, that everything was confusing, humiliating, and sudden. It had to be worse for Boris, who didn't have a clue why this was happening, merely that he was outside the reasons. Maggie knew how that felt, too. She'd tried to help him by starting to explain, but her throat had closed like a fist when she'd tried to say Vicente's name. Besides, the trails ran uphill and she needed her breath for fleeing. She'd promised to tell him everything later, tonight, when they could rest.

Forgive me, she thought, worried about Boris.

❖

He had been angry since the morning, when Doña Maggie's *loco* husband had shot off his pistol, and within a quarter of an hour all the other men had vanished into the forest, leaving him behind with Maggie. Comandante Oquendo had delegated him to escort the woman back to civilization. He'd even taken Boris's gun away and given it to Limbert.

Though he knew he was a soldier under orders, Boris could not understand why he'd been singled out for this inglorious errand. It smarted like a punishment, irrational, unjust, the last kind of treatment he'd expect from the Comandante. Wasn't Doctor Calzón responsible for Doña Maggie, was he not her husband? Had the Doctor not attacked the Comandante? That was treason. How could a *traidor* be permitted to remain with the expedition?

To make a bad thing worse, Doña Maggie, whom he liked, was crying and breaking down, just like his mother, Ema. Boris had hoped never to have to endure such racking tears again. Doña Maggie, who was usually good at explanations, at understanding people's feelings, and at making sense of things, had told him she could not yet explain what happened by the river. It had to do with sex, Boris knew that much. Maybe he didn't need her explanation.

Up to now, he had respected her. He'd asked her for advice. He'd even admired the way she'd wanted to come on this dangerous trip, then suffered without complaining, refusing to slow the men down. He would never make such a mistake again about a woman, Boris thought. The Rainbows never should have let her join them. Just as Don Sixto had said from the beginning, females were bad luck. They brought on jealousies and fights, just by their smell. True, and now Boris was her victim, while his brother, stupid little Limbert, had been permitted to go on and nobly risk his life.

Even the mine director had given him a look of pity.

It would be easy enough to push her off a rock, smash her head or something. He had not been able to do it yet, because of Comandante Oquendo's parting orders. "Take care of this woman. Respect her as if she were *mi propia persona,* my own person. Give your life for her, as I have already done." He'd smiled and clapped Boris on the back, chuckling as if Boris were a child who could not understand what was hidden behind his words. At first Boris had heard a prediction that all of them would die, because of the gringa. Then a flowery lie, a sweet sop. Finally he'd decided that the Comandante had been talking to himself. This was sufficiently mystifying that Boris had decided to obey, at least until he understood more clearly.

Maybe the Comandante did expect Don Calzón to shoot him in the back, and wanted Boris to save the woman. He'd spoken hurriedly, secretively, taking Boris aside amidst the handshakes and parting embraces, then immediately turned away and slipped out the cabin door into the rain, followed by the mine director, Limbert, the Doctor, and Don Sixto last. With their backpacks protected by plastic rain sheets, they'd looked like a parade of *jorobados,* hunchbacks, crossing the stream. But they'd disappeared into the forest as swiftly as a snake into its hole.

Minutes after that, a child, Roosevelt's eight-year-old son, Lenín, had led Boris and Maggie around the hill and to the far edge of the corn fields, to set their feet upon the trail. In two hours, on the right, they'd see another trail leading up to the Inca highway, Lenín said. Reaching that pavement, they should turn left, northwest. Given good weather, they'd emerge in three days in a settlement whose Quechua name meant Plain of Slime. Plain of Slime had no police post. People were unkind there, but they could mention Comandante Oquendo to an old woman at the edge of town. Her name was María Gracia Aliaga; she was Lenín's grandmother. She sold *chicha,* so her house was marked with an empty plastic bag on a stick.

After four hours, though, Boris and Maggie had to conclude that Lenín had overestimated their speed of travel. They hadn't found the second trail. Worse, they'd lost their own trail and been forced down onto the rocks of this riverbed, whose rocks were growing larger, more dangerously vertical. Water poured into their eyes and mouths. Often they had no choice but to wade in the torrent. It roared louder and louder, swelling with the rain, which had started again around noon, along with Maggie's tears when, after her bath, again and for the last time climbing the log fence into the foul muddy barnyard, she'd slipped and gotten more turkey shit on the heel of her right hand, which did not easily come off.

The tomb was a hundred yards straight up, held in a crack in the gray, stained cliff. Beside it was a reddish petroglyph, fifty feet across, a condor with spread wings. Silently she thanked Johnny Baines for training her to examine rock faces. The blurred drawing could have been a stain of iron oxide, the tomb a pile of broken stones.

"*Subamos,*" she suggested, pointing. "We cannot keep doing this." Boris hated the idea of resting, but in a few hours it would be dark, and finding any other dryness was unlikely. He offered his hand to help her climb, but she refused it.

Why had the settlers not mentioned this place, Maggie wondered as they scrambled up a tilted fault, covered with silt as fine as talcum. Perhaps it was a secret. The ledge was completely dry, hidden by plants and sheltered by the overhanging cliff. Yet turbulent footprints proved that the settlers must stop here, hunting or caught by rain. This trail to Plain of Slime was easier than the one up the Río Yatiri, so they usually came this way when they needed salt, batteries, alcohol, or medicine.

Boris pointed out a curled black bear turd, luckily dry and old. There was a long fire scar on the wall. Below it, cubical stones from the tombs had been set in a ring. More stones lay scattered down the slanted ledge. Cracks in the walls were filled with the sharp leaves of dead bromeliads. It was marvelous to find all this up here. Boris was surprised she'd seen the place, and said so. She'd always had good eyes, she answered, rather sharply.

At least she had stopped crying.

They took from their shoulders the squares of blue plastic that had so poorly sheltered them from the rain, and spread them over sticks to dry. Their packs were sagging, light. They'd given most of their food to the five men, whose trail was ten times longer and whose mission incalculably more dangerous.

All around were human bones, skulls, and shreds of white fabric with brown designs. "*Gentiles,*" Boris whispered. "Don't be afraid, they're well dried," she told him briskly. She looked at the dead things curiously, turning over an arm's connected bones, then walked up to the top of the ledge to see the tombs they had been taken from. The tombs were empty, stone houses full of wind. Their doors faced east.

From above, she watched Boris sit down on a cut stone, sticking his legs straight out, staring back the way they'd come.

The settlers' mummy might have come from this place. All last night it had watched them sleeping in the attic. Maybe it had guided them today. The settlers said the cliffs were full of tombs. They'd found feather crowns but they had dropped them, pots but they had broken them, and wooden carvings but they'd sold them one lean year. No gold. The mummy was all they had left. One day they'd sell it, too.

She wondered whether the settlers' mummy was a man or a woman. She stood inside its last house, looking out the window. Framed in the small stone cutout, the dreadful, steaming forest was suddenly a view. *"Mira,"* she called to Boris, "we're *higher* than the trail." From this tip of the ledge one could see the trail starting a hundred feet below, on the other side of the stream, a cut slanting upward through the bushes. And there, high up, was the Inca road running flat across the verdant mountain, like a crease in fat.

Boris came up to look. *"Qué bien,"* how great, he said grudgingly. *"Qué pasa?"*

"Nada, Señora." He was still angry with her.

"Let's sit down," she suggested. "We'll talk." To her relief, he agreed.

Their shoulders touching, they sat in the tomb's door and stared across the narrow valley, now clogged with fog and rain. Though it was not cold, steam rose from their pants and shirts. Maggie began to shiver. *Nu nununu,* her lips mumbled of their own accord, unwilling to form any better words. The backs of her hands were purple.

Boris took out the bag of fried corn kernels they'd been given at the cabin and silently offered its open mouth to Maggie. She ate two handfuls, then stopped herself. Boris ate one handful, then shoved the bag back into his shirt front. They stared at the rain a while longer. Maggie imagined them having escaped and celebrating, facing each other at a hotel restaurant, with a white tablecloth, a flower in a cut-glass vase. There would be piano music and, although it might be raining, the rain would be falling on a flagstone patio outside French windows. "Thank you for all you did for me," she'd say. "Now I will tell how everything came to pass." A chant began in her mind, the rhythm of a nursery rhyme. Because of a secret, because of a loss, because of two men. None of it was true anymore.

Instead, she told Boris, "Do not walk with me. I know you do not want to."

"I must, Señora. The Comandante said to keep you safe."

"I am safe. See? We found the trail, this ledge." She giggled. "What if *I* order you? Whom will you decide to obey? Me, the Comandante, or yourself? It's always your decision."

Boris was not sure what he would have said next, but instead the gringa told him that she was bearing Comandante Oquendo's child, and she had to save herself because of that. Didn't that make some things clearer? She loved the Comandante. She had never intended to betray her husband, because she loved him also, but in the end she had been forced to choose, not between two men, but which thing was most true inside herself. That was what she wanted to communicate to Boris. Did he know what she meant? Boris should feel free to do whatever he felt he must do. Stay. Go.

"I didn't know," he said helplessly. Though he was glad she'd clarified things, now he wished she would stop talking. Not only was he embarrassed to have this kind of conversation, but to speak of that which must be done had caused him to recall his father.

She continued, saying she'd always recognized this duty or mission in other people, but from the outside. She'd never believed it could exist in her. "A force in you that will never go away," Doña Maggie was insisting. "Which thing in you will never disappear, Boris?"

"My soul?"

"No," she told him flatly. "Not a word you memorized from some stupid priest. What part of you will be there, unchanging, till you die?"

Boris thought of the nameless rage that had made him search for vengeance, and train his little brother to do whatever Boris wanted. But that rage had diminished. Maybe he'd felt something eternal in those days at the clinic, long before the Doctores had arrived, when the older nurse used to take her clothes off, showing Boris her brown breasts hanging like two soft bells. "*No sé,*" he said, shrugging, I don't know.

Then he was ashamed of ever disrespecting Maggie, for she spoke beautifully to him, better than any preacher, telling him that he was a man and he had to find what his mission was or else he would die. He could call it soul if he wanted to, but she meant a power or an urge that already guided him whether he knew it or not. Actually, she thought Boris already knew what she meant and was too shy to admit it. It wasn't a concrete thing, so sometimes you needed someone else to point it out to you. She wanted Boris to know that she'd begun to observe this quality in him. Usually, she would never dare to talk to anyone in such a way, but today was a strange and extraordinary day, maybe the last day of their lives, and she believed that Boris would be interested in what she had to say.

Boris nearly invited her to go and get fucked. Normally he would have, but perhaps for some of the reasons she'd listed, today it didn't seem worth it. Instead, he considered what she'd told him. He was ashamed to agree with her out loud, but he had to admit that she was right. He too had admired this force in other people, mostly in Comandante Oquendo, but also in Doctor Calzón and Don Sixto. He too had seen it from the outside, doubting that it could exist inside himself, nor certainly in any woman.

His soul, he realized now, had taken form after the whipping. He'd been determined to endure it nobly. Through that resolve, somehow he'd learned, instead of more rage, respect for the justice that had overpowered him. The justice of the Black Rainbow, Comandante Oquendo, and Don Sixto, whose words had come true. "He feels in the flesh the wrongness of his acts." Afterward, rather than getting the better of the people around him, he'd desired more than anything to emulate those men who tried to do right and to enact rightness upon this earth, no matter what the cost.

He'd lacked the strength at first. Last month he'd gone to Comandante Oquendo to ask for help. His father had been lurking around the house, threatening to kill his mother. He'd beaten on the door, howling for Ema to come out. One night he'd chiseled off the lock and hinges, come in, and thrown Ema to the ground, kicking her several times in the head before the boys could stop him. She was lucky to be alive, according to Doctor Calzón.

"What can I do?" Boris had asked the Comandante.

"You know as well as I," the Comandante had said. "But you do not have to act alone."

Boris and Limbert had led the Rainbows to where their father had been sitting by the river, outside the shack he'd built. Drunk and drooling like an animal, he'd raised his head and regarded them all dully. "Who will strike?" Don Sixto had asked, and Boris had slowly raised an index finger. He had not wanted someone else to do this task. Don Sixto had handed him the *barreta,* and he'd given his father one blow on the back of the neck, direct, decisive, merciful. He'd killed a man who could not learn.

Afterward, he'd met with the Comandante, who had advised Boris to maintain a clear conscience, always remembering the necessity of what had been done. *Recto,* the Comandante had said, gesturing with the edge of his palm. Walk straight through all your sorrow, your regrets, your doubts. Don't let them pull you back. This will require more strength than you imagine.

The Comandante had been right. Sometimes it required more strength than Boris could summon.

While he pondered this, the Señora got up and walked around, then sat back down directly on the sand. Seeming nervous, she spoke as if she were talking to herself, worrying because the five men were getting thin in her mind's eye, like ghosts. She was afraid of a certain *malvado,* an evil person, following them, a soldier named Juan Carlos Yáñez. "Until we meet again," this man had said to her in the Cajamarca airport. Boris reassured her, saying she must not be superstitious. She must walk straight through her fears. He showed her his palm's rigid edge.

She knew, she said, lifting one hand limply. Tears came to her eyes, and she let the hand fall, saying that just now she felt as if she were not alive, but in the land of the truly dead.

Boris quickly asked her to stop talking in such a way. It was not good.

"Ay, disculpa," sorry, she said. Of course she was alive, and she was going to have a child, and she hoped it would be healthy. And did Boris realize they had succeeded? Now there was no way of stopping the campaign to clean the water of Piedras. Two hostages, a doctor and a general's son, held by the Black Rainbow. The whereabouts of the doctor's wife unknown. The world would hear it all. Her voice trailed off.

Depending on what happened, she might stay in Peru, or else get another job in a clinic, maybe far away, in la India. Boris could visit her there. She'd find a way to bring him, pay his ticket. In la India, men wore dresses and women wore pants. Would he like to see that? She would.

Boris said yes, only to please her, and then volunteered to get water from the stream. He suggested Maggie rest. She agreed, and went back a bit farther into the tomb, and lay down under the overhanging cliff, saying the sand was warmer there.

When the boy was gone she rested for a while without a thought in her head. Then she got up, left the little square building, and walked down the ledge to begin gathering dry sticks. She put them in several piles, planning to consolidate them later. Why was Boris taking so long? Maybe he was busy devising something to carry water in.

She regretted advising him to leave. Staying by her side hardly guaranteed his safety, but she hadn't realized how much more she'd worry when he was out of sight. She supposed she'd been relying on him, judging from the conviction she felt now, that their conversation had been truncated. She did want to talk more, especially about Vicente. Boris was one of the few people who would understand her feelings. He loved the Comandante about as much as she did.

Momentarily, she was visited by a fear that she'd driven him off. Could he have thought she didn't want him near her? What a speech she'd given him! Where had all that come from?

As she walked from one end of the ledge to the other, toting this and that twig and sorting them into piles by size, up to a small log that would have to be fed into the fire lengthwise (she was trying to accumulate enough wood to burn all night), she began to acknowledge a slight, odd feeling of confidence. Everything she'd said to Boris had been justified.

Now she had one of those weird retrospective experiences, discovering a translucent solidity inside herself. It had appeared, unnoticed, hours or days ago. It was subtle, but it was definite, which made it different from nearly all of Maggie's other feelings, which tended to be as turbulent as they were uncertain.

She'd had a similar experience back in August, but in reverse, when she'd felt a deep pull in her chest and belly upon seeing Vicente, Luz, and Lady Maggy standing together in the middle of the clinic's floor. At the time, she'd identified it as sheer dread, suppressing it, then forgetting it. The sensation had surprised her by resurfacing hours later, nudging at her consciousness as if requesting further attention. Weeks had elapsed before she'd recognized it fully: not simply dread, nor a terrified responsibility, but also desire, her first attraction to Vicente.

Today she could probably trace the instant this new solidity had been born — down on the riverbank, in the stillness just after Carson's gun went off. Now that it had returned, she could articulate it: she was there as a consequence of her own acts and thoughts, for better or worse. For some reason, this was freeing.

Clearly she'd brought herself to Piedras. She'd made choices all her life, but never felt before that she was a cause, even an influence, really on anything at all, not even on things inside herself. It was horrible to consider how she'd lived, so tractionless, until today when her existence had come together all at once, and out of the resulting thunderclap she'd created a turning point as concrete as any decision of Carson's. She'd sent Vicente and Carson off together, leaving her alone. She would have been amazed that they'd obeyed her, except that her decision had emerged from a logic so economical, swift, and complete that her mind could no longer repeat its path. In one gesture, she had overturned her previous life. She now understood that she'd lived as if she'd been a zombie, guided by someone else's thoughts. She'd adopted Althea's biography, because she couldn't find her own and was afraid of being swallowed up by Carson's.

Where this tendency had come from wasn't worth making the effort to determine. It had been a form of blindness. It had led her to do evil, pile mistake upon mistake. Because of it, she might never see Vicente again. She might soon have contributed to his death and Boris's and Carson's and at least a dozen more people, if she included herself and the settlers. She might be bringing to life a creature already poisoned, doomed to die before it would be born.

These things hadn't happened yet, she reminded herself. When, if, any of them did come to pass, she hoped someone or something would be able to forgive her. Just now she had to hold on to herself, keep moving forward, and not look back. The amazing thing was that she knew she could.

You might be able to trust me now, she told the child.

Walk out of the forest, get to the U.S. embassy in Lima, call journalists. She sat down again with her back against the cliff. The layers of mud under her feet had begun to suck her socks down. She unlaced her boots, pulled them off, and turned them over. A pint of water drained from each one, making Maggie almost proud. Next, she wrung out her socks, again producing an abundant juice, this one smelling of wet dog. It ran out in thin braids, dark brown with a yellow tinge, and disappeared instantly, drunk up by the earth. The water was mixed with blood, from that old blood blister she'd gotten dancing at the festival. It had never healed; now it had burst again. Good. The Earth Mother was always hungry, and was fond of blood, according to Fortunata.

Eat this, Maggie thought, and be satisfied.

It was becoming obvious that Boris would not return. In her mind she watched him running after the Rainbows. Slipping, jumping down ledges, running to join them, returning to their plan from which she had now been freed.

Good, she thought again, as solitude settled around her. He'd left her here, as she had asked, to go where he was most needed, where he wanted to be. That had been her lesson to Carson, too. Like a bad preacher, she'd been able to convince Carson of something she needed to learn herself. He was acting on it now, still being true to himself, the only way he would ever have of being true. She still loved him for that, but not in the way she would have liked to love him, not in the way she had loved Vicente. She'd loved Vicente completely.

Now they'd both slipped away from her. The idea that she'd never see Vicente again was leaden, hard to bear.

Their passion would always stay fresh and perfect, like Uncle Christopher, who would forever be a baby; like Althea's love for her priest, still blooming on her deathbed. There was something creepy about that. Maggie would have preferred to find out what would have happened next between them. Now there would be no next. Vicente had betrayed her — chosen a path that had been mapped for him, and glorified it with the name of destiny. She forgave him, though, considering. Just now she was unable to imagine ever loving anyone else.

He was still alive, she thought, wrenching back her thoughts. Alive, alive. She pushed Vicente on into the forest. Faster, she thought.

She wondered whose child hers would be.

She sat staring at the rain until she heard a shout, hollow and reverberating, then three quick, booming gunshots in the near distance. She snatched her blue plastic rain sheet off the twig just before the uniforms came into view, moving toward her. The soldiers were only a couple hundred meters away, downstream, walking toward her on the trail that she and Boris had strayed from. At this distance they looked toylike. She had a wacky impulse to jump out, let them kill her or forgive her.

If she stayed out of sight and didn't move, they'd pass right under this ledge and never see it. She was on the west side of the stream, directly above their heads; they'd be scanning the opposite hillside. As soon as they spied the Inca road, and the trail that led to it, she'd be safe.

Her cheek against the ground, she lay shivering, still, like a baby rabbit in a shallow burrow. She prayed for invisibility. May all of the confusion I have ever felt leave me, and surround Juan Carlos Yáñez and his men. Please let Boris not be dead. May all of them not die.

She prayed to saints and mummies and to God, and to all her ancestors and friends, and to the rocks and the dirt beneath her cheek. She squeezed the little claw in her pocket. The gold chain around her neck had snapped sometime today, probably when she'd been heaving herself up those ledges. It had slipped off, releasing Althea's ruby ring. Maggie tried to imagine where the ring lay now, glinting pink and gold in water, mud, or amongst green leaves. An offering.

Please let me live too, she added, and heard the men pass under where she lay, talking in urgent grunts and whoops among themselves.

She'd never know what happened to Boris. The shout had sounded like his raw, young voice. Again and again she replayed this cry, trying to hear whether it expressed terror, triumph, agony, or warning. Perhaps he'd yelled to warn her from a hidden place, and then escaped into the greenery, zigzagging and dodging bullets. In her mind's eye she could see his thighs pumping, his feet in rubber-tire sandals scrabbling, leaving skids and tread marks in the steep mud of a hillside. She gritted her teeth against other images. Yet if they hadn't succeeded in shooting him, why had the soldiers continued marching in such good order? Had they left others behind to search for Boris? In her fleeting glimpse of them, she had not registered Juan

Carlos Yáñez. The first man in line had been tall and gaunt, with a mustache like a brush for scrubbing floors.

She lay with her cheek against the soft powdery silt. Never had she loved the earth so much; it seemed to love her back. She decided not to stand up until nightfall, to stay pressed against the sweetness of the ground. She peed quietly, warmly, into her trousers.

Hours passed, during which dozens of versions of Boris's fate swept through her mind. Sometimes he escaped, and left the forest, and found love in Mollepata with an apple-cheeked *campesina* who bore a resemblance to Maggie's first patient, Ofelia. They lived a long and fruitful life.

Boris jumped down into the streambed to hide behind a rock, wondering what to do. They were coming from the direction of the cabin, four of them. Sinchis, anti-terrorist commandos. They'd extracted information from Marisol or Roosevelt. It would have been easy for them. Boris knew about Sinchis; that was the kind of unit his father had retired from. When he drank, Boris's father had raved about tearing out fingernails, setting fire to locked houses full of people, beheading little children in front of their parents to get one piece of information. As he beat Boris's mother, he'd always told her: "Be glad, woman. Thank me for this, my kindness. You don't want to know my wrath."

Sinchi platoons consisted of a dozen men. This group was only four. The rest must be chasing the Comandante. At least the other Rainbows all had guns, except Ignacio. Boris prayed for them, glad at last that Limbert had a weapon. Lord Jesus, help them. Help them to escape or kill the enemy. And please, make Limbert push the gun's bolt all the way to the bottom. Don't let him be nervous or the shell will blow up in his face.

He could have hidden there until they all had passed, but he remembered Doña Maggie, who had left her blue plastic drying on that stick. The Sinchis would surely see its bright, artificial color. Or what if she had left the ledge to look for Boris by the stream? He should have told her he was leaving her, but he'd felt a little bit ashamed. He was more ashamed now, of his petty cowardice.

The trail turned up, momentarily taking the Sinchis out of sight.

Boris darted from rock to rock, trying to get ahead of the soldiers, to get back up and warn her. Too soon, they came out again into the clear. They were still five hundred meters off, but they were walking like machines, not men. Evidently they'd fought in the Huallaga. Two carried rifles; one a light grenade launcher. The one in front was armed with a pistol only, flat and black, still snapped into its leather holster. He was fat, with sunglasses, a sauntering, cruel little father's son from Lima — obviously that same *malvado* who was looking for Maggie in particular.

Give your life, the Comandante had said. As I have done already. Love, Boris realized. That was clearly what the Comandante meant. Love was expressed as sacrifice, and the Comandante loved that thing in Maggie which she'd just described to Boris. The soul, or something. Her words had been better, but to Boris finding a word for the thing was not important. Whatever you wanted to call it, he knew it was alive in all three of them.

He thought of shouting "Save yourself!" and running, but then the soldiers would know that Maggie was nearby, and they'd probably manage to shoot him too.

If she heard gunshots, she'd recognize the danger.

Stealthily, swiftly, he advanced. From the stream, a rock the size of a melon came to his hands. With it he surely weighed a hundred kilos. Creeping farther along the streambed, he found a fallen log to shield him. Behind this he crawled up, until he was above the trail. He chose his place, and waited. All too soon the evil one came walking, crossing into the invisible circle Boris had drawn upon the dirt. The top of his head was there, exactly.

Boris drove his soul into the center of what it knew. I am not I, he thought, I am that instead. Inside a blinding shout he dropped, and smashed Juan Carlos Yáñez's skull.

Yes, that could be, Maggie thought. That story didn't contradict any of the evidence she had so far. It combined her highest hopes, her lowest impulses, and her worst fears. Boris probably hadn't actually killed Juan Carlos Yáñez, but if Boris had died, she wanted him to have had some kind of victory. His shout could very well have been intended to save her. Whether warning her had caused his death or not — that was a crucial question, but it came after other questions, all unanswerable just now. No matter what, Maggie reflected, she had no right to ask Boris to sacrifice his life, even in her imagination, solely to satisfy her need for logic.

She'd probably have to live with never finding out. Yet her story had one moral use: along with all the other things she was going to be responsible for facing, she might have to try to live up to this version of things, in case it was the real one.

There was comfort in not knowing. If she and the child survived, one day she'd tell the child that story. But she could also tell it another one, the tale that ended happily.

She could hear her child's piping voice, asking why she'd never bothered to learn the final facts.

I did all I could, she promised. If you aren't satisfied, then it is your turn to try.

Slowly, the roar of the small river again became inhuman, part of the silence of the forest. Maggie shifted onto her back, to gaze up at the softly clouded sky. She began to make a list for the child of things that contained the same tones of gray. The hindquarters of a circus horse, the lining of new sweatpants. The North Sea frozen solid, ten feet beneath the surface. Each item took a long time to explain, since the child had not yet seen anything whatsoever.

Much later, in a moonless darkness, hidden in an added density of fog, she would crawl up the inclined ledge toward the tomb, feeling her way in the dust until her dry fingertips touched cut stone. She would be so exhausted and numb that she'd be able to devise no better strategy than to knock her head gently and systematically against the stone wall of the tomb until she found a place of no resistance, a door. She would crawl through it, fall asleep.

She would live for several days and nights on this ledge, creeping down to the stream to drink, as furtive as an animal; eating fried corn grain by grain. At last she would dare to walk, cautiously, weakly, toward Plain of Slime. On its outskirts, María Gracia Aliaga would be waiting, pretending to hoe a potato field. She'd dress Maggie in a skirt and shawl woven from the wool of her two black llamas, and they'd walk into town. The soldiers would have marched in and out, leaving Plain of Slime wrapped in its ancestral silence, its inhabitants having offered nothing beyond the same bad impression they'd been perfecting for centuries. María Gracia's hut would be window-less, containing not a stick of furniture. In it, by the light of an alcohol lamp, Maggie would tell a group of María's friends what had happened to Comandante Oquendo; she'd hope they had no news for her in return. When she'd recovered from fatigue and sadness, enough to be able to walk, María Gracia would give her a handful of dirt to disguise the pallor of her face; and a filthy hat, mushroom-shaped and mushroom-colored, with two braids of real human hair sewn under its brim. Then she'd show her the trail for the coast.

Author's Note

This is a work of fiction, and I hope it will be read as such. With the exception of Atahualpa, no character or plot element in this book is intended to resemble any real person or event, living or dead, present or past. Some things in the book are based on real-life objects, but still I intended for them to be the objects in a fiction. Thus, for example, criticisms of governments, political movements, and institutions are not to be read as the author's opinions, but as those of given, invented characters.

For all errors of verisimilitude, fact, or feeling, the author holds herself solely responsible. However, details were invented and distortions deliberately perpetrated. There is no Rosario River. There is no Black Rainbow Movement. Dates of known earthquakes have been changed. The festival of Saint John's Beheading, though it does occur on a Sunday in late August, is not celebrated as described. Other cultural practices have been altered or reinterpreted as well. Atahualpa's death stone lies in the main plaza of Cajamarca, but no plaque describes the manner of his execution. What may seem melodramatic in this book is intended to be so.

I am indebted to the work of John Hemming, Mercedes López-Baralt, and David M. Guss for information about Atahualpa, and to López-Baralt for the Quechua text and the translation into Spanish of Atahualpa's poem in chapter 10. The translation into English is my own. For information on geologic theory, and facts and stories about earthquakes, I consulted books by Haroun Tazieff and Nicholas Hunter Heck and asked questions of my father, Charles B. Wheeler. From John Simpson's book *In the Forests of the Night*, I gathered information and impressions about the cocaine business in Peru.